ST. LOUIS RISING

Louis de Kerlérec

Ch.er de l'Ordre Royal et Militaire de S.t Louis, Capit.ne de Vaisseaux du Roy, et
Gouverneur de la Province de la Louisianne.

Sur les bons Témoignages

Qui nous (ont) donné de la fidélité, de la Capacité, et de l'attachement pour la Nation francaise, du nommé *Okana Stoté*
grand Chef de toute la Nation Cherakis, et de la grande loge du grand Village de Toute.

Nous l'avons Etabli

Et Etablissons Capitaine a la tête
de sa conduite de tous les partis qui iront en guerre contre nos ennemis, et pour le service de la Nation francaise, Ordonnons
à tous Commandants des postes de la Colonie, de le faire reconnaître en cette qualité tant par les Nations, les Francais, que
Sauvages à nos ordres, ou attachés à ce grade à S.A.M. le Roy, Jouissant des droits et prérog.es que le Service doit leur
Mandons en outre à tous officiers, Cadets, Soldats, Miliciens, armés ... ...
Okana Stoté ... Comme officier allié et devoué au Service de la Marine francoise
En foi de quoy Nous lui avons donné et donnons la présente Commission pour
... Voulons partout où besoin sera, Et a cette fin y avons apposé le sceau de nos armes, Et le contresing ...
Nôtre fidèle Secrétaire. Donné à la Nouvelle Orleans le 27 février 1761, fait le sceau de nos armes et
le contresing de notre Secrétaire.

Kerlerec

Par Monseigneur
Huisté

ST. LOUIS RISING

THE FRENCH REGIME OF
LOUIS ST. ANGE DE BELLERIVE

CARL J. EKBERG

SHARON K. PERSON

UNIVERSITY OF ILLINOIS PRESS
Urbana, Chicago, and Springfield

© 2015 by the Board of Trustees
of the University of Illinois
All rights reserved
Manufactured in the United States of America
1 2 3 4 5 C P 5 4 3 2 1
∞ This book is printed on acid-free paper.

Frontispiece: Kerlérec Indian commission. This exquisite tableau is the ornamentation on a commission tendered to the Cherokee chief Okana-Stoté by Louisiana governor Louis Billouart de Kerlérec in February 1761. The Cherokees were sometime enemies of the French, but Kerlérec took his diplomatic duties seriously and sought out their friendship. The French royal coat of arms is at the top, on the left is that of Louisiana, and on the right that of Kerlérec. Courtesy National Archives, Washington, D.C.

Library of Congress Cataloging-in-Publication Data
Ekberg, Carl J.
St. Louis rising : the French regime of Louis St. Ange de Bellerive /
Carl J. Ekberg and Sharon K. Person.
pages   cm
Includes bibliographical references and index.
ISBN 978-0-252-03897-6 (hardcover : alk. paper) — ISBN 978-0-252-08061-6 (pbk. : alk. paper) —
ISBN 978-0-252-09693-8 (e-book)
1. Illinois—History—To 1778. 2. Saint Louis (Mo.)—History—18th century. 3. Saint-Ange de Bellerive, Louis Groston de. 4. Frontier and pioneer life—Illinois. 5. Frontier and pioneer life—Missouri—Saint Louis. 6. French—Illinois—History—18th century.
I. Person, Sharon. II. Title. III. Title: Saint Louis rising.
F544.E39   2015
977.8'6602—dc23   2014031907

St. Ange has served since he was a child, and became a captain on October 15, 1748. He is an excellent officer for that region [Upper Louisiana], especially regarding the Indians, whom he leads and guides at his will. He's a man of absolute probity, a zealous servant of the king, and has always regarded commercial activities as beneath him.

—Governor Louis Billouart de Kerlérec, 1759

CONTENTS

List of Maps, Plans, and Illustrations   ix
Preface   xi
Chronology   xv
Introduction: Beyond the Laclède-Chouteau Legend   1

Part I. St. Ange de Bellerive and the Illinois Country
1. Fort d'Orléans and the Grotton–St. Ange Family   11
2. The Rise of Louis St. Ange de Bellerive   33
3. The Illinois Country in Transition, 1763–1765   50
4. Commandant St. Ange de Bellerive   72
5. The Village Emerges   96

Part II. Contours of Village Life
6. Logs and Stones: Early St. Louis Buildings   111
7. The *Coutume de Paris* Rules   127
8. Slaves: African and Indian   147
9. In Small Things Forgotten   165
10. Foundations of the St. Louis Fur Trade   187
11. End of An Era   206

Conclusion: St. Louis and the Wider World   217
Appendix A. St. Louis Counts   227
Appendix B. St. Louis Indian Slave Census, 1770   247
Notes   251
Index   315

MAPS, PLANS, AND ILLUSTRATIONS

Maps and Plans

Eastern North America, ca. 1770   2
The Illinois Country (*Pays des Illinois*), Jacques-Nicolas Bellin, 1755   3
Bourgmont's expedition to the Padoucas, 1724   21
Lower Ohio River valley, Jacques-Nicolas Bellin, 1762   37
The Illinois Country, Thomas Hutchins, 1766   54
Plan of Fort St. Charles, prince of Asturies, unknown draftsman, 1767   85
Plan of St. Louis, Antoine Soulard (?), 1804   102
Plan of New Orleans, Philip Pittman, 1770   102

Illustrations

Amos Stoddard letter, 1804   6
Robert Grotton de St. Ange marriage contract, 1718   13
Pierre St. Ange marriage contract, *New York Times*, 1876   28
St. Ange letter to Governor Vaudreuil, 1752   39
Signatures on Cerré-Giard marriage record, 1764   58
Antonio de Ulloa, governor of Louisiana, 1766–68   74
General Alejandro O'Reilly, interim governor of Louisiana, 1769–70   74
St. Louis census heading, 1766   77
Appellation "St. Louis" first appears, July 1765   98
Woodworking tools, France, eighteenth century   113
French Canadian houses, eighteenth century   117
Evolution of the Illinois Country Creole house   118
Threshing cereal grain, France, eighteenth century   120
Coutume de Paris, 1680   128
Code Noir, 1724   150
Dough-kneading trough (*pétrin*)   169
Walnut armoire from early St. Louis   173

ix

Caned chair from early St. Louis   180
French flintlocks, eighteenth century   182
Mississippi freight *bateau*, Joseph Warin   190
Signatures on St. Ange's last will and testament, 1774   209
Ordonnance du Roy, 1720   213
Creole house, Joseph Warin, 1795   220

Color Plates

Color illustrations follow page 216

Fort d'Orléans, Jean-François-Benjamin Dumont de Montigny
Missouri Indian, George Catlin, 1832
Kansas warrior, George Catlin, 1832
Comanche (Padouca/Plains Apache) village, George Catlin, 1846
Comanche (Padouca/Plains Apache) bison hunt, George Catlin, 1846
Osage woman and child, George Catlin, 1834
Young Osage warriors, George Catlin, 1834
Piankashaw-Miami Indian, George Catlin, 1830
Peoria Indian, George Catlin, 1830
Marie-Thérèse Bourgeois Chouteau
Marguerite Blondeau Guion
St. Louis with buildings depicted, Guy Dufossat, 1767
Confluence of Missouri and Mississippi Rivers, Guy Dufossat, 1767
St. Louis and environs, Guy Dufossat, 1767
Limestone quarry near St. Louis, Guy Dufossat, 1767
French Moustier-style faience, eighteenth century
Pharmaceutical mortar and pestle, colonial St. Louis
Early silverware

PREFACE

The roots of this book go back several years, when Helen Vallé Crist suggested that Sharon and Carl collaborate on a research project dealing with early St. Louis; our gratitude for this gesture of benevolence continues to inspire us. After dinner at Anne and Rodney Johnson's historic home in Webster Groves, Missouri, in June 2011, we began an e-mail conversation about the extraordinary 1766 St. Louis manuscript census. In our exchange of ideas, we soon concluded that it was a document worth scrutinizing, annotating, and publishing. Then there was the thought that the 250th anniversary of St. Louis's founding was coming up soon and that, as historians, we wished to make some contribution to the occasion. Deeper in our minds was the suspicion that the rich archives of the Missouri History Museum had manuscript collections pertaining to early St. Louis that had not been fully exploited. And, finally, working our way tentatively into recent historical literature about the American West, we discovered remarkable neglect of the colonial Illinois Country, of which St. Louis was a part and without the existence of which St. Louis would never have developed. For all these reasons, we decided to plunge ahead, and we began research on what we, with increasing confidence, envisioned as a major revisionary book.

At the outset, we must acknowledge that this study is an astringent critique of much that has been written about St. Louis's early years. The city's history has proved irresistible to writers of many stripes and varying degrees of talent, each of whom has told the story from his or her own perspective, with his or her own particular biases and prejudices. And the 250th anniversary of the city's founding (2014) has provoked a flurry of additional commentary, opinion, scholarship, and writing about early St. Louis. Whatever the diversity of views, however, all versions of early St. Louis history have one thing in common: they focus overwhelmingly on the importance of Pierre Laclède and Auguste Chouteau. The further we delved into original manuscripts, the more dubious we became of that standard formulation, for we discovered that Laclède's name appears but rarely, and Chouteau's even more rarely. The seeds of Chouteau's eventual prominence were surely there during the 1760s, but primary sources do not reveal them. After combing the archives for many months, we mutually agreed that the story of St. Louis's founding and early days cried out for retelling.

In 1910 the St. Louis Field Club, which had been founded in 1897 as a nine-hole golf club, reconstituted itself as a full-fledged eighteen-hole country club, and a controversy arose over selecting a name for it. "The matter of choosing a name for the new club had been under discussion for several months. Nearly every club member had his individual preferences and aversions. . . . It was apparent from the beginning that these divergencies of view could not be reconciled through discussion." To avoid an acrimonious debate, the club decided to conduct a secret poll, and 169 members participated. Bellerive (for Louis St. Ange de Bellerive) was their overwhelming preference for a name; Laclède ran a distant fourth (behind Brookwood and Pontiac), and Chouteau's name did not make the short list. It is apparent that those old duffers with their handlebar mustaches, plus-fours, and hickory-shafted golf clubs knew a little something about the history of early St. Louis and about the towering importance of the Canadian-born man who governed the French outpost during its formative years.

The book that follows is complex. It is a history of the Illinois Country between 1720 and 1770, an overview of the important Grotton–St. Ange family, a biography of Louis St. Ange de Bellerive, and a study of St. Louis's formative years as a French outpost—including the roles of women, slaves, farmers, carpenters, and fur traders. It is western history, southern history, midwestern history, and colonial history; although containing much about Indians, it is not a study in ethnohistory per se, for neither our sources nor our inclination took us in that direction. Because of our text's complexity, we have relied on assistance from a wide range of persons, without whose help the book would never have appeared in its present form. First, the indispensable archivists and librarians: Larry Franke at the St. Louis County Library; Dennis Northcutt, Molly Kodner, and Jaime Bourassa at the Missouri History Museum in St. Louis; Mary White and Sarah Elizabeth Gundlach at the Louisiana State Museum in New Orleans; Richard Day, authority on all things pertaining to colonial Vincennes; Emily Lyons at the Randolph County Courthouse in Chester, Illinois; Father Kenneth York at the diocesan archives in Belleville, Illinois; and Marie-Paule Blasini at the Archives Nationales d'Outre Mer in Aix-en-Provence. We bombarded these custodians of the past with many idiosyncratic requests, and they came through unfailingly and with good humor.

American Indian studies has become such a large, diverse, and contentious field that we were obliged to consult persons more expert than we. Many e-mail dialogues with linguists and cultural historians Carl Masthay and Michael McCafferty have proved endlessly useful. And Carolyn I. Gilman of the National Museum of the American Indian helped us sort out the George Catlin paintings that are reproduced in this book. Kathleen Duval generously took of her time to critique the chapter on slaves, African and Indian. Material culture—furniture, housewares, architecture, building practices, clothing—plays an important role in our book, and again we have relied on expert assistance: Robert F. Mazrim of the Illinois State Archaeological Survey; Anne Woodhouse of the Missouri History Museum; Maurice Meslans, with his formidable knowledge of early silversmiths and silverware; Peter Moogk, self-effacing cognoscente of French Canadian building ways; Jay Edwards of Louisiana State University, subtle anthropologist of Creole architecture and building practices. Gilles Havard lent his expertise regarding fur-trade complexities, as did U.S. Appellate Judge Morris S. Arnold regarding legal nomenclature.

Help has also arrived from abroad: Christine Knutson Beveraggi of Paris, an expert on domestic law in France, was especially useful concerning the intricacies of the *Coutume de Paris*, a subject so obscure in the United States that the mere mention of it raises eyebrows in the most erudite company. Daniel Beveraggi, etymologist *passioné*, explained to us the meaning of archaic phrases, such as the charmingly bucolic *toile herbée*. Jean Bruggeman, of Villeneuve d'Ascq, France, the world's leading expert on historic wind-, water-, and horse mills, helped us distinguish flour mills from tannin mills, a small topic that was of the utmost importance in early St. Louis. Google cannot help with this issue.

Finally, there is the text itself. We have reached out to a wide array of authorities: authorities on style, on history, on law, on slavery, on eighteenth-century sensibilities, and on storytelling, for in most languages (not English) *history* and *story* are identical words; if there is no story to tell, don't bother to tell it. We wanted our narrative to possess accuracy, energy, pace, and coherence. Many readers have helped us pursue our goal of telling the story of early St. Louis in a passionate and accessible manner, our obvious passion providing, we hope, easier access for the reader. William E. Foley and Robert M. Morrissey, read every syllable of the text and provided innumerable suggestions about both style and content; Gregory P. Ames, editor of Auguste Chouteau's "Journal," offered many constructive criticisms about arcane but important aspects of our book that no one else could have mustered.

This book has gone from conception to completion in a remarkably short period of time. This is in no small way due to the energetic and efficient team at the University of Illinois Press, a team led by Laurie Matheson and that included Dawn Durante, Tad Ringo, and Annette Wenda. Working with two authors made their task more difficult, but with patience and understanding we moved through the many intricacies of scholarly publishing briskly, albeit with a few warm discussions.

CHRONOLOGY

ca. 1685	Robert Grotton–St. Ange emigrates from France to Canada
1720	Grotton–St. Ange commandant at Fort St. Joseph (Niles, Michigan)
1721	Grotton–St. Ange accompanies Father Charlevoix down the Mississippi
1723	Robert and son Pierre St. Ange join Bourgmont expedition to the Missouri
1724	Élisabeth Chorel and Louis St. Ange de Bellerive join Robert and Pierre at Fort d'Orléans
1724–30	Robert St. Ange commandant at Fort d'Orléans
1730–34	Robert St. Ange commandant at Fort de Chartres
1730–36	Louis St. Ange de Bellerive commandant at Fort d'Orléans
1736	Pierre St. Ange burned alive during Chickasaw campaign
1736–64	Louis St. Ange commandant at Vincennes
1754–63	French and Indian War
1762	France cedes Louisiana to Spain (Treaty of Fontainebleau)
February 1763	France cedes east side of Mississippi to British (Treaty of Paris)
1763–65	New settlers arrive from the east bank of the Mississippi
1764–70	Louis St. Ange de Bellerive commandant of Upper Louisiana
July 1765	The new outpost acquires its name "St. Louis"
October 1765	St. Ange relinquishes Fort de Chartres to the British
	St. Ange moves across the Mississippi to St. Louis
1765–70	St. Ange and his notary, Joseph Labuxière, govern St. Louis
April 1769	Pontiac murdered by Peoria Indian and buried at Cahokia
May 1770	Pedro Piernas relieves St. Ange as commandant at St. Louis
Summer 1773	St. Ange and Angélique, his Indian concubine, move into an apartment in Mme. Chouteau's residence
December 1774	St. Ange dies and is buried in St. Louis

INTRODUCTION

Beyond the Laclède-Chouteau Legend

There is no history of early St. Louis, for history means the truth, and we have but phantoms that gibber in its stead.

—Oscar W. Collet, ca. 1890

The French adventure, or misadventure, in the immense colony named Louisiana began with the explorations of Jacques Marquette and Louis Jolliet in 1673 and did not end until Louis St. Ange de Bellerive relinquished his command to Spanish authorities at St. Louis in 1770.[1] St. Louis was the last of a series of French colonial communities to coalesce in the Illinois Country. Marquette and Jolliet commenced recorded European exploration of the region in 1673, when they descended the Mississippi as far as the mouth of the Arkansas River. And, a decade later, Robert Cavelier de La Salle led an expedition down, and ever down, the great river to the Gulf of Mexico and superbly claimed the entire Mississippi watershed on behalf of King Louis XIV. Francis Parkman captured the scene in his enchanting prose: "The Frenchmen were mustered under arms, and while the . . . Indians looked on in wondering silence they chanted the *Te Deum*, the *Exaudiat* and the *Domine salvum fac Regem*. Then, amid volleys of musketry and shouts of 'Vive le Roi,' La Salle . . . proclaimed in a loud voice: 'In the name of the most high, mighty, invincible, and victorious Prince, Louis the Great, by the Grace of God King of France and Navarre, Fourteenth of that name, I . . . have taken possession of this country of Louisiana.'"[2] An alluring strand of grandiosity ran through the thoughts and words of many early French explorers of North America, which is one reason their stories remain captivating, even intoxicating, for all those interested in the Mississippi frontier in colonial times.

Permanent European settlement of the Illinois Country (the settled portion of Upper Louisiana) began with the founding of Cahokia by Seminarian missionaries in 1699. It was followed in succession, during the next six decades, by Kaskaskia, Chartres, Saint Philippe, Vincennes, Prairie du Rocher, Ste. Genevieve, and finally St. Louis. Over time the last became first, as St.

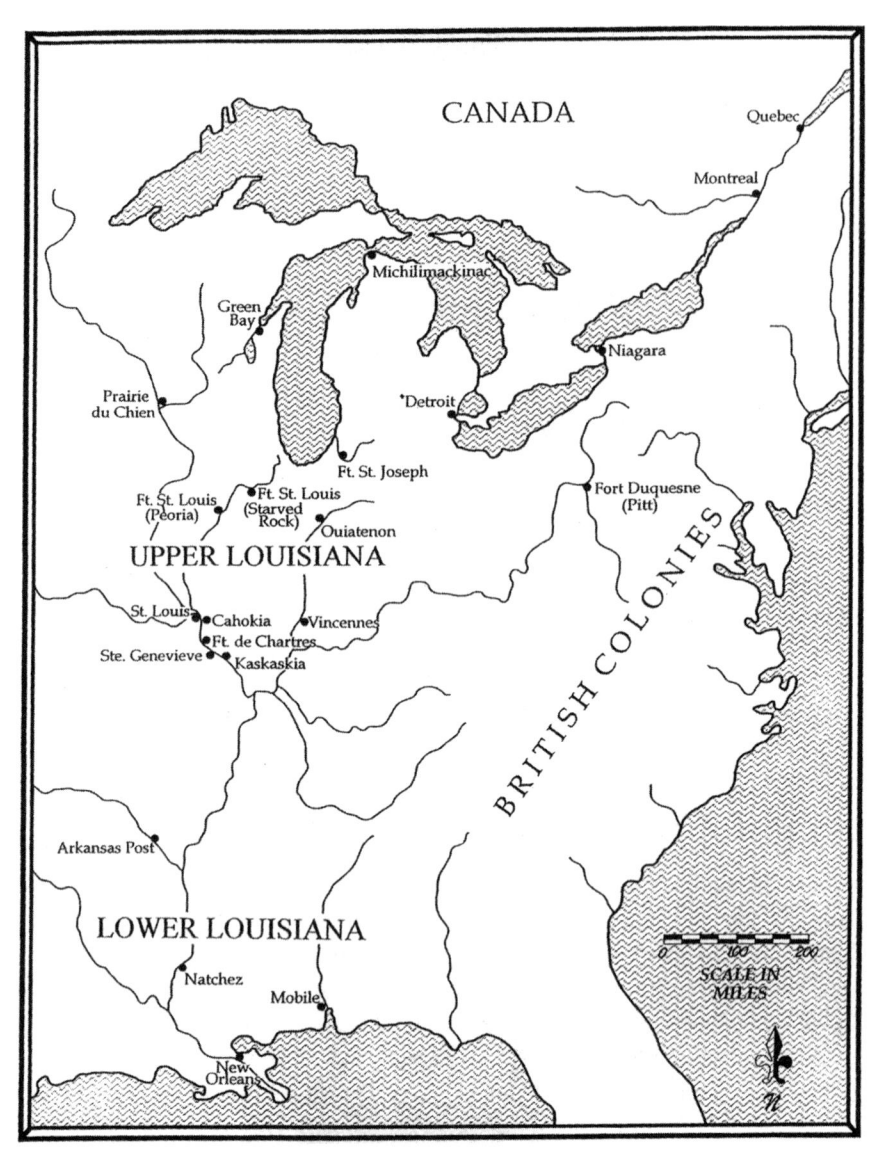

Eastern North America, ca. 1770. Notice the concentration of French villages in the settled portion of Upper Louisiana (the Illinois Country). St. Louis was the last of these villages to emerge (1764).

Louis vastly outstripped all other Illinois Country villages, ultimately to become the region's only metropolis. To have predicted this, even when Lewis and Clark arrived in the region in December 1803, would have demanded preternatural vision. Nevertheless, Auguste Chouteau claimed that his surrogate father, Pierre Laclède Liguest,[3] had foreseen St. Louis's immense prospects from the very beginning—indeed, quite literally, even before the beginning.

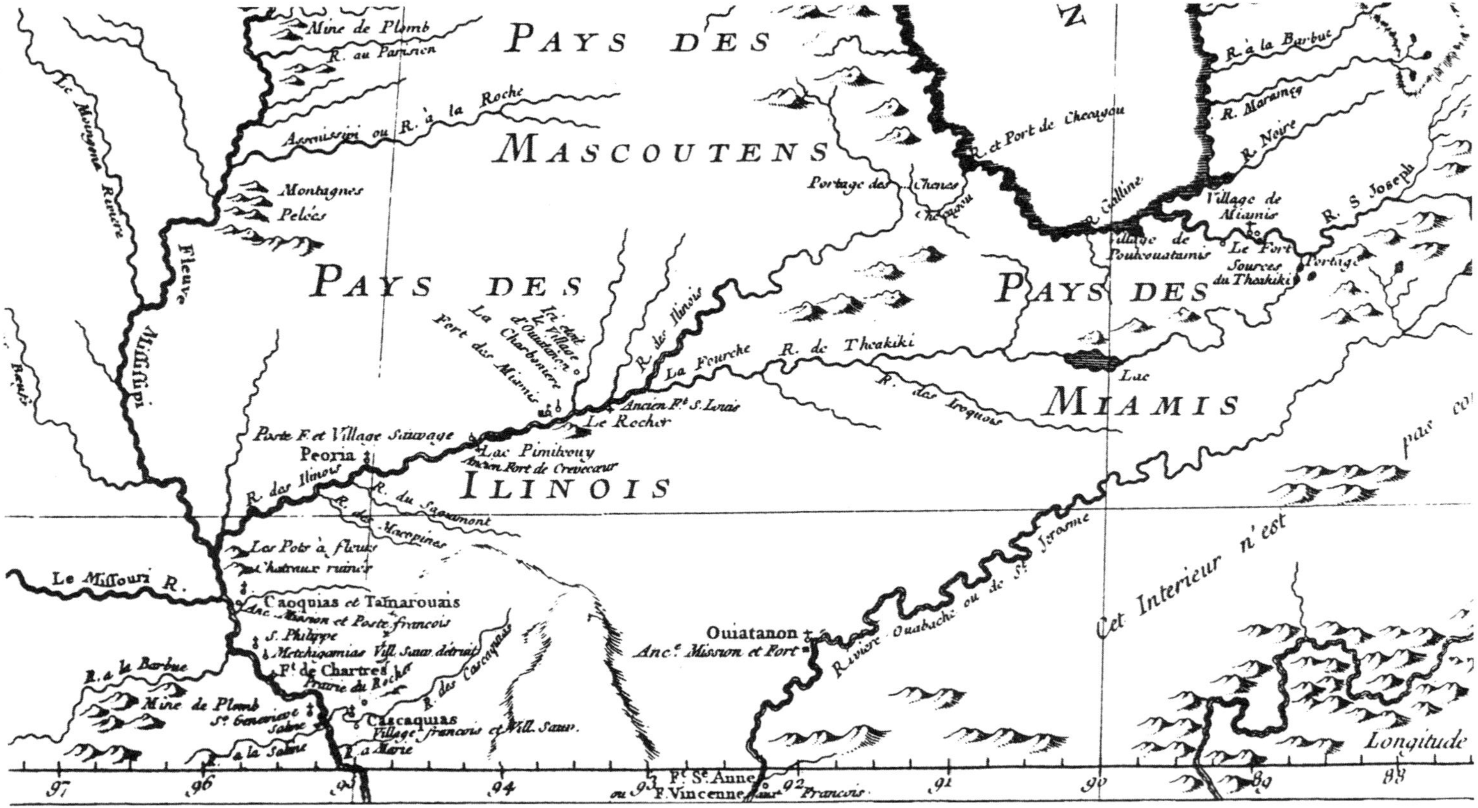

The Illinois Country (Pays des Illinois) drawn in Paris by Jacques-Nicolas Bellin, 1755. Notice the concentration of French settlements on the east side of the Mississippi. Ste. Genevieve, founded ca. 1750, was the only settlement in the region situated west of the river at the time. Courtesy of the Library of Congress, Maps and Geography Division.

Chouteau described in his "Journal" how Laclède had prophesied in December 1763 that the trading outpost he would establish in February 1764 was destined to become "one of the finest cities in America."[4]

This claim, as so much that Chouteau wrote about early St. Louis, is dubious. He was writing from a vantage point many decades later, by which time steamboats were plying the Mississippi River and St. Louis had become the grand riverine entrepôt of the American West. Chouteau's famous "Journal" has drawn a great deal of attention; it is the fountainhead from which most all interpretation of St. Louis's early years has flowed.[5] But his account must be viewed with an appropriately skeptical eye and used gingerly. The "Journal" is not a daily record of events as that name suggests, but rather a hodgepodge of souvenirs of events long past.[6] Moreover, Chouteau's narrative was fabled by a person who had a personal stake in construing history to cast a favorable light on himself, and on his stepfather, Pierre Laclède Liguest; it is a brief with an argument and a thesis rather than a disinterested source. Based on more reliable manuscript sources, this book posits that others, especially Commandant Louis St. Ange de Bellerive and royal notary Joseph Labuxière, were more important than either Laclède or Chouteau during St. Louis's earliest years.

⚜ ⚜ ⚜ ⚜

St. Ange de Bellerive looms large in part 1 of this book. Although consistently obscured by the long shadows of Laclède and Chouteau, he was demonstrably more important than they to St. Louis during the critical period 1765–70. As military commandant, he provided law and order and stability to a frontier settlement that was French, roots and branches, although technically situated in Spanish territory. St. Ange was an agent of European empires, first French and then Spanish, but no evidence exists that he viewed himself as an actor on a world stage. Étienne Veniard de Bourgmont, the explorer and adventurer whom St. Ange met when he was a youth, was motivated (as La Salle had earlier been) by grandiose visions of his own importance in global affairs; St. Ange was not. St. Ange resided for more than a half century in Louisiana but never once visited New Orleans, much less France. He was a public servant who served the public under his regional command, yet it was never far from his mind that he, and his ceremonial sword, represented the Bourbon monarchies of France and Spain in the upper Mississippi River valley.

Joseph Labuxière served as St. Ange's right-hand man in governing Upper Louisiana. For years they worked in tandem on a daily basis, although we have no evidence about their personal relationship. As a traditional military man, St. Ange may have had contempt for Labuxière as a learned scrivener; on the other hand, Labuxière may have smugly sneered at St. Ange's lack of book learning—indeed, his semiliteracy. But they depended upon one another and, from all evidence, worked smoothly together as a governing team. Labuxière looms large in part 2 of this book, for as royal notary he drafted the vast majority of the manuscripts upon which each chapter is based. Labuxière was unusually busy, and an unusually large number of manuscripts that he drafted have survived. His body of work constitutes an indispensable reservoir of sources for early St. Louis history.

St. Louis is the focus of this book, but it is not a narrow focus. Rather, we explore the importance of St. Ange and Labuxière within the larger context of Illinois Country history and society, how these men rose to prominence in a French colony that had existed for more than a half century before St. Louis came into being. Yet it is not our intention to fatuously replace shopworn heroes with newly burnished ones; as important as St. Ange and Labuxière were, that would simply not do. We therefore strive to bring to life scores of other persons, many of whom have never before appeared in any history book but who nevertheless played important roles in early St. Louis. This approach means that chapter 6 is dominated by woodcutters, carpenters, cabinetmakers, and stonemasons; chapter 7 is more concerned with women and children than with adult males; chapter 8 is about the one-fourth of the village's population, African and Indian, that was enslaved; chapter 9 presents windows, via material possessions, into the daily lives of a broad spectrum of early St. Louis denizens—from the most humble to the most well-to-do; and chapter 10 describes the many heretofore obscure men who initiated the fur trade that emanated from St. Louis. Our intention in these chapters is to arouse in the reader's imagination the warp and woof of village life—the sights, sounds, odors, the small triumphs and frequent tribulations—in a way that a top-down account of the "great men" who governed the settlement could never do.

The moral issue of colonization quietly suffuses our entire text; indeed, it must do so. If state-sponsored colonialism as an exploitative enterprise is reprehensible, morally wrong, we nevertheless accept the human claims of French colonists in the Illinois Country as equally valid as those of neighboring Indians, many of whom had only recently arrived in the region.[7] Nelson Mandela's moral and political greatness inheres in the fact that he understood Boers to be just as South African as Zulus or Xhosas. Indeed, the vast majority of Indians who inhabited the middle Mississippi River valley considered French settlers and traders to be just as indigenous as themselves, and they proclaimed as much, repeatedly, in council meetings (as discussed in chapter 3).

This book is about the Mississippi River frontier during the mid–eighteenth century. But it has little to do with Frederick Jackson Turner's paradigm of a linear frontier, with a phalanx of white settlers marching across the face of North America, inexorably pushing the line of settlement farther and farther

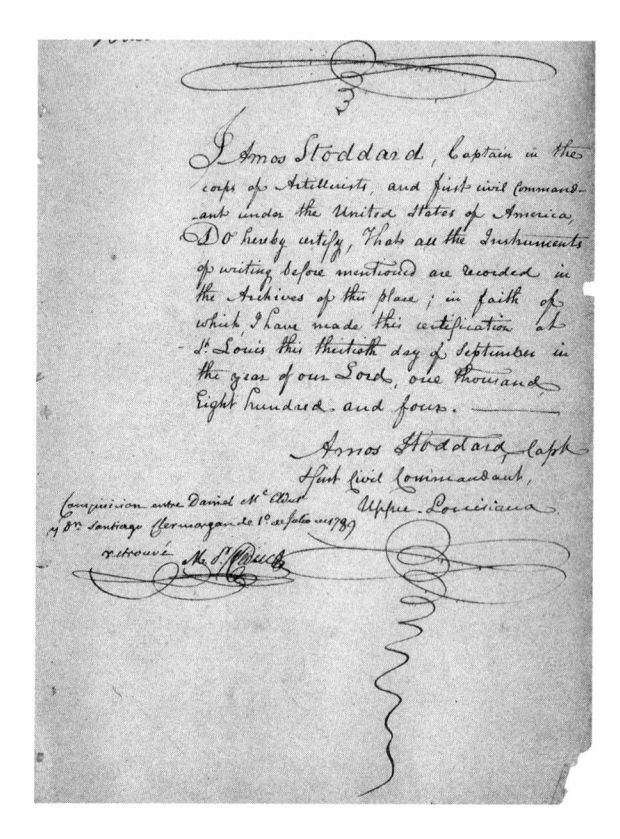

Captain Amos Stoddard arrived at St. Louis in March 1804 to take command of Upper Louisiana on behalf of the United States. In this memorandum, he discusses the archives, now largely housed at the Missouri History Museum, that form the basis of much of the following book. Courtesy of the Missouri History Museum, St. Louis.

west as they pursued cheap land and more abundant lives. French colonists pursued land, to be sure, but the cluster of settlements in the Illinois Country represented a *zone* of development rather than a *line*.⁸ And this zone of colonization, although expanding during the course of the eighteenth century, did not move appreciably farther west, other than that in 1800 French traders were penetrating somewhat farther up the Missouri River than they had been during the 1720s.

Throughout the eighteenth century, the Illinois Country zone of settlement was in constant, intimate contact with other North American zones of settlement. First was the geographically diffuse but ubiquitous zone represented by myriad Indian nations; then, other francophone zones existed, in Canada (especially Montreal and Detroit) and along the Gulf Coast (especially Mobile and New Orleans); and finally, by the end of the century, there was a new zone defined geographically by the Ohio River valley. This *zone* had been created as Turner's *line* of American settlement crossed the Appalachians and moved down the Ohio Valley following the American Revolution. During much of the eighteenth century, Kaskaskia was indisputably the hub of the Illinois Country zone, with the largest population, the most productive agriculture, and the most vibrant commerce. Following its founding in 1764,

St. Louis grew slowly, surpassing Ste. Genevieve (founded ca. 1750), its sister trans-Mississippian village, by 1790 and rivaling Kaskaskia in size and importance by 1800. But this book is about the deep background, the seeds, and the infancy of St. Louis. And our story about early St. Louis must begin a half century before the village was settled, must begin with the French Canadian Grotton–St. Ange family, how it arrived and then thrived in the Illinois Country during the first half of the eighteenth century. Chapter 1 is devoted exclusively to this family, focusing on Robert Grotton de St. Ange during the era before his son Louis St. Ange de Bellerive rose to prominence, eventually to become the region's most imposing figure and first commandant at St. Louis.

PART I

*St. Ange de Bellerive
and the Illinois Country*

CHAPTER 1

Fort d'Orléans and the Grotton–St. Ange Family

The Padoucas spread a bison robe on the ground and placed M. de Bourgmont on it with his son, M. de St. Ange, and M. La Renaudière. Fifteen men then bore them to the dwelling of the head chief.

—Philippe de La Renaudière, 1724

Louis St. Ange de Bellerive first came to prominence under the sponsorship of his father, Robert Grotton–St. Ange, a humbly born and illiterate Frenchman. This book asserts that the Grotton–St. Ange family was the most important political and military family in Upper Louisiana for the half century between 1720 and 1770. Although never before made, this assertion is not controversial because not enough has been written about this family to provoke debate; confusion rather than controversy tends to characterize the history of the Grotton–St. Anges in the Illinois Country.[1] Robert Grotton (his spelling, but also given as Groton or Groston) was born ca. 1665 in eastern France, in the picturesque town of Châtillon-sur-Seine in the Côte d'Or region of northern Burgundy.[2] Robert's father, Jean Grotton, was a master baker, although Robert, who persistently aspired to higher status, identified his father as "captain of the hunt for the royal waters and forests."[3] This was a fabricated title that had a vaguely aristocratic ring to it, conveying a sense of a rural aristocracy inhabiting a noble French landscape of woods and rivers. Robert immigrated to Canada at an early age, likely as a teenager, and quickly took up the military life as a way to advance himself and make his way in the New World. By 1686 he had attained the rank of sergeant and acquired the nickname St. Ange, meaning that he was called Robert Grotton *dit* St. Ange. This was slowly transmogrified into *de* St. Ange, putting a distinctly aristocratic spin on it that had no basis in his bloodlines.

Robert married Marguerite-Louise Crevier, widow of Laurent Beaudet in 1688, and the couple settled down at La Prairie, near Montreal. Although they experienced five barren years (1688–93), they finally produced eight children in less than ten years of childbearing. The formidable fertility of French Canadians, which produced more children than the harsh conditions and tenuous agriculture of the St. Lawrence Valley could sustain, was a major engine behind Canadian emigration to the Mississippi Valley.[4] Marguerite died in 1707, leaving Robert with a house full of children to feed and raise, which he seems to have done in an entirely responsible fashion. The selfless shouldering of responsibility was a hallmark of the Grotton–St. Ange family, and this characteristic would ultimately have major consequences for the frontier community of St. Louis.

After a decade of life as a widower tending to his children, Robert Grotton took a second wife, Élisabeth Chorel, the sixteenth of eighteen children produced by François Chorel and his wife, Marie-Anne Aubuchon, over a thirty-year period. Robert and Élisabeth married in March 1718, Élisabeth bringing into the marriage a "natural child," Jeanne, born only six months earlier, in September 1717.[5] Robert Grotton was a man with a highly developed sense of rectitude and honor, but taking for a wife a woman with Élisabeth's past (checkered by our standards but not necessarily by theirs) presented no obstacle to the marriage. If Élisabeth had made mistakes, Grotton knew human nature well enough not to dwell on them. Robert and Élisabeth were devoted to one another; she stuck by her man, and he by his woman, in settings and situations quite unimaginable to us.

By the time that Robert and Élisabeth signed their marriage contract (a prenup in modern American parlance) in March 1718 in the Montreal parish of Ville Marie, Robert's name had evolved from Grotton *dit* St. Ange to Grotton *de* St. Ange (see illustration). Despite this aristocratic affectation, however, Robert was still, after some thirty years in service, frozen in rank as sergeant in the French marines. Promotion to commissioned officer status was difficult in Canada for a man who had no certifiable noble lineage. This may well have been the reason that Robert chose to head West, where the *Pays d'en Haut* provided a more fluid social structure that would give him opportunities for advancement not available in the St. Lawrence Valley. Grotton chose wisely, as he most always did.

In the spring of 1721, we find Robert Grotton at Fort St. Joseph on the St. Joseph River, which flows into Lake Michigan from the southeast. This small French fort cum trading post was located where Niles, Michigan, now stands, and during the past quarter century historians and archaeologists have explored the site in remarkable detail.[6] On April 17, 1721, the stalwart Élisabeth Chorel Grotton, who had accompanied her husband westward through Canadian waterways, bore a son at Fort St. Joseph. The Grotton son was baptized François-Marie in honor of Élisabeth's father, François Chorel *dit* St. Romain, and Louis Grotton (Bellerive) stood as godfather.[7] But François-Marie did not survive the rigors of infancy in the wild place where he was born, and his

Robert Grotton de St. Ange's marriage contract with his second wife, Élisabeth Chorel, was signed and the marriage performed at Montreal in March 1718. Shortly thereafter, the couple, accompanied by Robert's two sons (Pierre and Louis) by his first wife, headed west to establish the St. Anges as a leading family in the Illinois Country. Kaskaskia Manuscripts, Randolph County Courthouse, Chester, Illinois.

baptismal record is the sole surviving document pertaining to his short life. Grotton St. Ange met Pierre-François Xavier de Charlevoix, the Jesuit father and famous epistolary, at St. Joseph. Charlevoix arrived there in August 1721 and remarked that "there is a commandant and a small garrison. The commandant's house, which is a very small affair, is called the fort because it is surrounded with a shoddy palisade."[8] No commissioned officers were posted at St. Joseph at the time, and it seems likely that St. Ange, as a senior sergeant, was in fact the commandant mentioned by Charlevoix and that the "fort" was the structure in which Élisabeth bore her son in April 1721.[9]

Charlevoix, a metropolitan Frenchman, regarded Canadians as a distinct species of human being, not quite French and not quite Indian. He posed the rhetorical question whether they had the mental capacity to engage in serious intellectual activities and was perhaps a bit taken aback by Grotton's gruff speech and illiteracy. Nevertheless, Canadians, even transplanted ones like Grotton, had certain virtues, of which Charlevoix had urgent need on his travels through the treacherous western waterways. He allowed that "their agility and dexterity are unequalled; the most skillful Indians do not handle their canoes better in the most dangerous rapids, and are not better marksmen."[10] In his travels on western waterways, Charlevoix required Canadian guides, and Grotton St. Ange evidently joined the Jesuit's entourage at Fort St. Joseph. Charlevoix wrote from Kaskaskia in October 1721 that he was accompanied by a well-armed and well-commanded escort, of which St. Ange was the commander.[11]

When St. Ange, his wife, and children left Fort St. Joseph and headed south via the Illinois and Mississippi Rivers to Kaskaskia, they had effected the transition from Upper Canada (*le Pays d'en Haut*) to Upper Louisiana (*le Pays des Illinois*). Robert and two of his sons (Pierre and Louis) would rise to positions of prominence there, and both Robert and his (second) wife, Élisabeth Chorel, would die and be buried there. That a man could manage successfully to accomplish this transition at what was for that time advanced middle age (probably fifty-five years) tells us that in the person of Robert Grotton de St. Ange, we are dealing with a man of remarkable vigor and determination.

⚜ ⚜ ⚜ ⚜

Jacques Marquette and Louis Jolliet were the first explorers to be captivated by the drama and mystery of the Missouri River. Passing the river's mouth in June 1673, Marquette remarked that "sailing quietly in clear and calm Water, we heard the noise of a rapid, into which we were about to run. I have seen nothing more dreadful. An accumulation of large and entire trees, branches, and floating islands, was issuing from The mouth of The river pekistanouï [Missouri], with such impetuosity that we could not without great danger risk passing through it. So great was the agitation that the water was very muddy, and could not become clear."[12] A decade later, Robert Cavelier de La Salle passed the mouth of the Missouri on his way to the Gulf of Mexico, and a member of his party commented that "we camped . . . close to a river that flows into the Mississippi and that makes it very turbulent and muddy. This river is called the Missouri and it flows out of the northwest. According to the Indians the valley is well populated, and the Panis live on this river a long way from its mouth."[13] The Panis (Pawnees) were already of special interest because they so often were caught up in the Indian slave trade.[14] Today, on satellite maps, the image of the Missouri as it flows into the Mississippi is much the same as seventeenth-century Frenchmen described it, the Mississippi running clear and the Missouri impenetrable with suspended sediments.

Étienne Veniard de Bourgmont (he signed this way, although the name sometimes appears as Bourgmond or Bourgmon) first ascended the Missouri River valley in 1714, the first known white man to do so. The presence of his outsize personality constituted something approaching an invasion of the valley. Bourgmont was one of the more flamboyant and fantastical characters to appear in colonial French North America, a region that was richly endowed with such larger than life individuals. Bourgmont was born in Normandy in 1679 and immigrated to Canada when he was about twenty years of age. All of the usual clichés—or perhaps truisms—that are generally applied to *coureurs de bois* apply to Bourgmont: adventuresome, restless, fearless, indefatigable, dissolute, but with Bourgmont there was also high intelligence and noble ambition. For four years, 1714–18, he lived in the Missouri River valley and drafted two lengthy reports that are replete with amateurish but valuable geographic and ethnographic information. He became an intimate of the Missouri Indians, resided for extended periods in one of their villages on the Missouri River, and fathered a son by a Missouri woman.[15]

By 1720 Bourgmont was back in France, which was then ruled by the regent, Philippe duc d'Orléans, on behalf of the minor king Louis XV. At the time, greater Louisiana was controlled by the Indies Company, with which Bourgmont contracted to return to the Missouri River valley as leader of a major expedition. Jean-Baptiste Le Moyne de Bienville was governor of Louisiana, and he explained that Bourgmont had "a commission as commandant and was under orders from His Highness the Regent to establish an outpost with the Missouris in order to reconcile, if possible, the Padouca [Plains Apache] tribe,[16] allies of the Spaniards in New Mexico, with the Missouris,"[17] and therefore with the French. This geopolitical issue had taken on increasing urgency as a consequence of the 1720 Villasur expedition into what is now Nebraska. Although Pawnees and Otos (perhaps aided by French traders) destroyed most of Villasur's command, this expedition reminded French officials of the frightening reach of Spanish ambitions on the western plains.[18] The vertiginous scope of Bourgmont's western ambitions as outlined in this letter is breathtaking. It possesses all the grandiosity of many of the regent's initiatives, which included John Law's risky financial schemes.[19] Bourgmont's expedition was destined to be Bourbon France's most ambitious attempt to stake out a permanent position in the remote trans-Mississippian West, out as far as the ninety-fifth meridian.

On February 1, 1723, Governor Bienville explained that Bourgmont was about to leave New Orleans with "a company of infantry, rations, munitions and merchandise to *endeavor* to fulfill his mission,"[20] Bienville's choice of words revealing that he was not terribly sanguine about the mission's chance of success. Bourgmont's convoy apparently arrived at Fort de Chartres in July, when Bourgmont's name appeared in a minor commercial transaction.[21] During his sojourn at the fort, Bourgmont strategized with the commandant, Pierre Dugué de Boisbriant, and discussed the impending western expedition. It was at that point that the trajectory of Bourgmont's life intersected that of Robert St. Ange's. Perhaps Boisbriant encouraged Bourgmont to add St. Ange to his entourage, but, in any case, St. Ange's association with Bourgmont during the following two years was fraught with significance for the history of the Illinois Country.[22] Bourgmont proceeded on up the Mississippi from Fort de Chartres to Cahokia, where he recruited Jean-Paul Mercier for the Missouri campaign. Mercier was a priest from the Seminary of Foreign Missions in Quebec, and he was head of the growing mission establishment at Cahokia. Bourgmont's determination to recruit Mercier, as well as Mercier's willingness to join the expedition, demonstrate that the proposed fort in the Missouri River valley was intended to be a substantive undertaking, the creation of a potentially permanent outpost that required a resident priest. Mercier remarked, without elaborating, that Bourgmont had "done so much for us that we could not refuse his request to have one of us [missionaries] ascend the Missouri with him and his garrison."[23]

Bourgmont spent roughly two months (July and August) in the Illinois Country before heading for the Missouri River valley. His overweening confidence that he could master that feral environment and engineer a lasting and ecumenical peace between Bourbon France and various Indian tribes bordered on the pathological. A band of Missouri Indians descended the rivers to meet with Bourgmont at Fort de Chartres, clearly revealing the affection with which the Missouris held the Frenchman. Something (perhaps a latitudinarian Roman Catholicism) in Bourgmont's upbringing in an ancient provincial family at Cerisy Belle-Etoile in central Normandy had endowed him with astonishing cross-cultural skills.[24] The Missouris presented Bourgmont with a female Indian slave as a welcoming gift, and a question arose as to whether she might be a Padouca (Plains Apache). In keeping with the French intention of establishing a lasting peace with the Padoucas, Illinois commandant Boisbriant had expressly prohibited trading in slaves from that tribe. Bourgmont explained that the confusion of mutually unintelligible languages made it impossible to determine from which tribe she had come, but, knowing that the Missouris were not at war with the Padoucas at that time (summer 1723), he assumed that she was not a Padouca. In any case, Bourgmont decided to wash his hands of the matter. He bartered away the slave to local habitants (apparently at Chartres) in return for salt and flour that he needed for his impending expedition up the Missouri.[25]

French officials were in earnest about abolishing trade in Padouca slaves, and in 1724 Bourgmont went to some pains to return captured Padoucas to their tribe.[26] But over the long term, Boisbriant's prohibition on trading in Padouca slaves was not effectively enforced. More than a decade later, Governor-General Charles de la Boische de Beauharnois of Canada informed Pierre Diron d'Artaguiette, who would later succeed Robert St. Ange as commandant at Fort de Chartres, that if warfare between Padoucas and Panis resulted in producing Indian slaves for sale, it was permissible for Frenchmen to acquire them so long as the French had had nothing to do with instigating the warfare that produced the slaves.[27] Beauharnois's casuistic approach to the issue was not in keeping with the original intentions of Boisbriant and Bourgmont, who had wanted to eliminate Padouca slaves from the French market in order to maintain a durable western peace with the Padouca tribe. In the event, Padouca slaves continued to be present in Illinois Country villages, including St. Louis, throughout the colonial era.[28]

Bourgmont's western expedition included Frenchmen, Canadians, Louisiana-born Creoles (very few) from the Mississippi Valley, officers, soldiers, and *engagés*. The widely disparate backgrounds and social statuses of the men made Bourgmont's command a veritable nightmare. Two young gentlemen lieutenants, Jean Pradel de La Masse and Seimar de Belisle, caused Bourgmont endless grief as they bristled at having to take orders from one they deemed their social inferior. Three bateaux and an unknown number of pirogues constituted Bourgmont's convoy, which reached the principal Missouri Indian village on November 9, 1723. Lewis and Clark required only a month to get from their encampment at Wood River to the site on the Missouri River where James Mackay's map placed the remains of Bourgmont's fort. Clark was interested enough and knowledgeable enough to search for the site: "Mr. Mackey has Laid down the rems. [remains] of an old fort in this Prarie, which I cannot find."[29] But the Americans, with their main vessel under sail, moved up the lower Missouri more swiftly than Bourgmont, whose expedition likely required two months to arrive at the site selected for the fort.

The season was getting late, the cottonwoods already dropping their leaves, when the expedition arrived at the site that Bourgmont had selected.

The men quickly disembarked and began work on a fort, close to the left bank of the Missouri River. Like the recently founded city they had left in February, the fort was named Orléans in honor of the duke regent of France who had promoted the expedition. Although always mentioned in the same breath as Bourgmont, this fort is more appropriately associated with the St. Ange family. In many respects, the fort's story is that family's story during the entire time that the fort was occupied, 1723–36. Moreover, the family's association with the fort was the making of three military careers—those of Robert Grotton de St. Ange and two of his sons, Pierre St. Ange *fils* and Louis St. Ange de Bellerive.

Debate continues about the location of Fort d'Orléans, and the physical remains of the fort are one of the holy grails of Missouri archaeology. According to W. Raymond Wood, distinguished professor emeritus of anthropology at the University of Missouri, Columbia, the site has been pursued with energy and eagerness, and with all available instrumentation, not excluding coat hangers in the quivering hands of witching experts.[30] When even this avenue has been pursued and has failed, one must reluctantly conclude that the errant and voracious Missouri River has indeed swallowed up the hallowed remains of the first more or less permanent European establishment in what is now the state of Missouri.

Serving under Bourgmont were three lieutenants—Pradel, Belisle, and Grotton St. Ange, just recently promoted. The first two were minor French aristocrats, educated, willful, and persuaded that they were, by pedigree, better suited for command than Bourgmont. St. Ange had come up through the ranks the hard way; he was illiterate and, after a false start, utterly loyal to Bourgmont. In December 1723, Pradel and Belisle drafted a letter damning Bourgmont's leadership from every possible perspective, and they persuaded St. Ange to sign on to something he likely could not read. St. Ange was at first impressed by the young lieutenants, who were cocky and confident and had the social status that he lacked.

A few days later, in early January 1724, Bourgmont and St. Ange met face-to-face, probably in the cabin in the Missouri village where Bourgmont was recovering from his nagging illness. Out of this meeting emerged a letter, which Bourgmont addressed to "Messieurs," meaning the directors of the Indies Company in Paris; they, after all, had sponsored the expedition. Copies would also have gone to Governor Bienville in New Orleans and likely Boisbriant, commandant at Fort de Chartres. Bourgmont wrote that he was forwarding St. Ange's affidavit to demonstrate that St. Ange had been "solicited by messieurs Pradel and Belisle to sign a letter that was full of suppositions."[31] Bourgmont also noted that St. Ange had been caught off guard, "surprised" by Pradel and Belisle, who had persuaded him to sign the harsh letter criticizing Bourgmont's command. But, Bourgmont continued, St. Ange had immediately reconsidered what he had done and had come directly to Bourgmont to set matters right. Bourgmont's language makes it clear that St. Ange had taken the initiative to rectify the situation; that is, St. Ange had come to him.

This little episode at a remote outpost on the Missouri River provides great insight into St. Ange's character, as his brief, but soul-searching, affidavit attests:

> I, the undersigned, confess to have signed the letter that these messieurs [that is, Pradel and Belisle] wrote to Monsieur Bourgmont, dated December 31, 1723. I found myself unwittingly engaged in the matter, without having reflected sufficiently on the consequences, and I didn't want to disappoint them [Pradel and Belisle]. I recognized all this immediately after I had done it.
> Village of the Missouri, January 2, 1724, signed St. Ange[32]

St. Ange was a generation older than Pradel and Belisle, but they were the dashing young gentlemen from France; they were secure in their positions as officers, while St. Ange, who had spent more than thirty years as a sergeant, was not. But St. Ange was honest, with himself as well as with Bourgmont. He understood his error in judgment in trusting Pradel and Belisle; he understood that loyalty to the command, the commander, and the service was more important than loyalty to men who certainly would not have stood loyal to him. These were difficult issues for any man to face, but Grotton–St. Ange dug deep and met them squarely as a good soldier, and in so doing saved his career, as well as those of his sons Pierre and Louis. This had long-term consequences for the history of the American West, for Robert Grotton de St. Ange rose to become commandant at Fort de Chartres and son Louis St. Ange de Bellerive went on to replace his father at Fort d'Orléans, before becoming commandant at Vincennes on the Wabash (Ouabache), then interim commandant at Fort de Chartres (1764–65), and finally the anchor of St. Louis during the critical period of the town's infancy, 1765–70. In the short term, Pradel and Belisle utterly disappear from the Fort d'Orléans saga, and pretty much from Louisiana history, whereas St. Ange emerges from the turmoil and misery of the 1723–24 winter as indispensable to the fort and, longer term, of major importance to French Louisiana.

When Commandant Boisbriant at Fort de Chartres received written confirmation of the shenanigans and perfidy of Pradel and Belisle at the Missouri outpost, he immediately recalled them.[33] Once Bourgmont rid himself of these difficult lieutenants and recovered, for the time being, his health, things went better at Fort d'Orléans. There had been too many officers, which muddled the chain of command. With Pradel and Belisle thankfully gone, the chain became clear; from the top down, it was Commandant Bourgmont, Lieutenant St. Ange *père*, Sergeants Roch and Dubois, and Corporals Gilbert *dit* Rôtisseur[34] and Gentil, with the priest, Mercier, playing an important adjunct role, although outside the military chain of command. Problems, of course, continued to arise, as they necessarily would in the savage, tumultuous world of the upper Missouri. A Missouri Indian killed, for reasons unknown, a Frenchman of Bourgmont's party, and Bourgmont felt compelled to make an example of the guilty party. He arranged to have the Indian's own brother execute him in his own village by bow and arrow, "à coups de flèches."[35] If Bourgmont's account is true, this episode demonstrates beyond any doubt his extraordinary power and influence with the Missouri tribe.

In the spring of 1724, Boisbriant dispatched from Fort de Chartres a convoy of reinforcements for Fort d'Orléans. It carried much-needed supplies for Bourgmont's new outpost, but the particular personnel aboard the bateaux were striking and consequential. Included were Philippe de La Renaudière and the bulk of Robert Grotton St. Ange's household—Pierre St. Ange, Louis St. Ange de Bellerive, and Robert's second wife, the resilient Élisabeth Chorel.[36] These names reveal important things about what was going to transpire up the Missouri River valley. La Renaudière, a mining engineer with some geographical knowledge, could help navigate in the uncharted western regions where Bourgmont proposed to conduct his Indian diplomacy.[37] Moreover, the planned expedition to the Padoucas would be heading in a southwesterly direction, that is, toward the Spanish outpost at Santa Fe. Everyone knew about the rich silver mines near Santa Fe, but no one knew just how far away they were. In any case, La Renaudière could keep an eye peeled for prospective mining sites. As it turned out, La Renaudière's most important, by far the most important, contribution to the Bourgmont expedition and to history was the invaluable journal he kept.[38]

Ensign Pierre St. Ange and Cadet Louis Bellerive serving with their father, Lieutenant Robert St. Ange, gave the St. Ange family complete control (under Commandant Bourgmont) of the commissioned officer corps at Fort d'Orléans.[39] St. Ange *père* had proved his loyalty to Bourgmont in the showdown with Pradel and Belisle, and the St. Anges were being rewarded. But the rise of the St. Ange sons Pierre and Louis was not purely political, for they possessed indisputable attributes; they, like their father, were tough, smart, loyal, and familiar with, if not fluent in, Indian languages—just the sort of fellows whom Bourgmont needed to support his audacious push into the unknown West. Finally, there was the remarkable Élisabeth Chorel. Her arrival at the fort in the spring of 1724 reveals that the place was intended to be more or less a permanent affair, a veritable *établissement*, a French settlement as well as a military and trading outpost. She bore a daughter, Élisabeth, at the fort, and when this daughter married François Coulon de Villiers at Fort de Chartres in 1740, she was identified in her marriage contract as a "native of the fort of the Missouri, Archbishopric of Quebec."[40] Surely, Bishop Jean-Baptiste de la Croix Chevrière de St. Vallier

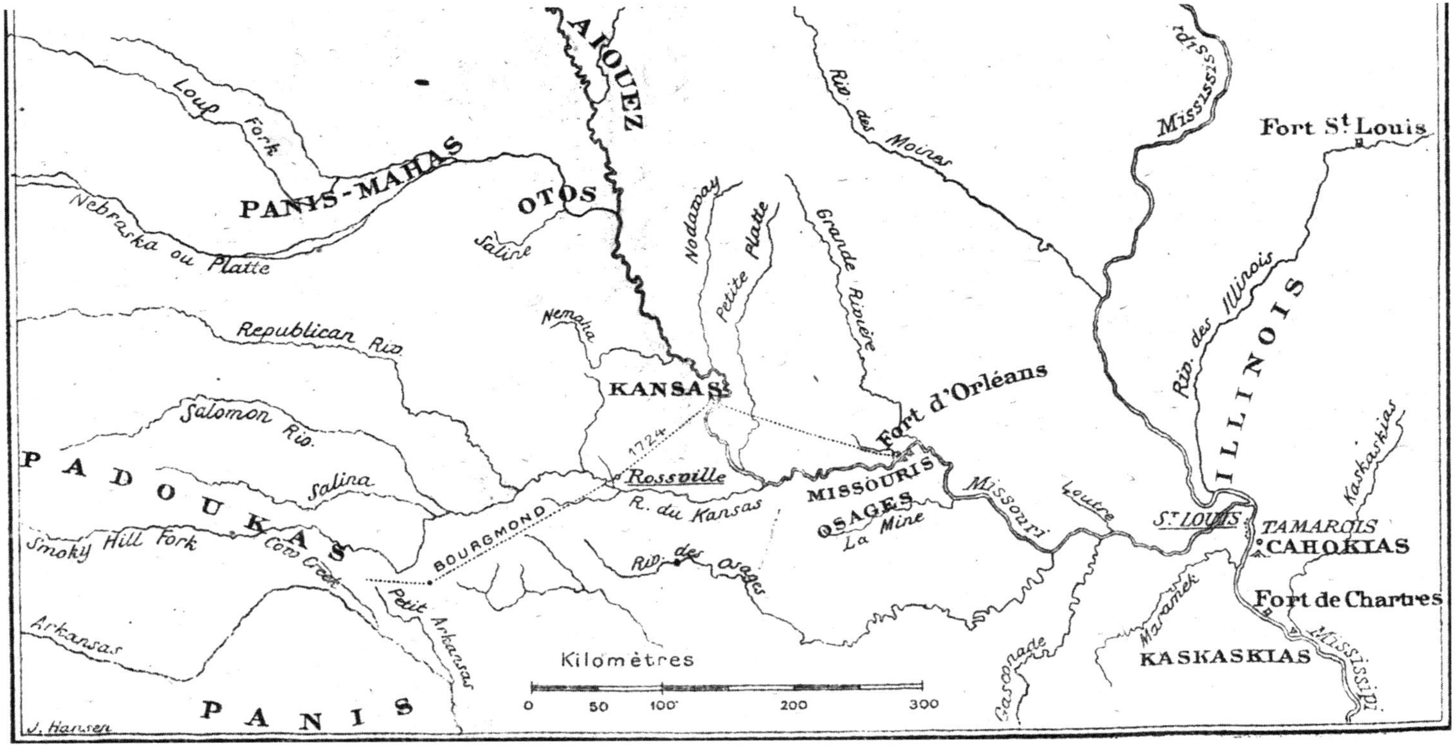

Étienne Veniard Bourgmont's Fort d'Orléans and the approximate route of his peacemaking expedition to the Padoucas (Plains Apaches) in 1724. St. Louis is depicted only as a later reference point. Reproduced from Marc Villiers du Terrage, La Découverte du Missouri et l'histoire du Fort d'Orléans, 1673–1728 (Paris: H. Champion, 1925).

in Quebec had no idea that his authority extended out to the ninety-fifth West meridian, a thousand trackless miles from Quebec City.

Between June and October 1724, two expeditions thrust westward from Fort d'Orléans in search of the main body of Padoucas. Peace with that tribe was the principal goal of Bourgmont's expedition, for that would facilitate French trading ventures in the Far West and help check Spanish advances from the southwest. On both occasions, Robert St. Ange *père* remained behind, being left in command at the fort. His older son Pierre played a major role in both expeditions, while the younger son Louis (Bellerive) was active during the first expedition but remained behind with his father during the second.[41] The first expedition was forced to turn back because Bourgmont's illness, which he had been fighting all year, became too much to cope with. But on October 18, 1724, Bourgmont's party of seventeen Frenchmen and twenty-four Indians (Padoucas, Kansas, Missouris, and several Otos and Iowas) finally reached their objective, a major Padouca encampment in what is now central Kansas (see map). From Paris, where Bourgmont had sworn he could do it, he had traversed—by land, sea, and rivers—more than four thousand miles. *Heroic* is surely not too strong a word for what he had accomplished, against long odds and while often wracked with fever. According to La Renaudière's journal, a bit improbable in this passage, Bourgmont, his *métis* son, Pierre St. Ange, and La Renaudière himself were ceremonially borne on a single bison robe to the dwelling of the principal Padouca chief.[42] On the expansive western plains, both bison robes and fables assumed large proportions.

Bourgmont's party spent four glorious days with the Padoucas, in fine autumnal weather, feasting and exchanging gifts and speeches. Multitudinous trade goods had been transported across the Atlantic from France to New Orleans, and from there laboriously carried by river and land out to the western plains. Despite some peripheral contact with Spaniards in New Mexico, the Padoucas were a technologically primitive people, and the metal items brought by Bourgmont—fusils, axes, hatchets, knives—captivated them. In return, the French got horses and hand-worked turquoise objects, but slaves were not mentioned. Slaves were the most valuable commodity that western tribes had to offer the French. If the Padoucas possessed slaves from western tribes (Panis, Wichitas, Arikaras, for example) that were not part of the French-sponsored alliance, none were offered as gifts. All in all, it seems as though the Padoucas got the better deal in the exchange of material things. But from Bourgmont's perspective, he received the most precious gift of all—promises from the Padoucas that they would remain at peace forever with the French and with all French allies among the western tribes. Bourgmont was serving the aggressive colonial interests of the Bourbon monarchy, but, at the same time, no doubt exists that he was at heart a peacemaker, a visionary, and a diplomat, not a warrior.[43]

Leaving the Apache encampment on October 22, and traveling more lightly than on the outgoing trip, Bourgmont's party proceeded rapidly back toward Fort d'Orléans across sun-drenched grasslands; the Frenchmen had never seen horse country the likes of it. Upon reaching the Missouri River, some members of the party fabricated skin boats ("bullboats")[44] on the spot and proceeded downriver to the fort. Pierre St. Ange commanded a mounted contingent that swam their horses across the Missouri and then proceeded to the fort down the left bank of the river. As Bourgmont approached the fort, St. Ange *père* and Bellerive had welcoming shots fired with fusils and cannons, according to La Renaudière. On November 15, Bourgmont had twelve Frenchmen sign a sworn affidavit that they had truly accompanied him on his fantastical journey to the Padoucas. Their experiences had indeed been stranger than fiction, and Bourgmont wanted them certified as reality, a peculiarly French colonial kind of reality. Pierre St. Ange as "adjutant," that is, second in command on the expedition, signed first, followed by La Renaudière.[45]

November 1724 at Fort d'Orléans saw the reunion of all members of the St. Ange family—Robert and his wife, Élisabeth Chorel, and his two sons Pierre and Louis by his first wife. They constituted the first family of the fort (Bourgmont not having one, other than his *métis* son), and they would have attended *en famille* the Te Deum mass celebrated by the Reverend Jean-Paul Mercier in his small chapel at the fort. No such mass had ever been celebrated by Frenchmen in North America that far west. The entire St. Ange family as described above remained at Fort d'Orléans when Bourgmont departed, and the fort was commanded by one or another member of the family until 1736.[46] During that time period, Fort d'Orléans served as the nerve center for French outreach and diplomacy with the western Indian tribes. This deep experience with and expertise in Indian affairs advanced the careers of the Grotton–St. Anges from the 1720s right on through the 1760s.

Bourgmont's last presence at Fort d'Orléans came on November 19, 1724, when a council of Missouris, Osages, and Otos met to agree on dispatching tribal emissaries to France with Bourgmont. The Missouris would send four chiefs and "the daughter of the great chief." The Osages also sent four chiefs and the Otos one. A convoy set off down the Missouri River from Fort d'Orléans immediately after the council, and Bourgmont's descent to the Illinois Country and then New Orleans proceeded with astonishing speed. Stopping briefly at Kaskaskia to pick up the Jesuit father Ignace Beaubois and five Illinois Indian chiefs, Bourgmont proceeded rapidly down the Mississippi to New Orleans. The end of the Bourgmont saga—his arrival in Paris with his Indian entourage and his eventual retirement to his family estate at Cerisy Belle-Étoile in Normandy—is utterly fascinating, but it has been told by Norall and others and is not germane to the remainder of the Grotton–St. Ange story.[47]

While posted at the remote Fort d'Orléans during the late 1720s, the St. Anges almost disappear from Illinois Country records, both civil and religious. But they sometimes emerge from obscurity in unexpected and sumptuous fashion. By letter Marie-Françoise, widow of Joseph Lamy, agreed to sell to "Monsieur [Robert] St. Ange, officer of the troops and commandant in the Missouri," the following items: "a complete woman's dress made of striped satin and lined with rose colored taffeta; a pair of silk stockings, slippers and a pair of fingerless gloves [mitaines],"[48] all for the price of eight hundred livres in peltries, which St. Ange promised to pay one year later, in October 1726. Joseph Lamy had served as head church warden of the parish of the Immaculate Conception in Kaskaskia but was "killed by a party of enemies [that is, Fox Indians] two steps from the village," in May 1725.[49] His widow, Marie-Françoise, faced uncertain prospects after the death of her husband, and she had three children plus a nephew in her household.[50] Although she later remarried, she did the responsible, though painful, thing as a newly widowed woman and chose to sell her finery in order to support herself and her family.

Commandants at frontier outposts were usually licensed to trade as a way to supplement their meager salaries, and it is apparent that St. Ange *père* made good use of his position at Fort d'Orléans.[51] St. Ange's wife, Élisabeth Chorel, would be attired in apparel worth as much as a modest dwelling house in the village of Kaskaskia at the time,[52] and thus adorned she could promenade along the bank of the Missouri River at Fort d'Orléans, watching feathered Missouris ride by, with mutual gazes of wonderment passing between Indians and the French woman. The Missouri River valley had never before witnessed such a scene. Sophie White has recently remarked that "colonists deployed clothing to uphold the fiction of a French moral and social order in the colony, allowing them to exert control over the hinterlands in a potentially dangerous and alien environment not yet subsumed to colonial rule."[53] Mme. St. Ange would have been baffled at the suggestion that she was "deploying" her satin, taffeta, and silk clothing for fictional purposes, for as a good French woman, she simply delighted in the touch of fine fabrics on her skin. In any case, St. Ange kept his promise, and in October 1726 the eight hundred livres in peltries were duly delivered to widow Lamy's new husband, Jean-Baptiste Lasource,[54] whom Marie-Françoise had married the previous March.[55] Lasource was a recently arrived Canadian who was willing to take on major family responsibilities right from the day of his marriage to the widowed mother.[56]

Indeed, as commandant at Fort d'Orléans, Grotton St. Ange carved out a veritable fiefdom on the bank of the Missouri River for himself and his wife during the mid-1720s. An illiterate former sergeant had risen into the officer ranks, and by virtue of his loyalty and service to Bourgmont had succeeded him as commandant at the fort. He lived there as lord and master of the manor. If Élisabeth wore fancy French clothes, Robert washed down his bison steak or short ribs with red wine transported from France.[57] Indian slaves from western tribes served Élisabeth and Robert as domestic servants, but the extent to which they affected daily life in the Grotton–St. Ange household cannot be determined.[58] As a youth and a commoner, St. Ange had observed how aristocrats lived in France, and now, by God, four thousand miles away in the remote Missouri River valley he was living like one—albeit in a landscape that bore little resemblance to his native Burgundy, with its carefully cultivated fields. For several years, St. Ange rarely left his comfortable, though remote, command post at Fort d'Orléans, and his sons Pierre and Louis were stationed there as well. Pierre was present at Fort de Chartres in October 1726, and he must then have delivered the peltries that his father had promised in payment for Élisabeth Chorel's rich attire.[59]

Robert St. Ange (accompanied by Élisabeth Chorel) and son Pierre came down to Fort de Chartres in 1727 to serve under Commandant Charles-Henri de Liette—Robert as lieutenant and Pierre as ensign.[60] This left Louis St. Ange de Bellerive in command at Fort d'Orléans with a token garrison of eight men, as well as the chaplain, Jean-Paul Mercier, who remained there for some years. Governor Étienne Périer was hoping that "the missionary could make some progress in preaching the gospels to the Indians." In April 1729, Périer wrote to Versailles that he had ordered the Missouri post abandoned because it was costing the Indies Company too much to maintain and was no longer of any real value.[61] The original purpose of Bourgmont's Fort d'Orléans had been as a diplomatic base for negotiating an enduring peace in the Missouri River valley, with the goal of facilitating western trade and commerce. This, according to Périer, had been achieved, and in truth Bourgmont's diplomatic initiatives had been astonishingly successful, at least in the short run. All the tribes of that "province" were at peace with one another and with the French. Moreover, the route up the Missouri Valley to Fort d'Orléans, "where all our men have been killed," was costly to defend;[62] Périer was referring to the deaths of lieutenants Pierre Mélique and Nicolas de Franchomme and their men, killed respectively in 1727 and '28 in expeditions against the Foxes. But, despite what Périer wrote, Fort d'Orléans was not abandoned at this time, and Bellerive maintained a St. Ange presence there until 1736, when he was brought down to become commandant on the Wabash.[63]

Services that the St. Anges rendered at Fort d'Orléans were important, but the St. Ange name rose to special prominence in the Illinois Country as a consequence of the Fox wars. The tenacity and audacity of the Foxes in opposing French colonization of the Midwest had been remarkable, but the fierce and independent Foxes had also made enemies with other tribes. In

1729 Chippewas, Ottawas, Winnebagos, and Menominees attacked Fox villages in what is now southern Wisconsin, killing scores of men, women, and children. Weakened and seemingly at violent odds with everyone, the Foxes (they called themselves Mesquakie, people of the red earth) in 1730 decided to flee eastward, hoping to find refuge with the Iroquois and the English. In June three hundred warriors and six hundred women and children moved southeastward out of the mixed hardwood forests north of the Illinois River to the high-grass prairie of what is now east-central Illinois.[64]

The French and their Indian allies—including Mascoutens, Kickapoos, Piankashaws, and Illinois—were, in the meantime, preparing a mortal blow against the Foxes.[65] Robert Grotton St. Ange (who had replaced de Liette as commandant at Fort de Chartres) advanced northward up the Illinois River valley, while Nicolas-Joseph des Noyelles came west from the Miami Post (later Fort Wayne) and Nicolas-Antoine Coulon de Villiers[66] south from Fort St. Joseph (southeast of Lake Michigan). The three French commanders, all accompanied by their respective Indian entourages from various tribes, converged on the Foxes in August 1730. A French officer reported several months later from Quebec that Monsieur de St. Ange had ninety Frenchmen (that is, royal marines and militia men) and three hundred Indians under his command, which would have made St. Ange's contingent the largest of total allied forces.[67]

The siege on the Illinois prairie drew to its inevitable and dreadful conclusion on September 9, 1730. A dark, rainy night persuaded the Foxes to risk a desperate breakout from their fort. It did not work. They were immediately tracked down, mostly by Indian allies of the French, "who were fresher and more vigorous" than the starving Foxes.[68] A slaughter ensued, and hundreds of men, women, and children were butchered, with only a few Fox warriors escaping. Captured Foxes (mostly women and children) were divided among the victorious tribes and then either enslaved or burned alive. No more doleful event has ever transpired within the territory that now constitutes the state of Illinois. Pierre-François Xavier de Charlevoix, a humane and intelligent Jesuit priest, later commented that St. Ange had "very much distinguished himself against the Foxes."[69] This remark was made a world-remove away, in Paris, and one wonders how Charlevoix would have felt about things had he been witness to that dark and sanguinary night on the Illinois prairie. In any case, his remark reveals how embittered the French, even the most cosmopolitan and civilized of the French, had become about the Foxes.

When, from their headquarters at the Hôtel Tubeuf in Paris, the directors of the Indies Company assessed Robert Grotton de St. Ange, they noted that he had helped defeat the Foxes and that he deserved to be treated with distinction.[70] In 1731 the company surrendered its Louisiana charter to the government of Louis XV, and for the duration of the French regime (that is, until 1762–63) Louisiana was a crown colony. St. Ange oversaw this transition in the Illinois Country, and an inventory of the company's possessions in the Illinois Country was compiled in the summer of 1732.[71] These possessions consisted of Fort de Chartres, "tumbling in ruins," and associated buildings, arms, munitions, merchandise, and furniture.[72] Inside the fort was a large structure built of black walnut logs that was divided into two equal apartments, one for St. Ange and one for his storekeeper. Each small apartment consisted of a living room, two bedrooms, and a kitchen, and was adorned with a walnut armoire, four *pieds* wide and eight high, shuttered with double doors. Madame Élisabeth Chorel St. Ange must have kept in their armoire the satin dress that Robert had purchased for her back in 1725. The St. Anges likely also had a more commodious residence outside the fort, for their household included six Indian slaves,[73] and they continued living at Chartres after Robert stepped down as commandant.

In July 1732, Commissaire-Ordonnateur Edme-Gatien Salmon wrote at length from New Orleans about the Illinois Country, expatiating on its virtues and its problems:

> The Illinois Post is rather considerable and becomes more so every day. I've learned that several families from Detroit have settled there. . . . Since the Illinois Country is fine and very fertile [*vivant*], it's not surprising that habitants from all regions have gathered there. In the last convoy, several voyageurs from New Orleans have gone up there, and I would not be in the least bit surprised if they decided to settle there, for that region is as easy to cultivate as this one is difficult. Moreover, a sort of freedom obtains there, for no stern officer maintains law and order. Sieur de St. Ange is a good officer, and he deserves credit for his services in the last war [against the Foxes]. All the officers in the colony speak well of him, but he's not really in command and everyone there is his own master. The *habitants* are insolent, for a sizeable proportion of them have had, and continue to have, [intimate] relations with the Indians. And this by necessity, for the voyageurs who settle there, not finding any women, have taken up with Indian girls. I've learned that these sorts of marriages have been authorized by the missionaries, who say there's no difference between an Indian and a white Christian.[74]

In short, Salmon thought that the Illinois Country had real potential, especially in the realm of agriculture, but that things were a bit out of control in the upper colony. Salmon was a stiff-necked French bureaucrat, and he thought that both civil and religious authorities, that is, Grotton St. Ange and the Jesuit missionaries, were too lax in exercising their authority. A larger military presence would be useful, and Salmon recommended establishing a major garrison of 250–300 men to keep a lid on things in Upper Louisiana, using Fort de Chartres as the principal base. During the autumn of 1732, St. Ange had a new, palisaded Fort de Chartres erected, based on plans drawn up by Philippe Renaut, the sometime mining engineer who also did surveying and drafting. Salmon described this fort as having a better defensive position, and it survived as the center of government in Illinois until the 1750s, when the stone version of the fort was built.[75] Over the twenty years following, the garrison at the fort was increased, agriculture flourished at the Illinois Country villages, and indispensable flour shipments to New Orleans grew apace.[76] The Illinois Country was the sine qua non of French Louisiana, and in no small measure the burden of responsibility for the region rested on the shoulders of the St. Anges.

Salmon, who never lived and breathed Louisiana beyond the confines of New Orleans, was profoundly ignorant about society in the Illinois Country. His premise that Frenchmen who married Indian women became "insolent," seemingly assuming some of the savagery of their *sauvagesse* wives, is dubious to the point of hilarity.[77] And after the 1720s, fewer Frenchmen in the Illinois Country married full-blooded Indian women, for more French and *métisse* women were available for matrimony, and these women had in effect been raised as French women. Indeed, just two months before Salmon bemoaned the sorry effects of mixed marriages in the Illinois Country, Pierre Grotton de St. Ange married Marie-Rose Tessier (or Texier), daughter of Louis

" On the 13th day of May, 1732, before us, notary in the Illinois, and the undersigned witnesses, appeared Mr. Pierre Grotton de St. Ange, officer of the troops detached from the marine serving in Louisiana, son of Sieur Robert Grotton de St. Ange, commandant in the Illinois, and Mme. Margaret Creine, his father and mother of the one part, and Marie Rose Tessier, daughter of the late Louis Tessier and Catharine Wabenaqueokoe, her father and mother of the other part, who by common accord and consent have made this agreement and convention of marriage, guided by the advice and counsel of their parents and friends here assembled in order to celebrate and solemnize before our mother, the holy church catholic, apostolic and Roman, as soon as it shall be advised by the aforesaid parents and friends, that is to say on the part of his friends Grotton du St. Ange his father, Mr. Robert Grotton Pierre du Bellerive, his brother Sieur Dutime, officer of the troops, and Sieur de St. Laurient; and on the part of Demoiselle Marie Rose Tessier, Mr. LaLande Le Jeune, her step-father; Mr. Lafatigue, her tutor. and Mr. Deucegentre, her assistant tutor. The aforesaid future spouses shall hold in community all goods movable and immovable, and acquisitions now held and to be acquired, according to the custom of the city, provost and viscompte of Paris.

As an article of historical curiosity, the New York Times *(July 30, 1876) published an English translation of the 1732 marriage contract between Pierre Grotton de St. Ange, older brother of Louis St. Ange de Bellerive, and Marie-Rose Tessier, an upper-class* métisse. *The unknown translator of the document erred in naming Pierre's brother Pierre rather than Louis. The original document has gone missing.*

Tessier and his wife, Catherine 8ebana8ic8e ("dawn-colored woman"), a full-blooded Illinois woman. This marriage, celebrated at Fort de Chartres in May 1732, brought the three Grotton–St. Ange men (father Robert and sons Pierre and Louis) together, Louis coming down to Chartres from Fort d'Orléans for the occasion of his brother's wedding.[78]

As commandant at Fort de Chartres, St. Ange was not quite so careless and lackadaisical as Salmon suggested. In the autumn of 1732, two members of the garrison at the fort, François Fretél *dit* Picard and Pierre Roston *dit* Langevin, got embroiled in a heated argument that turned violent. The fact that one was from Picardy and the other from Anjou (*Langevin* meaning "from Anjou"), which were different cultural regions where French was spoken quite differently, perhaps exacerbated the argument. In any case, the sad result was that Fretél shot Roston to death with a fusil at close range; powder burns were found on Roston's clothing. St. Ange ordered an extensive and detailed forensic investigation, one really worthy of comparison with a modern criminal justice process—extensive interrogations were conducted and depositions taken.[79] Finally, a war council was convened consisting of eight men, officers and soldiers, presided over by "Monsieur [Robert] de St. Ange commandant" and including "Sieur [Pierre] de St. Ange *fils* enseign." The French *Code Militaire* specified that war councils were supposed to be composed exclusively of officers,[80] but St. Ange had but few officers at his disposal, and he democratized his council by including enlisted men. In any case, this criminal case makes it apparent that St. Anges—Robert and Pierre, father and son—were the team that governed the Illinois Country during the early 1730s.

After a lengthy and solemn discussion led by St. Ange, the war council condemned Fretél to be "hung and strangled until dead." As a coup de grâce, Fretél's head would be smashed at 3:00 p.m. on October 16, 1732, outside the fort and in the presence of the troops assembled under arms. Executions having been extremely rare in the Illinois Country, there was no official executioner at Fort de Chartres to perform these unsavory but necessary tasks. However, if such an official had been present, Fretél would, as prescribed by French law, have been hideously tortured before being hung and strangled.[81] In this regard, the Illinois frontier, as violent and bloody as it was, was more sparing of human flesh than metropolitan France. Sergeant Hennequin (one of many Irishmen to serve the Roman Catholic king of France), a member of the war council, could not sign the mortal judgment document, but the other seven members of the council did, including the generally illiterate Robert de St. Ange *père*. This execution, one of the very few ever performed in the entire colonial history of the Illinois Country, cost the garrison at Fort de Chartres a treasure, its baker, for Fretél had occupied that position, and men from

Picardy, a bountiful wheat-producing region of northern France, were bakers by calling.

The Foxes to the north, having been mercilessly crushed in 1730, left the Chickasaws (occasionally allied with Natchez and Cherokees) to the south as the most intractable enemies of the French in Louisiana. In one important way, the Chickasaw threat to the French colonies in the Illinois Country was even more serious than that of the Foxes—the Chickasaws were provoked, and sometimes led, by British operatives, whose grand strategic plan was to seize control of the central Mississippi Valley and thereby sever the link between Louisiana and Canada. French overseas colonies were managed by the naval ministry (Ministère de la Marine), and in December 1735 Minister Jean-Frédéric Phélypeaux de Maurepas approved Louisiana governor Bienville's proposal to wage hot war against the Chickasaws.[82] The war's twin purposes were to thwart British encroachments from the east and keep the Mississippi River corridor safe for commerce between New Orleans and the Illinois Country. That commerce, with the transport of Illinois flour running south and European products north, was the lifeline of colonial Louisiana.[83]

In 1733 Pierre Diron d'Artaguiette replaced Grotton St. Ange as commandant at Fort de Chartres.[84] And after his father's retirement, Pierre St. Ange continued to serve under d'Artaguiette as a first lieutenant at the fort. Along with François-Marie de Vincennes, commandant on the Wabash, Pierre was a principal officer in the Illinois army that d'Artaguiette assembled early in 1736 for the Chickasaw campaign. The French grand strategy called for Governor Bienville to advance against the Chickasaws from Mobile and d'Artaguiette from Illinois, catching the Chickasaws between the respective French forces. D'Artaguiette's Illinois army consisted of 140 Frenchmen, 41 marines and 99 militiamen, in addition to 266 Indians, 190 Illinois and Miamis, 38 Iroquois and 38 Arkansas, making up a total force of 406.[85] The bitter enmity that generally characterized French-Iroquois relations did not prevent Iroquois splinter groups from attaching themselves to the French interest, from time to time.

D'Artaguiette's polyglot army proceeded down the Mississippi by bateaux and pirogues toward the end of February 1736. This flotilla was the largest armed force that the Mississippi Valley would witness during colonial times. The French and Indian warriors disembarked at Écores de Prudhomme (later called Chickasaw Bluffs, where Tennessee's Fort Pillow State Historic Park is now located)[86] on February 23 and two days later departed overland for the Chickasaw villages, some 60 leagues (perhaps 150 miles)[87] distant. The Illinois forces were supposed to meet up with Bienville's southern army of French and Choctaws coming north from Mobile, but this rendezvous was never effected—Bienville's army met defeat and d'Artaguiette's disaster quite independently of one another.

When Bienville appointed d'Artaguiette commandant at Fort de Chartres, he characterized him as "wise, judicious and of proven valor."[88] The last of these virtues prevailed when d'Artaguiette engaged the Chickasaws (supported by some Cherokees) at daybreak on March 25, not far from one of their villages. The Illinois and Miamis immediately panicked and fled the field of battle, leaving the French with their Arkansas and Iroquois allies to be either slaughtered or captured. Illinois Indians were natural and longtime allies of the French, but their loyalty and resolution could never be taken for granted. By nine in the morning, the French and their remaining Indian allies had been routed, and a score of captives—including d'Artaguiette, Pierre St. Ange, Vincennes, and the Jesuit father Antoine Sénat—were hauled off as trophies of war to the nearby Chickasaw village (near where Fulton, Mississippi, now stands). During the Chickasaws' victory celebration, which went on late into the night, all of these men were burned, the sickening stench of burning flesh sullying the vernal evening air.

This grisly event brought the debacle of the 1736 Chickasaw campaign to a mournful close. It had been Bienville's initiative, and whatever excuses he might adduce (and he adduced many),[89] this episode was a major blemish on his career. The campaign's abject failure raised questions about the very viability of French Louisiana in the face of so many strategic obstacles. Nevertheless, when Commissaire-Ordonnateur Salmon gave his account of the affair, he singled out the bravery of d'Artaguiette, St. Ange, and Vincennes for special praise.[90] By year's end 1736, Robert Grotton de St. Ange was living in geriatric retirement,[91] and his older son Pierre St. Ange had met his dreadful fate. This meant that hopes for the family's future, and to some degree for the future of French Illinois, lay in the hands of Pierre's younger brother Louis St. Ange de Bellerive.

Louis was born at La Prairie, just across the St. Lawrence River from Montreal, in 1702.[92] His surname appears in a variety of forms in eighteenth-century manuscripts (St. Ange [Holy Angel], Bellerive, St. Ange de Bellerive, Bellerive St. Ange), occasionally, but seldom, preceded by the Christian name Louis. Sometimes, until the death of his father, St. Ange *père* (father) in early 1740, he signed his name St. Ange *fils* (son), which confuses things because his older brother Pierre usually signed St. Ange *fils* as well. The Bellerive addition came from their mother, Robert de St. Ange's first wife, Marguerite-Louise Crevier, whose father styled himself sieur de Bellerive.[93] Bellerive was likely attached to Louis St. Ange to distinguish him from his brother Pierre. After Pierre's death in 1736, at which time only one St. Ange *fils* remained, Louis seldom used Bellerive in his signature. Yet the name persisted, and in his last will and testament (December 1774), he used the full "Louis Saint Ange de Bellerive" as his legal name.[94] Pronouncing "Louis St. Ange de Bellerive" in French fashion gives a distinctly iambic beat (da-dum) to his name, although from what we know of the man he would have been oblivious of such poetic resonances. St. Ange de Bellerive is the best-known member of the Grotton–St. Ange family. In profound chagrin, he relinquished Fort de Chartres to British troops in 1765, and in stoic resolution he guided St. Louis through the tumultuous years, 1765–70, finally dying in the house of Marie-Thérèse Bourgeois Chouteau in December 1774. The following chapter traces St. Ange's slow ascent to power during the three decades preceding the French and Indian War.

CHAPTER 2

The Rise of Louis St. Ange de Bellerive

St. Ange has commanded at the Wabash post for four years, where he has conducted himself very wisely. He is well-known, liked and valued by the tribes in that region.

—Governor Jean-Baptiste Le Moyne de Bienville, 1740

France's North American empire—the sweeping transcontinental crescent from the estuary of the St. Lawrence to the delta of the Mississippi—was a waterborne empire, and St. Ange de Bellerive was a creature of the rivers. His entire adult life revolved around them—living beside them, gazing across them, ascending them, descending them, traversing them, dreaming about them. From Fort St. Joseph (Niles, Michigan) on the St. Joseph River, to Fort d'Orléans on the Missouri, to Fort Vincennes (or St. Ange) on the Wabash, to Fort de Chartres on the Mississippi, and finally to St. Louis, St. Ange never lived beyond eyeshot of a river; he was as much at home in a pirogue as on terra firma. At all these locations he also lived in, or adjacent to, a fort (pitiable though some of them were), except at St. Louis, which had no fortification of any kind during St. Ange's tenure as commandant (1765–70). This reinforces the fact that St. Ange de Bellerive was first and foremost a military man. Yet he was a military man who never experienced the heat and tumult of battle, for his peculiar calling was Indian diplomacy. During the last decade of his life (1765–74), St. Ange became a friend to the young Auguste Chouteau when they were both residents of St. Louis. In his "Journal," Chouteau remarked that "Monsieur de St. Ange de Bellerive was Canadian, a former officer, who had made war against Indians since his tenderest days of youth."[1] In fact, no record exists of St. Ange *ever* having made war against Indians; rather, he spent his entire adult life conducting intricate, peaceful negotiations with them. This chapter deals with Bellerive's rise as an Indian diplomatist and important Illinois Country administrator during the nearly three decades that he commanded the outpost of Vincennes on the east bank of the Wabash (Ouabache) River.

The Chickasaw calamity in the spring of 1736 left two gaping holes in French leadership in the Illinois Country. Pierre Diron d'Artaguiette had to be replaced at Fort de Chartres and François-Marie Bissot de Vincennes (he spelled it "Vinsenne") at the Wabash post, these outposts being the two most important in the region. Governor Jean-Baptiste Le Moyne de Bienville moved quickly to fill the vacancies. For Chartres, he selected Alphonse de la Buissonnière, who had already served for three years as a captain in the Illinois Country. Indeed, Pierre de St. Ange had been a lieutenant in Buissonnière's company before he set out to his doom on the Chickasaw campaign.[2] Bienville explained that none of the officers at his disposal in New Orleans had the experience necessary for managing the three major constituencies in Upper Louisiana—Indians, habitants, and voyageurs.[3] Buissonnière knew these constituencies, and he would command at Fort de Chartres from 1736 until his death ("after six days of illness") in December 1740.[4]

Bienville continued his dispatch, remarking that Vincennes's death left a spot vacant for a *lieutenant réformé*, that is, at rank of lieutenant but on half pay, to command on the Wabash. After his father (Jean-Baptiste Bissot de Vincennes) died in 1719, François-Marie assumed the responsibility of serving as French liaison with the Miami Indians near the Miami portage (where Fort Wayne now stands).[5] In 1730 Vincennes relocated his outpost some 150 odd miles down the Wabash, and the *contrôleur général* of the Indies Company expressed his approval of the move: "It's good that Monsieur de Vincennes has taken the initiative of bringing down the Miamis, and it's absolutely necessary to fortify the place as soon as possible."[6] This new location, lower down the Wabash, brought Vincennes into close contact with the Piankashaws, which was likely his principal reason for effecting the move. By 1731 Vincennes was in a command of a small fort and embryonic settlement that would eventually evolve into present-day Vincennes, Indiana.[7] In relocating his base of operations to the lower Wabash, Vincennes had moved his outpost from Upper Canada to Upper Louisiana.[8] Throughout the remainder of the colonial period, there would be continuous contact between the Illinois settlements on the east bank of the Mississippi River and Vincennes. And the latter, as part of Upper Louisiana, was subordinate to Chartres within the Louisiana chain of command. Ouiatenon, on the other hand, farther up the Wabash River, was deemed to lie in the *Pays d'en haut*, Upper Canada, and was subordinate to Detroit.

Bienville, while ruminating about a new commandant for the Wabash post, sketched a brief history of the service that the St. Ange family had rendered to France over *decades*, rather than years: Robert de St. Ange *père* had served for more than fifty years, which was no exaggeration, for he had been a sergeant in Canada as early as 1686.[9] Robert's older son Pierre had just been burned by the Chickasaws on an expedition that Bienville himself had promoted, and Robert asked Bienville to appoint his remaining son (Louis St.

Ange de Bellerive) as commandant on the Wabash. Bienville noted that this son was already commanding a small outpost on the Missouri (that is, Fort d'Orléans) and that d'Artaguiette had long spoken of him as a "garçon brave et d'un grand méritte."[10] Bellerive got the job, and by the time of his death at St. Louis in 1774, he had served the French monarchy even longer than his father before him.

On June 22, 1736, Salmon wrote to Versailles that a convoy from the Illinois Country had arrived in New Orleans the evening before.[11] This convoy would have left the Illinois Country in mid- or late May, for with spring freshets surging the Mississippi the downriver trip required only three or four weeks. Ascending the Mississippi was a wholly different affair, convoys often requiring three or four months or more. Salmon noted that he tried to arrange things so convoys were not forced to winter over during the long upriver trip to the Illinois Country, adding that "Monseigneur can judge the pain that the soldiers and blacks [that is, slaves] must endure, having continually to row during all that time."[12] White men and black men worked shoulder to shoulder rowing and poling the bateaux against the Mississippi's current, sluicing one another off with river water when the heat and insects became unbearable.

In any case, the spring convoy that arrived at New Orleans in June 1736 carried news about St. Ange's outpost on the Wabash. This outpost was slowly acquiring the name Vincennes, in honor of its first commandant, and St. Ange must have been responsible for conveying this posthumous honorarium to an officer who had died with his brother. But things were not going well for the new commandant on the Wabash. Most of the Indians (apparently both Miamis and Piankashaws) who sustained the post had withdrawn to the Vermilion River (one hundred miles north), and the remainder (twenty-five men) seemed inclined to follow suit. St. Ange was thinking that the outpost was not of much value, and Salmon opined that it cost more to maintain than it was worth. However, Salmon added that if the French abandoned Vincennes, British traders would certainly move into the Wabash Valley via the Ohio River, which was totally unacceptable from the French strategic point of view. In the end, the French maintained their outpost on the Wabash, and St. Ange would spend the next twenty-eight years there as commandant.[13] His time was largely taken up with Indian affairs, which were of prodigious complexity and delicacy. But St. Ange's dozen years in the wilderness at Fort d'Orléans on the Missouri had well prepared him for the intricate and multifaceted tasks of Indian diplomacy.

In 1740 Governor Bienville evaluated all French military officers in Louisiana.[14] "St. Ange *fils* has commanded at the Wabash post for four years, where he has conducted himself very wisely. He is well-known, liked and valued by the tribes in that area. He's thirty-nine years old."[15] Bienville also assessed François Coulon de Villiers: "Son of a former captain of Canadian troops, he is wise, energetic, intelligent, and well-disposed to serve the colony well. He's twenty-five years old."[16] Villiers in fact came from one of the most distinguished military families in Canada.[17] His father, Nicolas-Antoine Coulon de Villiers, was longtime commandant at Fort St. Joseph near Lake Michigan, had dueled for many years with Fox Indians, and was finally killed by them in 1733.[18] François's brothers, Joseph and Louis, became famous when they confronted the young George Washington in the Allegheny Mountains of southwestern Pennsylvania in 1754, the confrontations being, in the famous words of Horace Walpole, the spark that "set the world on fire."[19]

François Coulon de Villiers arrived at Fort de Chartres as an ensign in the late 1730s, and in 1740 he married Louis St. Ange de Bellerive's half sister, Élisabeth Grotton de St. Ange. As noted above, Élisabeth had been born the daughter of Robert Grotton de St. Ange and Élisabeth Chorel at Fort d'Orléans on the Missouri River ca. 1725, which meant she was only fifteen years old when she married Villiers. This marriage, which linked two of the great military families of French North America, was arguably the most important marriage ever celebrated in the colonial Illinois Country, as the elaborate prenuptial contract abundantly reveals.[20] The marriage was celebrated at Fort de Chartres, where Joseph Gagnon was priest. But one priest was not adequate for this grand occasion, so Father René Tartarin was brought up from Kaskaskia to participate. Tartarin and Captain Jean-Baptiste Benoist de St. Clair[21] were witnesses in the marriage contract on the groom's behalf, and on the bride's side were Gagnon, Élisabeth Chorel (the bride's mother), and "Monsieur Louis de St. Ange Bellerive, officer commandant on the Wabash." The fathers of the bride and groom, Robert Grotton de St. Ange and Nicolas Coulon de Villiers, were both deceased,[22] but they had been friends and comrades in arms when they collaborated to crush the Fox Indians on the Illinois prairie in 1730.

⚜ ⚜ ⚜ ⚜

During the mid–eighteenth century, commerce between the major Illinois Country settlements (Kaskaskia and Chartres) and Canada was usually conducted via the Ohio and Wabash Rivers and the Miami portage, rather than the Illinois River and the Chicago portage, or the Illinois and Kankakee Rivers. Along the southern route, the confluence of the Ohio (Belle Rivière) and the Tennessee River (known to the French as Rivière des Cheraquis) was a volatile and dangerous region, for Cherokees and Chickasaws could quickly descend the north-flowing Tennessee to strike French commerce on the Ohio before it turned up the Wabash and headed upstream for St. Ange's outpost—and beyond to the Miami portage, Lake Erie, and Detroit. In October 1740, Chickasaws descended on five "voitures" (pirogues) loaded with pel-

Lower Ohio (L'Oyo) River valley by Jacques-Nicolas Bellin, 1762. Notice "F[ort] S. Anne ou Vincenne" on the lower Wabash River. The cartographer in Paris mistook St. Ange for St. Anne. St. Ange himself called his fort Vincennes to honor the founder of the outpost, François-Marie Bissot de Vincennes. Courtesy of the Library of Congress, Division of Maps and Cartography.

tries, tobacco, flour, and lead (all products of the Illinois Country) that were heading for Upper Canada via Vincennes. Seventeen of the French, including one Derozier, his wife, a daughter, and a son, were killed, as was one slave (perhaps an Indian); four others were badly wounded, and only four came through the ordeal unscathed, to make their way up the Wabash to safety at Vincennes.[23] This bloody incident was particularly worrisome because it turned out that Chickasaws (not Cherokees) had been the aggressors, and Bienville had ostensibly arranged a durable peace with them. Proposed forts were never built on the lower Ohio River, and the region remained a danger zone over which St. Ange had little control.

The extraordinarily unsettled and fragile nature of affairs on the Wabash River, and therefore of St. Ange's entire command there, was revealed when, in 1750, Charles de Raymond, commander at the Miami Post, reported that the Piankashaw Indians had totally abandoned Vincennes, apparently spurning St. Ange's pleas.[24] This essentially left St. Ange without a constituency at

Vincennes, and he repaired to Fort de Chartres to await orders from Governor Pierre de Rigaud de Vaudreuil-Cavagnal in New Orleans. Vaudreuil had set the northeastern boundary of Louisiana where the Vermilion River flows into the Wabash, some one hundred miles upstream from Vincennes, meaning that St. Ange's outpost at Vincennes indubitably lay within Vaudreuil's jurisdiction.[25] St. Ange had proposed that he could go up the Missouri Valley (a region that he knew intimately) and recruit Missouri Indians to follow him en masse eastward to Vincennes,[26] for that outpost was not viable without constituent Indians residing in the area. This was an altogether remarkable, verging on fantastical, proposal, and it was never implemented, but it does show the depth of St. Ange's affiliation with the Missouris. This close association was to stand St. Ange in good stead, when, in October 1765, he became commandant at the new outpost of St. Louis, a place that was often frequented by groups of Missouris.

While St. Ange was at Fort de Chartres in January 1750 awaiting orders from Vaudreuil, he also attended to some family affairs, for his half sister (Élisabeth St. Ange), his brother-in-law (François Coulon de Villiers), and his father's second wife (Élisabeth Chorel) all lived at or near the fort; the same group of folks had assembled for the Villiers–St. Ange wedding discussed above. On January 13, 1750, the Reverend Joseph Gagnon, who had performed the 1740 marriage, baptized at the fort the son of François Coulon de Villiers and Élisabeth St. Ange. "Monsieur Louis de St. Ange" stood as godfather at the baptism, and the infant was baptized Louis in his honor.[27]

In August 1751, Governor Vaudreuil dispatched a new commandant up the Mississippi to Fort de Chartres, Jean-Baptiste Macarty Mactigue. His tenure at the Illinois post, 1751–60, was longer and more eventful than that of any other commandant at Chartres; he compiled the remarkably detailed 1752 census of the Illinois Country villages and oversaw the building of the new stone Fort de Chartres. This was the first fort at Chartres to be designed by a professional military engineer, the capable François Saucier.[28] Vaudreuil presented Macarty with voluminous, detailed instructions for his Illinois command,[29] and he wrote specifically about St. Ange's responsibilities at Vincennes:

> He [Macarty] will give the Sieur St. Ange, who commands at Vincennes on the Wabash, such instructions as he thinks necessary in accordance with our intentions, as to the conduct he should pursue regarding the soldiers of the garrison, the inhabitants of that place, and the voyageurs who pass through those parts. We are further informed that the Sieur St. Ange has the confidence of the tribes of that region, among whom he is in good standing. Accordingly, it will be proper to keep him in command at that post and to have delivered yearly from the king's stores and sent to that officer the presents we are accustomed to give the Indians, in order to attach them to our interest and to retain them.[30]

Signature page of St. Ange's letter (February 28, 1752) to Governor Pierre de Rigaud de Vaudreuil. Notice St. Ange's inventive spelling (bottom left) of Vincennes, "Viencene." Commandant at Vincennes for nearly three decades (1736–64), St. Ange was so highly respected that he was seldom given orders from his superiors. No one in French Louisiana had a better grasp of the intricacies of Indian diplomacy. Courtesy of the Huntington Library, San Marino, California.

Vaudreuil was obviously well up to speed on the situation in his upper colony, and he recognized the increasing importance of the Wabash post as the geopolitical situation was evolving in eastern North America at mid–eighteenth century. The governor had confidence in St. Ange's ability to deal with Indians (especially Piankashaws and Miamis) in the Wabash Valley, having promoted him to "captaine réformé [half-pay]" in October 1748.[31]

By 1750 informed persons throughout North America were aware that renewed war between France and Great Britain was virtually inevitable and that friction in the American West (that is, west of the Appalachian Mountains) was a major source of escalating international tensions. In 1749 the governor-general of Canada, Roland-Michel Barrin de La Galissonière, dispatched Pierre-Joseph Céloron de Blainville[32] to buttress French claims to the upper Ohio River valley. In a justly famous expedition during the summer and autumn of 1749, Céloron proceeded from Lake Erie to the headwaters of the Allegheny River, descended it to its confluence with the Monongahela (future site of Pittsburgh), thence down the Belle Rivière (Ohio) as far as the mouth of Scioto (Portsmouth, Ohio), before returning northward to Montreal in November.[33] Céloron's party buried six engraved lead plaques along the banks of the Ohio (among others, one at the mouth of the Kanahwa and another at the mouth of Muskigum), claiming the Ohio Valley on behalf of King Louis XV. Céloron encountered English traders (working out of western Virginia) in the valley and peremptorily ordered them to leave territory that belonged, rightfully, to the French monarch. In other words, by the time that Macarty headed up the Mississippi toward the Illinois Country in the autumn of 1751, the game was on for control of the Ohio River valley, and the Wabash post commanded by St. Ange was the closest French outpost to that strategic valley until Fort Duquesne was built in the spring of 1754.

During the early 1750s, Indian affairs swirled with mind-boggling complexity in the region between the Ohio and Miami Rivers, an area today encompassing large swaths of western Ohio and eastern Indiana. Bands of Miamis and Piankashaws led by the Miami chief, La Demoiselle, and incited by English traders, had rebelled against French tutelage and gathered at Pickawillany on the Great Miami River (near present-day Dayton, Ohio). These rebels hoped to bring all of the surrounding tribes (including Kickapoos, Mascoutens, and even some Illinois) into a grand anti-French alliance, and it was St. Ange's responsibility to prevent this from materializing. Furthermore, "republicans" from the Great Miami were aroused because they had been attacked by a party of Nipissings (generally French allies) from Canada. "Républiquién," such a strange word (not to be found with this spelling in any dictionary) to discover in St. Ange's letter, fairly leaps off the page.[34] St. Ange surely did not use it in any sophisticated Madisonian sense of government conducted by assemblies of elected representatives. Rather, he was simply contrasting republicans and monarchists, and in this instance "republican" Indians were those who were rejecting the patronage of the French monarchy. Vaudreuil had earlier accused insidious Englishmen of having sponsored an Indian "république" on the Great Miami.[35] In any case, St. Ange was most disturbed by the absence of established, resident Indians at his Wabash outpost, "which induces some of our inhabitants to leave the place, as they can live only by the Indian trade."[36] Other villages in the Illinois Country (Kaskaskia, Cahokia, Chartres, Prairie du Rocher, and so forth) had vibrant agricultural economies, but St. Ange's post, while home to a small group of resident farmers,[37] was more heavily dependent on the Indian presence and the concomitant advantages that that offered for trade and commerce.

St. Ange and his post on the Wabash were important enough to the French strategic presence in Upper Louisiana that Governor Vaudreuil and St. Ange communicated directly with one another, rather than via Macarty at Fort de Chartres. St. Ange's settlement at Vincennes was expanding, and he wrote to the governor that he had extended with small pickets his fort's palisade so as to encompass the church, the presbytery, and the growing number of habitants.[38] St. Ange's fort was in a sad state, and Vaudreuil allowed that in the present tenuous circumstances, repairs had to be made, "but with the utmost economy and the least expense possible."[39] Vaudreuil was parsimonious regarding military expenditures, but he urged St. Ange to "spare nothing" on the diplomatic front. Sparing nothing in this case meant that St. Ange should exercise all of his formidable linguistic and persuasive powers to prevent the tribes of the Wabash Valley from swinging dramatically, and dangerously, into the clutches of the English. That would have exposed the entire northeastern flank of French settlement in the Illinois Country and severed the principal route to Canada that proceeded via the Miami-Wabash portage. Louis Billouart de Kerlérec, who replaced Vaudreuil as governor-general in 1753, quickly grasped and articulated the issue: "If they [Englishmen] become masters of the Wabash, communications will be cut off between that river and the Illinois and between Illinois and Canada."[40]

Charles-Michel de Langlade was a *métis* born in 1729 at Michilimackinac, son of an Ottawa mother and French Canadian father.[41] One of the more dashing and charismatic figures of eighteenth-century America, he was a partisan warrior of fearsome energy and manifold skills. In June 1752, he descended from the north on La Demoiselle's outpost at Pickawillany with a small force of Ottawas and Ojibways (Sauteurs) and quickly subdued it. La Demoiselle, to set an example, was slaughtered, cooked, and eaten by the Indians, some of whom were kinsmen of Langlade, with La Demoiselle's followers watching with rapt attention, they, in that manner, being informed of what harvest the seeds of rebellion against French sponsorship brought forth.[42] This grisly event worked wonders in discouraging the anti-French revolt that La Demoiselle had fomented and that St. Ange, Macarty, and Vaudreuil had been anxiously observing from their respective locations. Gros Bled (Big Corn) had been one of the leaders of the rebel Piankashaws (not all Piankashaws had joined the revolt), and he likely was present at Pickawillany for the cannibal feast in June. In July Gros Bled sent peace offerings (a hand-worked *capot* and a white shell) to St. Ange, accompanied by a message: Gros Bled and his rebel band of Piankashaws beg to be forgiven and wish to draw together in ever-closer friendship and alliance with the French.[43]

La Demoiselle's death and the gradual disintegration of the anti-French coalition left the Wabash Valley in relative peace (if not perfect harmony) during the French and Indian War. St. Ange's outpost was most often called Vincennes in honor of its first commandant, but it was also called Poste de St. Ange or Fort St. Ange (sometimes transformed into Ste. Anne), which, given St. Ange's long tenure there, was appropriate. Governor Kerlérec used the appellation "Poste St. Ange" regularly,[44] although St. Ange himself, apparently in a gesture of self-effacement, used "Viencene" when identifying his post. Vincennes rarely appears in Louisiana administrative correspondence during this time period, suggesting that St. Ange was fending for himself, without much direction or interference from either Macarty at Fort de Chartres or Governor Kerlérec in New Orleans. His track record of success in handling Indian affairs meant that he was left pretty much on his own to preserve Franco-Indian alliances in the Wabash Valley and maintain a bulwark against English encroachment from the East.[45]

Kerlérec, from his vantage point as Louisiana governor, sketched a profile of St. Ange in 1759: "He has served since he was a child, and became a captain on October 15, 1748. He is an excellent officer for that region [Upper Louisiana], especially regarding the Indians, whom he leads and guides at his will. He's a man of absolute probity, a zealous servant of the king, and has always regarded commercial activities as beneath him. He survives in straitened circumstances as commandant at Fort Vincennes. There, he encourages the habitants to cultivate wheat, which they are doing with success."[46] This brief profile serves as an abstract of Vincennes's history during most of the three decades that St. Ange served there: founded as a French fragile outpost for managing Indian affairs in the Wabash Valley, Vincennes, under St. Ange's long and skillful leadership, evolved into a stable agricultural settlement, permanent home to habitants as well as halfway house for traders moving between the Great Lakes and the Ohio and Mississippi watershed.[47]

Jacques-François Forget Duverger was a Seminarian priest who left Quebec in April 1754, heading west to assume his duties at Cahokia, which he finally reached on November 22. Descending the Wabash in a pirogue, Duverger arrived at Vincennes the evening of October 10 and quite fell in love with the place, remaining there for the remainder of the month. He was witness to a brilliant display of foliage, as the autumnal maple and sweetgums set ablaze the banks of the river. His description of St. Ange's outpost on the Wabash is our only known firsthand depiction of the community at that time; it is precious:

> The chaplain gladly offered me his hospitality. The fort is on the left bank of the Wabash River, . . . sixty leagues from its confluence with the Ohio or Belle Rivière. Monsieur de Bellerive de St. Ange is commandant of this fort. His disposition is extremely gentle and peaceful, and he possesses an uncommon piety. The chaplain, who also serves as missionary with the Indians, is a Jesuit, [Louis] Vivier, about age forty, who has both virtue and intelligence. This post is composed of twenty or twenty-five houses, without counting the Indians, who are present in large numbers. . . . I finally departed Thursday, the last day of October, with the commandant [St. Ange] and twenty-four men, traveling in pirogues to go to the Illinois.[48]

Duverger's idyllic description captures a community that St. Ange had built pretty much from scratch, and it was a quintessential Illinois Country village: a benevolent military commandant maintaining order, a resident Roman Catholic priest/missionary, and, most important, amicable relations between the village and surrounding Indians.

Because St. Ange was successful in maintaining good relations with neighboring tribes, his small settlement was free to grow and evolve from a mere trading outpost into a recognizable and identifiable village. Vincennes continued to be home to a large number of transient voyageurs, but a village with a resident commandant and priest implied a stable, albeit small, population of resident farmers (habitants).[49] Four years after Duverger's visit, Kerlérec wrote that "Fort St. Ange . . . has a garrison of forty men and there are eighteen or twenty good farmers [*bons habitants*] who raise wheat, tobacco and maize. The fort is a simple enclosure of stakes, and is very old. The Piankashaws, numbering eighty warriors, are settled there. . . . They're much attached to the French, and they merit consideration because they cover the Post of Vincennes or St. Ange. This post has prospects for growth, especially while Sieur St. Ange resides and commands there."[50] Governors came and went in New Orleans, but St. Ange's presence at Vincennes was continuous and continuously respected in Louisiana. And this respect would only grow, on both sides of the Mississippi and under both French and Spanish regimes, until 1770, when St. Ange went into well-deserved retirement at St. Louis.

A permanent settlement, as opposed to an evanescent trading post, necessarily entailed property ownership, and St. Ange conveyed no fewer than seventy land grants at Vincennes between 1749 and 1764.[51] This was his prerogative as post commandant, as it later would be when he served as commandant at Chartres and finally at St. Louis. Once Vincennes had become

British territory after the French and Indian War and St. Ange had departed, confusion arose over proprietorship in and around the settlement. Some unknown person contacted St. Ange, who was living in retirement in St. Louis and requested that he verify his role in conveying land grants at Vincennes. This he gladly did on August 30, 1773, sixteen months before his death. St. Ange explained that he had become commandant at Vincennes in 1736, that his commission was from His Most Christian Majesty, the king of France, and that he had served under the governments of four successive governors of Louisiana—Bienville, Vaudreuil, Kerlérec, and d'Abbadie.[52] In old age, St. Ange was waxing a bit grandiose. Bienville had appointed him to be sure, but it is most unlikely that Louis XV ever heard of St. Ange or signed a royal commission for him. Moreover, St. Ange casually neglected to note that his immediate superiors had been the various commandants at Fort de Chartres, whose sphere of governance included all posts of the Illinois Country, including Vincennes.[53] The old soldier may be forgiven a bit of grandiosity.

In any case, the important issue was that St. Ange had indeed conveyed land grants at Vincennes, both "Terres et Terrains," that is, both agricultural plots and town lots. Some of these concessions had been formally inscribed and signed by St. Ange. But others, especially for "terres," St. Ange had granted "verballement" in view of the fact that the cultivators had occupied and cultivated the lands for some period of time. We shall see that the same homesteading rules applied at early St. Louis, where St. Ange conveyed concessions verbally in consideration of tenants having put the land to productive use over a certain period of time. An enumeration of land concessions at Vincennes, together with St. Ange's written certification of the grants, made its way to New York City in 1774 and landed on the desk of General Frederick Haldimand, interim commandant of all British forces in North America. Haldimand's opinion was that it would be difficult and pointless to dispute French land claims at Vincennes and that the best thing was to "les laisser tranquille," just leave them in peace.[54] A particularly sound reason for adhering to this admonition was that by the early 1770s, many of the old village records had been lost due to "rain, rats and insects."[55]

Most early residents at Vincennes were of French Canadian background, but there were others as well. Take, for example, Étienne Philibert *dit* Orléans, who was born at Orléans on the River Loire in 1719. Étienne had a calling for public service, and he enlisted in the royal French marines as a teenager. He joined St. Ange's small garrison at Vincennes ca. 1740, and he was buried there nearly a half century later. Étienne spent his entire adult life on the Wabash River, which, lazy moving as it is, perhaps reminded him of his native silvery Loire. The first extant local records from Vincennes date from 1749, and Philibert's name appears almost immediately: in April 1750 he witnessed (as did "St. Ange, commandant") the marriage of a French Canadian and an

Indian woman,[56] and over the next thirty-five years no one's name appears so frequently as Philibert's in Vincennes's parish records.

In 1752 Philibert received St. Ange's permission to leave the French marines after fifteen years of service. Abandoning the military, Philibert became an ordinary habitant at Vincennes, but his devotion to public service persisted. He became *chantre* in the parish of St. François Xavier, he was witness at numerous marriages and baptisms, and he performed many provisional baptisms when a priest was not available; he became a veritable assistant priest, although he did marry on two occasions. Nothing is known about Philibert's first wife other than that she was a Charbonneau,[57] but following her death he married Angélique Gelibert-Gilbert in 1765 at Kaskaskia, his bride's hometown.[58] He seems to have had no children by either wife, but in 1761 St. Ange gave him a land grant that was certified by Louisiana governor Louis Billouart de Kerlérec. By the early 1770s, Philibert was, in addition to performing religious duties, also serving in a civil capacity as royal notary at Vincennes.[59] His spelling and grammar were better than most French officials in the Illinois Country (and, it most be noted, far better than St. Ange's), which means that he must have left home with a solid formal education; for an enlisted man in the French marines, this was a very rare asset. Philibert lived through several bloody occasions in Vincennes when the town changed hands times during the American Revolution, and continued serving his community through the violent upheavals. He had come to Vincennes as a subject of Louis XV, became a subject of George III following the French and Indian War, and finally a U.S. citizen after the American Revolution. These political changes would have meant next to nothing to Philibert, who remained throughout his life French in language, religion, and daily habits, and devoted to his community.

Philibert was buried by his close friend Father Pierre Gibault on April 26, 1786. In a highly unusual gesture, Gibault inscribed in Philibert's burial record that the "solemn burial service had been attended by the entire parish, of all ages and both sexes." And as a high honor, Philibert was buried under the floor of the parish church, "between the door and the holy water font."[60] If St. Ange was the pillar of Vincennes between 1736 and 1764, Philibert was that pillar between 1764 and 1786.

⚜ ⚜ ⚜ ⚜

In 1749 Father Sébastien-Louis Meurin arrived at Vincennes from the Jesuit establishment at Kaskaskia, and he was succeeded by other Jesuits, Louis Vivier in 1753 and Julien Devernay in 1756. Surely, it was St. Ange who first requested a priest for his community, which he had been nurturing almost single-handedly since his arrival in 1736. A fair scattering of sacramental records were kept at Vincennes during the 1750s, and St. Ange appears regularly in them. He was witness at no fewer than six marriages between 1749 and 1757, and in one instance (the marriage of Julien Trottier and Josette Marie) St. Ange and his entire (very small) garrison of French marines (including Étienne Philibert *dit* Orléans) stood up as witnesses in what was a very rustic chapel.[61] Monsieur Trottier surely stood the whole wedding party to drinks after the marriage ceremony was completed, the Jesuit father Meurin tippling with the best of them. Many, indeed most, of the slaves at Vincennes were Indians, and the four recorded slave marriages were all of Indians.[62]

St. Ange was unmarried, which meant that his household at Vincennes consisted only of himself and his domestics, who were Indian slaves. Fort d'Orléans on the Missouri River, where St. Ange had served for more than a decade, was an entrepôt for the western Indian trade, including commerce in slaves, and he perhaps brought Indian slaves with him to Vincennes in 1736. The most important of these was Lizette, who gave birth to three children at Vincennes before accompanying St. Ange to Fort de Chartres and then on to St. Louis. She appears a decade later as St. Ange's slave ("about forty years old") on the 1770 Indian slave census of St. Louis.[63] These circumstances compel us to consider the likelihood that Lizette was in fact the bachelor St. Ange's concubine, the mother of some of his children, and also a longtime manager of his domestic affairs, a veritable *maîtresse de sa maison*.[64]

In early July 1759, British and American forces laid siege to the French fort at the mouth of the Niagara River. A sizable contingent of French marines and militiamen from Fort de Chartres joined Canadians and their Indian allies in an attempt to relieve the siege. Luckily for St. Ange, he was indispensable as commandant on the Wabash and therefore was left out of this calamitous expedition. Captain François-Marie Le Marchand de Lignery led the combined French forces, assisted by Captain Charles-Philippe Aubry from Chartres. Abandoned by their Indian allies at the last minute, the French marched boldly, and foolhardily, into battle at La Belle Famille, outside Fort Niagara on July 24.[65] The French force was utterly routed, and the fort surrendered to the British the day following. This defeat, together with the even more momentous one on the Plains of Abraham outside Quebec City in September, sealed the fate of the French empire in North America, including the Illinois Country.

At Fort de Chartres, Macarty received word of the cataclysm at Niagara in late August and informed Kerlérec of heavy French casualties, including many marines and militiamen from Illinois.[66] Macarty claimed that both Aubry and François Coulon de Villiers,[67] who had married St. Ange's half sister, Élisabeth, in 1740 at Fort de Chartres, had been killed, but this turned out to be erroneous. Both officers were captured (Villiers badly wounded) and transported to New York City, where they were freed in an exchange of prisoners. Aubry and Villiers both eventually made their way to New Orleans, where

Aubry served as acting governor of Louisiana (1765–69). He and St. Ange communicated regularly after St. Ange installed himself as commandant at St. Louis in October 1765.[68]

Pierre-Joseph Neyon de Villiers (no relation to the Canadian Coulon de Villiers family) replaced Macarty Mactigue as commandant at Fort de Chartres in 1760. Neyon was an authentic French aristocrat, born in Lorraine, who had begun his military career in the elite regiment of duc Étienne-François de Choiseul, the greatest of Louis XV's ministers. Socially, he was a decided cut above most Canadian officers (such as St. Ange) with their manufactured aristocratic names, and to boot he was brother-in-law to Governor Kerlérec. At the close of the French and Indian War, he wrote to Governor Jean-Jacques Blaise d'Abbadie (who had replaced Kerlérec) in New Orleans about St. Ange's work at the Wabash post. "On October 24 [1763], M. de St. Ange informed me that he had assembled the Piankashaws and had explained to them the *parole* [promise] that I had given to all the tribes of the Ohio River valley. They accepted the peace pipes, and said that my assurances would suffice to maintain them in peace."[69] This passage makes it clear that between 1752, when several bands of Piankashaws were in revolt against the French alliance, and 1763, St. Ange had managed to pacify most, if not all, bands of that tribe. It also suggests that St. Ange had learned their language ("he . . . explained to them") well enough to communicate with them on a familiar basis. St. Ange's talent for communicating with Indians helped to make him the most successful, as well as the longest-serving, administrator in Upper Louisiana during the colonial era. Andrew R. L. Cayton, in his excellent survey of frontier Indiana, observed that "St. Ange was perhaps the most important figure in the history of frontier Vincennes."[70] Cayton's qualification, "perhaps," might well be replaced with "indubitably."

In 1764 the French, defeated on North American battlefields and bankrupt at home, were preparing to abandon Louisiana, and St. Ange was ordered to leave Vincennes. Neyon de Villiers, while commandant at Fort de Chartres (1760–64), came to respect St. Ange's skill at maintaining peace in the Wabash River valley, which required mastering a kaleidoscope of Indian affairs. Villiers knew his man, and he was the first to suggest that St. Ange should replace him as commandant at Chartres, remarking in December 1763 that he could turn the fort over to him with a garrison of forty marines.[71] Villiers had other officers in his command who could have filled his boots, but St. Ange was clearly his first choice. On April 20, 1764, Villiers dispatched orders to St. Ange, ordering him to leave Vincennes and report to Fort de Chartres in preparation for taking over as commandant.[72]

On May 18, St. Ange delivered his farewell proclamation to the assembled residents of Vincennes, a motley crowd of fur traders, farmers, and Indians from several tribes. This must have been an emotional moment for St. Ange, for he had nurtured the community for nearly three decades. But no emotions show through in St. Ange's words, which were all business, laid out in a curt military style:

> By virtue of the orders of Monsieur de Neyon, major commanding in the Illinois Country, to select a person to deal with policing and maintenance of good order among the residents, as well as among the *volontaires* [transient traders] and Indians of this post, we, acting captain, being on the verge of departing for the Illinois to receive orders from Monsieur de Neyon, have named Monsieur Drouet de Richardville [or Richerville], captain of the militia, and Sieur le Caindre, soldier from the garrison. Their first responsibility must be to maintain good relations with the Indians, preventing any disorders during the time that they have authority. When they receive an accusation against someone, they should assemble the most important [*plus notables*] residents of the community, who shall decide the issue by majority vote.
>
> Messieurs Drouet de Richardville and de Caindre cannot be too careful to make sure that the habitants maintain their fences, for it is in the public interest that the animals don't get into the grain fields. To the best of their abilities, they will suppress disorders that are often occasioned by [alcoholic] drinks. When they receive any news that may bear on the good of the service, they will let us know about it. And finally in all situations that we have not been able to predict we're counting on their good judgment and their commitment to the public good.
> Presented at the post of Vincennes, May 18, 1764.
> St. Ange[73]

This document tells us a great deal about St. Ange and the settlement at Vincennes. While he was building up a traditional Illinois Country settlement at Vincennes, St. Ange appointed Richardville captain of the militia. This power of appointment was always the prerogative of post commandants, and St. Ange appointed militia officers at St. Louis a few years later.[74] In any case, Richardville, as captain of the militia, was the most important man at Vincennes—after St. Ange himself—and it is significant that St. Ange named him ahead of the soldier de Caindre when creating the command structure he left behind.[75] St. Ange's emphasis on Indian affairs was to be expected, but his special attention to agricultural fencing is noteworthy. It reveals that a mature (though small) agricultural settlement had finally emerged at Vincennes, and it implies that the tripartite configuration of this settlement was the same as at the other Illinois Country villages—commons for pasturing livestock, enclosed plow lands for grain production, and a compact village of habitants and traders. From his time spent at Fort de Chartres, St. Ange knew this configuration well, and it evolved at Vincennes while he was commandant. St. Ange's concern about heavy drinking and public disorder reminds us, however, that Vincennes was still fundamentally a trading community. As such, it constituted a base for rowdy voyageurs who worked the waterways between Canada and the Illinois Country and who stopped over at Vincennes both going and coming. St. Ange's concern with keeping a lid on a turbulent frontier trading society at Vincennes was not misplaced. Daniel Bloüin, in his 1771 "Mémoire" to General Thomas Gage, remarked that "the post of Vincennes (named Post St. Vincent by the English) is a well-populated village on the Wabash. It's an ungoverned place where there is no respect for law and order."[76]

St. Ange departed Vincennes shortly after posting his proclamation on May 18, 1764. With substantial baggage and an entourage that included Indian slaves, he traveled via the rivers—down the Wabash, then down the Ohio, and finally up the Mississippi to Fort de Chartres. It is not known precisely when he arrived at the fort—likely it was about June 1, and surely it was before Neyon de Villiers, abandoning the Illinois Country, set out for New Orleans on June 15. Ultimately, Villiers had no personal loyalty to the region, and he abandoned it with insouciance. His convoy was perhaps the largest ever to descend the Mississippi River from the Illinois Country in colonial times—twenty-one bateaux and seven pirogues—but it moved unvexed and swiftly downriver, arriving in New Orleans on July 2.[77] Villiers was delighted to leave the doleful, yet volatile, situation in the Illinois Country in St. Ange's hands—doleful because the end of an era was clearly at hand and volatile because the embers of Pontiac's anti-British revolt still burned brightly. Villiers could not bail out of Louisiana quickly enough. Within two weeks after arriving in New Orleans, he had embarked for France, taking with him roughly half of his former garrison from Fort de Chartres (three officers and twenty-four enlisted men).[78] In a nice irony, Villiers's ship was the *Missouri*, a region in which Villiers had never evinced a scintilla of interest.

As for Louis St. Ange de Bellerive personally, the future was uncertain and riddled with contingencies. He knew that British forces were expected to occupy the Illinois Country east of the Mississippi and take possession of Fort de Chartres, but no one knew with certainty when this would occur. But, come what may, St. Ange was doggedly determined to remain loyal for the remainder of his mortal days to the region, to its francophone inhabitants, and to the ruling Bourbon family. As he departed Vincennes that early summer of 1764, he perhaps had not yet heard about the embryonic outpost emerging on the west bank of the Mississippi that would soon acquire the name "St. Louis," and he had no inkling that he would die and be buried there.

CHAPTER 3

The Illinois Country in Transition, 1763–1765

I have the honor to inform you that since my last dispatch Sieur Laclède has presented a request asking permission to establish a trading house [établissement] on the other side of the Mississippi, specifying that he has from you verbal permission to establish one in what he judges to be the best location.

—Pierre-Joseph Neyon de Villiers to Governor Jean-Jacques d'Abbadie, March 13, 1764

Étienne-François, comte de Stainville and duc de Choiseul, was Louis XV's chief minister during the 1760s. It was Choiseul who persuaded the French king to convey Louisiana to Spain in the secret Treaty of Fontainebleau (November 3, 1762) and he who negotiated the Treaty of Paris (February 10, 1763) that forfeited all French possessions east of the Mississippi River to Great Britain. The territorial cessions to Great Britain were a consequence of French losses on the battlefield, while the cession of Louisiana was rooted in Choiseul's lack of interest in, and knowledge of, the trans-Mississippian West. In Paul W. Mapp's succinct analysis, "French diplomats treated the unknown as expendable."[1] Even before news of these treaties reached North America, Pontiac's rebellion against British overlordship had begun to roil the western frontier (that is, west of the Appalachian Mountains), and within a year a new outpost was emerging on the west bank of the Mississippi River that would slowly evolve into the village of St. Louis. North America was in turmoil and transition during the 1760s as large, impersonal forces—economic, geographic, and cultural—provoked and shaped events; human beings were buffeted this way and that by powerful tides of change. Nevertheless, within these macro currents and cross-currents, the future of the middle Mississippi Valley was also being influenced by the decisions and actions of individual men. St. Ange de Bellerive was one of these individuals, and this chapter follows his career during the critical years 1764–65, as he moved his commandancy westward across the Illinois Country from Vincennes to Fort de Chartres and finally on across the Mississippi to St.

Louis. At the same time, other Frenchmen in Louisiana were eyeing the Illinois Country for purposes altogether different from those of St. Ange, and one of these men was Pierre Laclède Liguest. This chapter also traces his career, which tracked simultaneously with, but quite independently of, that of St. Ange. We must follow these two separate tracks, which ultimately, though unpredictably, converged in a raw, new settlement perched on a bluff overlooking the Mississippi River.

On August 2, 1763, the merchants Pierre Laclède, Gilbert-Antoine Maxent, and Jean-François Le Dée sat down in New Orleans to talk business. The unofficial document (never properly drawn up, notarized, and filed) reveals as none other the roots of Laclède's impending expedition to the Illinois Country, which was on the cusp of departing up the Mississippi from New Orleans. Maxent chaired the meeting, and the core clause of the resulting document is as follows:

> Sieur Maxent, having obtained an exclusive privilege for the Indian trade at the Illinois Post and its dependencies for the period of six consecutive years, dated ____ July last, acknowledges and stipulates by the present document that he has ceded one-fourth of the trade to sieurs Le Dée, Laclède and Company to enjoy the same privilege and benefit that he does, now and in the future, and they will also be subject to the same risks, costs and expenses that will ensue.[2]

Curiosities abound in this single run-on sentence. D'Abbadie's original intention had been to grant trading privileges for three years, not six, which suggests that Maxent had persuaded, or hoped to persuade, d'Abbadie to double the grant's term.[3] But the blank date also suggests that nothing was ever put down with ink and paper, and, indeed, no document entitled something like "Maxent's Exclusive Trading Privilege" has ever been found. Apparently, Maxent and d'Abbadie never got beyond verbal agreements when they discussed trading privileges in New Orleans during the summer of 1763. While chatting—perhaps in d'Abbadie's office, perhaps in a café, or perhaps on a street corner—d'Abbadie had said, "Sure, go ahead and find a good spot for your trading outpost up in the Illinois Country, put it anywhere you find convenient."[4] The colony of Louisiana was a loosely run ship, as Louis XV's government was preparing to scuttle an investment that had been a perennial loser for the French crown.

Significantly, nowhere in the August 2 document does Maxent mention the Missouri River, or the Missouri River valley, or the establishment of a new settlement on the west bank of the Mississippi River. None of the men gathered at the table had ever been upriver to the Illinois Country—a large, ill-defined region encompassing the middle Mississippi Valley and the lower valleys of the Illinois, Missouri, Ohio, and Wabash Rivers—and they knew precious little about the region. Where Laclède might establish his trading post was left entirely to his discretion, and either side of the Mississippi might do. The men who gathered that August in New Orleans were plungers, risk takers, and Laclède was assigned the riskiest task of all. He was to proceed upriver to the Illinois Country; he was to consult with the commandant there (Pierre-Joseph Neyon de Villiers at Fort de Chartres); he was to establish a trading house ("maison de traite") and then get on with the serious business at hand—namely, making money off the Indian trade.[5] At that business, Laclède turned out to be an abject failure, but then he did help to found a settlement that evolved, over time, into the celebrated city of St. Louis.

What Laclède knew about the geopolitical situation in Louisiana as his bateau pushed off from the docks at New Orleans in early August 1763 is an issue worth brief examination. A flurry of correspondence emanated from Versailles, King Louis's nerve center, on February 10, 1763, not coincidentally the same day that the Peace of Paris was signed that ended the Seven Years' War.[6] One dispatch went to Louis Billouart de Kerlérec, informing the outgoing governor-general of Louisiana that final peace treaties had been concluded and that Jacques-Blaise d'Abbadie was on his way to New Orleans to serve as general director of Louisiana as French rule in the province was winding down. A brief letter of appointment, signed by Louis XV, went to d'Abbadie and, under separate cover, a five-page "Mémoire" of instructions for his impending mission in New Orleans. Then, although undated but presumably written a short time later, a second set of instructions was addressed to d'Abbadie, twice as long as the first. By far the most important addition to the second set was the announcement, in the first paragraph, that western Louisiana had been ceded to Spain. For whatever reasons (Choiseul perhaps did not wish to violate an earlier agreement of secrecy with Spain), this thunderous news had been omitted in the first set of instructions.[7] In any event, after d'Abbadie arrived in New Orleans in June 1763, carrying both his instructions and the king's dispatch to Kerlérec, both men knew with certainty that the west side of the Mississippi, in addition to New Orleans on the east side, had been ceded to Spain and the east of the river to Great Britain.[8]

New Orleans was a small provincial city in 1763, with a tightly knit power elite of government officials, merchants (including Maxent and Laclède), and wealthy planters. On the city streets and in the cafés, these men rubbed shoulders, conversed, and exchanged information and gossip every day. It stretches credulity to believe that news about the cession to Spain did not leak out during these conversations. Indeed, there was nothing in the royal letters and "Mémoires" sent to Kerlérec and d'Abbadie that commanded them to keep this information secret. If Laclède knew that France had ceded the west side of the Mississippi to Spain, this knowledge likely did not bother him all that much. No one knew when, if ever, Spain would occupy its recently acquired territorial possessions, and even if it eventually did the Bourbon monarchies of France and Spain were bound tightly together by ties of royal blood, religion, and common interests, especially anti-British interests. Moreover, the immensity, the remoteness, and the savagery of Upper Louisiana overwhelmed Europeans who first encountered it, arousing in them an indelible sense that natural elements—endless prairies, primeval forests, and majestic rivers—governed human destiny, rendering impotent paltry lines that European diplomats sketched on crude maps of North America.

Heading up the Mississippi in August 1763,[9] Laclède left behind his pregnant concubine, Marie-Thérèse Bourgeois Chouteau, along with their three young children Jean-Pierre, Marie-Pélagie, and Marie-Louise.[10] Thirteen-year-old Auguste Chouteau, Marie Thérèse's child by her estranged husband, René, accompanied Laclède upriver. Given this fact and Madame Chouteau's strong personality, this high-risk venture must have had her blessing. Laclède's journey up the Mississippi went without a hitch and proceeded with remarkable swiftness, the trip consuming less than the three months usually required to ascend the river from New Orleans to the Illinois Country. Chouteau remembered that they arrived in the Illinois Country ("aux Illinois") on November 3 and that their first stop was Ste. Genevieve.[11] Ste. Genevieve was at the time the only village situated on the west side of the Mississippi in the Illinois Country, and it would have been a logical spot for Laclède to have set up a trading post—at least temporarily. But he soon discovered that Ste. Genevieve had no suitable place to accommodate his large stock of trade goods, which meant that he quickly moved on.[12] Laclède's most important accomplishment in Ste. Genevieve was meeting François Vallé, captain of the local militia and the wealthiest person in Upper Louisiana;[13] quite by accident, Laclède's first contact in the Illinois Country just happened to be one of the most important men in the entire region.

Concerning Laclède's activities during the autumn of 1763, we have four rock-solid, incontrovertible dates based on reliable sources: August 2, when Maxent, Laclède, and Le Dée met in New Orleans to strategize about their trading venture; August 10, when Laclède signed a notarial document in the city; November 6, when he was outbid at the auction of the Jesuit properties at Kaskaskia; and November 19, when he purchased a substantial property near Fort de Chartres. A plausible scenario would be that Laclède arrived in Ste. Genevieve in early November, crossed the Mississippi to Kaskaskia to participate in the Jesuit auction on November 6, and then moved on upriver to Chartres a few days after that.[14] Laclède apparently reached the fort only after November 8, or at least Commandant Neyon de Villiers made no mention of him when he wrote to d'Abbadie that day. Villiers, of course, had more important things on his mind as a group of Iroquois, Delawares, and Shawnees had just turned up at Fort de Chartres (November 2) displaying as trophies twenty English scalps and requesting military aid.[15] Villiers summarily rejected this request, making it

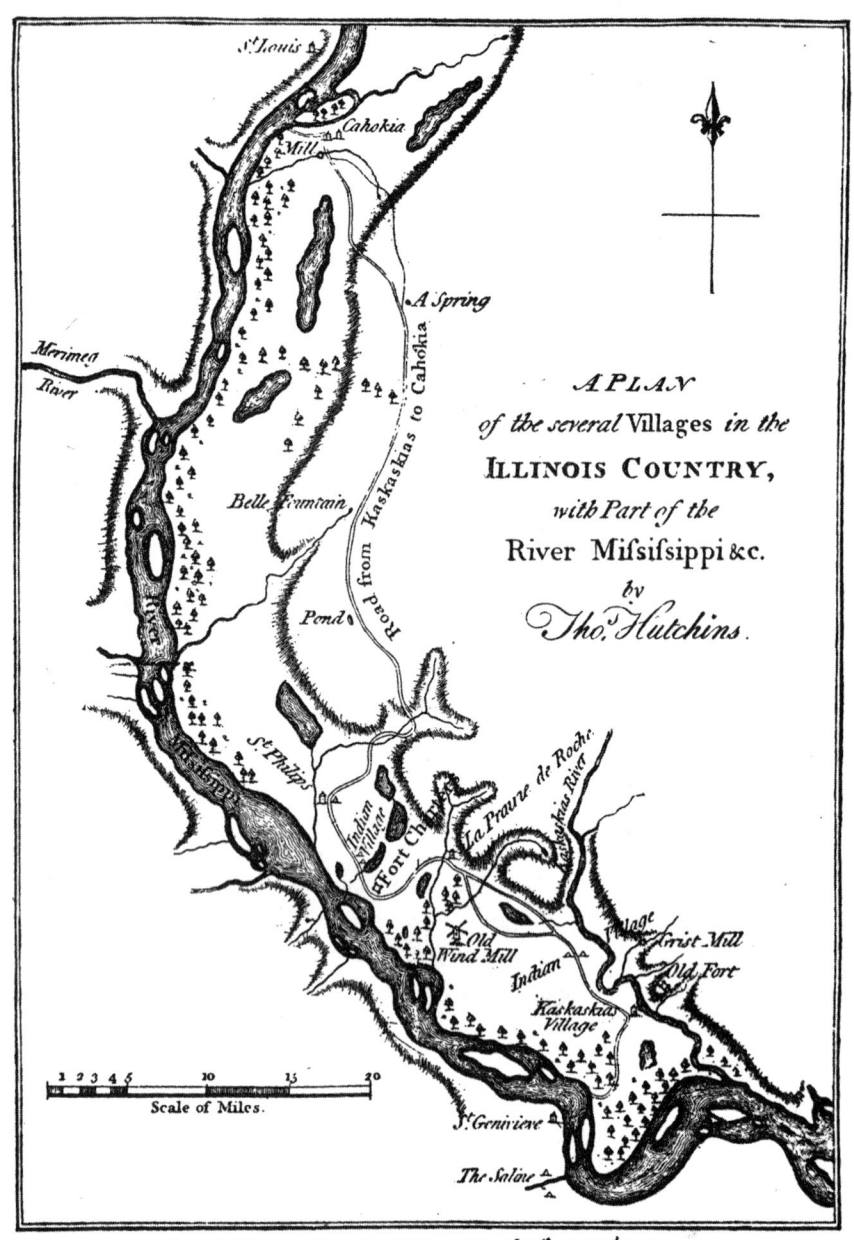

Lieutenant Thomas Hutchins's map of the Illinois Country, based on his exploration of the area in 1766. Notice St. Louis at the very top, of which Hutchins remarked that "it is the most healthy and pleasurable situation of any known in this part of the country. Here the Spanish Commandant [that is, St. Ange], and the principal Indian Traders reside." Reproduced from Frederick Charles Hicks, ed., A Topographical Description of Virginia, Pennsylvania, Maryland, and North Carolina, *reprint of 1778 ed. (Cleveland: Burrows Brothers, 1904).*

clear to the disappointed Indians that the French would not support Pontiac's continued resistance to British dominion east of the Mississippi River.[16]

The auction of the Jesuit properties was a signal event in the colonial history of the Illinois Country, but curiously Chouteau made no mention of it in his "Journal." Jesuit fathers had served—always conscientiously, often heroically—in the region for nearly a century, but their order was being suppressed by the government of King Louis XV. Although this action was welcomed by sophisticated Enlightenment courtiers at Versailles, it was a severe blow to the French habitants of the Illinois Country.[17] On the Mississippi frontier, the reverend fathers represented both the Roman Catholic Church *and* French civilization; they performed the holy sacraments but also participated in civic affairs, often drafting legal documents (in lieu of a notary) in a society that was largely illiterate. The black-robed fathers had been a ubiquitous presence in Kaskaskia, the very heart and soul of the community, from its founding in 1703 until 1763. The suppression of the Jesuit establishment marked a forlorn end of an era in the Illinois Country; it was almost as important as the treaty (February 1763) that conveyed to Great Britain the east side of the Mississippi River.

Auctions in the Illinois Country were traditionally held on Sundays, and the Jesuit properties in Kaskaskia were auctioned off on Sunday, November 6, 1763. This was done in front of the parish church of the Immaculate Conception just after Mass, as the parishioners (and a few visitors, such as Laclède) were flowing out of the front doors of the church. Laclède's losing but very substantial bid (thirty-nine thousand livres) on the Jesuit real estate reveals that, at that moment, he was seriously considering settling down there and that he had no preconceived idea of establishing a trading post on the west side of the Mississippi.[18] No one was making casual investments in real estate at Kaskaskia in 1763, and Laclède did not bid on the Jesuit properties as a side bet to his main commercial enterprise. Laclède must have thought that the ready-made Jesuit complex of buildings could serve him well as the main base for his trading operations. Indeed, who knows, in the long run Kaskaskia may have worked out better than St. Louis for Laclède, who failed to make his fortune trading out of St. Louis, whereas another fortune hunter, the Canadian Gabriel Cerré, became wealthy during the 1760s and '70s trading out of Kaskaskia in all directions—west, east, north, and south. It is noteworthy that Cerré visited St. Louis during the 1760s,[19] yet chose to remain in Kaskaskia for many years to come. The record of the Jesuit auction contains the first mention of Laclède's name in known sources from the Illinois Country. Laclède's presence at Kaskaskia in November 1763, and his hefty bid at the auction, must have set local tongues awagging—here was a flashy new guy in the neighborhood, French born and bred, and he had a lot of cash to throw around.

In the autumn of 1763, Laclède had his nose to the wind, sniffing about for an advantageous place to establish a trading outpost. Finding Ste. Genevieve unsuitable and failing in his bid for the Jesuit properties, Laclède quickly moved on to Chartres. Chouteau's narrative is credible about Laclède's searching-and-probing activities during this period. At Fort de Chartres, Neyon de Villiers commanded a shrinking garrison of French marines, a total of about thirty-five ill-equipped men. Villiers may well have permitted Laclède, who was a Frenchman (that is, neither Creole nor Canadian) like himself, to put up at the fort. On November 19, very soon after having reached Chartres, Laclède purchased a substantial property in the village close to the fort for seventy-five hundred livres.[20] Chouteau did not comment on this initiative, but Gilbert Maxent, Laclède's senior partner, did. Referring to himself in the third person, and not mentioning Laclède, Maxent wrote that "he then had [trade goods] transported at great cost to the village of Fort de Chartres; there, in the hope that there would be steady commerce, he created a very expensive establishment, which has since turned into a total loss."[21] Maxent was writing in 1769 and remarked that Laclède abandoned the trading outpost at Chartres only after British forces had occupied the region, which was manifestly untrue. Nevertheless, the substantial property that Laclède purchased at Chartres together with Maxent's account reveal that when Laclède made the purchase on November 19, 1763, he had every intention of establishing his trading outpost there and remaining for the foreseeable future. In any case, Laclède made no big impression at Chartres. Villiers sent a long, discursive dispatch to Governor d'Abbadie on December 1 and wrote not one word about Laclède's arrival at Chartres or his activities there and at Kaskaskia.[22] The newcomer from New Orleans had certainly not captured the commandant's attention.

Within a month after purchasing property at Chartres, Laclède, for reasons never explained, changed his mind. According to Chouteau's memories, Laclède, in December 1763 and "accompanied by a reliable young man [that is, Chouteau himself], set out to reconnoiter the entire vast region between Fort de Chartres and the Missouri country."[23] The region was vast but far from terra incognita. Since 1673 when Marquette and Jolliet became the first *known* white men to pass through it on their trip from Lake Michigan to the mouth of the Arkansas River, hundreds of explorers, missionaries, voyageurs, and *coureurs de bois* had viewed this region with interest and awe. Laclède had never ascended the Mississippi upriver from Fort de Chartres; he had never viewed the strategic region where the Mississippi, Missouri, and Illinois Rivers converge and where, thirty years later, Nicolas de Finiels would get drunk on the "indescribable spectacle" of the meeting of the three rivers.[24] Clearly, the reconnaissance of December 1763 was led not by Laclède but by men from Chartres who knew the region as well as they knew how to skin a white-tailed deer. The site selected was not so good for agriculture as Ste. Genevieve, but it was elevated enough to avoid flooding, it was close to the mouths of the Missouri and Illinois Rivers, it was intersected by several smaller sweet-water streams, and it had plentiful good timber for construction purposes. Given the favorable and well-known location of the site, it is also likely that cabins for seasonal dwellers—hunters, trappers, loggers, even quarriers of local limestone deposits—stood there.[25]

Laclède, after blazing some trees "with his own hand" (according to Chouteau) at the site, returned to Fort de Chartres and reported with "enthusiasm" to Commandant Neyon de Villiers that he had found the spot where he would build a settlement that one day would be one of the "plus belles villes de l'Amérique."[26] By the time that Chouteau penned these words decades later, he may well have been harboring grand thoughts about the future prospects of St. Louis, but it is unlikely that Laclède was dreaming that big in December 1763. More likely, he was merely hoping to get a modicum of return on his already substantial investment—in time, effort, and money—in the Illinois Country. And no evidence exists that Neyon de Villiers shared any of Laclède's enthusiasm about future development in the region. Rather, Villiers was already making personal plans in December to bail out of the Illinois Country and leave to St. Ange de Bellerive the anguish and chagrin of surrendering Fort de Chartres to British troops.[27]

Laclède's first recorded presence after the turn of the year 1764 came on January 24, when he witnessed the marriage of Gabriel Cerré and Catherine Giard in Kaskaskia.[28] It seems odd that Laclède would take the time to ride the five or six hours down from Fort de Chartres, spend several festive days in Kaskaskia, and then ride back to Chartres, just at the time that he was ostensibly ramping up to move his trading outpost across the Mississippi. Laclède had met most of the important men in Kaskaskia a few months earlier, when the Jesuit properties were auctioned off, and he was apparently determined to cultivate contacts with Kaskaskia's commercial elite. If young Auguste Chouteau accompanied Laclède to Kaskaskia for the Cerré-Giard wedding, which he likely did, he would have had an opportunity to acquaint himself with his future parents-in-law; Marie-Thérèse Cerré was born at Kaskaskia in 1769 and married Chouteau at St. Louis in 1786.

On February 3, 1764, Neyon de Villiers wrote to d'Abbadie, and he began with a topic that he deemed of the highest importance—the sterling personal qualities of François Vallé: "I have given permission to Sieur Vallé, captain of the militia in Ste. Genevieve, to descend to New Orleans to attend to his affairs, as well as those of some others." He is "one of the most energetic and wealthiest men in the region. Fortune seems to have rewarded him for being a good and honorable man [*honnête homme*]."[29] Indeed, Villiers was describing Vallé just as his fortunes were about to soar, making him the wealthiest

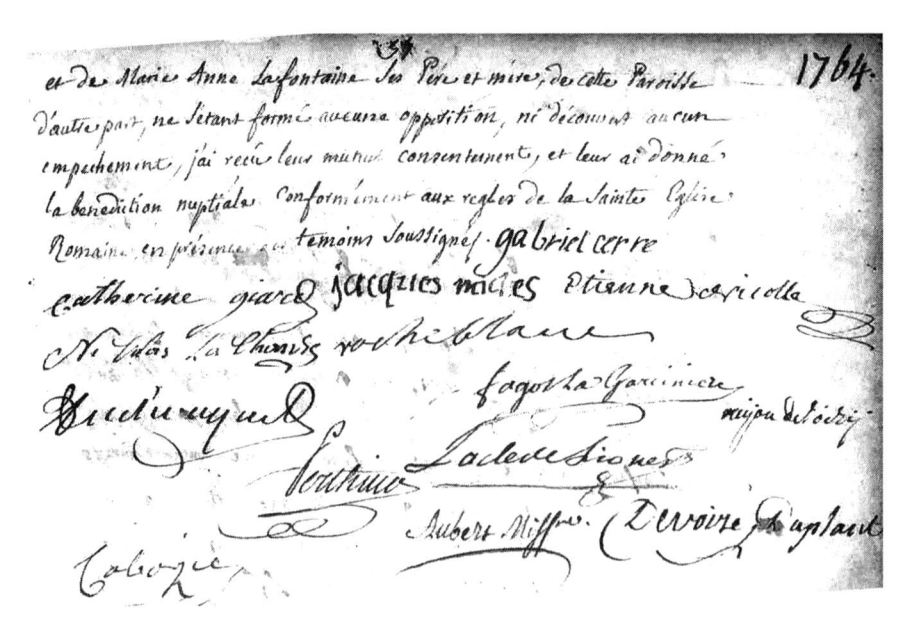

Gabriel Cerré and Catherine Giard marriage record (Kaskaskia, January 24, 1764), containing the signature of Pierre Laclède Liguest, among others. Laclède was establishing rapport with the Illinois Country's power elite. The young Auguste Chouteau was very likely present at this marriage of his future wife's mother and father. Courtesy of the Diocese of Belleville.

man within a five-hundred-mile radius of Ste. Genevieve; his assets, especially in slaves and agricultural land, dwarfed anyone else's in the region at the time.[30] After discussing Vallé's signal virtues, Villiers yawned before dryly noting, "Since my last dispatch, nothing much out of the ordinary has occurred in these parts. I learn only by itinerant French and Indians that the latter intend to recommence hostilities with the English as soon as they can get pulled together." Villiers wrote this just as (according to Chouteau's account) Chouteau was about to lead an expedition from Fort de Chartres to the hallowed ground on the west bank of the Mississippi that Laclède had selected for his trading outpost. But it was the continuing reverberations from Pontiac's rebellion that were on Villiers's mind, not anything that Laclède and Chouteau were planning, proposing, or executing.

As we have seen, Chouteau's accounts of events associated with St. Louis's founding must be handled gingerly. According to his "Journal," in early February 1764, Laclède fitted out a bateau, loaded it with thirty men, "almost all laborers," and put fourteen-year-old Chouteau in charge of the expedition.[31] He was to proceed up and across the Mississippi, to the site that had been selected two months earlier, and begin work on a seed settlement. John Francis

McDermott picked up the story at that point and, relying exclusively on Chouteau's narrative, painted this captivating scene: "It is the afternoon of the 14th of February more than 200 years ago. A bateau draws up at an opening in the low bluff on the western bank of the [Mississippi] river. A very young man—he is not yet five months beyond his fourteenth birthday—steps ashore followed by thirty men. Camp is made for the night. Supplies are unloaded. There is some talk, no doubt, about what is to come."[32] This enchanting scene, enough to tickle the soul of any former Boy Scout, stretches credulity, for the men who likely accompanied young Chouteau were in no way the sort of men to be taking orders from a fourteen-year-old greenhorn scarcely off the bateau from New Orleans.[33] The very notion of this is preposterous.

Take, for example, Jean-Baptiste Martigny, who was almost certainly a member of this expedition.[34] Martigny was born in 1718 at Varennes, just across the St. Lawrence River from Montreal, son of Jacques Lemoine, sieur de Martigny.[35] Unlike many French Canadians in the Illinois Country, Jean-Baptiste had a formal education and an elegant hand. Martigny emigrated to the Illinois County in the early 1740s and in 1745 married Marie Hébert, daughter of Ignace Hébert, longtime captain of the militia in the parish of Ste. Anne at Chartres. Martigny himself—intelligent, educated, and assertive—quickly rose to prominence in the Illinois Country, wheeling and dealing and trading in everything imaginable and inevitably becoming an officer in the Ste. Anne parish militia; all important leaders in every community in the Illinois Country during the entire colonial era served as militia officers. The tradition, going back to Canada and even further back to France,[36] of militia officers as community leaders and not just military leaders was very strong in the Illinois Country. François Vallé, leading citizen in Ste. Genevieve, was captain of the militia there; Martigny would be the first such captain in St. Louis; and thirty years later, Auguste Chouteau would be captain in St. Louis. In short, there was no way on earth that a man like Martigny would have taken orders from a fourteen-year-old lad, even one as precocious as Auguste Chouteau. Frederick H. Hodes has pointed out that Martigny in fact got the choicest residential lot in the embryonic outpost on the west bank of the Mississippi,[37] and it is not unlikely that Martigny was in charge of the expedition that traversed the icy river that fateful February 1764.

Indeed, Martigny, along with his high-status wife, Marie Hébert, and formidable *métisse* mother-in-law, Hélène Danis, might well have initiated the entire project of forming a new settlement on the west bank of the Mississippi. As a militia officer, he had survived the French military calamity at Belle Famille, outside Fort Niagara, in July 1759, but he had witnessed the horrors as Iroquois warriors, British allies, tracked down wounded Frenchmen, scalped, and killed them.[38] No Frenchman in North America detested the English more than Jean-Baptiste Martigny, and by 1763 he knew with certainty that British troops were preparing to occupy *his* Illinois Country, that portion of the region lying east of the Mississippi. Martigny and his fellow militiamen were the obvious men to organize an amphibious move from Chartres to the west side of the Mississippi—they had the knowledge, the skills, and the motives. Laclède, invited by these men, likely threw in his lot and joined the expedition pretty much at the last minute. That is, the energy and initiative to settle across the river did not come from New Orleans via Laclède but rather from habitants and militiamen at Chartres.[39] Such a scenario clears up many inconsistencies and confusions in the traditional story of St. Louis's founding, including the issue of Laclède's abrupt, and puzzling, abandonment of his newly bought property at Chartres. Settlement at St. Louis did not proceed as a consequence of a capricious decision by Laclède but rather progressed as a result of evolving circumstances in the Illinois Country.

The best source—indeed, the only known independent, contemporary source—concerning events in the Illinois Country during the early spring of 1764 is Commandant Neyon de Villiers's letter to d'Abbadie of March 13, 1764.

> I have the honor to inform you that since my last dispatch [that of February 3] Sieur Laclède has presented a request asking permission to establish a trading house [*établissement*] on the other side of the Mississippi, specifying that he has from you verbal permission to establish one in what he judges to be the best location. He has accomplished this, at least the plan [*dumoins le projet*]; and therefore, has begun having trees cut [et en conséquence, il a fait mettre hache en bois]. I've been content to tell him . . . that he can go ahead while we await your response concerning the objectives of which we have had the honor to inform you.[40]

The tenor of the letter suggests that when Villiers was writing on March 13, Laclède had just heard from the men (including Martigny and young Chouteau), who were engaged at the site on the west bank of the Mississippi. Villiers's dispatches of early 1764 inform us that he had little interest in what Laclède was doing, and d'Abbadie in New Orleans apparently had none at all. He never bothered to respond to Villiers's dispatch of March 13, and he never once mentioned Laclède or his commercial plans in the detailed "Journal" that he kept between June 1763 and December 1764.[41] Once Laclède had departed New Orleans in early August 1763, he was gone, out of sight and out of mind to administrators in Louisiana's metropole. Laclède appears briefly in Villiers's dispatch in March and then disappears, like a wraith. When Villiers again wrote to d'Abbadie on April 20, 1764, he was preoccupied with Pontiac, who had just arrived at Fort de Chartres and whose provocations were keeping Villiers busy "day and night."[42] The fact that Laclède had recently left Chartres to join Martigny and Chouteau across the Mississippi was of no interest to Villiers. Laclède emerged from total obscurity only two years later—first, when he showed up at Ste. Genevieve as a fur trader in April 1766 and then when St. Ange enumerated him (along with Marie-Thérèse Bourgeois Chouteau and her unnamed children) on the St. Louis census of May 1766.[43]

Madame Chouteau's role in the settlement of St. Louis is one of the enduring mysteries left by the scarcity of reliable sources from the early 1760s. Curiously, Auguste Chouteau, neither in his "Journal" nor in his deposition to land commissioner Theodore Hunt, ever once mentions his mother and her role in the events of 1764–65. Marie-Thérèse Bourgeois Chouteau's last child, Victoire, was baptized at New Orleans in May 1764, having been conceived shortly before Laclède departed New Orleans in August 1763.[44] On June 12, 1764, a convoy of three bateaux left New Orleans on June 12, "sent by Illinois and Missouri traders," and headed up the Mississippi.[45] Along with seventy-two crew members, five passengers were in the convoy, and these were almost certainly Madame Chouteau and her four children by Laclède—Jean-Pierre, Marie-Pélagie, Marie-Louise, and the suckling infant, Victoire. Jean-Baptiste Rivière claimed that his father, Antoine Rivière, brought Marie-Thérèse Chouteau and her four children northward from Kaskaskia in a cart, accompanied by Laclède, who was presumably on horseback.[46] Once arriving at Cahokia, this party would then have crossed the Mississippi to the new settlement in a pirogue or bateau. Given the usual time required to ascend the Mississippi, Rivière's cartage of Madame Chouteau and her children must have occurred in early autumn 1764. Pierre Chouteau's later testimony, that he had arrived (as a six-year-old) in St. Louis six months after the settlement's founding,[47] more or less affirms that chronology, placing madame in St. Louis by September of that year. Despite Auguste's failure to discuss his mother, Marie-Thérèse Chouteau quickly established a formidable presence in the early settlement, partly because she was Laclède's consort, but more important because she possessed substantial assets—physical, intellectual, emotional, and financial—in her own right.

The history of St. Louis during the two years between the spring of 1764 and that of 1766 will remain forever a frustrating enigma, for only bits and scraps of reliable sources remain from which to reconstruct the story. Historians Richard Edwards and M. Hopewell honestly confessed, when they had arrived at 1765 in their narrative of early St. Louis, that "it becomes now necessary to break off the thread of the narrative, which cannot be pursued any farther at the present time with lucidity."[48] A scattering of sources for that time period do exist, however, and they do not reflect well on Laclède. Billon recounts that in April 1765, "a boat loaded with merchandise for the Indian trade of the Missouri River, before the establishment of any government here [St. Louis] under the charge and management of one Joseph Calvé, a clerk of the owners Messrs. John [Jean-Baptiste] Datchurut and Louis Viviat, merchants of Ste. Genevieve, was seized by employees of the government, at the instance of Pierre Laclède, as violating the laws of the Indian trade, and more especially the claims of the firm of Maxent, Laclède & Co. to the exclusive trade with the Indians of the Missouri."[49] After acknowledging that no government existed in St. Louis at the time, Billon did not explain how *government* agents materialized to seize the boat on behalf of Laclède.

Datchurut and Viviat did not take Laclède's seizure of their valuable merchandise in good humor, but rather sued in French Louisiana's highest tribunal—the Superior Council in New Orleans.[50] Laclède was the loser, and on May 25, 1767, he signed two promissory notes, one for Datchurut and one for Viviat, each representing one-half the total value (6,485 livres, 8 sols) of their confiscated merchandise.[51] Two years later, Maxent wrote that he had been "grievously damaged by the loss of a lawsuit, in which he was of necessity involved in order to protect the privileges granted him [that is, exclusive trading privileges] by a commandant [d'Abbadie] duly authorized by the king, which the [Superior] Council has nonetheless decided not to respect."[52] The Superior Council records for this case have not survived, and it is a bit of a mystery why the court decided against Maxent and Laclède. Perhaps it was because (as suggested earlier) the Maxent-Laclède trading grant was never formalized in writing, and by the time the case came before the Superior Council (likely not until 1766), d'Abbadie was dead (February 1765) and could not explain to the councilors what he had done regarding trading privileges back in 1763.[53]

Laclède launched his first recorded fur-trading venture in the autumn of 1765, when he provided a group of three voyageurs from Ste. Genevieve merchandise for trading with Shawnee Indians, whose villages were located along the lower Ohio River.[54] Laclède's decision to trade out of Ste. Genevieve must have been based on his earlier contacts (starting in November 1763) with François Vallé, who worked closely with local and regional Indian tribes.[55] The trade goods that Laclède brought to Ste. Genevieve may well have been those that he had confiscated from the bateau of Datchurut and Viviat earlier that same year. In any case, Laclède was apparently imprudent enough not to formalize with a written contract his business relationship with the voyageurs, and this venture turned into a total disaster. Rather than trading Laclède's merchandise for peltries in the Shawnee village, our merry voyageurs used the trade goods to purchase sexual favors from Shawnee women, quite "abandoning themselves to libertinage." The women, for their part, were apparently free to negotiate their own terms in the sex-for-trade-goods bartering that transpired, not requiring permission from anyone to conduct the business at hand.[56]

In April 1766, Laclède invited a group of Shawnee men, in addition to an upright trader who had also been present in the Shawnee village, to appear in Ste. Genevieve and testify about the voyageurs' licentious and larcenous behavior. The Shawnees were duly sworn in, and their testimony was recorded by a notary and witnessed by St. Ange and François Vallé, among others.[57] This is the only recorded instance when these two men, French Canadians by birth but at the time the two most powerful persons in Upper Louisiana, ever met face-to-face. The swearing-in ceremony presented an exotic tableau in old Ste. Genevieve, provoking wonderment about just what the Shawnees were thinking when they placed their hands on the Bible for the swearing-in process. No further paper trail exists about this affair, and it is not known whether the Shawnee deposition helped Laclède recoup from the *voyageurs debauchés* any of his losses. Vallé seems to have served Laclède's interests poorly in Ste. Genevieve, setting him up with dissolute and unreliable voyageurs and failing to advise him to secure a written contract with them.[58] One must wonder whether the wily (though illiterate) Vallé, fearing competition from the sophisticated Frenchmen's apparent wealth, had lured the greenhorn into this hopeless quagmire. As it turned out, Laclède drifted slowly toward insolvency, while Vallé's wealth and influence continued to grow by leaps and bounds until his death in 1783.[59]

This entire episode begs a puzzling question about Laclède and his intentions. If, as conventional wisdom has it, Laclède founded his St. Louis trading outpost where he did in order to engage in the Missouri River fur trade, why was his first recorded fur-trading venture with Shawnees who frequented the Ohio River valley? And this question in turn raises further significant issues: Was it in fact Laclède who selected the site upon which St. Louis would slowly arise? If Laclède did indeed select the site, what was his purpose in doing so? Why did Laclède, a Frenchman located in what was technically Spanish territory, choose to trade with Indians who were located in British territory east of the Mississippi River? A single manuscript located in the civil records of early Ste. Genevieve provokes all of these important questions that are yet to be satisfactorily answered, even as the 250th anniversary of St. Louis's founding is being celebrated.

Laclède was surely not dominating the fur trade in Upper Louisiana during the mid-1760s (see chapter 10). He took a loss on the property that he had impulsively acquired at Chartres, according to Maxent. Then he was aggressive in seizing Datchurut's and Viviat's trade goods, only to lose that case at the Superior Council in New Orleans and suffer the consequent financial penalty. And finally, he botched the trading venture with Shawnees outside of Ste. Genevieve. Laclède's erratic behavior during the mid-1760s certainly was not an auspicious beginning to a fur-trading career.

⚜ ⚜ ⚜ ⚜

During the mid-1760s, French administrators in the Illinois Country were consumed with affairs east of the Mississippi—Pontiac's rebellion and the imminent arrival of British forces in the region. No French officer or administrator in Louisiana of any stature supported Pontiac's quixotic rebellion against British occupation of the West. In October 1763, Villiers flatly rejected an invitation to provide assistance to Pontiac, and Governor d'Abbadie quickly affirmed that Villiers had done well to do so; France wanted a smooth and tranquil transfer of power in the Illinois Country.[60] In April 1764, Villiers and Pontiac squared off face-to-face at Fort de Chartres. According to one first-person account, when Pontiac offered Villiers a wampum belt of alliance (Villiers's acceptance of which would have violated formal treaty obligations signed in Paris and taken the French garrison at Fort de Chartres back into an unwinnable war against the British), Villiers kicked the belt from Pontiac's hand and demanded of the once fearsome chief if he was hard of hearing.[61] Villiers's contemptuous gesture was either one of the more foolhardy acts ever committed on the Mississippi frontier or Villiers sensed that Pontiac's once mighty stature was already beginning to wilt.

In April 1765, an Indian arrived at Detroit from Illinois and reported that "their Father [St. Ange at that time] is there and holds the Hatchet by the middle of the Handle, but as soon as the strawberries are Ripe he will take it by the proper end."[62] This report was patently untrue. After his arrival at Fort de Chartres about June 1, 1764, St. Ange adhered punctiliously to Villiers's policy, although this did not allay British suspicions of him. General Thomas Gage wrote from New York that St. Ange was "greatly to be Suspected,"[63] as indeed were all French commandants in the West. Gage, who (along with George Washington) had narrowly escaped death when French-led Indians demolished General Edward Braddock's army near the Monongahela River in 1755, harbored an abiding distrust of Frenchmen. But, in truth, St. Ange positively discouraged any Indian resistance to British occupation of the Illinois Country. In his first dispatch to Governor d'Abbadie as commandant at Fort de Chartres, St. Ange told of how the tribal chiefs from the Wabash Valley, men he had surely met when he was commandant at Vincennes, came to him begging assistance for their impoverished tribes. St. Ange coldly admonished them that if they had quit fighting the British as Villiers had earlier advised them, they would not find themselves in such desperate straits.[64] When d'Abbadie wrote to Gage protesting accusations that the French were complicit in Indian opposition to British occupation of the Mississippi Valley, he appended a copy of St. Ange's dispatch to prove his point.[65]

Charles Gayarré, a Creole historian of deep French sympathies, thought that Villiers (and by implication St. Ange) had carried "Christian humility and charity" too far in working "to dispose the Indians favorably towards the English."[66] The fact that neither Villiers nor St. Ange evinced any sympathy whatsoever for Pontiac or his cause is perhaps a bit surprising, and Parkman saw fit to comment on the issue: "Perhaps in his secret heart, Saint-Ange would have rejoiced to see the scalps of all the Englishmen in the backwoods fluttering in the wind, . . . but his situation forbade him to comply with the solicitations of his intrusive petitioners."[67] Villiers and St. Ange, as *bons français*, properly despised the English (as Gayarré bloody well thought they should), but as French officers of honor, they felt a deep obligation to adhere to the international political order as arranged in peace treaties signed in Europe. This obligation trumped any vision of a continuing concord in the old Illinois Country (that is, east of the Mississippi River), with French settlements governed by the Bourbon monarchy existing more or less harmoniously with diverse Indian nations.

St. Ange, in anticipation of the approaching parleying season, wrote to d'Abbadie on February 21, 1765, assuring the governor that he "would punctually obey his orders to strive at reconciling the Indians and the English."[68] In early April 1765, with various bands of Illinois Indians returning from their winter hunt, St. Ange convened at Fort de Chartres a large assembly of Indian chiefs. Representatives were present from most all divisions of the Illinois nation (Kaskaskia, Peoria, Cahokia, Michigamea), as well as from the Missouris and the Osages. St. Ange's delegation also included several officers from his garrison, plus the captain of the local militia and Joseph-François Lefebvre. Lefebvre was chief magistrate in the Illinios Country. He worked closely with St. Ange at Chartres during the final year of the French regime there, and this collaboration continued during their first critical year together at St. Louis. The assembly's guest of honor, as it were, was Lieutenant John Ross of the Thirty-Fourth Regiment, who had come up overland from the newly installed British garrison at Mobile. Ross had arrived at Fort de Chartres on February 18 and reported that St. Ange received him "very agreeably."[69]

St. Ange's long-term purpose in holding this ecumenical conference was to maintain peace with, and among, the various Indian tribes, but his immediate goal was to tamp down any possibility of Pontiac's rebellion flaring up anew.[70] St. Ange began the proceedings with a long exhortation about how peace would serve the best interests of all Indian nations. Repeatedly addressing the Indians as "chers enfants rouges," St. Ange understood that they had no objection to being metaphorically identified as his children.[71] St. Ange argued his case—articulately, conscientiously, and sincerely—for peace and tranquillity. He closed by referring (no doubt also gesturing) to Lieutenant Ross, insisting that he had come to the Illinois Country in peace and was willing to listen to the Indians' side of things. St. Ange went so far as to claim that the English were brothers to the French, who were brothers (if not fathers) to the Indians. These words must have stuck in St. Ange's craw, but he was merely doing his duty as an official emissary of the French crown.

St. Ange's we're-all-brothers speech did not gain any noticeable traction with the assembled Indians. A Kaskaskia chief, Tamarois, gave an eloquent but combative reply on behalf of the entire Illinois nation: The Illinois wanted nothing to do with the English. Tamarois was glad that Ross had come to hear him out, and Ross had nothing to fear as St. Ange's guest. But the English were wicked, they did not have the pure heart ("coeur blanc") of the French, and they were not welcome in the Illinois Country. Shaking Ross's hand, not in friendship but as a gesture of ultimate rupture, Tamarois advised him to get out, depart, and do not return. An unnamed chief representing the Missouris and Osages then spoke, and his words echoed those of Tamarois. The Missouris and Osages knew only the French as their fathers. The English should remain on their own lands and leave Indian lands to the Indians. In clasping Ross's hand, he admonished the Englishman to "depart, depart, depart." Significantly, in his discussion of real estate, this Indian spokesman accepted as legitimate the French presence (as opposed to the English) in the region, believing that it presented no threat to traditional Indian tribal lands. This is all the more interesting because the permanent villages in the region were, of course, French.

St. Ange's report about this grand convocation was studiously factual, but he was glad enough that Ross was preparing to leave the Illinois Country, which he soon did. Ross's report from New Orleans a few weeks later was more pessimistic, and he recounted an episode at Fort de Chartres that had startled and frightened him. Ross and St. Ange were in conference in St. Ange's office when an Osage chief burst in and demanded an audience with the commandant. Upon seeing Ross, he flew into a rage and, according to Ross, would have attacked him with his tomahawk if St. Ange and the interpreters present had not intervened.[72] As he had in arriving at the fort, Ross complimented St. Ange, noting that he was obliged to say that the French commandant had treated him in "a very friendly manner during my Stay in Illinois." Indian responses to St. Ange's plea that they accept British dominion with tranquillity did not bode well for British Illinois, and in truth British rule, or at least the semblance of rule, in the region (1765–78) turned out to be difficult, troubled, problematic—and brief. Pontiac did not attend the early April 1765 conference held at Chartres (he appeared there shortly afterward), but his spirit hung heavy over the gathering. The Osage chief who had threatened Ross in St. Ange's office vouched for his undying loyalty to Pontiac and his hatred of all things English.

Ross was soon followed to the Illinois Country by Lieutenant Alexander Fraser, who left Fort Pitt in late March and arrived at Fort de Chartres a month later.[73] Fraser moved quickly by disembarking from his "batteau" at Fort Massac on the lower Ohio River and cutting northwestward overland to Kaskaskia (the same route that George Rogers Clark made famous in 1778). Fraser spoke passable French, and he learned from local habitants about Ross's narrow escape at Chartres several weeks earlier. The dramatic story making the rounds in Kaskaskia was that St. Ange had only with difficulty saved Ross's life and that if Ross had remained at Chartres until Pontiac arrived, he would have been forthwith seized and burned by Pontiac's retainers.

The road between Kaskaskia and Fort de Chartres (trunk road of the Illinois Country) had been improved over the decades, and Fraser hired a calash and driver to carry him up to the fort in relative comfort. When he arrived, St. Ange repeated the Ross incident to Fraser and warned him to move about only at night so as to avoid detection as a British officer. That evening Fraser was at dinner with St. Ange at the fort when Pontiac burst in like a raging (and perhaps drunken) bull with eight retainers and seized the Englishman, with the apparent intention of hauling him off to endure God only knows what torments. But St. Ange rose to the occasion as an officer and gentleman, daring Pontiac to kill him first and declaring that he was determined to die rather than surrender his guest.[74] The Indians released Fraser, whose pants were perhaps soiled, but Pontiac had nevertheless been squarely faced down. This was a galvanic moment, and emblematic of the beginning of the end of his power and influence. Fraser reported that "Pontiack and his Ruffians are mostly always drunk. He himself is too sensible to abuse me but his followers, who are a set of idle, abandond Rascals, strike me and threaten at times to scalp or burn me."[75] Sadly, the former charismatic warrior was now mostly drunken bluster, more a gang leader rather than a war chief. Pontiac's aim of preserving a modicum of Indian power in the swath of wilderness between Ohio River and the Great Lakes had been a noble goal, but as the tide turned against him he had to face defeat from which he knew no recovery was possible. Ultimate defeat rarely brings out the best in a man, and in Pontiac's case it diminished him as a person. The pathos that inhabits the trajectory of Pontiac's rise and decline makes for a rueful epilogue to the French and Indian War.

Nevertheless, during the spring of 1765, Pontiac was still a man of many faces, and over a period of several weeks Fraser's attitude toward him changed dramatically: "He is the Person who seems most inclined to peace amongst any of them, and it is to be wished that He may be prevail'd on to make a Peace, as it will probably be of a longer duration than any made without him. He is in a manner Ador'd by the Nations hereabouts, and He is more remarkable for His integrity and humanity than either French Man or Indian in the Colony [that is the Illinois Country]."[76] Pontiac's enthusiasm for continued war was flickering out, and he told Fraser that one of the reasons he was inclined toward peace was that his French father, St. Ange, had recommended it.[77] Pontiac (when he had his demons under control) was obviously an accomplished diplomat as well as a warrior, and his mollifying words quite captivated Fraser. The British officer was less sure, however, about the Frenchman, St. Ange, bluntly informing him that he ought do a better job of managing the Indians.[78] St. Ange, who had saved Fraser's life a few weeks earlier, must have tossed the lieutenant's letter into his fireplace with a wry smile about the ungrateful nature of the human race.

In any event, the prolonged efforts of the British to install a garrison at Fort de Chartres were about to pay off. George Croghan, frontiersman extraordinaire, played a major role in these efforts. He deserves to be better known—Indian agent, guest in the Onondaga Council, land speculator, fur trader, adventurer of vertiginous ambitions—Croghan was the most important Britain in the Ohio Country for the twenty-five years preceding the American Revolution. He turns up everywhere: at Pickawillany on the Big Miami River in 1752, at Winchester for the big Indian-white conclave in 1753, at Braddock's defeat on the Monongahela in 1755, at the British conquest of Fort Duquesne (Fort Pitt) in 1758. Narrowly escaping death on numerous occasions, his presence was ubiquitous on the trans-Appalachian frontier. In May 1765, Croghan set out down the Ohio River from Fort Pitt for the West, and in June Kickapoos and Mascoutens attacked his party near the mouth of the Wabash River. Croghan "got the Stroke of a Hatchet on the Head, but my Scull being pretty thick, the hatchet would not enter, so You may See a thick Scull is of Service on some Occasions."[79] By June 15, Croghan had arrived at Vincennes on the Wabash, where St. Ange had commanded for nearly three decades, and remarked: "The French Inhabitants hereabouts are an idle lazy people a parcel of Renegadoes from Canada and much worse than the Indians."[80] Well, anyone who has even briefly followed Croghan's frenetic career understands that *everyone* else is idle and lazy. Croghan certainly knew that St. Ange had commanded at Vincennes, and he wrote to him from his former post in June. Unfortunately, that letter has not survived, but it must have pertained to St. Ange's intercession that saved Croghan's life when Indians in the Wabash Valley had threatened to burn him, this act of mercy tendered despite the fact that Croghan was a notorious Francophobe.[81] While in the central Wabash Valley, Croghan met with Pontiac, "a shrewd Sensible Indian of few words," and was largely successful in persuading the great Ottawa chief to accept British occupation of the Illinois Country.[82]

In September 1765, General Thomas Gage, commander of all British troops in North America, wrote of the vexatious problems in the Mississippi Valley. "The takeing Possession of the Illinois, . . . and relieving the French troops posted there . . . has been attended with a good deal of Difficulty and very great risk. . . . The French Traders and Inhabitants, found means privately to obstruct our Endeavors."[83] Gage's assessment was accurate, but he was careful not to claim that French officers had also conspired to thwart British efforts to take possession of Illinois, as prescribed in the Treaty of Paris (1763). Taking possession was inherently a difficult task, for only two avenues existed for bringing a serious British force to Fort de Chartres—up the Mississippi River from New Orleans or down the Ohio River from Fort Pitt. Individuals (Ross, for example) might thread their way overland from Mobile, but large expeditions required the big rivers for transport of men and matériel. And both major river routes were tenuous and dangerous, for if Louis XV's government, and the French command in Louisiana, had reconciled itself to a British takeover, many Indians had not.

Governor d'Abbadie in New Orleans permitted British troops to use his city (never British territory) as a jumping-off point for an upriver expedition to Illinois, and Major Arthur Loftus attempted this ascent in 1764.[84] But Loftus's expedition foundered after being attacked by Tunica Indians, conceivably incited by French traders, several hundred miles upriver from New Orleans. In 1765 the British decided on a two-pronged attack. Major Arthur Farmar, who brought troops over from his Thirty-Fourth Regiment at Mobile, set out from New Orleans in late June.[85] Meanwhile, Croghan sent word from Detroit to Fort Pitt that Pontiac had accepted peace, which made the Ohio River avenue to the Illinois Country somewhat less dangerous than it had been. This news encouraged Captain Thomas Stirling of the famous Forty-Second Regiment (the Black Watch) to set off down the Ohio River from Fort Pitt on August 24 with some 111 men, plus two interpreters, in seven "Battoes."[86]

During the colonial era, river travel from the forks of the Ohio (Fort Duquesne, Fort Pitt, finally Pittsburgh) to the Illinois Country was always more swift than from New Orleans. Stirling's party made remarkably good time in its long descent of the Ohio (and shorter ascent of the Mississippi), taking only six weeks to get to Fort de Chartres and arriving nearly two months before Farmar coming up from New Orleans. Although of lesser rank than Farmar, Stirling was empowered to accept the transfer of Illinois from French to British hands. On September 30, the British troops completed their descent of the "very clear" waters of the Ohio River and commenced the tedious ascent of the "thick, dirty, clay-coloured" waters of the Mississippi. On October 9, the convoy proceeded upriver past Ste. Genevieve, and the British surgeon's mate, Lieutenant James Eddington, remarked on the "very pretty Girls" who gazed in wonderment from the right bank of the Mississippi.[87] These Roman Catholic maidens had no idea that they were witnessing the first major influx of Protestants to the Illinois Country; indeed, they likely did not know exactly what sort of strange creatures Protestants were, other than that they were reputed to be a vengeful enemy.

By three in the afternoon, the British arrived at Fort de Chartres, where they were "receiv'd very politely at the landing by Monsr. St. Ange, a very Gentlemanly looking old man."[88] The necessary official proceedings moved along apace the next day. The heart of the matter was the cession of the fort and all its buildings, and a remarkably detailed description of these structures was drawn up, both in French and in English. Stirling and St. Ange had a minor disagreement about the disposition of the "Ammunition and Artillery Stores" at Fort de Chartres, but that was soon resolved in Stirling's favor because St. Ange with his pathetic garrison of French marines had no leverage with which to bargain.[89] The cession was officially signed on October 10, 1765, by Stirling, James Rumsey (Stirling's commissary), St. Ange, and Joseph Lefebvre, *garde magasin* (storekeeper) at the fort. British officers were noticeably impressed with the fort. "One of the Prettyest Stone Forts I ever Saw,"[90] Eddington remarked, and capable of housing two hundred troops, according to Stirling.[91] Captain Harry Gordon went further, "the Barracks are . . . commodious and elegant. This Place is large enough to contain 400 men."[92]

Back in December 1763, Neyon de Villiers claimed that he was prepared to turn Fort de Chartres over to St. Ange with a garrison of forty marines in the spring of 1764.[93] But by October 1765, that number had dwindled to twenty men and one officer; some had perhaps deserted, and some may have gotten permission to move across the Mississippi to Ste. Genevieve or St. Louis.[94] The British newcomers were not impressed by the quality of these troops, for the garrison at Chartres had been painfully neglected for years. Destitute French officials in New Orleans simply did not have the resources to keep the Illinois garrison properly supplied and accoutered. Eddington snottily observed that "the French troops we relieved here might be called anything else but Soldiers, in Short I defy the best drol comick to represent them at Drury Lane."[95] The English lieutenant could not get over the scruffy appearance of the French marines, and he remarked in his "Journal" that they looked like "Invalids without any sort of uniform. Most of them had on Jackets of different colours and slouch'd Hats."[96] The sad portrait Eddington drew of St. Ange's French marines is reminiscent of photos taken of disconsolate, ragtag Confederate soldiers at the close of the American Civil War.

When St. Ange died in December 1774, he owned a handful of books, including Pierre de Briquet's *Code Militaire*.[97] Stirring are the words that St. Ange would have read, perhaps put to memory, from Briquet's preface: "The French nation has always been considered warlike and bellicose. It is by arms that she has distinguished herself since the time of the Gauls, and her reputation antedates her existence." With these words engraved on his heart, St. Ange could not countenance having one of his own French troops strike the "Pavilion Francois [sic]," under which he had served for a half century (and his father for a half century before that). Captain Stirling finally ordered one of his own soldiers to bring down the Bourbon flag, the last French flag ever to fly over Fort de Chartres. Stirling's laconic reporting of this incident, with no hint of triumphalism, suggests that he had a certain grudging respect for St. Ange's obstinate loyalty to France.[98] Stirling was a Scot, after all, and he had heard from childhood about the Auld Alliance between Scotland and France that went back through many desperately fought battles to the thirteenth century.[99] As for St. Ange, until his death in December 1774, he simply could not help himself—he would continue to consider the territory that he governed as French, and, in truth, in most respects that is exactly what it was.

CHAPTER 4

Commandant St. Ange de Bellerive

Lieutenant Governor Piernas shall preserve the best of relations with Monsieur de St. Ange, whose practical knowledge of the Indians will be very useful to him. He shall do whatever he can to gain his friendship and confidence, and shall listen to his opinion attentively on all matters.

—Governor-General Alejandro O'Reilly, February 1770

Frederic Louis Billon correctly observed that as of the spring of 1765, no government existed at what would eventually become St. Louis.[1] This would change dramatically by the end of year, when Louis St. Ange de Bellerive brought a governing organization with all the personnel—lock, stock, and barrel—over from the east side of the Mississippi. St. Ange established this civil government at St. Louis six months before there was any ecclesiastical presence in the settlement, for the itinerant Father Sébastien-Louis Meurin did not record his first baptisms there (in a tent) until May 1766.[2] First and foremost, St. Ange's government was a military organization, because St. Ange was an officer and accustomed to a hierarchical command structure. But he also brought with him ancient French customary laws and habits that could not be violated willy-nilly and could not be ignored by the commandant. British lieutenant Alexander Fraser remarked that St. Ange enticed French habitants from the east side of the Mississippi to join him at St. Louis "for the Advantages of Enjoying their Ancient Priviledges and Laws."[3] Traditional privileges included freedom from direct taxation and the right to peacefully assemble and petition the government, and laws included the Customary Law of Paris (see chapter 7).

Once Fort de Chartres had been relinquished to British forces on October 10, 1765, St. Ange had no reason to tarry on the east side of the Mississippi. But on October 11, he did ask of Captain Thomas Stirling that French marines be permitted to remain in the fort for a few days until he could secure lodgings for his men on the other side of the river.[4] On October 17, Lieutenant Eddington stated categorically that "the French Commandant removed his Garrison to the other side of the Messisipi."[5] Stirling later wrote that "Monsr St Ange withdrew on the 23d [of October] with all the French Troops in this

Country, to a village called St Louis."[6] Patching these disparate comments together, the following scenario seems likely: St. Ange left most of his garrison at Fort de Chartres on October 11, while he proceeded on across the Mississippi to start arranging for the arrival of his troops in what everyone agreed was still French-governed territory. The slight disagreement between Eddington and Stirling regarding dates is perhaps because St. Ange's marines left Chartres in several groups—some on October 11, more on the seventeenth, and the remainder on the twenty-third. Finding quarters for them in St. Louis at that time would have been no easy matter, and St. Ange may well have moved them across and up the Mississippi in several batches. In any case, all French marines had certainly departed Chartres for St. Louis by the end of October 1765.

Auguste Chouteau claimed that St. Ange arrived in St. Louis in July 1765, adding that "after his arrival St. Louis was considered as the capital of upper Louisiana."[7] It is possible, even likely, that St. Ange made reconnaissance trips to St. Louis starting in the late summer of 1764, although not establishing himself there permanently until October 1765. St. Ange never explained why he selected St. Louis to be the seat of his government (*chef lieu*) in Upper Louisiana, but several good reasons existed. St. Ange was thoroughly familiar with the geography of the area, having passed the site on innumerable occasions during the preceding forty years. Surely he recognized the strategic value of St. Louis's location close to the mouth of the Missouri River, which was true for both commercial and military reasons. Furthermore, it was convenient for St. Ange to remove himself from Chartres to St. Louis, while he arranged with Philippe Rastel de Rocheblave, another French officer, to move from Kaskaskia to Ste. Genevieve.[8] This arrangement provided an integrated command structure of French officers on the west side of the Mississippi that lasted until 1770, and because St. Ange was Rocheblave's superior St. Louis became, de facto, capital of Upper Louisiana.

No need existed for St. Ange to be *appointed* commandant at St. Louis. Once he had taken command at Fort de Chartres in June 1764, he was ipso facto commandant of Upper Louisiana, which included, on the west side of the Mississippi, adolescent Ste. Genevieve and embryonic St. Louis. After British occupying forces arrived at Fort de Chartres in October 1765, the east side of the Mississippi was no longer deemed to lie in Louisiana, which meant that St. Ange at St. Louis remained commandant of all Upper Louisiana. When Antonio de Ulloa arrived in Louisiana as the first Spanish governor in March 1766, he accepted this situation without thought or question. And when the usually fast-moving General Alejandro O'Reilly became interim governor of Louisiana in September 1769, he was in no rush to replace St. Ange at St. Louis, for the Irish Spanish general appreciated the virtues of the old French captain. After deliberating for six months, O'Reilly appointed Captain Pedro

Antonio de Ulloa was an accomplished intellectual but a generally hapless Spanish governor of Louisiana (March 1766–October 1768) before being pushed out of the colony by rebellious Frenchmen. However, he did dispatch an expedition to St. Louis commanded by Francisco Morales y Ríu, which resulted in the splendid maps drawn by Guy Dufossat. Courtesy of the Missouri History Museum, St. Louis.

General Alejandro O'Reilly arrived at New Orleans in September 1769 to crush the anti-Spanish revolt that had erupted there and to establish Spanish authority and government in Louisiana. Understanding St. Ange de Bellerive's importance in Upper Louisiana, O'Reilly was slow to replace him, finally appointing Captain Pedro Piernas in 1770. Courtesy of the Missouri History Museum, St. Louis.

Piernas to replace St. Ange, and Piernas finally arrived to take command at St. Louis in May 1770.

In any case, the government that St. Ange brought en bloc to St. Louis in late 1765 was the self-same government that had existed at Fort de Chartres during his tenure there. St. Ange himself was, of course, commandant, and Joseph Lefebvre chief civil magistrate and storekeeper. His full name was Joseph-François Lefebvre Desruisseau, he was a Frenchman (rather than a Creole or Canadian), and he had come up to Illinois from New Orleans in 1762.[9] Lefebvre had been in place at Fort de Chartres as the highest-ranking civilian official for more than a year before St. Ange took over as military commandant there in June 1764, and he maintained that position after he and St. Ange crossed to the west side of the Mississippi in October 1765. Lefebvre, with his classical French education, was an important adjunct to St. Ange while he was establishing the first government at St. Louis. Lefebvre died at St. Louis on April 3, 1767, apparently after a lingering illness.[10]

Crossing the Mississippi along with St. Ange and Lefebvre came the notary Charles-Joseph Labuxière, also French born and educated. It is difficult to exaggerate the importance of notaries in the French Illinois Country. They were the highest-ranking legal officials, for lawyers had been outlawed in Louisiana early on. French-Illinois society would not have held together without notaries, and historians today could not reconstruct the region's history without the rich array of extant notarial documents. After Captain Stirling arrived in the Illinois County, he remarked that "the only Judges here, was one LeFevre [sic] who was judge, King's commissary, and Garde du Magazin, and another who acted as procureur du Roi [royal attorney]."[11] This "procureur du Roi" was none other than the notary Labuxière.

Labuxière was born at Bénévent, diocese of Limoges, ca. 1727, the son of Charles-Léonard and Renée Cleret.[12] He was educated locally and taught to draft legal documents in proper notarial form, likely apprenticing with a notary.[13] How and why he came to Louisiana are unknown, as are why and under whose auspices he was sent up to the Illinois Country from New Orleans in the mid-1750s. When Jean-Baptiste Bertlot *dit* Barrois died, Labuxière replaced him, becoming the most authoritative notary in Upper Louisiana.[14] With his newly acquired status, Labuxière decided to marry a local woman, and on June 30, 1757, he and Anne-Catherine Vifvarenne married in the parish church of Ste. Anne at Chartres,[15] with Commandant Jean-Jacques Macarty Mactigue as one of the witnesses. Labuxière had entered the ranks of the power elite in the Illinois Country, and he would remain there, first at Chartres and then at St. Louis, beginning in 1765.

St. Ange, in one of his first dispatches to New Orleans after becoming commandant in St. Louis, wrote that Labuxière has "always performed his duties with zeal" and "is useful to the region."[16] St. Ange might have said "indispensable." When Labuxière wrote to New Orleans in December 1767, justifying his position at St. Louis, he could rightly claim, "I've been known in this region for twelve years, and I've always been employed in the service of His Most Christian Majesty."[17] Labuxière, like everyone else in St. Louis at the time, continued to think of Upper Louisiana as French territory; His Most *Christian* Majesty was Louis XV, while Carlos III was His Most *Catholic* Majesty. The history of early St. Louis simply cannot be comprehended without digesting the scores of notarial documents that Labuxière drafted between 1766 and 1770.[18] He was the custodian of French legal traditions in St. Louis, and he knew the proper words and phrases for real estate transactions, marriage contracts, wills, inventories, auction proceedings, and so forth. These documents—carefully filed by one of Labuxière's assistants, either François Cottin as *huissier* (bailiff) or Pierre Pery as *greffier* (court clerk)—contain much of St. Louis's early history. When Cottin occasionally filled in for Labuxière and drafted legal documents, he styled himself, rather grandly, as "huissier en la jurisdiction royalle des Illinois."[19] The traditional, indeed medieval, French titles applied to these assistants reveal the deep French mental structures that pervaded all legal affairs in early St. Louis.[20]

With Lefebvre on his deathbed in August 1766, Labuxière replaced him as St. Ange's right-hand man for *all* civil affairs and began signing land grants along with St. Ange. In addition to serving as notary, Labuxière was "assistant to the royal procureur général, serving as judge in Illinois."[21] The *procureur général* (district attorney) was the highest-ranking legal official in New Orleans, and Labuxière, subject to New Orleans, was the same in St. Louis. As if these civil offices were not enough, he was also lieutenant in the local militia. Labuxière was perhaps as important to early St. Louis as St. Ange himself, and infinitely more so than Laclède, not to mention Auguste Chouteau.[22] Chouteau would have his day (poor Laclède never really had his), but that is a much later story.

Other important members of Captain St. Ange's team at St. Louis were Lieutenants Pierre-François d'Hautemer de Volsey and François-Louis Picoté de Belestre, each married to a niece of St. Ange;[23] Jean-Baptiste Martigny, captain of the militia; André-Auguste Condé, surgeon; Louis Deshêtres, interpreter; Jean-Baptiste Hervieux, gunsmith; and Sébastien-Louis Meurin, chaplain. Meurin had been one of the Jesuits packed off to New Orleans when the Society of Jesus was suppressed in 1763, but he returned to the Illinois Country under the auspices of the Capuchins in 1764 and served conscientiously—indeed, heroically—on both sides of the Mississippi until his death in 1777. Respective salaries for this group of officials reveal something about their relative importance in Upper Louisiana. St. Ange, Lefebvre, Condé, and Deshêtre all received one thousand livres per year, Hervieux seven hundred, and Meurin six hundred.[24] Maintenance of a civil society at St. Louis was evidently more important than saving souls. Interestingly, Labuxière, important as he was as notary, was not a salaried official. At that early time, he was remunerated exclusively by "emoluments [fees]" that came from drafting legal documents, for which he often received five livres (or one and one-half piastres) per document.[25] Doing piecework for a living, Labuxière was often scribbling fast and furious, for which historians can be grateful.

McDermott considered it worth noting that "Laclède at no time held any military or civil office."[26] One minor exception to this appeared on St. Ange's May 1766 census of St. Louis, in which Laclède appears as "premiro commisario," first commissary. In this case, "commissary" was applied to Laclède because he was supplying bread to St. Ange's small garrison, for which he was paid six hundred livres per year.[27] But McDermott was fundamentally correct: Laclède never held any official position of leadership. He never even served as a militia officer, which was something community leaders in the Illinois Country had always done. Post commandants appointed militia officers, and why St. Ange chose to pass over Laclède in this regard will never be known. Laclède certainly did not lack physical courage. Perhaps, for some reason, he did not inspire confidence in others; he simply was not a recognized leader. Or perhaps, as we saw earlier, his lack of acumen in commercial affairs reflected poorly on him as a manager.

St. Ange, while getting a government up and running at St. Louis, was also active recruiting habitants for the new settlement. Lieutenant Alexander Fraser wrote on December 16, 1765, that St. Ange was "very busy among the Inhabitants," persuading them to cross to the west side of the Mississippi, where

Padron y Lista de los Milicianos y Habitantes DE EL LUGAR NUEVO NOMBRADO San Luis en dho territorio de los Ylinoises FECHA EN 3J DE MAYO 1766.

St. Louis census heading, 1766. This remarkable document, compiled by St. Ange in French during the spring of 1766 and forwarded to New Orleans, where it was translated into Spanish, provides the first detailed portrait of the early settlement's residents. Courtesy of the Ministry of Culture, Archivo General de Indias, Audiencia de Santo Domingo, Seville, Spain.

they could enjoy "their Ancient Priviledges and Laws."[28] That is, Frenchmen (and women) could continue being French, as they always had been. St. Ange certainly viewed the west side of the river as a continuation of *French* Illinois, French in every respect—language, religion, customs, laws, and privileges. He knew that the west side of the river had technically been conveyed to Spain, but who knew when, if ever, Spanish authorities would arrive in the area. And, even if they did, the Roman Catholic Borbón king of Spain, Carlos III, was first cousin to the Roman Catholic Bourbon king of France, Louis XV, and so how much difference were Spanish authorities going to make to the lives of folks living in St. Louis and Ste. Genevieve anyway? Well, as it turned out, very little indeed.

Don Antonio de Ulloa arrived in Louisiana in March 1766 to assume command of the province on behalf of King Carlos III. Charles-Philippe Aubry had been acting French governor of Louisiana since 1765, and after Ulloa's arrival a curious shared governorship developed. Ulloa was technically governor, but Aubry generally handled correspondence between New Orleans and outlying posts, like St. Louis, where French officers continued to command. In April 1767, Aubry wrote to St. Ange that "Monsieur de Ulloa recognizes your merit, and you can expect good treatment and a good salary."[29] Ulloa gave no thought to replacing St. Ange as commandant in Upper Louisiana, but he soon developed plans to establish a Spanish presence in the region, for as of 1767 none whatsoever existed—not a single soldier or official, farmer, or merchant. In mid-April 1767, a small convoy under the command of Captain Francisco Ríu y Morales left New Orleans and headed for Illinois.[30] Ríu's convoy consisted of two large bateaux with a total of forty to fifty men, mostly Spanish soldiers but also including workmen and, most important, Captain Guy Dufossat, a French military engineer who had joined the Spanish service in New Orleans. Ulloa's instructions to Ríu were long (seventy-seven articles), complicated, and replete with plans and ambitions that never came to fruition.[31] A wonderful and telling detail—revealing of Ulloa's meticulous, pious, and impractical mind—included precise orders about how the rosary should be recited when the convoy pulled over to the riverbank each evening.

Aubry's letters to St. Ange in April 1767 demonstrate beyond any reasonable doubt that Aubry was making a good-faith effort to help the Spaniards get established in Louisiana. He spelled out at length what Ulloa intended regarding St. Ange's relationship with Ríu. The Spanish captain had orders to assume command at St. Louis, but *only* if St. Ange's French troops agreed to serve under Ríu, accepting him as their commandant. Aubry wrote with point-blank honesty: "Taking possession of your post depends on the will [*volonté*] of your garrison."[32] If the garrison chose not to serve under Ríu, St. Ange would remain in command at St. Louis, and Ríu would command, with his own Spanish troops, only at the forts to be built at the mouth of the Missouri River. Ulloa's instructions to Ríu acknowledged that St. Ange was commandant in "Ylineuses" (St. Louis), but conveyed command of the "Misuri" to Ríu.[33] Things were complicated in Spanish Illinois, and both Aubry and Ulloa were fully aware of St. Ange's importance in the region. Aubry wrote to Ulloa (significantly, *after* he had written to St. Ange) and informed him that he had been presumptuous enough to inform St. Ange that Ulloa intended to retain him as commandant at St. Louis. Aubry noted that St. Ange was "a good old man, who owns nothing, and who has served in the Illinois Country for forty years."[34] St. Ange was indeed getting old (sixty-five years), had never had pecuniary ambitions of any sort, and had served the Bourbon monarchy in Upper Louisiana for more than four decades.

As commandant of Upper Louisiana, St. Ange was responsible for a huge swath of North America. Indeed, this territory encompassed a large portion of what would eventually be included in the Louisiana Purchase. In 1767 a French trader working far up the Arkansas River took it upon himself to write a letter of complaint to St. Ange. How a trader working in that remote area would have found pen and paper to write such a letter and then somehow get it delivered to St. Louis will remain an abiding mystery. In any event, this trader was literate (a rare capacity among traders), had an urgent complaint, and knew that it should be addressed to St. Ange. Big Osages from the Missouri Valley had traversed over into the Arkansas Valley (Indian mobility over great distances continues to astonish one) during the winter of 1766–67, killed two Frenchmen, wounded one, and killed three Indian slaves belonging to the French. They also killed a black chief ("chef noire") that the commandant at Natchitoches had sent out on reconnaissance, revealing that French traders were working far northward out of Natchitoches. St. Ange had faced many strange situations since arriving in Upper Louisiana ca. 1720, but the convoluted goings-on in the Arkansas Valley were too much to grasp, even for him. He addressed Aubry in exasperation: "Voilà, Monsieur, the grand chaos (*dérangement*) among the Indian tribes. I await with impatience the arrival of Monsieur Ríu."[35] St. Ange was old, he was ill, and he was finally getting tired of the interminable job of handling multitudinous Indian affairs in a territory whose geographical limits remained unknown.

A rare bit of good news came from the far other end of St. Ange's jurisdiction, the valley of the Rivière St. Pierre (Minnesota River), a full seven hundred miles from the valley of the Arkansas. Representatives from three Sioux villages had come to St. Louis, asking that St. Ange send French traders north to their tribe and pledging their loyalty to the French and Spanish nations. French traders had been working with the Sioux for a century or more, and this nation's avowed loyalty to France was apparently deeply felt.[36] As of 1767, the border between Spanish Louisiana and British Canada had in no way been fixed—indeed, would never be during the colonial era. But the Rivière

St. Pierre entered the Mississippi from the west (now at St. Paul, Minnesota), meaning that its valley was indisputably part of Spanish Louisiana and therefore within St. Ange's range of authority.

In the spring of 1767, Lieutenant Volsey (second in the military chain of command at St. Louis) corresponded with Aubry on behalf of a seriously ill St. Ange, and the news he sent down to New Orleans was not good. Volsey was concerned that if St. Ange died, Volsey might not be able to hold things together in St. Louis, which seemed to be on the verge of spinning out of control. The place was full of "vagabonds and mutineers," and there were not enough troops to maintain discipline and good order. Volsey promised to do all he could to keep a lid on things with the help of "some reliable militiamen,"[37] but he was not sure that he could handle it. Transients, rootless men, Indian traders, and boatmen had little or no stake in seeing an orderly and well-governed settlement develop on the west bank of the Mississippi River; they were not invested in building a stable, viable community. Alcohol made things worse. Soon after becoming governor, Antonio de Ulloa (1766–68), principled and impractical man that he was, decided to crack down on traders who were supplying Indians with "eau de vie et tafia." Knowing that the Illinois Country was a center of the fur trade, he wrote to St. Ange in July 1767, admonishing him to severely punish traders who dealt excessively in alcohol.[38] This was a difficult issue, for how could St. Ange effectively prevent freewheeling voyageurs from using spirits in the Indian trade? Moreover, according to St. Ange, English traders were supplying plentiful quantities of tafia (low-grade but powerful rum) to Indian tribes, and French traders were obliged to do the same if they wished to compete on an equal footing.[39] Ulloa would not let go of the issue, however, and he instructed Ríu, who was about to depart upriver for St. Louis, to prevent the purveyance of liquor to Indians, "although it is the thing they desire the most."[40]

The last week of April 1768, drunken Indians ran riot on the streets of St. Louis, according to Ríu, even banging on the door of St. Ange's lodgings, demanding "aguardiente." This episode thoroughly rattled Ríu, who was happy to defer to St. Ange, for he had "worked with the tribes for forty years."[41] St. Ange himself never mentioned the affair of the riotous Indians in his dispatches to New Orleans, likely taking such affairs all in good stride and not getting overly agitated by them. Nevertheless, events of late April 1768 did account for a citizens' petition to St. Ange and Labuxière, who were viewed (accurately) as a two-man government in St. Louis.

Illinois Country villages were traditionally governed by military commandants, but village assemblies had always served various purposes in these communities; they elected parish wardens and syndics for communal projects (such as agricultural fencing), and they were the source of petitions and appeals addressed to commandants.[42] May 1768 was a hectic month for village assemblies in St. Louis, and the result was two petitions that demonstrated townspeople's insistence on maintaining local control over local issues. Early in the month, eighty-nine townsmen signed their names or affixed their marks (fifty-four such) to a petition addressed to St. Ange and Labuxière, respectively "commandant" and "judge and district attorney."[43] Signatures included those of all substantial citizens who happened to be in town at the time: René Kiercereau, Joseph Taillon, André-Auguste Condé, Jean-Baptiste Hervieux, Louis Deshêtres, Jean-Baptiste Papin, Louis Chancellier, Picoté de Belestre, and Pierre Laclède.

The complaint broadly addressed the baleful effects of purveying distilled liquors ("eaux de vie") to local Indians (mostly Peorias, but with an admixture of others, such as Kaskaskias, and occasionally Missouris and Osages), which had grievous effects on commerce, peace, religion, and even the local Creole children: "Indians have always considered pernicious liquor their divinity, finding their greatest happiness in offering sacrifices on its altars." Unbridled drunkenness "corrupted hearts that were already barbarian," and consequently the Indians could neither support themselves nor serve as reliable partners in commerce, that is, the fur trade. Drunkenness not merely rendered the Indians indolent and useless; it also aroused criminal instincts that provoked "perpetual disorders and brigandage, pillaging and burning." The prospect was even raised of a bloody Indian uprising, fueled by alcohol and divested of all reason. The petitioners seized upon Ulloa's concern that purveying alcohol to Indians was a bad practice and carried it much further, making it a truly unmitigated evil. But—the petitioners concluded—Ulloa no longer need worry about it, for the petitioners themselves would serve as a vigilante force to crack down hard on the alcohol trade; it was a local issue that could be dealt with locally.

On May 8, 1768, St. Ange and Labuxière responded to the townsmen's petition, first abjectly acknowledging that their government had failed and that a serious problem existed. Then they slapped an absolute prohibition on trading, retailing, or purveying any and all intoxicating beverages to Indians, with a five-hundred-livre fine for first-time offenders and even more severe penalties for repeat infractions; proceeds would go to the parish, as was customary in Illinois Country communities.[44] Taken together, there is something fishy about these two documents, the citizens' petition and St. Ange's and Labuxière's response to it; they emit a distinct odor of contrivance. The petition's language is too extreme, the assent to the petition too unanimous, and St. Ange's and Labuxière's unreserved acknowledgment of their own failures too odd. Furthermore, men who signed the petition had themselves been providing alcohol to Indians and would continue to do so[45]—all this suggests that the documents were trumped up to mollify Spanish authorities who, themselves not being invested in the fur trade, were afflicted with naive scruples about the Indian-booze trade.[46] Everyone in St. Louis had an interest in keeping Ulloa out of their hair by claiming that the problem could be handled locally, without interference from New Orleans. And everyone quite understood, the petition notwithstanding, that liquor would continue to flow to Indians in exchange for peltries, which likely meant that our petitioners were more interested in who provided the liquor than in prohibiting its use.

Then, and not coincidentally, a second village assembly gathered in St. Louis later the same month of May 1768. And this second assembly had precisely the same purpose as the first—let's do everything possible to keep the pious busybody Ulloa out of our business. In February Ulloa had written to St. Ange suggesting that each trader be limited to just one tribe and, even worse, be required to obtain a trading permit in New Orleans. Labuxière took detailed notes about the villagers' complaints, and St. Ange used them as the source for his letter to Aubry on May 16.[47] St. Ange declaimed that all St. Louis citizens—traders, habitants, and *négociants,* as one body ("tous en corps")—had the strongest objections to Ulloa's proposals. "The traders who go out to the Indian tribes are for the most part men without resources, without houses or possessions, and their circumstances preclude their making a trip of 500 leagues [that is, back and forth to New Orleans] to ask permission to engage in trade with the Indians." This would entail time, expenses, and inconveniences that traders simply could not endure and remain in business. Moreover, Indians, who had become utterly dependent on European trade goods, would be traumatized and would descend on St. Louis en masse, provoking huge disorder. "The Indian knows only his own caprice, and it matters little to him that there may be reasons for standing in his way." Permitting only one trader per tribe would arouse jealousy and "zizanie [discord]"[48] in the Indian; it would precipitate a war that would make Upper Louisiana uninhabitable. "Frustrated Indians will take out their rage on Frenchmen as well as on Spaniards, for a promise is a promise and one violation is for the Barbarian what fraud and perfidy are for us." Never had circumstances been so favorable for a reconciliation between Indians and Englishmen, which was absolutely the worst nightmare that French and Spanish officials in Louisiana could imagine. This was the most overtly emotional letter that St. Ange ever wrote, as he faithfully communicated the St. Louisans' distress to Aubry in New Orleans. No sentient official in Louisiana could ignore opinions about the Illinois Country that came with the weight of St. Ange de Bellerive behind them.

Aubry must have immediately persuaded Ulloa to abandon his one-trader-per-tribe proposal, for it was never again mentioned. St. Louis traders (*commerçants* and voyageurs) were not compelled to descend to New Orleans in the summer of 1768 to get permits for the upcoming hunting, trapping, and trading season. Rather, *négociants* in New Orleans who wished to transport trade goods upriver would apply to cogovernor Antonio de Ulloa for permits to trade with the Illinois Country.[49] This did not incommode *négociants* as it would have St. Louis traders, and the rigid proposal to permit only one trader per tribe was abandoned. Among applications for trading permits that came into Ulloa's office during July and August 1768, several mentioned the Big Osages, several more mentioned the village of the Missouris, another the upper and lower Missouri Valley, yet another wanted to trade with "the villages of the Sioux, on the right side [that is, west bank] of the Mississippi," and one simply mentioned "the region that extends out to the Indian tribes."[50] When *négociants* rather than traders became responsible for obtaining permits, regulation at the grassroots was forgotten. Once *négociants* in St. Louis had farmed out their trade goods to voyageurs, these latter went on their merry way and traded wherever they wanted and with whomever they wanted to maximize their profits.

⚜ ⚜ ⚜ ⚜

Ríu's trip up the Mississippi from New Orleans during the summer of 1767 had been a comedy of errors and mishaps, requiring five months instead of the usual three to get as far as Ste. Genevieve.[51] The story of Ríu's adventures, and many more misadventures, in Upper Louisiana has been well told, most recently by Patricia Cleary.[52] As Ulloa was not taken very seriously in New Orleans, so it was with Ríu in St. Louis. St. Ange mentioned that Ríu had arrived in St. Louis on September 7, but his men were restless and unruly. St. Ange averred to Aubry that "it was sad to see Monsieur Ríu stuck with such an insubordinate group to command."[53] When Ríu could not maintain order and discipline among his own Spanish troops, no way in heaven or hell that St. Ange was going to turn his command over to the Spaniard. Ríu was so pathetic a figure that no one in St. Louis believed that the Spaniards were serious about occupying Upper Louisiana. During the entire time that Ríu was in and around St. Louis (September 1767–April 1769), with the potential of becoming Spanish commandant of Upper Louisiana, all legal documents drafted in St. Louis referred to the region as "the French part of Illinois," and Ríu was never identified as commandant. It may be reckoned as one of Ríu's virtues that he accepted all this in good grace, never once questioning St. Ange's position of authority.

As of 1766, no fortification of any kind existed in Spanish Illinois, and, given the volatility in the region, this situation was deemed unacceptable. St. Ange recommended building a fort on high ground close to St. Louis,[54] which could serve as his headquarters. But Ulloa had directed Ríu to build at the mouth of the Missouri River, and Ríu's engineer, Dufossat, oversaw the building of Fort Don Carlos el Señor, Príncipe des Asturies, on the south side of the river's mouth. This was a crude log structure, eighty feet square, containing a small garrison and some light artillery.[55] By 1778 Fort Don Carlos was in ruins, and in the spring of 1780 Lieutenant Governor Fernando de Leyba, desperate to bolster his defenses, sent militiamen to fetch five small cannons down to St. Louis.[56] Entirely abandoned, the fort was soon swallowed up by floodwaters and shifting sands, leaving no physical remains. The Spanish attempt to fortify the mouth of the Missouri River turned into an expensive folly. To study the Ríu interlude in St. Ange's tenure as commandant of Upper Louisiana is to discover its general lack of significance for St. Louis's early history. The most important result of Ríu's abortive expedition was the three splendid maps that Dufossat produced while in St. Louis (see color plate section).

St. Ange's dispatch of November 19, 1767, offered a sweeping *tour d'horizon* of affairs in Upper Louisiana and explained how he was attempting to manage them.[57] Droves of Indians were expected to pour into St. Louis during the spring of 1768 seeking gifts, and St. Ange was wracked with anxiety that he would not have presents enough to go around. Up the Missouri River, a party of Missouris had attacked a French trader and his Illinois Indian partner; the trader had successfully fled into the woods, but the Indian was killed, the Missouris having no pity for an Indian working with a Frenchman. St. Ange had known the Missouris intimately since the 1720s, but he could not fathom what was occurring up the Missouri Valley, what was motivating whom—and if St. Ange could not understand what the Missouris were up to, no white man in Upper Louisiana could. If the Missouri Valley was difficult to manage, the Arkansas Valley was even more intractable. Clermont, chief of a major band of Osages ("who have always been friends of the French"), came into St. Louis to avow his loyalty to Ríu, and by implication to Spain. Clermont insisted that he was doing everything he could to keep his Osage band at peace, but that the "disorder" in the Arkansas Valley was quite beyond his sphere of influence.[58]

Pivoting from west to north, St. Ange noted that three years earlier (that is, in 1764), he had effected a peace between the Sacs and the Foxes and the Illinois tribes. The more northern tribes had been inveterate enemies of all branches of the Illinois nation since the Illinois had participated in crushing the Foxes on the Illinois prairie in 1730.[59] For the sake of French traders working north up the Mississippi and its various tributaries, St. Ange thought it "essential" that peace be made with the Sacs and Foxes. Nevertheless, during the summer of 1767, a war party of the Sacs and Foxes descended the Mississippi and struck the Peoria village just outside St. Louis (see color plate section), killing fourteen or fifteen. This was a smaller replay of the notorious Fox attack on the Illinois (Metchigamea) village near Fort de Chartres in 1752.[60] Complicated and bitter enmities of long duration provoked intertribal bloodshed, which frustrated and sometimes baffled St. Ange, who much preferred to see no blood spilled, that of Frenchmen or that of Indians. In any case, he was doing his damnedest to prevent a full-scale war from bringing chaos to the region, "which would be destructive to our traders working up the rivers."

The ill-considered revolt against Ulloa and Spanish rule in Louisiana erupted at New Orleans in October 1768, and the much-abused governor fled the colony on November 1, under an expulsion decree from the Superior Council. This revolt was instigated and led by a Creole elite in New Orleans that did not exist at the time in Upper Louisiana, and St. Ange would never, ever, have supported anything of the kind in St. Louis.[61] Although French born and bred, Aubry in New Orleans had prudently refused to support this anti-Spanish revolt, for he had little in common with the Creole jurists and planters who fomented it. From November 1768 until July 1769, when General Alejandro O'Reilly arrived in New Orleans, affairs in Louisiana drifted along under Aubry's anxious hand. Aubry was apologetic about his inability to support the Illinois post, for he had no money or soldiers or merchandise (for the Indians) to send upriver.[62] All Aubry could do was commiserate with St. Ange and ask him to hang on as best he could. What remained of Ríu's

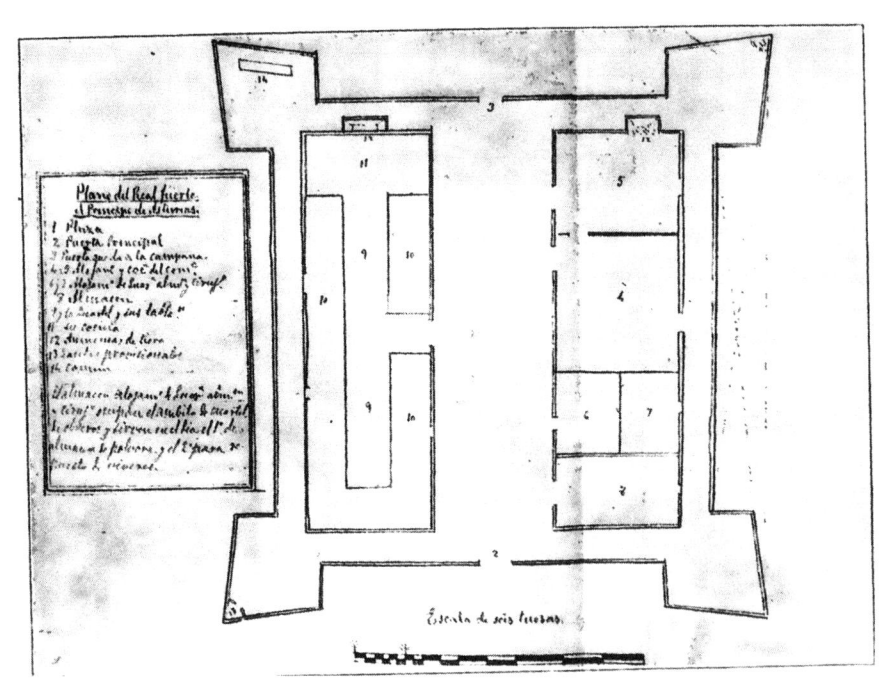

Plan of Fort St. Charles, prince of Asturies, likely drawn in 1767 (Guy Dufossat?). Located on unstable alluvial ground at the mouth of the Missouri River, it was totally abandoned in 1780. Reproduced from Louis Houck, comp. and ed., The Spanish Regime in Missouri: A Collection of Papers and Documents Relating to Upper Louisiana Principally within the Present Limits of Missouri during the Dominion of Spain *(Chicago: R. R. Donnelly, 1909), vol. 1.*

small force abandoned Illinois in early April 1769, leaving St. Ange with the unwelcome task of trying to maintain Fort Don Carlos el Señor, Príncipe de Asturies, at the mouth of the Missouri River.[63]

Suddenly, unexpectedly, dramatically, Pontiac's murder by a Peoria Indian on April 20, 1769, threw the entire Illinois Country into turmoil. Peoria villages were located close to St. Louis on either side of the Mississippi, and Peorias were not hospitable when members of other tribes appeared in the area. They viewed intruders as competition for the gifts that St. Ange distributed on behalf of the Spanish government and they had no intention of sharing their special relationship with the French establishment at St. Louis. Bloodshed between members of various Indians tribes, either inhabiting or visiting the St. Louis area, was endemic and unsettling. Pontiac's murder at Cahokia by a Peoria was part and parcel of persistent intertribal rivalry, friction, and bloodshed in the region, and it was St. Ange's job to curtail such destabilizing violence. Ríu had earlier reported that St. Ange was "both practical and intelligent in dealing with the Indians."[64]

Howard Henry Peckham's account (based largely on Daniel Blouin's manuscript "Mémoire") remains the standard account of Pontiac's death and burial.[65] Peckham's prose does not possess the luxuriant romantic panache of Francis Parkman's, but his account of the famous Ottawa chief's demise is more painstaking and accurate. According to Peckham (that is, Blouin), the Peorias, after deliberating on the issue in council, decided to have Pontiac assassinated for motives never explained. An unnamed nephew of a Peoria chief, Makatachinga (Black Dog), was selected to carry out the foul deed on behalf of the entire tribe.[66] After feigning friendship with Pontiac, the young man visited with him in Cahokia at the trading post of Baynton, Wharton, and Morgan, where they likely swigged tafia. As they left the store on April 20, Pontiac was clubbed down from behind and then stabbed, expiring on the muddy street almost immediately. Word of the murder was forthwith taken across the Mississippi to St. Ange, and his account of it in a letter to Aubry on April 21 is the freshest known account, that closest to the time of the murder. This heretofore unknown document must be presented in full:

> After I wrote my letter, I was informed of the death of the famous Pontiac (whom you knew) in Cahokia yesterday. He was cowardly assassinated by the Peoria tribe in the middle of Cahokia. From what I've heard, this was a premeditated blow. Although committed against Pontiac personally, it is nevertheless being regarded as a general action against all the [northeastern] tribes, as a consequence of their great esteem and consideration for him. An Iroquois, who was in the area, proclaimed that "the Illinois [Peorias were Illinois] have done a fine day's work, for with a single blow they've killed many tribes." What I definitely believe is that they [the Illinois] will have time to ruminate over this, and that truly they will suffer repercussions, as will the English. I regard them as a nation destroyed, whichever side they choose.

The French, although having nothing to fear for their lives, could nevertheless suffer, and I could as well.[67]

St. Ange's account confirms several points made later by Bloüin, most important that the assassin was not a lone lunatic but had served as a designated killer on behalf of the Peorias. No satisfactory explanation, no specific motive, for the killing has ever been proposed. The Peorias had never been deeply devoted to Pontiac or his cause, and in that sense, foul though the murder was, they had not cravenly betrayed their leader.[68] Bloüin largely dismissed the notion that the British officers in the Illinois Country had instigated the murder, for Pontiac was no longer a threat to British occupation of the region. Gratuitously to inflame things by instigating the murder would have been the height of folly for the British command. Nevertheless, some Peorias, attempting to shift blame, were busy spreading the word that Englishmen were behind the murder. Bloüin advised Gage to get to the bottom of it and punish any errant persons (definitely not English officers) in British Illinois who may have been involved in the affair.[69]

Concerning St. Ange's involvement from just across the river in St. Louis, Peckham claimed that St. Ange, after being implored by the Peorias to help them shift blame for their crime, had "sent out messages to the northern tribes that the English had set on an Indian to kill their chief and champion."[70] There is no evidence that St. Ange did this, and such deviousness does not comport with what we know about his character, which was blunt and forthright rather than sly and conniving. According to Bloüin, after St. Ange had heard the Peorias out in "a public audience," he was "too prudent to get mixed up in an affair concerning a neighboring power, and ordered them to leave for fear of having the region he governed enveloped in the fallout from their crime."[71] Prudence of this sort had characterized St. Ange's entire long and successful career in Illinois Country Indian affairs.

Most observers in the region, including many Illinois Indians, thought that Pontiac's death demanded revenge and that a massive bloodletting would ensue. Lieutenant Colonel John Wilkins, British commandant at Fort de Chartres, claimed that five to six hundred Illinois had gathered at the fort seeking protection from those who wished to avenge "Pondiack."[72] St. Ange went so far as to predict with some precision when (either July 18 or 19) tribes with persisting loyalty to Pontiac (Sauteurs [Ojibways], Ottawas, Piankashaws, Miamis, Potawatomies, Kickapoos, Mascoutens, and so forth) would strike the Illinois.[73] St. Ange, to be sure, was caught in tight spot. Peoria villages were situated close to St. Louis on both sides of the Mississippi, and the Peorias considered St. Ange their patron and protector. On the other hand, tribes with which St. Ange had been intimate when he was commandant at Vincennes, especially the Piankashaws and Miamis, had been loyal to Pontiac. In any event, the galloping fears and dire predictions turned out to be largely baseless. Residual power and influence of once great men are often exaggerated, and so they were with Pontiac. By 1769 few Indians from any tribe were willing to kill, or to die, to avenge him and thereby honor his memory. Many in fact probably thought "good riddance" to a man who had become a caricature of his former self.[74]

Wilkins ordered a trader at Cahokia to see to it that Pontiac's body was properly buried. Parkman, based on conversations he had in St. Louis with the aged Pierre Chouteau, claimed that "Saint Ange, mindful of his former friendship, sent to claim the body and buried it with war-like honors near his fort of St. Louis."[75] No solid evidence exists to support this heartwarming story; indeed, there is no evidence that Pontiac and St. Ange were ever friends, and St. Ange never had a fort to command at St. Louis. The tenor of St. Ange's writings during the spring and summer of 1769 reveals no inclination further to stir things up by having Pontiac's body disinterred and brought to St. Louis for reburial.[76] Bestowing such an honor on the dead chief would have angered the Peorias, with whom St. Ange had to deal on a daily basis, and would likely have appeased no one. St. Ange repeatedly referred to Pontiac as "famous," but never as "great" or "my friend" or "our comrade in arms," and he evinced no particular affection for him. The scary confrontation with Pontiac over the fate of Lieutenant Fraser, when St. Ange, at his dinner table, had dared Pontiac to kill him, was no doubt etched in St. Ange's memory. St. Ange's last known mention of Pontiac came in a letter of November 1769: "Regarding the death of Pondiaque, the Peorias have yet to feel the vengeance of the different tribes [loyal to Pontiac], although they have turned up in several large parties. . . . I have nothing to fear because these tribes are not accusing us of anything, knowing that he [Pontiac] was a friend to the French."[77]

Blouïn remarked in his 1771 "Mémoire" that several "large parties of Ottawas and allied tribes" turned up in the Illinois Country seeking revenge and that some Peorias, "more bold in assassinations than in warfare," sought protection from the British at Fort de Chartres. Blouïn also noted that in 1770, "le Grand Sauteur," a chief of the Sauteurs and a kin of Pontiac, had appeared in Cahokia with two warriors looking for a clerk of Baynton, Wharton, and Morgan Company, whom they suspected of having been involved in Pontiac's murder. Not finding the clerk whom they sought, they killed and scalped two other employees of the company.[78] But all in all, Pontiac's demise was anticlimactic, for, well before his death, he was cutting a figure of pathos, a leader with few followers and a cause with no future.

⚜ ⚜ ⚜ ⚜

Spanish Louisiana was in disarray during the summer of 1769. St. Ange wrote to Aubry, commiserating with him about his doleful situation in New Orleans: "I hope as you do that the king [Carlos III] will soon relieve you of the crushing weight of governance, which agitates and torments you in both mind and body and which may shorten your days."[79] Aubry's days on earth were in fact numbered, for he was drowned in a shipwreck off the coast of Bordeaux in February 1770, before getting a chance to set foot once again on his ancestral soil.[80] If governance was a burden for Aubry in New Orleans, so also was it for St. Ange in St. Louis, where disorder reigned thanks to the "libertinage of the mass of vagabond traders."[81] But St. Ange also knew that his town depended on these dissolute vagabonds, for trade was the economic lifeblood of the settlement; if the commandant couldn't do with 'em, he also couldn't do without 'em.

But help was on the way—from Havana. A flotilla containing two thousand Spanish soldiers commanded by the redoubtable General Alejandro O'Reilly was crossing the Gulf of Mexico as St. Ange's letter of July 18 was making its way down the Mississippi. When O'Reilly's ships dropped anchor in the Mississippi facing the Place d'Armes on August 18, no one in New Orleans had a mind to voice any opposition to Spanish rule. O'Reilly (who was made of much sterner stuff than Ulloa) immediately set about prosecuting the leaders of the 1768 revolt, five of whom were finally executed and six sent to prison in Havana.[82] No doubt existed that they had engaged in treason, and by the standards of the time O'Reilly's sentences were stiff but not excessive. The sobriquet he acquired in New Orleans, "Bloody O'Reilly," was neither accurate nor fair. The new governor, a straight-up military man, carefully balanced rigor and justice. The Superior Council was replaced with the Cabildo as the highest-governing body of Louisiana, but French law was modified rather than scrapped wholesale. The French Black Code was preserved, while future commerce in Indian slaves was outlawed with a view to the eventual extinction of Indian slavery, to which Spanish jurists had been objecting since the sixteenth century.[83]

The Aubry–St. Ange correspondence during 1768–69 reveals a mental and emotional exhaustion (and with St. Ange also physical decay), a sort of bewildered hopelessness. The war had been lost, Louisiana had been lost, British occupiers on the left bank of the Mississippi were abusive bullies, financial resources were depleted, and there were not even sufficient troops to maintain domestic law and order. Aubry's reaction to O'Reilly's arrival in New Orleans supports the great-man thesis of historical causation. Everything changed dramatically and for the better with the arrival of the Spanish general with the Irish name and the iron will. Less than two weeks after O'Reilly's arrival in New Orleans, Aubry wrote that "it is surprising that the presence of a single person can reestablish in so little time good order, peace and tranquility. If the colony had had the good fortune of having Monsieur the General arrive earlier, we would not have witnessed all the calamities with which we have been afflicted."[84] Aubry had never read Thomas Hobbes's *Leviathan*, but he understood from experience that rigorous government is always preferable to chaos.

In New Orleans, Aubry observed that O'Reilly had taken notice of St. Ange in Illinois and that he had been serving there for fifty years. O'Reilly had confidence in St. Ange's experience and his integrity, and he knew that St. Ange had had no truck with the anti-Spanish rebellion of 1768. On August 24, less than a week after having arrived in New Orleans, O'Reilly wrote to St. Ange, his letter reaching St. Louis on November 16, and St. Ange responded, at length, on November 23, addressing O'Reilly as "Your Excellency."[85] No French governor of Louisiana had ever been addressed with such a grand title. St. Ange's long letter is one of our best sources for getting a lay of the land at St. Louis during the transitional period, 1769–70, when Spanish rule was gaining traction in Louisiana.

First things first, St. Ange presided over a ceremony in which all available citizens of St. Louis swore an oath of allegiance to His Most Catholic Majesty, Carlos III. St. Ange reported that his fellow citizens understood, as of course he did, that this was a change in name only (that is, from Louis XV to Carlos III), meaning that the fundamental allegiance to the Bourbon family remained intact. This dynastic conception of political loyalties was mainstream Old Regime thinking. The oath taking in November 1769 occurred exactly seven years after France had conveyed Louisiana to Spain in the secret Treaty of Fontainebleau. French people who inhabited Upper Louisiana (that is, mostly citizens of Ste. Genevieve and St. Louis) surely had had some awareness that they were en route to becoming subjects of Carlos III; Ríu's bumbling expedition had been concrete proof of that. But the oath that St. Ange administered brought geopolitical facts squarely home to each and every resident. Before the oath, Ríu's expedition notwithstanding, Spain's sovereignty in Upper Louisiana had not been taken seriously. By the spring of 1770, legal documents in St. Louis that had once referred to "la partie française" of the Illinois Country began to refer to "la partie espagnole."[86]

St. Ange would be "eternally grateful" that O'Reilly had offered him (on Aubry's advice) official commandancy of Upper Louisiana. This had not been done previously, and during the years 1765–69 St. Ange functioned as commandant on the basis of implied (and universally acknowledged) powers brought with him from Fort de Chartres in October 1765. St. Ange admitted forthrightly that, given his physical disabilities, he was not confident of his ability "punctually to fulfill the duties" required of him as commandant. He would be happy to fade away into retirement as a simple officer, as his father had done at Chartres thirty years earlier. In the event, St. Ange governed until May 1770, when Captain Pedro Piernas took over as lieutenant governor of Upper Louisiana with his headquarters at St. Louis. The "ten or twelve unfortunate soldiers" who made up St. Ange's garrison in St. Louis (Ste. Genevieve had no garrison of any kind until 1770) were in a similar situation. They were the remnants of the group of French marines that had crossed the Mississippi with St. Ange in 1765. Once they took the oath to Carlos III in November 1769, they technically ceased to be French marines and became Spanish soldiers. Surely, there were tears in their eyes when they took that oath, for they had been the last surviving and serving French marines in North America.

In several concentrated pages, St. Ange attempted to convey to O'Reilly the complexity of Indian affairs in Upper Louisiana. Gifts could not merely be distributed wholesale, tribe by tribe, or even chief by chief. Things were more complicated than that. Tribes were divided into bands, and in addition to the "grand chef" there were multiple war chiefs, and all these divisions and individuals required dedicated, individualized attention. Interestingly, St. Ange claimed that when an Indian chief died in the environs of St. Louis, it was the commandant's obligation to "cover him [*le couvre*]."[87] "Covering" was a stock expression used to describe gifts tendered as compensation for the death of an important leader—if the death was natural, it was a sign of empathy and goodwill; if a murder had occurred, "covering" might assuage bitterness and prevent acts of revenge.[88] And when Indians arrived in St. Louis, they demanded more than just gifts, for they had to be housed and fed and even provided with firewood should the season require it. Indians' urgent needs were a burden without end for the commandant in St. Louis.

St. Ange claimed that he was vexed most by Indians from the British side of the Mississippi. "It would be natural," St. Ange opined, "to leave them to the generosity of the prince [George III] who possesses them [curious phrasing]." But the practice had always been to treat all Indians who came to St. Louis equally, from wherever they came; furthermore, "Messieurs les Anglais" (St. Ange's use of "Messieurs" here seems ironic) were attempting to seduce with gifts Indians situated on the west side of the river. St. Ange thought that it would be imprudent to abruptly stop cultivating the eastern tribes, for they might prove useful someday. When in May 1769 St. Ange compiled a list of Indian tribes accustomed to receiving gifts at St. Louis, the tally included more tribes from the east side of the Mississippi than the west.[89] If fur traders from St. Louis were working on both sides of the Mississippi, which doubtless they were, it made a good deal of sense to be distributing presents ecumenically.[90] Recently, ethnohistorian Daniel K. Richter has written that following the Treaty of Paris (1763), "the ability of Native North Americans to play one imperial power off against another—a defining characteristic of the eighteenth-century Atlantean world—virtually ceased to exist."[91] In fact, precisely the opposite was true in the Illinois Country, for British occupation of the east bank of the Mississippi provided surrounding Indian tribes with the perfect opportunity to play Spain off against Great Britain.

As for the Missouri River valley, the defensive works that Ríu and Dufossat had constructed on either side of the mouth of the Missouri were already decaying. By the late 1760s, this issue was becoming increasingly important, for, according to St. Ange, English traders operating from east of the Mississippi were already penetrating the Missouri River valley. But the unstable alluvial sand at the mouth of the Missouri provided a poor foundation for fortifications, and St. Ange recommended building a fort a bit farther upstream, where the river was narrower and the shoreline more stable. The Spanish regime in Louisiana never had the resources, or the will, adequate to implement St. Ange's prudent recommendation, and pesky English interlopers were a vexation in the Missouri Valley throughout the colonial era.[92]

St. Ange then discussed his citizens at St. Louis, their strengths and their weaknesses. Habitants (St. Ange using the word in the traditional sense of resident-farmers) "might be useful for defending the settlement but they are saddled with many burdens. They must sow their crops in order to survive. Everything is extraordinarily expensive and the cost of labor very high. A worker demands eight to ten livres, plus board, per day, which is hardly enough to support him, especially if he has a family.[93] Many young men frequent the Indian tribes and they prefer that life style above all others. It's impossible to find anyone to guard the Spanish fort (Don Carlos el Señor, Príncipe de Asturies), and even if volunteers were available they wouldn't abide the daily grind of military service."[94] St. Ange was nevertheless quick to say that in an emergency, in case of an enemy attack, these young men would jump to and do their duty, but on a day-to-day basis they were just too free-spirited and independent to be counted on. When the Anglo-Indian attack did come, in 1780, St. Ange was proved correct. The citizen militia companies of St. Louis and Ste. Genevieve saved St. Louis and in so doing altered the course of North American history.[95]

In November 1769, St. Ange was too infirm to travel down to Ste. Genevieve and administer to the citizens the oath of allegiance to His Catholic Majesty, Carlos III, king of Spain. Labuxière went instead, and he was absolutely delighted with this responsibility. With great relish, he wrote to O'Reilly ("Your Excellency") from Ste. Genevieve, explaining how well he had handled the formalities in Ste. Genevieve. Town commandant Rocheblave assembled the parish militiamen, "under arms," to hear proclaimed the details concerning the "change of dominion" in Upper Louisiana, after which Labuxière, "serving as judge," administered the oath. Anyone who refused to take it would be obliged to leave "this part," meaning the west side of the Mississippi River, Spanish Illinois.[96] Normally, St. Ange handled communications between Upper Louisiana and New Orleans. But Labuxière had, with some justification, concluded that his responsibilities in Ste. Genevieve licensed him to write directly to O'Reilly, and he included a long paragraph about himself. Labuxière's various titles—*notaire, subrogé procureur général*, and *juge*—were French titles, and Labuxière was concerned that with the coming of the Spanish regime, he might well lose his influential offices. "If, however, Your Excellency deigns to permit me to continue exercising these functions, I assure him that my zeal for the royal service and for the administration of justice will never cause him to regret it."[97] But Labuxière's plea fell on deaf ears, and once Piernas assumed command at St. Louis in May 1770, Labuxière's demotion was fast and sure.

During the six months between November 1769 and May 1770, St. Louis hung in limbo. Everyone in town knew that a Spanish administration was on its way, but they did not know exactly when it would arrive or what it would bring. After decisively putting down the anti-French revolt in New Orleans during the fall of 1769, General O'Reilly spent the following winter reading and ruminating; the general was a man of thought as well as of action. He knew that his tenure in Louisiana would be brief (in the event, it lasted just seven months), and a multitude of decisions had to be made and rapid-fire orders given. Among other things, O'Reilly decided how Upper Louisiana would be governed after he left Louisiana, and the system of government that he created for the upper colony remained intact until Captain Amos Stoddard assumed control on behalf of the United States in March 1804. Most important, there would be a Spanish lieutenant governor at St. Louis, who would exercise both civil and military authority. Ringleaders of the infamous rebellion at New Orleans in 1768 had been legal officials, and O'Reilly was wary of such men. He therefore abolished notarial positions at all outlying posts, including St. Louis and Ste. Genevieve. Henceforth, the signature of the lieutenant governor, rather than a notary (like Labuxière), would render documents legal and official in St. Louis.[98] Geographic boundaries for the vast reaches of Upper Louisiana remained unknown, but in principle they extended westward to the Rocky Mountains and northward to British Canada. O'Reilly spoke specifically of St. Louis, Ste. Genevieve, the districts of the Missouri River, and that portion of Illinois that belonged to King Carlos III. These areas, the more or less settled parts of Upper Louisiana, constituted what may be called Spanish Illinois.[99]

Piernas arrived in St. Louis on May 18, 1770, armed with O'Reilly's detailed instructions about how he was to govern the upper colony.[100] Piernas had been sharply critical of St. Ange in October 1769, informing O'Reilly that he was "good-for-nothing."[101] But O'Reilly flatly ignored Piernas's assessment, admonishing him in no uncertain terms: "The lieutenant governor shall preserve the best of relations with Monsieur de St. Ange, whose practical knowledge of the Indians will be very useful to him. He shall do whatever he can to gain his friendship and confidence, shall listen to his opinion attentively on all matters, and shall defer to him in so far as possible without prejudice to the service."[102] No one else in all Louisiana warranted this kind of endorsement from O'Reilly, and Laclède received no mention whatsoever. Louis St.

Ange de Bellerive was the pillar that supported St. Louis in 1770, and Piernas would be well advised to understand that before he arrived in town. And in a major gesture of confidence in St. Ange's judgment, O'Reilly ordered Piernas to keep the militia officers whom St. Ange had appointed in St. Louis: Captain Jean-Baptiste Martigny, Lieutenant Louis Lambert *dit* La Fleur, and Sublieutenant Eugène Pourré would all remain in place. This was an issue of vital importance, for the small contingent of Spanish regulars (approximately 30) that Piernas was bringing to St. Louis was only a fraction of the size of the local militia (approximately 125). As Niccolò Machiavelli observed in his infamous little book, *The Prince*, a successful ruler must know how to organize an effective militia.[103] O'Reilly's instructions must have stung Piernas, but he took them to heart, and all the evidence suggests that he and St. Ange got along well together during the early 1770s—Piernas as lieutenant governor and St. Ange as councilor sans portfolio.

⚜ ⚜ ⚜ ⚜

The Black Legend (*la leyenda negra*) was an accumulation of propaganda and Hispanophobia that alleged that Spanish colonialism was monstrously cruel, bigoted, and exploitative. It took root in northern Protestant Europe (especially in England and the Netherlands) during the sixteenth century and persisted for centuries.[104] This legend remained alive and well during the eighteenth century, and after 1765 it came to color British views about affairs in Upper Louisiana. Who could possibly wish to live under the dark reign of His Catholic Majesty of Spain when territory ruled by his enlightened Protestant majesty of Great Britain was just across the river? General Thomas Gage wrote of "a Strange Mixture of French and Spanish Government on the opposite side [that is, west] of the Mississippi, so that there is no knowing to whom the Country belongs. . . . The French Inhabitants appear to be so much disgusted, that it was expected many of them would become British subjects."[105] Gage persisted in this delusion and wrote in June 1770 that "the French on the opposite shore by no means relish the Spanish Government, and it's thought many will come over to our Side."[106]

Gage's thinking was indulgently fanciful and rooted in the hoary, Hispanophobic Black Legend, and migration throughout the 1760s and '70s was always preponderantly westward across the Mississippi rather than vice versa. Take the case of François Lalumandière *dit* La Fleur, who petitioned St. Ange for a land grant in November 1766. La Fleur wished to move from Kaskaskia to Ste. Genevieve in order "to take refuge in his fatherland" because Kaskaskia had been "ceded to enemies of the religion [Roman Catholicism] and the fatherland."[107] Lalumandière probably was not sure which European state, France or Spain, "owned" the west side of the Mississippi, but he knew what he knew, which was that Ste. Genevieve was a Roman Catholic community and was governed by the Bourbon family. That was good enough for a Roman Catholic Anglophobe like Lalumandière. St. Ange, of course, was delighted to grant Lalumandière's request, which validated his government in Upper Louisiana and reinforces the premise of this chapter—which is that St. Ange governed the region well in difficult circumstances. Firmness, prudence, and tolerance were his hallmarks, and his ability to prevent a single recorded bloody incident between Indians and his town's people or members of his garrison is utterly remarkable.

And, make no mistake about it, St. Ange's St. Louis was governed. Shannon Lee Dawdy recently argues for a freewheeling, insubordinate, quite lawless early New Orleans—"rogue colonialism," as she puts it in a memorable epigram.[108] Royal officials, whether in France or in French colonies, habitually whined and wailed about insubordinate, intractable subjects and unsolvable problems, as St. Ange himself did. Nevertheless, in early St. Louis, contracts were drafted and honored, justice was meted out,[109] censuses were taken, estates were probated, minor children and the infirm were protected, prenups were registered, sacraments were performed, and the level of interpersonal physical violence was generally low. Concerning the last point, however, it must be acknowledged that sexual coercion, particularly with slave women, was apparently not uncommon. The demographic profile of early St. Louis, with a high proportion of unmarried males, surely contributed to this problem (see chapter 8). In the Illinois Country, sexual morality was generally deemed to be the parish priest's responsibility, and during the 1760s St. Louis had no resident priest. Nevertheless, and all in all, St. Ange's government functioned remarkably well, in one of the most remote outposts of Western civilization. St. Ange could not govern the village as tightly as he would have liked, that is, like a disciplined company of French marines, but St. Louis, although home to many rogues, was certainly no rogue colony.

CHAPTER 5

The Village Emerges

The situation of the town is elevated. . . . It has two long streets running parallel with the Mississippi, with a variety of others intersecting them at right angles.

—Captain Amos Stoddard, 1804

After British forces finally occupied the Illinois Country east of the Mississippi River in October 1765, that region was no longer deemed to be part of Louisiana; it was simply British Illinois. West of the Mississippi lay Upper Louisiana, of which St. Louis became the seat of government the moment of St. Ange's arrival there (October 1765), auspicious though the arrival of his dispossessed, tatterdemalion French marines certainly was not. Early St. Louis was a small military outpost, was intermittently home to a missionary priest, and was an important fur-trading center—but its physical configuration was that of a classic Illinois Country agricultural village; that is, the town and its environs evolved in accordance with a long-established pattern in the region.

As with all other Illinois Country villages, the settlement pattern that emerged at St. Louis during the 1760s was distinctly tripartite, consisting of nuclear village, plowlands for sowing grain, and commons for pasturing livestock, gathering firewood, and shooting rabbits and squirrels.[1] This pattern had developed at Cahokia and Kaskaskia during the first two decades of the eighteenth century, before any provincial government existed in the Illinois Country and before local civil records were being kept. Soon after the founding of New Orleans in 1718, French officials and military officers were dispatched up the Mississippi to Illinois, the first Fort de Chartres was erected (1719), and soon French-trained notaries were drafting civil records—land grants, marriage contracts, real estate transactions, business agreements, and so forth. The civil records drafted in the Illinois Country during the early 1720s reveal, unmistakably, that the distinctive tripartite settlement pattern was already fully developed in the region. A certain mystery inheres in the fact that this pattern of occupying and tilling the land was radically different from the dispersed settlement pattern in the St. Lawrence Valley, despite the fact that a clear majority of early Illinois Country settlers were Canadian.

Throughout the Illinois region, for whatever reasons, Canadian settlers opted to create a system of village agriculture that was modeled after that in northern France. Precisely the same thing occurred at St. Louis.

Charles E. Peterson, in his slim but irreplaceable book, *Colonial St. Louis: Building a Creole Capitol*, observed that whatever claims Indians may have had to the land on which St. Louis was built were never formally extinguished. When Louis XV of France conveyed all of Louisiana west of the Mississippi to Carlos III of Spain in the secret Treaty of Fontainebleau (November 1762), European diplomats surely did not consider any possible Indian claims to that vast territory.[2] Peterson went on to add that it is unknown by "what specific authority" land grants were conveyed in the new settlement. Frederic Louis Billon in *Annals of St. Louis* claimed that Pierre Laclède was by 1765 considered the "legal proprietor" of the land containing the new outpost and that he conveyed land grants verbally to the newly arriving settlers.[3] Billon, valuable though his work often is, was incorrect on both of these important points. The real estate concessions contained in the *Livres Terriens* (land books), the first entries of which were made on April 1, 1766, make it abundantly clear that the land upon which St. Louis was slowly rising was the "domaine du roy," the king's domain. It may be debated precisely to which king this consistently used phrase referred, Louis XV of France or Carlos III of Spain (almost certainly the former), but surely Laclède was not, had never been, and would never be proprietor of the real estate upon which the new settlement was emerging.

Furthermore, no evidence exists that Laclède was ever empowered by any authority to convey land grants at St. Louis.[4] Louis St. Ange de Bellerive was commandant of the entire region, first from his post at Fort de Chartres (July 1764 to October 1765) and then from St. Louis, where he arrived in October 1765. If unoccupied land at St. Louis was part of the king's domain, St. Ange was the indisputable custodian of that domain. On July 17, 1743, King Louis XV of France issued a declaration "concerning land grants in the French colonies of America," which affirmed the authority of colonial governors and intendants to convey grants.[5] On July 4, 1766, bachelor Jean Prévost requested a town lot in St. Louis, for he wished to settle down in the budding community of *négociants*, voyageurs, artisans, farmers—and slaves. Commandant St. Ange and civil judge Lefebvre forthwith conveyed to Prévost a lot of what had become the standard dimensions for in-town properties—120 pieds (1 pied = 12 pouces = 12.79 inches) frontage and 150 pieds deep, and they did so "by virtue of the authority of the governors and intendants of Louisiana."[6] St. Ange was more specific in his 1774 affidavit concerning concessions that he had earlier granted at Vincennes: he had conveyed land in the name of the king and under the authority of Louisiana governors going all the way back to Bienville and including Vaudreuil, Kerlérec, and

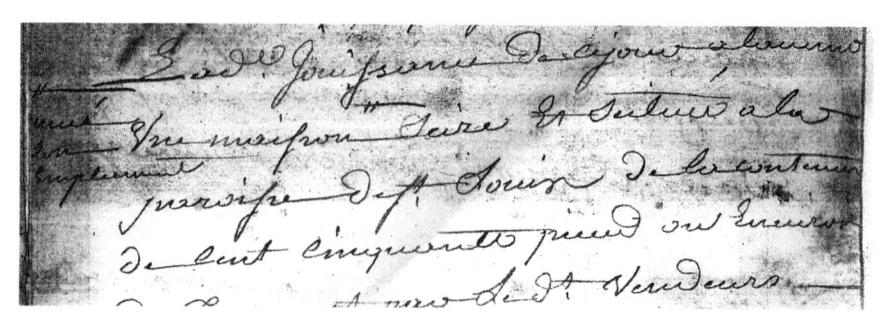

This real estate transaction, drafted in Cahokia on July 27, 1765, contains the first known usage of the appellation "St. Louis." The notary, Joseph Labuxière, erred in calling St. Louis a parish (paroisse), for the village did not achieve canonical status as a parish until 1774. Nonetheless, this record demonstrates that the new settlement had taken firm root. Kaskaskia Manuscripts, Randolph County Courthouse, Chester, Illinois.

d'Abbadie.[7] This reference, and deference, to French authorities was occurring in what, by the Treaty of Fontainebleau, had technically become Spanish territory; St. Ange and Lefebvre were functioning as though that treaty had never been concluded, although they were surely aware that it had been. In any event, no one—in the Illinois Country, in New Orleans, in France, or in Spain—ever questioned St. Ange's authority to convey land grants while he was commandant at Vincennes (1736–64), Fort de Chartres (1764–65), and St. Louis (1765–70).

But who was conveying town lots in St. Louis before St. Ange arrived on the scene in October 1765? On the east side of the Mississippi, John Reynolds later remarked that "the French villages were laid out by common consent,"[8] and this may have been the case at St. Louis. Or perhaps the most important heads of household got together and decided things as a group. A long tradition in the French Illinois Country had village assemblies making local decisions as syndics or church wardens.[9] Indeed, when St. Ange was preparing to leave Vincennes in May 1764, he advised the captain of the militia there to decide all important issues by convening an "assembly of the most important habitants, who would then settle things by majority vote."[10] After St. Ange arrived at Fort de Chartres about June 1, 1764, he may well have admonished Jean-Baptiste Martigny, a militia officer, to do this on the west side of the Mississippi, or, conceivably, St. Ange himself crossed the Mississippi from time to time to convey land grants.[11]

"St. Louis" first appeared as a village containing residential property on July 27, 1765, when Jacques Lacroix sold to François Cottin a house and town lot situated in the "paroisse de St. Louis."[12] As noted earlier, St. Louis did not become a canonical parish until 1776, but in any case the bill of sale describes Lacroix's property as "about 150 pieds," without bothering to provide an approximate second dimension. The haziness of the property description likely reveals that no accurate surveying had yet been done at the new settlement. This sales contract was drafted in Cahokia, but six months later, on January 21, 1766, occurred the first real estate transaction in St. Louis for which a written record remains; indeed, this is the earliest known document of *any* kind drafted in St. Louis, by a St. Louisan, on behalf of St. Louisans.[13] Jacques Denis, master woodworker (*menuisier*),[14] was selling to Antoine Hubert and Company (*Société*) half a town lot (that is, 60×150 pieds) containing a small house. Hubert was a *négociant* and had business associates, hence the inclusion in the sales contract of "Company." St. Ange's notary, Joseph Labuxière, explained that the house belonged to Denis because he had built it, and the lot belonged to him because it had been "granted to him following the practices and customs of the said place [the Illinois Country], being from the king's domain, and having no fees, rents or obligations attached to it." The last phrase made it clear that Denis had unencumbered proprietorship of the land, that is, it was burdened with no manorial dues. This was an important point because much real estate in Canada was still entailed with such traditional dues, which *roturiers* (commoners) owed to landholding seigneurs.[15] Denis was a new kind of French American, whose ownership of his land was not impinged upon by old habits carried over from Europe. No seigniorial or manorial system was ever implanted at St. Louis, or for that matter anywhere in the Illinois Country.[16]

The Denis-Hubert contract of January 21 made no attempt to explain how Denis had acquired the half lot he was selling, other than to note that he had done it via the usual practices and customs of the region. But, on March 15, Denis sold the other half of his lot to Hubert, and on this occasion Labuxière spelled out that the land had been granted to Denis "verbally by the commandant and *commissaire* of the post."[17] Verbal land grants were common in French Louisiana, and Denis's situation at St. Louis was not all that rare.[18] Indeed, as Denis was selling one town lot in St. Louis, he was simultaneously buying another from Lambert *dit* Bonvarlet, a marine in St. Ange's small French garrison, and Bonvarlet had acquired the parcel in precisely the same way—it had been "accordé verballement."[19] The commandant of the post was of course St. Ange, and the *commissaire* (storekeeper) was Joseph Lefebvre, whose full title was "assistant to the ordonnateur and judge in the region."[20] We saw in chapter 3 that Lefebvre was a senior official at Fort de Chartres during the last years of the French occupation and that he and St. Ange had worked as a team, as commandant and judge, conveying land grants on the east side of the Mississippi.[21] They continued this practice on the west side of the Mississippi, and the first grants recorded in the *Livres Terriens* were certified with their signatures. A virtually identical situation arose in September 1767, when Jean Comparios, another of St. Ange's marines, was in the process of selling his house and town lot. St. Ange had earlier given Comparios a verbal grant ("permission verballe") to occupy the lot, but to make everything proper at the time of the sale, St. Ange provided him with a formal, written title.[22]

Surviving records provide no hint as to when Bonvarlet, Denis, and Comparios received their verbal grants. All that can be said is that St. Ange and Lefebvre likely conveyed them shortly after moving across the Mississippi in late October 1765, which was a hectic time, demanding quick decisions and immediate action, especially with winter fast coming on. Even if St. Ange and Lefebvre had had pen, ink, and paper at hand, they could not be bothered to stop and do paperwork. However, it is also conceivable that St. Ange and Lefebvre were conveying land grants on the west side of the Mississippi *before* they left Fort de Chartres, for their writ to govern and convey such grants *unquestionably* extended across the river before they left the fort and moved to St. Louis.

But some occupation of town sites in early St. Louis occurred with no official authorization whatsoever, verbal or written. That is, the first occupants were purely and simply squatters. On May 1, 1768, St. Ange and his notary, Labuxière, conveyed to Louis Beor a standard town lot (120×150 pieds).[23] But Beor was not the first person to occupy this parcel, for one Joseph Dubé had earlier built a small house on the lot and had even encircled the property with pickets, "sans concession," without a grant. Dubé then decided to convey the property to Beor and his Indian wife (who just happened to be Dubé's former slave),[24] but he had no written title to convey. This issue was resolved by a grant cum title issued by St. Ange on May 1, the ambiguity of the situation requiring that the grant be entitled "Beor or Dubé." This is the only such case recorded in book 1 of the *Livres Terriens*, but these land books are far from complete, and no doubt other such instances occurred of individuals occupying a parcel of land, improving it, and later acquiring official title by virtue of the time and labor they had invested in it.

St. Ange conveyed many land grants in early St. Louis containing an explicit homesteading provision, which stated that the grantee was required to occupy and improve the land within one year and one day from the date of the grant before gaining clear title to the property.[25] This homesteading provision had in fact been employed in the Illinois Country since the early 1720s, when a government structure was first established in the region.[26] And at Ste. Genevieve on the west side of the river, the one-year-and-one-day requirement was used from the earliest days of the settlement in the early 1750s.[27] Moreover, the repossession clause included in King Louis XV's 1743 declaration was also implemented in early St. Louis. On April 31, 1766, St. Ange and Lefebvre granted Joseph Calvé adjoining town lots, making for a total parcel 240 pieds wide and 150 pieds deep. But Calvé improved only one of these lots, and therefore St. Ange repossessed the second lot and reintegrated it with the royal domain. And this was done despite the fact that Calvé's original grant had not spelled out the one-year-and-one-day provision. The homesteading template was so deeply embedded in the collective consciousness of the community that the provision did not have to be explicitly articulated in order to be enforced. After repossessing the parcel, St. Ange and Labuxière granted it to Jean-Baptiste Valeau, a royal surgeon with the marine garrison in St. Louis.[28]

As new settlers moved into St. Louis and more town lots were conveyed, the configuration of the new settlement began to emerge. Like Ste. Genevieve, some sixty-five miles downriver, early St. Louis was a string town, with its two main streets (Grandes Rues) running more or less parallel to the Mississippi and its side streets ("rues de traverse") intersecting at right angles. This basic configuration was already in place by the summer of 1767, remained the same throughout the colonial period, and was observed by Captain Amos Stoddard when he arrived in St. Louis in February 1804: "The situation of the town is elevated. . . . It has two long streets running parallel with the Mississippi, with a variety of others intersecting them at right angles."[29] The town's more or less elongated configuration was dictated largely by its location along the right bank of the Mississippi River.

Peterson was perhaps the first to remark that, as St. Louis developed, its plan came to resemble that of New Orleans in several ways—a gridiron configuration, laid out along the Mississippi, with rectangular residential plots and a central public square facing the river.[30] In New Orleans, this public space was the well-known Place d'Armes, while in early St. Louis it was simply the "place publique," where, among other things, auctions were held.[31] For a brief period, resemblances between New Orleans and St. Louis went beyond the general to the specific, for in 1766 two of St. Louis's main streets were named Bourbon and Royale.[32] This interesting aping of New Orleans did not persist for long, however, and the appellations referring to the French royal family soon disappeared. Furthermore, while residential lots in the older French towns in the Illinois Country (Kaskaskia and Ste. Genevieve) tended to be more or less square and were measured in either arpents or toises, St. Louis, like New Orleans, had rectangular lots measured in French pieds. Despite these details, the general configuration of St. Louis during the 1760s only vaguely resembled that of New Orleans. Moreover, St. Louis's general layout was that of an agricultural village, which New Orleans never was.

Auguste Chouteau claimed in his "Journal" that Laclède had originated the plan for the early village.[33] Given Laclède's familiarity with New Orleans, it is conceivable that he was responsible for the vaguely similar plans of the two French colonial towns. But in his deposition to Theodore Hunt, recorder of land titles, Chouteau told a rather different story, claiming that he, Chouteau,

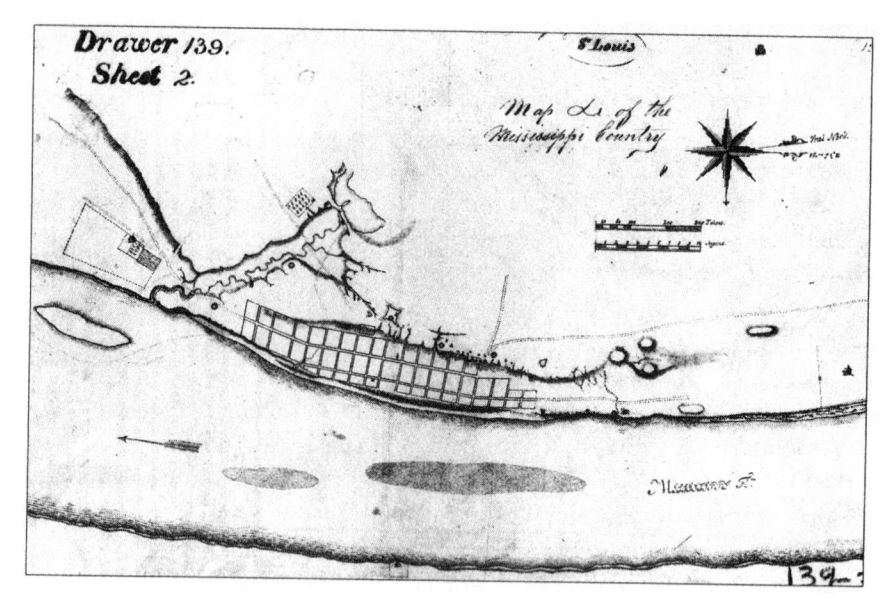

This carefully done map, dated 1804 and likely drawn by Antoine Soulard, a French-trained engineer, depicts the configuration of St. Louis that had developed during the 1760s. Notice the two principal streets paralleling the Mississippi, the mill stream, and the Indian mounds outside of town. Reproduced from Charles E. Peterson, Colonial St. Louis: Building a Creole Capital *(St. Louis: Missouri Historical Society, 1949).*

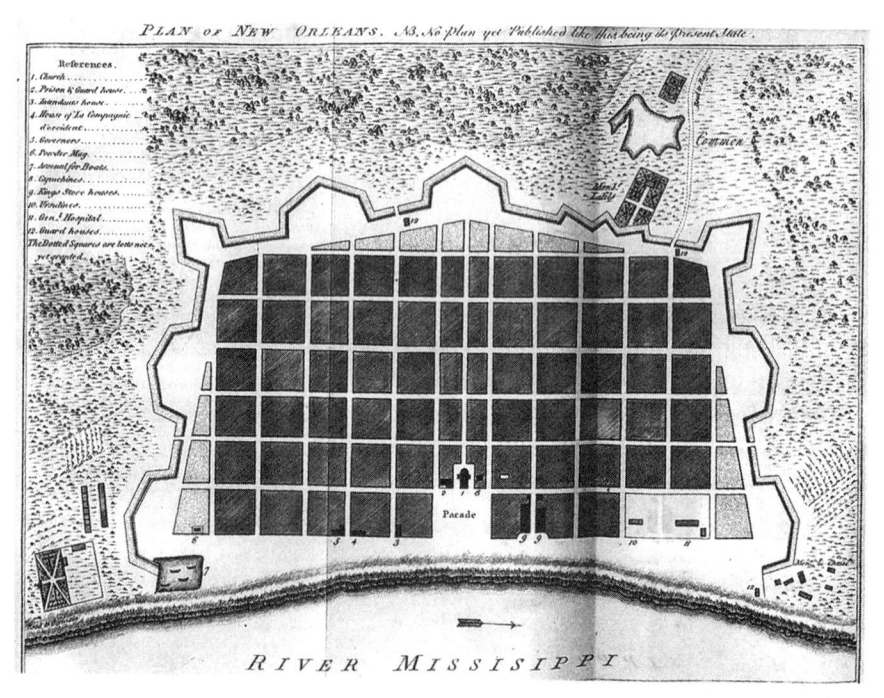

Philip Pittman's plan of New Orleans (1770). Early St. Louis, with main streets running parallel to the Mississippi and a centrally located public square, vaguely resembled New Orleans. Reproduced from Philip Pittman, The Present State of the European Settlements on the Mississippi *(London, 1770).*

personally surveyed the town site in 1764, laid out the streets and residential blocks, and drafted a plat of the whole.[34] This claim, made some sixty years later, is hardly credible, for Chouteau, at age fourteen, would have had neither the skills nor the instruments necessary to undertake such an engineering project. Furthermore, none of the early real estate records mentions a surveyor (*arpenteur*) or surveying, although the uniform dimensions of the town lots suggest that some form of crude measurements were being made. When two French engineers, Guy Dufossat and Martin Duralde,[35] arrived in St. Louis in September 1767, as members of Francisco Ríu's expedition, more exact surveying was conducted. A comparison of Dufossat's two maps of the St. Louis area from 1767 suggests that a clearly discernible town grid for the nascent village perhaps emerged only at that time. In any case, the grid that appears on Dufossat's map (see the colored plates section) is the first depiction of the geometric nucleus of St. Louis, which remained intact until the mid–twentieth century, when the Jefferson National Expansion Memorial development project obliterated it.

After Lieutenant Governor Pedro Piernas arrived at St. Louis in May 1770, he appointed Duralde surveyor general of the entire region (later, that honor would fall to Antoine Soulard, of Soulard Market fame). Duralde explained how he proceeded with his work at the time of his appointment: "Survey report done by me, Martin Duralde . . . and deposited in the government archives in the form of official minutes in order to designate the various land concessions given in the king's name to the inhabitants of the post of St. Louis—some with written titles and some done only verbally by the leaders who governed the place since its foundation—which I have surveyed."[36] In other words, Duralde used what written records were available going back to early 1766 and also likely interviewed people (most especially St. Ange and Labuxière), physically surveyed all the town lots such as they were in 1770, and then compiled his reports to be inscribed in the *Livres Terriens*.

If any serious town planning was done at early St. Louis, was it inspired by aesthetic, political, or sociological conceptions that went beyond merely making St. Louis somewhat resemble New Orleans? Did St. Louis's grid of main streets and cross streets reflect *l'esprit géométrique*, which permeated Enlightenment thinking in everything from cosmology to constitution writing to urban planning? Was it thought that a geometric framework would promote orderliness, obedience, and social cohesion in a ragtag frontier community? Were separate neighborhoods planned for different functions (residential, commercial, military, religious) or different classes (*négociants*, *commerçants*, habitants, voyageurs) of the population? Shannon Lee Dawdy claims that all of these issues influenced the development of early New Orleans, but there simply is no evidence that they bore on the planning of early St. Louis, insofar as it was planned;[37] whatever town planning was conducted in the early days was ad hoc and on the ground, not at a drafting table with precise instruments and sophisticated preconceptions. Dawdy further suggested that Spanish conceptions of colonial town planning influenced New Orleans's early development. Although St. Louis developed in what was technically Spanish territory, any Spanish aspects of St. Louis's emergent plan would only have been a consequence of its being modeled, if indeed it was, on New Orleans.

St. Ange did not convey town lots democratically to all residents. Important folk—French marine officers, civil officers, and big-time *négociants*—almost always wanted more than one parcel. Laclède got an entire block, as did Labuxière, Pierre-François de Volsey, and François-Louis Picoté de Belestre. Not only were Volsey and Belestre marine officers, but each was married to a niece of St. Ange, both daughters of his half sister, Élisabeth St. Ange, and her husband, Lieutenant François Coulon de Villiers. French marine officer blood was deployed all over early St. Louis, making the settlement *very* French and with a military-aristocratic elite dominating the top of the social (not economic) scale. Other important men, such as the surgeon André-Auguste Condé and the major slave owner Joseph Taillon, got half blocks of residential property.[38] At least in principle, those who received large parcels of town property had to possess the resources to improve the land, or they could lose it as a consequence of the homesteading provision on which land grants were premised. Residential property could be improved with—in addition to residences—stables, barns, pig sties, slave cabins, poultry sheds, orchards, kitchen gardens, and, occasionally, free-standing kitchens. Alexis Marié was a very early resident of St. Louis, and he appears in the May 1766 census. Marié was married, owned an Indian slave boy, and had an indentured child living in his household.[39] On March 2, 1770, he sold to Jean-Baptiste Sarpy what may be considered a typical St. Louis residential property at the time.[40] The lot was the standard 120×150 pieds, which contained a vertical-log house with a stone fireplace and chimney. Further improvements included a small (slave?) cabin, a barn or stable, and some additional conveniences, including a cellar and a garden. Although modern socioeconomic terminology does not usually work very well when examining colonial St. Louis, this was a typical "middle-class" family dwelling during the settlement's earliest years.

The first baptism performed in St. Louis, that of Marie Deschamps, was done in the spring of 1766 (likely in May) by Sébastien-Louis Meurin. Meurin had, along with five fellow Jesuit fathers, descended to New Orleans in the autumn of 1763 after Louis XV's government officially suppressed their mission at Kaskaskia. But Meurin returned to the Illinois Country in 1764 as a Capuchin, all the while maintaining faithful to the tenacity and fearlessness of the Society of Jesus.[41] The record clearly states that Marie's baptism was done in a tent, for lack of a more substantial facility. But Meurin had performed baptisms in meadows and under trees, for a sacrament's efficacy had nothing whatsoever to do with the surroundings in which it was performed. When St. Ange repossessed Calvé's town lot in January 1768 and reassigned it to Jean-Baptiste Valeau, the parcel was identified as facing a large street leading to "the chapel." On the other hand, when St. Ange had granted that parcel to Joseph Calvé back in April 1766, the street was not so identified, suggesting that a chapel had not yet been built.[42] But Dufossat's map of October 1767 clearly shows a religious edifice at St. Louis, meaning that the first chapel was erected sometime between the summer of 1766 and the autumn of 1767. And by the time that St. Louis became an official parish in 1776, the community certainly had a proper church, which may have looked like the restored vertical-long Church of the Holy Family at Cahokia. By 1770, when Eugène Pourré *dit* Beausoleil bought residential property facing the church property, a presbytery was planned but had not yet been built.[43] This meant that when Father Meurin, making his rounds in the region, visited St. Louis, he was dependent on the hospitality of the local citizens. An advantage of this was that Meurin could take the pulse of the community, even discovering which recently born slave babies needed baptizing.

⚜ ⚜ ⚜ ⚜

In 1716, two years before New Orleans was founded, Louis XV's government, under the regency government of the duc d'Orléans, promulgated a land ordinance for Louisiana that had pervasive influence in the colony during the entire colonial period.[44] One clause of the ordinance decreed that agricultural land was to be conveyed "in the proportion of two to four arpents front by forty to sixty in depth." The edict likely reflected practices that were already being employed in the colony, but, in any case, the ordinance's guidelines were applied with remarkable consistency at all communities in the Illinois Country, including St. Louis.[45] Agriculture was not so important to St. Louis's economy as it was to Kaskaskia's or Ste. Genevieve's, but the settlement pattern at St. Louis bore all the signs of an agricultural community.

When, on April 31, 1766, Joseph Calvé received his concession for a town lot, he also received a strip of agricultural land.[46] This is the first official record for an agricultural land grant at St. Louis, and Calvé's strip of plowland was two arpents wide and forty deep. Whereas town lots (*terrains*) were always measured in pieds, plowlands (*terres*) were measured in arpents (roughly 192 English feet). Calvé's parcel fitted nicely within the guidelines established by the 1716 royal land ordinance, as did the vast majority of *terres* granted in the first *Livre Terrien* (1766–70). These agricultural lands spread out around the village, and, over time, they developed into seven discrete compounds of plowlands, including that at outlying Carondelet (see the color plates section). The compound closest to the village ("derrière le village") was parceled out first and appropriately named "Prairie St. Louis."[47] The expanses of land surrounding the village that were converted from prairies to clusters of plowlands were called "Common Fields" by early American surveyors. This was because no fencing separated the various parcels, even though the individual strips were individually owned. Each compound was, however, surrounded by a *commonly* maintained fence, crops were planted and harvested in accord with community rules and regulations, and a communal ethos governed the tilling of the land.[48] In 1825 Jean-Baptiste Rivière described the fencing he had seen as a boy outside the village: "The fence was made in various modes, some was of the Picket fashion, some Worm fence [split rail], some with Trees of their full length and small Stakes with riders on the Top."[49] The fence was an ad hoc affair and slapdash in appearance, but it was absolutely essential for protecting the grain crops. It was the single most important structure in the settlement, more important than the village church, for without fencing to protect the crops there could be no grain harvest, and with no harvest the entire village would have faced imminent starvation.

Conveyances proceeded apace in Prairie St. Louis, and on May 30, 1766, François Bissonet was granted a one-by-forty-arpent strip of plowland there.[50] Bissonet soon wished to add to his plowland in the prairie, and on October 28, 1766, he acquired a second one-by-forty-arpent strip adjacent to the one he had been granted in May. Bissonet purchased this from Louis Desnoyer and his wife, Agnès Pichard (or Pichart), and they had acquired it "by taking it from the royal domain and clearing it at the time the settlement was emerging."[51] That is to say, back in 1764, when folk were squatting on town lots with no formal titles, they were also unofficially taking up lands outside the village, clearing them for agricultural purposes, and thereby acquiring undocumented, but valid, proprietorship. Indeed, the St. Louis census dated May 31, 1766, indicates that a large quantity of agricultural land had already been assigned ("tierras assignadas"),[52] almost all of which had been done before any official land books were being kept. In the original census, which was surely done in French and which has not survived, St. Ange likely used the phrase "terres concédées," by which he meant that he had put his blessing on ownership acquired by dedicated occupation and improvement. The notion that improving the land conveyed ownership was deep and pervasive, and agricultural lands were subject to the same one-year-and-one-day rule that applied to residential plots. On August 12, 1766, Joseph Labuxière, the royal notary, was granted a two-by-eighty-arpent tract of land in Grand Prairie. But earlier, likely back in 1764, Pierre Texier had staked off ("marquée") this same tract, with no mention of any surveying or measuring.[53] When Texier abandoned the land rather than improving it, this tract reverted to the royal domain, and St. Ange, as custodian of this domain, then conveyed it to Labuxière.

As St. Ange did not convey *terrains* in town democratically, he proceeded in the same fashion in conveying *terres* outside of town. Men of status received preferential treatment. Laclède is usually thought of as a fur trader, but his highest priority was to establish himself as a landed gentleman. On August 11, 1766, he received a grant for a huge tract of land "situated in the prairie behind the village," that is, Prairie St. Louis. The parcel was eight arpents wide ("and more on the southern side if there's room running over to the Petite Rivière") and eighty deep, which was four times the standard width and double the depth. And on the same day, Laclède received a second large *terre* situated in the Grande Prairie, lying farther out from the village, measuring six by eighty arpents.[54] The reference line for this parcel was to be "established by the one who will be charged with surveying the *terres*." This telltale phrase was used repeatedly when St. Ange conveyed agricultural land, and it is not clear when accurate surveying was finally conducted on the prairies. But surveying or no surveying, the land grants that St. Ange and Labuxière conveyed created an archetypal Illinois Country settlement, consisting of nuclear village, fixed compounds of elongated plowlands, and a commons.

Cahokia, Kaskaskia, and Ste. Genevieve all went through gestation periods of at least a decade before emerging as distinct compact villages. St. Louis emerged quickly, in the three years between 1764 and 1767, very much as New Orleans had done between 1718 and 1721. The initial founding surge of settlers, which included Laclède and Chouteau and, most important, Jean-Baptiste Martigny, came between February and April 1764, and a second surge came in October 1765 when St. Ange led his French marines to the west side of the Mississippi.[55] Both groups had large entourages that included women, children, and slaves, both black and Indian. And between those surges came a steady trickle of random newcomers who were associated with neither Laclède nor St. Ange but who were nevertheless welcome in the embryonic settlement. Many of these newcomers were habitants arriving from other Illinois Country villages, but some were simply vagabonds and voyageurs coming in off the riverine thoroughfares, finding grateful refuge in the new settlement.

Louis Billon remarked that St. Louis was at first called "Laclède's Village,"[56] but no evidence of this has ever come to light. Chouteau claimed that Laclède immediately christened St. Louis in honor of the reigning king of France, Louis XV,[57] but this seems unlikely for several reasons: first, that name does not appear in any known source document during the first eighteen months of the settlement's existence; second, humiliating French losses in the Seven Years' War had made Louis XV a thoroughly unpopular figure, hardly one to be honored in such a fashion; and, finally, Laclède never occupied a post of civic authority in the early village. As noted above, the earliest known use of the appellation "St. Louis" appears in a document drawn up at Cahokia (because there was no notary in St. Louis at that time) in July 1765. On October 18, 1765, Captain Stirling mentioned by name the only two Illinois Country villages situated west of the Mississippi, Ste. Genevieve and St. Louis, although he erred in noting that St. Louis was larger than Ste. Genevieve; this would not be true for another twenty years.[58] It may not be coincidental that the July 1765 document first mentioning St. Louis jibes with Chouteau's remark that St. Ange first came to town that same month. It is entirely plausible that *Louis* St. Ange de Bellerive, commandant of Upper Louisiana, named the new outpost after his patron saint, St. Louis (King Louis IX), and that he did so in the summer of 1765.

PART II

Contours of Village Life

CHAPTER 6

Logs and Stones: Early St. Louis Buildings

Pierre Rougeau, resident of St. Louis, promises to complete to perfection for Thomas Blondeau on his lot a house built of poteaux-en-terre *measuring 20 pieds square. . . . This contract concluded for the sum of 500 livres in beaver or other peltries.*

—Building contract, 1766

Charles Emil Peterson was one of the founding fathers of preservation architecture in the United States. After taking his bachelor's degree in architecture at the University of Minnesota in 1929, Peterson found employment with the National Park Service (NPS) and was posted to St. Louis, Missouri. On weekends during the early 1930s, he began to visit Ste. Genevieve, some sixty-five miles down the Mississippi from St. Louis; Peterson was fond of the chicken dinners served at the Hotel Ste. Genevieve after Sunday Mass.[1] Strolling through the town's historic center after dinner, Peterson became captivated by the surviving French-built vertical-log houses. These strolls had far-reaching consequences, for Peterson was moved to submit a memo to the director of the NPS outlining a plan to create an inventory of important historic buildings in the United States. In that way, French colonial architecture in Missouri was a catalyst for the creation in 1933 of the now renowned Historic American Buildings Survey.

Peterson went on to write three seminal pieces about colonial architecture in the middle Mississippi Valley.[2] Since he wrote, more than a half century ago, a number of authors have broached the subject, but no comprehensive study has ever been done of Illinois Country architecture.[3] This is surprising, both because of the fame of the still-standing colonial houses in Ste. Genevieve and because the documentary record concerning this unique architecture, going all the way back to Kaskaskia during the early 1720s, is exceedingly rich. The following chapter, building on Peterson's work, is confined to building techniques and architecture in St. Louis during its earliest years, 1766–70. Based largely on extant manuscripts in the archives of the Missouri History Museum, this chapter examines how St. Louis's early buildings were similar to, but also different from, those in other Illinois Country communities (Kaskaskia and Ste. Genevieve), those on the Gulf Coast, and those in French Canada.

Most houses in early St. Louis were, by modern American standards, astonishingly small. Some residences measured a scant 15×12 pieds, in which case they were sometimes identified as "cabanes" or "maisonnettes."[4] Even the house of François-Louis Picoté de Belestre, a distinguished marine officer and husband to St. Ange's niece, measured only 25×20 pieds, outside dimensions.[5] Belestre's house, like the great majority in the early village, was constructed with exterior walls erected *poteaux-en-terre* style. This was the fastest and cheapest way of erecting house walls, the exterior shell, and settlers arriving in early St. Louis were hard-pressed to get living quarters of some sort thrown up quickly. A quadrilateral trench was dug about 3 pieds deep, roughly dressed posts (preferably of rot-resistant red cedar or white oak) were set upright in the trench, the trench was back-filled, and the spaces between the posts were filled in, either with mud (*bouzillage*) or stone fragments (*pierrotage*). Joseph Lefebvre's *poteaux-en-terre* house measuring 25×20 pieds required sixty posts, from which we may gather that the posts (probably 10–12 pouces [1 pouce = 1.066 inches] thick) were set fairly close together; after all, there was no shortage of suitable timber in the area. The Bequette-Ribault House in Ste. Genevieve is a notable surviving example of French-colonial *poteaux-en-terre* construction, and recent archaeological excavations in St. Louis near the Arch have revealed the remains of several early structures of this type.[6]

A more sophisticated and time-consuming method of construction was to build on wooden sills, which in turn rested on stone foundations. Sometimes this method was identified as *en charpente*, meaning framed with large timbers; other times, the phrase *en colombage* or *poteaux-sur-sole* was used, meaning that vertical posts were mortised into sills rather than set in the ground.[7] The historic Bolduc House in Ste. Genevieve is a remarkable surviving example of *poteaux-sur-sole* construction, a treasured and unique example in North America. Finally, some houses in early St. Louis had exterior walls made of stone; Laclède's town house was one of these. Outcroppings of fine limestone were everywhere in the area, but the best was located a short way up the Missouri River. Dufossat's map of 1767 (see colored plates section) shows a quarry (*carrière*) in that location, near where Cold Water Creek (Rivière de l'eau froide) now enters the Missouri River;[8] from this location, stone building blocks could be brought into town conveniently on rafts and barges. Illinois Country residents may have exploited this quarry even before the founding of St. Louis, and, remarkably, it has been worked *continuously* ever since.

Jacques Denis owned the first house in St. Louis for which we have written records, and on January 21, 1766 (as noted in chapter 5), he sold it to An-

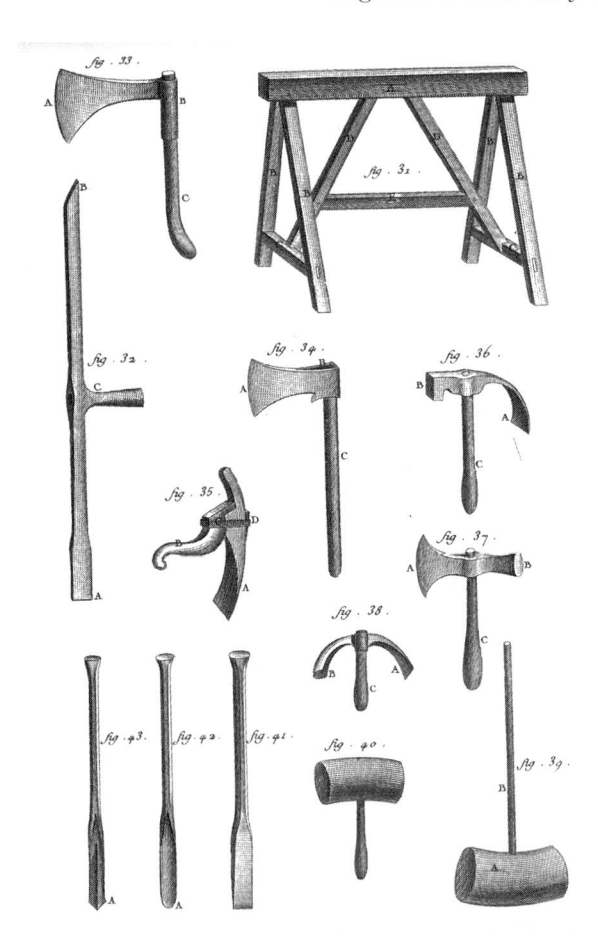

Most early St. Louis houses were of timber-frame construction (that is, vertical logs). Local carpenters used all of these tools when erecting a house, which generally required about six months of labor. Reproduced from Denis Diderot and Jean le Rond d'Alembert, comps. and eds., Dictionnaire raisonnée des arts, des sciences, et des métiers, Planches, *vol. 2 (1763).*

toine Hubert and Company. The sales contract provides no dimensions for the house, but likely it was very small, perhaps with a footprint of 400 square pieds or so. It was built in *poteaux-en-terre* fashion, "pierrotée" (meaning broken-stone nogging between the posts),[9] had a stone chimney, and was roofed with hand-split wooden shingles ("bardeaux"). Denis had not quite completed the house, however, and he committed himself to finish the structure by installing a ceiling of ax-hewn planks ("plancher d'en haut en madrier ecary a la hache [sic]"). The hand-hewn planks reveal that there was no water-driven sawmill in the settlement at that early time. Cottonwood (*liard*) was a favorite for ceiling planks, for it was plentiful, fine-grained, soft, and easy to hew.

Most houses in early St. Louis were roofed, as the one above, with *bardeaux*. But some were thatched with straw ("en paille"), some were covered with planks ("madriers"), and a few were even roofed with bark ("en écorce"). Louis Briard *dit* La Roche, one of St. Louis's earliest settlers, had a bare-bones dwelling of vertical logs with a clay chimney and bark roof to shelter his wife and two children from the elements.[10] Birch was not available in the St. Louis region, but the bark of other trees (oak, hickory, elm, and chestnut) could have been used. In any case, the diverse roofs on early St. Louis houses gave the village a corrugated, picturesque skyline—not that anyone at the time and in that place was concerned with the romantic attributes of their built environment.

Erecting a *poteaux-en-terre* house required some knowledge and skill, to be sure, but raw muscle was most important, for the most onerous task in building such a house was the pick-and-shovel work of digging wall trenches. On August 7, 1766, Pierre Rougeau contracted to build such a house at St. Louis for Thomas Blondeau. Rougeau's defined status, "garçon volontaire," meant that he was unmarried,[11] had no specific vocation, and owned no land of his own, all of which placed him toward the bottom of the socioeconomic scale in the community. But he was young and strong and willing to work, qualities that helped one survive in early St. Louis. Blondeau's status, "commerçant," on the other hand, placed him toward the top of the scale, although not as high as *négociants* like Laclède or Hubert. In any case, Blondeau's house was to be 20 pieds square with an interior dividing wall of dressed vertical logs. These posts were all to be of oak or "French walnut," which must have meant American black walnut, as opposed to the wood of some other nut-bearing tree, such as hickory or butternut. Blondeau contracted to pay Rougeau 150 livres in beaver or other peltries, and Rougeau committed himself to have the house completed by May 1767. He set to work immediately with pick and shovel digging the requisite trenches, for they needed to be completed before heavy frost arrived in Upper Louisiana.[12]

Hubert, among his many other enterprises, functioned as a general building contractor, and on July 17, 1769, he contracted to build a house for a fellow *négociant*, Louis Lambert.[13] The contract identifies Lambert as "ordinarily a resident of New Orleans," but he had been operating in and out of St. Louis as a trader since at least as early as 1766.[14] Lambert was a particular man, he wanted things just so, and his contract with Hubert contains our most detailed contemporary description of a *poteaux-en-terre* structure. Lambert's house would be 30×22 pieds, with an "apentie [*appentis* = shed]" addition (kitchen?) on one end, a double stone chimney (that is, two fireplaces with one stone flue) connecting the house and the "apentie," and wooden shingles covering both portions. The "master posts," those in the corners and on either side of the windows and doors, would be of red cedar[15] (very rot resistant), the remaining of squared-up white oak (quite rot resistant). A window would be located in each of the four corners, and the floor and ceiling fashioned of well-planed, tongue-and-groove ("embouvetés") planks. The floor was to be a mere 1 pied above street level and the ceiling 8 pieds above the floor.

An interior wall divided the main floor of Lambert's house into two basic components, a *salle* and a *chambre*, the first intended to serve as his office and the second as his bedroom. More than anything else, this house would serve as Lambert's business headquarters, where he could crash when not on the move, which he was incessantly; the man seldom slept. Two exterior doors faced one another across the *salle*, and near one of these an interior door connected the *salle* into the *chambre*. The "apentie" would have one exterior door and one window, with floor and ceiling finished as in the main dwelling. Under the house, Lambert had a cellar, 20×14 pieds and 6 pieds deep. Hubert finished the job by slathering the entire structure, inside and out, including the "apentie," with a thick coat of lime-based whitewash ("lait de chaux"). Many years later, Timothy Flint, the itinerant preacher, visited Ste. Genevieve and remarked about the French buildings that "the greater proportion of the houses have mud walls, whitened by lime, which have much the most pleasant appearance at a distance."[16] Flint, although Harvard educated and observant, was ignorant of the complex carpentry and joinery that underlay the whitewash.

Hubert was to have Lambert's house ready, "keys in hand," in May 1770 for a price of twelve hundred livres worth of peltries. But he could not deliver. Lambert, who was often out of town, had specified in the contract that "experts" would examine all details of the construction project as it proceeded, and perhaps the demands of these inspectors had become too much for Hubert; or perhaps Hubert's Indian slave, Joseph, who was a trained woodworker, did not get the help he needed to finish the project.[17] In any case, on August 7, 1771, Lambert and Hubert agreed to terminate their agreement with the house incomplete, the price being reduced to 855 livres.[18] Lambert died a few months later in Ste. Genevieve, and when his estate inventory was compiled in August 1772 his St. Louis house was described as missing the interior wall and the "planking," for the ceiling. Nevertheless, the structure was appraised at 1,000 livres, which constituted only a minuscule portion of Lambert's total estate.[19]

Jacques Denis was one of several prominent woodworkers in early St. Louis. On April 21, 1770, he contracted to build for Jacques Chauvin, *négociant*, a house 20×25 pieds, outside dimensions, with two doors and four windows (including shutters [*contrevents*]).[20] Wall construction was to be "en charpente," with vertical posts, of red and white oak, set on sills. The contract is unusual and valuable for its details, such as specifying that the joists ("solivaux") would be affixed to the top plate ("sablières") with swallow-tail joints ("pris en queue d'[h]irondelle")—what we call dovetail joints. Such joinery, by securely tying together the top plates, prevented bow out at the cornice of the building. As a *menuisier* (joiner) Denis had no trouble doing the fine chisel work required for these intricate joints. This house would have a stone chimney and fireplace ("cheminée en pierre"), as did most early St. Louis residences, for good limestone abounded in the area. A few modest houses, however, had clay chimneys ("cheminée en terre"),[21] which were widely used in Lower Louisiana, where good stone was scarce.[22] Clay chimneys were best adapted for gabled houses (*maison à pignon*), where the chimney stood outside the exterior wall of the house. Houses with hipped roofs invariably had interior stone chimneys, as may be seen at the historic and iconic Bequette-Ribault and Bolduc houses in Ste. Genevieve.

Hand-wrought nails were brought up the Mississippi to the Illinois Country in large quantities. In 1768 the *négociant* Daniel-François Fagot de la Garcinière brought 300 livres of nails (along with a mass of trade goods) upriver from New Orleans.[23] Nails may also have been fashioned by local blacksmiths from pig-iron stock, but in any case they were doled out carefully for construction purposes. When Jean-Marie Toulouse, *commerçant-voyageur*, contracted with François Thibault to build a small (18×20 pieds) *poteaux-en-terre* house, Toulouse supplied Thibault with three pounds of small nails ("cloux à latte"), three pounds of medium nails ("cloux à aretier"), and 150 spikes "pour les poteaux."[24] Bent nails were saved, not casually tossed over one's shoulder, and recycled for various purposes.

Poteaux-en-terre houses were often built by men who were not specialized craftsmen, but stone houses always required professional masons. On July 13, 1767, *commerçant* Joseph Labrosse contracted with Jean-Baptiste Papin *dit* La Chanse, *maçon*, to build a stone house 25×30 pieds, outside measurements.[25] The gabled house was to have a stone fireplace at either end, two doors, and five windows and to be elevated 1 pied above ground level. The ground floor ceiling would be 8 pieds high, standard height for houses in early St. Louis. Papin agreed to supply all the materials and labor and deliver the finished product to Labrosse in April 1768. As payment, Papin received 1,400 livres worth of beaver pelts, reckoned at 40 sols per livre, or deerskins reckoned at 20 sols per livre, standard equivalences.

Laclède's residence was one of the first stone houses built in St. Louis. No building contract has survived, but its dimensions and features may be determined with some precision because there was a copycat residence in town. On August 6, 1767, René Buet, *commerçant-voyageur*, struck an unusual contract with Laclède. Laclède would serve as Buet's general contractor for constructing "a house, built of stone, like, and following the same dimensions, proportions and arrangement of that which Sieur Laclède has had built on the right side of his own lot in St. Louis."[26] Laclède was to have his workmen complete the house, inside and out, including a walnut door and window frames, and deliver the keys ("la clef à la main") to Buet by the spring of 1768. Buet wanted a house identical to Laclède's, with one small reservation—he did not want Laclède's "pigeonniers [dovecotes]." *Pigeon-*

niers were distinctly aristocratic appurtenances to residences, in Louisiana as well as in France, but they were unusual features in the Illinois Country.[27] Often, *pigeonniers* were freestanding structures, and at châteaux in France they could assume architectural qualities of scope and significance.[28] But Laclède's *pigeonniers* were integral to his house, apparently consisting of dormers built into the roof, with the *grenier* (attic) serving as the pigeons' roosting place. Although modest by French standards, Laclède's *pigeonniers* marked him as an aspiring aristocrat, self-styled though he was. Buet wanted none of that pretension—or perhaps he simply was not fond of pigeon breast at his Sunday dinner table.

At a cost of 2,000 livres in peltries, Buet's was one of the pricier houses built in St. Louis during the 1760s—and one of the larger. It was described in detail when, after Buet's death in 1773, it was auctioned off in front of the parish church: "Built of stone, about 40×30 pieds, chimneys at each gabled end, roofed with shingles, cellar underneath, a main room (*grande salle*), one large bedroom (*chambre*) and two small ones (*cabinets*), windows and doors with shutters."[29] The Laclède and Buet residences were large for their time and place, but certainly not grandiose. Joseph Labuxière's stone house was larger, measuring "about 66 pieds long" (no width provided), and Laclède's fellow *négociant* Louis Perrault purchased it on July 4, 1772, for 3,000 livres in peltries.[30] The stone houses of Laclède, Buet, and Labuxière were the finest residences in St. Louis during the 1760s, by a long shot, but they were widely

Whether constructed of vertical logs or stones, most houses in early St. Louis resembled these French Canadian houses in form, and only later were Creole features, such as galeries, *introduced from Lower Louisiana. Original drawings by Peter N. Moogk and Carole Richards, reproduced from Peter N. Moogk,* Building a House in New France *(Toronto: McClelland and Stewart, 1977), with permission of the author.*

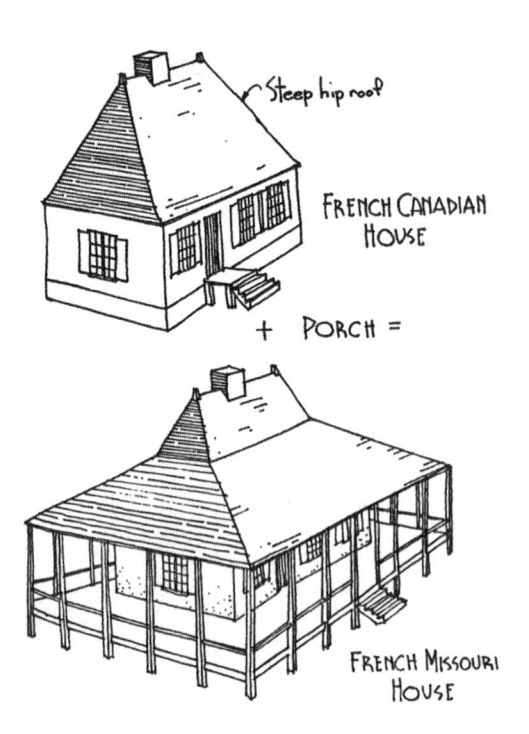

Charles E. Peterson's rendition of the evolution of the Illinois Country Creole house, placing a traditional Canadian structure at the core. This evolution took place in St. Louis between 1770 and 1780. Reproduced from Charles E. Peterson, "Early Ste. Genevieve and Its Architecture," Missouri Historical Review 35 (January 1941).

dispersed and did not constitute a fashionable neighborhood; neighborhoods based on socioeconomic status did not exist in the early village.

Galeries (porches) are engraved in the historical memory as ubiquitous features of Illinois Country houses. They stand out on the remarkable colonial houses that still stand in Ste. Genevieve and may be seen in early illustrations and photographs of long-gone early St. Louis houses. Remarkably, in examining more than fifty building contracts and bills of sale for the period 1766–70, we have found no mention of any *galerie*, of any sort, on any residence in St. Louis. This could not conceivably have been mere oversight by Labuxière, who drafted all the property descriptions in early St. Louis. The contracts for Lambert's and Labrosse's houses contain another seeming oddity—the first floor was to be elevated merely 1 pied above street level. That is, the houses were not erected on a raised platform in typical Creole fashion, as all the earliest (1790–1820) Ste. Genevieve houses are. All in all, it seems that early St. Louis houses were, in appearance, markedly more Canadian than Louisianan, which may reflect the fact that roughly one-half the adult male residents at St. Louis in 1766 had been born in Canada.[31] Charles Peterson observed that "the porch or *galerie* was much in evidence at St. Louis, and seems to have been used on one, two, three or all sides of most houses."[32] but this Creolization of domestic architecture in St. Louis occurred *after* 1770. The issue of *galeries* is important, for it bears directly on our understanding of the texture of daily life and social interactions in the village, as in who was gossiping with whom and about what from the strategically located front *galerie* of their house facing la Grande Rue. A comprehensive study of architecture in colonial St. Louis begs doing, and this chapter is merely a source-based beginning to the subject.

The village was soon dissected with a multitude of fences (*clôtures*), producing a crazy-quilt pattern across the landscape. Buet's double lot, 120×300 pieds, was completely enclosed with a fence of rot-resistant mulberry posts. Many lesser plots had lesser fences, erected with stakes (*pieux*) rather than posts. Louis Dubreuil sold a 40×150-pied parcel in 1771 (the standard 120×150 lots were already being subdivided) that had "pieux sur toutes les faces," stakes on all sides.[33] But early St. Louis customs required fencing within town lots, as well as encircling them. Fernand Braudel has remarked about European villages that "the towns urbanized the countryside, but the countryside 'ruralized' the towns too.... In fact, town and countryside never separated like oil and water."[34] Nothing could be more true for colonial St. Louis, where rich rural sights, sounds, and smells pervaded the atmosphere—bulls breeding, calves bawling, and pigs shitting. According to Jean-Baptiste Rivière, who arrived on the west bank of the Mississippi with Auguste Chouteau in 1764, Auguste's mother had a fenced enclosure on her property in which she confined her cattle.[35] Virtually every household in town had some chickens, pigs, and at least one milk cow on their residential property. Manure was close at hand for the kitchen gardens, which adorned every plot. No evidence exists that residential fencing in early St. Louis was intended for defensive purposes, that is, as defense against Indians or Englishmen, and no attack of any kind occurred on St. Louis until the British instigated the infamous, unsuccessful attack in 1780.

The ruralized town properties in early St. Louis often had small barns on them, situated behind the dwelling houses. When in January 1767 Julien Le Roy sold his house and lot, which faced la Grande Rue and ran back to the bluff ("échor")[36] above the Mississippi, the property included a barn measuring 32×18 pieds covered with thatch ("en paille"). But town properties had only limited room for major outbuildings, and a solution had to be found. As early as May 1768, Prairie des Granges (Barn Prairie) appears in St. Louis real estate records.[37] This area, dedicated to barns, was squeezed in between the town residential grid and Prairie St. Louis, and the name was soon changed to Côteau des Granges (Barn Hill). On February 2, 1770, Jean-Baptiste Langoumois received a real estate concession on that hill measuring 40×60 pieds,[38] which he had requested for the purpose of erecting a barn. Less than three weeks later, Langoumois sold this property to Jean-Baptiste Sarpy (a wealthy *négociant*) for 180 livres in peltries. At sale time, the property was described

120 Contours of Village Life

Threshing scenes like this one from eighteenth-century France occurred every autumn in the barns that occupied the Côteau des Granges outside early St. Louis. Reproduced from Denis Diderot and Jean le Rond d'Alembert, comps. and eds., Dictionnaire raisonnée des arts, des sciences, et des métiers, *Planches, vol. 1 (1762).*

as improved with a barn measuring 30×20 pieds with a thatched roof.[39] Likely, Langoumois had already built a barn on the site when he went to St. Ange and requested official title to the property. Such a sequence of events would have been entirely in keeping with the organic, ad hoc evolution of early St. Louis: paperwork followed development on the ground. St. Louis was unique among Illinois Country settlements in having an entire neighborhood devoted exclusively to barns, which added an additional rural aspect to the village.

⚜ ⚜ ⚜ ⚜

Traditionally in the Illinois Country, the fenced-in compounds of plowlands contained no buildings, not even tool sheds or slave quarters. St. Louis was traditional in many ways, but some structures were erected within the plowland compounds that surrounded the town to the west, east, and north. Indeed, during the late 1760s, Laclède developed a very substantial plantation on his 6×80-arpent parcel in the Grande Prairie. The dwelling house was a *poteaux-en-terre* structure, covered with wooden shingles, 80 pieds long, and divided into several apartments (*logements*).[40] This semirural residence was extravagant by Illinois Country standards, and the *habitation* complex also included several slave cabins ("cabannes à nègres"), a barn, an orchard, and a kitchen garden. It was a full-scale plantation of a type rarely seen in the Illinois Country and was situated "about a league" from town, or about an hour's brisk walk across the agricultural fields. Peterson called the establishment "Laclède's country place," as though the hamlet of early St. Louis was not country enough. But perhaps Peterson was correct, and Laclède and his consort Madame Chouteau retired to this residence when on weekends the braying of drunken voyageurs along the St. Louis waterfront became too much for them to endure. The slaves, who were apparently permanent residents at the plantation, served both as agricultural laborers and as domestic servants. Fifty years later, Pierre Ménard developed a similar *habitation* outside of Kaskaskia, with the important difference that Ménard had no residence in town.

After Laclède's death in 1778, Madame Chouteau bought Laclède's plantation at auction on Sunday, July 4, in front of the parish church as the congregation spilled out of Mass. In Illinois Country villages, auctions were conducted on Sundays just as religiously as the Masses that preceded them. Sieur Moreau started the action with a lowball bid of 350 livres, then came Sieur Cambas with 400 livres, Sieur Labadie with 500 livres, Sieur Descharmes (?) with 600 livres, back to Cambas at 650, Labadie at 700, and finally the bailiff François Demars knocked off the property to Madame Chouteau for 750 livres, payable in either deerskins or beaver pelts at current St. Louis values.[41] Laclède had died insolvent, but Madame Chouteau had financial resources in and of her own right, and these were managed and deployed altogether independently of Laclède, for the couple had never married and therefore a *communauté* of worldly possessions was never established (see chapter 7). This meant that Laclède's insolvency did not adversely impinge on Marie-Thérèse Bourgeois Chouteau's assets.

A handful of other upper-class families also had country places in addition to their town residences in St. Louis. As revealed on the Dufossat maps (see color plates section), the early village was bracketed by two small streams—on the south by "Rivière de Pain Court ou St. Louis" (later Mill or Chouteau's Creek), and on the north by "Rivière de la Joie" (later perhaps Gingras Creek). And just north of this latter little stream, running along the west bank of the Mississippi, was a large swath of land known as the "Prairie de la Joie." These two geographical features were named after Jean Salé Lajoie, one of the area's first settlers, who likely had built a cabin on the bank of his namesake creek before Laclède ever visited the area. In any event, unlike the other prairies flanking the town, Prairie de la Joie was not fenced in and converted into plowland. On this prairie, the wealthy *négociant* Sieur Antoine Hubert built his country place called "Habitation de la Prairie de Joie."[42] Like Laclède's country place, Hubert's was a large parcel of land, 6×40 arpents, which was improved with a house, barn, gardens, and fencing. The house was rustic, constructed *poteaux-en-terre* style with a thatched roof, and though of unknown dimensions was enlarged with an "appenti" on one end. Hubert's country property faced Belle Fontaine Creek, meaning that it was located quite some distance from town, at the north end of Prairie de Joie. This would place it near the famous, historic Bellefontaine Cemetery; indeed, the cemetery may precisely occupy the site of Hubert's "habitation."

The Laclède and Hubert cases reveal a lifestyle that was, with the advent of St. Louis, new to the Illinois Country, that of having two major residences, a town house and a country estate. It may well suggest a certain aristocratic ethos stemming from Europe (both Laclède and Hubert were immigrants from France), where high-ranking aristocrats, and of course royalty, traditionally had both town residences and country hunting lodges or châteaux. Even the wealthiest families in Ste. Genevieve at the time, those of François Vallé and Henri Carpentier (both French Canadians), did not indulge in this rather extravagant, aristocratically inspired residential practice.

⚜ ⚜ ⚜ ⚜

Ensuring a food supply was a major and perennial problem at early St. Louis, and foodstuffs often had to be brought in from Ste. Genevieve, which had a more productive agricultural economy.[43] Philip Pittman observed in 1766 that "the village of St. Louis is supplied with flour and other provisions" by Ste. Genevieve.[44] Indeed, during the period 1764–66, most flour consumed in St. Louis was likely imported, and early settlers were preoccupied with procuring enough of it. It is not known when the first wheat crop was harvested from the plowlands outside St. Louis, but once taken in this wheat had to be ground into flour; gristmills had to be built.

Harnessing water- and wind power for driving gristmills requires engineering skills and relatively (that is, relative to the Illinois Country ca. 1765) complex technology. These essential elements sometimes coalesced in the Illinois Country, but for the entire colonial period horse mills were much more common than either water- or windmills. Antoine Hubert was a *négociant* who had a finger in many enterprises, and in December 1768 he hired a master woodworker, Pierre Lupien *dit* Baron, to construct a horse mill.[45] It would be a wooden frame structure, 40×35 pieds outside dimensions, erected on a sturdy stone foundation and roofed with wooden shingles. Baron would also assemble the milling apparatus within the building and supply all the materials for it—"millstones, gears, iron fittings, and everything else required." Hubert's share of the project was to have the masonry foundation laid up and provide twenty pounds of nails. Furthermore, timber for the building was to be cut on Hubert's land, and he would provide two men (possibly slaves) and a team of oxen for hauling and dressing the timbers. This was a major construction project, and Baron agreed to have it completed, with the mill up and running and producing flour, by the end of May 1769. Given that the contract was struck in December 1768, Baron did not have much time to complete the project, but he was being paid a handsome 1,200 livres in peltries for less than six months of work, and he likely subcontracted part of the job. Baron was a woodworker, not a stonemason, and it would have made sense for him to hire a mason to quarry and shape the millstones. These tasks alone would have required several months of labor, both arduous and highly skilled.

Early St. Louis boasted a number of fine woodworkers (*menuisiers*), but Baron was at the top of the class. His knowledge and skills were well known, and just before Christmas 1769 Pierre Dumay Jr. indentured himself to Baron to learn the woodworker's craft.[46] Pierre was still a minor at age twenty-two,[47] and therefore his father, Pierre Dumay, had to authorize the *contrat d'engagement*. The contract ran for three consecutive years, commencing immediately, December 22. Pierre Jr. was to "learn the occupation of cabinetmaking," but at the same time he committed himself to doing everything that Baron ordered him to do pertaining to "cabinetmaking, carpentry, and the dressing of timber." Baron committed *himself* to do "everything possible to teach [Pierre] everything that he knows, and promises to pay him at the end of three years sixty livres worth of peltries so that he can buy cabinetmaker's tools." Furthermore, Baron would provide Pierre board, room, clothing, laundering, and medications in case of illness. Pierre Dumay the elder was an integral part of the contract, and he promised not to aid his son, the apprentice, should he attempt to flee Baron's service. Neither of the Dumays could sign their names, while Baron, the master craftsman from Montreal, signed with a flourish.[48]

Horse mills were used for grinding wheat into flour, but they also had an important role in crushing oak bark to extract tannin for curing leather. St. Louis had fresh hides in abundance (from both domestic and wild animals) for tanning, and leather was in demand for multitudinous purposes in the frontier settlement. A February 1769 contract provides us with a rare view into the intricacies of these specialized tannin mills. Paul Sigle *dit* Maltais (apparently of Maltese descent) was a tanner by profession, and he contracted with Antoine Sans Souci, a master mason, to do the fundamental and exacting stonework required for a mill.[49] Using limestone from the local quarry, Sans Souci agreed to fashion a round upper millstone ("une meule") nine pouces thick with a diameter of three pieds, eight pouces. In the center of this stone would be a hole eight pouces square that would eventually accommodate the axle of the mill. The bottom stone ("le lit"), which would remain stationary, was of the same thickness but would be four pieds, six pouces, square and made in two sections (probably because of the size and weight). The upper stone ("meule") would be mounted vertically and move circumferentially on its axle to crush the oak bark placed on the *lit*. For the heavy lifting, Sigle agreed to supply additional manpower, and he also provided Sans Souci with meals during the two months (February 26 to April 30) required to get the job done. Sans Souci's wages for his highly skilled labor were two hundred livres in beaver pelts or deerskins, half due in May and half in September.[50]

Part of being a landed aristocrat, both in France and in French Canada, was the right to own a gristmill and reap modest profits from having a local milling monopoly.[51] Profits, however, were not so important as symbolism, mills serving as traditional symbols of aristocracy. Such seignorial rights, dating back to medieval times, did not exist in the Illinois Country, but mills nevertheless continued to be emblematic of aristocracy. This meant that Pierre Laclède Liguest simply could not do without one. On August 11, 1766, St. Ange granted Laclède a tract of land that was defined as "running up to the stream called la Petite Rivière [also called Rivière de Pain-Court or St. Louis]."[52] And a year later, Laclède contracted with Jean [John] Hamilton, "maitre charpentier," to build a water-driven gristmill on this property.[53] But the deal quickly fell through, and Hamilton never built the mill. This was perhaps because Joseph Taillon, a more astute agricultural entrepreneur than Laclède, had already seized the best site on the stream and built a mill there. Guy Dufossat, whose draftsmanship was better than his spelling, delicately inked in this mill as "Moulain de Talion" on his splendid 1767 map of the St. Louis area (see color plates).

Laclède, rather than building a mill and competing with Taillon, chose instead to buy out Taillon. He purchased Taillon's mill on the Petite Rivière, and the bill of sale (December 1767) is unusually informative. Taillon was removing all of the milling machinery from the building and selling only the immovable real estate—land and buildings. The "mill belonged to Taillon because he had built it at his own expense within the royal domain, although without any official concession."[54] Taillon built his mill very early on, perhaps as early as 1764, before St. Ange arrived on the west bank of the Mississippi and began conveying official concessions. Taillon had occupied the land for more than a year and a day, had improved it, and had thereby acquired title to it by customary right. No dimensions were given for the tract of real estate involved, which was defined simply as the land associated with the mill. It is possible that the mill site actually fell within the boundaries of land ("running up to the Petite Rivière") that St. Ange had granted Laclède back in August 1766, no one being aware of the anomaly at a time when accurate surveying was not being conducted. In any event, Laclède was to take possession of the mill property on March 22, 1768, a date with no apparent meaning other than it was the time of the vernal equinox, another way of saying "next spring." The price of four hundred livres in hard cash ("argent réel," which was very rarely used in early St. Louis) suggests that the mill was a modest establishment. But even before he took possession of the property, Laclède was making preparations to rectify that; modest simply would not do for St. Louis's self-styled aristocrat. Moreover, St. Louis had an urgent need for flour from a major local gristmill.

François Delin was a master carpenter, born in Limoges, who arrived in St. Louis early on.[55] On January 7, 1768, he contracted to supply Laclède with a very large quantity of construction timber.[56] American white oak (*Quercus alba*) is native only to North America, but European settlers, including Laclède, soon came to prize its strength and durability. White oaks grew (and grow) in abundance in the St. Louis area, and Laclède specified in the contract that the timbers he wanted would be exclusively of white oak. No sawmill existed in St. Louis at this time, which meant that Delin dressed the timbers with an ax or adze. Many of the largest pieces (*soles, soliveaux, lambourdes, sablières,* and *poteaux*)[57] weighed more than a half ton apiece, reckoning unseasoned white oak at forty-six pounds per cubic foot. Like blocks of limestone from the Cold Water Quarry, large timbers were most easily brought into St. Louis via the Mississippi, and Delin was bringing Laclède's oak into town on a "cajeu," a raft.[58] Significantly, Delin was to deliver the oak timbers to Laclède's Landing ("*embarquement de Laclède*") below the bluff on the Mississippi's bank in March, not coincidentally the same month (March 1768) that Laclède was to take possession of the mill he had purchased from Taillon. As in his purchase of the mill from Taillon, Laclède paid Delin cash money, "argent de la caisse royalle [*sic*]."

Once Delin's raft arrived at the Mississippi landing, Laclède agreed to supply two black slaves to help lug the timbers up to the public square near Laclède's house. So, our earliest view of the St. Louis waterfront suddenly comes into focus: Delin maneuvering his bulky raft into the shoreline; Laclède giving orders to his slaves; the slaves, torsos convulsed (re: Michelangelo's sculpture *Unfinished Slaves*), loading the oak, piece by piece, onto a *charrette* (a heavy, two-wheeled conveyance); and finally teams of oxen struggling to draw the *charrette* up the hill to the town center. After being stockpiled near Laclède's house, the massive timbers would eventually be hauled out to the mill site. Significantly, the road to the Taillon-Laclède mill was the first-mentioned road to penetrate out into the surrounding countryside beyond the compact village.[59]

Laclède's investment in the mill on the Petite Rivière was substantial—400 livres in his original purchase, plus 1,720 livres for all the new construction timber, plus whatever he had to pay craftsmen to accomplish the total rebuilding of it. When finished the mill was the largest structure in the St. Louis area, dwarfing the small chapel situated at the center of town, as today's Ralston-Purina complex off Chouteau Avenue dwarfs the St. Louis Old Cathedral complex. After Laclède's death, Auguste Chouteau purchased the mill at auction for 2,000 livres and made further improvements at the site, which included a dam that created Chouteau's Pond.[60] This mill remained the only *water* mill in the St. Louis for the entire colonial period, and by the 1790s Chouteau's millpond was a prominent feature of the St. Louis landscape.

Construction timber in early St. Louis was dressed either with broad axes and adzes or, rarely, laboriously hand sawn. Jean-Baptiste Martigny and Joachim (?) Roy[61] understood that this situation was an obstacle to progress, and, being quintessential Americans (that is, frontiersmen yearning and learning to master the North American environment), they wanted to improve things. On January 2, 1770, they applied to St. Ange for a concession of 4×40 arpents on which to build a "moulin à planches," a water-driven sawmill for cutting planks.[62] This, the applicants argued, would be "advantageous for the public welfare." As custodians of the public welfare, St. Ange and Labuxière, in order to "support their good intentions," honored Martigny's and Roy's request and granted the concession. The land was situated on the Petite Rivière above the Prairie La Joie, meaning that it was far enough upstream not to interfere with Laclède's flour mill. Whether this mill was ever built to serve the public good and produce profits for Martigny and Roy is doubtful—sawmills required even more complicated technology than gristmills. Lieutenant Governor Francisco Cruzat later reunited this real estate to the royal domain before granting it to Jacques Clamorgan.[63]

The St. Louis of 1764–70 was a humble village, neither as large nor as wealthy as Kaskaskia or Ste. Genevieve among the villages of the Illinois Country. Most residences in town were mere vertical-log cabins, but a rich diversity of folk resided in them: Canadians, Frenchmen, and Creoles (a distinct minority); Indian slaves and black slaves; merchants, voyageurs, blacksmiths, carpenters, cabinetmakers, farmers, millers, tanners, and others. The following chapters will explain more fully just who these folk—of many colors and hues and backgrounds—were and how they set about fashioning, even improving, their lives in a raw, new environment.

CHAPTER 7

The *Coutume de Paris* Rules

The future couple will hold in common all moveable property and all acquired real estate in accordance with the Coutume de Paris, *according to which their marital community will be managed.*

—Marriage contract, St. Louis, 1767

The first sentence of Claude de Ferrière's magisterial *Nouveau Commentaire sur La Coutume de la Prévosté et Vicomté de Paris*[1] provides a good working definition of customary law: "It is a legal practice of which the people approve, which is introduced by their tacit consent and which is observed over a considerable period of time." Hodgepodge agglomerations of customary laws emerged in France during late medieval times, and jurists began to codify them during the sixteenth-century Renaissance. Feudal fragmentation meant that individual French provinces developed their own respective congeries of customary laws, but the *Coutume de Paris* governed domestic life in much of northern France (not just Paris) and in all North American French colonies. The *Coutume* was definitively established in Canada in 1664, just before traders and missionaries from the St. Lawrence Valley began to penetrate, via the Great Lakes, into the greater Mississippi River valley.[2]

French Canadians who settled early at Cahokia and Kaskaskia adhered loosely to many provisions of traditional French customary law, but it took a while for the *Coutume de Paris* to be fully institutionalized in the Illinois Country. A printed text of the *Coutume* finally arrived in the Illinois Country in 1719, when French administrators arrived from New Orleans to establish a Provincial Council and framework for government in the region. But it was a complaint that arose in 1723 at Kaskaskia that established the *Coutume*, in theory and practice, as the law of the land in the Illinois Country.[3] The case began when the stepson of the wealthiest resident of Kaskaskia, Jacques Bourdon, contested Bourdon's will. The Illinois Provincial Council adjudicated the case at Fort de Chartres and determined that Bourdon's carelessly drafted will violated several sections of the *Coutume*. The council's decision brought Bourdon's succession, which his will had muddied, into compliance with the *Coutume*'s fundamental provisions. This case settled the issue once and for all: henceforth, the *Coutume* would be the governing authority regarding domestic legal issues in Illinois.

When, starting in early 1766, St. Louis's French-trained notary Joseph Labuxière drafted legal documents, he adhered to the *Coutume*—down to the last detail. The most important of these documents were marriage contracts, ancient French versions of prenuptial agreements.[4] When examined in the light of the *Coutume*, they reveal much about the roles of respective family members, bringing us into direct contact with Illinois Country women—as minors, wives, and widows—in unprecedented ways. Much more than dull, legalistic boilerplate, early St. Louis marriage contracts enrich our understanding of that French colonial society in remarkable fashion.

Before a village couple stood in front of the Roman Catholic priest to be united in the holy sacrament of matrimony, they met with Labuxière in a civil ceremony to draw up a marriage contract. Parents, relatives, and friends assembled with the couple and the notary, usually in the home of the bride. The notary penned the intricate document starting with the names of the spouses, parents, and witnesses, continued with strings of legalistic terms and

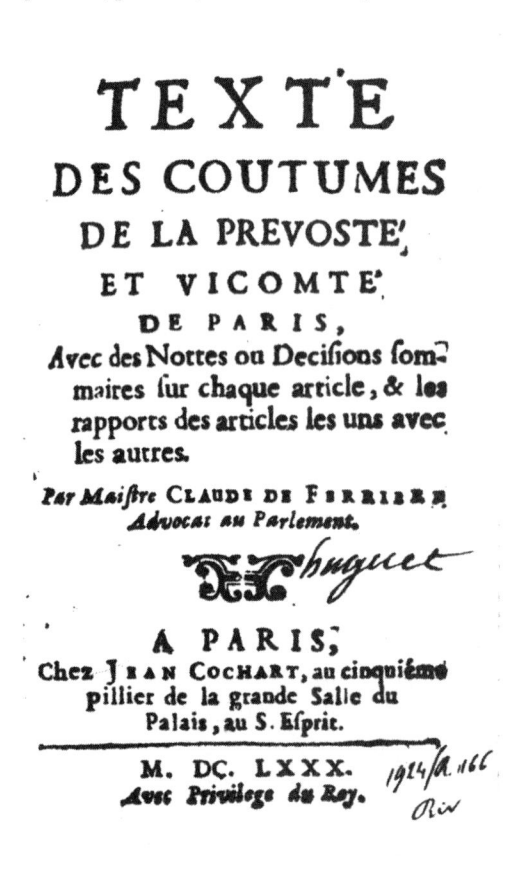

The Coutume de Paris *(Customary Law of Paris) governed domestic affairs, especially inheritance practices, in a large swath of northern France, as well as in French colonies. Beginning in the 1720s, the* Coutume *was regularly cited in Illinois Country legal documents, and St. Ange's French-educated notary, Joseph Labuxière, was the strict custodian of French law and legal traditions in St. Louis.*

left space at the end for the signatures (or crosses of the illiterate). Such civil marriage contracts stood at the very heart of domestic life in French Illinois. The profane always preceded the sacred, for marriage contracts declared that marriage in the "Holy Mother Church, Catholic, Apostolic and Roman" would take place as soon as the sacrament could be arranged, or when either party requested it. In St. Louis during the 1760s this also depended on the perambulations of an itinerant priest, for the village had no resident curate until Valentin (his only known name), a Capuchin priest, arrived in 1772.

The *Coutume* staked out its wide authority in the "choice of law" clause in marriage contracts.[5] Every early St. Louis contract declares that the *Coutume de Paris* would be the governing legal authority for the marriage no matter where the couple lived, even if they later moved to a place where different laws reigned.[6] This was a bold assertion of French legal folkways and culture in a frontier outpost of the Spanish empire where, looking out his window, a St. Louis villager could see British Illinois just across the Mississippi River. The various British colonies were experimenting with how to handle women's property rights in marriage, and "depending on the talents, inclinations, and prejudices of influential men in any given colony, laws developed in one direction or another." In general, however, under English law prenuptial agreements were rare, and married women enjoyed only minimum financial safeguards.[7] In French St. Louis, on the other hand, prenuptial contracts explicitly laid out the inheritance terms, and in all contracts during St. Ange's tenure the surviving spouse could take full possession of the community property if there were no children (referred to as the mutual donation clause).[8]

Acquisition, preservation, and disposition of family property were the principal aims of the *Coutume*, and under its terms women secured certain explicit property rights at the outset of marriage.[9] Marriage contracts defined the marital community of goods, the *communauté*, which commenced automatically when the marriage was solemnized. All personal property that each spouse possessed and whatever the couple acquired during their married life, both personal (movable) and real (immovable) property, normally became part of the *communauté*.[10] Slaves fell in the category of personal, movable property,[11] just as livestock, furniture, and housewares did. On the other hand, all buildings—residences, barns, poultry sheds, and so forth—were immovables. Movable, personal property that a spouse wished to exclude from the *communauté* had to be stipulated in a specific clause in the contract.[12] Such clauses requested by brides appear in several early St. Louis contracts, demonstrating that even the youngest (with the advice of parents and friends) knew how to utilize the legal options available to them.

The *Coutume* afforded wives certain protections, and a husband could not alienate (sell or mortgage) property that his wife had brought into the marriage. Neither spouse was responsible for the other's premarital debts, and the premarital-debt clause appears in every St. Louis contract. Contracts stipulated, in detail, how the *communauté* would be settled after the death of either spouse. If a marriage produced no children, the mutual-donation clause guaranteed that the surviving spouse inherited the entire *communauté*. If there were children and a husband died first, the widow was eligible for two fixed sums as specified in the premarital contract: First was the *douaire préfix*, which the wife might claim immediately upon her husband's death, and which the husband had to guarantee with his own property.[13] Second was the *préciput*, a sum due to *either* surviving spouse following the death of the other and was generally one-half the amount of the *douaire préfix*. These sums (or sum in the case of a widower) were subtracted from the inventoried estate before the surviving spouse received her or his one-half of the remaining community property. Children from the marriage were entitled to receive the other half, divided into equal parts among them, regardless of gender or age.

The *douaire préfix* and *préciput* provided wives with a certain degree of financial protection, and so also did the renunciation clause often included in marriage contracts. This clause allowed a widow whose husband had managed the *communauté* poorly (accumulating excessive debts, for example) formally to renounce her stake in the *communauté* and take the guaranteed *douaire* and the possessions with which she came into the marriage.[14] Indeed, the *Coutume* guaranteed a wife's right to renounce even if no such clause had been specifically incorporated into the marriage contract. Divorce as we know it was not admissible in Roman Catholic St. Louis, which meant that the marital *communauté* typically ended only with the death of one of the spouses.[15] Upon such a death, a team of appraisers appointed by the commandant, usually in consultation with the surviving spouse, conducted an inventory and appraisal of the community property, all the movables and immovables. A written marriage contract was not a prerequisite for the *Coutume* to function: even couples who, for whatever reason, had not drafted a contract had their successions settled in accordance with the *Coutume*.[16]

Sixteen marriage contracts have survived from the four years of St. Ange's government, and these captivating artifacts from the early village transport us into the very heart of the living and breathing community. All these contracts include specific features of the *Coutume* as described above, but they also reveal its pervasive influence in St. Louis society at every level. Marriage contracts and inventories were not just means for the wealthiest families, the social elite, to manage their property, and inventories exist for estates as small as 500 livres (not enough to purchase a house) and as large as 54,000 livres (enough for more than twenty houses).[17] The remainder of this chapter presents early St. Louisans going about marrying, buying and selling property, and making arrangements for old age and death. The chapter is not legal history per se, but rather is intended to illuminate the human dimensions of the *Coutume* as it was implemented in St. Louis. The following case histories permit us to explore precisely how this was done to help guide village families in the management of their mortal affairs.

⚜ ⚜ ⚜ ⚜

The first marriage to occur in St. Louis, the union of Marie-Josèphe Beaugenou and Toussaint Hunaud, deserves special attention. A picturesque account of the marriage, written decades later, highlighted the "frontier" attire of the nuptial couple and the rowdy drunkenness of the wedding party afterward.[18] But the sober marriage contract that Labuxière penned for the couple is a far more important historical document, for it established the fixed precedent that marriages in the new settlement would follow traditional French customs. At two o'clock in the afternoon, Joseph Labuxière, formally attired in culottes, hose, jacket, and cravat, arrived at the Nicolas Beaugenou home—quill, ink, and paper in hand. Eighteen-year-old Marie-Josèphe Beaugenou, born across the Mississippi in the village of Chartres, was to wed twenty-five-year-old Toussaint Hunaud, who had come down to the Illinois Country from the St. Lawrence Valley. Following the pattern of many other French Canadian transplants, he found a local bride.[19]

The marriage contract contained the fundamental elements described above: definition of the *communauté*, absolution for premarital debts, the *douaire préfix* and *préciput*, and the renunciation and mutual-donation clauses. *Douaire préfixs* and *préciputs* were generally reliable indicators of the matrimonial principals' wealth and status.[20] The 500 livres *douaire préfix* promised by Hunaud, which Marie-Josèphe could claim upon his death, was modest. The largest *douaire préfix* among St. Louis early contracts was 2,000 livres, enough to buy a large stone house, while the usual amount was 1,000 livres. The *préciput* was usually half the *douaire préfix*, and ranged from a high of 1,000 livres down to 150 livres, which was relatively small but still not paltry.[21] In the Beaugenou-Hunaud contract, the *préciput* was set at 250 livres, precisely half the *douaire préfix*.

The signing-of-the-marriage-contract gathering at the Beaugenou home included a multitude of family and friends, as was usual for these affairs.[22] The bride's mother, Marie-Anne Henrion, acting on behalf of herself and her husband, Nicolas Beaugenou Sr., presented her minor daughter and accepted the contract's various clauses on her behalf. Nicolas was too ill to participate and died before the census of May 1766, on which Marie-Anne appears as a widow. Three witnesses stood up on behalf of the bride: First was Gilles Chemin, family friend to the Beaugenous and sergeant in the village militia. The two families had been neighbors at Chartres on the east side of the river, and

Marie-Josèphe's mother was godmother to the Chemins' son Charles.[23] Marie-Josèphe's uncles, Gilles and Nicolas Henrion, both unmarried, completed the bride's party. Toussaint likewise had three witnesses: his uncle Antoine Hunaud from Ste. Genevieve;[24] Jean-Baptiste Martigny, captain of the St. Louis militia; and Toussaint's friend Louis Briard *dit* La Roche, a married man with several children. (All the legal witnesses were men in this case, but women, most especially Marie-Anne Henrion, were a major presence on the occasion.)[25]

The *Coutume*, a major but generally unseen presence in villagers' daily lives, asserted itself overtly when marriages and deaths occurred. Marie-Anne Henrion survived her husband only by a few years, and after her death specific provisions of the *Coutume* protected the interests of the minor children: Guillaume Bizet, a prominent and successful businessman,[26] became the minor children's *tuteur*, a financial guardian, and another of the widow's brothers, François Henrion, was the assistant, or *subrogé tuteur*.[27] The two men together arranged for an auction of agricultural land from the Beaugenou parents' *communauté* as a means of providing sustenance for the minor children. François Henrion himself purchased one parcel of land, receiving formal title to his deceased sister's property in return for his financial support of his nieces and nephew.[28]

The first St. Louis marriage contract included all the common, conventional clauses of contracts from the 1760s, yet others from St. Ange's administration are more compelling in important details—of promises made, of conditions imposed, and of family intimacies revealed.

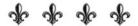

⚜ ⚜ ⚜ ⚜

On May 10, 1766, Joseph Michel *dit* Taillon and his wife, Marie-Louise Bossett, formally requested that Labuxière draw up a marriage contract for their firstborn daughter, Marie-Josèphe, age eighteen, and Paul Kiercereau, of legal age.[29] This second St. Louis marriage united two of the wealthiest families in the village, and seventeen years later the sole surviving child of Marie-Josèphe and Paul, Pélagie, married Pierre Chouteau, natural son of Pierre Laclède and Marie-Thérèse Bourgeois Chouteau. Again, wealth attracted wealth, and the bride was an excellent catch for the Chouteau family. The Taillons were the most prosperous St. Louis family in 1766—as measured by their real estate and their slave and livestock holdings, which were good indicators of wealth and status in the village. The bride's father, an Illinois Country miller since the 1740s, had built the first water-driven gristmill in St. Louis. In virtually every regard Taillon was a wealthier man than Laclède. Laclède attended the contract ceremony as a witness for Marie-Josèphe, revealing that he had become friends with his more prosperous neighbor.[30] If he was a jealous friend, we will never know.

The Taillon-Kiercereau marriage contract of 1766 is unique among early St. Louis contracts because it includes specific provisions for the groom's mother, Gillette Le Boure. Gillette had already outlived at least two husbands,[31] and how she would be cared for in old age seemed to be on everyone's mind when her younger son married. The respective parties in the Taillon home that Saturday hammered out an agreement for Gillette that was incorporated into Marie-Josèphe and Paul's marriage contract. Paul's mother, who was of an "advanced age," would be fed and cared for in health or sickness from the couple's community of goods, and in return for this care Marie-Josèphe would be "mistress" of the family community of possessions. Paul's mother appears to have donated her own estate to the community in return for this guaranteed care. The commitment would be binding whether or not Marie-Josèphe and Paul had children, and even in the event that her son died.[32] Such long-term care arrangements were common in early St. Louis, but this is unique in being incorporated into a marriage contract. The Taillon-Kiercereau contract nicely demonstrates that marriage contracts could serve a variety of purposes and were employed to deal with a wide range of vital family affairs. Gillette Le Boure apparently engineered this arrangement out of enlightened self-interest, and her prudence proved wise, both for herself and for her future granddaughter.

That May a tent served as St. Louis's only religious edifice, and after the marriage ceremony the Taillon-Kiercereau families may have celebrated alfresco on the bluff overlooking the Mississippi River. Within a month or so, Marie-Josèphe Michel became pregnant, and in mid-March 1767 daughter Pélagie was born. During his second visit to St. Louis, on May 7, 1767, Father Sébastien-Louis Meurin baptized Pélagie Kiercereau and five other infants, four girls and one boy.[33] These six children were among the earliest known native-born (Creole) St. Louisans. Five French mothers with their husbands, and one Indian slave mother (Angélique)—with her master Commandant St. Ange, the likely father of her child[34]—assembled with their relatives and friends who served as godparents. The itinerant Father Meurin may have come to St. Louis on this occasion to consecrate the first church building, as well as perform baptisms, for by 1767 the village had outgrown the tent.[35] Marie-Josèphe was the youngest mother on that day, and she became pregnant with their second child about January 1769. This time the child was a boy, christened Paul after his father, but Marie-Josèphe did not survive long after her son's birth. To her brother-in-law René Kiercereau, church sexton, fell the task of arranging the burial in the absence of a resident priest. By late 1770, Kiercereau had begun registering burials, and one of his first records (March 1771) was for his nephew—Paul Kiercereau, age about eighteen months. Paul Kiercereau *père* followed his wife and son in death the next year.[36] His mother, the durable Gillette Le Boure, had outlived the people who had been designated as her caretakers.

Pélagie's immediate family had died all around her, leaving her an orphan at age five, a situation that demanded attention. As per the *Coutume*, Gillette Le Boure requested an inventory of her son's estate soon after his death.[37] Joseph Taillon became the financial caretaker (*tuteur*) of his granddaughter's inheritance, which now supported both Pélagie and her paternal grandmother, in accord with the 1766 marriage contract; Taillon kept careful records on the matter. After four years, Madame Kiercereau, Gillette Le Boure, who had buried so many of her loved ones, died in August 1776 at the age of seventy-nine, a very advanced age for that time and place.[38] With Labuxière's assistance as an inscriber of legal documents, she had provided herself security for growing old in young St. Louis. At her age and with her presence, this matriarch must have been a revered figure in the village.

Grand-père Joseph Taillon managed young Pélagie's finances, and in 1778 he decided to sell off some of her assets, most notably one of the two slaves.[39] Paul was about forty years old, and while he was too old to be considered prime (*pièce d'Inde*, in Louisiana parlance), the merchant Louis Dubreuil paid 1,325 livres in peltries for him. This was a very substantial amount (a fine house in town could be had for that sum) and would provide for Pélagie's living expenses for years to come. In 1780 Joseph Taillon called for a detailed inventory of Pélagie's assets, and he calculated the expenses charged to the Kiercereau estate during his seven-year guardianship.[40] However tight-fisted wealthy Taillon may have been, young Pélagie received schooling from Madame Barsalou (Madeleine Le Page).[41] Moreover, her fourteen outfits, six pairs of shoes, silver earrings, and two gold rings (undoubtedly inheritance from her mother and grandmother) made her the best-dressed young lady in town.

Upon completion of his accounting, Taillon created an annuity of 160 livres in peltries for Pélagie until she married. This occurred three years later, when Taillon presented her in marriage to Pierre Chouteau; Pélagie was sixteen and Pierre just a few months shy of his twenty-fifth birthday. This sixteen-year-old orphan brought an inheritance of 6,750 livres in peltries into the marriage with Chouteau, a very considerable sum, more than forty times Pélagie's yearly annuity. The marriage contract of Pélagie's parents in May 1766 had been the initial mechanism for preserving the wealth that husband Pierre Chouteau now managed. Foley and Rice remarked that the sum Pélagie brought to her marriage with Chouteau, as stated in the contract, "1,600 silver dollars" of possessions made her "a young woman of considerable means," and it was her inheritance that constituted the major portion of her wealth. Joseph Taillon duly conveyed the sum, which they had not yet calculated on the day of the marriage contract, to Pierre Chouteau after the marriage.[42]

⚜ ⚜ ⚜ ⚜

Thérèse Hervieux was a "natural" daughter, born of an intimate liaison between Canadian-born Jean-Baptiste Hervieux, the village gunsmith, and his married lover, the *métisse* Agnès Hulin.[43] Thérèse's father was a literate, high-status member of the community, often serving as a witness to notarial transactions at Fort de Chartres. Thérèse's illegitimate status presented no impediment to the execution of a civil marriage contract between Thérèse and her fiancé, Nicolas Dion, which was done in St. Ange's chambers rather than in Hervieux's home.[44] Thérèse did not live with her father, and this venue perhaps allowed Thérèse's mother to attend discreetly without raising eyebrows about her presence in the home of her former lover. In their marriage contract, Thérèse and Nicolas declined to describe any currently owned property, meaning that the *communauté* would consist exclusively of property acquired *after* their marriage.

As an illegitimate child, Thérèse could not inherit from her parents through the succession process prescribed in the *Coutume*. Jean-Baptiste Hervieux nevertheless made some effort to ensure his natural daughter's future well-being. Six months after her marriage, he provided a "caution," a guarantee, when Nicolas Dion purchased an arpent of agricultural land outside the village. In all likelihood, given the depth of Hervieux's pockets and the shallowness of Dion's, Hervieux put up the money for this purchase, the land then becoming part of his daughter's marital *communauté*.[45] And in 1774, Hervieux helped Dion with the legal work that enabled him to collect his share of his parents' succession back in Canada.[46] Financial and legal paperwork regularly moved back and forth between the Illinois Country and the St. Lawrence Valley, geographic obstacles notwithstanding.

Hervieux died in November 1775, leaving no marriage contract because he never married and leaving no final testament (his death was apparently sudden and unexpected) through which his natural daughter and son-in-law might have inherited at least part of his estate.[47] This left Thérèse completely dependent on Nicolas Dion and the *communauté* they had begun to build together.[48] Thérèse was pregnant when her father died, but when Father Bernard de Limpach baptized her child, Céleste, on July 27, 1776, Thérèse had also died, likely succumbing to postpartum complications; compounding Nicolas's misery, infant Céleste was buried just two months later,[49] leaving her father to wonder, like Job, about the mercy of divine justice. On September 2, 1776, as Céleste was fast failing, it was officially reported to Martin Duralde (the appointed executor of Jean-Baptiste Hervieux's estate) that four pigs and one calf from Hervieux's estate had mysteriously gone missing and that no one knew anything whatsoever about their disappearance.[50] Likely, some sense of community justice permitted Nicolas Dion to take the law into his own hands and make off with a small piece of his deceased father-in-law's estate. Everyone but everyone knew this, including those who had reported the missing livestock, and no one was going to utter a word about it to anyone.

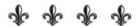

⚜ ⚜ ⚜ ⚜

The *Coutume* decreed that husbands were to manage the marital *communauté*, but this did not leave wives totally powerless and bereft of legal authority. Hans Baade outlined three exceptions to wives' general inability to initiate legal transactions. First, the wife always had the power of "the purse and key," meaning that she could make the arrangements necessary to run the household without her husband's consent on every detail. These everyday activities could cover a wide range of domestic issues, but they usually generated no notarial records, depriving historians of paper trails. Second, the wife might represent the couple, "duly authorized" with her husband's permission. Third, under certain specific conditions, she could operate as a merchant in her own right, with her own assets, as a *femme marchande publique*.[51] This last, with the woman in "full legal capacity," empowered women very substantially, but these cases were rare. Therefore, it is in "duly authorized" transactions that we most often see women participating in the management of the *communauté*, often buying and selling real estate.[52]

Commerçante (in the feminine form) served as a convenient synonym for *femme marchande* in the Illinois Country. *Commerçantes* were more than wives who now and then represented their husbands, as when Marie-Anne Henrion represented her ailing husband at the marriage contract ceremony of their daughter. Labuxière chose the word *commerçante* to describe just two women in early St. Louis documents: Véronique Panissé and Marie-Thérèse Bourgeois Chouteau.[53] Véronique's business dealings, which proceeded for more than twenty years at both Chartres and St. Louis, went far beyond issues of "purse and key." Indeed, she seemed consciously to be pushing the envelope, testing the rules of the *Coutume* to their (and Labuxière's) limit.

Panissé's first husband, Jean Prunet *dit* la Giroflée ("the wallflower")[54] was a master mason. She married him sometime prior to April 12, 1758, when they bought a house together in the village of Chartres, near the fort.[55] Véronique and Jean bought and sold property together in and near Chartres in 1758, 1759, and 1760—three transactions in 1760 alone. These purchases variously included both movable (livestock and farm implements) and immovable (land and buildings) acquisitions that became part of the couple's *communauté*. A husband's permission for his wife to enter by herself into a business agreement was articulated in the phrase "duly authorized," following her name in the opening lines of a document. La Giroflée *repeatedly* gave Véronique such authorization. In December 1759, she represented the couple, authorized by her husband, to purchase for six thousand livres (a fair sum of money) from the widow Hervy, Renée Drouin, all the movables and immovables related to her property at Chartres. Included were a house with a double stone chimney, a barn, stable, garden, agricultural implements, livestock, land, and generally everything that was in the house.[56] This was one of the most substantial residential properties in Chartres, and the real estate deal was struck between two savvy women.[57] In January 1760, Véronique, again legally representing herself and her husband, sold this same house and the land it was on (minus the movables—livestock, furniture, and farm implements) to Paul Labrosse.[58] Why La Giroflée chose to let his wife represent the couple in these transactions is unclear, but it was undoubtedly she who conducted the negotiations and closed the deals.

Véronique Panissé sold another property at Chartres that has since gained some fame because Pierre Laclède purchased it in November 1763. The complicated context of the sale is far more compelling than the simple fact that Laclède was involved.[59] Laclède purchased the property (consisting of land, buildings, farm implements, and livestock) from a French marine, Jean Gerardin, who had bought it from Panissé in December 1762. Her husband, La Giroflée, had purchased the land and buildings from Joseph Labuxière, the notary, for just over ten thousand livres the year before.[60] The normal string of property titles was disrupted, however, because no notarized sales contract between Panissé and Gerardin was ever drafted. Rather, an informal note dated December 20, 1762, stated that Panissé had sold it to Gerardin in a verbal agreement and that she had received a payment of fifteen thousand livres. Further, and importantly, the note stated that she had struck this deal without prior authorization from her husband, a technical violation of the *Coutume*. When Labuxière drafted the sales contract between Girardin and Laclède, these awkward issues meant that he had to employ an entire arsenal of legalese to make the transaction legitimate. Susan Boyle's study of activities in colonial Ste. Genevieve suggested that "*coverture,* the control of women's legal activities by their husbands, was not strictly enforced," and the Véronique Panissé case supports this observation.[61]

In April 1764, when work had just begun on the new settlement on the west bank of the Mississippi (embryonic St. Louis), Panissé entered the real estate market in Chartres again, purchasing property from Joseph Hennet. Labuxière did not require spousal authorization for Véronique in the sales contract[62]—perhaps because she, in the notary's opinion, had established a solid presence as *commerçante (femme marchande publique)*, or perhaps because her husband was absent, already working as a master mason across the river.

Jean La Giroflée was present for the first census of St. Louis in May 1766, but by November of that year he had died.[63] In the short time that Panissé was a widow, she had the legal right to act independently in financial transactions, but there are no extant records to demonstrate that she did this. The legal status of Véronique, Veuve Giroflée, would soon be altered once again when she acquired a new husband. "Kiery" Louis Marcheteau Jr. was from the second generation of one of the largest extended families that moved early on to St. Louis from the east side of the Mississippi. In November 1766, when the Marcheteau family gathered for the marriage contract ceremony between the widow La Giroflée and Kiery Marcheteau, they assembled at her home, "*chez Véronique Panissé.*"

Documents involving Véronique Panissé are often idiosyncratic, and her position as a *commerçante* forced Labuxière to keep on his toes as he wrote. In 1776 and in 1777, Kiery Marcheteau, while ill, dictated two wills, the first in Spanish and the second in French, both drafted by Labuxière. Donation clauses stating that if there were no children, the survivor (either spouse) would have full ownership of the estate, movables and immovables, were inscribed in almost all marriage contracts. Kiery's will referred directly to his and Véronique's donation clause and recapitulated its terms.[64] Their marriage contract, furthermore, had been registered and "insinuated" (copied and filed separately), the final step in making the donation legal beyond any doubt.[65] The motivations behind the two wills are therefore unclear, but perhaps other events in their lives had prompted Marcheteau and Panissé to reiterate the donation. An agreement through which they had leased out their farm for the previous three years was about to end,[66] and so their property and the disposition of the *communauté* may have been on their minds. Panissé perhaps felt that members of the large, extended Marcheteau clan would contest her full right to the community property if she survived her husband.

In the second (French) will, Marcheteau commended his soul to God the Creator, Father, Son, and Holy Spirit and, with the intercession of the Virgin Mary and St. Louis his patron saint, pleaded that his soul might take its place in the kingdom of heaven among the blessed. Marcheteau wanted his debts paid, and he wanted to be buried in the cemetery among the faithful. He declared that his wife, Véronique Panissé, had demonstrated her attachment to him throughout their marriage, had cared for him every day *in an equal and perfect union* (interesting, even touching, words). The couple had no children (she had none by either husband), and Kiery stipulated that Véronique should receive all his possessions and acquisitions, wherever they may be. His wife was to be his universal and general heir, exercising full ownership and use of all his property from the day of his death, without having to make any direct or indirect accounting for it to anyone. At his death, she could also determine the appropriate prayers and services to be said for the repose of his soul, and no one, not even the priest, could constrain her in this matter.

But it was not yet Kiery's time to meet his maker. Several years later, in 1780, we find the Marcheteaus selling a house in St. Louis, and once again it was Véronique who represented the couple, authorized by her husband.[67] She sold a town lot with house, barn, pigeon house, henhouse, hay shed, plus an agricultural plot in the Prairie Desnoyers. Also included in the sale were extensive household furnishings, which Panissé stated she had acquired from "Sr. Barré" in a transaction that had been duly recorded and filed.[68] This cross-referencing of notarial documents reveals a civilized seriousness about generating paper trails that could connect properties and people across time and often place. Even illiterate residents—neither Marcheteau nor Panissé could sign their names—understood the necessity of drafting proper legal documents. Panissé and Labuxière had been conducting business together for twenty-two years, but this was their final transaction and the last appearance of Véronique Panissé in St. Louis records. From Panissé's unauthorized, virtually scandalous sale of the property at Chartres to the seemingly superfluous wills that her second husband dictated to Spanish authorities, Véronique Panissé often had a fractious relationship with the rules of the *Coutume*.

⚜ ⚜ ⚜ ⚜

The documents relating to Véronique Panissé are unique. No similar sources exist for Madame Chouteau, although Labuxière also identified her as a *commerçante*. Because her legal husband, René Chouteau, was "absent" in New Orleans, she could not obtain the necessary "duly authorized" permission to participate in legal transactions as Panissé and other married women did. Pierre Laclède and Marie-Thérèse Bourgeois Chouteau were an unmarried couple, and as such they could neither create a legal *communauté* of possessions nor accumulate an estate to divide. Laclède had to use an alternate avenue for dealing with his property and providing for his illegitimate family. In 1768 he conveyed very substantial assets to the children of Madame Chouteau via *donation*, a method of conveying property that was fully sanctioned by the *Coutume*.[69] Laclède gave to Auguste (Marie-Thérèse's son by her husband, René, and whom Laclède referred to as his clerk), Pierre, Pélagie, Marie-Louise, and Victoire Chouteau (all natural children of Marie-Thérèse and Laclède) a village lot with a stone house "new and in good condition." In addition, he gave them five slaves, equal to the number of siblings, two of whom, Manon and Thérèse, were Indian girls.[70] The other slaves were two black women, one with a two-year-old son. The last item in the donation was a parcel of agricultural land of standard size (two arpents by forty arpents) on the Grand Prairie outside the village. Madame Chouteau's role in the donation, in the absence of her husband, was to accept the gifts on behalf of her children, who were all legal minors. Because Madame Chouteau was intended to have usufruct (lifetime use) of these gifts, this was, in essence but not in law, a donation to her, and not to her children.

The complicated intertwined issues of illegitimacy and inheritance came up in the lives, and deaths, of both Jean-Baptiste Hervieux (as seen above) and Pierre Laclède, and it must be said that Laclède dealt with them much more effectively. Perhaps with help from Marie-Thérèse Chouteau (she does seem to have had the better foresight of the two), Laclède perpetuated a legal fiction, namely, that young Pierre Chouteau and his sisters were all the legitimate children of Marie-Thérèse and René Chouteau (eight-year-old Pélagie slipped up in her first appearance as a godmother when she gave her name to Father Meurin as Pélagie Laclède),[71] never admitting that he was their father. Madame Chouteau did not give birth to any additional children after arriving in the Illinois Country, which kept their story line intact. When Laclède died intestate in 1778, his concubine, Thérèse, and their children were already in legal possession of a significant amount of property that he wanted them to have.

Laclède's mechanism for transferring property to the next generation fell within the rules of the *Coutume*, but it was unusual. The standard form of succession was via the estate inventory and partition of the *communauté* among the children and the surviving spouse. The following cases explore egalitarian partition of both small and large estates, and the significant roles that widows played in implementing important provisions of the *Coutume* after the death of a husband.

⚜ ⚜ ⚜ ⚜

Marie-Josèphe Quebedot was already once-widowed when she married the cobbler Alexander Thomas Laville *dit* St. Germain in 1749.[72] For whatever reasons, she and Laville did not have a marriage contract drawn up; nevertheless, when Laville died, the *Coutume* governed the modest marital *communauté* they had built. When widow Laville remarried once again (to Claude Tinon, a marine at Fort de Chartres), Labuxière recorded the inventory of goods from the widow's marriage with Laville, which facilitated the division of the community property into simple halves.[73] The widow received no *douaire* or *préciput*, which came only as prescribed in a marriage contract. The Quebedot-Tinon marriage transpired, and the Laville inventory was compiled on the east side of the Mississippi. Then, the next year, in October 1765, Tinon, along with the rest of the French marines from Chartres, traversed the river with St. Ange. Labuxière, in his punctilious fashion, transferred the recorded inventory to the new *greffe* (records depository) that he was establishing at St. Louis. What Labuxière was doing, and he full well knew it, was transporting French civilization, as represented in documents that sustained a civil society, to the new settlement on the west bank of the Mississippi.

Marie-Josèphe Quebedot was part of the extended Chemin (sometimes Duchemin) family, consisting of several married couples and several single adult males.[74] Despite the presence of an extended family, the premature death of Laville had serious consequences: Quebedot and her new husband put the children from her marriage with Laville out to service. On September 25, 1767, the couple signed an indenture agreement (*contrat d'engagement*) with Jean-Baptiste Bidet *dit* Langoumois for Quebedot's daughter Madeleine Laville, seven years old, to live with the Langoumois family until age eighteen.[75] They were to feed and raise her like their own child, but she was to render all the services she was capable of. The contract was binding, Madeleine was no longer a free person, and Quebedot and Tinon had no legal right to terminate her servitude and take her back into their household.

The Tinon and Langoumois homes in the village were located adjacent to one another in 1770,[76] which meant that Madeleine's separation from her family was likely not a wrenching experience. Two days later (September 27), Tinon and Quebedot similarly indentured Madeleine's nine-year-old brother, François, to Alexis Marié and his wife, Renée Guilgaut.[77] The indenture contracts for these children are rather different from apprenticeship contracts, which ordinarily specify trades, tools, and training.[78] Indenturing of young children strikes a modern sensibility as inhumane, but it was surely not seen as such at the time, and it could provide distinct material and emotional benefits. On the practical side, Tinon and Quebedot may have viewed the inheritance from Laville (125 livres for each child) as insufficient to provide for their children until, eventually, each could marry. At a time when so many children succumbed to disease before reaching adulthood, we know that Madeleine made it through the dangerous, difficult years. On July 28, 1777, just at the end of her indenture, Madeleine St. Germain, daughter of Alexander Laville *dit* St. Germain and Marie-Josèphe Quebedot, married Joseph Rivet in St. Louis. And on the 1787 census, the Rivet nuclear household was intact, consisting of two parents and three daughters, the family representing an early St. Louis success story.[79]

⚜ ⚜ ⚜ ⚜

Widows, by delaying the inventory of the marital *communauté*, could enhance and prolong their power and authority. Delaying would perpetuate the *communauté*, and the widow had the right to manage it until either she or other heirs of majority age requested that the succession be settled.[80] Alternatively, a widow could turn over management of the *communauté* to a close male relative, relieving herself of the responsibility.[81] St. Louis widows sometimes extended their authority as financial managers, cooperating rather than competing with close male relatives, some of whom often lived under the same roof.[82]

Gabriel Dodier was a blacksmith and interpreter of Indian languages at Fort de Chartres.[83] Marie-Françoise Millet and Dodier married in 1736, producing one son and four daughters before Gabriel's death, sometime in the early 1760s.[84] Gabriel died as the Seven Years' War was inexorably ending the French regime in North America, yet we can trace the continued implementation of French customary law across time and space in the Illinois Country. The Dodier family presents a case in point, as an extended series of family documents takes us on a fascinating excursion, from Chartres to St. Louis, and from French to Spanish administrations in Louisiana.

Under the *Coutume*, once an inventory was properly requested, it had to be conducted and the estate settled within three months.[85] Gabriel's death date is not known, but his widow was ready by August 4, 1763, to settle the estate. Marie-Françoise exercised her right personally to select the men she wished to appraise the community property: Louis Métivier, Henri Carpentier, and Guillaume Bizet, all prominent residents at Chartres and undoubtedly family friends.[86] She then requested Judge Jean Valentin Bobé-Descloseaux to come to her home to conduct the inventory, in which he listed all the real and personal property of the Dodier household, including the forge, with a value in livres assigned to each item by the appraisers. Bobé-Descloseaux saw to it that the appraisers conducted an exhaustive inventory, including the bedding and clothing of *each* of the family members. After finishing the household items, the appraisers moved on to the forge and blacksmith tools, then the livestock, the slaves, and, last, some of that year's wheat harvest, "found in the barn." The total value of the inventory was 29,214 livres. After subtracting the widow's *douaire* and Gabriel's medical expenses, 27,110 livres remained in the estate. This was a large estate, more than fifty times that of Laville.

Six days later, August 10, 1763, Bobé-Descloseaux returned with the appraisers and witnesses to determine the partition of the goods as per the *Coutume*: half of the community of goods for the widow, and from the other half a three-fifths portion for the minor daughters and a one-fifth lot each for Gabriel Jr. and for his sister Marie-Françoise, married to Jean-Baptiste Becquet. The three-fifths partition for the minor daughters was left intact with their mother, who was their financial guardian. The mathematical division of the ca. 27,000-livre estate was simple and clear. Apportioning the estate's human property, however, two slave families and three single slaves, was more complicated and revealed a nuanced approach to implementing the law.[87] One slave family, François and Catteau (diminutive of Catherine) and their two children, remained in the widow's share. The other family, Jacob and his wife, Fanchon, and son, Jean-Louis, became part of the three minor daughters' lot, which their mother, their guardian, retained. Also in the minors' lot was the slave Baptiste, a trained blacksmith. After the daughters married, they could claim the slaves in their portion and appropriate them from their mother's household.[88] For the time being, however, the widow followed the intent of the *Coutume* that property be distributed in an egalitarian manner, while she kept the slave families intact within her own household. Each adult Dodier child received one unmarried adult slave: to the son, Gabriel, a male slave and to daughter Marie-Françoise a female slave.[89] As much as we might want to ascribe humanitarian motives to Millet, keeping legitimately married parents and children together represented both adherence to the *Code Noir*[90] and shrewd judgment in managing the financial asset that slaves represented.

Still in charge of the bulk of the estate, the widow needed to manage her resources prudently. Baptiste, the skilled blacksmith, rather than being "apportioned" to son Gabriel, who was a blacksmith as his father had been, remained in Millet's household. Some of the forge tools, however, went to Gabriel in the partition, which meant that Gabriel managed the operation and Baptiste worked with him—black man and white man, equally skilled smithies, sweating together at the forge mending plowshares and hammering out hardware. The rewards, however, were not equal, for Baptiste's slave labor was done for the benefit of the widow's household; in this twisted sense, Baptiste replaced Dodier Sr. as a family breadwinner.[91]

Gabriel Dodier Jr., one year following the partition of his father's estate, married Marie-Marguerite Becquet, sister of his brother-in-law, in the village of Chartres.[92] In fact, the widow may have conducted the inventory precisely so that Gabriel could use his portion of the estate to establish his own household. The entire extended family relocated to the new settlement across the Mississippi in time to get listed on 1766 St. Louis census. The census enumerated the three daughters and seven slaves in widow Dodier's household, and the remainder of the *communauté* that had existed with her husband manifested itself in ten parcels of agricultural land, a horse, and five head of cattle and oxen. The three Dodier households (the widow, her son, and daughter and son-in-law) combined ranked second in landownership in the new village—only Joseph Taillon, the miller, agriculturist, and major slave holder, owned more. Both Baptiste, the black slave, and Gabriel Jr. may have continued to work at the forge, but by 1772 the widow and her son harvested an amount of flour second only to the Taillon family.[93] The village of St. Louis carried the nickname "Paincourt" (short of bread), but there was never a shortage of good wheat bread in the extended Dodier family.

On August 15, 1768, Élisabeth Dodier married Alexis Cotté, the first Dodier family marriage to be celebrated in St. Louis.[94] Cotté, of legal age, had been born near Quebec and was only recently arrived in the Illinois Country,[95] while Élisabeth was still a minor. The entire Dodier clan was present for the nuptial ceremonies: Élisabeth's mother; her older brother, Gabriel; her brother-in-law and deputy guardian, Jean-Baptiste Becquet; and Louis Dodier, who was her cousin. Two old friends of her mother, Joseph Taillon and Guillaume Bizet, both prominent residents, also attended. The Dodier-Cotté marriage contract stipulated that any property that would come to Élisabeth from her father's succession would become part of the *communauté*. This makes clear that the distribution of a daughter's rightful inheritance generally took place only *after* her marriage, or when she reached the age of majority. The *douaire préfix* from Alexis to Élisabeth was 400 livres, and the reciprocal *préciput* to the surviving spouse was 200 livres, to be taken from the movable goods. These were not large amounts, which indicated that Cotté was making an advantageous match, moving up socially, when he married a Dodier.

Four years later, Cotté and Élisabeth requested Élisabeth's share of her inheritance, and Labuxière pulled the 1763 inventory and partition papers from his files in order to settle the account. The widow agreed *amiablement* to give up the services of Baptiste, the blacksmith slave, to her daughter and son-in-law. They also received one arpent of agricultural land on the Grand Prairie of St. Louis as a substitute for an equal plot of land near Chartres (part of the original inventory), and a pair of oxen, essential for plowing. Just two years later, in 1774, Élisabeth and Alexis Cotté sold Baptiste, now age thirty-five to forty, for 863 livres in processed deerskins.[96]

In January 1776, Marie-Françoise Millet dictated her will.[97] Her youngest daughter, Thérèse, along with her husband, Simon Coussat, had moved into the widow's house. Thérèse had not yet received her share of her father's estate, and therefore Millet decreed in her will that her son-in-law Coussat could take Thérèse's share, 2,900 livres, in slaves and other goods. Indeed, that is precisely what occurred—Labuxière again amended the original 1763 inventory to show that Coussat and his wife took three slaves: Pierre, age twelve, son of Jacob and Fanchon; Jean-Louis, age fourteen (and for the first time identified as of mixed race); and Marie-Josèphe, age ten, who had not yet been born at the time of the original partition. Nothing more was taken, but Millet stipulated in her will that Thérèse and Coussat should have her house. Further, Millet desired that her black slave François be freed at her death because she was grateful for how well and faithfully he had served her.

When Marie-Françoise Millet died in 1783, her will automatically went into effect, and her remaining possessions, including the slaves (excluding François), were sold at public auction, the profits to be divided into equal portions among her surviving heirs. Like Cotté and Élisabeth's sale of Baptiste, the sale to an outsider of the slave couple Jacob and Fanchon, now approaching old age, seemed at odds with the widow Dodier's earlier effort to keep the slave families intact and within her household. This second generation of Dodiers was perhaps living in more straitened circumstances,[98] and financial exigencies may have weighed on the heirs. Fittingly, a woman purchased both Jacob and Fanchon, and henceforth they would serve Marie-Josèphe Goudeau, the wife of Eugène Pourée *dit* Beausoleil, an important trader and militia officer.[99]

Also sold at the Millet auction was Françoise, daughter of François, the slave freed in Millet's will, and Catteau, deceased. Françoise's younger brother, twenty-three-year-old Louis, was sold separately. This was the slave family that the widow had kept in her own share of the division of the *communauté* she had originally built with her husband. Since the siblings' mother, Catteau, had been an Indian, and since status derived from the mother, manumission of Françoise and Louis would have been in keeping with the intention of the Spanish regime in Louisiana to curtail Indian slavery. The sale of Françoise and Louis demonstrates the frequent disregard of Governor Alejandro O'Reilly's 1769 decree that forbade commerce in Indian slaves.[100]

Marie-Françoise Millet never remarried, and she survived her husband by two entire decades. Managing the remainder of her marital *communauté*, she became one of the most productive agriculturists in St. Louis. She also provided her daughters with their appropriate inheritances intact—Thérèse, the younger daughter, claiming her portion approximately thirteen years after her father's death. A woman of uncommon strength, tenacity, and intelligence, Veuve Dodier was buried in St. Louis on February 10, 1783, surely one of the truly grandes dames of the early settlement.[101]

The remarkable integrity of the Dodier family documents elucidates not just traditional French customs but also widely understood expectations about transferring property to the next generation. The *Coutume de Paris* governed this process, with minor modifications accommodated by inserting dedicated clauses into marriage contracts.[102] During the marriage, the husband was to be a responsible manager of an accumulating estate, but the *Coutume* did not allow him to be a sovereign patriarch, and women, whether they were wives or widows, had an undeniable presence in the management of estates. Each of the Dodier daughters could expect a portion of their parents' estate equal to their brother's share because the *Coutume* required equal portions for each child, of whatever age or either gender, explicitly forbidding the privileging of the eldest son. The only requirement for obtaining an equal portion of the estate was being born. In theory, then, children had some freedom to function as individuals, less constrained by parental and societal demands and expectations.[103]

⚜ ⚜ ⚜ ⚜

Reverberations from the Bourdon case in the 1720s carried on down the generations to the time of the settling of St. Louis, as French families in the Illinois Country faced the sober facts of marriage, old age, inevitable death, and family assets. The region was shaken to its roots as a consequence of the French and Indian War, which brought British sovereignty to the east side of the Mississippi and Spanish to the west side. The early citizens of St. Louis were all deracinated francophones, and they sought order, continuity, and security wherever they could find it. The *Coutume* provided an ancient and proven framework for domestic life in the new settlement, a framework without which villagers would have felt confused and adrift in a rapidly changing world. Other than the French language itself, no aspect of culture in early St. Louis was so French as the *Coutume*. And, looking forward, marriage contracts done at St. Louis in accordance with the *Coutume* during the colonial era remained valid and binding after the American government arrived in Upper Louisiana in 1804; a valid contract was a valid contract. When Auguste Chouteau died in 1829, his succession was handled in accordance with the terms of his 1786 marriage contract with Marie-Thérèse Cerré, which in turn was based on provisions of the *Coutume de Paris*.[104] In that fashion, legal customs from medieval France worked their way down through the centuries and influenced life in nineteenth-century Missouri.

CHAPTER 8

Slaves: African and Indian

On May 7, serving as curate, I baptized Constance, daughter of Angélique, Indian belonging to the Captain Commandant.

—Sébastien-Louis Meurin, 1767

Slaves, both African and Indian, had been present in French Illinois villages since the early eighteenth century,[1] and they were present—men, women, and children—at the founding of St. Louis in 1764; their bound labor helped lay the foundations of the original settlement. Slaves appear only marginally in most studies of colonial St. Louis, which tend to dwell on the fur trade and commercial relations with Missouri Valley Indians. In this chapter we examine the village's slave population during the first decade of the settlement's existence. During those years, the numbers of both Indian and African slaves increased, and slaves became thoroughly integrated into the life of the growing village.

Indians had practiced slavery long before European explorers, traders, and colonizers arrived on North American shores. Slaves were sometimes captives of war, but they were also seized specifically to be used in intertribal trade. Some captives, usually women and children, were integrated as full-fledged members of their captors' societies, while others became human commodities in far-reaching networks of commerce and exchange.[2] Evidence suggests that Indians treated their slaves harshly, the word for dog and slave (*nitaïa*) being identical in the Illinois language.[3] French traders acquired Indian slaves early on from Missouri Valley tribes, and during the 1720s administrators in Louisiana sought to limit the Missouri Valley slave trade in order to promote alliances with certain western Indian nations.[4] But no attempt was ever made to suppress the Missouri slave trade completely, and the trade continued throughout the duration of the French regime, and beyond.[5]

Indian slavery was well established in Illinois Country settlements before African slaves were brought to the region. But soon after New Orleans was founded in 1718, commerce began between Louisiana's new capital and the Illinois Country, and slaves were part of that commerce. Between 1719 and 1731, the transatlantic slave trade introduced more than five thousand black slaves to French Louisiana,[6] and some of these wound up in the Illinois Country. By 1720 the Jesuits at Kaskaskia, among the earliest and largest slaveholders in the region, owned sixteen to eighteen slaves, both African and Indian.[7] Over the decades persistent demands for more slaves emanated from the Illinois Country. In 1720 Pierre Dugué de Boisbriant, commandant at the recently erected Fort de Chartres, mused that a contingent of "100 negros would be marvelous for this settlement [the Illinois Country]" to help develop and expand its agriculture. But in 1744 Governor Pierre de Rigaud de Vaudreuil scoffed at Illinois Country habitants' demands for more black slaves, explaining that lazy white agriculturists simply needed to work harder.[8] Still, the number of slaves grew from 164 (more than one quarter of the total population) in 1732 to 595 (43 percent of the total population) in 1752. At St. Louis, St. Ange noted in 1766 the continued scarcity of slave labor and asked Governor Antonio Ulloa to help villagers purchase slaves on credit. The Spanish governor recommended that St. Ange pursue the matter directly with Bordeaux traders, which he seems never to have done.[9]

Profitable, market-oriented agriculture developed in the Illinois Country as early as the 1720s, and slaves (especially Africans) were used as field hands.[10] By the 1750s, Antoine Bienvenu was the largest slave owner and landholder in the region, with fifty-nine slaves and many arpents of arable fields.[11] He had migrated as a young man from New Orleans to the Illinois Country and established himself as a farmer and trader. He used his profits to purchase additional African slaves and then took his accumulated wealth back to Lower Louisiana and set himself up as a major planter. François Vallé, in contrast, became the wealthiest man in Upper Louisiana during the 1760s and lived out his mortal days in Ste. Genevieve. Vallé's slave holdings increased more than twelvefold in the space of fourteen years, from five slaves in 1752 to sixty-three in 1766. Five years later, Vallé produced as much wheat and flour as the entire village of St. Louis.[12] Slaves were critical to his commanding position in agriculture, and over thirty years priests baptized nearly one hundred slaves from the Vallé household.[13] In St. Louis in 1766, the most prosperous resident on the village's first census was Joseph Taillon, who owned twelve slaves to work his forty parcels of plowlands and his flour mill. In 1771 Taillon produced double the amount of flour that most other St. Louis habitants did (although still just one-tenth of what Vallé produced in Ste. Genevieve).[14]

Slaves, especially Indians, were also used occasionally in the fur trade, but few slaves were trained as highly skilled craftsmen; only two instances emerge from early St. Louis records. Joseph, an Indian belonging to Antoine Hubert, was an apprenticed joiner, and Baptiste, a black man in the Dodier household, was a blacksmith like his master Gabriel. Manual skills clearly mattered a great deal in determining the value of slaves. Joseph, having completed his apprenticeship, and in his prime at age twenty-five, was appraised at twenty-four hundred livres,[15] making him one of the highest-valued slaves in the 1770 Indian slave census. Of comparable value was Baptiste, the thirty-three-year-old blacksmith, appraised at twenty-five hundred livres.[16] Pierre Laclède reported the value of his Indian slave Cupidon, age twenty-two in 1770 and with no apparent special skills, at sixteen hundred livres. Madame Chouteau bought Cirille, a black slave age thirty-four, for a very substantial four thousand livres in 1786, but whatever skills he may have possessed were not noted in the bill of sale.[17] Historians of slavery have long debated its profitability,[18] and evidence from the eighteenth-century Illinois Country suggests that slaves were a sought-after investment, whether for agriculture or the fur trade.[19] Slaveholding was a good index of wealth in St. Louis, and village farmers and entrepreneurs utilized slaves to help sustain and promote their economic ventures.

The French *Code Noir*, or Black Code, of 1685 was part of an effort by Louis XIV's minister Jean-Baptiste Colbert to provide France's Caribbean colonies with a comprehensive legal code.[20] In 1724 the code was revised somewhat and introduced in New Orleans as the *Code Noir de la Louisiane*.[21] Among its fifty-five provisions, the code spelled out requirements for, among other things, religious instruction, baptism, and marriage. One provision forbade cohabitation or concubinage between white subjects and black slaves and stipulated fines for violations. Slave owners were also forbidden to sell young children away from legitimately married parents, or to sell old, infirm slaves, while manumission of a slave required permission from the Superior Council in New Orleans.[22] In August 1766, Nicolas Chauvin de La Frenière, attorney general for the Superior Council, sent a stern reminder to St. Louis about the *Code Noir*. He ordered, in no uncertain terms, that notary Labuxière and Judge Lefebvre annul a sale that had separated a legitimately married male slave from his wife and children.[23] In spite of La Frenière's admonition, it is clear that many provisions of the code were at best laxly enforced in Upper Louisiana. Concerning remote St. Louis, this much may safely be said: priests baptized most slaves, very few slave couples married, and manumissions were effected locally, without consulting with provincial authorities in New Orleans.[24] No fines or punishments were ever meted out to Frenchmen who cohabited with or had children with slave women, and only rarely did fathers recognize, and manumit, the children they had by slave women.

The biographies of individual slaves presented in this chapter are for the most part mere abstracts, fashioned from a scattering of civil and religious records. Recent studies on the French slavery in the French Caribbean treat

EDIT DU ROI,

Touchant l'Etat & la Difcipline des Efclaves Négres de la Loüifiane.

Donné à Verfailles au mois de Mars 1724.

LOUIS, par la grace de Dieu, Roi de France & de Navarre : A tous préfens & à venir, SALUT. Les Directeurs de la Compagnie des Indes Nous ayant reprefenté que la Province & Co...

The French Code Noir, *or Black Code, of 1685 was part of an effort by Louis XIV's government to provide France's Caribbean colonies with a comprehensive legal code. In 1724 the Code was revised and introduced in New Orleans as the* Code Noir de la Louisiane. *Reproduced from* Recueil des édits, déclarations et arrests de Sa Majesté concernant l'administration de justice et la police des colonies françaises de l'Amérique *(Paris, 1744).*

slave resistance, revolution, and emancipation with wide-ranging sources that permit multifaceted narratives and analyses. Gwendolyn Midlo Hall and Daniel H. Usner Jr. adduced Superior Council records, memoirs, and official correspondence to develop their studies of slave culture and intercultural exchange in Lower Louisiana,[25] but historians of early St. Louis have fewer available sources.

⚜ ⚜ ⚜ ⚜

Public auctions in the Illinois Country were generally festive occasions, providing opportunities for the entire village to come together, with both women and men calling out their bids. St. Louis's first recorded public auction took place on Sunday, February 9, 1766. A young black slave named Lorine was on the auction block, villagers bidding for one year of her labor. Slaves were often rented out in the Illinois Country, but auctioning of slave labor was uncommon. The record of this auction is one of our earliest manuscript sources on St. Louis history, and it contains the first mention of a black slave's presence in St. Louis. Lorine is one of the best-documented slaves in early village history, but her riveting story has heretofore remained in the shadows.

> February 9, 1766
>
> Lorine, belonging to the minor daughter of La Ferne, whose guardian was Condé, was taken to the public square on Sunday February 9, 1766 to be auctioned off for one year for the profit of the minor daughter. The public being assembled, there were a number of bids, and the winner was Michel

Rolet *dit* La Déroute. He is to pay twenty-four livres per month for a term of one year. He is to keep her and provide her with food, and should she become ill provide her with treatment for a period of eight days.[26]

Lorine, the black slave of Marguerite La Ferne, was sixteen when Michel Rolet *dit* La Déroute and other early St. Louisans bid for her services. Lorine was part of the estate left to sisters Marguerite and Marie-Anne La Ferne, whose parents had died at Chartres. When Marie-Anne married André-Auguste Condé, the royal surgeon, at Chartres in July 1763,[27] the newlyweds took Marguerite and the La Ferne slaves into their household, and Condé became the financial guardian of his young sister-in-law. During the week leading up to the Sunday auction, the bailiff read the announcement in the customary form, shouted out in public in a high and audible voice. La Déroute, the successful bidder, was a *volontaire* in the militia, a group of generally single and landless men, but he had ambitions to improve his status. He had married Marguerite Le Grain in June 1765,[28] and their daughter Catherine was baptized in St. Louis in March 1767.[29] La Déroute was moving up in the fur trade, as seen in a 1768 contract that described him as a *commerçant*, one who might hire others (voyageurs, *engagés*) to travel upriver for the Indian trade.[30]

As part of the La Ferne household, Lorine may have lived in Kaskaskia, New Orleans, and Ste. Geneviève before arriving in St. Louis; her distant past is obscure.[31] But there is no mistaking the course of her life during the next twenty-three years, for unlike other slaves whose appearance in the records is usually fleeting, Lorine's name appears again and again. After La Déroute returned her to the Condé household, Lorine was written into the 1768 marriage contract of Marguerite La Ferne and Pierre-François Brunot Joseph d'Inglebert Lefebvre. More commonly known as Joseph Debruisseau, Marguerite's new husband was the son of Joseph Lefebvre, deceased judge and royal storekeeper. Taking advantage of property provisions in the *Coutume de Paris*, Marguerite declared a large portion of her inherited wealth—mostly her human property—as her own, to be excluded from the *communauté* of her marriage. This required that Labuxière note the name of each slave in the marriage contract: Lorine and her five-month-old son, Lambert; Marianne, age about forty; and her two daughters, Marguerite, age ten, and Louison, about five. The slaves, together with the declared inanimate objects, were valued at a total of five thousand livres. This was a very substantial sum, unmatched in kind or amount among early St. Louis marriage contracts, and Marguerite received from Debruisseau the contractual guarantee that their value would be protected from losses the married couple might incur. Debruisseau was marrying well, but he was required to guarantee that he would be a responsible custodian of the assets his wife brought into the marriage.[32]

Itinerant priest Pierre Gibault baptized two children of Lorine's, Lambert and Julie, in 1770. Marguerite La Ferne stood as godmother to Lambert, keeping the baptismal ceremony largely within the family and affirming the household hierarchy.[33] Julie's godmother was Marie-Louise Taillon, the daughter of Joseph Taillon. The Joseph Michel *dit* Taillon family members were the most frequent early sponsors of other persons' slaves, placing them, in this sacramental way, at the center of the slave-owning network. In each baptismal record, Gibault noted that the child was not born of a legitimate marriage and that the father was unknown. In later documents, the word *mulatto* further identified the children, but a father's name never appeared.[34]

Marguerite's husband, Joseph Debruisseau, in fact died within several years, and the specific clause in the marriage contract defining Marguerite's property should have secured her ownership of the slaves.[35] But losses from her husband's felonious mismanagement of the king's assets threw the succession into confusion, and it took several years to set things straight.[36] Lorine and Julie were seized as part of Debruisseau's goods to compensate the king's losses, but they returned to the La Ferne family when Condé purchased the two slaves in 1776; he may have recognized that Lorine's productive and reproductive potential could still benefit his family.[37] Auguste Condé soon died, and Lorine and Julie were conveyed to the minor daughters in the settlement of the estate. Marguerite remarried and moved to France, while Lorine lived out her complicated life in Upper Louisiana.

In January 1779, Lorine physically assaulted a slave named Marianne, who belonged to Lieutenant Governor Fernando de Leyba. In order to set a public example, de Leyba took the matter to court, rather than handling the issue privately.[38] Joseph Labuxière dutifully recorded the depositions of the witnesses—two female slaves and a teenage white boy, Joseph Cotté: Slave women were doing laundry in Mill Creek, which served as the community's *lavoir*, and they began to argue over the best spot at the creek, which on this day was merely a hole in the ice. The argument escalated when Lorine attacked Marianne, pushing her into the water, even attempting to drown her. Other women pulled Marianne out of the water, but still the incensed Lorine went after her again, shoving her into the fire that had been built to help keep them (and the laundry water) warm.[39] Washing laundry in January in an icy creek was an unforgiving task that may have provoked unforgivable words. None of the witnesses, slave or white, excused Lorine's violent actions or defended her, and they all agreed that Lorine and Marianne had never had any previous "difficulties" that might justify Lorine's outrageous behavior. Perhaps Lorine had a long-standing history as a troublemaker, or perhaps Marianne had disrupted the spontaneous hierarchy that had developed among village washerwomen. A doctor's examination of Marianne revealed no life-threatening injuries, but Lorine was sentenced to one hundred lashes in the same public square where her labor had been auctioned off in 1766.[40] Lieutenant Governor de Leyba, who was only six months into his tenure, evidently had no tolerance for slave-on-slave physical violence and decided to use a draconian sentence to set an example with Lorine.

Lorine was still nursing her youngest child when the incident at the creek occurred,[41] meaning that execution of the sentence with its corporal trauma would come down heavily on both mother and child. Although no records survive to reveal the conclusion of the case, it seems unlikely that the harsh sentence, virtually a death sentence, was carried out. In 1767 Ste. Genevieve's commandant, Philippe-François de Rastel de Rocheblave, had issued the same sentence of one hundred lashes to each of seven slaves in a curious case involving the accidental drowning of an eighth slave, but the punishment seems not to have been meted out. These cases raise a serious question about whether barbarously severe sentences were ever executed on the valuable bodies of slaves in the Illinois Country.[42]

But the Mill Creek incident was not the end of Lorine's story. In 1786 Marie-Anne La Ferne and Gaspard Roubieu (her second husband) sold thirty-five-year old Lorine and her three youngest children to La Ferne's daughter Marianne and her husband.[43] Roubieu and Marie-Anne were liquidating their most precious assets, in part to manage the Condé daughters' share of their father's estate. Eight years earlier, when the couple sold many items from Condé's estate "to the account of the children," Lorine had not been included in the sale.[44] Then, in 1789, Lorine was removed from the family that had owned her for most of her life. She and two young "mulatto" sons were sold to Charles Taillon, son of Joseph Taillon, the largest slaveholder in early St. Louis.[45] Lorine was sold with no guarantees (explicitly stated "sans garantie") regarding either her title as property or her physical condition.[46] She had given birth to at least seven children from 1768 through 1789—a twenty-one-year span of childbearing—and at thirty-eight she was nearing the end of her reproductive years. Taillon paid seven hundred piastres (or thirty-five hundred livres) for the mother and two sons, a debt that he paid in full five years later.[47]

Lorine's tumultuous life suggests some commonalities in the lives of early St. Louis slaves: First, they were mobile—the French Illinois villages were interconnected networks of families and businesses, and slaves moved among the villages with their owners or those who had rented them.[48] Second, common subjugation to white masters did not necessarily generate bonds of mutual dependence and affection among slaves, as Lorine's altercation with Marianne at Mill Creek demonstrates. Third, close interaction among village whites and blacks (perhaps particularly children) was a ubiquitous feature of life in early St. Louis, as young Joseph Cotté's presence at the creek demonstrates. Finally, succession processes and family strategies meant that slaves, both black and Indian, could remain within extended families for long periods of time.[49] Five persons from *three* generations of the La Ferne–Condé family held title to the flesh-and-blood property that was Lorine: the widow of Ignace Bardet de la Ferne, *both* daughters Marguerite and Marie-Anne, Andre-Auguste Condé, and one of Marie-Anne's daughters and son-in-law.

Yet observing Lorine move from one owner to the next does little to illuminate the complexities, the many pains and few joys, of her daily life. Those seven illegitimate children, most of whom were mulatto, urgently bring the realities of slavery and sex to our attention. In 1766 St. Louis, there were at least eighty unmarried Frenchmen, and reliable documents reveal that these men were regularly engaging in sex with slave women. Roughly one-third of the households enumerated in 1766 contained unmarried men living with their slaveholding married sisters and brothers. Obviously, the potential for various and sundry sexual relationships within slave-owning households existed, and apparently white men were little constrained from taking advantage of slave women. By the late 1770s, more than half of the children born to black and Indian slave women (representing about three dozen households) were of mixed race.[50] The Black Code discouraged sexual relations with slaves, but St. Ange's government (or any other government in colonial St. Louis) did little or nothing to curtail such relations. In the racially tolerant atmosphere of the village, no one wished to see government interfering with sexual matters that did not come to bear directly on maintaining public order.[51]

Lorine's repeated pregnancies inevitably invite questions about slave child raising. Lorine bore children in the same cycle that wives in elite French families did—a child every two or three years. The presence of Lorine's children in the baptismal register and in sales contracts suggests that the general conditions of her life, in particular her diet and her work, allowed her to carry her pregnancies successfully to term. Moreover, she was able successfully to nurture through infancy most of the children she bore.[52] This was altogether remarkable in a society where the rate of white infant mortality ran more than 30 percent.[53] Lorine's obvious fertility made her a valuable slave, even if her pugnacity was sometimes bothersome. Her success in bearing robust children, and surviving the traumas of childbirth, may well have been the reason that the La Ferne family held on to her for more than two decades. This was an exceedingly long time for any kind of human relationship to endure in the Illinois Country, a region where life was brief and contingencies many.

⚜ ⚜ ⚜ ⚜

The absence of a resident parish priest in St. Louis during the 1760s surely contributed to lax sexual morals of villagers and especially transient traders. Nevertheless, when Sébastien-Louis Meurin or Pierre Gibault turned up in town, villagers brought their slaves, and mixed-race slave children, in for the baptismal rite that protected their souls. For the French residents of St. Louis, slaves were most certainly not soulless, less than human creatures.

From 1766 through the end of 1770, more than half of the baptisms performed by Fathers Meurin and Gibault in St. Louis were for slaves (forty-nine of eighty-five). With baptism, these slaves indubitably became part of an ecumenical Roman Catholic community in the village.

> October 20,1767
> I the undersigned missionary priest . . . baptized with all the prescribed ceremonies for adults six slaves. First, Pierre, black, age about thirteen years, belonging to Mr. Pierre-François de Volsey Lieutenant of a detached company of the French marine, resident of the Illinois at St. Louis. His godfather was Mr. Louis de St. Ange commandant of the Illinois Country and godmother Dame Elisabeth de Villiers, wife of Volsey, who signed with me.
> S. L. Meurin[54]

Father Meurin first visited St. Louis in the spring of 1766, and, as he made his circuit around the Illinois Country villages, he stopped there five times during St. Ange's tenure as commandant. On this third visit, he baptized thirty-one persons, children and adults, of whom twenty-five were slaves, both Indian and African. Meurin's records for this day alone testify to the racial diversity of the village, for the remaining six baptisms included four French Creole children, a son of Jeanette and Grégoire,[55] legitimately married free blacks, and a *métis* child born to an unnamed, unbaptized Indian woman and a vagabond trader, one Baudoin. Slave owners in Meurin's 1767 baptismal records include many of the village's elite: the merchant Guillaume Bizet, the widow Dodier, militia captain Jean-Baptiste Martigny, Commandant St. Ange, Lieutenant de Volsey, Madame Chouteau, and Pierre Laclède. Laclède's infant Indian slave, Antoine, was the same age as the *métis* Antoine Chouteau who later claimed that Auguste Chouteau was his father.[56] From what is known about Auguste's sexual habits and tastes,[57] this claim was likely well founded. Even as the priests performed many slave baptisms, not every adult slave converted to Roman Catholicism. In October 1767, for example, the daughter of Bizet's "infidelle" black slave Courtette was baptized, and in 1770 Courtette had still not accepted Christianity.[58] When priests engaged unconverted adults in a tug-of-war over religious beliefs, the holy fathers scored their victory over recalcitrant pagans in the coming generation, for the abiding Roman Catholicism of St. Louis could not be denied interminably.

During St. Louis's earliest years, slave godparenting roles brought members of the village elite together. Commandant Louis St. Ange and his niece Élisabeth Coulon de Villiers, Madame de Volsey, stood as godparents both to Volsey's adult slave Pierre and to Madame Chouteau's slave child, who were baptized the same day. Eventually, following 1770, slaves began to appear in baptismal records as godparents to other slaves, resuming a practice seen in earlier Illinois Country villages.[59] In May 1772, for example, Father Valentin recorded a mulatto slave and a free black woman as the godparents to a mulatto slave of

Guillaume Bizet, and a free mulatto and a slave *mulatresse* were godparents to a mulatto slave. These godparenting practices suggest a maturing slave population, within which small social networks were crystallizing.

Nuclear slave families appear but rarely in early St. Louis records, although the Black Code encouraged the formation and maintenance of such families.[60] At least in principle, the Bourbon monarchies of both France and Spain valued stable, Roman Catholic families, whether free or slave. Of the 150 individual slaves identified in this study, just twenty-four were members of identifiable two-parent families.[61] Four slave families were black, one was Indian,[62] one consisted of a black father and Indian mother,[63] and two were not identified as either black or Indian. Through the end of the 1770s, legitimately married slaves belonged to the widow Dodier, the Volseys, Father Bernard de Limpach, and Sylvestre Labbadie, and a stable couple, though unmarried, belonged to Eugène Pourée *dit* Beausoleil, a militia captain, and his wife.[64] In Ste. Genevieve, by comparison, the François Vallé household over a period of thirty years contained twenty-six legitimately married slave couples.[65] Slave marriages could not be performed without consent of the owners, the priest, and the slaves themselves, but some owners were evidently more inclined to allow or encourage marriages among their slaves. Philip D. Morgan remarked that in the Chesapeake Bay region, slaves sometimes had family ties not easily identified in succession documents,[66] and it is conceivable, even likely, that slave unions existed across households in St. Louis. Nevertheless, the paucity of identified slave fathers in St. Louis records suggests that slave unions were tenuous at best. While slave families seldom appear in the sources, mother-child relationships abound. Documented association of slave children with their mothers was essential because a child's status, free or slave, was determined by the mother's status.

✣ ✣ ✣ ✣

Records are replete with references to children born of liaisons between white men and slave women, but the intangible and intimate details of these relationships are difficult to tease out of the documents. Few fathers formally manumitted the children they had with slave women, but a scattering of manumission records reveals complex and interesting human situations that arose when children were born of such liaisons.

> January 20, 1767
>
> Was present Jacques Quevedot dit L'Espagnol of the post of St. Louis of the Illinois country, who recognizes having a daughter with an Indian slave woman belonging to Sr. Gilles Chemin. The woman died about eighteen months ago, and (Quevedot) bought the child named Marianne age about three years from Chemin for the sum of five hundred livres. Quevedot dit L'Espagnol recognizes Marianne as his child, free by means of the purchase

and payment which he made to Chemin. Quevedot has been in ill health for some time without much hope of recovery and agreed before me the notary in the presence of the witnesses as follows: Quevedot leaves to Gilles Chemin Marianne Quevedot his daughter for Chemin to raise in the Catholic faith in health and sickness until the age of fifteen, at which time Marianne Quevedot will be free.[67]

Jacques Quevedot and his *métisse* daughter Marianne lived in an extended-family household that also included Jacques's brother Charles; his sister Marie-Jeanne; her husband, Gilles Chemin; and the Chemin's two children. Such complicated households were common in early St. Louis, the 1766 census revealing that fewer than half the village households consisted of a simple nuclear family. Gilles Chemin owned Marianne, as he had owned her deceased mother, with whom Quevedot had had an intimate relationship.[68] Once purchased by her father, Marianne was a free person, but her father's contract with Chemin constituted a type of indenture by which Marianne would be a bound servant until age fifteen. But Chemin was also bound by the agreement, obliging himself to raise Marianne in the Catholic faith and care for her if she became ill. Marianne, born a slave, became free when her father purchased her and was then indentured with the prospect of becoming free again at age fifteen. These transformations in Marianne's status likely changed little about the immediate circumstances of her quotidian existence.

In 1783 at age twenty, and as a free person, Marianne married a French Canadian, Joseph Vaillancourt.[69] The Chemins had adhered strictly to their contract, raising Marianne as a good Roman Catholic and eventually releasing her from her indenture as stipulated. The marriage record finally informs us that Marianne's long-deceased Indian mother, Jacques Quevedot's partner, was named Catherine, but we learn nothing more about her. Marie-Jeanne Quevedot lived just long enough to attend her niece's wedding, and Gilles Chemin, Marianne's uncle, died the next year, as the family in which the *métisse* child Marianne had grown and thrived finally reached its mortal end.

⚜ ⚜ ⚜ ⚜

Deep in Indian lands on the Missouri River at Fort d'Orléans during the 1720s, the Grotton–St. Ange family had experienced firsthand the Indian slave trade.[70] They surely acquired slaves there, for soon after settling at Chartres, St. Ange *père* and his wife, Élisabeth Chorel, had six Indian slaves in their household, five women and one man.[71] In 1743 Élisabeth (Louis St. Ange's stepmother) had Father Joseph Gagnon baptize two children of a black slave father and Indian slave mother, and in 1746 her thirty-year-old Indian slave Marie Patoka was buried in Chartres.[72] For thirty years, Madame St. Ange had used Indian slaves as domestic servants, but according to the 1752 census of Chartres, she had but one left to draw her water, cook her meals, and soon sit in death vigil at her bedside.[73] If madame's conversations with her slaves had been recorded, they would have provided historians with an utterly novel perspective on the history of the Illinois Country and the Missouri River valley. Alas, Madame St. Ange, though literate, left no such record.

Louis St. Ange de Bellerive's voluminous official correspondence as commandant at St. Louis—reports on Indian tribes, gifts, and diplomacy for the French and Spanish governments—reveals none of his personal thoughts concerning Indian slavery, concubinage, and *métissage*. A deep tradition, going back at least as far as Homer's heroic Greek warriors, has military leaders taking captured women as slave concubines. Mighty Agamemnon, king of the Mycenaeans, received Chryseis "of the lovely cheeks" in the division of booty after a victory over the Trojans. Taking the girl as his slave, Agamemnon acknowledged that she was finer than his wife and staked his claim on her life, her work, and her body: "I intend her to grow old in Argos, in my house, a long way from her own country, working at the loom and sharing my bed."[74] And when Agamemnon finally acceded to the pleas of Chryseis's father to release her, Agamemnon took his rival Achilles's slave girl Briseis as a replacement, insulting Achilles and provoking a feud that ended the two warriors' tenuous alliance. No Indian fathers stepped forward to ransom slave concubines in eighteenth-century St. Louis, and their owners were free to realize Agamemnon's ambition of complete possession.

St. Ange stated in his last will and testament that he had never married, and historians have regularly referred to him as a bachelor.[75] Some soldiers have a priest-like calling to the profession of arms and lead largely celibate lives; Frederick the Great of Prussia, St. Ange's younger contemporary, was apparently one such. It is conceivable that this was the case with St. Ange, but the authors of this book believe the evidence points almost incontrovertibly in another direction. Indeed, it seems likely that St. Ange fathered as many as five children by two Indian slave women, Lizette and Angélique, that St. Ange was, mutatis mutandis, an eighteenth-century Agamemnon, although lacking the mighty Greek's hubris. The origins of St. Ange's Indian slave women are obscure, yet there is enough evidence to present an outline of their lives with him.

Lizette was perhaps born into a slave family belonging to the St. Anges when they governed Fort d'Orléans. Or she may have come to him via the estate of his nephew Pierre St. Ange Jr., who died in 1757.[76] Whatever her early history, she belonged to St. Ange at Vincennes in 1758, when her first child was baptized. She named a former soldier as the father. Lizette gave birth to two additional children at Vincennes, and the absence of a father's name in their baptismal records allows us to speculate that the father was St. Ange.[77] Angélique, born about 1740, was St. Ange's only other adult female slave and seemingly appeared out of nowhere (as did many early villagers and slaves) in St. Louis baptismal records during the mid-1760s. Angélique was the mother of Charlotte (1765), Constance (1767), and Antoine, *métis* (1773).[78] Fathers' names do not appear in the extant baptismal records. Lizette bore no children from the time of Angélique's arrival until 1770, when she had a child with François, an Indian slave also belonging to St. Ange. This complicated time line suggests that Angélique replaced Lizette as St. Ange's concubine. The succession of sexual partners may have evolved through delicate negotiations, but as with the rest of St. Ange's personal relationships (including his friendship with Laclède), there are very few sources with which to sort things out clearly or satisfactorily.[79] Lizette did not bear any children after 1770, and she died in August 1774, her spare burial record revealing nothing of her complicated life story.[80]

The pattern of births to St. Ange's Indian slave women points toward their role as his sexual partners; his final testament does as well.[81] He bequeathed Angélique to his niece Joachine Coulon de Villiers de Belestre and stipulated that her two children, Charlotte and Antoine, be manumitted. The case of Charlotte, Angélique's daughter, however, cries out for further consideration in light of her absence from the 1770 Indian Slave Census (appendix B). Charlotte's only appearance in historical records is in St. Ange's 1774 will, which stated that she was about nine years old. She could have appeared on the 1770 Indian slave census as the five-year-old daughter of Angélique, but she did not, and her absence is startling. For the census, St. Ange provided only the names of six slaves: the family of François, Lizette, and Louis, plus Jean-Baptiste, Angélique, and Ignace.[82] St. Ange must have omitted Charlotte because he considered her exclusively his daughter and not a slave. On his deathbed, habitant Jacques Quevedot explicitly acknowledged his sexual relationship with the Indian slave woman in the household where he lived, but St. Ange made no similar admission. The Spanish crown opposed Indian slavery in principle, yet Carlos III never made a definite decision regarding ownership of Indian slaves in Louisiana. St. Ange was at liberty to emancipate Angélique's children in his will, but he was under no legal obligation to manumit Angélique.[83] She remained in the Belestre household until her death in 1781, when she was buried in the same consecrated ground as St. Ange and her son, Antoine.[84]

St. Ange's domestic arrangements, and those of his slaves, are not fully documented, but this much is known. At St. Louis, he never owned residential property, and while commandant he lived in the "government house" rented from Pierre Laclède. St. Ange may have lodged some of his slaves close by, but he kept Angélique even closer. The inventory of items in his chambers after his death clearly suggests that Angélique shared his living quarters at least in his last months, cooking for him and tending to his daily needs as his once formidably strong body ineluctably gave way to old age. The single most intriguing item in St. Ange's inventory, out of place among the items that identify him as a military man, is a fancy red skirt—almost certainly Angélique's. In the Illinois Country, Indian women who became wives to Frenchmen became thoroughly "Frenchified," as Sophie White argues, and the acculturation process occurred "with the consent of the women themselves."[85] Indian slave concubines very likely underwent a similar cultural transformation. In any case, the appraisers of St. Ange's estate were apparently not taken aback at finding a fancy skirt among his possessions, but casually inventoried it to be sold along with the mundane array of cooking pots, faience plates, and linen shirts.[86]

Female Indian slaves working as domestics in Illinois Country households, including those in St. Louis, were sexually exploited, just as female servants were exploited in upper-class households in eighteenth-century Europe. That is, Indian women were exploited not so much because they were Indians, or even because they were slaves, but rather because as subordinate members of a household they were there and available for exploitation.[87] Shortly after arriving in Upper Louisiana, Pierre Laclède acquired two Indian slave girls, Thérèse and Manon, who were likely brought into St. Louis by a Missouri River trader. In 1768 Pierre Laclède presented them (as discussed in chapter 7), along with other slaves and real estate, as gifts to the children of Madame Chouteau, meaning that they became part of madame's household. Two métis children were born into Madame Chouteau's household, Aléxis in 1775 and Jean-Baptiste in 1779. Jean-Baptiste was Manon's son, and Alexis likely was, too, but neither baptismal record names a father. We know that young Auguste had a taste for Indian slave women, and the likelihood must be entertained that the two métis boys were Auguste's children. Better than any other male in St. Louis, he was in a position to exploit his mother's slaves.[88]

⚜ ⚜ ⚜ ⚜

The two slave manumissions recorded and filed in St. Louis during St. Ange's commandancy were for Indian slaves, and they were handled locally, without reference to legal authority or precedents in either France or New Orleans. Furthermore, these manumissions antedated Governor Alejandro O'Reilly's famous decree from late 1769, which outlawed commerce in Indian slaves, meaning that manumissions were definitely not a consequence of new Hispanic legal principles seeping into Louisiana.

> This day May 9, 1767, before me Jos. Labusciere [sic] acting as Judge and Substitute of the King's Attorney-general in the Illinois, appeared Joseph Dubé, travelling trader, now living in this Post of St. Louis, who, in the absence of Mr. de St. Ange, sick, and the death of Mr. Lefebvre, Judge, declared that he had received valuable services from his Indian Slave Marie Marguerite, for which reason as he has always found her a faithful and attached servant, he now gives her her freedom, as also to her female child

Victoire aged about 2 years, declaring said slaves now free, to enjoy all the rights and franchises of free persons, requesting that all persons may recognize and consider them as such, the child to remain with the mother until the age of 14 years &c.&c.&c. Said Dubé not being able to write has affixed his cross.[89]

Five months later, Dubé drew up a contract with Louis Beor, the husband of Dubé's former slave Marguerite, in which Dubé conveyed to the couple all his movable possessions and real estate, including cattle, pigs, and a small house, in return for their caring for him during his last days on earth. Dubé would "do whatever work he judges to be appropriate, and the said Beor and his wife cannot force him to do anything more. The above enumerated possessions will become the property of Beor and his wife from this day forward, for such has been agreed upon and stipulated by the respective parties."[90] On May 1, 1768, all three were still living together, and Dubé requested that St. Ange formalize the title to his house and property, making the agreement fully legal.[91] These actions taken together—the manumission, the "long-term care" agreement for Dubé in his retirement and infirmity, and the land cession—reveal that humane, amicable, practical relations could indeed exist between owner and slave. In effect, Marguerite became the mistress of the property that she had previously maintained as a slave. And she would continue to care for Dubé, although as the legitimate wife of Louis Beor.[92] This combination of manumission and marriage was an uncommon occurrence in colonial St. Louis,[93] as it was in all slaveholding societies in North America and the Caribbean.

The death in St. Louis of Nicolas Henrion prompted Louis Métivier to cross the Mississippi from his home in British territory in 1768. His purpose in St. Louis was to make official a previous verbal agreement he had made with the recently deceased Henrion. The document that Métivier had drafted confirmed the emancipation of five-year-old Marie, who was the daughter of Henrion and Métivier's Indian slave woman named Agnès.[94] The verbal agreement, according to Métivier, included three provisions: Henrion had accepted Marie as a free gift with no payment required (as in the case of Marianne Quevedot above); he promised to take care of her "like a good father," which would have included raising her in the Catholic faith, finding a husband when the time came, and providing the funds for a *préciput;* and, finally, that Marie would be freed, a condition Métivier stipulated before he had agreed to relinquish the child to her father. Métivier was confirming Marie's manumission in writing so that she should not fall into slavery again, and the document included a clause stipulating that none of Nicolas Henrion's heirs had any claim to her services. This was an important statement, since it would require local officials (St. Ange and Labuxière) to uphold her status as a free person for the foreseeable future. Métivier's motivations for this timely act cannot be sorted out with certainty. Did he take the extraordinary measure on Marie's behalf as a result of his friendship with Henrion, in consideration of the intimate relationship between Henrion and Marie's mother, Agnès, or possibly just out of some vague, unarticulated sense of doing the right thing?

⚜ ⚜ ⚜ ⚜

St. Ange, Henrion, and Quevedot, three bachelors, did not marry the Indian slave mothers who bore their children, but they did arrange to have their children emancipated. Two emancipations for children of black slave mothers also occurred in early St. Louis.[95] In 1771 Pierre-François de Volsey and his wife, Élisabeth de Villiers (St. Ange's niece), drew up a will that made Françoise, Volsey's nine-year-old "natural" daughter by a mulatto slave woman, a legal heir, the couple not having any children of their own.[96] The occasion of the will was Volsey's impending trip to New Orleans, and the will included directions for the distribution of their *communauté* (see chapter 7) should both he and his wife perish before his return. Françoise had been living in the Volsey household for seven years, and the couple "mutuellement considered her their child." Madame de Volsey evinced an exceedingly generous spirit, accepting Françoise into her home and making her her legal heir. As it turned out, Volsey returned home safely, rendering the will null and void. The Black Code prohibited *donations* to slaves, but Françoise was soon emancipated, and, decades later, she inherited what remained of the Volsey estate.[97]

The first known St. Louis emancipation of a black slave mother and child occurred in 1772, when Joseph Papin, a Canadian fur trader, manumitted his twenty-five-year-old slave, Flora, and her two-year-old son, Charles. This unusual manumission was confirmed the next day, with St. Ange lending his considerable authority as a witness to the proceedings. Papin declared that he was grateful to Flora for her faithful services (standard phrasing in many slave emancipations) and then, his gratitude having been duly recorded, died five days later. If the young Charles was Papin's son, a distinct possibility, no one saw fit to remark on it.[98] By 1787 Flora lived in her own household, with two additional sons and a daughter, one of just two households headed by free black women on the census of that year.[99] Extant sources tell us virtually nothing about the human context of the sexual encounters that produced *métis* and mulatto children. Surely, many of these encounters entailed troubling elements of coercion, overt and covert,[100] but some master-slave sexual relationships contained elements of genuine compassion and care, as well as lust. This seems to have been the case with Jean Comparios, who lived for some years, unmolested by anyone, with his black slave Marguerite.[101] Tolerance of such concubinage trumped narrow adherence to Black Code prohibitions of such relationships and reveals a relaxed racial climate in early St. Louis.

⚜ ⚜ ⚜ ⚜

Runaway slaves (maroons) were uncommon in Upper Louisiana, for the region's dog-eat-dog environment was in no way hospitable for maroons.[102] On rare occasions, however, we catch glimpses of them. Two who decided to run for their freedom were Aiken and Julien, teenage sons of Marie-Louise, an Indian slave of Joseph Taillon. Marie-Louise had been with the Taillons since they lived at Chartres,[103] and, after the family moved to St. Louis, Taillon included her and her sons on the Indian slave census of 1770. Interestingly, both slaves and slaveholders in St. Louis discussed the meaning of O'Reilly's 1769 decree banning commerce in Indian slaves, and conflicting interpretations confused the issue of Indian slavery for decades.[104] Joseph Taillon's daughter Madame (Marie-Louise) Chauvin related in an 1806 legal deposition that Aiken and Julien "ran away and passed for freemen at the commencement of the Spanish Government,"[105] believing that O'Reilly's 1769 decree abolishing commerce in Indian slaves had indeed freed them.[106] The ultimate fate of Marie-Louise's two sons is unknown, but Madame Chauvin believed that they were headed for New Orleans. There, they would have found the city, with a large population of free people of color and a decidedly cosmopolitan environment, a more hospitable place to live.[107]

But Aiken and Julien were not the first St. Louis runaways. In 1769 Indian interpreter Louis Deshêtres did the sums on his financial account with Pierre Laclède and Madame Chouteau and concluded that Laclède owed him for seven days' work chasing runaway slaves.[108] Deshêtres's knowledge of Indian languages and ease moving among the local tribes made him an ideal bounty hunter.[109] Deshêtres spent a mere three days working to recapture the runaway slaves, which likely meant he succeeded in bringing them back into town. Slaves were well integrated into village society in both St. Louis and Ste. Genevieve, and Indian maroons would not have been welcomed by neighboring Indian tribes. These tribes themselves dealt in slaves, and they had absolutely no interest in taking in refugees from alien, perhaps even hostile, tribes. Moreover, to have done so would have alienated French villagers with whom they had constant, essential relations. This was a fortiori true for black maroons, who would have been even more bereft than Indians of succor and resources in the wilderness of Upper Louisiana.

⚜ ⚜ ⚜ ⚜

The *Code Noir*, the *Coutume de Paris*, peripatetic Roman Catholic priests, and eventually O'Reilly's 1769 decree all governed official relations between masters and slaves in early St. Louis. As the foregoing vignettes demonstrate, however, unpredictable actions of idiosyncratic individuals shaped the contours of slavery in complicated and intimate ways, some of which may be discerned by historians. Existing manuscripts, which bring us as close to St. Louis's slaves as we can come, reveal certain similarities in the lives of black and Indian slaves: priests penned baptismal and burial records with the same formulaic language, and white French residents stood as godparents. Villagers reckoned the value of slaves on the basis of their skills, not their origins or skin colors. Slaves appeared as movable, heritable property on estate inventories, and no comment or distinction set black apart from Indian. This chapter has largely presented the stories of black and Indian slaves together, as though they constituted a single undifferentiated bloc of bound humanity. Yet traditional divisions of labor in the Illinois Country and the paucity of black-Indian couples (and offspring) suggest that black and Indian slaves, in both the economic and the social realms, led daily lives that were largely separate.[110]

Slaves in early St. Louis were indisputably chattels, scarce and valuable property. Nevertheless, the language of emancipation documents conveys an affecting sense of a common humanity, ultimately bringing slaves and masters together (ironically, as they were simultaneously separating) in affective bonds that are elusive but were nevertheless real.[111] As more light is cast on the lives of early St. Louis slaves, African and Indian, the essential interdependency of all the village's residents comes into sharper focus. C. Van Woodward's statement about American southerners and blacks holds equally true for masters and slaves in remote St. Louis: "They . . . shaped each other's destiny, determined each other's isolation, shared and molded a common culture. It is in fact, impossible to imagine the one without the other, and quite futile to try."[112]

CHAPTER 9

In Small Things Forgotten

A wood-framed bedstead with two feather mattresses and one of fur, a calicoe quilt, one large, worn bedspread and two small ones. An armoire containing sundry items, with lock and key and royal-seal latch.

—Estate inventory of Nicolas and Madeleine Barsalou, 1778

His surname was Querseret, sometimes rendered as Kerceret or Carsseret, but he was generally known by his *dit* name, Comparios or Compariot or Comparisot. He was a longtime French marine, and his name on muster rolls usually appears as "Comparios."[1] His Christian name was sometimes Jean, sometimes Étienne, sometimes Auguste (or Augustin). The notary Labuxière used all these forms when dealing with many legal issues involving Comparios—when he was alive and well, when he was desperately ill and confined to his bed, and, finally, when he was dead and buried. Adding to the confusion, his common nickname was "Gascon," either because he had come from southwestern France or because he was a braggart, a raconteur of *gasconnades*.[2] In the great geopolitical events of his time, such as the transfer of Louisiana from France to Spain, this illiterate man played no role. He never married and had no known children. He was so insignificant that people could not get his name straight,[3] yet he must be recognized, even honored, as one of St. Louis's founding settlers.

Comparios was born about 1725 in Toulon, a great seaport city, where he likely joined the French marines. He was deployed to Louisiana early during the French and Indian War and posted up the Mississippi to Fort de Chartres. When St. Ange commanded there in June 1765, Comparios was listed as a "fussillier" in the small French garrison remaining at the fort.[4] When British forces arrived four months later, Comparios, along with his fellow marines (perhaps twenty-five men), moved across the Mississippi to St. Louis with St. Ange. Comparios, with sobriety, discipline, and hard work, carved out a not uncomfortable niche for himself on the Mississippi frontier. Cultivating his land (*not* the land of any seigneur) with a *charrue* and team of oxen was hard work, but all the grain he could produce found a ready market in a community that was often short of foodstuffs. Comparios's life at St. Louis was immeasurably better than that of most French peasants at the time. If he had joined the French marines in order to see the world, he had finally settled down in a rather sunny, fruitful, and pleasant part of that world.

Comparios had arrived on the west bank of the Mississippi with nothing, but he scrapped and pinched, scrimped and saved, to accumulate enough wealth to acquire a black female slave, Marguerite. In 1773 Comparios fell seriously ill and dictated a last will and testament.[5] For married couples in the Illinois Country, marriage contracts usually sufficed for dealing with the disposition of family property, but for single persons wills were essential. On November 17, six residents of St. Louis, led by the lieutenant governor, Captain Pedro Piernas, repaired to Comparios's house. Labuxière, former royal notary, served as scribe and the others as official witnesses ("témoins d'assistance"). Comparios was in bed, ill in body but sound in "mind, memory and understanding." His testament was not complicated. Concerning the spiritual part, he commended his soul to God, the Virgin Mary, and his patron saint, Augustine; concerning the earthly part, after Comparios's debts were settled, he wanted his estate divided into two equal parts. One-half would go "for the adornment and other urgent needs of the church," which in 1773 was merely a crude log chapel, in dire need of adornment; the bishop of Santiago de Cuba did not elevate St. Louis to canonical parish until 1776. Comparios was devout and earmarked the other half (an unusually large percentage) of his estate for services and Masses to ensure the repose of his soul.

But Comparios disappointed death in 1773 and survived for five more years. He never fully recovered his health, however, and he wished to live out the remainder of his life in a modicum of comfort. Comparios worked out a reasonable plan, and on January 11, 1775, he went to the same officials who had done his will, Piernas and Labuxière, and had the plan done up in proper legal form as a "Donnation [sic]."[6] By that time, Comparios's household consisted of three persons—Comparios himself; Marguerite, his black slave; and a single white man, Étienne Bray, and the document drafted that January day was in fact an elaborate contract involving all three. Comparios had come to trust Bray, and he therefore annulled the will he had dictated in 1773 and in the new document conveyed to Bray all of his possessions, except Marguerite. At the time of Comparios's death, Marguerite would be free to go wherever she wished, or she could continue to serve Bray voluntarily, "without that he can prevent her from being free to leave." But in the meantime, she would remain in the household as a slave. Bray, in return for becoming Comparios's sole legatee, agreed to live with Comparios and to feed, lodge, care for, and provide medications for him for the remainder of his life. Comparios remained master of the household despite his frailty, however, and should

Bray not live up to Comparios's expectations, Comparios specifically reserved the right to renounce the contract.

This unusual legal document served multiple purposes and was called a donation simply for lack of a more inclusive name for a complicated document: it was a makeshift will that replaced Comparios's earlier, more formal, one; it was a *contrat d'engagement* (using many of the standard phrases for such contracts) that bound Bray to serve Comparios in specific ways, and it was, ultimately, a bill of manumission for Marguerite. The document was carefully, humanely, and intelligently drafted, and all three parties stood to benefit from it. But things did not work as planned, and within months Comparios went to the new lieutenant governor of Upper Louisiana, Francisco Cruzat, and had a new document done up, in which "all of the clauses in the said donation are annulled."[7] The parting of ways between Comparios and Bray seems to have been more or less amicable, and both Comparios and Bray affixed their marks to the annulment document. With the annulment duly recorded, the Comparios household was once again reduced to two, Comparios himself and his slave, Marguerite. For several years, she had her hands full managing the household and taking care of her sickly master. Nevertheless, Marguerite surely knew of Comparios's benevolent intention that she should ultimately gain her freedom.

In 1778 Comparios suffered a stroke, or more likely a series of strokes, and they ravaged him. He had no family, other than, in some sense, Marguerite, and he was hand-carried to the home of Louis Marcheteau *dit* Desnoyers. Comparios was a former French marine and a respected yeoman farmer, and his desperate situation demanded attention. None other than Lieutenant Governor Ferdnando de Leyba stepped in and assigned a physician, Antoine Reynal, to examine Comparios. Reynal, a relative newcomer to the community, forthwith set about examining a man he called simply "Gascon." Reynal reported on July 15, 1778, that Comparios had experienced an "appoplexie," which paralyzed his right side and broke his mind ("esprit totallement dépravé").[8]

Within two days, things were worse, much worse; Comparios's mind had been reduced to that of an infant, and his body was debilitated. Something had to be done—and quickly. De Leyba, "captain in the infantry regiment of Louisiana and commander in chief of the western part of Illinois and lieutenant governor of that part," sprang into action—a Spanish army officer working on behalf of a former French marine in one of the most remote parts of the civilized, or almost civilized, world. Three highly respected citizens were assigned to assess the value of all Comparios's earthly possessions, the total of which would be allocated to support the desperately ill man for the remainder of his earthly days. Pierre Pery had come over to St. Louis with St. Ange, and Comparios, that fateful autumn of 1765.[9]

In 1778 he was identified as a "commerçant," he was a literate, and served as "greffier [court clerk]" when Labuxière was royal notary. Jean Gibert *dit* La Fontaine was also a literate and was identified as a potter (perhaps St. Louis's first) on the 1780 militia muster roll.[10] Antoine Rivière *dit* Bacanet (also Baccané, devoted to Bacchus) was an illiterate Canadian whose fondness for wine did not adversely affect either his good judgment or his longevity; he died at St. Ferdinand in 1816, age 110.[11]

The three assessors went to work on July 17, 1778, with Labuxière serving as De Leyba's scribe to record the inventory.[12] Comparios's residential property was improved with some fruit trees, a poultry house, a pigsty (facing the street, to delectate all passersby), and the residence itself. Again, we are reminded how rural life intruded right into the center of early St. Louis. The house was described as "a small poteaux-en-terre structure, somewhat rundown, measuring approximately 25×18 pieds, and with an "apenty [shed]" addition." This residential real estate the three assessors appraised at 500 livres, whereas Comparios's 1×40-arpent strip of plowland was valued at only 80 livres.

Comparios's most valuable possession, by a long stretch, was Marguerite, his forty-year-old black slave, who was appraised at 800 livres. She must have been in robust good health and was worth nearly half the aggregate value of his worldly possessions, 1,969 livres, 6 sous. To say that Marguerite was his most treasured possession vastly understates it. The meager evidence we have suggests that she was Comparios's concubine: they had coexisted in very close quarters under one roof, and apparently in one bed. Comparios had likely never seen a black person until he arrived in New Orleans ca. 1755, but he seems to have adjusted to Louisiana's tolerant and accommodating racial climate with perfect aplomb. There is no way to ascertain Marguerite's feelings as Comparios's body crumbled and his mind disintegrated. Was she distraught because her "husband" was dying, or was she delighted that her oppressor was getting his just deserts? If they were indeed living, for all intents and purposes, as husband and wife, more likely the former than the latter.

Labuxière's inventory provides a snapshot of the lifestyle that Comparios and Marguerite had once enjoyed. The house's spare furnishings consisted of a buffet without locks, appraised at 15 livres; a table with turned legs and a drawer at 5; three chairs together at 4; and a bed at 5. Not much, but when a neighbor stopped by for a glass of wine, the third chair was there to accommodate him. The "apenty" addition to Comparios's house was likely a kitchen, and Marguerite cooked at the fireplace, for no stoves of any sort existed in St. Louis at the time, and Marguerite employed four vessels over the fire: a large iron kettle and a small one, a small copper kettle, and a frying pan, with an aggregate value of 23 livres. She also made bread, for there was

Pétrin *and* huche *were used interchangeably in the Illinois Country for a dough-kneading trough. There was no baker in early St. Louis, and even humble households owned a* pétrin *or* huche *for kneading and storing bread dough. Reproduced from* Petite Larousse Illustré *(Paris: Larousse, 1911).*

a kneading trough ("pétrin") with its cover.[13] Marguerite seems to have been a homemaker, jarring though that term may seem when applied to a black slave living in St. Louis during the 1760s.

The couple's diet was not very varied—eggs, milk (they had a milk cow with a calf), chicken, pork, whole-wheat bread, peas (two minots of dried were on hand), and apples, sometimes leavened with fresh venison or fish—but it was tasty, wholesome, and quite superior to the diets of most Frenchmen at the time, and very likely to those of most Africans as well. On their table at dinnertime, Comparios's prized piece was a baking dish ("tourtière") with its cover, appraised at 15 livres, the high value because it was made of copper. Of their three plates, two were faience and one earthenware, and if Marguerite made a potage they had earthenware bowls in which to serve it. Their friend La Fontaine the potter perhaps fashioned these earthenware vessels right there in St. Louis.[14] Comparios and Marguerite had no cups and saucers but drank their breakfast coffee out of earthenware bowls ("pots à boire")—as Europeans often do to this day—and, given their milk cow, Marguerite could whip up a rich *café au lait* in the morning. A Frenchman from Languedoc and a woman from Africa taking their morning coffee together at home in a vertical-log house perched on the west bank of the Mississippi River is not our usual image of an American West peopled by cowboys and Indians or by French officers in knee britches and tricornes; nevertheless, it presents a plausible and engaging tableau of early St. Louis.

Comparios's earthly possessions were inventoried on July 17, 1778, and on the eighteenth de Leyba had to decide how to utilize these resources to provide a modicum of comfort for the poor man whose "body was infirm and his mind alienated." So, who in St. Louis would be willing to assume the responsibility of caring for Comparios in return for receiving his entire estate? De Leyba was advised that the blacksmith Pierre Roy was a good, reliable man, and with the consent of Comparios's caretaker ("curator"),[15] La Fontaine, the following contractual terms were worked out: Roy would take Comparios into his home to care for as though he were his own son; he would provide him with food, lodging, and clothing; he would do everything in his power to assist and comfort Comparios. Should, however, Comparios somehow miraculously recover, regain his senses, get back on his feet, and become independent again, then Roy would be paid at the rate of 20 livres per month for his time, efforts, and expenses in providing care for Comparios. Labuxière drafted the documents in accordance with ancient French customary laws, and all of these intricate proceedings for taking care of a broken member of the community could just as well have occurred in fourteenth-century France—except that Comparios's firearm, "un gros fusil," and his slave would not have appeared on the inventory of his possessions.

Within ten days, Jean-Etienne Querseret *dit* Comparios *dit* Gascon was dead, and he was buried in the rich Missouri soil of the St. Louis parish cemetery on July 27, 1778, a very long way from his home on the arid earth of Languedoc.[16] As he had left no blood relatives, no one rose to dispute the fairness of Roy receiving the entire Comparios estate for only ten days' worth of service. With this boost to its fortunes, the Roy household—Pierre, his wife, Jeanne, and their four children—prospered and endured.[17] Within a decade the slave Marguerite was gone (likely had died), but perhaps she was not forgotten, especially by the Roy children whom she had perhaps suckled and had certainly helped to raise.

⚜ ⚜ ⚜ ⚜

But not everyone in early St. Louis drank out of rustic, earthenware bowls like Jean-Etienne Querseret. Joseph-François Brunot Lefebvre Desruisseau came to St. Louis with St. Ange in 1765 and served as both *garde de magasin* (official storekeeper) and judge until his death in April 1767. St. Ange immediately appointed his son, Pierre-François Brunot D'Inglebert Lefebvre Desruisseau, to replace his father. On November 10, 1768, Lefebvre *fils* contracted an excellent marriage with Marguerite La Ferne, daughter of the deceased surgeon-major at Fort de Chartres, Pierre-Ignace Bardet de la Ferne, and Commandant St. Ange witnessed the civil marriage contract.[18] Lefebvre was twenty-five years old, meaning that he had achieved majority and was fully in charge of his own affairs. But Marguerite was just fourteen years old, meaning that (in keeping with the *Coutume de Paris*) she had a *tuteur*, a guardian to look after her affairs and represent her during the signing of her marriage contract.[19] Marguerite's *tuteur* was the medical doctor André-Auguste Condé, who was married to Marguerite's older sister, Marie-Anne. Because the parents of the two La Ferne sisters were both dead, Marguerite was residing with the Condé family in St. Louis, and the civil marriage contract was concluded in Condé's residence on November 10, 1768.

As was customary, the sacramental ceremony of marriage took place several days after the civil contract was signed, and Pierre-François and Marguerite began married life in handsome style—moving into a substantial *poteaux-en-terre* house situated on a double lot (150×240 pieds), facing la Grande Rue, and just across a side street from the large residence of Labuxière, the royal notary.[20] It was a tony quarter of early St. Louis, and the bluff behind their properties afforded Labuxière and Lefebvre a splendid panorama of the Mississippi, although it is not at all clear whether romantic vistas provided people of that time and place with a frisson of delight. Although no children were forthcoming, young Lefebvre occupied an important official post, and the couple occupied a place at the very top of St. Louis's social structure. When streets were merely ankle-deep in dust and not knee-deep in mud, they moved about in what was perhaps the only four-wheeled carriage (*calèche*) in the village. Then, quite suddenly, things went completely to hell.

As soon as Captain Pedro Piernas assumed command at St. Louis in mid-May 1770, he faced a serious problem. The longtime notary, Labuxière, had lost that official position as soon as Piernas arrived in town, but his services as scribe were still essential. Piernas summoned Labuxière to his office, and the two men drafted a dispatch for Lieutenant Colonel John Wilkins, commandant of British Illinois in residence at Fort de Chartres.[21] It was a bit awkward, a Spaniard dictating a dispatch to a Frenchman that would be sent to an Englishman, but such was the nature of life in the Mississippi Valley in 1770. Piernas reasoned, probably correctly, that Wilkins was more likely to read French than Spanish. In any case, the gist of the dispatch was that the storekeeper Pierre-François Brunot Lefebvre had fled St. Louis, apparently crossing the Mississippi (an international frontier) for the British side of the river. Indeed, Lefebvre had fled twice in the span of several days. On the first occasion, he had returned under his own volition ("volontairement"), but after his second flight he disappeared for good. Lefebvre's erratic comings and goings certainly suggest a man in profound mental and emotional turmoil.

Piernas was not in the least concerned with Lefebvre's mental problems, however, but rather with "the confusion in which he has abandoned the property and the interests of the king [Carlos III], of which he had been in charge, which is very prejudicial to the king, as well as to the public." Lefebvre had engaged in, or was at least strongly suspected of engaging in, peculation as royal storekeeper. Under this cloud, he had abandoned his duties and his teenage wife and fled, leaving behind in St. Louis a very messy situation. Piernas desperately wanted Colonel Wilkins's assistance in apprehending Lefebvre, and he argued that the "happiness, tranquility and security" of both sides of the Mississippi depended upon cooperation between the British and Spanish commandants. It is unlikely that Wilkins (well known as churlish) paid much attention to Piernas's plea, but, in any event, Lefebvre, with two companions, eluded capture and succeeded in fleeing downriver to New Orleans.

Marguerite, Lefebvre's young wife, did the prudent thing: she moved back into the Condé household, with her sister and her former *tuteur*, leaving her residence in the care of a housekeeper, one Monsieur Beland, and her six black slaves. In May 1772, Piernas decided that some sort of reckoning must be done, and he ordered that a complete inventory of the Lefebvre estate be compiled—residential land, agricultural land, slaves, and all personal property right down to a pair of silk stockings, "rather worn."[22] This inventory provides us with a window into an early St. Louis lifestyle much more refined and elaborate than that of Comparios and his black slave. Second Lieutenant Antonio de Oro of the Spanish garrison was officially in charge of the inventory, but "Louis St. Ange de Bellerive, former commandant," and "Sieur Labuxière, former royal attorney," performed the duties.

The house had *poteaux-en-terre* walls and a stone chimney and was roofed with split wooden shingles. The walls were pierced by two doors (presumably front and back) and five windows. The structure was divided into three spaces with internal walls fashioned of vertical planks: a central hall with small rooms ("cabinets") on either side, one of which would have been the couple's bedroom. Projecting off one end was an "apenty" addition that served as a kitchen. This arrangement was the same as at Comparios's house, and the use of *appentis* for kitchens seems to have been common practice in town. All substantial homes in the Illinois Country had slave quarters situated on the residential property, rather than in outlying fields. Lefebvre's quarters were small (15×15 pieds) but solid, with *poteaux-en-terre* walls and a wooden shingled (rather than straw or bark) roof. This structure was apparently room enough for the six slaves, two women and four children, who made up Lefebvre's holdings, for it is very unlikely that any slaves lived within the main residence. Interestingly, the two women, aged forty and twenty, were identified as "negresses,"[23] while all four children were identified as "mulattoes." This suggests that the pattern of intimate relations common between white men and Indian women in St. Louis also included white men and black women.[24]

The major pieces of furniture within the Lefebvre residence included two doe-footed tables (popular in early St. Louis), a walnut buffet, a walnut daybed, a feather bed, eleven caned chairs, and an armoire, placed next to the fireplace. Which of these pieces was locally made remains an intriguing but unanswerable question, although the black walnut certainly suggests local provenance.[25] Large armoires were ubiquitous in France and all its colonies, serving, in lieu of closets, as multipurpose storage places. In Lefebvre's armoire were, among other odds and ends: two dozen faience plates (eleven "cassé" by rats), five faience plateaux (two broken, with no identified culprits), eighteen pewter plates, a pewter bowl, three pewter cups, a pewter teapot, a table knife with a silver handle, and five Beaufort (linen) bedsheets. For some reason, not secured in the armoire were seven coffee cups and saucers (Lieutenant de Oro had borrowed two others), six coffee spoons of white metal, small tongs "for taking sugar," and eleven crystal goblets (de Oro had borrowed the twelfth). De Oro would eventually distinguish himself as commandant in Ste. Genevieve (1784–87),[26] but he first appears in Upper Louisiana borrowing utensils for his dining table.

The Lefebvre kitchen in the main residence had fallen into desuetude. Nevertheless, two items remaining in the abandoned facility are instructive: as in Compario's kitchen, there was a dough-kneading trough ("pétrin"), but there was also a "pelle à feu [long-handled wooden paddle]," used for inserting and retrieving bread loaves from a bake oven. Similar instruments may be seen today in pizza shops where traditional wood-burning ovens are

Armoires were ubiquitous in the Illinois Country from the earliest days of French settlement, and cabinetmakers (menuisiers) were fashioning them in St. Louis as early as the 1760s, often of black walnut. Photo by the authors from the collection of the Missouri History Museum, St. Louis.

used. These items convincingly demonstrate that there were no bake shops in town, each home having to bake its own bread, unless neighbors sometimes shared a bake oven.

Marguerite La Ferne Lefebvre, having quit her residence to live with her sister and brother-in-law, took all her clothing with her. Her husband, on the other hand, had bolted out of town, abandoning most of his wardrobe. All his remaining clothing was stored in the buffet:

Culottes[27] of crimson velvet, almost new

Two scarlet culottes, half new

Two camel hair [*camelot*][28] culottes, half new

Red camel hair culottes, half new

Two camel hair suits, one black and the other sky blue, half used

Dress jacket of silk with silver flowers on a white background, half used

Linen jacket and culottes, half used

Crimson wool riding coat, half used

The material culture that surrounded the young Lefebvre couple in their home at St. Louis was far more varied and luxurious than that of Comparios and his slave, Marguerite. Young Lefebvre had apparel suitable to promenade in Parisian boulevards on a Sunday afternoon, and with his penchant for crimson he must have cut quite a figure among the mud-spattered voyageurs, habitants, artisans, and slaves on the muddy streets of early St. Louis. But the rich fabrics clothed a man of craven character, and his giddy flight from St. Louis to New Orleans did not liberate him but only led to an early death.

The abandoned Lefebvre residence, where rats had the run of the place, presented a forlorn scene, emblematic of the end of a family for which there had been high expectations when the Lefebvres married in 1768. Toward the end of the inventory, the scrupulous appraisers dutifully recorded two items that bring the scene—doleful sights and odors of death—vividly to the reader's attention: "a staved-in pirogue at river's edge" and "a kid goat—dead."

⚜ ⚜ ⚜ ⚜

Louis Deshêtres ("of the beech trees") was one of the more interesting characters to occupy the stage of early St. Louis history, and thankfully substantial sources remain to tell us a good deal about his life (and early death) in the fledgling village. Deshêtres was born and baptized on January 26, 1731, the son of Antoine and Charlotte Chevalier, at post St. Joseph des Miamis in what is now far southwestern Michigan (Niles).[29] He was named after his godfather, Louis Coulon de Villiers, who, twenty-three years later, would gain fame by capturing and humiliating George Washington at Fort Necessity in southwestern Pennsylvania. Growing up at the remote St. Joseph outpost, Deshêtres did not learn to read or write (even his signature), but he had a God-given talent for languages and soon became adept in several Indian tongues.

The extended Deshêtres family likely moved eastward to the Detroit area early in 1751. Louis married Marie-Thérèse Damours de Louvières at the parish of Ste. Anne de Détroit on February 18, 1760. At the time, the bride had not yet reached her fourteenth birthday.[30] The couple's first child was born and baptized (Thérèse) in Detroit on March 7, 1762, but died shortly thereafter. Deshêtres was active on both sides of the Detroit River and received a land grant on the southern shore "near the village of the Ottawas of whom he is the interpreter,"[31] and Charlotte, second daughter of Louis and Marie-Thérèse, was born July 11, 1763, on the South Coast of Detroit (Sandwich).[32]

Because of Pontiac's uprising, the situation at Detroit during the first half of 1765 remained volatile and dangerous.[33] It is difficult to know what French Canadians like the Deshêtres thought about Indian affairs, other than to say that they were heartily fed up with perpetual turmoil and uncertainty. The Deshêtres family appears on the August 1765 census of Detroit,[34] but soon thereafter they abandoned that British-occupied area and headed west, for the Illinois Country, where Louis had connections and Marie-Thérèse had family. What can be said of this westward journey across the American wilderness is largely conjectural. Louis Deshêtres was certainly in charge of the family that included Louis and his wife, Marie-Thérèse Damours de Louvières Deshêtres;[35] the couple's two-year-old daughter, Charlotte; Marie-Thérèse's sister, Charlotte; and the sisters' mother, Marie-Josèphe, widow of Louis Damour de Louvières. Louis Deshêtres, although a man of many and diverse talents, would have had his hands full, what with a sickly two-year-old, his much pregnant wife, his mother-in-law, and his sister-in-law. Perhaps the extended Deshêtres family headed west within a larger group that was fleeing Upper Canada for Upper Louisiana across a western frontier still reverberating with the lingering effects of Pontiac's Rebellion.

These Canadians, with all their worldly possessions in hand, likely followed the Wabash River route to the Illinois Country, for during the mid–eighteenth century this was the most common route. Descending the Detroit River in spruce-framed and bark-covered canoes, they could have followed the western shoreline of Lake Erie around to the mouth of the Maumee River and ascended that river to the portage that led to the headwaters of the Wabash (now Fort Wayne, Indiana). This portage (often called Miami) would have been the most difficult part of the trip. George Croghan described it in August 1765, perhaps a month before our Canadians traversed it: "We Arrived at the Carrying Place between the River Maimes & the Cuabache which is about nine Miles long in dry seasons but not above halfe that Length in Freshes."[36] Of course, Croghan was not discussing canoes loaded with men, women, and children and all of their worldly possessions.

After stopping briefly at Ouiatenon, the Wabash River carried the Canadians quickly downstream to Vincennes, where Joseph-Antoine Drouet de Richardville, captain of the militia, gave them a hearty welcome. Richardville was himself from a distinguished Canadian military family,[37] and the Deshêtres would have known other families in Vincennes, many of which had Canadian roots.[38] Richardville may well have tried to persuade the Deshêtres family to settle down at Vincennes, but Louis and Marie-Thérèse had laid down other plans: they were headed for Prairie du Rocher near Fort de Chartres, where Marie-Thérèse had scads of relatives—close, blood relatives—within the Damours de Louvières family. The Deshêtres family's move to the Illinois Country was typical of French Canadian chain migrations, with groups of immigrants following clusters of other extended family members.[39]

The Deshêtres family probably arrived at Prairie du Rocher about mid-October 1765, having buried their two-year-old daughter, Charlotte, somewhere along the way.[40] Nevertheless, they had beaten the arrival of winter to the Illinois Country, and Marie-Thérèse had endured the hardships of the journey without miscarrying the child she was carrying. What an enormous relief it must have been for her to be met on the eastern bank of the Mississippi by her cousin Pierre Damours de Louvières, who gave Marie-Thérèse a hand out of the pirogue and escorted her to a comfortable home in Prairie du Rocher.[41] At nearby Fort de Chartres, British forces had just arrived from Fort Pitt, and St. Ange was hurriedly preparing to remove his French marines to the west side of the Mississippi. The Deshêtres family had fled British-occupied Detroit only to arrive in the British-occupied Illinois Country; such was the dispiriting plight of Canadian refugees during the 1760s.

Marie-Thérèse gave birth to a son on January 2, 1766, at her cousin's residence in Prairie du Rocher.[42] Louis, the father, may not have been present for the birth (a women's affair at the time, in any case), for he likely followed St. Ange to St. Louis to take up his position as interpreter, as well as to prepare lodgings for his family. It is not known when Marie-Thérèse, her newborn child, her sister, and her mother made their way to the west side of the Mississippi. On May 16, 1766, Sébastien-Louis Meurin, the former Jesuit turned reluctant Capuchin, baptized in the chapel of St. Joseph in Prairie du Rocher Pierre, born of the legitimate marriage of Marie-Thérèse and Louis Deshêtres, explaining that the child had been born January 2. Priests were in short supply in the Illinois Country at the time, and Meurin had not been available before May to baptize the child.[43] Marie-Thérèse Deshêtres was in temporary residence with her cousin in Prairie du Rocher at the time of this baptism, and very likely Marie's mother and sister were as well. This was a comfortable situation for all involved, for the Damours de Louvières family was one of the largest and wealthiest in the community.

The Deshêtres family settled seamlessly into the emerging French community at St. Louis, which at the time was more Canadian than Creole. On St. Ange's May 1766 census, they already owned a substantial parcel of agricultural land, a horse, and two head of cattle (likely Deshêtres's team of draft oxen).[44] Deshêtres was illiterate (could not sign his marriage record)[45] but had an annual salary of one thousand livres as "interprète pour les sauvages," identical to that of commandant St. Ange de Bellerive.[46] Upon arriving in St. Louis, Deshêtres attained high status, certainly more than he could ever have hoped to achieve in Detroit. Louis also had entrepreneurial instincts, and on June 18, 1766, he and his business partner, Nicolas LeCompte, bought a horse mill for crushing oak bark to extract tannin for curing leather;[47] on June 30, they received from St. Ange a land grant upon which to place their newly bought machinery.[48]

Moreover, Deshêtres family affairs proceeded apace. As soon as the family arrived at St. Louis in the spring of 1766, a neighbor, Jean-Baptiste Gamache, liked what he saw—fellow Canadians, including a very eligible young lady, Charlotte, sister to Deshêtres's wife. The Gamaches had immigrated to Canada from Montes–le Jolie, situated just down the Seine Valley from Paris, in the late seventeenth century.[49] They settled at Cap St. Ignace, across the St. Lawrence River from Quebec City, where Jean-Baptiste was born in 1734. He seems to have arrived in the Illinois County just in time to become one of St. Louis's earliest citizens. Gamache immediately became friends with Louis Deshêtres and began to court Charlotte. On May 3, 1767, the civil marriage contract of Jean-Baptiste Gamache and Charlotte Damour de Louvières was drawn up in the Deshêtres home as prescribed by the Customary Law of Paris.[50] Charlotte's mother signed the document as witness, for she, unlike her two daughters and their husbands, was literate. The young couple married in May, and over the centuries the Gamaches proved to be one of the most prosperous and fertile French families in St. Louis. Recently, this distinguished family erected a monument in the city's historic Calvary Cemetery to honor these early families.

Nothing is known about the Deshêtres family's original dwelling in St. Louis. Certainly it was small, certainly it was crowded (almost beyond our comprehension), and certainly it was built of vertical logs. But Louis Deshêtres was an important person in town, with a substantial salary and a respectable family. Appropriately, on December 4, 1767, he contracted with Louis Des Loriers and Antoine Sans Souci, "master masons," to build the stone shell for a new house.[51] The Canadian Roussel *dit* Sans Souci family was originally from Normandy,[52] which had been producing master stonemasons since early medieval times.

The building contract for this house is chockablock with information about an abundance of issues pertinent to this study and is worth a brief digression. The house was to be 25×35 pieds, which was large by early St. Louis standards—roughly twice as large as the average *poteaux-en-terre* residence in town. It was to have gabled ends, with stone chimneys on either end, and walls 18 pouces (1 pouce = 1.066 inches) thick—in other words, a very sturdy structure. Deshêtres obligated himself to provide the two masons with all the stone and the wood necessary for scaffolding, plus "food for the workers during the time of their work." The contract was only for the masonry, which meant that all the woodwork had to be done later. Des Loriers and Sans Souci were to commence laying stone "the first days of spring" (1768) and when they had completed their work would be paid five hundred livres in peltries. "First days of spring" could mean many things in early St. Louis: spring perhaps arrived when the ice broke up on the Mississippi or, as one observer remarked, "when the strawberries were ripe."[53] Marie-Thérèse Damours de Louvières Deshêtres may have packed some fresh strawberries in the lunches, which, as per the building contract, the masons were to receive.

As this building project evolved, the house became larger, and—being large, built of stone, and facing la Grande Rue—it would have made a fitting residence for the royal interpreter with his extended family. But Deshêtres could not afford to keep it, and in April 1769 he sold it for twelve hundred livres in peltries to Joseph Motard, a French-born goldsmith.[54] Between the summer of 1768, when the house was to have been completed, and the summer of 1770, when Louis died, things quite unraveled for the illiterate Canadian linguist with big ambitions. Deshêtres farmed, served as interpreter, and performed other odd jobs, such as pursuing runaway slaves and castrating horses, delicate work this last.[55] But he could not seem to make ends meet, and then fickle luck completely abandoned him—Deshêtres went deeply into debt and was then struck down by a mortal illness or illnesses. His succession papers tell us a good deal about his financial affairs, including those involving Jean-Baptiste Sarpy.[56] Sarpy arrived in St. Louis in 1769 and immediately assumed a role as major *négociant*, bringing large quantities of trade goods up the Mississippi from New Orleans. Sarpy and Deshêtres did a good deal of business together, selling, among other things, tafia to the local Peoria Indians—Sarpy supplied the booze, and Deshêtres, who knew the Peoria language, served as intermediary with the Indians.

Deshêtres's accounts reveal in detail how business and legal affairs were conducted in St. Louis at the time. On May 3, 1769, Deshêtres went to the notary, Labuxière, and had him draft an official IOU that obligated Deshêtres to pay Pierre Montardy the sum of four hundred livres in peltries during the month of October next. Deshêtres affixed his mark to the document, which was witnessed by Louis Lambert and Michel La Déroute. On October 29, Montardy signed the note over to Joseph Motard, the local tradesman and goldsmith who had a "boutique" associated with his large house on la Grande Rue.[57] When Motard was unable to collect from Deshêtres on his note, he appealed to Commandant St. Ange and Judge Labuxière on December 2, 1769. Labuxière dealt with the matter by dispatching his *huissier* (bailiff), François Cottin, to Deshêtres's home to face him directly. Life in St. Louis absolutely depended upon men honoring their financial notes, which were in effect a form of currency. If notes were not honored, commerce, indeed civil society itself, would collapse; it was as simple as that.

Huissier Cottin relished getting a chance to perform his official functions. Before noon on Saturday, December 2, he marched directly to Deshêtres's "domissille," where he found Louis and Marie-Thérèse Deshêtres chatting. Interrupting the conversation, Cottin confronted Deshêtres with Motard's complaint, and Deshêtres responded that he knew nothing of the matter. Cottin had been anticipating this response, and he forthwith issued Deshêtres a summons ("assigniasson" [*sic*]) to appear in court. Court consisted of St. Ange and Labuxière seated in the "chambre du gouvernment" (St. Ange's office), which served as the seat of government for the small village of St. Louis as well as for the entire vast region of Upper Louisiana. Court convened on December 4, 1769, and Deshêtres was ordered to "settle the note as prescribed." It is not clear whether Deshêtres fulfilled this obligation during the eight months that he had left on earth.

By June 1770, Deshêtres was on his deathbed, consuming large quantities of cough syrup ("sirop pectoral") and "kina," a word derived from *Cinchona* (Jesuit's bark); by the mid–eighteenth century, the utility of Jesuit's bark in battling malaria was widely known.[58] Deshêtres died on Sunday, August 12, 1770, and was buried quickly, probably on August 13. No priest was available at the time, but when the itinerant Father Pierre Gibault showed up in town almost two months later he performed a memorial service for Louis in the crude chapel that served as provisional church. Either because the Deshêtres family had been pretty much wiped out financially trying to cover Louis's debts or because he had had an official position as interpreter, new Commandant Piernas paid Gibault three livres for performing the service. Piernas likely also paid for the sixteen candles (eight livres) that were consumed during the service to help propel Deshêtres's soul upward toward heaven.[59]

On Monday, August 13, Labuxière compiled the inventory of Deshêtres's estate.[60] The family's house was the usual *poteaux-en-terre* affair, with a footprint of sixteen by eighteen pieds. This was pretty small even by early St. Louis standards, although it was enlarged a bit with shed-like addition ("apenty") on one end. We saw above precisely the same configuration on Comparios's somewhat larger house. The double stone chimney would have been in the center of the Deshêtres dwelling, providing two fireplaces, which suggests a layout of two equal-size rooms on the main floor, plus the addition. Given the size of the Deshêtres family, and the smallness of its house, the attic likely provided sleeping quarters.

180   Contours of Village Life

Assuming that only a few personal possessions had been brought from Canada, the Deshêtres family had accumulated a substantial mass of material possessions in less than three years of living in St. Louis. Some of these possessions—a folding walnut table, a walnut armoire, and six caned chairs—were probably fashioned in St. Louis, although not the lock ("fermante à clef") on the armoire. Other items—a copper serving dish, nine faience plates, a faience platter, and a mirror with a broken glass—would all have come from France. The twenty pots[61] of bear's oil listed on the inventory stands out and suggests that Deshêtres was trading in oil. His close associations with Indians as an interpreter perhaps gave him easy access to a regular supply of oil. Butter was preferred in Canada for cooking but was difficult to conserve in Louisiana, where bear's oil was highly esteemed. Paul Alliot observed that hunters in Upper Louisiana "find in their forests bears prodigiously fat and large, the oil from which is much sought after by the inhabitants, even those of New Orleans. Although it is very bitter to the taste, it is preferred to the poor oil of Provence."[62] It is hard for modern Americans to swallow the idea of bear's oil as preferable to olive oil, but the former was a constant component in the diets of Lewis and Clark's men in the Corps of Discovery. On May 5, 1805, they rendered six gallons of oil from one bear, which must have been as prodigious as those that inhabited Alliot's imagination.[63]

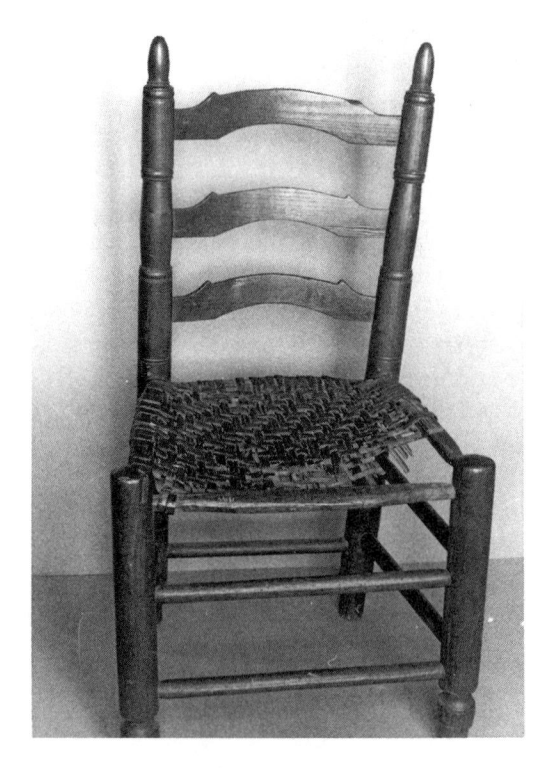

Caned chairs (chaises empaillées), often with turned legs, were standard household items in the Illinois Country, including St. Louis (stuffed armchairs being virtually unknown). Photo by the authors from the collection of the Missouri History Museum, St. Louis.

Louis Deshêtres owned a half-dozen pairs of culottes, but unlike Lefebvre's that were fashioned of fancy fabrics Deshêtres's were all of plain cotton. Many St. Louis men strode through St. Louis's Place Publique wearing culottes, but the different cuts, colors, and fabrics of these pantaloons made visible a rudimentary frontier social and economic hierarchy. Sociologists frequently comment on clothing as markers of class that help to define social orders.[64] And Deshêtres had only two pairs of knee-high cotton stockings to go with his culottes—the pair he wore to his grave and the pair itemized on his inventory. Being a woodsman, he had two *capots*, the one made of "cadix" suggesting an origin of fine Spanish merino wool.[65] These longish, hooded garments were as ubiquitous on the French frontier as "hoodies" are on many urban streets today. The three shirts (either of linen or cotton) included in the inventory were all well worn, but Marie-Thérèse had two flat irons to keep them well pressed. Likely, Deshêtres wore one such shirt when he went to face St. Ange and Labuxière in court on Monday, December 4, 1769.

We saw above that a worker of precious metals, Joseph Motard, was already a resident of St. Louis by 1769. Perhaps he fashioned the one sterling silver soup spoon owned by the Deshêtres family. Or, more likely, this object of utility and beauty was a family heirloom that had been carefully packed near Detroit and then transported via water and portage down to the Illinois Country. Canadians had been bringing silver tableware to the region since the early 1700s.[66]

Louis Deshêtres was only thirty-nine years old at the time of his death, but it is apparent that he died of a lingering illness, or combination of illnesses—pneumonia, tuberculosis, and malaria all likely possibilities. He was hardly cold in his grave when his creditors submitted their bills to the estate. The major *négociant*, Louis Lambert, had provided the family with imported items for domestic use and consumption. Marie-Thérèse received two packets of fancy French thread ("fil d'Épinay"), worth six livres per packet, and twelve bars of soap, worth eighteen livres, fifteen sols. Everyday soap was produced locally, but refined, perfumed soap came from France via New Orleans. Louis Deshêtres had gotten four pots of tafia at five livres each, and one bottle for his brother Antoine at two livres, ten sols. A bottle of white wine had the same value, meaning that tafia provided more kick for the livre. Lambert's claim against Deshêtres's estate was fifty-five livres, fifteen sols, which could be paid off either in deerskins or beaver pelts.

Deshêtres's largest creditor was Sarpy, his sometime business partner, and he submitted detailed and fascinating bills to the estate. Between September 1769 and February 1770, Sarpy had provided Deshêtres with seventy-three bottles of tafia, which wound up in the hands of diverse denizens of St. Louis and environs: two went to an Indian named Mercier, four to an Indian who had supplied meat to Deshêtres, eight to another unnamed Indian, one to Picard's black female slave (one is permitted to hope that this was for her own consumption), one to Hervieux's black slave, one to Deshêtres's brother Tranquille (nickname for Antoine), two to an Indian who had accompanied Tranquille, and many more to brother Tranquille, who, like Louis himself, was apparently retailing the fiery refreshment. Evidently, everyone in town of whatever color or status was drinking the stuff.

⚜ ⚜ ⚜ ⚜

Pierre-Jean-Baptiste Hervieux was born and baptized in Montreal on April 29, 1706. He was the first child born to Léonard *dit* Jean-Baptiste and Catherine Magnan, and his father was identified as a merchant and "maître arquebusier" (master craftsman of arquebuses),[67] what we would today call a gunsmith. Jean-Baptiste (he dropped the Pierre) turned up in the Illinois Country sometime in the mid-1750s, serving as a witness at the marriage of Étienne Gauvereau in 1755.[68] Gauvereau was a master blacksmith, and it seems likely that Hervieux, a gunsmith like his father, was friend to a man who worked in a related field; they both heated, hammered, and shaped metals. But as a gunsmith, Hervieux was, in the hierarchy of men who worked with their hands, situated

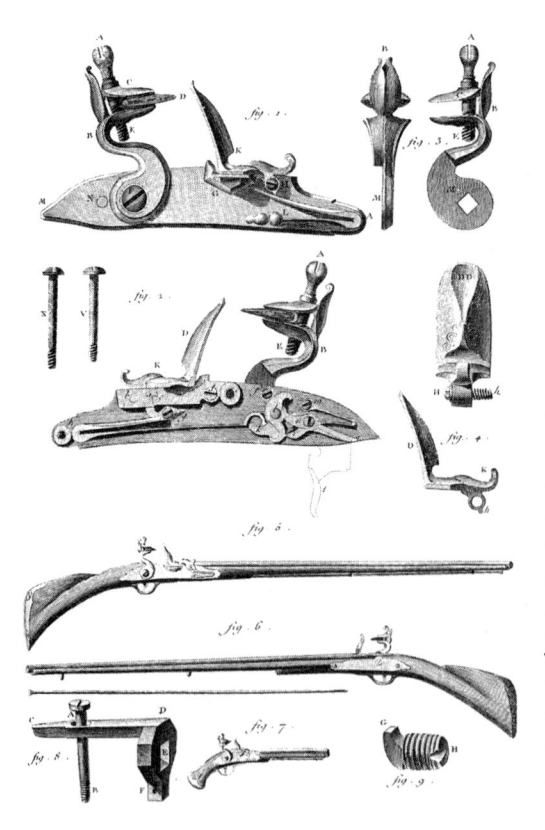

French flintlocks were considered superior firearms during the eighteenth century. Early St. Louis boasted a Canadian-trained master gunsmith, Jean-Baptiste Hervieux, who kept in good order the weapons of St. Ange's small garrison and of the village militia. Reproduced from Denis Diderot and Jean le Rond d'Alembert, comps. and eds., Dictionnaire raisonnée des arts, des sciences, et des métiers, Planches, vol. 1 (1762).

at a higher level than a blacksmith, for he was an artisan, which in traditional French society placed him very close to the realm of artists.

Hervieux knew another master blacksmith in Kaskaskia as well, Louis Normand *dit* La Bruyère.[69] In 1747, well before Hervieux arrived in Kaskaskia, Normand had married Agnès Hulin, a *métisse*, and they had at least one child together, Raimond.[70] But almost immediately upon Hervieux's arrival in the community ca. 1754, he and Agnès Hulin Normand *dit* La Bruyère began an intimate affair that led to the birth of a child, Thérèse, *une fille naturelle*, in traditional French legal parlance.[71] It was unusual for married women in the Illinois Country villages to bear "natural" children, and this created an uncomfortable situation in a community where everyone knew everyone else's business. Agnès Hulin's sexual adventures led to further notoriety before she died at Ste. Genevieve in February 1774.[72]

Fallout from Hervieux's illicit relationship with Madame Hulin may have provided the motive for his flight from Kaskaskia to Chartres. By June 1756, Hervieux was in residence at Chartres, and in 1759 he had sufficient financial resources to bid 8,500 livres on a large house with three stone fireplaces located near the fort (Hervieux lost out when the property was knocked off for 10,475 livres).[73] At Chartres Hervieux served frequently as a witness in civil records, perhaps because the notary Labuxière appreciated seeing Hervieux's ornate signature on documents he drafted in a community that was mostly illiterate. Hervieux and Labuxière became colleagues working on official documents together, and they were both present in Kaskaskia on November 6, 1763, to help manage the auction of the Jesuit properties.[74] (Laclède was, as we have seen, an unsuccessful bidder at that auction.) After Labuxière and Hervieux moved to St. Louis, the two men remained friends and lived near one another in the new village.[75]

At the Jesuit auction in November 1763, Hervieux was identified as "the king's gunsmith," which means that, although not a French marine, he was attached to St. Ange's garrison at the fort. Hervieux was present at Chartres in April 1764, and in July 1765 he stood as godfather at a baptism in Kaskaskia.[76] When precisely Hervieux established a residence at St. Louis is unknown, but certainly he was there when St. Ange came over with his marines in late October 1765. At the new outpost on the west side of the Mississippi, Hervieux maintained his official position as gunsmith, for his skills were absolutely essential for St. Ange's marines and the local militiamen. Hervieux's name first appears in St. Louis sources on the May 31, 1766, census, and on the July militia muster roll he was listed as "armurier du roi," royal gunsmith. When Captain Pedro Piernas arrived as Spanish commandant in May 1770, St. Ange and Labuxière both lost their official positions (commandant and notary), but Hervieux retained his, and at the time of his death in 1775 he was still identified as "harmero del Rey."[77]

On October 30, 1766, St. Ange granted Hervieux a standard village lot (120×150 pieds), which faced the Grande Rue to the west and overlooked the Mississippi to the rear.[78] On this property, Hervieux had a house built of wooden timbers ("casa de madera"), which probably meant *en charpente*, that is, fashioned of large dressed timbers set vertically on sills. The house had a stone chimney, was divided into three parts, and was roofed with split wooden shingles. Likely, the floor layout of Hervieux's house consisted of a large central hall, which served as a commons and his work space, that was flanked by two secondary rooms. Hervieux seems to have lived alone, and this was an adequate facility for his residence and his atelier, his gun shop. Furthermore, the town lot was improved, as were many residential properties in St. Louis, with a stable.[79]

The man who had seduced Agnès Hulin (or had she seduced him?) in Kaskaskia ca. 1754 was the Beau Brummel of the Illinois Country. A large portion of Hervieux's estate inventory was taken up with his clothing, and he required *two* armoires, one large and one small, to accommodate his mountain of clothes: a silk and cotton suit with red and white stripes; two dress coats, one brown with gold buttons and the other with white taffeta lining; many pairs of culottes of different colors; four dress jackets, three of cotton flannel and one of blue and white *polonesa* (*polonaise*);[80] two waistcoats, one of white cotton and the other of flowered silk; three linen shirts; two pairs of silk stockings; two pairs of (shoe?) buckles, one silver and one brass; silver cuff links; and a silver tie clasp. An artisan of Hervieux's status and tastes and bearing did not have to make way for any *négociant* on the muddy streets of early St. Louis, and when an ordinary habitant or *volontaire* appeared in Hervieux's shop to get his fusil repaired he doffed his cap in deference to the master gunsmith, "S'il vous plaît, monsieur l'armurier."

In Hervieux's shop when he died were many firearms awaiting his attention, "eighteen fusils, large and small, many without stocks." Hervieux worked with wood as well as metal, for much of his work consisted of repairing and replacing guns' stocks; he had eight on hand roughed out and ready to be adapted and finished to fit individual fusils. If someone wanted a fancy gun, Hervieux had on hand a silver escutcheon that could be set as ornamentation into a wooden stock. His inventory of gunsmithing tools and materials was, of course, extensive: hammers, files, tongs, planes, saws, chisels, scissors, an anvil, a bellows, stocks of raw iron, copper and lead, and borax (sodium borate for flux in soldering). As a gunsmith, Hervieux had, as one would expect, a bullet mold, but he also had one for casting crucifixes ("un molde para hasen Cristos"). Crucifixes were likely cast, cheaply, in lead and disseminated to Indians by traders and missionaries, ad majorem Dei gloriam. Indian-made molds for casting crosses are well known from Illinois Country archaeological contexts, and Hervieux's mold may have been Indian made. Hervieux also enjoyed taking his tobacco in an Indian-made Micmac pipe ("un calumete con su cara en carnado"), the red face meaning that the pipe had been carved from catlinite, commonly called pipestone.[81] Hervieux perhaps puffed on this pipe while reading and rereading his "four old books," rare possessions in an Illinois Country inventory. Frustratingly, we cannot use these books to peep, even a short way, into Hervieux's mental habits because titles were not provided.[82]

Piernas appointed Martin Duralde, an educated Frenchman and engineer, executor of Hervieux's estate. Two claimants came forward: Jean-Louis Lacroix claimed that a number of items included on the inventory belonged to him—a tomahawk, a mirror, a pair of silver buckles, and a hat. Duralde himself claimed four pigs and a pair of scissors. These claims were apparently settled quickly and amicably. In accordance with French customary law, Thérèse, Hervieux's natural daughter, had no legal claim on any part of her father's succession, unless Hervieux had so provided in a will, and no such document has survived, if indeed he ever wrote one.[83]

⚜ ⚜ ⚜ ⚜

In February 1769, Nicolas Barzalou (or Barsalou or Barsaloux) and his wife, Madeleine LePage, acquired a fine residence from Antoine Hubert, who was constantly wheeling and dealing in St. Louis real estate. The house—built by a Frenchman, Julien Le Roy, for a Frenchman, Hubert—was constructed "sur sole ou colombage [on sills or of half-timbers]."[84] In appearance, this house was perhaps more like a house in Normandy than one in Kaskaskia or Ste. Geneviève. By 1778 the Barsalous, husband and wife, were dead and buried, and their estate inventory contains a multiplicity of personal and household goods, including two grand beds, raised on wooden platforms and complemented with feather ticks.[85] But here we wish to focus on Madame Barsalou's clothing, for male attire has already been discussed.

In two words, Madeleine LePage Barsalou was a fashion plate, beyond any doubt the most chic woman in town, and her apparel occupies a significant portion of the Barsalou estate inventory. Women as well as men wore *capots*, and Madame Barsalou had at least four: of blue damask with white silk flowers, of purple taffeta, of calico ("Indiana") lined with blue *polonaise*, and of white muslin. She had two shawls, one of black taffeta and another of black flannel; a half-dozen skirts (one of calico with red and green flowers); many blouses, petticoats, stockings (of linen and cotton); and a yellow camel-hair corset. In addition to clothes, madame had other adornments for her body—sterling silver earrings and bracelet, all set with stones; three gold rings, one set with a ruby and the others with "French stones"; a sterling silver crucifix; nine silk ribbons of various colors; and three black necklaces. At Mass on Sunday mornings, Madame Barsalou lighted up the somber interior of St. Louis's rude log chapel like a roman candle. We do not know enough about burial customs at that time and place to know whether she carried with her into the grave in 1778 jewelry that might otherwise have been listed on the Barsalou inventory.

✧ ✧ ✧ ✧

Marriages, illnesses, and deaths of early St. Louis denizens required paperwork that casts light onto their daily lives. Although most lived in conditions that strike us as unimaginably crowded, they, even the most humble, were not starved for material possessions. Houses in early St. Louis were generally tiny, but they were jammed full of a wide assortment of goods and home furnishings. Some of these were produced locally, likely the black walnut armoires and tables, but a vast quantity of goods had come from Europe via New Orleans, and some had arrived from Canada via the waterways (surely that treasured silver spoon in the Deshêtres household). An extraordinary array of fabrics—wool, cotton, linen, and silk, rendered as flannels, muslins, worsteds, serges, taffetas, brocades, both plain and brightly colored—appears in the clothing of early St. Louisans. All fabrics were imported from Europe, for no spinning or weaving was done locally, or even regionally. Pierre Laville was a "tailleur habits [tailor of clothes]" at St. Louis in 1770, but he may have specialized in male attire.[86] Tantalizing evidence exists that some women in town were doing their own sewing. The Barsalou inventory lists six pieces of linen, various fabrics designated for mending and patching, and a case of small silvered tools (scissors, thimbles, needles?).[87] Madame Barsalou was unquestionably doing needle work, but whether madame's skills elevated her to the level of seamstress, who fabricated some of the fine garments kept in her wardrobe, cannot be known, although we would like to believe that she did precisely that.

On balance, early St. Louisans lived better at the material level than their counterparts back home in France. Their *armoires* were stuffed with all manner of clothing, both utilitarian and Sunday-go-to-meeting, and their homes had full complements of furniture and cookware. St. Louisans certainly had more calories at their daily disposal than Frenchmen, and their diets were more varied and better balanced because of their diverse and plentiful supply of proteins. King Henry IV's supposed remark that he wanted every French family to have "a chicken in the pot [*poule au pot*]" was a far greater likelihood in St. Louis than in France. During the colonial era, life was easier for Frenchmen in America than in Europe, and for the black slaves in St. Louis likely easier in America than in Africa. The Mississippi frontier was a frontier of relative bounty for all who dwelled there.

CHAPTER 10

Foundations of the St. Louis Fur Trade

> *Guillaume L'Espérance, voyageur, commits himself to Jean-Marie Toulouse,* commerçant, *to serve him as a faithful* engagé *and to row his vessels destined for the fur trade of the Mississippi and other rivers. . . . The present contract done for the sum of 350 livres in peltries, which Sieur Toulouse promises to pay to L'Espérance.*
>
> —St. Louis, May 1766

Hiram Martin Chittenden's classic study, *The American Fur Trade of the Far West*, was the first serious, modern study of the subject, and the author portrayed Pierre Laclède and Auguste Chouteau as the founders of the St. Louis fur trade. Chittenden was a personal friend of Pierre-Sylvestre Chouteau (grandson of Jean-Pierre, Auguste's half brother) and relied heavily on Chouteau manuscripts as sources for his work.[1] Chittenden's original portrait has been altered remarkably little over the past one hundred years, merely painted in brighter colors. The early St. Louis fur trade is generally portrayed as having been dominated by Laclède, and Captain Harry Gordon's isolated remark to that effect is religiously cited to prove the point.[2] But Gordon spent little time in the Illinois Country, and his offhand comment in August 1766 is of dubious weight and value for assessing the early fur trade and Laclède's role in it. Far and away the most important sources for examining the early St. Louis trade are manuscripts housed at the Missouri History Museum in St. Louis and the Archivo General de Indias in Seville. These heretofore neglected sources bring to center stage an entirely new cast of characters (*négociants, commerçants,* and voyageurs) that animated the early St. Louis fur trade, bringing to it imported trade goods, energy, and entrepreneurial skills.

Trade in peltries[3] had been an important part of New France's economy since the early seventeenth century, and fur traders had first penetrated into the Illinois Country from Canadian settlements in the St. Lawrence Valley.[4] Father Jacques Marquette's partner, Louis Jolliet, was a trader, and Robert Cavelier de La Salle, while pursuing fame and glory, also envisaged opening the greater Mississippi Valley as a vast trading zone. Two of his closest associates, Henri de

Tonti and François Dauphin de La Forest, became major traders, who worked in the Illinois River valley. Gilles Havard has brilliantly illuminated their respective roles in the early fur trade of the *Pays d'en haut* (Upper Canada).[5] Montreal was the base of operations for these early traders, and archives in Canada are replete with contracts pertaining to trade canoes heading west to the Illinois Country.[6]

But once a settlement was established at Mobile in 1702 and, more important, at New Orleans in 1718, the orientation of the Illinois fur trade turned decidedly southward. Louis Tessier and Jacques Bourdon were both Canadian traders living in Kaskaskia, and if they had begun trading through Montreal, by the early 1720s their commercial entrepôt had become New Orleans. The large inventories taken after their respective deaths reveal the scope of material things, including Indian trade goods, that were being brought up the Mississippi to the Illinois Country from New Orleans almost immediately after the city had been founded.[7] Tessier in fact died in 1721 at Natchez when returning from a commercial expedition to New Orleans, just as Pierre Laclède died in 1778 near Arkansas Post while on a similar expedition. Traders working out of Montreal continued throughout the colonial era to be active in the villages of the Illinois Country, including St. Louis, but by the time St. Louis had emerged, New Orleans was indisputably the major commercial entrepôt for the Illinois Country.

During the French regime, Illinois-based traders (like Bourdon and Tessier) brought trade goods up the Mississippi to Illinois Country settlements, and from these local entrepôts the goods were transshipped farther up the Mississippi and its tributaries to Indian villages. But following the French and Indian War, major *négociants* from New Orleans, and from France, settled in Ste. Genevieve and St. Louis and revolutionized the nature and scope of the fur trade in Upper Louisiana. Newly arriving English merchants were eager to compete, but Sir William Johnson, superintendent of Indian affairs for the northern British colonies, complained about a natural advantage French traders possessed: Indians, because of longtime association with the French, were willing to pay more for French trade goods coming out of New Orleans than British goods coming into the Illinois Country via the Great Lakes. French traders "are constantly sending very large Cargoes up the Missisipi, the better to maintain their Influence."[8]

St. Louis's earliest known fur-trading documents date from April 1766. The brothers Desgagné, Antoine and Jean, both identified as *commerçants*, teamed up for a fur-trading expedition that spring. They intended to ascend the Mississippi to Sioux villages (likely on what is now the Minnesota River) with 1,772 livres' worth of trade goods, and for this purpose they pooled their resources, forming "une Société," a partnership. Antoine had fronted 300 livres' worth of peltries as an advance to acquire the merchandise, which they would have purchased from a *négociant* in either New Orleans or St. Louis. *Commerçants* were often the link between *négociants* and voyageurs in the commercial hierarchy of the fur trade. Once the Desgagné brothers returned to St. Louis in the spring of 1767, Antoine would take his 300 livres off the top of the profits, before the remainder was split fifty-fifty between them.[9] The gist of this partnership document is that the two brothers were working on their own, without any supporting *engagés*, and probably taking on the challenge of the Mississippi and Minnesota Rivers together in a two-man pirogue. Nicolas de Finiels mentioned bark canoes at St. Louis late in the eighteenth century, but dug-out pirogues were far more common in the Illinois Country.[10]

The Desgagné brothers were early small-time traders working out of St. Louis. But Jean-Marie Toulouse ran a larger operation, requiring more manpower. In April–May 1766, Toulouse was preparing for a trading expedition up the Mississippi River and its tributaries, and he set about engaging men to work for him. First was Antoine Bouquet, "garçon volontaire [unmarried hired hand]," who signed a contract to serve Toulouse for the period of one year—May 1766 to May 1767—doing everything that Toulouse asked of him that was "legal and honest." The trading trip would ascend "streams and rivers [rivières et fleuves]," but Bouquet also committed himself to work on terra firma to maximize Toulouse's profits and minimize his losses. At the end of the specified year, when Toulouse and his men brought their pirogue loads of skins and furs into St. Louis, Bouquet would be compensated with 300 livres' worth of peltries.[11]

After engaging Bouquet in April 1766, Toulouse signed on two more men in May. François Cayolle (he signed Cailhol), unmarried voyageur, agreed to ascend "the Mississippi and other rivers, to row and to guide [Toulouse's] trading vessels [*pirogues*], and to do everything he was ordered to do that was legal and honest." Cayolle's term of engagement was also one year (usual in fur-trading *engagements*), for which he would receive 350 livres' worth of peltries, 50 livres more than Bouquet. Cayolle seems to have been an experienced pirogue handler ("to row and to guide"), which made his services more valuable.[12] And the same was true of Guillaume Billaud *dit* l'Espérance (the hopeful one), who signed on the following day for the same 350 livres.[13] Labuxière, the notary, identified both Cayolle and l'Espérance as "voyageurs," while Bouquet was simply a "volontaire," and at a higher level yet was Toulouse himself, the *commerçant*. "Coureurs de bois," with its overtones of illegality, is a phrase that does not appear in early St. Louis fur-trading records, although such characters often flitted in and out of town, cutting small-time commercial deals that left no paper trails drafted by Labuxière.

The *contrats d'engagements* signed at St. Louis in the spring of 1766 are significant for the details they provide about the internal mechanisms of the fur trade, but they also inform us about several larger external issues. First, the geographic descriptions of Toulouse's trading activities (the upper Mississippi and all its tributaries) contain no mention of any political boundaries whatsoever. Toulouse was conducting his business as though no treaties had been signed in European capitals in 1762–63. Toulouse, a Frenchman, was working throughout territories that were technically Spanish and British without so much as batting an eye. Moreover, Toulouse was operating without any license from any authority, French, Spanish, or English. He was free to go wherever he wished and to trade with whomever he wanted with no concern for constrictive regulations or government interference. General Thomas Gage remarked that English merchants were often forced to use French traders as intermediaries in Indian villages situated in British territory "thro' fear of exposing their own Persons"[14] to the hazards of conducting business with Indians face-to-face, for such business was a French *spécialité*. The laissez-faire atmosphere of the mid-1760s would wane as the Spanish regime in Louisiana began to gain traction after 1770.

During June and July 1768, merchants in New Orleans were preparing to send bateaux loaded with trade goods up the Mississippi to the Illinois Country. Some of the merchandise was intended for residents of Ste. Genevieve and St. Louis and some for the Indian trade. Rowing, cordelling, and cursing a ba-

Flat-bottomed freight bateaux like this one carried produce from the Illinois Country (peltries, flour, lead, and apples) to New Orleans and returned with products from Europe and the Caribbean (fabrics, clothing, wine, sugar, coffee, brandy, tafia, guns, and so forth). Travel time downriver from St. Louis to New Orleans was usually three to four weeks, upriver three to four months. Copper-plate engraving based on a sketch by Joseph Warin, reproduced from Victor Collot, A Journey in North America . . . Illustrated *(Paris, 1826).*

teau up the Mississippi was the most backbreaking labor in Louisiana, and it made plowing, harvesting, and woodcutting seem like child's play. Both hired hands (*engagés*) and slaves worked as boatmen, ordinarily more of the former than the latter. The *engagés* were generally white men, but free blacks also signed on as rowers; the slaves were always blacks and mulattoes, for Indian slaves, for some reason, were not generally used for the New Orleans trade.

On July 30, 1768, Daniel Fagot de la Garcenière (usually called simply Fagot) asked Governor Ulloa's permission to send his bateau upriver from New Orleans.[15] Fagot had been a French marine officer before going into commerce, and having been posted for a time at Fort de Chartres he knew the Illinois Country firsthand. He married Charlotte-Constance Olivier de Vézin in New Orleans and named his bateau, *La Charlotte*, after her.[16] This was a large bateau and was loaded with four lots of merchandise belonging to four respective merchants, including Fagot himself. His share consisted of:

- 8 *barriques* (large barrels) of wine
- 6 *barriques* of tafia, including two for the crew
- 16 *quarts* (small barrels) of brandy
- 2 *quarts* of coffee
- 1 *quart* of sugar
- 1 *barrique* of loaf sugar
- 1 *barrique* of salt
- 1 piece of cordage
- 3 *jarres* (large earthenware jars)
- 4 cases of soap
- 6 bales of trade goods
- 2 bales of French goods
- 2 *quarts* of tar
- 1 case of goblets

Of special interest are the two *barriques* of tafia reserved for Fagot's crew of twenty *engagés* and four slaves. Boatmen, apparently both free and slave, were given daily rations of tafia to energize them and buffer the pain of rowing. Reckoning a *barrique* to contain 255 liters and reckoning ninety days for the trip upriver, each of Fagot's crew member received 7 or 8 ounces of spirits per day.[17] This level of refreshment kept the crew members content but also ensured that they would arise each morning ready to go—not wracked with headaches or nausea.

Fagot was asking permission not only to take his boat upriver, but also to trade with the Little Osage tribe during the year 1769. The six bales of trade goods included in his manifest were obviously intended for the Indian trade, and likely some of the lower-end alcohol (tafia) was as well. On the other hand, the soap, goblets, and French merchandise were all intended for the residents of St. Louis. Fagot's brother-in-law, Olivier de Fourcelles, would command *La Charlotte* for the trip to St. Louis, and he had a similar but smaller load of merchandise on the vessel. His manifest also included a case of wine, which was probably good claret, bottled and corked in Bordeaux— obviously not for the Indian trade. Lafitte cadet (probably from the important Natchitoches Lafitte family)[18] was also sending a mixture of merchandise to St. Louis, including nails, sun-bleached linen cloth ("toile herbée"), and woolen fabric. And finally, the New Orleans business partners Fournier and Saintpé were sending, among other things, four bales of dry goods, very likely an assortment of Indian trade goods.

Other bateaux in the 1768 convoy to the Illinois Country carried a larger proportion of Indian trade goods. One Monsieur Devin asked permission to take a boatload of goods to St. Louis and from there dispatch an agent ("un commis," that is, a voyageur) up the Missouri River to trade with the Missouri tribe. Devin was a relatively small-time merchant and his cargo consisted of the following:

10 pieces of Limbourg [woolen cloth]
80 white blankets
200 pounds of gun powder
400 pounds of lead balls
150 pounds of kettles
1 gross [twelve dozen] knives
20 fusils
20 pick axes
20 axes[19]

Gilbert Maxent was the senior partner in his business association with Pierre Laclède, and, moreover he was situated in New Orleans. On May 8, 1769, Maxent requested that Governor Ulloa convey to him and Laclède exclusive trading rights with the Oto and Big Osage tribes and be permitted to send a huge shipment of trade goods upriver to St. Louis.[20] In theory, Laclède would eventually arrange contracts with voyageurs in St. Louis to proceed up the Missouri, Osage, and Kansas Rivers and conduct trade with the specified tribes. But no evidence exists that this grandiose plan was ever effected. No bill of lading for a bateau to transport the trade goods up the Mississippi has come to light, and early St. Louis records contain nothing about such a shipment of goods arriving there. Moreover, on the same day that Maxent petitioned Ulloa, he and Laclède formally dissolved their partnership—perhaps because Ulloa had for some reason rejected Maxent's petition, or perhaps for reasons internal to the Maxent-Laclède partnership.[21] The dreams and ambitions of Maxent and Laclède always transcended their capacities, and their luck, to bring them to fruition.

The men (usually *négociants*) who brought trade goods up the Mississippi to St. Louis stockpiled their merchandise in preparation for the next step, which was to find specialists (*commerçants* and voyageurs) to carry the trade goods up the rivers to far-flung Indian trading grounds. Before arriving at their final destinations, goods sometimes passed through several hands in St. Louis. In June 1767, for example, Laclède worked through a *commerçant* (Thomas Blondeau), who in turn dealt with a voyageur (Charles St. Pierre), who loaded his pirogue with merchandise to be carried upstream to Indian villages.[22] Laclède chose not to shake the callused hand of the voyageur who paddled his pirogue into the Indian trading zones, for Laclède was a Frenchman with pretensions, even though his family lineage was bourgeois rather than aristocratic. Moreover, when he had attempted to work directly with voyageurs in Ste. Genevieve during the 1765–66 trading season (see chapter 3), he had gotten his fingers badly burned.

Laclède was reluctant to engage directly in the hurly-burly of the fur trade, but there were other St. Louis *négociants* who immersed themselves deeply in it, and in doing so made money. One such was Jean-Louis Lambert *dit* La Fleur. Lambert, "ordinarily a resident of New Orleans," turned up in Ste. Genevieve in March 1766 after a harrowing trip up the Mississippi. Lambert and one Sieur Cazeau must have left New Orleans in the autumn of 1765, headed for St. Louis in a bateau loaded with trade goods. Somewhere along the route, they were attacked by Indians, likely Chickasaws (perennial bugbears of the French) at Chickasaw Bluffs.[23] Cazeau was snatched and dragged off, never again to be heard from, but Lambert and his crew finally fended off the attack and brought their bateau safely into port at Ste. Genevieve. Lambert recovered quickly from this setback and soon made his way on up the Mississippi to St. Louis, where he settled in as a *négociant* to engage in the Indian trade.[24]

On June 17, 1768, Lambert concluded two deals that illuminate an important nexus of the fur trade at the intermediate level. He provided to Michel Rolet *dit* La Déroute, *commerçant*, 3,525 livres and 10 sols' worth of "bonnes et loyalles [sic]" trade goods and equipment, for which La Déroute promised to pay the following May in good peltries, giving Lambert preference above all other creditors.[25] Despite La Déroute's not altogether reassuring nickname, Lambert would not have dealt with him unless he was a good risk. It is conceivable that La Déroute as a *commerçant* might in turn have struck a deal with some voyageur, providing him with the goods and equipment to trade in distant Indian villages while La Déroute himself never left St. Louis. La Déroute would then have taken a cut of the peltries before making good on his debt to Lambert. Sources do not exist to resolve this issue, but in any case La Déroute acquired his anticipated peltries and paid off Lambert on June 29, 1769, a month late but apparently without incurring any financial penalty. In something as freighted with dangers and contingencies as the fur trade, some flexibility had to be admitted by all parties involved.

During the late 1760s, Lambert was the most active *négociant* in St. Louis, and on June 17, 1768, he struck a second contract, this time with Pierre Montardy and Jean Perin *dit* Boucher.[26] Montardy, originally from Languedoc in southwestern France, had come to St. Louis as a corporal in St. Ange's company of marines, and St. Ange promoted him to sergeant.[27] But Montardy's contract with Lambert also identified him as a "commerçant," while his partner, Jean Perin *dit* Boucher, was simply a voyageur. This contract was for a whopping 6,907 livres and 15 sols' worth of "bonnes et loyalles" trade goods and equipment, which advance they agreed to pay off the following May with peltries, this time specified by type: beaver pelts, doe- and buckskins (differentiated in this contract), as well as otter, prairie wolf, and bear skins. They brought their peltries into St. Louis on June 29, 1769, the same day as Déroute, likely revealing that they all brought their peltry-laden pirogues down the Missouri or the Mississippi together in a late-spring convoy. This contract, more than any other known document, reveals the truly large sums of money involved in the early St. Louis trade, as well as the high risks run by *négociants*. Lambert's substantial investment in Montardy and Boucher was based on the expectation that they could survive and succeed in the daunting wilderness of the Upper Louisiana. The large sums and high risks involved meant that *négociants* like Lambert were in fact high-stakes gamblers, who rolled the dice every time they outfitted a voyageur in the autumn and trusted him to return to town the following spring. It is utterly remarkable how often this routine bore fruit, but as we saw with Laclède's earlier misadventure in Ste. Genevieve, trust was sometimes violated and serious losses incurred.

In a later era, *négociants* like the Chouteau brothers and Manuel Lisa themselves ascended the Missouri River to negotiate directly with Indian tribes.[28] But during the 1760s, *négociants* working in St. Louis were not that intrepid; rather, they simply supplied the goods and equipment to *commerçants* and voyageurs, who then set out in their pirogues for distant Indian villages. Lambert, for example, never sojourned north or west out of St. Louis. It is not always possible to sort out the various roles played by different participants in the complex fur-trading business. In the Montardy-Boucher partnership, perhaps only Boucher, the voyageur, sallied forth to do the trading, while Montardy remained in town managing the finances of the partnership. On August 7, 1769, for example, Montardy in his role as *commerçant* supplied the voyageur Bazile Denoyé with 193 livres' worth of trade goods.[29] In this instance, Montardy was functioning as a sort of low-level *négociant*, perhaps actually as an intermediary between someone like Lambert and the voyageur Denoyé. And to complicate matters still more, Montardy was sometimes identified as a "commerçant-voyageur," suggesting that he at least sometimes took up a paddle himself, left whatever comforts St. Louis provided, and ascended the rivers.[30] Montardy and his trading associates, Boucher and Denoyé, all owned Indian slaves,[31] which suggests a relationship between Indian slavery and the early Missouri fur trade. That is, the traders had contacts in Indian villages where slaves were sold.

Lambert invested large amounts with *commerçants,* but he was not above dealing with small-time traders as well. Antoine Malet was a young bachelor ("garçon voyageur") working out of St. Louis, and on September 27, 1768, Lambert advanced him trade goods and equipment for a fur-trading venture. Their idiosyncratic contract is of particular interest because it reveals an important point about monetary values. Lambert provided Malet with 446 livres of "trade goods and equipment, of which he has need to conduct his commerce."[32] Malet agreed to pay this amount back in the spring of 1769 (no specific date given) in peltries at the going rate in St. Louis. However, should Malet choose to settle up in Spanish currency (piastres gourdes), he would be required to pay Lambert double—892 livres' worth of piastres at an exchange rate of 5 livres/piastres, or 178 piastres and 4 reales. In other words, Spanish currency was highly devalued relative to peltries, and in fact was very rarely used in Upper Louisiana at the time.

Lambert never returned home to New Orleans, but became an important resident of St. Louis and lieutenant in the militia, despite the fact that his wife, Catherine Lépine, remained in New Orleans. Newcomers and outsiders seldom became militia officers in the Illinois Country, and St. Ange's appointment of Lambert reveals the commandant's respect for him. Lambert also conducted a good deal of business in Ste. Genevieve, where he died on December 26, 1771. Lambert's estate (only the Upper Louisiana portion), which was finally tallied up in July 1772, was very large (63,820 livres) and reveals him to have been one of the most successful of early St. Louis traders.[33] Because he was a *négociant,* substantial portions of his estate were paper obligations, and one such obligation was 3,422 livres, 10 sols, still owed by the fur traders, Montardy and Boucher, on an original advance of 7,774 livres, 10 sols, that Lambert had provided them in August 1770. These two men continually functioned as essential commercial middlemen, receiving their trade goods from Lambert in St. Louis and transporting them to Indian villages located far up the river valleys.

Scores of persons who had done business with Lambert appear in his massive estate inventory (thirty manuscript pages)—Labuxière, Lefebvre, Martigny, and Segond in St. Louis; Daniel Blouïn and Mathew Kennedy in Kaskaskia; Jean-Baptiste Datchurut in Ste. Genevieve; François Francoeur at

Arkansas Post; and even Juan José de Loyola, Spanish treasurer in New Orleans—but not Laclède.[34] Laclède apparently functioned within a very restricted circle of his own making, not generally mixing his business interests with those of other *négociants*. Lambert's house in St. Louis was a very modest *poteaux-en-terre* structure, evaluated at 1,000 livres, and he did not own a single arpent of agricultural land (*terres*) outside of town. A compulsive trader, he threw all of his time, energy, and resources into commerce. When Lambert died at Ste. Genevieve in December 1771, his wife was still a resident of New Orleans. One wonders who, if anyone other than the officiating priest, bothered to attend the burial of one of St. Louis's most important earlier residents—sic transit gloria mundi.

Louis Perrault had, like Lambert, come up to St. Louis from New Orleans early on, perhaps in 1766, to pursue the fur trade and make money. He wisely struck up a business association with a young, connected, local merchant, Joseph Papin, whose son eventually married Marie-Louise Chouteau, daughter of Madame Chouteau and Laclède.[35] Perrault's association with Papin gave him immediate and intimate entrée to the Illinois world of commerce, finance, and the fur trade. During the summer of 1769, Perrault's bateau ascended the Mississippi from New Orleans carrying not only trade goods but official letters from acting governor Aubry to St. Ange. Several "bold smokers of tobacco" on the bateau were sucking furiously on their clay pipes near a barrel of gunpowder that had been "imprudently" stored on the deck under a canvas awning. Live ashes blew from the clay pipes to the awning to the gunpowder, and puff!—Aubry's letters were burned, Perrault's trade goods damaged, and his bateau put out of commission.[36] Perrault, ever the resourceful *négociant*, enlisted another bateau and managed to get the undamaged portion of his merchandise on into St. Louis in time to conclude the all important contracts for the 1769–70 hunting and trapping season. Let us be clear, it was these essential autumnal contracts, pure and simple, that floated the economy of early St. Louis.

On September 5, 1769, "Louis La Traverse,[37] voyageur, native of Sorel in Canada but presently residing at St. Louis in the French part of Illinois [no one in St. Louis took Spanish claims to Upper Louisiana seriously until late in the year 1769]," struck a deal with "Messieurs Perrault and Papin, associated *négociants* presently at St. Louis in Illinois."[38] The *négociants* would immediately provide La Traverse with "handsome and excellent [*belles et bonnes*] trade goods and equipment," as well as an advance on the wages of his *engagés*. In return for this La Traverse obligated himself to pay Perrault and Papin, on April 1, 1770, precisely 4,892 livres, 15 sols, and 4 deniers in peltries. Such precision indicates that this was an advanced trading society; approximations simply would not do. To secure what amounted to a very large loan (a good stone house could be built in St. Louis for 2,000 livres), La Traverse mortgaged everything he owned, both real estate and personal property—in the Illinois Country, in the village of Sorel, and anywhere else in Canada. Moreover, Perrault and Papin would have first choice of La Traverse's pelts when he brought them into St. Louis the following spring. The two *négociants* signed the contract, Papin with an elegant flourish, while La Traverse could not sign at all. It is worth noting that two of three men involved in this contract were not permanent residents of St. Louis, which had become important enough as a fur-trade entrepôt to attract enterprising outsiders, traders who gravitated to it as a temporary location from which to turn a profit. These French Roman Catholic merchants were just as interested in making money as any enterprising English Puritan of Boston, the latter supposedly energized by the Protestant work ethic.

Perrault and Papin were busy *négociants* in the autumn of 1769, and on September 18 they struck a deal with Antoine Desgagné (the same Desgagné as above), who was identified as a "commerçant-voyageur," placing him in the Illinois Country trading hierarchy a half notch above a simple voyageur.[39] When the notary Labuxière drafted fur-trade contracts he used the nomenclature—*négociant, commerçant, voyageur, commerçant-voyageur, engagé*—with some precision; that is, he was thinking about the sometimes fine distinctions as he was writing. In any case, in this contract the advance was for 3,449 livres, 7 sols, and 4 deniers worth of "belles et bonnes" trade goods and equipment, in return for which Desgagné would, like La Traverse, deliver pelts of that value to Perrault and Papin on April 1, 1770. The delivery date in both of these contracts meant that La Traverse and Desgagné had to get their peltries-laden pirogues down into St. Louis as soon as the ice broke up on the upper rivers. Spring was a hectic time of year, as a multitude of pirogues pushed up to the St. Louis river landing in preparation for voyageurs and *négociants* to assemble and get the peltries sorted out and appraised. The haggling over values must have been an animated and often contentious affair, but those face-to-face exchanges on the bank of the Mississippi, between the men who brought in the pelts and the men who had supplied the trade goods, were the very heart and soul of the early St. Louis fur trade.

The fur-trading contracts struck in St. Louis constituted a sort of regional paper currency, for most contracts included a clause stipulating that whoever carried the signed document ("porteur des présentes") had a right to present it and demand payment in peltries. The IOUs were paper backed not by gold but by something just as precious in colonial Louisiana—good peltries—and this makeshift currency was an essential lubricant for the machinery of commerce in the Mississippi Valley.

Voyageurs, illiterate or not, could sometimes be major businessmen in the Illinois Country, and their reputation for integrity permitted them to assume large financial obligations. Beneath the voyageurs in the fur-trading hierarchy stood the *engagés,* whom voyageurs hired to accompany them up the rivers and into the grassroots Indian trading zones. On July 29, 1766, Joseph Texier, blacksmith, signed on with Jean-Baptiste Hamelin, voyageur, for a term of engagement lasting until the end of June 1767.[40] By signing a *contrat d'engagement,* Texier became something more than merely a hired hand in our sense of those words, for he in effect signed away his freedom for a fixed period of time. Texier obligated himself to accompany Hamelin on a trading expedition up the Missouri River and its tributaries, to do anything that Hamelin ordered him to do that was "honest and legal," and to strive to maximize Hamelin's profits and minimize his losses. And, more specifically, Texier would work at his profession as a "blacksmith [*forgeron*] in the villages where they would be trading." The image of a French blacksmith setting up his forge in remote Indian villages of the Missouri River valley is picturesque to the point of puzzlement, but in somewhat similar circumstances a blacksmith and his forge were part of Lewis and Clark's Corps of Discovery. Texier's work in Indian villages was more likely as *armurier* (gunsmith) rather than traditional *forgeron.*

Texier had specific contractual obligations, but so did Hamelin, the voyageur-entrepreneur. He would supply Texier with all the equipment for his forge, with the exception of his files (gunsmithing again comes to mind). Hamelin would also provide Texier with a blanket, a shirt, a breechcloth, and a pair of leggings, whereas Texier would supply his own undergarments, leaving us to imagine just what these might have been. And at the end of June 1767, Hamelin obligated himself to pay Texier's wages of 600 livres in peltries. This was not a trifling sum, and it demonstrates that the wealth generated by the fur trade did trickle down to some extent, even to those, like blacksmiths, who had only their skilled labor to invest.

Texier headed up the rivers to Indian villages, but stay-at-home blacksmiths in St. Louis were also vital to the fur trade. Sylvestre Labbadie was French born, like many of St. Louis's early power elite, and he apparently arrived at St. Louis in 1769. His reason for being there was purely and simply to make money in the fur trade, and he started out as a *commerçant*-voyageur, only later matriculating to the ranks of the *négociants*. In October 1770, Labbadie struck a business deal with Martin Baram, a leading blacksmith in St. Louis. Labbadie provided Baram with 682 pounds of pig iron and 169 pounds of steel, which would have arrived in St. Louis from France via New Orleans. Baram's task was to convert these metals into objects for the Indian trade ("traite sauvages"), mattocks, axes, and knife blades, of equal numbers each. The unusual Labbadie-Baram contract was for piecework, meaning that Baram would receive 25 sols (20 sols = 1 livre) in peltries for each "perfected" piece. At the time of the contract, Labbadie was about to head out of St. Louis for the 1770–71 hunting and trapping season, and Baram obligated himself to finish the job by the time that Labbadie returned the following spring (probably in May).[41] The mattocks, axes, and knives would go out to the Indian tribes when Labbadie once again set out on the rivers in the autumn of 1771 for the new hunting and trapping season.

Blacksmiths were skilled labor, and unskilled workers did less well financially. On June 12, 1768, Pierre Marcil signed on with Urbin Morice *dit* La Fantazie (the dreamer) to ascend the Missouri all the way to the villages of the Otos and Panis, which were probably located on the lower Platte River.[42] Marcil was young and unmarried ("garçon voyageur") and had no specific skills other than that of being able to man a pirogue. La Fantazie was a "commerçant-voyageur," evidently with unfulfilled dreams, and he must have done business in St. Louis with some *négociant* like Lambert or Perrault to get the supplies and equipment required for his trading sortie. Marcil agreed to do anything required of him that was "honest and legal," but, rather curiously, no terminal date was set for his contract. Rather, Marcil committed himself to wintering over with La Fantazie and remaining with him until he had finished his trading affairs and was ready to return to St. Louis. This kind of an open-ended labor contract (task rather than date defined) was unusual in the Illinois Country and likely reflects Marcil's lack of bargaining power because he was unskilled. Moreover, his wages were only 300 livres in peltries and his clothing allowance just "one blanket large enough to make a capot." Until Marcil managed to find himself a bison robe, it was going to be a mighty cold winter for him on the lower Platte River.

Unskilled *engagés* also worked in and around St. Louis. For example, in February 1767, Laclède engaged one Louis Desfond, an unmarried young fellow ("garçon volontaire"), for a one-year term. Desfond had no identified skills but would do everything required of him, apparently working on Laclède's properties in and around town. Unskilled, Desfond would receive 480 livres in peltries at the end of his term of service, but any sick days taken off work would extend his term commensurately. In addition to wages, Laclède would provide Desfond with board and lodging "in the manner usual for *engagés* in this settlement."[43] This intriguing and unusual phrase reveals that at early St. Louis, *engagés* were considered a distinct class of human being, for they were neither entirely slave nor entirely free. What this implied for their clothing, food, and shelter may only be imagined.

Some peltries harvested in Upper Louisiana made their way, on the rivers and through the lakes, out to Montreal, which had been the major entrepôt for the Canadian fur trade since mid–seventeenth century. But by the mid–eighteenth century, most furs and skins from the Illinois Country were shipped down the Mississippi to New Orleans. The first loads of peltries brought into St. Louis from the 1769–70 hunting and trapping season were sent downriver in July 1770. Captain Pedro Piernas had just assumed command as lieutenant governor in St. Louis (May 1770), and, being the officious Spaniard that he was, he required all bateau commanders heading for New Orleans to get written permission, in effect a passport or license, before departing downriver.[44] Piernas himself issued the licenses in St. Louis, while town commandant Lieutenant Louis Villars issued them in Ste. Genevieve. During the mid–eighteenth century, bateaux ascending the Mississippi from New Orleans to the Illinois Country usually traveled in convoys. Those going downriver had less incentive to do so because running with the current made them less vulnerable to attack by Indians, or riverine freebooters of whatever variety.

On July 14, 1770, Piernas issued Antoine Bêrard, "commander of a boat that Monsieur Laclède was sending to New Orleans," a commercial license, which is worth examining in some detail.[45] Bêrard was in command, and immediately under him was the "patron," the skipper, Francisco Marin (François Marin), who in turn bossed, bullied, and cursed ten crew members: Pedro (Pierre) Bernier, Pedro Quenel, Jacobo (Jacques) Budinon (?), Jorge (George) Soeper (?), Macarte (Macarty), Francisco Huruois (Michel Huron?), Juan Baptista Vien (Jean-Baptiste Vien), Francisco Larroche, Jorge Chiller, and Taxoye (Texier?); Piernas had some difficulty dealing with French and English names. The cargo was composed exclusively of peltries—320 bales of them, mostly of white-tailed deer, but also 30 of bear, 12 of beaver, and 7 of *chat* (raccoon).[46] These were Laclède's peltries, but it is not clear how he had acquired them, for there are no surviving contracts between Laclède and voyageurs during the summer of 1769, when, logically, they would have been struck to produce pelts for shipment to New Orleans in 1770. Perhaps the documents have simply not survived, or perhaps Laclède purchased pelts from freelance voyageurs who had worked in Indian villages with no contracts from *négociants*. Finally, Bêrard's bateau carried "un esclavo Indio reyo," a male Indian slave belonging to the Spanish government. This mysterious slave was not part of the crew, but was merely a passenger (perhaps an unwilling one), with no known origins and no known fate, in his person subsuming the destiny of many colonial Louisianans—black, red, and white; free and slave; female and male.

Heading downriver from St. Louis, Bêrard ordered the skipper to bring the bateau into Ste. Genevieve for several days of layover. Crew member Jorge Chiller took advantage of this opportunity to desert, and he was replaced by two other Englishmen, John Brown and John Smith. Bêrard likely recruited these men from Kaskaskia, which after the arrival of British forces in 1765 had developed a small English population of merchants and boatmen, vagabonds, deserters and desperadoes. Ste. Genevieve commandant Lieutenant Louis Villars authorized the changes in personnel for Bêrard's bateau (also changing Jorge Chiller's name to Georges Shills), and also added

69 bales of peltries, mostly deerskins, to Bêrard's manifest.[47] Young Auguste Chouteau happened to be in Ste. Genevieve at the time serving as Laclède's proxy, and he must have purchased the additional peltries from local suppliers who were looking for a practical way to get their goods downriver to New Orleans.

In addition to handling the peltries, Chouteau had another responsibility in Ste. Genevieve. Most of Bêrard's crew members were working within the terms of labor contracts negotiated in St. Louis before the bateau headed downriver. For whatever reason, this had not gotten done for one crew member, Jean-Baptiste Vien, and Chouteau had to get the matter rectified in Ste. Genevieve. Vien contracted to serve as a boatman under the orders of François Marin, Bêrard's skipper, for the purpose of going to New Orleans, and agreed to do everything that Marin ordered him to do that was legal and honest.[48] This contract was exclusively for the trip downriver, which required at most four weeks, and Vien's wages, due in New Orleans, would be 65 livres. Vien would have to find his own way back to St. Louis, likely by signing another labor contract in New Orleans that would pay, given the arduous three-month trip upriver, substantially more. Chouteau signed the contract,[49] which spelled out that he was doing so only as proxy for Laclède. Leaving Ste. Genevieve on July 23, Bêrard's bateau would have arrived in New Orleans no later than the end of August.

We know more about Vien's quotidian existence than that of any other boatman from early St. Louis. In February 1770, "Jean-Baptiste Vien, billiard master," leased a complete billiard outfit—table, felt cover, cues, and balls—to Louis Vigé, "commerçant," for a period of three years.[50] Vigé was intending to operate a lucrative entertainment center, for he agreed to pay Vien 600 livres in peltries each year for the billiard setup. Billiard parlors, rather than taverns, served as entertainment centers in the Illinois Country, and of course gambling and drinking accompanied the billiards. Vien was illiterate, but he was a savvy businessman, and his investments were working for him in St. Louis while he labored on the Mississippi. And as a "billiard master," he may have been able to hustle novices in New Orleans and get into their pockets. Vien soon gained enough experience on the river to get promoted from boatman to *patron*. In 1771 he skippered Bêrard's *berge* (a smaller version of the flat-bottomed bateau) loaded with 14,300 livres of flour and three packets of peltries from Ste. Genevieve to New Orleans.[51] Vien was a fellow who made his way, who earned success with energy, discipline, and good luck in the small, dangerous, and complex, world of the eighteenth-century Mississippi River.

On July 28, 1770, Piernas presented a passport to "Señor Luis Perrault, Bourgeois."[52] Piernas used "Bourgeois" here in a vaguely Marxist sense, meaning a person who lived by capital investments rather than physical labor. Louis Perrault, who is always identified as a *négociant* in French documents, wanted to take a bateau load of peltries down to New Orleans. These would have been the pelts and skins that La Traverse and Desgagné had contracted to deliver to Perrault at St. Louis in April (as seen above). Perrault's skipper was (Louis?) Lecompte, who had a crew of three *engagés* (Rivet, Renault and Jan[?]), six black slaves, and one mulatto. The cargo consisted of 112 bales of assorted peltries—doeskins, beaver, bear, and cat—and 300 bales of buckskins. In addition, there was one large barrel of flour and 500 pounds of flour in sacks headed for Arkansas Post. It was not at all unusual for Arkansas Post to need imported flour, but it was usually furnished by Ste. Genevieve rather than St. Louis, for St. Louis itself often needed more flour than its fields and mills could produce. In 1770 Joseph Tellier shipped 22,700 pounds of flour from Ste. Genevieve to New Orleans in two pirogues, which provides us with some idea of the impressive size of eighteenth-century freight pirogues. New Orleans had an insatiable appetite for Illinois flour from its founding throughout the colonial period—and beyond.[53]

As Laclède's bateau had done several weeks earlier, Perrault's bateau laid over for several days at Ste. Genevieve, and local commandant Villars authorized additions to the bateau's load: 2 bales of beaver pelts, 2.5 bales of doeskins, 1 of otter pelts, 28 buckskins, and 500 pounds of flour for Arkansas Post.[54] Leaving Ste. Genevieve on August 11, and with a stop at Arkansas Post, probably put Perrault's bateau into the docks at New Orleans late in November 1770.

While peltry-laden bateaux were preparing to descend the Mississippi from the Illinois Country to New Orleans in the summer and early fall of 1770, contracts were being struck in St. Louis regarding the peltries that would be brought into town during the spring of 1771, following the winter's hunting and trapping season. The former notary, Labuxière, was kept frenetically busy as scribe drafting these contracts on behalf of Lieutenant Governor Pedro Piernas, whose signature on the completed documents made them official. On one day, August 22, 1770, Labuxière drew up four trading contracts, as *négociants, commerçants,* and voyageurs concluded their haggling and deal making and came to Piernas's office ("chambre du government") to get things written up in proper legal fashion.[55] Three of these contracts involved Louis Lambert, who was advancing a hefty 8,370 livres and 17 sols' worth of merchandise to various traders.

Also on August 22, Laclède struck a contract with two men, Jacques Chauvin, a *négociant* like Laclède himself, and Pierre La Déroute (brother to Michel above?), a simple trader, advancing them 828 livres and 10 sols' worth of trade goods.[56] As we saw above, Laclède preferred working through an intermediary, in this case Chauvin, rather than directly with the individual, La

Déroute, who would ascend the rivers to the Indian villages. Lambert, on the other hand, dealt directly with La Déroute, advancing him 173 livres' worth of merchandise on the same day.[57] One imagines an animated group of *négociants, commerçants,* and voyageurs gathered near the center of St. Louis on that sultry August day, cutting deals this way and that, La Déroute, for example, doing business with Laclède and Lambert virtually simultaneously. A few days earlier, Lambert and Laclède had cooperated to provide Nicolas Royer *dit* Sans Quartier with 3,332 livres and 7 sols' worth of trade goods.[58] Lambert had struck the original deal with Sans Quartier, but Laclède wanted in on the action, and Lambert obliged and cut him in to the tune of 1,691 livres, 10 sols, roughly half the total value of the merchandise advanced to Sans Quartier. Again, we see Laclède functioning one step removed, letting Lambert do the face-to-face haggling with the *commerçant*-voyageur, in this case Sans Quartier. Lambert's total investment in fur-trading futures during one week of August 1770 (8,370 livres, 17 sols) was more than ten times what Laclède put up.

The routine of shipping peltries down the Mississippi to New Orleans in 1771 was very much the same as in 1770, although, somewhat oddly, two merchants usually based in St. Louis, Perrault and Lambert, dispatched their respective bateaux downriver from Ste. Genevieve. This meant that Lieutenant Villars, rather than Lieutenant Governor Piernas, drafted the passports. On November 18, Louis Perrault *père* (senior) received his papers to send a bateau to New Orleans, but this time rather than going himself, his son, Perrault *fils* (junior), would accompany the crew. As in 1770, Perrault's skipper was Lecomte, under whose command were two *engagés*, Dubut and Baudouin; five slaves (likely all blacks);[59] and one black lad ("négrillon"), all belonging to Perrault. And in 1771 Perrault's bateau had a more diverse and interesting cargo than in 1770—in addition to the usual deer, otter, beaver, and bear pelts, there were two bales of buffalo robes, three kegs of onions, 9,000 pounds of flour, and numerous cases of fruit, each with a specific address attached. During the colonial era, apples were often shipped from Ste. Genevieve to New Orleans, sometimes in small quantities as gifts and sometimes in bulk as commercial products.[60] In this instance, it appears that Perrault was sending apples as gifts to various personal friends and business associates in New Orleans. Upon arriving in New Orleans, Perrault's slaves would be delivering the welcome Illinois Country apples just before Christmas baking season began. Perrault's bateau checked in at Manchac (situated on the isthmus between the Mississippi and Lake Pontchartrain) on December 18 and would have arrived in New Orleans just one day later.

On November 28, 1771, Villars issued a passport to Louis Lambert, "lieutenant in the St. Louis militia," but for the time being conducting business out of Ste. Genevieve.[61] Lambert was sending "une berge" to New Orleans with a load of peltries—doe, bear, and buffalo hides; raccoon and *pichoux* (lynx or bobcat)[62] skins; as well as 1,300 pounds of flour, this likely destined for Arkansas Post. François (?) Durcy was skipper of Lambert's bateau, which had a crew of four *engagés* (Germain, Boucher, [Jean-Baptiste] Vien, and Michel Huron *dit* Lorette), and three black slaves (two men and one woman) all belonging to Lambert. Presumably, the female slave came along as cook and laundry woman, for no evidence exists that female slaves, either blacks or Indians, were compelled to perform arduous labor of any kind in the Illinois Country. This bateau's progress down the Mississippi to New Orleans may be followed with some exactitude. Pushing off from Ste. Genevieve on November 28, it checked in at Arkansas Post on December 19, at Pointe Coupée on the twenty-ninth, and at Manchac on the thirty-first. Durcy was a hard-driving skipper, and likely the bateau proceeded on into New Orleans on Wednesday, January 1, 1772, just in time for the crew to celebrate New Year's. The boat's owner, Lambert, did not survive to see 1772, however, for he had died the week before in Ste. Genevieve. His widow, Catherine Lépine, was left (with her six children) to sort out her late husband's complicated affairs, including the boatload of skins and furs that had just arrived from the Illinois Country.[63]

A commercial network between the Illinois Country and the Gulf Coast (especially to Mobile) had commenced soon after Kaskaskia was established in 1703. This meant that even before New Orleans was founded in 1718, Illinois merchants were connected with the wide world of Atlantic trade and commerce. Shipping records from the very early eighteenth century have not survived, but the old habit of using the expression "à la mer" (to the sea) when pirogues and bateaux descended the Mississippi to the Gulf Coast region on commercial ventures continued on into the 1720s. After 1718 "to the sea" from the Illinois Country meant to New Orleans, even though the expression was not precisely accurate.[64] By the 1760s, this commercial network had become routinized, it had become safer, and the time required for the round trip had been somewhat reduced. Pirogues and bateaux may have been improved over the decades, and boatmen had perhaps become more specialized and therefore more skilled. Surviving labor contracts from the 1760s reveal that the young men who worked the route between the Illinois Country and New Orleans were a different set than those who worked from St. Louis up the rivers to the Indian villages. Perhaps this was a matter of the different skills demanded, or perhaps it was a consequence of individual tastes—some men preferred to embrace the challenges of trading in the remote wilderness; others had a hankering to luxuriate for a few days in the cafés and bordellos at New Orleans before they had to face the daunting task of ascending the Mississippi.

Recently, historian Daniel K. Richter has written that following the Treaty of Paris (1763), "a substantial French *population* remained [in the Illinois

Country], but no French *government* or trading connections provided a counterbalance to British hegemony."[65] Well, during the period 1766–70, a French government most decidedly did function in St. Louis, and an agent of that government, the French notary Labuxière, was indispensable for facilitating the complex trading connections that pullulated in the settlement. And the multiplicity of traders who sustained these connections meant that the very notion of a British trading hegemony in the Illinois Country is ludicrous. If this chapter has no other purpose, it should serve as a counterbalance to pervasive misconceptions about the Illinois Country that infest much historical scholarship, even the most recent and best known.

Finally, a word about Indians and their involvement in the early St. Louis fur trade. A large and growing body of literature exists about Indians, including Indian women, and the fur trade,[66] and indubitably they were indispensable to the St. Louis trade. Traders who sallied forth up the rivers each autumn usually wintered over in Indian villages. Joseph Texier, the blacksmith mentioned above, did not set up his temporary forge in a vacuum, but certainly in an (Osage?) Indian village. And certainly Texier's master, Jean-Baptiste Hamelin, depended largely on Indians for harvesting and processing the peltries with which his pirogue was loaded when it pulled into the riverbank at St. Louis in the spring of 1767.

Furthermore, Indians (mostly from Illinois tribes) sometimes accompanied traders working out of St. Louis, but these Indians do not appear in the notarial contracts inscribed in St. Louis. Sometimes this was because the Indians were slaves and their labor was subsumed within legal agreements made by their masters; chapter 4 recounted the furor provoked in 1767 when Big Osages killed three Indian slaves working with French traders in the Arkansas River valley. Sometimes, perhaps often, free Indians functioned as unofficial and silent partners to white or métis traders, as when in 1768 Missouri Indians killed an Illinois Indian, partner of a French trader, far up the Missouri River.[67] This unnamed trader had very likely struck a contract with a *commerçant* or *négociant* in St. Louis before setting off upriver with his trade goods, but his Indian partner would not have appeared in the contract. Indians were omnipresent in and around St. Louis during the 1760s, but surviving documents tell us very little about their precise roles within that colonial village society. Assumptions must sometimes suffice, and assumptions are often seductive and always dangerous for historians striving to re-create a past that is necessarily imagined but for which empirical data must place limits on the imagination.

CHAPTER 11

End of an Era

Monsieur Louis St. Ange de Bellerive, former captain in the infantry, just died at the residence of Madame Chouteau in this post of St. Louis. We went forthwith to the room in which he died and found the deceased recumbent on his bed.

—Joseph Labuxière, 9:00 a.m., Tuesday, December 27, 1774

In 1768 Governor Ulloa drafted a careful evaluation of St. Ange for the Marqués Jerónimo de Grimaldi, Carlos III's minister of war and navy. "Yes, he's an old man, but he's very well known among the tribes. He's been at Pencur (that is, Paincourt [St. Louis]) since Fort de Chartres passed to the British. He must be kept in command there, not only because of the way he handles himself but because of his credit and reputation among the Indians."[1] Significantly, Ulloa's praise of St. Ange focused on his skills as an Indian diplomatist. From the time that St. Ange de Bellerive was stationed with his father at Fort St. Joseph (1720–21) until he arrived at St. Louis as commandant in October 1765, not a day passed that he did not have dealings of one sort or another with Indians of one tribe or another. His entire adult life was all about Indians, and not only in the public arena, for we must also reckon with the Indian women who bore his children.

In discussing Indian affairs, St. Ange never once, ever, suggested employing force of any kind as an instrument of policy. Although a military man, his passion, his knowledge, and his skill lay in diplomacy, not warfare. In this regard, he was perhaps the best the American West would ever see. He succeeded in maintaining the peace (and relative tranquillity) under trying circumstances at Fort d'Orléans during the 1720s and '30s, at Vincennes during the '40s and '50s, and at Chartres and St. Louis during the '60s. Compare St. Ange to other soldiers of the North American West, Philip Henry Sheridan ("The only good Indian is a dead Indian") or George Armstrong Custer (Washita Massacre) as examples, these two spilling Indian blood wantonly, even gleefully. This was never, ever, the modus operandi of St. Ange; it would have revolted him. It stretches credulity to think of a white military man serving in the midst of Indian territory in the American West, yet having no blood on his hands. But such seems to have been the case with St. Ange.

Yet, regretfully, we know almost nothing about St. Ange's innermost feelings about Indians. He was not a man given to discussing feelings, those of his own or those of others, for he was always more concerned with action and results rather than ruminations and reservations. From what we know of his life, this much may be safely said: St. Ange was certainly at heart no Indian killer, in the manner of George Rogers Clark. Indeed, not a scintilla of evidence exists that he ever killed an Indian, as Daniel Boone did, or even fired a shot at one in anger or in fear. Surely, he would not have agreed with George Washington's chilling assessment that Indians were like wolves that should best be exterminated.[2] St. Ange was surely no racialist. The word *race* appears in no known manuscript from the eighteenth-century Illinois Country, and discussion of racial attitudes in the region is a problematic exercise.[3] Indeed, the very notion of race as it came to be elaborated in the nineteenth century was alien to St. Ange, as it generally was to all persons of French extraction living in the Illinois Country.[4]

Whether St. Ange had any interest in or respect for Indian culture that went beyond what was useful to him in his diplomatic work with various tribes is unknown. What he discussed with the Indian women with whom he had intimate relations is far beyond the reach of historians who must rely on written sources that carry us into St. Ange's bedroom on only one occasion—when he was on his deathbed in his apartment *chez* Madame Chouteau. Surely, St. Ange was no proto-anthropologist, imbued with a sense of cultural relativism that led him to view all cultures as fundamentally equal. St. Ange remarked about how Indians had become dependent on European trade goods, noting that if the fur trade emanating from St. Louis got disrupted, "the Indian tribes, who are accustomed to the same things we have, will come and attack us. These barbarians [*barbares*] do not listen to reason when there is nothing to give them, and the best way to keep them at a distance is to take things out to them."[5] Captain Franciso Ríu used identical language when he praised St. Ange's abilities in dealing with Indians, claiming that he was "both practical and intelligent handling the barbarians [*varvaros*]."[6] But it is hard to say precisely what St. Ange and Ríu had in mind when employing the word *barbarian*. Probably, they meant people who lacked European manners, mores, and customs. That is, both St. Ange and Ríu used the word pretty much as Greeks had originally, in reference to people who did not participate in their civilization, someone who did not speak their language. In this regard, Juliana Barr has observed that Spanish "officials might refer rhetorically to 'indios barbaros' or other generic groupings of Indians, yet even then the label was not used to convey a racial or cultural identity but rather a political one designating Indians independent of Spanish rule."[7] Or, as David

J. Weber has recently noted, "While Spanish scholars created taxonomies and examined shades of meaning, in popular parlance Spaniards of the late eighteenth century used barbaros, salvajes, bravos, and gentiles interchangeably to describe Amerindians who lived beyond the pale of Christendom."[8]

French colonial officials frequently employed the phrase "for the good of the service." "Service" was often qualified as that "of the king," or, occasionally, "of his majesty," and missionary priests sometimes expanded the phrase to "the good of the service and the progress of religion [that is, the Roman Catholic religion]."[9] When St. Ange referred to his devotion "to the service," the phrase generally meant for him the regime of government represented by the Bourbon monarchy, whether it was that of Louis XV or that of Carlos III. But on two occasions, he employed the phrase "the good of the service" in a manner that enlarged, and perhaps altered somewhat, the definition of the phrase. When in the spring of 1764 St. Ange was preparing to depart Vincennes in order to assume command at Fort de Chartres, he crammed into one brief paragraph "good of the service [bien du service]," "public good [bien du publique]," and "public interest [l'interait du publique]."[10] No royal or religious entity was added to qualify any of these phrases. And three years later, St. Ange wrote on the same subject to Philippe Aubry, acting French governor of Louisiana. Concluding a letter to Aubry, whose political views and attitudes were similar to his, St. Ange explained his "zeal for the good of the service and the public interest [zèle pour le bien du service et l'interêt publique]."[11] In principle, St. Ange was serving an old-fashioned divine-right, absolute monarchy, but in practice his political views were more modern and more secular, although he would never have used those particular words. The fundamental purpose of any government, including the one that St. Ange was serving, was to serve the public interest. This placed St. Ange squarely within the political sensibility of the eighteenth century, during which enlightened opinion in the Western world turned aggressively in the direction of demanding that government be justified on utilitarian grounds, that is, precisely on how well it served St. Ange's "public good."[12]

⚜ ⚜ ⚜ ⚜

By the spring of 1770, St. Ange de Bellerive wanted nothing more than to be relieved of his command at St. Louis; he had been pleading this case for years. He had enjoyed a very long life, living to a much riper age than the vast majority of his fellow citizens in colonial St. Louis. This may have been due in part to favorable genes (his father, Robert Grotton de St. Ange, had lived into his mid-seventies), in part to good luck, and perhaps in part to having practiced a healthy lifestyle—active, temperate, and disciplined. Ruminating over his long life, St. Ange could not help but conclude that it had been a successful one and that his professional successes—at Fort d'Orléans, Vincennes, Fort de

Chartres, and St. Louis—had been earned achievements. This in turn likely led him to spend his last months on earth somewhat comforted by a justified sense of satisfaction about his life as a whole, even though he had never married and left no legitimate children to carry on his distinguished name.

During the last seventeen months of his life, St. Ange lived in the residence of Marie-Thérèse Chouteau. Other than the bare fact of this residential arrangement, however, we have no evidence about their personal relationship. Madame Chouteau (her estranged but legitimate husband, René Chouteau, did not die in New Orleans until 1776) was a full three decades younger than St. Ange. She appears so maternal and commanding in her portrait from later years that it is difficult to image her as a daughter, but she may well have assumed a filial attitude toward the old captain, one of the few persons in St. Louis more formidable than she. Lieutenant Governor Piernas repaired to Madame Chouteau's house early in the afternoon of Monday, December 26, 1774, to witness the last will and testament that St. Ange dictated as he lay on his bed, "dangerously ill but sound in memory and understanding." Five men accompanied Piernas, including Jean-Baptiste Martigny (captain of the militia), and Joseph Labuxière, St. Ange's former notary. With St. Ange on his deathbed staring at eternity, Labuxière inscribed his spoken words, and the final testament that resulted is one of the most precious manuscripts in the archives of the Missouri History Museum.[13] Over the preceding decade, Labuxière had drafted hundreds of documents on behalf of St. Ange; this would be his last.

Signatures on St. Ange's last will and testament, drawn up by Joseph Labuxière in St. Ange's bedchamber on the afternoon of December 26, 1774. St. Ange's hand was shaky but his mind clear when he dictated the will, which documents his final thoughts about death and the disposition of his worldly possessions, including his Indian slaves. He died early the next morning. Courtesy of the Missouri History Museum, St. Louis.

First came the boilerplate: St. Ange, as "a good Christian, Catholic, Apostolic and Roman has consigned his soul to God, to the Holy Virgin, and to all the saints in the heavenly court, supplicating them to intercede on his behalf with the All Mighty One." Although these were stock phrases, no doubt exists that St. Ange was serious about every word. Next, St. Ange, in orderly fashion, arranged to have minor debts paid off from the proceeds of his estate. He owed Madame Chouteau for board and room going back to August 1, 1773; (Joseph) Deschênes for twenty-five loads of firewood; and Laville, a tailor, for a riding coat, a dress jacket, a vest, and two pairs of knee britches (*culottes*).[14] St. Ange had some cash reserves on hand, somewhat surprising in a community that depended almost exclusively on peltries as currency. He bequeathed three hundred livres in French money (*en argent*) to his friend Antoine Bêrard and three hundred livres in Spanish currency (*en piastres*) to his niece Élisabeth Coulon de Villiers de Volsey.

Because St. Ange had no wife, no legitimate children, and no real estate, his most valuable possessions—by a huge margin—were his Indian slaves, and there is no hint in his will that "as good Christian" he had any scruples about owning slaves. Only on rare occasions did Roman Catholic clergy in the Illinois Country voice any objections to Indian slavery,[15] and newfangled Enlightenment ideas from the Atlantic world that questioned the morality and even the utility of slavery had not yet seeped into Upper Louisiana. Indeed, even on the Atlantic Seaboard, people of St. Ange's generation were morally complacent about slavery. Peter Jefferson (born 1708) suffered none of the tortured moral qualms about slavery that his son (born 1743) did. In any case, as we saw in chapter 8, St. Ange conveyed three "red" slaves, a mother and two children, to his niece Joachine Coulon de Villiers de Belestre.[16] This was perfectly legal, for Indian slaves that Louisianans had acquired before Governor Alejandro O'Reilly's 1769 decree banning commerce in Indian slaves continued to be heritable property and could be conveyed from one owner to another through succession documents.[17]

What transpired in St. Ange's room at his bedside in Madame Chouteau's house during the few hours (less than twenty-four) that lapsed between the time he signed his will, at 2:00 p.m., December 26, with a shaky but legible hand, and the hour of his death may be pieced together with some accuracy. Father Valentin performed the last rites of the Roman Catholic Church, as per his burial record,[18] but there is no evidence that St. Ange and Valentin were on intimate, or even friendly, terms. Although Angélique appears in St. Ange's final testament merely as property to be transmitted, she was the flesh-and-blood entity physically (and emotionally?) closest to the dying man. And given the virtual certainty that she was resident within St. Ange's allotted space in Madame Chouteau's house, she likely kept a bedside death vigil. Angélique would have been the last person to see St. Ange alive, and she was the last person with whom he ever communicated—a squeeze of the hand or a flicker of eyelids by candlelight. It was fitting and proper that this should be so, for they had been through much together during the preceding decade. St. Ange's death scene in St. Louis—a French marine officer being comforted by his Indian slave concubine—distills many essences about life, and death, in the eighteenth-century Illinois Country; our reimagining of that time and that place would not be complete without it.

Only on very rare occasions do sources from the Illinois Country tell us the exact time of a person's death,[19] and the moment when St. Ange's "soul separated from his body" (how he defined death in his will) is not known. Piernas, Laclède, and Labuxière arrived at Madame Chouteau's at 9:00 a.m., Tuesday, December 27, and found St. Ange dead in his bed. They forthwith removed the body and secured his room and his "grande armoire" with strips of white paper sealed with red wax.[20] Gravediggers (probably village militiamen) worked quickly, perhaps having to break through the earth's frozen crust in the small churchyard, and St. Ange was buried the same day, rigor mortis perhaps not having yet set in. When François Vallé was buried at Ste. Genevieve in September 1783, the conscientious and alcoholic priest Pierre Gibault took the time and trouble to note in the burial record that the entire parish had turned out at the interment to pay their respects.[21] In contrast, when Valentin buried St. Ange, he simply noted that St. Ange had been a captain in the Louisiana battalion (of the Spanish army); the brevity of the burial record for a man of large stature and many accomplishments is cold and unsatisfying.[22] If St. Ange had had his way, the priest would instead have recorded that St. Ange, like his father before him, had served France as a marine officer for a half century, with loyalty to the Illinois Country that never wavered. Without doubt, a sizable crowd, if not the entire parish, attended St. Ange's burial, although December 27 may have been a blustery, bitter day on the bluff overlooking the Mississippi River. The assembled mourners included all of St. Ange's former marines, whom he had led out of Fort de Chartres in October 1765 and guided on their mission of destiny, to cross the Mississippi and secure, for the Bourbon monarchy and for French civilization, the new settlement on the west bank of the river.

St. Ange's will states that he wished to dispose properly of the few worldly possessions ("peu de biens") that God had seen fit to grant him. On Friday, December 30, Pierre Laclède, whom St. Ange had designated executor of his estate, appointed two sharp moneymen, Jean-Baptiste Sarpy and Joseph Segond, to appraise St. Ange's possessions.[23] Sarpy and Segond, *négociants* who traded regularly with New Orleans, knew the value of material things as well as anyone in Upper Louisiana. The compilation of worldly goods that resulted from their appraisal casts light on the daily life of a professional, disinterested military man, a man devoted to his calling who had absolutely no interest in pursuing riches. Virtually all of St. Ange's material possessions were contained within his rented quarters *chez* Madame Chouteau.

St. Ange's apartment within this residence was a relatively commodious space. The stone house that Laclède had given her in 1768 measured 50×34 pieds, and if St. Ange occupied, say, one-half of the second floor, that gave him (and Angélique) approximately 450 square feet of living space; this was more floor space than characterized many houses in St. Louis at the time. St. Ange's space was perhaps informally divided into three distinct areas based on use: St. Ange's sleeping area, Angélique's sleeping area, and a commons area for cooking, eating, and socializing. Ornamenting the walls, St. Ange had a framed mirror (a common feature in Illinois Country residences) and, intriguingly and much more rare, "un tableau representant d'un personage." Who was this "personage"? Obviously, it was not St. Ange himself, or someone well known such as Louis XV, but perhaps St. Ange's father, Robert Grotton, who had visited New Orleans in 1722 with Father Pierre-François Xavier de Charlevoix and where perhaps Robert could have had a crude portrait done.

The very large array of cooking equipment (pots, kettles, frying pans, even a serrated pot hanger for the stone fireplace) and eating utensils (sterling-silver place settings and faience plates) leaves no doubt that cooking and eating occurred within St. Ange's chambers. Angélique must have prepared the food, and one can only imagine the ingredients—likely heavy on bread, meats (including venison), and dairy products, for St. Ange owned a milk cow and her calf that were pastured on Madame Chouteau's spacious residential property as well as a bull, who was "errant in the woods." The lactating cow provided them with rich cream for their morning coffee, which Angélique served at a black walnut table with doe-foot legs. The subjects of their breakfast conversation would take us as deep into the manners and morals and mores of the French Illinois Country as any that may be imagined.

St. Ange was fond of powdered tobacco, having no fewer than five receptacles (two silver boxes, one cardboard box, and two flasks) from which to dispense a favored (for both men and women) eighteenth-century delicacy. He would have placed a pinch of tobacco on the back of his hand and then snorted it, with the accompanying pleasure, up his nose. If this small indulgence provoked a paroxysm of sneezing, St. Ange had ten red cotton handkerchiefs (fabric of Rouen) with which to muffle the squall. St. Ange generally had fastidious personal habits: he owned four washbasins, a brick and a half of fancy soap (appraised at 6 livres), a faience shaving dish, and several razors. His twenty-one linen shirts were his most valued material possessions (appraised at an aggregate of 365 livres), worth more than his five sterling-silver place settings and large silver ladle (together 195 livres). Each morning before conducting official business, St. Ange slipped on a fresh linen shirt, then a vest of silver-based fabric ("fond d'argent"), and completed his attire with a burgundy suit (jacket and culottes) fashioned of silk serge. The value of this entire outfit, minus the shirt, was 120 livres. And on special dress occasions, and perhaps at Mass, St. Ange carried a dress sword with a roped silver handle. Laclède paid 60 livres for this sword when St. Ange's effects were auctioned off on January 30, 1775.[24] The sword had reified Ange's political and military authority in St. Louis, but animistic forces had no effect in this instance, and the sword's soul never conveyed that authority to Laclède. In any case, a royal ordinance of 1720 forbade bourgeois like Laclède from carrying swords in the colonies, as they were also in France.[25]

St. Ange had three pairs of spectacles for use when writing or reading, and to facilitate writing he had a faience inkstand that incorporated a small caddy containing blotting sand. St. Ange's library consisted of a mere handful of books: Paul de Briquet's *Code Militaire* was a professional handbook that became a classic and went through multiple editions during St. Ange's lifetime; Pierre-François-Xavier de Charlevoix's *Histoire de l'Isle espagnole ou de S. Domingue* in two volumes was a luxury edition, bringing a whopping 16 livres and 10 sols at auction;[26] and the two nameless "livres de piété," which, on the other hand, brought only a paltry 15 sols.[27] St. Ange's library was minuscule compared to the two hundred volumes owned by Laclède when he died in 1778,[28] but then St. Ange was a provincial French Canadian military man, whereas Laclède was a cosmopolitan French merchant. When St. Ange's effects were auctioned off, his bull was still "errant in the woods," relishing the exhilarating freedom of movement that many of God's creatures, both bestial and human, enjoyed in the Illinois Country. St. Ange's personal possessions

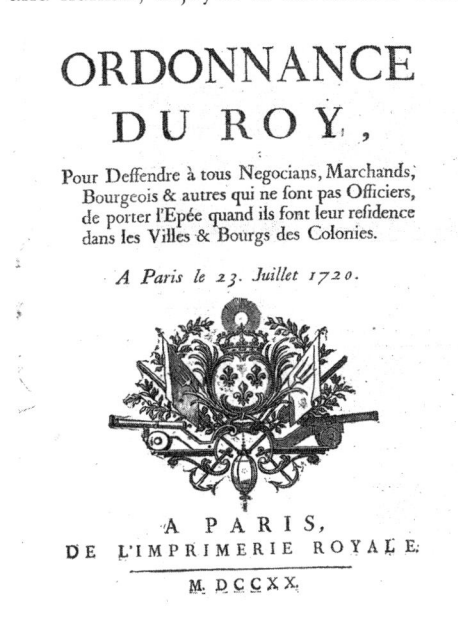

ORDONNANCE DU ROY,

Pour Deffendre à tous Negocians, Marchands, Bourgeois & autres qui ne font pas Officiers, de porter l'Epée quand ils font leur refidence dans les Villes & Bourgs des Colonies.

A Paris le 23. Juillet 1720.

A PARIS,
DE L'IMPRIMERIE ROYALE.
M. DCCXX.

Ordonnance du Roy, 1720. This royal ordinance prohibited the carrying of swords in French colonies by men who were not officers. Pierre Laclède's purchase of St. Ange's sword at the dead man's estate auction has a pathetic quality, for a man of bourgeois stock could never properly wear this emblem of aristocracy. Reproduced from Recueil des édits, déclarations et arrests de Sa Majesté concernant l'administration de justice et la police des colonies françaises de l'Amérique *(Paris, 1744).*

could just as well have been those of a provincial official in metropolitan France. A recent analysis has it that members of the Lewis and Clark Expedition became "Indianized" during the course of their epic western trek. And in the same vein, Carolyn Gilman has subtly suggested that "to take on the clothing of another culture was to surrender part of themselves."[29] Little or no evidence of such Indianization appears among St. Ange's material possessions—perhaps the two beaver-skin robes, although North American furs and beaver-felt hats were ubiquitous in Europe. St. Ange's sole possessions that reveal him definitively to have been an American man whose long life had transpired on the remote and exotic eighteenth-century Illinois Country frontier, and in everyday contact with Indians, were not material but rather human—his three Indian slaves. Labuxière, noting their presence at the head of the inventory, laconically remarked that the "slaves have been turned over to Madame Belestre in accordance with the intention of the deceased, and are therefore not eligible for valuation." Labuxière was, of course, thinking in strictly monetary terms, but even if he had wished to expand his vision and sensibility to include social and emotional values, he would not have been able to put a price on them—nor perhaps could St. Ange have done so.

⚜ ⚜ ⚜ ⚜

Joseph Labuxière plays a large role in this book—indeed, in some chapters a larger role than St. Ange himself. Manuscript sources conclusively demonstrate Labuxière's importance in holding St. Louis together as a community that adhered to French customary laws and legal practices. Between 1766 and 1770 he virtually single-handedly created the paper trail of documents necessary to maintain a cohesive and thoroughly French society at the frontier outpost. When Lieutenant Governor Piernas arrived in St. Louis in May 1770, Labuxière's positions as notary and judge were quickly suppressed, in accordance with General O'Reilly's orders.[30] Henceforth, Spanish commandants rather than notaries would exercise all legal authority in St. Louis, and Piernas's presence immediately became ubiquitous in the village's official business. Legal documents, including marriage contracts, consistently began, "Before us, Don Pedro Piernas, captain of infantry and lieutenant governor of the province of Illinois and its dependencies that belong to His Catholic Majesty."[31]

Piernas had once sneered at Labuxière, calling him a "notorious drunk,"[32] but when he arrived in St. Louis Piernas must have summoned Labuxière, sat down with him, and learned the correct formulas and phrases for drafting documents in proper French form, for they continued to be done in that fashion, whether drafted in French or in Spanish, for the remainder of the colonial regime.[33] After Piernas's arrival, Labuxière continued to serve as scribe for drafting documents (including St. Ange's last will and testament), for he possessed unsurpassed knowledge of St. Louis's legal affairs; his signature appears frequently as a witness—but never again as notary, attorney, or judge.

Curiously, in July 1772, Labuxière applied for permission to move back to the east side of the Mississippi River. Piernas relayed the request to Governor Unzaga, who found Labuxière's request "out-of-bounds, frivolous, contrary to principles of loyalty and therefore not admissible."[34] Unzaga considered the British side of the river already as enemy territory, although Spain and Great Britain would not officially go to war until 1779; the governor did not wish to lose a valued subject of Spain. In order to supplement his income as a scribe in St. Louis, Labuxière decided to try his hand at the fur trade. In August 1774, he struck a contract with Louis Dufresne (Labuxière drafted the contract, which was rendered official by Piernas's signature) to conduct three thousand livres' worth of commerce with the Big Osages.[35] Labuxière acknowledged that he could not personally conduct trade with Indians because of his lack of experience in that exacting trade, but rather he would supply an *engagé* to accompany Dufresne up the Missouri River to the Osage villages. Labuxière apparently enjoyed some success in the Indian trade, for in 1777 he received a license (in partnership with Michel Lamy) to conduct twenty-two hundred livres' worth of commerce with the Missouri tribe.[36] Yet trade was not Labuxière's natural *métier*, and he continued to draft (but not notarize) documents for the francophone residents of St. Louis until 1780.[37] Soon after that, he finally succeeded in moving across the Mississippi to the American-occupied side of the river, and in 1782 he appeared in legal papers as state's attorney ("procureur de l'état") in Kaskaskia.[38] Interestingly, the same year, the inhabitants of Kaskaskia petitioned the district magistrates to require all who lived there to adhere to French domestic law, that is, the *Coutume de Paris*.[39]

The peripatetic Labuxière eventually reestablished his home in Cahokia, just across the Mississippi from the village whose infancy he had done so much to nurture. In 1790 the new American governor of the Northwest Territory, General Arthur St. Clair, appointed him notary for the District of Cahokia. In this role, Labuxière was responsible for what he did best: guaranteeing the authority of French customary law to those who made contracts and agreements under its terms. The Northwest Ordinance of 1787 provided for the "descent and conveyance of property" according to the laws and customs of the "French and Canadian inhabitants, and other settlers of the Kaskaskies, St. Vincents and the neighboring villages."[40] Fittingly, one of the first estates to be administered under this guarantee was Labuxière's own, for he died at Cahokia in April 1791.[41] The timeless Pierre Gibault (he had arrived in the Illinois Country in 1768) officiated at Labuxière's burial. As Gibault was wont to do for important persons, and to gladden the hearts of future historians, he inscribed an extended burial record: Labuxière had served as notary in the region, he had been born in Limoges or close by (in fact, in the parish of Bénévent, diocese of Limoges), and a large crowd attended the solemn service sung in the presence of Labuxière's corpse before it was interred.[42] Labuxière and Catherine Vifvarenne had married at Chartres in 1757,[43] and she asserted her contractual rights (in accordance with the *Coutume de Paris*) in the distribution of the Labuxière estate. Catherine had but a short while to enjoy these assets, however, for she followed her husband in death the year following, leaving what remained of the Labuxière estate to their children.[44] Neither Joseph Labuxière nor Catherine Vifvarenne could have dreamed at the time of their marriage that they would die as citizens of a young, rambunctious American republic.

An embellished depiction of Fort d'Orléans drawn by Jean-François-Benjamin Dumont de Montigny, but based on information (a sketch?) provided by someone else, possibly Bourgmont himself. The outlying residences of Bourgmont (no. 6), Robert Grotton de St. Ange (no. 11), and his elder son Pierre de St. Ange (no. 16) are depicted. Younger son Louis lived with his father and mother. Courtesy of the Archives Nationales, Outre Mer, Aix-en-Provence, France.

Missouri Indian (Haw-che-ke-sug-ga, Kills Osages) cradling a catlinite pipe, adorned with a bear effigy, depicted by George Catlin in 1832. Bourgmont's Fort d'Orléans was built on the Missouri River in the midst of a major Missouri Indian settlement. St. Ange de Bellerive had a long, peaceful, and productive association with the Missouri tribe, starting in 1724. Courtesy of the Smithsonian American Art Museum, Washington, D.C.

Imperious Kansas warrior (Sho-me-kas-see), depicted by George Catlin in 1832. Bourgmont used a Kansas village as a jumping-off point on his westward expedition to the Padoucas in 1724, and a Kansas chief was part of the Indian delegation that accompanied Bourgmont back to France in 1725. Notice the medal that Sho-me-kas-see is wearing. St. Ange conveyed such "sovereignty tokens" to important Indian leaders. Courtesy of the Smithsonian American Art Museum, Washington, D.C.

Comanche village, depicted by George Catlin in 1846. The Comanches were associated with the Plains Apaches (Padoucas), and the Padouca village where Bourgmont held his grand peace parley in October 1724 looked rather like this, though on a much larger scale. Notice the impressive size of the bison skins being processed. Courtesy of the Smithsonian American Art Museum, Washington, D.C.

The Padoucas (Plains Apaches–Comanches) that Bourgmont's expedition visited in 1724 had an expansive economy that revolved around horses and bison but included slave trading. The Padoucas had acquired large numbers of Spanish horses during the late seventeenth century, and Bourgmont's party received Comanche horses in exchange for French trade goods. Courtesy of the Smithsonian American Art Museum, Washington, D.C.

"She [Chief Clermont's wife] was richly dressed in costly cloths of civilized manufacture, which is almost a solitary instance among the Osages, who so studiously reject every luxury and every custom of civilized people," depicted by George Catlin in 1834. Osages made up part of Bourgmont's Indian entourage during his expedition to the Padoucas in 1724, and an Osage chief accompanied Bourgmont back to France in 1725. Courtesy of the Smithsonian American Art Museum, Washington, D.C.

Three young Osage warriors (Mun-ne-pús-kee, He Who Is Not Afraid; Ko-ha-túnk-a, Big Crow; and Nah-cóm-ee-shee, Man of the Bed), depicted by George Catlin in 1834. During the second half of the eighteenth century, the Osages supplanted the Missouris as the dominant tribe of the lower Missouri River valley and became major partners of St. Louis fur traders. Courtesy of the Smithsonian American Art Museum, Washington, D.C.

Piankashaw-Miami Indian (Men-són-se-ah, Left Hand), "a fierce-looking and very distinguished warrior," depicted by George Catlin in 1830. The Piankashaws were a subgroup of the Miami tribe, and during the mid–eighteenth century a large group of Piankashaws lived near Vincennes on the lower Wabash River. During St. Ange de Bellerive's tenure as commandant there (1736–64), he dealt with the Piankashaws on a daily basis. Courtesy of the Smithsonian American Art Museum, Washington, D.C.

Peoria Indian (Pah-mee-ców-ee-tah, Man Who Tracks), depicted by George Catlin in 1830. While St. Ange de Bellerive was commandant in St. Louis (1765–70), Peoria villages lay close to town on both sides of the Mississippi, and the Peoria and French settlements had a symbiotic relationship. After a Peoria Indian murdered the Ottawa Pontiac at Cahokia in 1769, St. Ange helped to prevent a bloodbath of revenge in the region. Courtesy of the Smithsonian American Art Museum, Washington, D.C.

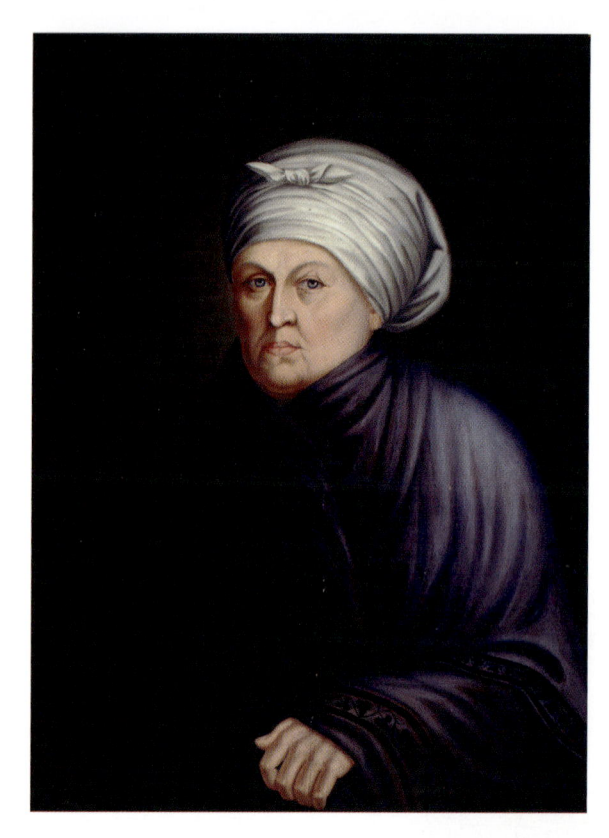

Marie-Thérèse Bourgeois Chouteau, as this portrait manifestly reveals, was tougher—in mind, body, and soul—than her more famous consort, Pierre Laclède Liguest. But she was only one of many remarkable women—black, red, and white—who helped build early St. Louis from the ground up. Early-nineteenth-century portrait by an unknown artist. Courtesy of the Missouri History Museum, St. Louis.

Marguerite Blondeau Guion crossed the Mississippi from Cahokia to the fledgling village of St. Louis in June 1764 to join her husband, Amable Guion. She was nineteen years old and carried with her their infant son. Marguerite was one of many remarkable (but oft-forgot) women who anchored family life in the early community. Courtesy of the Missouri History Museum, St. Louis.

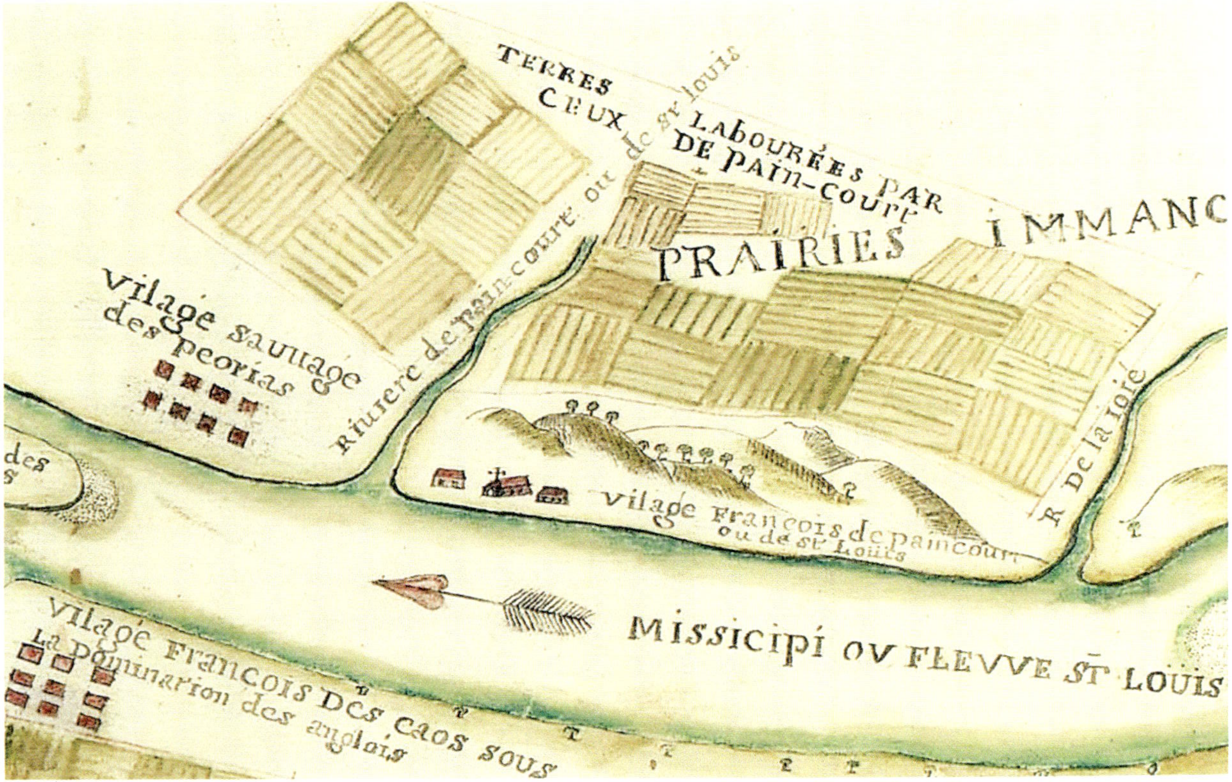

St. Louis (or Paincourt) region, depicted by French engineer Guy Dufossat in 1767. The church had just been built, replacing a canvas tent that had earlier served for sacramental purposes. The two residences depicted may have been those of Pierre Laclède and Joseph Labuxière, the royal notary. Notice the close proximity of the Peoria Indian village and British-controlled Cahokia (Caos) across the Mississippi. Courtesy of the Biblioteca Nacional de España, Madrid.

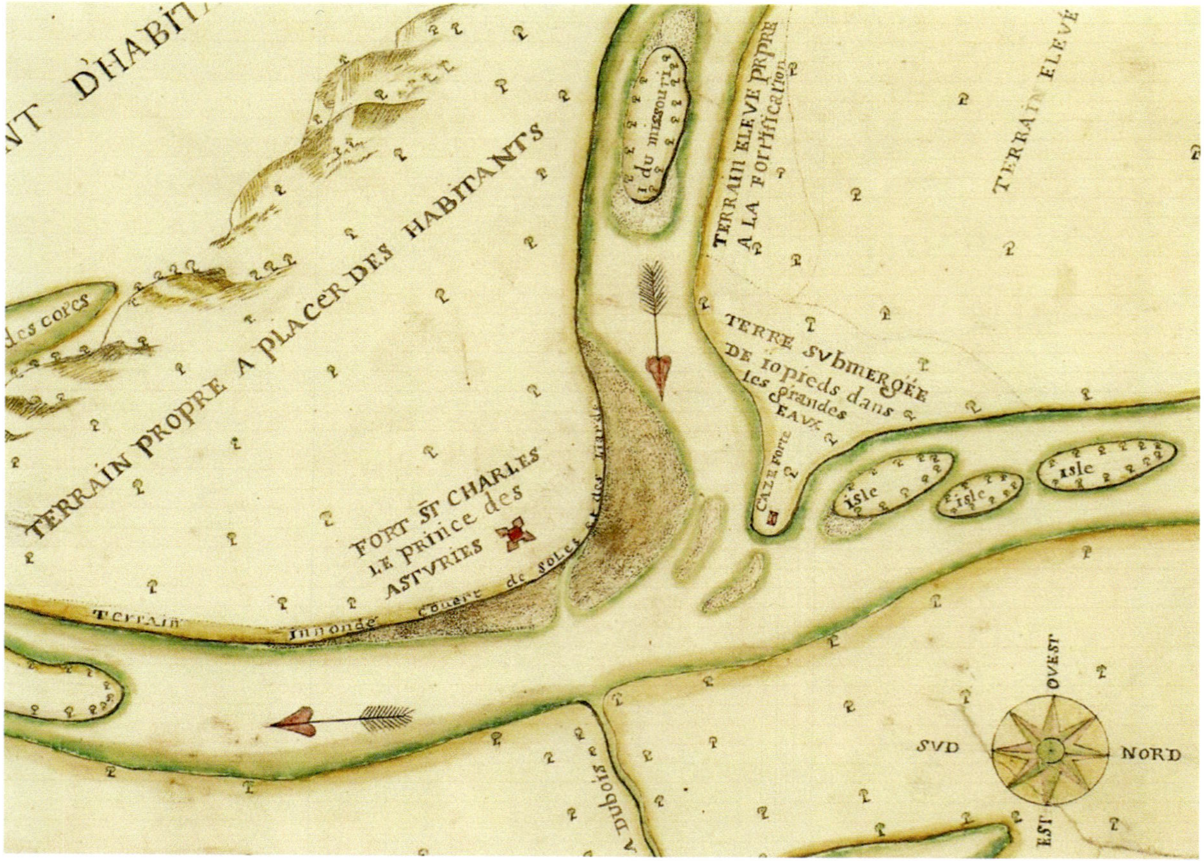

Confluence of the Missouri and Mississippi Rivers, depicted by Guy Dufossat in 1767. Notice "Fort St. Charles, le Prince des Asturies," which was intended to keep British interlopers out of the Missouri Valley. This fort contained a small garrison until 1780, when it was removed to St. Louis in preparation for the infamous Anglo-Indian attack. Courtesy of the Biblioteca Nacional de España, Madrid.

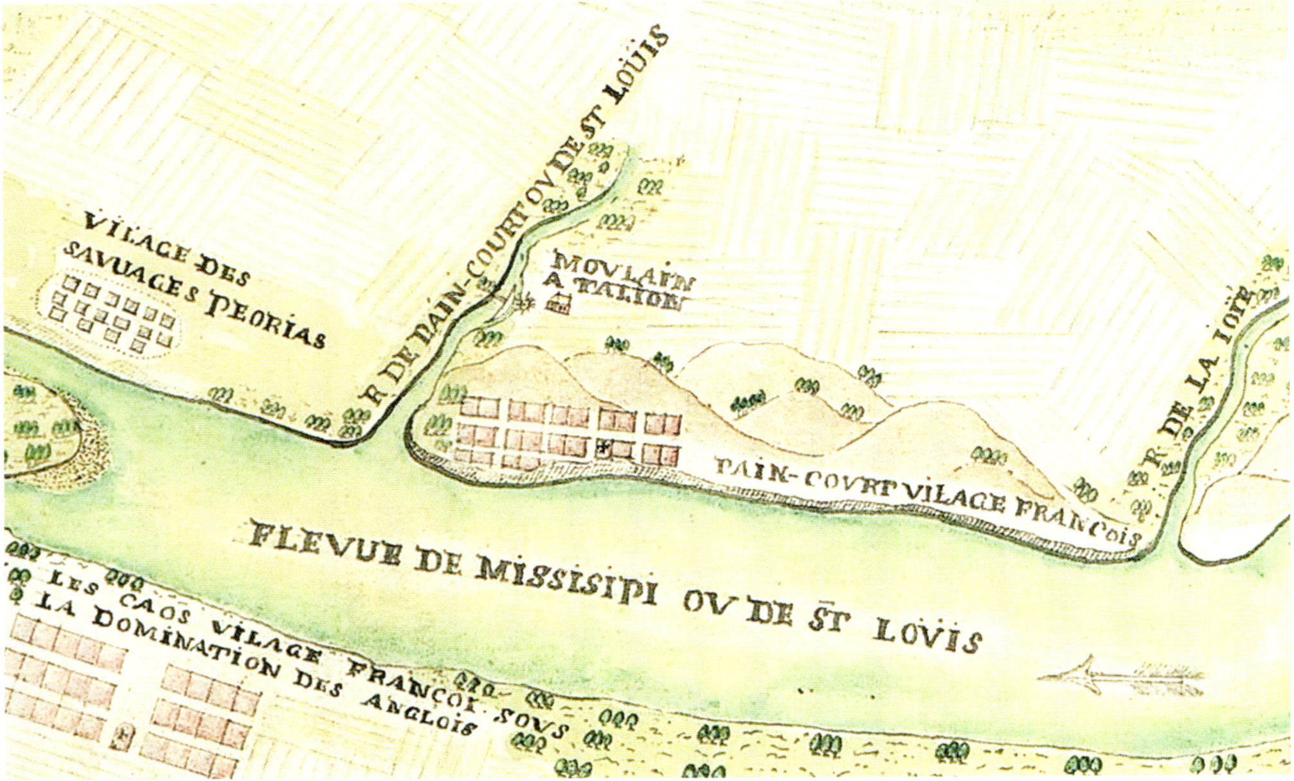

Detail of a map drawn by Guy Dufossat in 1767, depicting the street grid of early St. Louis, with the main streets (grandes rues) running parallel to the Mississippi River. Notice the water mill built by Joseph Taillon, which be sold to Pierre Laclède and which was later acquired by Auguste Chouteau. Some of Dufossat's hills are Mississippian Indian mounds, although he was unaware of that. Courtesy of the Biblioteca Nacional de España, Madrid.

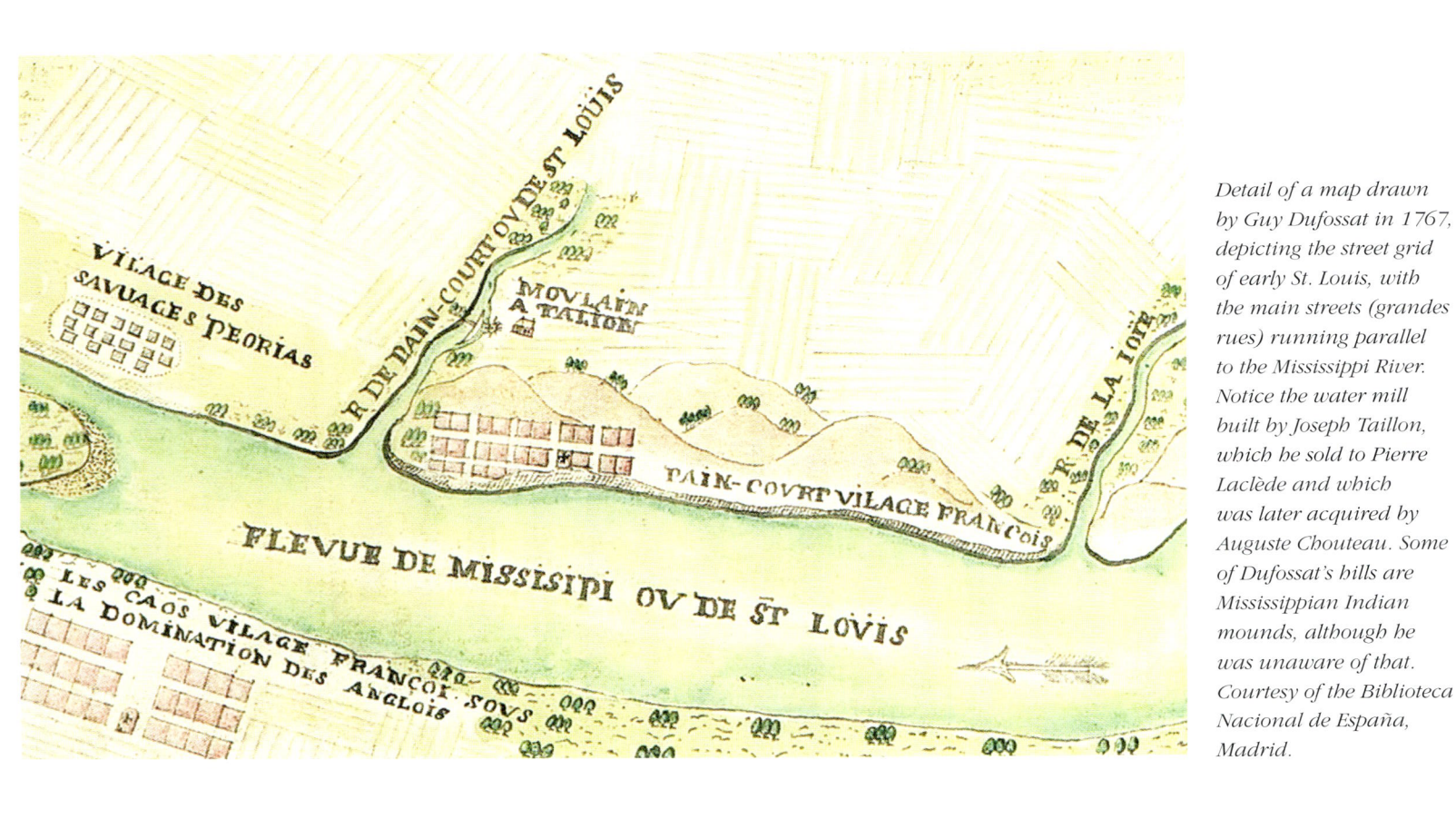

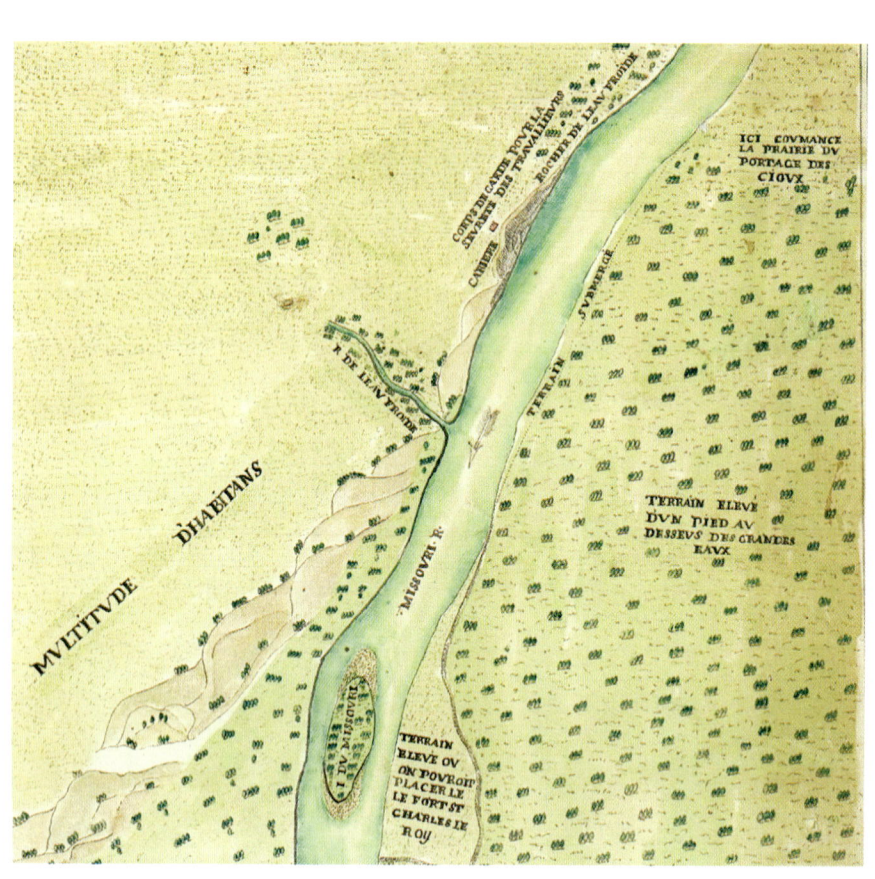

Cold Water Creek Quarry (CARIERE), where limestone was quarried for construction in St. Louis. This quarry (now the Central Stone Company) is today located just across Cold Water Creek (R DE LEAU FROIDE) from Fort Belle Fontaine County Park and has been in continuous operation since, or perhaps before, 1764. Across the Missouri River lies the famous Portage des Sioux (PORTAGE DES CIOUX). Courtesy of the Biblioteca Nacional de España, Madrid.

French faience in the Moustier tradition. Fragments coming from Illinois Country archaeological contexts. Every household in early St. Louis had some object made of imported faience. St. Ange, in addition to owning faience dinner plates, had a faience inkwell. Courtesy of the Illinois State Archaeological Survey, Urbana.

This pharmaceutical mortar and pestle, cast in bronze, was owned by St. Louis's first medical doctor, André-Auguste Condé. Condé could have used this to prepare Jesuit bark (from the South American cinchona tree), among other medications, as an antidote for malaria, which was endemic in the Illinois Country. Condé's descendants recently presented this rare object to the Missouri History Museum. Courtesy of the Missouri History Museum, St. Louis.

Silverware fashioned by French and Canadian craftsmen was common in early St. Louis, and by 1769 the village had its own French-born gold- and silversmith (orfèvre), Joseph Motard. None of his work has ever come to light, however, and the pieces shown here are later examples from the region. Louis Robitaille, a French Canadian craftsman, fashioned the ladle, and the sugar box came to St. Louis from Bordeaux, where it was made by Jean Cheret. Courtesy of the Missouri History Museum, St. Louis.

CONCLUSION

St. Louis and the Wider World

The commerce and trade of the Missouri would produce—without imposing any burden on the royal treasury and without and extraordinary effort—immense wealth for Louisiana.

—Governor Francisco Luis Hector de Carondelet, 1794

The collapse of the French empire in North America, ordained by the peace treaties of Fontainebleau (1762) and Paris (1763), ironically led to the development of what was the most thoroughly French community in the Mississippi River valley—early St. Louis. The village was a remnant of that collapsed empire, a veritable distillation of the French colonial civilization that had developed in North America during the seventeenth and eighteenth centuries. Between its first settlement and the arrival of a Spanish lieutenant governor in May 1770, no community in Louisiana was so convincingly French as St. Louis, not excepting New Orleans. New Orleans was a cosmopolitan community, which, almost from its founding in 1718, was substantially influenced by non-French elements—Spanish, English, German (la Côte des Allemands), and even by mid-eighteenth-century Sephardic Jewish. Remote and provincial St. Louis, at least at the level of language, laws, and customs, was more markedly French. Indians of various nations (especially Illinois, Osages, and Missouris, but also Sioux and Iowas) and languages (Algonquian and Siouan) passed through the village on a regular basis, and numerous Indian and black slaves resided in the village. Blacks and Indians surely influenced daily life in St. Louis, but whether as transients or residents their impact on the community's culture remains obscure and difficult for the modern historian to discern.

The cohesiveness that French language, laws, and customs provided remained intact during the 1760s—the admixture of black, red, white, mulatto, and *métis* peoples in the village notwithstanding. Tanis C. Thorne observed about the Illinois Country, including St. Louis, that "the inculcation of Indianized skills among the Creole youth of all classes provides some oblique evidence of the strong influence that Indian mothers exerted in shaping gender-role perceptions and expectations within the Catholic communities."[1] As more, and more refined, empirical data about Indian wives and mothers in French colonial settlements accumulate, this sort of earnest multiculturalism (appealing though it is) appears increasingly removed from a historical reality that may be documented and examined. Robert Michael Morrissey's recent penetrating research reveals the manner in which Illinois Indian wives of early French colonists adapted themselves to European culture, and Morrissey questions the entire premise of "Indianization" in Illinois Country settlements, of which St. Louis was the last to emerge.[2]

⚜ ⚜ ⚜ ⚜

During the first half of the twentieth century, four classic studies of the Illinois Country, encompassing both sides of the Mississippi River, appeared: volume 1 of Louis Houck's *History of Missouri* (1908), Clarence W. Alvord's *The Illinois Country, 1673–1818* (1920), Natalie M. Belting's *Kaskaskia under the French Regime* (1948), and Charles E. Peterson's *Colonial St. Louis: Building a Creole Capital* (1949). Nowhere in the first three books does the word *Creole* appear, perhaps because in the vulgar mind the word had become associated (incorrectly) with racial mixing and the authors did not wish to get muddied in that quagmire, or perhaps because the authors were simply acknowledging that *Creole* very rarely appears in manuscript sources from Upper Louisiana. For its time, Peterson's slim and idiosyncratic volume was innovative both in its subject matter (the built environment) and its definition of colonial St. Louis as "Creole." But, despite his subtitle, Peterson did not provide a succinct, working definition of *Creole* or address the complex issue of creolization in St. Louis, other than to observe: "This truly Creole architecture was in use throughout the Illinois Country before the founding of St. Louis and it was brought across the river by the first settlers in 1764."[3] Reading between Peterson's lines, however, one may discern that by "Creole," he meant specific building practices that evolved into a unique architecture in the upper Mississippi Valley.

John Francis McDermott, in his *Glossary of Mississippi Valley French, 1673–1850* (1941), defined *Créole* as "a white person born in America of European ancestry. As a noun this word is never applied to a mixed blood." This definition is a bit confused and confusing. What McDermott apparently meant was that *Créole* was never used specifically as a racial term, which was true, but there were indeed mixed bloods (*métis*) in the Illinois Country who were identified as "Créoles." As an adjective, McDermott opined that "créole means anything produced by Creoles. . . . The adjective was applied to blacks, as to other native growths: un nègre creole was a negro born in the colonies as distinct from one born in Africa."[4] McDermott's particular phrasing is curious, but the statement is generally accurate. During the eighteenth century, *Creole* was used as an identifying term more frequently in Lower Louisiana than in Upper Louisiana. Nevertheless, the word was properly understood in the

Illinois Country, and when Pierre-Charles Delassus de Luzières compiled the 1797 census of New Bourbon he used "Créole" correctly and consistently to identify heads of household born in the Mississippi Valley; these were, for de Luzières, distinct from Frenchmen, Canadians, and Americans. On rare occasions, the word was also applied (adjectively, as per McDermott) to persons of African ancestry born in the Illinois Country, as when at St. Louis in 1783 Madame Chouteau sold a "nègre Créol."[5]

The 1766 St. Louis census (see appendix A) reveals that Creoles, including Madame Thérèse Chouteau and her children, were a distinct minority within the village's population, and this condition persisted in the village throughout the French regime (that is, until 1770). As of 1766, roughly 50 percent of St. Louis's white male population were native French Canadians—including Commandant Louis St. Ange de Bellerive, captain of the militia Jean-Baptiste Martigny, and Indian interpreter Louis Deshêtres. Many of the town's leading citizens had metropolitan French origins, including civil judge Joseph Lefebvre, royal notary Joseph Labuxière, and of course Pierre Laclède. As the remainder of the colonial era unfolded, St. Louis's population became increasingly Creole (as indeed did that of the entire Illinois Country), despite a continuing influx of Frenchmen, Canadians, and Americans.[6]

Creole's derivatives *creolized* and *creolization* have become common in academic discourse in the past twenty-five years and are increasingly fashionable.[7] Without getting mired down in all the intricate issues (syncretism, pluralism, marginality, multiculturalism, *métissage*, and hybridization) that now inform usages of these words, one may fairly remark that culture in St. Louis became increasingly creolized during the last decades of the eighteenth century as its Canadian and French roots produced new products in new soil.[8] Architecture provides a convenient approach for studying cultural stasis and cultural change, and no evidence exists that Creole-style buildings existed in St. Louis during the 1760s: as seen in chapter 6, the houses had no *galeries* and featured main floors close to ground level (elevated merely 1 pied), rather than jacked up Creole style, making them distinctly French Canadian in appearance. Early St. Louis houses present us with a perfect example of local syncretism—*poteaux-en-terre* construction in traditional Illinois Country fashion, but assembled in a way that resulted in a distinctly Canadian form. The three buildings that Guy Dufossat depicted on his 1767 map of St. Louis (see the color plate section) have a markedly St. Lawrence Valley look about them, and given the large proportion of French Canadian blood in the village that makes perfect sense.

But after 1770, building practices and architecture evolved in St. Louis, and this evolution offers a clear window into the process of creolization in the community. Jay Dearborn Edwards of Louisiana State University is today's leading authority on Creole architecture in America, and its evolution

220 Conclusion

This 1795 illustration of an Illinois Country Creole-style house may have been based on a residence seen in either St. Louis or Ste. Genevieve. Notice the surrounding galeries and the raised-platform construction. Copper-plate engraving based on a sketch by Joseph Warin, reproduced from Victor Collot, A Journey in North America . . . Illustrated *(Paris, 1826).*

in colonial Louisiana. He provides a succinct working definition of the style: "Any distinctive architectural style or type historically derived from a synthesis of Western European and non-European architectural traditions in coastal W Africa, Latin America, the Caribbean, Louisiana, and the Gulf and Tidewater coasts of the southern U.S."[9] Descending from the general and abstract to the particular and concrete, Edwards remarks that "by the last decade of the eighteenth century, the term Creole house was popularly used in referring to those raised houses with full-length or encircling galleries." The distinguishing features were the raised platform construction and the galleries—generally full-length on houses with gabled ends and fully encircling on those with hipped roofs. The late-eighteenth-century Illinois Country house depicted by Charles Warin displays all the elements required to make it a Creole house as defined by Edwards. This Creole residential style began to emerge in the Illinois Country only *after* the mid–eighteenth century, and it eventually arrived at St. Louis, but not until after 1770.

Louis Bissonet owned a stone house facing "la deuxième grande rue" in St. Louis, that is, the second major street running more or less parallel to the

Mississippi River, and in February 1778 he was selling the house to Louis Dubreuil and his wife, Suzanne Saintous.[10] The residence had a cellar composed of two rooms, requiring an elevated first floor, and it had fully encircling *galeries*, thereby featuring two essential features of the Creole house as defined by Edwards. Adding to the Creole character of the property was a freestanding kitchen, not a common feature of earlier St. Louis houses. Bissonet agreed that a walnut armoire in the house's "grande chambre"[11] would be left in place, likely because it had been installed during the house's construction and was too massive to be removed easily. Interestingly, the Dubreuils agreed in return to provide Bissonet with hinges and a lock exactly like those on the armoire that he was leaving behind. All that Bissonet needed to do was take the hardware provided by the Dubreuils to a *menuisier* like Pierre Lupien *dit* Baron or Jacques Denis and order a new armoire, which would be fashioned from the abundant supply of black walnut in the St. Louis area.[12] The metal components of the new armoire would be French, whereas the wooden components were Illinois Country American; once completed, Bissonet's armoire exemplified nice pluralism at an elemental level.

⚜ ⚜ ⚜ ⚜

During the French regime of St. Ange de Bellerive, St. Louis established itself as the most important commercial entrepôt of the Upper Mississippi Valley. Defining it as an early Gateway to the West, which is often done, is not very accurate or satisfying. The important commercial axis was rather more north-south than east-west. Southward lay New Orleans, which was indispensable to St. Louis's growth both as a provider of trade goods and as a market for northern peltries. And northward lay the regions in which the trade goods were exchanged for peltries, the far-flung and diverse Indian trading zones. St. Louis's fur trade is generally thought of as having a western orientation—that is, west, or at least northwest, up the Missouri River. But during the 1760s, as many St. Louis–based voyageurs and *commerçants* headed pretty much straight north, up the Mississippi and Illinois (and even Minnesota) Rivers, as went northwest, up the Missouri. Sir William Johnson remarked, "The French inhabitants of that Country [Illinois] . . . engross not only all the Trade in that Quarter but also draw away the greater part of the Furr Trade from the [Great] Lakes to the Illinois."[13] Johnson saw the long reach of French traders extending northward rather than westward, which worried him because Canada, including the *Pays d'en Haut*, had become British with the Treaty of Paris in 1763.

In any case, during its earliest years, St. Louis was more Gateway to the Northern Fur Trade than Gateway to the West. Kaskaskia had earlier played this role, going all the way back to the early years of the eighteenth century, and to some extent it continued to do so after the founding of St. Louis. But the fact that major *négociants* like Louis Lambert and Louis Perrault and (a bit later) Gabriel Cerré gravitated to St. Louis was a harbinger of things to come. St. Louis's presence near the confluences of the Mississippi, Missouri, and Illinois Rivers certainly increased the volume of the Mississippi Valley fur trade. By the end of the colonial era, St. Louis dominated commerce between the upper Mississippi watershed and New Orleans, as it continues to do to this day, although the products of this commerce are somewhat different.

St. Louis's continuous and intimate contact with New Orleans meant that it participated, albeit indirectly, in the broad world of Atlantic trade and commerce, including that in slaves. In *French Colonial Louisiana and the Atlantic World*, edited by Bradley G. Bond, Daniel H. Usner Jr. contributed an elegant lamentation about the particular state of colonial Louisiana studies within the general field of American history. He argued that American historians, not excluding those from the state of Louisiana, have distorted, marginalized, and minimized colonial Louisiana, and continue to do so: "The regional otherness of eighteenth-century Louisiana, so deliberately written into national history over the nineteenth century, would continue to influence twentieth-century literary and popular impressions. . . . At the national level, the one-dimensional and subordinate role assigned long ago to non-English colonies by Bancroft, Parkman, and others still appears in the U.S. history textbooks and continue to privilege the English and eastern regions."[14] In a lengthy review of Bond's volume, Sophie White carried Usner's arguments right to the doorstep of colonial Louisiana historians, not excluding Usner and Bond. White underscored "a core problem with the current state of scholarship on French colonial Louisiana, namely the focus on lower Louisiana to the exclusion of upper Louisiana (or Illinois country)." Bond, for example, "highlights Louisiana's peripheral place in American and Atlantic history, yet . . . he denies the Illinois country formal inclusion within the colony of Louisiana."[15] White was adamant that the Illinois Country must be included not merely in American history but within the larger, increasingly visible field of Atlantic history.

Since Usner's essay appeared in 2005, the Atlantic world during the colonial era has become a favorite historical topic. Cambridge University Press recently released John K. Thornton's *A Cultural History of the Atlantic World, 1250–1820* (2012), touting the volume as a product of "deep learning and full immersion in source documents from four continents and many languages." The book's front cover is emblazoned with a portion of Alexandre de Batz's celebrated depiction of Indians (and one African) drawn at New Orleans in 1735 (Usner used a portion of the same de Batz composition on the cover of an earlier book),[16] but Thornton scarcely mentions Louisiana, which belies the promise of his book's cover. And it goes without saying that the French Illinois Country does not appear in Thornton's book, although the "Illinois nation" makes a brief appearance.

Thornton's general neglect of colonial Louisiana, and total disregard of the Illinois Country, is reflected in most recent books about Atlantic history.[17] Minor exceptions occur in *Atlantic History: A Critical Appraisal*, a collection of essays edited by Jack P. Greene and Philip D. Morgan.[18] Laurent Dubois's contribution, "The French Atlantic," takes note of Bond's volume about colonial Louisiana and about how its history is generally absent from Atlantic studies. Quoting Bond, Dubois notes that "the history of Louisiana poses as one of its challenges understanding how 'Native Americans, Africans, Canadians, Frenchmen and women, and Caribbean Islanders' managed to create 'polyglot and fluid societies that ultimately prevailed longer than the French colony.'"[19] Neither Bond nor Dubois mentions the Illinois Country, but their remarks are certainly applicable to that region, most especially early St. Louis. Dubois also opined that "in Louisiana, as in the Caribbean, the approaches of Atlantic history are central to the understanding of the roles and history of African individuals and communities."[20] But Dubois's formula may be instructively reversed: an understanding of roles of African individuals and communities, including those in the Illinois Country, is central to approaching Atlantic history, if that history is going to reflect a geographically inclusive approach.

Slavery in eighteenth-century Louisiana was a very different institution from that in the Caribbean islands. In the West Indies, sugar-cane monoculture led to "prototypes of modern assembly-line production,"[21] characterized by a division of labor and highly organized gang functions. The Caribbean climate and diseases and the generally oppressive conditions on the islands meant that the slave population grew not by natural increase, but only through continuous importation of African slaves. Although slavery in Louisiana began as an import from the Caribbean, including the importation of the *Code Noir,* French planters in the lower Mississippi River valley never replicated the Caribbean system, never fully realized a grinding, thoroughly dehumanizing plantation regime.[22] Planters in Lower Louisiana were slaveholders with aspirations, but managed, in the end, merely to create, in the well-known words of Ira Berlin, "a would-be slave society."[23]

Gilbert C. Din's remark that slavery in French Louisiana "evolved along its own lines" also holds true for slavery in the Illinois Country. The powerful French planter elite of Lower Louisiana had no parallel in the Illinois Country, where slaveholdings were generally small (minuscule by Lower Louisiana standards).[24] Habitants at St. Louis never even attempted to institute large-scale plantation-style agriculture, and it is instructive that one of the few large slaveholders at Kaskaskia, Antoine Bienvenu, eventually abandoned the Illinois Country and removed his plantation-style operations to Lower Louisiana.[25] In the Illinois Country, including St. Louis, slaves, even those who performed agricultural labor, generally lived in the villages and in many ways were integrated rather fully into village life. Indeed, slave fertility rates, as may be discerned in baptismal records, suggest a material standard of living little or no different from the white population of the village. Slaves (including both Indians and Africans) constituted only about one-quarter of the total population in early St. Louis, whereas in New Orleans slaves outnumbered whites.[26] And by the 1770s, New Orleans was evolving into a mature urban environment, characterized by a substantial free colored population. Gwendolyn Midlo Hall appropriately remarked about New Orleans that "being black did not necessarily mean being a slave."[27] At that time, St. Louis, despite being the seat of government for Upper Louisiana, remained an adolescent fur-trading and agricultural village, where few free blacks were able to carve out a niche. Even on the 1787 Spanish census, St. Louis's free black and mixed-race populations represent less than 3 percent of the total.[28] Within a decade, however, this figure had risen to 9 percent,[29] as St. Louis began slowly to approximate New Orleans as a gathering place for diverse free persons of color.

⚜ ⚜ ⚜ ⚜

Peter H. Wood, also writing in *Atlantic History: A Critical Appraisal*,[30] draws the North American heartland into the larger discussion of Atlantic studies. He asks rhetorically whether American colonial history should include "all parts of the North American continent, and all people living there before 1800," and responds with an emphatic, "Yes!" Ethnohistorian Daniel K. Richter declares that he was "facing east from Indian country" when gazing across the Mississippi River from his St. Louis hotel room, construing the great river as a distinct line of demarcation, with Indians on one side and the nebulous East on the other. But Richter evinces no particular interest in the early history of the Mississippi Valley itself, and he is oblivious of the early French settlements, including colonial St. Louis, that had once occupied the ground on which his hotel stood.[31] This region was without doubt a geographical middle ground, as Richter has it, but it was also a distinct cultural zone, which is often neglected, not only in Atlantic studies but in North American historiography generally. This is apparent in Paul W. Mapp's recent *The Elusive West and the Contest for Empire, 1713–1763*. In fine Anglocentric fashion, Mapp declares that the entire Mississippi River valley, including the Illinois Country, was merely "*putatively* French territory," the curious phrase suggesting that French colonies were somehow spurious, not real.[32] But they *were* real, although the Illinois Country is merely a flyover zone for Mapp. When he discusses Étienne Veniard de Bourgmont's 1724 expedition to the Padoucas, he neglects to mention that the Illinois Country provided an indispensable base camp (Fort de Chartres) for Bourgmont's ascent of the remote Missouri River valley.[33]

Wood's larger continental West by definition included the Spanish borderlands of Upper Louisiana, which encompassed the expanse of territory that may be glimpsed from a hotel window in Cahokia, gazing westward across the Mississippi. These eastern *Spanish* borderlands, including colonial St. Louis, made up the western portion of the *French* Illinois Country. And St. Ange de Bellerive, assisted by his notary, Labuxière, governed a community that became, over time, the first great city of the *American* West. Auguste Chouteau claimed that Pierre Laclède had foreseen this boundless future in 1764, but when Chouteau made this claim (ca. 1825) steamboats from New Orleans, Pittsburgh, and Cincinnati were already nosing up to the landing at St. Louis's riverfront.[34] If Laclède's prediction was as prescient as his protégé claimed, it demonstrates beyond any reasonable doubt that Laclède's imagination was the largest province in the realm of his mental faculties.

APPENDIX A
St. Louis Counts

In the days leading up to Saturday, May 31, 1766, the habitants of the village of St. Louis took time from their fields and household chores to stop for a few minutes at the government office, answering Commandant St. Ange's call for a census.[1] He had received instructions from Don Antonio Ulloa, the recently arrived Spanish governor in New Orleans, to enumerate the residents, their families, and their property—land, slaves, and livestock.[2] Censuses were becoming increasingly important instruments of government for European states during the eighteenth century, and Ulloa was a progressive thinker. St. Ange's notary, Labuxière, very likely gathered the requisite information from village residents and drafted the document for St. Ange's approval. This local census, done in French, was then sent on to the provincial capital, New Orleans, to become part of a comprehensive census of the eighteen *departamentos* of the Spanish colony of Louisiana. The anonymous scribe (a gifted calligrapher) in New Orleans must have had to peer closely at Labuxière's handwriting as he rendered the unfamiliar French names into their Spanish equivalents. Even with its creative versions of a few of the residents' names, this census included some of the first critical, official information about the settled territories Spain had acquired with the 1762 Treaty of Fontainebleau. The "new place," *el lugar nuevo nombrado San Luis* and *Sta. Genoveva,* were the colony's two northernmost settlements and the only ones that existed in Spanish *Ylinoises.*

The 1766 census authoritatively identifies the earliest families of St. Louis.[3] In his narrative of the settlement of St. Louis, Auguste Chouteau remembered that he first arrived on the west bank with thirty workmen, no names given. Pages later he named thirty habitants who began to give some substance to the village. Although Chouteau's story suggested that these were two different groups of thirty,[4] nineteenth-century historian Frederic L. Billon applied the names of the settlers to the first unnamed group of workmen. Then Billon added his own rhetorical flourishes to proclaim that "those thirty worthies, who, conducted by Laclede [sic], were the pioneers that led the way in opening up to settlement a boundless territory then inhabited but by a few roving savages and the wild animals of the forest."[5] And St. Louisans have been confused ever since about founders and firsts. The beautifully crafted, intriguing census document does not name of all the individuals living in the village, but it is far more accurate and historically compelling than Chouteau's nostalgic recollection or Billon's florid phrases.

St. Ange's next major task to complete for Ulloa was a militia muster roll, divided among sections for officers, habitants, and *volontaires*, laborers available for duty when present.[6] The census lists fifty-six households and the militia muster roll 120 names, and together these two documents provide astonishing and heretofore unexamined information about the population of the embryonic village. The following description of 1766 St. Louis draws on an analysis of the census, supplemented by the militia muster roll and genealogical information gleaned primarily from the French and Spanish archives, the Kaskaskia Manuscripts, and Illinois Country sacramental registers.

The census enumerated 332 residents in St. Louis,[7] including 75 slaves. In Ste. Genevieve, already more than a decade old, there was a total population of 547, of which 228 were slaves. The arms-bearing men who served as the villages' citizen militia totaled 118 in St. Louis and 162 in Ste. Genevieve.[8] In his report to Spanish Governor Alejandro O'Reilly in 1769, Pedro Piernas remarked that the resident population of St. Louis was slightly larger than that of "Misere," Ste. Genevieve, but by the time of Piernas's 1772 census, the combined white and slave population of St. Louis was still smaller than that of Ste. Genevieve.[9]

Following is the summary of the 1766 census:[10]

	St. Louis	Ste. Genevieve[11]
Households	56	58
Militia men	118	162
Women (wives, widows, etc.; see above)	38	44
Older males[12]	14	25
Older females	13	12
(Younger) Sons	37	35
(Younger) Daughters	37	41
Total	257	319
Slaves	75	228
Grand Total	332	547
Lands	401	1201
Horses	78	145
Large livestock	243	884
Small livestock	167	638

As commandant, St. Ange appears first on the enumeration (see census table below), followed by Judge Lefebvre and then the king's attorney and notary, Labuxière. "LaClede" is next, identified as *primero comissario,* quartermaster. Laclède never used this title, but he was paid by the Spanish government for supplying bread and housing troops.[13] The military surgeon (André-Auguste) Condé is identified, as is (Jean-Baptiste) Martigny, captain of the militia. (Louis) Dubreuil *Neg.t* is the only person designated as a merchant,[14] and no other occupations appear on this census. St. Louis had no resident priest at the time, but was served sporadically by the itinerant Father Sébastien-Louis Meurin. St. Ange's troops and officers were not considered "habitants" of the village, and therefore their names do not appear even though many had established residences in town.[15]

Thirty of the 49 male heads of household were married, and among the unmarried men there were several widowers.[16] The single men who were minors or at the age of majority (twenty-five years old according to the Customary Laws of Paris) usually married within a few years. Bachelors often had sexual partners and in some cases children.[17] The census captures most of the married couples in the town,[18] and where household enumerations do not reflect nuclear families, extended families were surely present. Mixed-family types, extended and blended, all existed without any special notice in 1766 St. Louis.

In the Illinois Country, widows were considered heads of household, and the May 1766 census confirms this for St. Louis. The presence of such matriarchs dramatically alters traditional accounts of early St. Louis, which have generally focused only on Madame Chouteau. Five widows appear on the census: Hélène Danis, the widow of Ignace Hébert; Marie-Françoise Millet, widow of Gabriel Dodier Sr.; Marie-Anne Henrion, widow of Nicolas Beaugenou; Marie-Françoise Pinot, the widow Charon; and Marie-Jeanne Illeret, the widow of Nicolas Maréchal. The widows Hébert and Dodier each managed more land, livestock, and slaves in 1766 than many of the male heads of households. Moreover, the widows, their siblings, their children and grandchildren, and their slaves formed extensive social networks within the town. Three of the widows, Maréchal, Dodier, and Hébert, lived into the 1780s, making a substantial contribution to the settlement during its formative first two decades.

Madame Chouteau's name immediately follows Laclède's on the census, revealing both her association with him and her high status. All five of Madame Chouteau's children were also enumerated, without names, just as the children of other families were. Madame Chouteau did not own real estate or livestock, but in association with Laclède their amalgamated household resembled that of other families. Thirteen unmarried postpubescent females and 37 girls appear on the census, but they were far outnumbered by around

80 unmarried adult men. With such an imbalance in the sex ratio, the bleak prospects for marriage with a French girl led these men to pursue other options, occasionally celibacy, but much more often slave women, or, for fur traders, Indian women living in distant villages. Under these circumstances, the pitiable efforts of itinerant priests to convince their male parishioners to confine sexual relations to legitimate marriage were utterly futile.

The remaining female "head of household" barely qualified as a woman, and certainly had no household of her own. Marguerite La Ferne, age twelve or thirteen, was one of two daughters of the (deceased) royal surgeon Pierre Ignace Bardet de la Ferne.[19] Marguerite's sister, Marie-Anne, had married André-Auguste Condé, another royal surgeon, on the east side of the Mississippi in 1763. They married not long after the girls' mother died, leaving the young Marguerite without parents and not old enough to marry. By November 1766, the legal paperwork was completed for Condé to become her guardian,[20] but in May her status was ambiguous, and this may account for her name appearing separately from her sister's family on the census. The fact that she owned four slaves may also have required that she be listed as a head of household.

Parents with children made up more than half of the households.[21] The number of families with young children (future heirs of property) must have lent stability to social and business interactions and tempers the notion that single men with unruly behavior dominated the social mores of the village.[22] Several households consisted of married couples with no children: the militia captain Jean-Baptiste Martigny and his wife, Marie Hébert;[23] Eugène Pourée and Marie-Josephe Goudeau; and Jean Prunet *dit* La Giroflée and his wife, Véronique Panissé. Toussaint Vaudry and his wife, Marie Anne Du Pré, were "empty nesters" by 1766, but Du Pré's daughter and family were also in St. Louis.[24]

Enslaved Africans and Indians accounted for 23 percent of the population in 1766, and they were integral to the St. Louis settlement from the start. Earlier French Illinois censuses (1732 and 1752) had listed black slaves by age and gender, and black and Indian slaves separately, but the 1766 census has but a single category for slaves. Twenty-four of fifty-six households owned slaves, making slave owning fairly democratized, yet half of those owned just one or two slaves. St. Ange, Madame Chouteau, and Laclède each owned three to five slaves. The three households with the most slaves were the Bizets (brothers Guillaume and Charles), who owned seven; the widow Dodier, also with seven; and the Joseph Taillon household, with twelve. Names of some of the slaves can be determined from sacramental records and notarial documents, and slaves whose presence in 1766 was likely have been added by name in the census table that follows.

A free black population developed in St. Louis early on, but free blacks do not appear on the 1766 enumeration. Jeannette *Forchet*, who acquired her surname from Abbé *Forget*, was manumitted by him in Cahokia in 1763 and may have been in St. Louis as early as 1766. In any event, she was one of the first free blacks in St. Louis, first appearing in land records in August 1767 as the owner of a town lot. Jeannette is a historical figure of some significance and has already been the subject of substantial research.[25]

Some of the first St. Louis settlers were descendants of local French-Indian marriages, and more Indian women—some wives, many slaves—would follow in later years. In earlier decades, French-Indian sacramental marriages in the Illinois Country accounted for as many as 20 percent of all marriages.[26] Two early St. Louis women were within one generation of their Indian origins. Hélène Danis, the widow Hébert, was the daughter of an Indian woman.[27] Agnès Pichart, wife of Louis Desnoyer, was the daughter of a woman with the family name *Patoka,* a variation of *Padoucah,* a tribe of Plains Apaches that was a frequent target of Indian slave traders.[28] Véronique Panissé, wife of Jean Brunet *dit* La Giroflée, has been called an Indian, but no solid evidence of any kind has been adduced to support this claim. She and her father (Marie-Jacques) spelled their name Panissé,[29] and it is abundantly clear that neither she nor her father was Indian.[30]

Agricultural land west of the village of St. Louis was being granted (also bought and sold) well before the census was taken in May 1766. Official, land grants began April 1, 1766, and all entries included the owners of neighboring, thus preexisting, grants. Four hundred one lots had already been assigned by the time the census was compiled, and twelve slave-owning households (one-half) had no agricultural landholdings. This might mean that some slaves were used exclusively for household duties or perhaps were rented out to neighbors.[31] Conversely, some households that had no slaves had large agricultural holdings. For example, the Guion and Le Roy families each owned twenty parcels of plowland, but owned no slaves.[32] Nine residents owned neither slaves nor agricultural land in 1766, including the widow Charon and the teenager François Cottin (Labuxière's assistant, identified as "greffier," record keeper and son of a schoolteacher);[33] neither had the resources to develop farmland.

In Ste. Genevieve, agriculture was well established at the time St. Louisans were just clearing their plowlands. In the older village, slaves made up about 42 percent of the approximate total population of 547. More than half of the residents owned slaves, and those who owned the most land also owned the most slaves. François Vallé of Ste. Genevieve was by far the largest slave owner in all of Upper Louisiana: he had 63 slaves, most of whom worked his large agricultural holdings.[34] No habitant in St. Louis was remotely comparable to Vallé as an agricultural entrepreneur.

The census also listed livestock in broad categories of horses and large (oxen and cattle) and small animals (probably pigs), and most St. Louisans, including Madame Chouteau, owned some livestock. Laclède had the most cattle, followed by Jean-Baptiste Hervieux, the royal *armurier*, and the Taillons. After Captain Thomas Stirling took command on the east side of the Mississippi in October 1765, he complained to General Thomas Gage that the inhabitants "drove off their cattle in the night and carried off their effects and grain" across the river. If this was true, starting a new life in St. Louis was still a slow process.[35] The meager livestock totals in St. Louis in 1766, when the village was two years old, suggest that few animals were taken across the Mississippi.[36] Spanish-era censuses would detail the extractive, productive results of the inhabitants, including packs of furs, flour, and lead, but that lay in the future.

A wide spectrum of ages characterized the village's first residents.[37] Most of the men listed on the census were in their forties and fifties in 1766. The two elders of the village were Commandant St. Ange, sixty-four, and Antoine Rivière *dit* Baccané, sixty. The two youngest were sixteen-year-old François Cottin and fourteen-year-old Louis Chancellier.[38] Similarly, among the female heads of households and wives, whose ages are known from other sources, the age distribution was wide, from twelve (Marguerite La Ferne) to midfifties (Hélène Danis and Marianne Du Pré). With at least a dozen women over age forty, including four widows, the village of St. Louis did not lack competent, experienced hands for running households and raising families. The first two marriages in St. Louis took place in April and May 1766, and each of the young wives gave birth the next year.

The age difference between husbands and wives was in many cases more than ten years. This might signal a second marriage after the death of a first wife, but extant records are not clear on this issue. Antoine Rivière at sixty was twenty years older than his wife, Marie-Barbe Eloy. Several couples were close in age, such as Jean-Baptiste Martigny, thirty-eight, and wife Marie Hébert, thirty-four. More documentation exists for widows who remarried than for widowers. Marie-Josèphe Lacroix, married to Alexandre Langlois in 1756, was the widow Gouin.[39] René Kiercereau married Madeleine Robillard, widow of Antoine Rivière.[40] Young widows often remarried soon, as Véronique Panissé married Kiery Marcheteau in St. Louis, within months, perhaps weeks, after the death of her husband Jean Brunet *dit* La Giroflée.[41]

Most men with identified birthplaces were born in Canada, and many wives were natives of the Illinois Country. About a dozen men were born in France, representing a higher percentage than in the older French villages in the region. Three women were born in New Orleans—Marie-Thérèse Bourgeois Chouteau, Marie-Marguerite Becquet, and Marie-Barbe Eloy. Mobile, Michilimackinac, and St. Joseph were also birthplaces given in the records for the first residents. All in all, though, early St. Louis was decidedly more Canadian than Creole in composition.

According to various British reports, about forty families settled at St. Louis in its first two years.[42] This comports well with the census, but in addition to nuclear families, extended family *networks* provided St. Louis with a running start at social and economic development. Some extended families are immediately recognizable on the census, such as the widow Dodier and son Gabriel Dodier and Louis Marcheteau and brother François Marcheteau. Others emerge from the militia muster roll, which permits us to place male relatives in particular households. Joseph Lemoine-Martigny, the brother of Jean-Baptiste, the militia captain, was almost certainly living with him (and still was in the 1787 census!). They had been partners in various ventures prior to their move to St. Louis.[43] Similarly, the unmarried Bizet (sometimes Bissette) brothers, Guillaume and Charles, made up a household by themselves. The adult Hébert sons, Auguste and François, were both part of their widowed mother's household; Ignace and Joseph La Roche were militiamen in Louis La Roche's home, and Noël Langlois lived with his brother, Alexandre, who appears on the census.

When we include wives and their families, the community networks light up. The brothers Charles and Nicolas Henrion surely lived with their widowed sister, Marie-Anne Beaugenou. Marie-Anne Gérome Roussilliet was the wife of census resident Louis Briard *dit* La Roche and the daughter of Marie-Anne Du Pré, whose second husband was resident Toussaint Vaudry. Joseph Calvé's residence is linked through his wife, Marie Maréchal, to her widowed mother's, Marie-Jeanne Illeret. The Guion household with Amable and his wife, Marguerite Blondeau, may have included her father and mother, Thomas Blondeau and Marie-Josèphe Duclos.[44] Thomas Blondeau contracted with Pierre Rougeau (*dit* Berger) to have a house built for himself just two months after the census.[45] In fact, those *without* extended family connections can be assumed to be new arrivals from either France or New Orleans, such as the merchants Antoine Hubert and Antoine Bêrard and Pierre Laclède and the Chouteaus. Laclède served as a witness at several marriages, including those of the parents of both Auguste's and Pierre's future spouses. In his first years in the Illinois Country, Laclède was establishing connections for his own family that would carry into the next generation.[46]

The three-generation extended family of the Marcheteau brothers, with deep roots in Canada, constituted a veritable mini-village within the village. Joseph, Louis, and François and their adult married children with spouses accounted for twelve persons in 1766, and all the married children had at least one child.[47] The Marcheteau family seems not to have been directly involved in the fur trade, for its male members were never identified as voyageurs or *commerçants*. Louis worked as a mason, François was a master carpenter, as was his son-in-law Louis Ride. Joseph Marcheteau's sons-in-law had other trades: Jean-Baptiste Becquet was a miller, and Charles Routier raised livestock. Among the six related families listed separately on the census (two brothers and four sons-in-law),[48] fifty-one agricultural lots were owned, but quite remarkably not a single slave—not in 1766 at any rate. Large scale, slave-labor agriculture never developed at St. Louis as it had earlier at Kaskaskia or Ste. Genevieve.

The census depicts St. Louis's merchant class at its very origins. A household with modest beginnings was that of "Dubreuil Negt," the merchant Louis Chauvet Dubreuil, who was born in France ca. 1736.[49] In 1766 he was unmarried and represented a single-member household on the census. Dubreuil had one slave and one bovine animal (cow or ox), so at this point his fortune lay in the future. He would, over time, marry Suzanne Saintous (also born in France) in 1772, have numerous children, and become one of St. Louis's most prosperous merchants.[50] When Dubreuil died in 1794, the priest noted the names of the important citizens who paid their respects by attending his burial—Cerré, Chouteau, Roubidoux, and Sanguinet, all leading businessmen. Newly arrived French-born merchants Antoine Hubert and Antoine Bêrard each owned two slaves but held no agricultural parcels in May 1766.[51] They became wealthy in frontier St. Louis but remained unmarried, for they had come to town not to put down roots but simply to get rich.

The gap between the haves and the have-nots was large in early St. Louis. Take the case of the widow Charon. Her name was Marie-Françoise Pinot, widow of François Blotte *dit* Charon, and living with her was just her daughter Thérèse. Blotte and Pinot had had three children: François, interred at Fort Chartres in 1758, Thérèse, and Noël, baptized on Christmas Day in St. Philippe in 1762.[52] Mother and daughter had no slaves, no land, no livestock, and no militia men in their household. We must conclude they did not even live in their own separate household, as there is no mention of her in the land records. The usual provision in land grants was that the grantee must improve the lot within a year and a day or lose title to it. Pinot's absence from these normal transactions indicates that she had little chance to make good on such a commitment. In 1776 eighteen-year-old "Theresa Charron" signed a marriage contract with Jean-Baptiste Petit in the presence of her mother. Amable Guion and Charles Bizet, both respected habitants, served as witnesses for Thérèse at the contract.[53] Widow Charon and her daughter appear on the census to have been living a lonely existence, but likely had extended family in the new village.

The census showed relative wealth by conventional standards: as a single man, Pierre Laclède looked attractive on paper, with three slaves, ten tracts of agricultural land, four horses, and thirty head of cattle. Amable Guion and his wife had one young son, twenty lots of agricultural land, and twenty-two animals. Most prosperous, though, was the household of *el nombrado Taillon*. This was Joseph Taillon, whose family consisted of his wife, Marie-Louise Bossett, and five children. His many assets in 1766 included twelve slaves, forty lots of agricultural land, seven horses, and thirty-two other animals. The next year Laclède would buy out Taillon's mill property, totally rebuild the mill, and pursue the flour business with more success than he did the fur trade.

Whatever its inconsistencies, even contradictions, this first official census showed St. Louis poised to become a permanent asset to the Spanish North American empire. A government structure was in place, and the local militia turned out in numbers (most households had at least one man in its ranks) for the muster roll in July 1766. There were enough women to bear children, to manage households, establish domestic economies, and maintain a semblance of social order. A new generation was growing and thriving, despite the high rate of infant mortality. Thirty-four households were engaged in improving assigned lands, growing crops and feeding livestock. More than three hundred men, women, and children, free and enslaved, black, red, and white, populated the French village that had become a remote outpost of the cosmopolitan Spanish global empire. The residents who moved across the Mississippi from the village at Chartres were determined to retain their French (Roman Catholic) religion, customs, and mores, which they considered at risk on the British side of the river.[54]

From Commandant Louis St. Ange de Bellerive, age sixty-four, to Catherine Bissonet, just twenty-five days old on May 31,[55] the demographics behind the 1766 census reveal a village of fully and partially transplanted family networks, lending an essential cohesiveness to St. Louis society. The census document is indispensable as the first objective view of St. Louis *from that time,* not re-created or remembered. It shatters the hegemony of the Chouteau narrative, a long overdue demolition, and it is a reminder that the history of French St. Louis is neither quaint nor unknowable.

⚜ ⚜ ⚜ ⚜

The May 1766 census named only the head of household (underlined below). The seven additional categories for people used ciphers, not names. The authors have added the names of family members from source documents that would reasonably place them in St. Louis in May 1766: the July 1766 Militia Muster Roll, documents from the St. Louis French and Spanish Archives, and baptismal, marriage, and burial registers. The categories for enumerated persons were (1) arms-bearing men, (2) wife, (3) adult males, (4) adult females, (5) (young) sons, (6) (young) daughters, and (7) slaves. Where the census showed a "0" in one of these categories, we omitted it.

Preferred records for filling in the census and identifying names in the militia muster roll were manuscript source documents. Transcriptions and translations such as *The Village of Chartres* are noted. Genealogical compilations were used for some birth years and for birthplaces outside the Louisiana colony.[56] Conflicting information is duly noted, as ages and birth years are particularly susceptible to variation. Many alternate spellings appear in the notes as well. The notes do not provide complete family genealogies; this is only an attempt to flesh out the household enumerations in the 1766 census.

Appendix A

St. Louis Census, May 31, 1766

Louis St. Ange de Bellerive, Commandant   Canada   1702–1774[57]

Arms-bearing men	1	
Slaves	4	Angélique, Lizette, Jean-Baptiste, François[58]

Joseph d'Inglebert Lefebvre, Assistant to the Ordonnateur and Judge   France   d. 1767[59]

Arms-bearing men	0[60]	
Slaves	3	

Joseph Labuxière, Royal Attorney and Notary   Bénévent, France   ca. 1727–1791[61]

Arms-bearing men	1	self
Wife	1	Catherine Vifvarenne, 1742?–1792[62]
Adult females	1	Marie-Françoise Vifvarenne[63]
Sons	1	Antoine-Joseph (Charles-Joseph?)[64]
Daughters	1	Marie-Anne[65]
Slaves	1	Louison?[66]

Pierre Laclède, Quartermaster   Béarn, France   1729–1778[67]

Arms-bearing men	6[68]	self
Slaves	3[69]	

Madame Chouteau (Marie-Thérèse Bourgeois)   New Orleans   1733–1814[70]

Arms-bearing men	1	Auguste Chouteau b. 1749[71]
Wife	1	self
Adult males[72]	0	
Sons	1	Pierre b. 1758[73]
Daughters	3	Pélagie b. 1760,[74] Marie-Louise b. 1762,[75] Victoire b. 1764[76]
Slaves	4	Marie-Catherine[77]

Antoine Bêrard   Bordeaux, France   ca.1740–1776[78]

Arms-bearing men	1	self
Slaves	2	Leveille?[79]

Antoine Hubert   d. by Aug. 3, 1778[80]

Arms-bearing men	1	
Slaves	2	Joseph[81]

André-Auguste Condé, surgeon[82]   Bordeaux, France   d. 1776

Arms-bearing men	1	
Wife	1	Marie-Anne Bardet de la Ferne[83]

Adult females	1	Marguerite La Ferne[84] [?] see next entry
Daughters	1	Marie-Anne[85]
Slaves	5[86]	

Marguerite La Ferne[87]   Mobile   b. ca. 1754

| Slaves | 4 | Marianne b. ca. 1728, Marguerite b. ca. 1758, Louison b. ca. 1763, Lorine b. ca. 1750[88] |

Jean-Baptiste Martigny, Officer of the Militia   Canada   ca. 1728–1792[89]

Arms-bearing men	2	self, Joseph Lemoine Martigny[90] b. ca 1724
Wife	1	Marie-Hélène Hébert[91] b ca. 1732
Slaves	2	Lizette b. ca. 1735 and daughter Élisabeth b. ca 1764[92]

Guillaume Bizet   Montréal, Canada   d. 1772[93]

| Arms-bearing men | 2 | self, Charles Bizet[94] |
| Slaves | 7 | Courtette, François, Maillet, Charles, Manegin, Maricadieu, Jacob, Lizette, Catin[95] |

Widow Hébert (Hélène Danis)   ca.1709–1784[96]

Arms-bearing men	3	François b. ca. 1750,[97] Auguste b. ca. 1742,[98] Joseph? b. ca. 1741[99]
Wife	1	self
Adult males	2	?
Adult females	1	Thérèse b. ca. 1746[100]
Slaves	4	Janette?,[101] Madeleine b ca. 1734,[102] Luis? b. ca 1765[103]

Widow Dodier (Marie-Françoise Millet)   Montréal   1721–1783[104]

Wife	1	self
Adult females	2	Jeanne,[105] Élisabeth b. ca.1753[106]
Daughters	1	Marie-Thérèse[107]
Slaves	7	Baptiste, (Catteau), François, Jacob, Françoise, Louis, Marie-Joseph, Jean-Louis[108]

Jean-Baptiste Deschamps[109]

Arms-bearing men	1	self
Wife	1	Marie Pinot[110]
Sons	2	
Daughters	2	Cécile,[111] Marie-Louise b. 1765[112]

Louis Ride   Canada   1727–1787[113]

| Arms-bearing men | 2 | self |
| Wife | 1 | Véronique Marcheteau *dit* Desnoyers[114] |

238 Appendix A

Sons	2	Louis,[115] Laurent[116]
Daughters	2	Véronique[117]

Amable Guion   ca. 1742–1780[118]

Arms-bearing men	4	
Wife	1	Marguerite Blondeau, 1745–1832[119]
Sons	1	Amable b. ca. 1764[120]

Jean-Baptiste Becquet (locksmith)   Chartres   1725–1797[121]

Arms-bearing men	2	self, Pierre Becquet[122]
Wife	1	Marie-Françoise Dodier, ca. 1744–1785[123]
Sons	2	Gabriel b. ca. 1758[124]
Daughters	2	Marie b. ca. 1759,[125] Marguerite[126]
Slaves	1	Manon[127]

Julien Le Roy   d. by 1779[128]

Arms-bearing men	2	self, Alphonse Roy?[129]
Wife	1	Marie-Barbe Saucier d. by 1793[130]
Adult females	1	
Sons	2	Julien b. ca. 1760,[131] Charles b. ca. 1756[132]
Daughters	1	Madeleine b. ca. 1764[133]

Louis Desnoyers   d. by 1798[134]

Arms-bearing men	1	self
Wife	1	Agnès Pichart ca. 1748–1798[135]
Sons	1	

Louis Dubreuil, négociant   La Rochelle, France   ca. 1736–1794[136]

Arms-bearing men	1	self
Slaves	1	Louis?[137]

Jacques Noisé (*dit* Labbé)   Illinois Country   b. ca. 1740[138]

Arms-bearing men	6	self, Alexis[139]
Wife	1[140]	
Adult males	1	
Daughters	1	
Slaves	1	

Louis Marcheteau (*dit* Desnoyers)   Montreal, Canada   1711–1773[141]

Arms-bearing men	4	Pierre Marcheteau,[142] Joseph Marcheteau[143]
Wife	0[144]	
Adult males	2	Louis Jr., (Kiery) b. ca. 1734[145]
Sons	4[146]	

Widow Charon (Marie-Françoise Pinot)[147]

| Wife | 1 | self |
| Daughters | 1 | Thérèze b. ca. 1758[148] |

Gabriel Dodier   Illinois   ca.1740–1805[149]

Arms-bearing men	3	self, Louis Dodier
Wife	1	Marie-Marguerite Becquet, 1733–1813[150]
Adult males	1	
Sons	1[151]	
Daughters	2	Suzanne b. ca. 1763?,[152] Marie-Jeanne, b. 1765[153]
Slaves	1	Laveille b. ca. 1745[154]

La Giroflée (Jean Brunet)   1725–1766/7[155]

| Wife | 1 | Véronique Panissé[156] |
| Slaves | 2[157] | |

Toussaint Vaudry   1707–1773?[158]

| Arms-bearing men | 1 | self |
| Wife | 1 | Marie-Anne Du Pré b. 1710[159] |

Louis Briard *dit* La Roche   d. 1773[160]

Arms-bearing men	3	Ignace La Roche,[161] Joseph La Roche[162]
Wife	1	Marie-Anne Gérome Rousilliet b. ca 1729[163]
Sons	2	Louis b. 1763[164]
Daughters	1	Marie-Anne b. ca. 1758[165]

Charles Parant   ca.1716–1771[166]

| Arms-bearing men | 3 | self[167] |
| Wife | 1 | Marie-Barbe Vicomte ca. 1725–1780[168] |

Widow Beaugenou (Marie-Anne Henrion)   1721–1769[169]

Arms-bearing men	5	Charles Henrion ca. 1723–1783,[170] Nicolas Henrion,[171] Nicolas Beaugenou Jr., "Fifi" b. 1747[172]
Wife	1	self
Adult males	1 (?)	
Adult females	1	Hélène b. ca. 1751[173]
Sons	1	Charles b. ca. 1761[174]
Daughters	4	Élisabeth,[175] Agnès Françoise,[176] Thérèse,[177] Marie?[178]

Gilles Henrion   d. 1789?[179]

Arms-bearing men	1	self

Gilles Chemin   Paris, France   ca. 1714–1784[180]

Arms-bearing men	5	self, Jacques and Charles L'Espagnol (Quebedeau),[181] Charles Duchemin bp. 1751[182]
Wife	1	Marie-Jeanne Quebedeau d. 1783[183]
Adult males	1	
Daughters	0[184]	
Slaves	1	Marianne? b. ca. 1764[185]

François Desnoyers   Montreal   bp. 1719[186]

Arms-bearing men	1	self
Wife	0[187]	
Adult females	1	Marie-Josèphe b. 1750[188]
Sons	1	Joseph b. ca 1753[189]
Daughters	2	Marie-Geneviève b. 1757,[190] Véronique[191]

Toussaint Huneau   Canada[192]

Arms-bearing men	1	self
Wife	1	Marie-Josèphe Beaugenou 1750–1799[193]

Alexandre Langlois (*dit* Rondeau)   Quebec   d. by 1778[194]

Arms-bearing men	2	self, Noël Langlois ca. 1722,[195] Joseph-Marie Langlois[196]
Wife	1	Marie-Josèphe Lacroix ca. 1712–1779[197]
Slaves	1	Marie-Josèphe?[198]

Eugene Pourée (*dit* Beausoleil)   d. 1783[199]

Arms-bearing men	1[200]	
Wife	1	Marie-Josèphe Goudeau d. 1785[201]
Slaves	2	Victoire[202]

François Eloy   Illinois Country   b. ca. 1737[203]

Arms-bearing men	7	self

Jean-Baptiste Hervieux   Montréal   d. 1775[204]

Arms-bearing men	1	self
Adult females	0[205]	
Slaves	0[206]	

Louis Chancellier   St. Philippe   ca. 1752–1785[207]

Arms-bearing men	2	self

François Cottin   Canada   ca. 1750–1810[208]

Arms-bearing men	1

Antoine Rivière *dit* Baccané   Canada   1706–1816[209]

Arms-bearing men	1	Antoine Baccané b. ca. 1745[210]
Wife	1	Marie-Barbe Eloy b. ca. 1726[211]
Sons	3	Jean-Baptiste b. ca. 1752,[212] Philippe b. ca. 1757,[213] Joseph?[214]
Daughters	2	Marie-Thérèse b. ca 1759,[215] Marie-Jeanne b. ca. 1760[216]

Joseph Michel *dit* Taillon   Canada   b. ca. 1717–1807[217]

Arms-bearing men	5	self, Roger Taillon[218]
Wife	1	Marie-Louise Bossett ca. 1730–1799[219]
Adult females	1	Marie-Louise?[220]
Sons	2	Charles,[221] Joseph?[222]
Daughters	2	Marianne,[223] Hélène[224]
Slaves	12	Marie-Louise,[225] sons Aiken and Julien b. ca. 1757 and 1759,[226] Marie-Jean Scypion[227]

Alexis Marié   France   ca. 1737–1797[228]

Arms-bearing men	1	self
Wife	1	Renée Guilgaut, b. ca. 1748[229]
Sons	1	Michel Alexis, b. ca. 1764[230]

Jean-Baptiste Langevin (*dit* Baguette)   d. by 1792[231]

Arms-bearing men	5	self
Wife	1	Marie-Anne Charbonnet[232]

Alexis Picard   Canada   bp. 1722 d. by 1787[233]

Arms-bearing men	3	self
Wife	1	Marie La Roche, ca. 1729–1787?[234]
Sons	1	
Daughters	2	Geneviève, b. ca. 1760,[235] Marie[236]
Slaves	4	

Jean-Baptiste Becquet (the miller)   b. Chartres, Illinois[237]

Arms-bearing men	2	self, Pierre Becquet[238]
Wife	1	Élisabeth Marcheteau *dit* Desnoyers b. 1734–1790[239]
Sons	4	Jean-Baptiste, b. 1755;[240] Joseph, b. ca. 1758; André, b. ca. 1761; Charles, b. ca. 1763[241]
Daughters	2	Élisabeth b. ca. 1753,[242] Marie[243]

Charles Routier   Canada   1703–1777[244]

Arms-bearing men	4	self, son Charles b. 1747[245]
Wife	1	Jeanne Marcheteau *dit* Desnoyers d. 1773[246]
Adult males	1	Charles?
Adult females	1	Geneviève bp. 1749[247]

Jean-Baptiste Bidet *dit* Langoumois   d. by 1776[248]

Arms-bearing men	1	self, marked "absent"
Wife	1	Marie-Catherine Noisé b. ca. 1738[249]

Jean-Baptiste Gamache   Canada   1734–1805[250]

Arms-bearing men	1	self

Louis Deshêtres   Fort St. Joseph   1731–1770[251]

Arms-bearing men	1	self
Wife	1	Marie-Thérèse d'Amours de Louvière d. 1776[252]
Adult females	1	Marie-Josèphe de Tonty[253]
Sons	1	Pierre b. 1766[254]
Daughters	1	Charlotte, sister of Marie-Thérèse?[255]

René Kiercereau   France   ca.1733–1798[256]

Arms-bearing men	3	self, Grégoire fils,[257] Paul Kiercereau[258]
Wife	1	Marie-Madeleine Robillard, d. 1783[259]
Adult males	1	Grégoire?
Daughters	1	Marie-Madeleine[260]

Joseph Calvé   Canada   173?–1815?[261]

Arms-bearing men	1	self
Wife	1	Marie Maréchal, 1740–1791[262]
Sons	1	Joseph, b. ca. 1763[263]
Daughters	1	Marie-Thérèse, d. 1828[264]
Slaves	1	

Widow Maréchal (Marie-Jeanne Illeret)   Fort de Chartres, Illinois   1720–1784[265]

Arms-bearing men	3	Jacques,[266] Nicolas, and Antoine Maréchal b. ca. 1744[267]
Wife	1	self
Adult males	3	
Adult females	1	Catherine[268]
Sons	2	Joseph, François[269]
Daughters	1	Marie-Élisabeth[270]

François Bissonet Canada ca. 1741–1787[271]

Arms-bearing men	2	self[272]
Wife	1	Marie-Catherine Marcheteau *dit* Desnoyers 1740–1808[273]
Sons	1	
Daughters	1	Marie-Catherine[274]

François L'Arche Quebec[275]

Arms-bearing men	3	self
Wife	1	Élisabeth Dauphinet[276]
Adult females	1	Hélène b. 1750[277]

Philibert Gagnon *dit* Laurent[278]

Arms-bearing men	2	self-volontaire

François Delin Limoges, France[279]

Arms-bearing men	1	self

Militia of St. Louis, July 27, 1766[280]

Officers

Messieurs	Martigny*[281]	(Jean-Baptiste)	Captain
	Labuxière*	(Joseph)	Lieutenant
	DesBruisseau	(Joseph, Jr.)	Ensign

Sergeants

	Chemin*	Gilles	
	Legrain[282]	Ignace	

Militia Habitants

Négociant	Laclède*	Le Sr.	
	Bêrard*	Le Sr.	
	Chouteau*	Le Sr.	
Négociant	Dubreuil*	Le Sr.	
	L'arche*	François	absent
	Marié*	Alexis	
	Butaud *dit* Brindamour	Jean	
	Langevin *dit* Baguette*	Jean-Bte	
	Hervieux armurier du Roy*	Jean-Bte	
	Chancellier*	Louis	

Deschênes[283]	Joseph	
Taillon*	Roger	
Picard*	Alexis	
Laroche*	Ignace	
Roy*	Alphonse	abs
Bequet*	Jean-Bte	
Routier, pere*	Charles	
Routier, fils*	Charles	
Pitre	Joseph	
Deshêtre*	Louis, interprète	
Kiercereau*	René père	
Kiercereau*	Gregoire fils	
Robert[284]	Louis	
Dubé[285]	(Joseph)	
Calvé*	Joseph	
Papin[286]	Le Sr.	
Langoumois*	Jean-Bte	abs
Gamache*	Jean-Bte	
Bissonnet*	François	
Maréchal*	Jacques	
Maréchal*	Nicolas (Jr.)	
Maréchal*	Antoine	
Langlois*	Alexandre	
Langlois*	Noel	
Taillon*	Joseph	
Kiercereau[287]	Paul	
Deschamps*	Jean-Bte	
Martigny*	Lemoine (Joseph)	
Ride*	Louis	
Guion*	Amable	
Le Roy*	Julien	
Noisé*	Jacques	abs
Noisé	Alexis	
Loise	Paul	abs
Marchetaud*	Louis	
Vaudry*	Toussaint	
Laroche*	Joseph	
Parant*	Charles	
Hunaud*	Toussaint	
Marchetaud*	François	
(Rivière *dit*) Bacanet*	Antoine	
Dodier*	Gabriel (Jr.)	

Bequet*	Jean-Bte	
Bequet[288]	Pierre	
Boujenau*	(Nicolas, Jr.)	
Henrion*	Gilles	
Henrion*	Charles	
Henrion*	Nicolas	
Duchemin	fils (Charles)	
(Quebedeau *dit*) Lespagnol*	Jacques	
(Quebedeau *dit*) Lespagnol*	Charles	abs
Hebert*	François	
Hebert*	Auguste	
Bizet*	Guillaume	
Eloy*	François	
Delin*	François	
Bizet*	Charles	
Desnoyer*	Louis	
Marchetaud*	Pierre	abs
Marchetaud*	Joseph	

Volontaires

La Chapelle[289]	Bazile	abs
Tourignan	Pierre	
Choret[290]	Nicolas	
Lamontagne	Antoine	
Lamontagne	Jean	abs
Bormet	Jean-Bte	
La Caboihe	Pierre	
Pichet[291]		
Lavergne[292]		
Desnoyer[293]	Bazile	
Laberge	Andre	
Bequet	Pierre[294]	
St. Amand[295]		
Jus (?)		abs
Dufresne[296]		abs
Langlois	Joseph-Marie	
Pitre	Alphonse	
Germain	Bte	
Germain	Jacques	
Des Biens		
Provenché[297]	(Jean-Bte)	
La Chanse		

Appendix A

Gaignon*[298]		
Pitre	Michel	
Michon	Alexis[299]	
Michon	Joseph	
Barsalous[300]	(Nicolas)	abs
Varoquier		abs
Pinaud[301]		abs
La Croix[302]	(Pierre or Jacques?)	
Desfond	(Louis)	
Prevost[303]	Jeannot	
Ladéroute[304]	(Michel Rolet *dit*)	
Deschêne (?)[305]		
Istre?		
Gervais[306]		abs
Berger[307]	(Pierre Rougeau *dit* Berger)	
Carrier		
Chartrand[308]		
Lavoye[309]	(Jean Salé *dit* Lajoye)	
Texier[310]		
Clavier		
Denis[311]	(Jacques)	
Gingras		
Dodier*[312]	Louis	
Laverdure[313]	François	
Cornaud[314]		
Sanschagrin[315]		
Sanssoucy[316]	(Antoine)	
Hortes[317]		
Boutillte[318]?		
Blondin[319]		
St. Cloux[320]		

APPENDIX B
St. Louis Indian Slave Census, 1770

Unnamed slaves are designated with an *X*; ages, where given, follow the names. Some of the younger slaves enumerated here appear in the baptismal registers of the Archdiocese of St. Louis Archives and Records. For example, Louis St. Ange de Bellerive's young Indian slave, Louis, son of two of St. Ange's other slaves, François and Lizette, was baptized on June 25, 1770, just before the census was completed on July 8. Slaves under the age of fifteen years are listed as children.

Appendix B

	Men	Women	Male Children	Female Children
Sieur [Joseph] Labuxière		Louison, 24, not bapt.		
Sieur [Antoine] Hubert	Joseph, 25			
Sieur [Louis] Dubreuil		Jeanette, 15, not bapt.		
Estate of Chevalier Doriocourt		Rose, 35		
Estate of [Jean?] Valeau		Susanne, 28		
Joseph Taillon		Marie-Louise, 35	[her sons][1] X, 13 X, 11	Marie-Roze, 11
Alexandre Langlois *dit* Rondeau		Josephte, 16, not bapt.		
François Marcheteau			Pierre, 13, not bapt.	
Dame [Marie-Thérèse] Choutaud [Chouteau]		Thérèse, 16		Manon, 13
[Eugène] Pourré *dit* Beausoleil	Jacob, not bapt.	Rozete, 16, not bapt.	François, 11	Angélique (11)[2]
Jean-Baptiste Langevin *dit* Baguette	Hypolite, 17, not bapt.			
Lambert [*dit*] Bonvarlet				Madeleine, 12, not bapt.
Nicolas Royer				Marie-Jeanne, 12
Michel Rolet				Rozette, 9 not bapt.
Charles Carier				Angélique, 13, not bapt.
Louis Dufresne			Pierrot, 7, not bapt.	Marie, 8, not bapt.

St. Louis Indian Slave Census   249

Jean-Baptiste Martigny	Baptiste, 15	Lizette, 35	[her children] Joseph, 4 [and] Elizabeth, 6
Widow Dodier		Françoise, 15	Louison, 12
Michel Lamy	Jacob, 30	Ursule, 23	Catherine, 12, not bapt.
			Charlotte, 9, not bapt.
Guillaume Bizet	Jacob, 15, not bapt.		
René Buet		Lizette, 40	[her son] Pierrot, 15
Louis Bissonnet			Joseph, 14, not bapt.
Joseph Farlardeau			Charlotte, 10, not bapt.
Silvestre Labadie			Marie, 13, not bapt.
Pierre Montardy			Angelique, 12, not bapt.
			Jacob, 11, not bapt.
Alexis Marié			Castor, 8, not bapt.
Gerard Barssalou			Fanchon, 8, not bapt.
Jean Salé			Louis, 13, not bapt.
			Jeanette, 13, not bapt.
[Louis] de St. Ange [de Bellerive]	François, 28	Lizette, 40	Jean-Baptiste, 11
		Angélique, 30, not bapt.	Louis, 3 months, son of Lizette [and François]
			Ignace, 9 not bapt.

	Men	Women	Male Children	Female Children
Pierre Laclède [Liguest]	Cupidon, 22	Lizette, 27	Paul, 5 months, son of Lizette	
		Françoise, 24	Louis, 5, son of Françoise	
			X, 3 months, son of Françoise	
[?] Bérard			Le Veillé, 13, not bapt.	
Joseph LaBrosse				Angélique, 13
Jean-Baptiste Belisle			Jean-Baptiste, 11, not bapt.	
[Pierre] de Volsay [Volsey]				Thérèse, 12
Nicolas Barsalou		Marion, 30, not bapt.		Lizette, 11, not bapt.
				Catot, 12, not bapt.
				Peronelle, 6, not bapt.
Véronique Desnoyer			Joseph (*métis*), 13	
Laurent Trudeau			Jacob, 12, not bapt.	Charlotte, 11, not bapt.
Totals	8	17	21	23
Grand Total	69			

NOTES

Abbreviations

ACJ *Auguste Chouteau's Journal: Memory, Mythmaking, and History in the Heritage of New France,* edited by Gregory P. Ames (St. Louis: Mercantile Library, 2010)

AGI Archivo General de Indias, Papeles de Cuba, and Audiencia Santo Domingo, microfilm in Historic New Orleans Collection, New Orleans, and Missouri History Museum Archives, St. Louis

Annals Frederic Louis Billon, *Annals of St. Louis in Its Early Days under French and Spanish Dominations* (St. Louis: privately printed, 1886; reprint, Charleston, SC: Bibliolife, 2010)

ANOM Archives Nationales d'Outre Mer, Aix-en-Provence, France

Coutume Claude de Ferrière, *Nouveau Commentaire sur La Coutume de la Prévosté et Vicomté de Paris,* 2nd ed. (Paris: Jean Cochart, 1688)

CP Clarence Walworth Alvord and Clarence Edwin Carter, eds., *The Critical Period, 1763–1765,* Collections of the Illinois State Historical Library no. 10 (Springfield: Illinois State Historical Library, 1915)

CR *Cahokia Records, 1778–1790,* Clarence Walworth Alvord, ed., Collections of the Illinois State Historical Library, 2 (Springfield: Illinois State Historical Library, 1907)

DCB *Dictionary of Canadian Biography,* edited by Ramsay Cook and Réal Bélanger, http://www.biographi.ca/.

DGFQ René Jetté, comp., *Dictionnaire généalogique des familles du Québec des origines à 1730* (Montreal: Les Presses de l'Université de Montréal, 1983)

FDC Diocese of Belleville, Catholic Church Parish Records, 1729–1956, Fort de Chartres Register (parish of Ste. Anne) online at https://familysearch.org

FFL Carl A. Brasseaux, ed. and comp., *France's Forgotten Legion: Service Records of French Military and Administrative Personnel Stationed in the Mississippi Valley and Gulf Coast Region, 1699–1769* [CD-ROM] (Baton Rouge: Louisiana State University Press, 2000)

FSA French and Spanish Archives, Missouri History Museum Archives, St. Louis

HMLO Huntington Manuscripts, Loudoun Collection

IOE Theodore Calvin Pease and Ernestine Jenison, trans. and eds., *Illinois on the Eve of the Seven Years' War, 1747–1755,* Collections of the Illinois State Historical Library no. 29 (Springfield: Illinois State Historical Library, 1940)

ISC   Indian Slave Census, 1770, ms. M-M 508m, Louisiana Collection, Bancroft Library, Berkeley, CA

KM   Kaskaskia Manuscripts, Randolph County Courthouse, Chester IL

KPR   Diocese of Belleville, Catholic Church Parish Records, 1729–1956, Kaskaskia Parish Records (parish of the Immaculate Conception) online at https://familysearch.org

LT   *Livres Terriens*, manuscript copy, Missouri History Museum Archives, St. Louis

MHMA   Missouri History Museum Archives, St. Louis

NR   Clarence Walworth Alvord and Clarence Edwin Carter, eds., *The New Régime, 1765–1767*, Collections of the Illinois State Historical Library no. 11 (Springfield: Illinois State Historical Library, 1916)

SLAR   Archdiocese of St. Louis Archives and Records; microfilm at the St. Louis County Library Headquarters, Special Collections; references are for the St. Louis Old Cathedral sacramental registers unless otherwise noted

SRM   Louis Houck, ed., *The Spanish Regime in Missouri: A Collection of Papers and Documents Relating to Upper Louisiana Principally within the Present Limits of Missouri during the Dominion of Spain*, 2 vols. (Chicago: R. R. Donnelly, 1909)

St. Louis 1787 Census   Manuscript copy, Missouri History Museum Census Collections; nineteenth-century copy of original Spanish manuscript

TP   Clarence Walworth Alvord and Clarence Edwin Carter, eds., *Trade and Politics, 1767–1769*, Collections of the Illinois State Historical Library no. 16 (Springfield: Illinois State Historical Library, 1921)

VC   Margaret Kimball Brown and Lawrie Cena Dean, trans. and eds., *The Village of Chartres in Colonial Illinois, 1720–1765* (Ville Platte, La.: Provincial Press, 2003)

Introduction

1. That is, if one ignores the brief Napoleonic interlude.

2. Francis Parkman, *La Salle and the Discovery of the Great West* (New York: Signet Classic Edition, 1963), 228.

3. Laclède signed his name "Laclede Liguest," never using a grave accent, but for 150 years the accent has been used and omitting it now looks awkward in print.

4. For Chouteau's account of Laclède's vision of St. Louis's future success, see *ACJ*, facsimile ms., 2.

5. In addition to publishing a lavish edition of the "Journal" (n. 4), the Mercantile Library, which owns the original ms., hosted a conference about the "Journal" in June 2014.

6. William H. Leckie Jr. ("Commentary Column," *St. Louis Post-Dispatch*, February 26, 1989) made a credible case that Chouteau's "Journal" was written no earlier than 1825. Oscar W. Collet, an early secretary of the Missouri Historical Society, was the first to point out that the "Journal" was more a collection of memories than a journal properly understood ("Preface to the Chouteau Journals," Collet mss., St. Louis History Collection, MHMA). Gregory P. Ames followed suit and chose to characterize the Chouteau document as a narrative ("Introduction: Why a New Translation of Chouteau's *Narrative*?" in *ACJ*, 43).

7. See Robert Michael Morrissey, *Empire by Collaboration: Indians, Colonists and Governments in the Illinois Country, 1600–1774,* Early American Studies Series (Philadelphia: University of Pennsylvania Press, 2015).

8. Concerning the issue of zones in colonial development, see the stimulating essay by Jay Gitlin, "On the Boundaries of Empire: Connecting the West to Its Imperial Past," in *Under an Open Sky: Rethinking America's Western Past,* edited by William Cronon, George Miles, and Jay Gitlin (New York: W. W. Norton, 1992), 71–89.

Chapter 1. Fort d'Orléans and the Grotton–St. Ange Family

1. The confusion began with Auguste Chouteau's "Journal" (*ACJ,* facsimile ms., 9–12), in which the brothers, Pierre and Louis, are conflated. Francis Parkman (*Conspiracy of Pontiac and the Indian War after the Conquest of Canada,* 6th ed., 3 vols. [Boston: Little, Brown, 1898], 2:275) conflated Louis and his father, Robert. Marc Villiers du Terrage (*La découverte du Missouri et l'histoire du Fort d'Orléans* [Paris: H. Champion, 1925], 84) mentioned Louis St. Ange de Bellerive but was unaware that Robert Grotton St. Ange even participated in Bourgmont's Missouri-River venture. Frank Norall (*Bourgmont: Explorer of the Missouri, 1698–1725* [Lincoln: University of Nebraska Press, 1988]) confused the three Grotton–St. Ange men who participated in Bourgmont's expedition.

2. In *DGFQ,* 531, compiler René Jetté notes that Grotton–St. Ange was a sergeant in a Canadian company of marines in 1686, which means that he couldn't have been born much, if at all, after 1665. See also *DCB,* s.v. "Groston (Grotton) de St. Ange, Robert," by John Francis McDermott.

3. Marriage contract in KM, 18-3-24-1, meaning the first inventoried document dated March 24, 1718. Margaret K. Brown and Lawrie C. Dean performed the Herculean task of sorting out, collating, and indexing this remarkable collection of manuscripts. All of us who are interested in Illinois Country history are indebted to these two scholars.

4. See Hubert Charbonneau, *Vie et mort de nos ancêtres: Étude démographique* (Montreal: Université de Montréal, 1975).

5. Jeanne seems to have died in infancy. Her father was one Jean Maillot, merchant of Ville Marie. See Ancestry.com, Joseph Drouin Collection, Quebec Vital and Church Records, 1621–1967 (database online). We are indebted to Pat Weeks of Dana Point, California, for calling this vital record to our attention.

6. See Rachel B. Juen and Michael S. Nassaney, "The Fur Trade," Fort St. Joseph Archaeological Project Booklet Series, no. 2, Western Michigan University, 2012; and the website http://www.ci.niles.mi.us/ . . . /fortstjosephmuseum/overviewfortstjosephmuseum.htm.

7. *DGFQ,* 532.

8. Pierre-François Xavier de Charlevoix, *Journal d'un Voyage* (Paris, 1744), 312. The remains of this fort have not yet been discovered.

9. See the short muster roll (eight men) of soldiers at St. Joseph in Joseph L. Peyser, trans. and ed., *Letters from New France: The Upper Country, 1686–1783* (Urbana: University of Illinois Press, 1992), 114–15.

10. Charlevoix, *Journal d'un Voyage,* 173–74.

11. Ibid., 390.

12. Reuben G. Thwaites, ed., *Jesuit Relations and Allied Documents,* 73 vols. (Cleveland: Burrow Brothers, 1896–1901), 59:139.

13. Pierre Margry, ed. and comp., *Découvertes et établissements des Français dans l'ouest et dans le sud de l' Amérique septentrionale, 1614–1754* (Paris: Imprimerie D.

Jouaust, 1875), 1:549–50. This account was likely that of Nicolas de La Salle (see *DCB*, s.v. "La Salle, Nicolas de," by C. E. O'Neill), no relative of the more famous La Salle.

14. Concerning the Pawnees, see Douglas Parks, "Pawnee," in *Plains*, edited by Raymond J. DeMallie, vol. 13 of *Handbook of North American Indians*, edited by William C. Sturtevant (Washington, D.C.: Smithsonian Institution Press, 2001), 514–17.

15. This paragraph is based largely on accounts in Villiers du Terrage, *La découverte du Missouri*, chap. 4; Norall, *Bourgmont*, chap. 2; and *DCB*, s.v. "Véniard de Bourgmont, Étienne de," by Louise Dechêne.

16. According to Douglas Parks, a leading expert on western Indians, "prior to mid-eighteenth century, the term Padouca and its many variants were used by the French to designate Plains Apacheans. After the Comanches displaced the Plains Apacheans in mid-eighteenth century, Padouca (Dhegiha Siouan in origin) came to designate the Comanches" (e-mail communication, August 23, 2004). See also Mildred Scott Wedel, "Claude-Charles Dutisné: A Review of his 1719 Journeys," pt. 2, *Great Plains Quarterly* 12 (Spring 1973): 158–59.

17. See Bienville to Indies Company commissioners, February 1, 1723, ANOM, C^{13A} 7:184.

18. See http://www.nebraskastudies.org/0300/frameset_reset.html?http://www.nebraskastudies.org/0300/stories/0301_0114.html.

19. On John Law, see especially Marcel Giraud, *Histoire de la Louisiane française*, vol. 3, *L'Epoque de John Law (1717–1720)* (Paris: Presses universitaires de France, 1966).

20. See note 17 (emphasis added).

21. KM, 23-7-20-1 (that is, document no. 1 for July 20, 1723).

22. Norall (*Bourgmont*, 42) states that St. Ange joined Bourgmont's expedition at Cahokia, but Fort de Chartres seems much more likely for this fateful event. Norall's book is essential for studying Bourgmont, but it also presents problems. Norall didn't understand that there were three St. Anges (indeed, four, counting Élisabeth Chorel Grotton St. Ange) involved in the Fort d'Orléans enterprise and didn't understand the family's importance at the fort. Second, he got his source references mixed up, so that his notes are sometimes confusing (see notations in the notes below). Louis Houck (*A History of Missouri from the Earliest Explorations and Settlements until the Admission of the State into the Union*, 3 vols. [Chicago: R. R. Donnelly & Sons, 1908], 1:260–67) provides a rather good account of Bourgmont and Fort d'Orléans but does not focus on the Grotton–St. Ange family and is unaware that Bellerive was a member of that family. Floyd C. Shoemaker's article "Fort Orleans: The Heritage of Carroll County," *Missouri Historical Review* 2 (January 1957): 105–12, curiously does not mention the Grotton–St. Ange family at all.

23. Mercier to Dominique-Marie Varlet, November 27, 1723, "Relations inédites des missions de l'Illinois," *Église et Théologie* 8 (May 1977): 280.

24. Norall discusses this welcoming party of Missouris (*Bourgmont*, 42) without citing a source and also claims that Bourgmont had with him his *métis* son by a Missouri woman who was named "Petit Missouri." It is clear (Bourgmont [at Fort d'Orléans] to Directors of the Company of the Indies, January 2, 1724, ANOM, C^{13A} 8:210–18) that a band of Missouris did in fact come down from their village to meet Bourgmont in the Illinois Country. Norall (*Bourgmont*, 170nn13, 15) incorrectly cites this letter as ANOM, C^{13C} 4: fols. 210 ff. Another version of this letter may be found in ANOM, C^{13C} 4:116 ff.

25. Bourgmont [at Fort d'Orléans] to Company of the Indies, January 2, 1724, ANOM, C^{13A} 8:215–16. Concerning some of the complexities surrounding Indian slav-

Notes to Chapter 1 255

ery in the Missouri River valley during the 1720s, see Carl J. Ekberg, *Stealing Indian Women: Native Slavery in the Illinois Country* (Urbana: University of Illinois Press, 2007), 16–22.

26. See La Renaudière's "Journal" in Norall, *Bourgmont*, 128, 132, 138.

27. Extract of letter from Beauharnois to d'Artaguiette, dated only 1735, ANOM, C¹¹ᴬ 63:259.

28. See Ekberg, *Stealing Indian Women*, 48; Sharon Person, *Standing Up for Indians: Baptism Registers as an Untapped Source for Multicultural Relations in St. Louis, 1766–1821*, Extended Publication Series no. 8 (Naperville, Ill.: Center for French Colonial Studies, 2010), 62.

29. Clark's "Journal," June 16, 1804, online at http://lewisandclarkjournals.unl.edu/index.html. Editor Gary E. Moulton's note to this entry states that "Sieur Etienne Véniard de Bourgmont established Fort Orleans in 1723. The site was in Carroll County, Missouri, above the mouth of the Grand River and nearly opposite the Little Osage village on the opposite side of the Missouri. . . . Mackay's map (*Atlas*, map 5) shows a 'vieux fort' some miles above the mouth of the Grand; Clark might have been using the map or Mackay's journal." See also http://www.jamesmackay.us/Map.html.

30. E-mail communication, October 10, 2011.

31. ANOM, C¹³ᴬ 4:111–12.

32. Ibid.

33. Bourgmont to Indies Company, February 18, 1724, ANOM, C¹³ᶜ4: 128. Pradel continued to serve for several years at Fort de Chartres and appears frequently in local civil records. Belisle, a brilliant though erratic officer, went straight on downriver to New Orleans, where he rose to the rank of major (1752) in the marine ranks and became a chevalier in the Order of St. Louis. However, in 1769 he was cashiered and sent back to France (ANOM, D²ᶜ 54).

34. Rôtisseur came from the parish of St. Leu in Paris. The parish church stands on rue St. Denis, just east of where the old central market, Les Halles, was located. One likes to think that Rôtisseur ("one who roasts") acquired his nickname roasting chickens in one of the *rôtisseries* at Les Halles. He died at Fort de Chartres in 1762.

35. Bourgmont to Messieurs (of the Indies Company), February 18, 1724, ANOM, C¹³ᶜ4:127.

36. La Renaudière stood as witness at a wedding in Kaskaskia on Saturday, April 22, 1724 (KM 24-4-22-1), and the convoy that bore him and the St. Anges up the Missouri must have left shortly thereafter, perhaps indeed the following Monday. All we know for certain is that it arrived at Fort d'Orléans well before June 25, when the first component of Bourgmont's expedition departed westward for the Kansa village.

37. He appears on the 1725 Illinois census as married and with two children (ANOM, G¹ 464).

38. Margry (*Découvertes et établissements des Français*, 6:398–449) was the first to publish La Renaudière's important "Journal," and Marc Villiers du Terrage was the first to identify it as La Renaudière's (*La découverte du Missouri*, 109). A signal contribution of Norall's book (*Bourgmont*, 125–61) is that it presents the first complete English translation of the "Journal."

39. Both of these sons were born at La Prairie, outside Montreal, Pierre in 1693 and Louis-Daniel in 1702 (*DGFQ*, 532). Jetté identifies the Louis born in 1698 as Bellerive, but later reports on Bellerive's age strongly suggest that he was the Louis-Daniel born in 1702. See also *DCB*, s.v., "Groston de St. Ange et de Bellerive, Louis," by Donald Chaput.

40. KM 40–4–25–1. François Coulon de Villiers was the brother of the two Coulon de Villiers brothers who fatefully encountered George Washington in western Pennsylvania in 1754 to ignite the French and Indian War (*DCB*, s.v. Villiers, François Coulon de; see also *DGFQ*, 282).

41. Norall (*Bourgmont*, chap. 7) and Villiers du Terrage (*La decouverte du Missouri*, chap. 9) present confused accounts of the respective roles of the St. Ange men, neither author being particularly interested in the St. Ange involvement in Bourgmont's ventures.

42. Norall, *Bourgmont*, 150.

43. This paragraph is based on La Renaudière's "Journal," in ibid., 151–58. See also this journal in Margry, *Découvertes et établissements des Français*, 6:440–46.

44. Norall's discussion of bullboats (*Bourgmont*, 79, 175n14) seems accurate but is impossible to verify because he provides no sources for his discussion.

45. ANOM, C^{13A} 4:130–158.

46. Norall (*Bourgmont*, 89) wrote that Fort d'Orléans was abandoned in a few years, but, as we shall see below, Bellerive remained there as commandant until1736.

47. ANOM, C^{13A} 4:159–160. See also Richard N. Ellis and Charlie R. Steen, "An Indian Delegation in France, 1725," *Journal of the Illinois State Historical Society* 67, no. 4 (1974): 385–405. This Indian woman eventually became known in historical accounts as Françoise Missouri or the Princess of the Missouris. Her life after she returned to the Missouri Country has been told by a descendant of hers, Pat Weeks of Dana Point, California (*Le Journal*, 7, no. 3 [1991]).

48. KM 25–10–13–1. *Mitaines* can be either mittens, in the American sense of the word, or fingerless gloves. In this instance, the latter seems more likely.

49. He was buried May 16, 1725, "Illinois, Diocese of Belleville, Catholic Parish Records, 1729–1956," images, FamilySearch (https://familysearch.org/pal:/MM9.3.1/TH-266-12338-134441-65?cc=1388122&wc=M99B-QMF:n480064976), Randolph > Kaskaskia Island > Immaculate Conception > 1695–1833 Baptisms, Marriages, Deaths > image 21 of 62.

50. Illinois census of 1725, ANOM, G^1 464.

51. See Joseph L. Peyser, trans. and ed., *On the Eve of the Conquest: The Chevalier de Raymond's Critique of New France in 1754* (East Lansing: Michigan State University Press, 1997), 9, passim.

52. See Bourdon estate documents (KM 23–7–1–1) in which a small house was valued at seven hundred livres.

53. Sophie White, *Wild Frenchmen and Frenchified Indians: Material Culture and Race in Colonial Louisiana* (Philadelphia: University of Pennsylvania Press, 2012), 227.

54. ANOM, G^1 464.

55. Marriage record March 5, 1726, "Illinois, Diocese of Belleville, Catholic Parish Records, 1729–1956," images, FamilySearch (https://familysearch.org/pal:/MM9.3.1/TH-266-12338-134145-62?cc=1388122&wc=M99B-QMF:n480064976), Randolph > Kaskaskia Island > Immaculate Conception > 1695–1833 Baptisms, Marriages, Deaths > image 24 of 62).

56. *DGFQ*, 1072.

57. Bison short ribs were a favored delicacy in the Illinois Country (see KM 23–11–8–4). It is also possible that grapes for wine were being grown at the fort. La Renaudière claimed that the French were raising grapes for wine near the Kansa village in the autumn of 1725 ("Journal," in Norall, *Bourgmont*, 129), and Terrisse de Ternan said that some wine was being produced at Fort de Chartres in 1729. See

Carl J. Ekberg, "Terrisse de Ternan: Epistoler and Soldier," *Louisiana History* 23 (Fall 1982): 404.

58. The six Indian slaves listed in the St. Ange household on the 1732 Illinois Country census (ANOM, G¹ 464) were surely brought down from Fort d'Orléans.

59. "St. Ange fils" (Pierre in this instance) signed an affidavit on another matter at the fort in October 1726 (KM 26–10–15–1), and presumably he took care of other family business as well.

60. Périer and de La Chaise to Company of the Indies, March 30, 1728, ANOM, C¹³ᴬ 11:90–91. Robert and Pierre were both given "réformé" ranks, which meant that they had the responsibilities of the specified rank but at reduced pay. Robert's annual salary was 480 livres and Pierre's 300.

61. ANOM, C¹³ᴬ 12:16.

62. The Foxes likely used the famous Portage des Sioux, an overland route between the Mississippi and Missouri Rivers, to strike at traffic on the Missouri River. See William E. Foley, *The Genesis of Missouri: From Wilderness Outpost to Statehood* (Columbia: University of Missouri Press, 1989), 87, 192, 227, 229, 233–34.

63. Bienville to Minister, June 29, 1736, ANOM, C¹³ᴬ 21:184. Bienville states clearly in this letter that Bellerive was being taken from "a small outpost on the Missouri" and sent to replace Vincennes on the Wabash. Both Villiers du Terrage (*La découverte du Missouri*, 115–16), and Norall (*Bourgmont*, 89) erroneously claim that Fort d'Orléans was abandoned before 1730.

64. Much discussion has taken place about the precise location of this Fox fortification. See especially Joseph Peyser's two articles "The 1730 Fox Fort: A Recently Discovered Map Throws New Light on the Siege and Its Location," *Journal of the Illinois State Historical Society* 73 (Autumn 1980): 201–13; and "The 1730 Siege of the Foxes: Two Maps by Canadian Participants Provide Additional Information on the Fort and Its Location," *Journal of the Illinois State Historical Society* 80 (Autumn 1987): 147–54.

65. The best account, by far, of the Fox Wars is R. David Edmonds and Joseph L. Peyser, *The Fox Wars: The Mesquakie Challenge to New France* (Norman: University of Oklahoma Press, 1993). Concerning the siege of the Fox fort, see especially chap. 5. The late Joseph Peyser was the reigning expert on this frightful episode in the history of the Illinois Country.

66. This was the father of the brothers, Joseph Coulon de Villiers, sieur de Jumonville, and Louis Coulon de Villiers, who famously engaged the young George Washington in southeastern Pennsylvania in 1754, humiliating Washington and igniting the French and Indian War. See Peyser, *Letters from New France*, chap. 7. Yet another Villiers brother, François, married St. Ange's daughter, Élisabeth, at Fort de Chartres in 1740 (marriage contract in KM 40–4–25–1).

67. Charles-François-Marie d'Auteuil de Monceaux, letter dated November 7, 1730, ANOM, F³24:197.

68. Beauharnois and Hocquart to Minister, November 2, 1730, ibid., 113.

69. Charlevoix, *Journal d'un Voyage*, 390.

70. ANOM, D²C 51. The Hôtel Tubeuf, facing the rue des Petits Champs in Paris's Second Arrondissement, is now the oldest portion of the Bibliothèque Nationale de France.

71. ANOM, C¹³ᴮ 1:139–46.

72. This fort was the one constructed in the spring of 1725 and was the second in a succession of Forts de Chartres.

73. This according to the 1732 census of Chartres, which Robert compiled (ANOM, G¹ 464).

74. Salmon to Minister, July 17, 1732, ANOM, C¹³ᴬ 15:166–68. Salmon was of course correct that Jesuit priests in the Illinois Country were countenancing mixed marriages (Ekberg, *Stealing Indian Women*, 26–27).

75. See Salmon to Minister, Jan. 31, 1733, ANOM, C¹³ᴬ 17:17–18. Robert Mazrim and Margaret K. Brown are conducting excavations at St. Ange's 1732 fort. Earlier excavations done at the site resulted in a publication (Edward B. Jelks, Carl J. Ekberg, and Terrance J. Martin, *Excavations at the Laurens Site: Probably Location of Fort de Chartres* I [Springfield: Illinois Historic Preservation Agency, 1989]) that incorrectly identified the fort as the one built by Pierre Dugué Boisbriant in 1719. Thirty years ago, it was not understood that St. Ange had built a fort in 1732. Brown and Mazrim posit that St. Ange's fort was located farther from the encroaching Mississippi River and to complement an expanding agricultural economy and concomitant growth of the village of Chartres.

76. See Carl J. Ekberg, *French Roots in the Illinois Country: The Mississippi Frontier in Colonial Times* (Urbana: University of Illinois Press, 1998), esp. chaps. 5 and 6.

77. Sophie White (*Wild Frenchmen and Frenchified Indians*, 135) ascribes "racial motives" to Salmon, which is debatable, but in any case she is careful not to confuse Salmon's motives with those of Illinois Country habitants.

78. Strangely enough, the only surviving record of this marriage appears in the *New York Times* of July 30, 1876 (see illustration). Pierre was killed in the infamous Chickasaw campaign of 1736, and his widow, Marie-Rose, married Nicolas Boyer on November 20, 1741. "Illinois, Diocese of Belleville, Catholic Parish Records, 1729–1956," images, Family Search (https://familysearch.org/pal:/MM9.3.1/TH-267-11765-123751-85?cc=1388122&wc=M99B-QMN:n2031332824), Randolph > Kaskaskia Island > Immaculate Conception > 1741–1834 Marriages > image 5 of 118).

79. ANOM, C¹³ᴬ 14:225–29.

80. Paul de Briquet, *Code militaire; ou, Compilation des ordonnances des roys de France concernant les gen de guerre* (Paris: Prault père, 1734 [also 1728, 1741, and 1761]), 384.

81. François Lange, comp., *La nouvelle pratique civile, criminelle, et beneficiale* (Paris: François le Breton, 1719), 803.

82. Peyser, *Letters from New France*, 157–59.

83. Many of the French source materials for the 1736 Chickasaw campaign were translated by Caroline and Eleanor Dunn and published in Indiana Historical Society Publications, vol. 8, no. 2 (Indianapolis: Wm. B. Burford, 1921), 73–143. The original mss. are mostly to be found in ANOM, F³ 24. The best secondary accounts may be found in Peyser, *Letters from New France*, 147–77; and James R. Atkinson, *Splendid Land, Splendid People: The Chickasaw Indians to Removal* (Tuscaloosa: University of Alabama Press, 2004), chap. 3.

84. Salmon to Minister, January 31, 1733, ANOM C¹³ᴬ 17:17–18, 212–13.

85. Report of September (?) 20, 1736, ANOM, F³ 24:256. Peyser (*Letters from New France*, 159) presents slightly different numbers using a different source.

86. Also sometimes called Écores à Margot by the French.

87. Estimated distances varied widely, even wildly, in colonial Louisiana.

88. "Remplacement d'officiers de guerre," May 18, 1733, ANOM, D²ᶜ 51.

89. ANOM, C¹³ᴬ 21:188–95.

90. Several accounts are found in ANOM, F³ 24:252–58. See also Salmon to Minister, June 15, 1736, ANOM, C¹³ᴬ 21:269.

91. From New Orleans on June 14, 1740, Bienville reported St. Ange's death, of which he had just heard (ANOM, C^{13A} 25:94).

92. *DGFQ*, 532, gives the births of a Louis Grotton, sieur de Bellerive, in 1698 and a Louis-Daniel Grotton in 1702. See also *DCB*, s.v. "Groston (Grotton) de Saint-Ange et de Bellerive, Louis," by Donald Chaput. Chaput suggests that the Louis St. Ange de Bellerive who appears throughout this book was in fact Louis-Daniel. We agree and conclude that the Louis born in 1698 died as an infant and that Louis-Daniel was his replacement in the Grotton–St. Ange family and took on the name Bellerive after the death of his brother. This conclusion is based on information provided by master genealogist Pat Weeks of Dana Point, California.

93. *DGFQ*, 293.

94. FSA, no. 2187.

Chapter 2. The Rise of Louis St. Ange de Bellerive

1. *ACJ*, facsimile ms., 10.

2. See muster roll from Fort de Chartres in 1735 in ANOM, D^{2C} 51.

3. Bienville to Minister, June 29, 1736, ibid., C^{13A} 21:181.

4. Salmon to Minister, Apr. 26, 1741, ibid., C^{13A} 26:142.

5. Concerning the Vincennes family, see *DGFQ*, 743; *DCB*, s.v. "Bissot de Vinsenne (Vincennes), François-Marie," by Yves F. Zoltvany; *DCB*, s.v. "Bissot de Vinsenne (Vincennes), Jean Baptiste," by Yves F. Zoltvany; Pierre-Georges Roy, *Sieur de Vincennes Identified*, translated by Mrs. Charles W. Moores, Indiana Historical Society Publications, vol. 7, no. 1 (Indianapolis: Indiana Historical Society, n.d.), 3–130; and Edwin C. Bearss, *Sieur de Vincennes: Founder of Indiana's Oldest City* (Vincennes: Vincennes Historical and Antiquarian Society, 2007), 1–15.

6. Contrôleur Général to Périer, November 1, 1730, ANOM, C^{13A} 12:344.

7. See "Projet de l'Estat des Depense pour l'année 1731," printed in Jacob Piatt Dunn, *Mission to the Ouabache*, Indiana Historical Society Publications, vol. 3, no. 1 (Indianapolis: Indiana Historical Society, 1895), 297. Also Minister Maurepas to Beauharnois, July 20, 1734, ANOM, Série B, fol. 568 (available online at Library and Archives Canada, http://www.collectionscanada.gc.ca/index-e.html).

8. Already in 1726 Vincennes's annual salary of three hundred livres was being paid out of New Orleans (see Governor Étienne Périer's instructions from the Compagnie des Indes, September 30, 1726, C^{13B} 1:93).

9. *DGFQ*, 531–32.

10. Bienville to Minister, June 29, 1736, ANOM, C^{13A} 21:184.

11. Salmon to Minister, June 22, 1736, ibid., 22:192.

12. Salmon to Minister, ibid., 21: 275.

13. Bearss (*Sieur de Vincennes*) presents a good survey of early Vincennes, but gives very short shrift to St. Ange.

14. Bienville to Minister, 1740?, ANOM, C^{13A} 25:86–93.

15. He was in fact thirty-eight, having been born February 13, 1702, and baptized February 20 (*DGFQ*, 532).

16. No baptismal record for him survives, but he was born sometime between 1712 and 1715 (ibid., 282).

17. See *DCB*, s.v. "Coulon de Villiers, François"; Gilbert C. Din, "François Coulon de Villiers: More Light on an Illusive Historical Figure," *Louisiana History* 41, no. 3 (2000): 345–57.

18. See Peyser, *Letters from New France* (see chap. 1, n. 9); and Edmonds and Peyser, *Fox Wars*, 177–78 (see chap. 1, n. 65).

19. For the latest detailed account of this famous episode on the early Ohio frontier, see Fred Anderson, *Crucible of War: The Seven Years' War and the Face of Empire in British North America, 1754–1766* (New York: Alfred A. Knopf, 2000), chaps. 4 and 5.

20. Marriage contract in KM 40–4–25–1. The sacramental record of the marriage has not survived.

21. He was acting commandant at the fort while La Buissonnière was engaged in Bienville's second Chickasaw campaign, that of 1739.

22. Robert Grotton de St. Ange signed a legal document pertaining to his grandchildren (of whom he was *tuteur*) on December 30, 1738 (filed by date in Illinois State Archives, Perrin Collection), but was not alive to be present at his daughter's wedding in April 1740. From New Orleans on June 14, 1740, Bienville reported St. Ange's death (ANOM, C^{13A} 25:94).

23. Report by Jean Jadard de Beauchamp (at Mobile) to Minister, April 25, 1741, ANOM, C^{13A} 26:207. For a listing of casualties, see ibid., C^{11A} 75:216.

24. Charles de Raymond (commandant at the Miamis Post) to Governor of Canada, Jacques-Pierre de Taffanel de La Jonquière, January 5, 1750, in *IOE*, 154–55. St. Ange's report on this development has not survived.

25. Vaudreuil, "Mémoire," November 9, 1745, ANOM, C^{13A} 29:85.

26. This according to Raymond in his letter to La Jonquière cited above, *IOE*, 153–54.

27. "Illinois, Diocese of Belleville, Catholic Parish Records, 1729–1956," images, Family Search (https://familysearch.org/pal:/MM9.3.1/TH-267-11882-151755-26?cc=1388122&wc=M99B-QMV:n408136662), Randolph > Fort de Chartres > St. Anne (transferred to St. Joseph) > 1721–1840 Baptisms, Marriages, Deaths, First Communion, Confirmations > image 67 of 603.

28. Concerning Saucier, see Walter J. Saucier and Katherine Wagner Seineke, "François Saucier, Engineer of Fort de Chartres, Illinois," in *Frenchmen and French Ways in the Mississippi Valley*, edited by John Francis McDermott (Urbana: University of Illinois Press, 1969), 199–230.

29. Macarty, "Order of Command," August 8–11, 1751, *IOE*, 293–322.

30. Ibid., 309.

31. ANOM, D^{2C} 54.

32. *DCB*, s.v. "Céloron de Blainville Pierre-Joseph," by W. J. Eccles.

33. See Pierre-Jean de Bonnecamps, "Relation du voyage de la Belle rivière fait en 1749, sous les ordres de M. de Céloron," in *Jesuit Relations and Allied Documents*, edited by Thwaites, 69:149–98 (see chap. 1, n. 12).

34. See Macarty's long dispatch to Vaudreuil, January 20, 1752, in *IOE*, esp. 444, 465; and St. Ange to Vaudreuil, February 28, 1752, ibid., 483–87.

35. Vaudreuil to Rouille, October 10, 1751, ibid., 404. On Indian republics, see also Richard White, *The Middle Ground: Indians, Empires, and Republics in the Great Lakes Region, 1650–1815* (Cambridge: Cambridge University Press, 1991), 186–240.

36. St. Ange to Vaudreuil, February 28, 1752, *IOE*, 485.

37. On French-style agriculture at Vincennes, see Ekberg, *French Roots*, 87, 115, 127, 243, and passim.

38. St. Ange to Vaudreuil, February 28, 1752, *IOE*, 485.

39. Vaudreuil to St. Ange, April 28, 1752, *IOE*, 613.

40. Kerlérec to Minister, October 1, 1755, ANOM, C^{13A} 39:35–36.

41. Concerning Langlade, see *Wisconsin Historical Collections* (Madison: Wisconsin Historical Society), vol. 3 (1857) and vol. 7 (1876).

42. R. White, *Middle Ground*, 230–31.

43. *IOE*, 674–75.
44. See Kerlérec to Minister (December 17, 1754, ANOM, C^{13A} 38:118; and December 12, 1758, ibid., 40:140). In later years, Fort St. Ange was sometimes transmogrified into Fort St. Anne by English speakers. See Edwin C. Bearss, *George Rogers Clark: Vincennes Sites Study and Evaluation* (Washington, D.C.: Department of Interior, 1967), 37n57.
45. We know that couriers did travel (apparently overland) between Chartres and Vincennes. In September 1752, Macarty wrote to Vaudreuil that he had sent "two couriers at once to travel day and night to inform M. de St. Ange of what is happening in these parts" (*IOE*, 671). However, no correspondence between Macarty and St. Ange has ever surfaced.
46. Service sheets of French officers in Louisiana, 1759 (ANOM, D^{2}C 50).
47. Charles de Raymond, St. Ange's sometime counterpart as commandant at the Miami Post (Fort Wayne), profited handsomely by engaging in the fur trade (see Peyser, *On the Eve of the Conquest*, 4–6 [see chap. 1, n. 51]).
48. Duverger, "Relation d'un voyage intéressant au Canada," Library and Archives Canada, microfilm reel F-651 (original ms. in Bibliothèque de l'université de Rennes), 80. Concerning Duverger, see *DCB*, s.v. "Forget Duverger, Jacques-François," by Noël Baillargeon.
49. Concerning Vincennes and its relationship to the other French villages of the Illinois Country, see Ekberg, *French Roots in the Illinois Country*, 83–84 (see chap. 1, n. 76).
50. Kerlérec to Minister, December 12, 1758, ANOM, C^{13A} 40:140.
51. Jacob Piatt Dunn, ed. and comp., *Documents Relating to the French Settlements on the Wabash*, Indiana Historical Society Publications, vol. 2, no. 11 (Indianapolis: Bowen-Merrill, 1894), 425–27.
52. Ibid., 429.
53. In any case, that is surely the gist of Vaudreuil's orders to Macarty, as seen above.
54. Frederick Haldimand to Thomas Gage, January 5, 1774, quoted in *Documents Relating to the French Settlements on the Wabash*, edited and compiled by Dunn, 431–33.
55. Haldimand to Earl of Dartmouth, January 5, 1774, quoted in Paul C. Phillips, "Vincennes in Its Relation to French Colonial Policy," *Indiana Magazine of History* 17 (December 1921): 335.
56. Marthe Faribault-Beauregard, ed., *La Population des forts français d'Amérique* (Montreal: Éditions Bergeron, 1984), 2:19.
57. Ibid., 26.
58. Ibid., 96.
59. Dunn, *Documents Relating to the French Settlements on the Wabash*, 428.
60. Faribault-Beauregard, *Population des forts français*, 2:68.
61. Ibid., 25.
62. Ibid., 26.
63. ISC. Original ms. census in Louisiana Collection, Bancroft Library, Berkeley, CA.
64. More on this issue in chapter 8.
65. Anderson, *Crucible of War*, 335–37.
66. Macarty to Kerlérec, August 30, 1759, ANOM, C^{13A} 41: 103
67. On Aubry, see *FFL*, s.v. "Aubry, Charles-Philippe." On Villiers, see *FFL*, s.v. "Coulon de Villiers, François"; *DCB*, s.v. "Coulon de Villiers, François; and Din, "François Coulon de Villiers."
68. See chapter 4.

69. Villiers to d'Abbadie, December 1, 1763, in *CP*, 52.
70. Andrew R. L. Cayton, *Frontier Indiana* (Bloomington: Indiana University Press, 1998), 47.
71. Villiers to d'Abbadie, December 1, 1763, *CP,* 55.
72. Villiers to d'Abbadie, April 20, 1764, ANOM, C^{13A} 44:93.
73. Dunn, *Documents Relating to the French Settlements on the Wabash*, 407 (our translation).
74. See chapter 4 and appendix A, Militia Muster Roll.
75. We are indebted to Diane Sheppard, Suzanne Boivin Sommerville, and Gail Moreau-DesHarnais for helping me sort out the complicated and important Drouet de Richardville family. The Richardville mentioned by St. Ange was baptized Joseph-Antoine Drouet at Sorel (on right bank of the St. Lawrence just below Montreal) on March 30, 1723. Cayton (*Frontier Indiana*, 48–49) discusses the Richardville-Outelas family and its importance in Vincennes after St. Ange's departure from the post.
76. Bloüin, "Mémoire," July 9, 1771, Thomas Gage Papers, 138:16, Clements Library, Ann Arbor, Mich.
77. D'Abbadie, "Journal," ANOM, C^{13A} 43:269.
78. D'Abbadie to Minister, July 16, 1764, ANOM, C^{13A} 44:99–100.

Chapter 3. The Illinois Country in Transition, 1763–1765

1. Paul W. Mapp, *The Elusive West and the Quest for Empire, 1713–1763* (Chapel Hill: University of North Carolina Press, 2011), 385. Mapp provides (chap. 13) an excellent recent analysis of Choiseul's diplomacy.
2. A photostat of this important document may be found in the John Francis McDermott Collection (Box 48, file 37) in the archives of Southern Illinois University at Edwardsville. The location of the original ms. is not known.
3. See d'Abbadie's marginal notes on a petition presented to him by New Orleans merchants (June 7, 1764, ANOM, C^{13A} 44:65); also Commissaire-ordonnateur Nicolas Foucault to Minister of Marine, Étienne de Choiseul, August 2, 1765, ibid., 45:138. Further confusing things, Chouteau, in the first sentence of his famous "Journal" (*ACJ*, facsimile ms., 1), claimed that Laclède's trading privilege was to last for eight years, but no other known source supports this claim.
4. For more on these issues, see Carl J. Ekberg, "The Exclusive Maxent-Laclède Trading Grant," *Missouri Historical Review* 106 (July 2012): 185–97.
5. See note 2.
6. Letters and instructions in ANOM, C^{13A} 43:216–224.
7. This has generated confusion, since Marc de Villiers du Terrage (*Les dernières années de la Louisiana française* [Paris: E. Guilmoto, 1903], 157) printed only the *first* set of d'Abbadie's instructions and remarked that the Treaty of Fontainebleau had been intentionally kept a secret from d'Abbadie.
8. Indeed, Kerlérec knew about the cession of Louisiana to Spain a month before d'Abbadie arrived in New Orleans (Kerlérec to Minister, May 2, 1763, ANOM, C^{13A} 43:196).
9. Ekberg, "Exclusive Trading Grant," 189.
10. See genealogical table in William E. Foley and C. David Rice, *The First Chouteaus: River Barons of Early St. Louis* (Urbana: University of Illinois Press, 1983), 211. Victoire, fourth child born of the liaison between Laclède and Madame Chouteau, would be born at New Orleans in March 1764 and baptized in May (see *Archdiocese of New Orleans Sacramental Records*, vol. 2, *1751–1771* [New Orleans: Archdiocese of New Orleans, 1988], 57).

11. *ACJ*, facsimile ms., 1.

12. Ibid.

13. See Carl J. Ekberg, *François Vallé and His World: Upper Louisiana before Lewis and Clark* (Columbia: University of Missouri Press, 2002), esp. chap. 7.

14. John Francis McDermott ("Myths and Realities Concerning the Founding of St. Louis," in *The French in the Mississippi Valley,* edited by McDermott [Urbana: University of Illinois Press, 1965], 9) tacitly accepted this chronology of Laclède's activities.

15. The most legible version of Villiers's November 1763 letter is a contemporary copy online from Canadian archives at http://collectionscanada.gc.ca/pam_archives/index.php?fuseaction=genitem.displayEcopies&lang=eng&rec_nbr=3073555&title=%5bRéponse%20de%20Pierre-Joseph%20Neyon%20de%20Villiers,%20commandant%20du%20fort%20de%20 . . . %5d.&ecopy=e000876039. Villiers's original ms. is given the date November 8 (available online at Louisiana Digital Archives).

16. Villiers to d'Abbadie, December 1, 1763, ANOM, C^{13A} 43:353–56.

17. Concerning the suppression of the Jesuit establishment at Kaskaskia, see *CP,* 62–133, especially Father Philibert Watrin's remarkable justification for the work that the Jesuits had done in the Illinois Country over many decades.

18. For details about this auction, see ibid., 125–32.

19. See, for example, KM 66-7-30-1.

20. *VC*, 788–89. Concerning this property, see Robert F. Mazrim, *At Home in the Illinois Country: French Domestic Site Archaeology in the Midwest, 1730–1800* (Urbana: Illinois State Archaeological Survey, 2011), 11–12, 214–16. See also chapter 7.

21. Maxent to Ulloa, n.d., AGI, PC, 188A.

22. Villiers to d'Abbadie, December 1, 1763, ANOM, C^{13A} 43:353–56.

23. *ACJ*, facsimile ms., 2.

24. Nicolas de Finiels, *An Account of Upper Louisiana,* edited by Carl J. Ekberg and William E. Foley and translated by Carl J. Ekberg (Columbia: University of Missouri Press, 1989), 83.

25. See Carl J. Ekberg and Sharon K. Person, "The 1767 Dufossat Maps of St. Louis," *Gateway* 32 (2012): 8–25.

26. *ACJ*, facsimile ms., 2.

27. Villiers to D'Abbadie, December 1, 1763, in ANOM, C^{13A} 43:353–56.

28. "Illinois, Diocese of Belleville, Catholic Parish Records, 1729–1956," images, Family Search (https://familysearch.org/pal:/MM9.3.1/TH-267-11765-123279-72?cc=1388122&wc=M99B-QMN:n2031332824), Randolph > Kaskaskia Island > Immaculate Conception > 1741–1834 Marriages > image 33 of 118.

29. Villiers to d'Abbadie, February 3, 1764, online with Louisiana Digital Library (http://louisdl.louislibraries.org/cdm4/index_LPC.php?CISOROOT=/LPC).

30. Concerning Vallé's importance in Upper Louisiana, see Ekberg, *François Vallé and His World.*

31. *ACJ*, facsimile of ms., 2.

32. John Francis McDermott, "Auguste Chouteau: First Citizen of Upper Louisiana," in *Frenchmen and French Ways in the Mississippi Valley,* edited by McDermott, 1 (see chap. 2, n. 28).

33. The issue of whether Auguste Chouteau was born in September 1749 or September 1750 has not been conclusively resolved. See Foley and Rice, *First Chouteaus*, 2.

34. Chouteau (*ACJ*, facsimile ms., 8) listed a "Baptiste Marligni" as one of the original settlers, and Frederic Louis Billon (*Annals,* 17–18) followed suit by including "Jno B. Martigny" among the "thirty worthies" who constituted St. Louis's first pioneers.

35. *DGFQ,* 713.

36. See Jacques Mathieu, *La Nouvelle-France: Les Français en Amérique du Nord, XVIe–XVIIIe siècles* (Quebec: Presses de l'université Laval, 1991), 100; Marcel Marion, *Dictionnaire des institutions de la France aux XVIIe et XVIIIe siècles* (Paris: A. & J. Picard, 1969), 376–79.

37. Frederick A. Hodes, *Beyond the Frontier: A History of St. Louis to 1821* (Tucson: Patrice Press, 2004), 72–73.

38. Concerning the battle at Belle Famille, see Brian Leigh Dunnigan, *Siege—1759: The Campaign against Niagara* (Youngstown, N.Y.: Old Fort Niagara Association, 1996), 83–97; and Pierre Pouchot, *Mémoires sur la dernière guerre de l'Amérique septentrionale* (Yverdon, Switzerland: n.p., 1781), 40, 91, 124. Fifty-four militiamen, mostly from Illinois communities, perished at Belle Famille (see Macarty's report to New Orleans, ANOM, C^{13A} 41:103).

39. Martigny's last appearance in the civil records of Chartres came in March 1763 (KM 63-3-1-1).

40. Villiers to d'Abbadie, March 13, 1764, online at Louisiana Digital Library (http://louisdl.louislibraries.org/cdm4/index_AAW.php?CISOROOT=%2FAAW). John Francis McDermott, ed., *Early Histories of St. Louis* (St. Louis: St. Louis Historical Documents Foundation, 1952), 33, presents this passage in French, taken from an early typescript. *Établissement* can mean a variety of things in French. In this instance, we have opted for "trading house" to make it conform to what was agreed upon in New Orleans on August 2, 1763, as described above.

41. D'Abbadie, "Journal" in ANOM, C^{13A} 43:249–282.

42. Villiers to d'Abbadie, April 20, 1764, ANOM, C^{13A} 44:92–93.

43. Ste. Genevieve Civil Records (microfilm MHMA), Miscellaneous 2, no. 80. See below for more on Laclède at Ste. Genevieve. Census in appendix A.

44. *Archdiocese of New Orleans Sacramental Records,* 2:57.

45. D'Abbadie, "Journal," ANOM, C^{13A} 43: 268.

46. Rivière deposition in July 29, 1825, Theodore Hunt, "Minutes," 2:102–03, MHMA.

47. Pierre Chouteau in Hunt, "Minutes," 3:100.

48. *The Great West and Her Commercial Metropolis* (St. Louis: published in the office of "Edward's Monthly," 1860), 243.

49. *Annals,* 50. Calvé was Canadian born and raised and a sometime resident of St. Louis. See 1766 St. Louis census in appendix A; and Houck, *History of Missouri,* 2:39–40 (see chap. 1, n. 22).

50. Both Datchurut and Viviat were literate, educated Frenchmen who traded out of Ste. Genevieve, sometimes as partners, until the early 1780s. Concerning Datchurut, see Carl J. Ekberg, *Colonial Ste. Genevieve: An Adventure on the Mississippi Frontier* (Gerald, Mo.: Patrice Press, 1985). For an interesting description of Viviat, see Robert G. Carroon, ed., *Broadswords and Bayonets* (n.p.: Society of Colonial Wars in the State of Illinois, 1984), 89.

51. FSA, nos. 1505A and 1508.

52. Maxent to Ulloa, May 8, 1769, AGI, PC, 188A.

53. Ekberg, "Exclusive Maxent-Laclède Trading Grant"; John Francis McDermott, "The Exclusive Trading Grant of Maxent-Laclède and Company," *Missouri Historical Review* 29 (July 1935): 272–78.

54. Document dated April 18, 1765, in Ste. Genevieve Civil Records (microfilm MHMA), Miscellaneous 2, no. 80. From this document's date, it may be inferred that Laclède had brought his trade goods to Ste. Genevieve the previous autumn.

55. In March 1766, Vallé received a government contract to house and feed Indians passing through Ste. Genevieve (FSA, no. 2836).

56. Henri Joutel recorded in his journal for October 1767 that Illinois Indian women, among whom he included Shawnees, unabashedly carried on sexual affairs with French traders (*Journal historique du dernier voyage que feu M. de laSale fit dans le Golfe de Mexique* [Paris: Etienne Robinot, 1713], 345). Michael McCafferty of Indiana University provided this reference.

57. See note 54.

58. If Laclède had had a written contract, it logically would have been mentioned in the deposition document cited in note 54 Fur trade contracts between merchants and voyageurs were standard operating procedure in the Illinois Country (see chapter 10).

59. Ekberg, *François Vallé and His World,* chap. 7.

60. Villiers to d'Abbadie, December 1, 1763, ANOM, C^{13A} 43:353–56; d'Abbadie to Villiers, January 1, 1764, *CP,* 233–34. See also Carl A. Brasseaux and Michael J. LeBlanc, "Franco-Indian Diplomacy in the Mississippi Valley, 1754–1763: Prelude to Pontiac's Uprising," in *The French Experience in Louisiana,* edited by Glenn R. Conrad, Louisiana Purchase Bicentennial Series in Louisiana History, vol. 1 (Lafayette: Center for Louisiana Studies, University of Southwestern Louisiana, 1995), 339; d'Abbadie to Villiers, January 1, 1764, *CP,* 233–34.

61. This according to firsthand intelligence gathered by Colonel Gladwin at Detroit, June 9, 1764. See *Papers of Sir William Johnson,* 14 vols. (Albany: State University of New York Press, 1921–65), 11:226.

62. "Journal of William Howard," ibid., 698. Dating events based on when strawberries ripened was popular in the Illinois Country (see Ekberg, *Colonial Ste. Genevieve,* 459).

63. Gage to Bouquet, November 9, 1764, *CP,* 353.

64. St. Ange to d'Abbadie, July 15, 1764, *CP,* 289–90.

65. D'Abbadie to Gage, August 16, 1764, Thomas Gage Papers, American Series 23, Clements Library, Ann Arbor, Mich.

66. *History of Louisiana,* 3rd ed. (New Orleans: Armand Hawkins, 1885), 2:98.

67. Parkman, *Conspiracy of Pontiac,* 2:276 (see chap. 1, n. 1).

68. St. Ange to d'Abbadie, February 21, 1765, ANOM, C^{13A} 45:53.

69. Ross to Farmar, February 21, 1765, *CP,* 442.

70. St. Ange report to d'Abbadie, April 7, 1765, *CP,* 471–81.

71. *CP,* 472–76.

72. Ross to Farmar, May 25, 1765, *CP,* 481–83.

73. See Fraser's lengthy report (twenty-nine pages) to General Thomas Gage, April 27, 1765, in Gage Papers, American Series, vol. 32, no. 4, Clements Library, Ann Arbor, Mich.

74. Ibid., 11.

75. Ibid., 21.

76. Fraser to Gage, May 18, 1765, *CP,* 494–95.

77. Fraser to Gage, April 27, 1765, see note 73, 17.

78. Fraser's letter to St. Ange has not survived, but Fraser reported its contents to Lieutenant Colonel John Campbell, British commandant at Detroit (Fraser to Campbell, May 17, 1765, *CP,* 493–94).

79. Croghan to William Murray, July 12, 1765, in *Papers of Johnson,* 11:841.

80. Croghan, "Journal," *NR,* 32.

81. See Stirling to Gage, October 18, 1765, *NR,* 110.

82. Croghan to William Johnson, November 1765, *NR,* 53.

83. Gage to Conway, September 23, 1765, *NR,* 85.

84. Concerning Loftus's expedition, see *CP,* 205–39.

85. Farmar to Stuart, December 16, 1765, *NR,* 127.

86. Stirling commanded the Black Watch during most of the American Revolution, became baron of Ardoch when his older brother died, and died himself at his home in Perthshire, Scotland, in 1808. (Carroon, *Broadswords and Bayonets,* 7). Description of Stirling's departure from Fort Pitt, *NR,* 26.

87. James Eddington, "Journal," *NR,* 75, 82. Thirty years later, Nicolas de Finiels wrote of "the naïve beauties of Ste. Geneviève" (*Account of Upper Louisiana,* 67).

88. Eddington, "Journal," in *Broadswords and Bayonets,* edited by Carroon, 83.

89. Stirling to Gage, October 18, 1765, *NR,* 110.

90. Eddington to ?, October 17, 1765, *NR,* 105.

91. Stirling to Gage, October 18, 1765, *NR,* 109.

92. Gordon, "Journal," *NR,* 298. Concerning Gordon, see biographical note in *NR,* 67n2.

93. Villiers to d'Abbadie, December 1, 1763, ANOM, C^{13A} 43:353–56.

94. Stirling to Gage, October 18, 1765, *NR,* 109.

95. Eddington to ? October 17, 1765, *NR,* 106. Drury Lane was the most famous playhouse in mid-eighteenth-century London.

96. Eddington, "Journal," in *Broadswords and Bayonets,* edited by Carroon, 83.

97. FSA, no. 2325. Briquet, *Code militaire,* first page of unpaginated preface (see chap. 1, n. 80).

98. Stirling, "Journal," in *Broadsides and Bayonets,* edited by Carroon, 45.

99. The Battle of Culloden (1745) ended forever Jacobite uprisings against Hanoverian England, and French troops supported the Scots on behalf of Charles Edward Stuart, pretender to the throne.

Chapter 4. Commandant St. Ange de Bellerive

1. *Annals,* 50.

2. SLAR, Baptism.

3. Fraser to General Gage, December 16, 1765, *NR,* 130.

4. Eddington, "Journal," in *Broadswords and Bayonets,* edited by Carroon, 84 (see chap. 3, n. 50).

5. Eddingstone [sic] to unknown person, October 17, 1765, *NR,* 106.

6. Stirling to Gage, December 15, 1765, *NR,* 124.

7. Theodore Hunt "Minutes," 1:125, typescript copy in MHMA.

8. Concerning Rocheblave's career at Ste. Geneviève, see Ekberg, *Colonial Ste. Geneviève,* 336–40 (see chap. 3, n. 50); and Ekberg, *François Vallé and His World,* 50–52, 99–102 (see chap. 3, n. 13).

9. Kerlérec to Minister, March 21, 1762, ANOM, C^{13A} 43:26.

10. See FSA, no. 2297. Lefebvre's son, Pierre-François Brunot Joseph d'Inglebert Lefebvre, immediately took over as storekeeper but not as judge. Several years later, he fled St. Louis under a cloud of suspicion about peculation. See chapter 9.

11. Stirling to Gage, December 15, 1765, *NR,* 124.

12. *VC,* 197–200. Also Labuxière's burial record at "Illinois, Diocese of Belleville, Catholic Parish Records, 1729–1956," images, FamilySearch (https://familysearch.org/pal:/MM9.3.1/TH-266-11132-133558-56?cc=1388122&wc=M99B-Q7X:893567332), St. Clair > Cahokia > Holy Family > 1783–1819 Deaths (originals) > image 9 of 57.

13. In addition to being of the Roman Catholic faith and of good morals, French notaries were supposed to pass an examination administered by jurists at the Châtelet

in Paris (Marion, *Dictionnaire des institutions de la France,* 400 [see chap. 3, n. 36]). It is entirely possible that Labuxière had gone through that process, or something very similar.

14. His first work as notary came in 1757 (*VC,* 623–65).
15. *VC,* 197–200.
16. St. Ange to Ulloa, June 16, 1766, AGI, PC, 2357.
17. Labuxière to Aubry, December 14, 1767, AGI, PC, 187A.
18. These are mostly in the FSA.
19. See FSA, no. 51, for an example.
20. Cottin, as "huissier," occasionally drafted legal documents that Labuxière then signed to make them official. Cottin was a Canadian and arrived in the Illinois Country ca. 1760. He sold his house in Kaskaskia in October 1765 (KM 65-10-30-1), apparently in preparation for moving to St. Louis with St. Ange.
21. These titles are spelled out in FSA, no. 2297.
22. Labuxière eventually moved back to the east of the Mississippi, first to Kaskaskia and then to Cahokia, dying there in April 1791. See chapter 11.
23. Volsey, as we saw in chapter 2, was married to Robert de St. Ange's granddaughter, Élisabeth Coulon de Villiers.
24. Abraham P. Nasatir, "Government Employees and Salaries in Spanish Louisiana," *Louisiana Historical Quarterly* 29 (October 1946): 914–15. Lieutenant Volsey was also on salary, perhaps six hundred livres per year. It is not clear, however, when, if ever, these salaries were paid, as will be seen below.
25. See FSA, nos. 1513, 1518. The usual rate of exchange was five livres per piastre.
26. McDermott, "Myths and Realities," 10 (see chap. 3, n. 14).
27. Nasatir, "Government Employees," 915. See also St. Ange to Aubry (September 15, 1769, AGI, PC, 187A) in which St. Ange mentioned Laclède as a supplier of foodstuffs for St. Louis.
28. Fraser to Gage, December 16, 1765, *NR,* 130.
29. Aubry to St. Ange, April 6, 1767, AGI, PC, 187A.
30. Throughout the colonial period, St. Louis was always deemed to be part of Illinois. "Missouri" referred only to the river and its valley.
31. *SRM,* 1:1–28.
32. Aubry to St. Ange, April 6, 1767, AGI, PC, 187A.
33. *SRM,* 1:5, 22.
34. Aubry to Ulloa, April 14, 1767, AGI, PC, 187A.
35. St. Ange to Aubry, June 27, 1767, AGI, PC, 107.
36. See Gilles Havard, *Empire et Métisssages: Indiens et Français dans le Pays d'en Haut, 1669–1715* (Sillery and Paris: Septentrion/Presses de l'Université de Paris, 2003), esp. chap. 7.
37. Aubry quoting Volsey in Aubry to unknown person, June 3, 1767, AGI, PC, 187A.
38. Ulloa to St. Ange, July 26, 1767, AGI, PC, 107.
39. St. Ange to Aubry, November 19, 1767, AGI, PC, 2357. It is not always clear which of St. Ange's letters were addressed to Ulloa and which to Aubry, but in this case it seems to have been Aubry.
40. *SRM,* 1:11.
41. Ríu to Ulloa, May 2, 1768, AGI, PC 109. This was Ríu's second letter to Ulloa of May 2.
42. Concerning village assemblies in the Illinois Country, see Ekberg, *French Roots in the Illinois Country,* 124–28 (see chap. 1, n. 76); and Ekberg, *Colonial Ste. Genevieve,* 376–77.

43. Early-nineteenth-century copy of the original French ms. in MHMA, St. Louis History Collection, Box 1, folder 1.

44. Ibid., attached.

45. See the succession papers of Louis Deshêtres (FSA, no. 2302), which reveal that Deshêtres and Jean-Baptiste Sarpy were purveying alcohol to Indians.

46. Patricia Cleary (*The World, the Flesh, and the Devil: A History of Colonial St. Louis* [Columbia: University of Missouri Press, 2011], 94–95) has a rather different take on this complex episode, arguing that riotous Indians were indeed an existential threat to St. Louis and that the petitioners of May 8 were in earnest.

47. St. Ange to Aubry, May 16, 1768, AGI, PC, 187A. A list of complaints offered by the "habitants" and "négociants" of St. Louis is appended to this letter.

48. Ibid. Lovely onomatopoeia!

49. These requests presented by *négociants* to Ulloa during July 1768 may be seen in AGI, PC, 188A.

50. Ibid.

51. Ríu to Ulloa, November 12, 1767, AGI, PC, 109; Ríu to Vallé, December 14, 1767, AGI, PC, 187A.

52. Cleary, *The World, the Flesh, and the Devil*, chap. 3; Gilbert C. Din, "Captain Francisco Ríu y Morales and the Beginnings of Spanish Rule in Missouri," *Missouri Historical Review* 94 (January 2000): 121–45. See also the detailed account by Jacqueline T. Trenfel-Treantafeles, "Spanish Occupation of the Upper Mississippi Valley, 1765–1770" (master's thesis, University of California, 1941). Trenfel-Treantafeles did her bachelor's degree under the direction of Abraham P. Nasatir at San Diego State University before moving on to Berkeley to pursue her master's degree under the direction of Herbert E. Bolton, who had earlier been Nasatir's Ph.D. dissertation director.

53. AGI, PC, 107. This dispatch seems to have been sent to Ulloa rather than Aubry.

54. St. Ange to Aubry, August 4, 1766, AGI, PC, 2357.

55. For a detailed description of the fort, see *SRM*, 1:49–53.

56. De Leyba to Governor Gálvez, June 8, 1780, AGI, PC, 193A. See also Gálvez to De Leyba, January 13, 1779, *SRM*, 1:166.

57. AGI, PC, 107.

58. AGI, PC, 107. See also Gilbert C. Din and Abraham P. Nasatir *The Imperial Osages: Spanish-Indian Diplomacy in the Mississippi Valley* (Norman: University of Oklahoma Press, 1983), 61–62, where it is remarked that St. Ange suggested giving Clermont an honorary medal as a means of ensuring his loyalty.

59. See Edmonds and Peyser, *Fox Wars*, chap. 5 (see chap. 1, n. 65).

60. On this attack, see Raymond E. Hauser, "The Fox Raid: Defensive Warfare and the Decline of the Illinois Indian Tribe," *Illinois Historical Journal* 86 (Winter 1993): 210–24; and Jean-Bernard Bossu, *Travels in the Interior of North America, 1751–1762*, translated and edited by Seymour Feiler (Norman: University of Oklahoma Press, 1962), 76–90.

61. Concerning this misguided revolt, see Carl A. Brasseaux, "Plus Ça Change, Acte Second: The Aubry-Foucault Clash and the New Orleans Rebellion of 1768," in *French Experience in Louisiana*, edited by Conrad, 603–9 (see chap. 3, n. 60); "Old and New Interpretations of the Rebellion of 1768," in *French Experience in Louisiana*, edited by Conrad, 610–17; Shannon Lee Dawdy, *Building the Devil's Empire: French Colonial New Orleans* (Chicago: University of Chicago Press, 2008), esp. 219–25.

62. Aubry to Minister, March 8, 1769, ANOM, C^{13A} 49:10. Aubry seems to have sent off his overland courier from New Orleans on March 18, and he arrived in St. Louis the middle of July (see St. Ange to Aubry, July 18, 1769, AGI, PC, 187A).

63. Din, "Francisco Ríu," 142.

64. Ríu to Ulloa, November 12, 1767, AGI, PC, 109.

65. Howard H. Peckham, *Pontiac and the Indian Uprising* (Princeton, N.J.: Princeton University Press, 1947), 310–13; Blouin, "Mémoire," July 9, 1771, Thomas Gage Papers, 138:16, Clements Library, Ann Arbor, Mich.

66. "Makatachinga" is Blouin's spelling of the Indian name, which Peckham rendered as "Black Dog." Black Dog as a Peoria chief appeared in British correspondence at the time (see *TP,* 406–7), but linguistic specialists (David Costa and Carl Masthay, e-mail communications, December 11, 2011) claim that Makatachinga could not possibly mean Black Dog. Costa: "I assume the word REALLY represents meehkateesinka, very literally 'it lies black.' This would be a reference to some natural phenomenon or other which was black in color. This is a fairly common strategy for personal names. As for Makatachinga supposedly meaning 'Black Dog,' I think someone is confusing this word with mahkateehsimwa 'black dog, black animal,' with -*hsimwa* the 'dog' final (meehkateehsinka is not a possible form)."

67. St. Ange to Aubry, April 21, 1769, AGI, PC, 187A. Aubry may have known Pontiac from the period (1757–59) when he was posted at Fort de Chartres. Gregory Evans Dowd proposed (*War under Heaven: Pontiac, the Indian Nations, and the British Empire* [Baltimore: Johns Hopkins University Press, 2002], 261) that Pontiac's murder occurred in the Indian, rather than the French, village of Cahokia, but by 1769 no discrete, independent Cahokia Indian village existed.

68. Neyon de Villiers claimed (Villiers to Loftus, April 20, 1764, *CP,* 244) that the Illinois nation as a whole vacillated in their loyalty to Pontiac.

69. Blouin, "Mémoire."

70. Peckham, *Pontiac,* 312.

71. Blouin, "Mémoire."

72. Gage to Hillsborough, August 12, 1769, *TP,* 577.

73. St. Ange to Aubry, July 18, 1769, AGI, PC, 187A.

74. Richard White (*Middle Ground,* 313 [see chap. 2, n. 35]) describes the failed attempt of the British to promote Pontiac to alliance chief in 1767. And Dowd (*War under Heaven,* 258–59) notes Pontiac's repudiation by young warriors of his own village in 1768.

75. Parkman, *Conspiracy of Pontiac,* 3:186 (see chap. 1, n. 1). Peckham (*Pontiac,* 313–14) accepted the notion that Pontiac was buried at St. Louis, but he was deceived by a letter in the *Papers of Sir William Johnson* (7:93–94 [see chap. 3, n. 61]) in which Pontiac's burial is mentioned. The editors of these published papers mistakenly filled in a lacuna in the manuscript, which contained only the final letter *s,* with "St. Louis." Almost certainly it should have been "Caokias," or "Caos," which were usual English names for Cahokia at the time.

76. Parkman relied on the unreliable testimony of Pierre Chouteau to place Pontiac's burial in St. Louis.

77. St. Ange to Aubry, November 15, 1769, AGI, PC, 187.

78. Blouin, "Mémoire."

79. St. Ange to Aubry, November 15, 1769, AGI, PC, 187.

80. FFL, s.v. "Aubry, Charles-Philippe."

81. St. Ange to Aubry, July 18, 1769, AGI, PC, 187A.

82. Concerning O'Reilly and the anti-Spanish revolt of 1768, see note 61; and Gilbert C. Din, *Spaniards, Planters, and Slaves* (College Station: Texas A&M University Press, 1999), 40–42.

83. This paragraph is based largely on the meticulous work in ibid., chap. 3. See also Ekberg, *Stealing Indian Women* (see chap. 1, n. 25); and Person, *Standing Up for Indians* (see chap. 1, n. 28).

84. Aubry to Minister, September 1, 1769, ANOM, C[13A] 49:85.

85. St. Ange to O'Reilly, November 23, 1769, AGI, PC, 187A. O'Reilly seems to have dispatched a special courier bateau or pirogue upriver to St. Louis, for Aubry wrote on September 1 that it was too late in the season to send a convoy to Illinois.

86. See, however, FSA, no. 62, in which as late as May 11, 1770, Labuxière continued to refer to the west side of the Mississippi as "la partie française."

87. St. Ange to O'Reilly, November 23, 1769, AGI, PC, 187A.

88. Concerning "covering," see R. White, *Middle Ground*, 90–93.

89. *SRM*, 1:44.

90. British officials complained incessantly about French illicit traders. See, for example, Hillsborough to Gage, June 11, 1768, *TP*, 298.

91. Daniel Richter, *Before the Revolution: America's Ancient Pasts* (Cambridge, Mass.: Harvard University Press, 2011), 406.

92. See Trudeau to Carondelet, July 3, 1796, in *Before Lewis and Clark*, translated and edited by Abraham P. Nasatir, 2 vols. (1952; reprint, Lincoln: University of Nebraska Press, 1990), 2:440–42.

93. Concerning wages at St. Louis, see also chapter 5. St. Ange's figure for wages seems somewhat exaggerated. A female black slave rented at St. Louis in 1770 for four livres per day (see FSA, no. 2302), and of course she would have required board. And Louis Deshêtres received only three livres per day for tracking down Laclède's runaway slaves (FSA, no. 2302).

94. St. Ange to O'Reilly, November 23, 1769, AGI, PC, 187A.

95. See Carolyn Gilman, "L'Année du Coup: The Battle of St. Louis, 1780," *Missouri Historical Review* 103 (April and June 2009).

96. Labuxière to O'Reilly, November 25, 1769, AGI, PC, 187A.

97. *SRM*, 1:73.

98. See "Ynstruccion a que se arreglaran los Tenientos de Governado," January 26, 1770, AGI, PC, 2357. The press of business in a city as large as New Orleans meant that notaries were a continuing necessity there, and they soon began to draft documents in Spanish as well as French. In Ste. Geneviève, the stature of François Vallé could not be denied, and O'Reilly created a unique position, that of special lieutenant, for him. Vallé's signature in Ste. Geneviève had the same weight as that of the lieutenant governor in St. Louis, even though Vallé technically shared power with a resident Spanish lieutenant. See Ekberg, *François Vallé and His World*.

99. Herbert Eugene Bolton at the University of California at Berkeley coined this term, and it was popularized by students of his, most important Abraham P. Nasatir.

100. "Ynstruccion a que se arreglaran los Tenientos de Governado," in AGI, PC, 2357. This appointment was confirmed by King Carlos III in 1772, and Piernas was granted an annual salary of 372 pesos (*SRM*, 1:110–12).

101. Piernas to O'Reilly, October 31, 1769, *SRM*, 1:73.

102. February 17, 1770, ibid., 83.

103. See "The Duties of a Prince with Regard to the Militia," chapter 14 in *The Prince and the Discourses*, edited by Max Lerner, Modern Library ed. (New York: Random House, 1950), 53–55.

104. Charles Gibson, *The Black Legend: Anti-Spanish Attitudes in the Old World and the New* (New York: Alfred A. Knopf, 1971). The term was not coined until early in the twentieth century. See also David J. Weber, *The Spanish Frontier in North America* (New Haven, Conn.: Yale University Press, 1992), 336.

105. Gage to Hillsborough, October 9, 1768, *TP,* 414–15.

106. Gage to William Johnson, June 10, 1770, in *Papers of Johnson,* 7:722.

107. Ste. Genevieve Civil Records, Concessions, no. 57, microfilm in the MHMA.

108. See Dawdy, *Building the Devil's Empire,* 3–5.

109. When, on September 17, 1770, Pedro Piernas banished one Jeanot for ten years, for, among other things, having stolen a blanket and two petticoats from his black female slave, with whom he had had intercourse, it was noted that St. Ange had earlier banished the "good-for-nothing" (MHMA, St. Louis History Collection, B1, f1).

Chapter 5. The Village Emerges

1. See Ekberg, *French Roots in the Illinois Country,* esp. chap. 2 (see chap. 1, n. 76).

2. Charles E. Peterson, *Colonial St. Louis: Building a Creole Capital* (Tucson: Patrice Press, 1993), 10n27; Mapp, *Elusive West,* esp. chaps. 13 and 14 (see chap. 3, n. 1).

3. *Annals,* 25, 36.

4. Oscar W. Collet, longtime secretary of the Missouri Historical Society, was the first to point this out, which he did in the strongest possible language ("Critique of Joseph N. Nicollet's *Sketch of the Early History of St. Louis,*" in Collet mss., St. Louis History Collection, MHMA).

5. Manuscript in Mémoires et Documents, series Amérique, vol. 8:261, Archives des Affaires Etrangères, Paris.

6. *LT,* 1:fol. 3.

7. Dunn, *Documents Relating to the French Settlements on the Wabash,* 429 (see chap. 2, n. 51).

8. John Reynolds, *The Pioneer History of Illinois* (Belleville, Ill.: N. A. Randall, 1852), 70.

9. See Ekberg, *French Roots,* 123–28.

10. Dunn, *Documents Relating to the French Settlements on the Wabash,* 407.

11. Auguste Chouteau (Theodore Hunt, "Minutes," typescript copy, 1:125, MHMA, St. Louis) claimed that St. Ange arrived in St. Louis in July 1765.

12. Bill-of-sale in KM 65-7-27-1.

13. FSA, no. 6.

14. Charles van Ravenswaay ("The Creole Arts and Crafts of Upper Louisiana," *Missouri Historical Society Bulletin* 12, no. 3 [April 1956]: 243) calls Denis a "joiner."

15. Mathieu, *La Nouvelle-France,* 85–86 (see chap. 3, n. 36).

16. Ekberg, *French Roots,* esp. chap. 2.

17. FSA, no. 4.

18. The same practice obtained in Lower Louisiana (Aubry to Ulloa, February 14, 1767, AGI, PC, 187A).

19. FSA, no. 2.

20. Lefebvre used this title when he and St. Ange granted land to Pierre Laclède on August 11, 1766 (Chouteau Collection, MHMA). The *ordonnateur* worked in tandem with the governor-general in Lower Louisiana, as Lefebvre did with St. Ange in Upper Louisiana.

21. See grant to Pierre-François de Volsey, September 9, 1765, *NR,* 81–84. This land grant, made shortly before the British garrison arrived at Fort de Chartres, was later confirmed by British officials.

22. *LT,* 1:fol. 1.
23. *LT,* 1:fol. 18.
24. See chapter 8.
25. *LT* is replete with such grants.
26. See, for example, a grant made to Jacques Catherine at Fort de Chartres on May 2, 1724 (*VC,* 340).
27. See especially the Heneaux and Lasource land grants of January and April 1752 in the Jacques Guibourd Collection, MHMA.
28. Regarding this case, see *LT,* 1:fols. 1, 16. From April 1, 1766, through August, Lefebvre cosigned land grants with St. Ange. Beginning in September, Lefebvre was replaced by Labuxière as St. Ange's assistant. Concerning the respective functions and titles of Lefebvre and Labuxière, see chapter 4.
29. Amos Stoddard, *Sketches, Historical and Descriptive, of Louisiana* (Philadelphia: Mathew Carey, 1812), 218–19.
30. Peterson, *Colonial St. Louis,* 6–7.
31. First use of the appellation "place publique" seems to have occurred in February 1766 (FSA, no. 2841).
32. See *LT,* 1:fol. 3.
33. ACJ, facsimile ms. 3.
34. Chouteau deposition of September 8, 1825 in McDermott, *Early Histories,* 95 (see chap. 3, n. 40).
35. Dufossat was a longtime officer in Louisiana, his service record going back to 1747 (FFL, s.v. "Dufossat, Guy"). Duralde (*Annals,* 447) was born in Biscaya, Spain, and after coming to St. Louis with Piernas married Marie-Josèphe Perrault, daughter of Louis Perrault, a wealthy French-Canadian merchant.
36. Duralde's description is on the first page of *LT,* 2.
37. Dawdy, *Building the Devil's Empire,* 67–74 (see chap. 4, n. 61).
38. See plat maps in Hodes, *Beyond the Frontier,* 84–87 (see chap. 3, n. 37).
39. The slave appears on Piernas's 1770 census of Indian slaves in St. Louis (ISC) and the indentured child in a contract of indenture (FSA, no. 2848).
40. FSA, no. 77.
41. Meurin died at Prairie du Rocher in 1777, but his remains were later moved, first to the former Jesuit seminary of St. Stanislaus in Florissant, Missouri, and finally to Calvary Cemetery in St. Louis.
42. Hodes's map of early St. Louis (*Beyond the Frontier,* 86) shows Valleau's lot facing the street that ran more or less south to the church.
43. *LT,* 1:fol. 33.
44. See this edict in *Louisiana Historical Quarterly* 14 (July 1931): 347.
45. Ekberg, *French Roots,* chap. 2.
46. *LT,* 1:fol. 1.
47. "Prairie" in standard French means meadow, but at early St. Louis the word was used more in the American sense of a broad grassland.
48. Ekberg, *French Roots,* chap. 3.
49. Theodore Hunt, "Minutes," 2:102. Rivière also recollected (ibid., 3:99) that St. Ange had created the commons, thereby establishing the fundamental tripartite configuration of land usage at the new settlement that had been customary in the Illinois Country since the early 1720s.
50. *LT,* 1:fol. 1.
51. FSA, no. 7.

52. AGI, Audiencia de Santo Domingo, legajo 2595.
53. *LT,* 1:fol. 5.
54. Ibid.
55. Hodes, *Beyond the Frontier,* 70–80.
56. *Annals,* 22.
57. *ACJ,* facsimile ms., 3.
58. Stirling to Gage, October 18, 1765, *NR,* 108.

Chapter 6. Logs and Stones
1. E-mail communication, Charles E. Peterson.
2. "Early Ste. Genevieve and Its Architecture," *Missouri Historical Review* 35 (1941): 207–32; *Colonial St. Louis: Building a Creole Capital,* expanded ed. (1949; reprint, Tucson, Patrice Press, 2001); "The Houses of French Saint Louis," in *The French in the Mississippi Valley,* edited by McDermott, 17–40 (see chap. 3, n. 14).
3. See Ekberg, *François Vallé and His World,* 62–88 (see chap. 3, n. 13); Ekberg, *Colonial Ste. Genevieve,* 284–96, 440–44 (see chap. 3, n. 50); Melburn D. Thurman, *Building a House in 18th Century Ste. Genevieve* (Ste. Genevieve: Pendragon's Press, 1984).
4. FSA, nos. 51, 61.
5. FSA., no. 1519.
6. Concerning the methodology of *poteaux-en-terre* construction, see Thurman, *Building a House.* E-mail communication, Michael J. Meyer, senior historic preservation specialist, archaeologist, Missouri Department of Transportation.
7. What distinctions may have existed between various framed structures erected on sills of dressed logs or ax-hewn timbers are not altogether clear, although the issue is of some importance for architectural history.
8. Fort Belle Fontaine Park is now located at the mouth of Cold Water Creek.
9. Nogging between vertical logs could be either of stone (pierrotage) or cow dung (bousillage, from *bouse,* cow dung). See Jay Dearborn Edwards and Nicolas Kariouk Pecquet du Bellay de Verton, comps. and eds., *A Creole Lexicon: Architecture, Landscape, People* (Baton Rouge: Louisiana State University Press, 2004), 32.
10. FSA, no. 2326. Louis, his wife, Marie-Anne, and their two children were enumerated on the 1766 census (see appendix A).
11. In 1767 he married Thérèse Hébert, daughter of the prominent Widow Hébert, FSA, no. 2011.
12. Cedar is more rot-resistant than oak, either white or red, and there are eighteenth-century *poteaux-en-terre* structures with cedar posts still standing in Ste. Genevieve.
13. Contract in FSA, no. 2864.
14. See chapter 10.
15. *Mûrier* means "mulberry" in standard French but also occasionally meant "cedar" in Louisiana French (see *Dictionary of Louisiana French,* edited by Albert Valdman and Kevin J. Rottet [Jackson: University Press of Mississippi, 2009], 409), and in this case it must have had the second meaning. Red cedars large enough to provide posts for *poteaux-en-terre* structures were relatively scarce in the St. Louis area, and this scarcity drove up the price of cedar, which by the 1780s cost three times as much as oak (see document dated October 2, 1781, MHMA, François Vallé Collection, Box 1).
16. Timothy Flint, *Recollections of the Last Ten Years* (Boston: Cummings, Hilliard, 1826), 100.
17. Concerning the Indian slave Joseph, see chapter 8.

18. Addendum to FSA, no. 2864.
19. FSA, no. 2311. Concerning Lambert's death, see chapter 10.
20. FSA, no. 1538.
21. See building contracts in FSA, nos. 17 and 40.
22. Edwards and Bellay de Verton, *Creole Lexicon*, 54–55.
23. See bill of lading for Fagot's *bateau* in AGI, PC, 188A. Concerning Fagot's life in Louisiana, see *FFL*, s.v. "Fagot de la Garcinière, Daniel."
24. House contract, June 26, 1767, in FSA, no. 2850.
25. FSA, no. 2842.
26. FSA, no. 2851.
27. Interestingly, the house that Laclède bought at Chartres in 1763 had a free-standing "pigeon house." See *VC*, 788–90.
28. Edwards and Bellay de Verton, *Creole Lexicon*, 156.
29. FSA, no. 130. According to Billon (*Annals*, 149), the two stone houses on Laclède's property when it sold in 1789 had footprints, respectively, of 1,380 and 1,500 square pieds. And the stone house that Laclède gave to Madame Chouteau in 1768 was described as 50×34 pieds (FSA, no. 9B), but this house seems to have been located on a piece of property independent of Laclède's main town lot. In 1767 Laclède was renting a house to the Spanish government in which were housed the commandant (St. Ange), the storekeeper (Lefebvre), and some troops. See Nasatir, "Government Employees," 915 (see chap. 4, n. 24).
30. FSA, no. 111.
31. See appendix A. On French-Canadian architecture, see the award-winning and indispensable book by Peter N. Moogk, *Building a House in New France* (Toronto: McClellan and Steward, 1977), esp. chaps. 2 and 3.
32. Peterson, *Colonial St. Louis*, 26 (see chap. 5, n. 2).
33. FSA, no. 87.
34. Fernand Braudel, *The Structures of Everyday Life*, translated by Siân Reynolds (New York: Harper & Row, 1982), 486.
35. Hunt, "Minutes," 2:187
36. FSA, no. 18. *Échor* (also *écore* or *écor*) was an antique French word often used in early documents to describe the bluff line at St. Louis. Concerning this word, see also John Francis McDermott, comp., *A Glossary of Mississippi Valley French, 1673–1850*, Washington University Studies, n.s., no. 12 (St. Louis: Washington University, 1941), 71.
37. *LT*, 1:fol. 18.
38. *LT*, 1:fol. 34.
39. FSA, no. 75.
40. FSA, no. 264.
41. Proceedings of auction in FSA, no. 264.
42. FSA, no. 90.
43. Ekberg, *Colonial Ste. Genevieve*, 127, 137.
44. Philip Pittman, *The Present State of European Settlements on the Mississippi*, facsimile of 1770 edition (Gainesville: University Press of Florida, 1973), 50.
45. FSA, no. 1520. Concerning Baron, see van Ravenswaay, "Creole Arts and Crafts," 245 (see chap. 5, n. 14).
46. FSA, no. 2856.
47. Age of majority according to French customary law was twenty-five. François Lange, *La nouvelle pratique civile, criminelle, et bénéficiale*, 139 (see chap. 1, n. 81).
48. Peter N. Moogk (e-mail communication, August 10, 2012) encountered Baron in Montreal notarial records.

49. FSA, no. 1522. We are much indebted to Jean Bruggeman of Villeneuve d'Ascq, France for explaining the details of such a mill. Bruggeman has devoted his entire adult life to the study and restoration of old mills and has written extensively about them. See http://asso.nordnet.fr/aramnord/jean_bruggeman_qui_est_il.htm. See also FSA, no. 11, for the sale of what was also apparently a horse mill used for crushing bark to obtain tannin for tanning leather.

50. St. Ange claimed (St. Ange to O'Reilly, November 23, 1769, AGI, PC, 187A) that workers at St. Louis were demanding eight to ten livres, plus board, per day. San Souci's wages were evidently not that high.

51. The seignorial mills in Canada took by right one-fourteenth of the grain that came to them (Mathieu, *La Nouvelle-France*, 85).

52. *LT*, 1:fol. 5.

53. Contract dated August 9, 1767, in FSA, no. 2843.

54. Contract dated December 2, 1767, FSA, no. 22.

55. Birthplace is given as "Delimoch" in his will (FSA, no. 2234), written in Spanish. See also van Ravenswaay, "Creole Arts and Crafts," 243.

56. FSA, no. 2845.

57. All these itemized construction components may be seen in illustrations in Edwards and Bellay de Verton, *Creole Lexicon*, facing 1 and 64.

58. Ibid., 40.

59. *LT*, 1:fol. 23.

60. *Annals*, 147.

61. See van Ravenswaay ("Creole Arts and Crafts," 247) concerning Joachim Roy, who was a carpenter.

62. *LT*, 1:fol. 31.

63. Ibid., marginal notation.

Chapter 7. The *Coutume de Paris* Rules

1. Paris: Jean Cochart, 1688.

2. See Mathieu, *La Nouvelle-France* (see chap. 3, n. 36); and Peter Moogk (*La Nouvelle France: The Making of French Canada—a Cultural History* [East Lansing: Michigan State University Press, 2000], 143–81, for a lively discussion of the Coutume in New France.

3. Carl J. Ekberg, "The Nicolas Peltier de Franchomme Affair and the *Coutume de Paris*," unpublished ms.

4. Hans W. Baade, "Marriage Contracts in French and Spanish Louisiana: A Study in 'Notarial' Jurisprudence," *Tulane Law Review* 53 (December 1978): 43. The authors defer to Baade's judgment on the legal aspects of the Coutume. Ecclesiastical law governed the form of marriage, and secular *coutumes* governed marital property.

5. Term from ibid., 15–16.

6. Except, oddly, not in the contract of Panissé and Marcheteau, although the rest of the clauses conform. FSA, no. 2015.

7. Marylynn Salmon, *Women and the Law of Property in Early America* (Chapel Hill: University of North Carolina Press, 1986), 5, 13, 146.

8. All contracts save one, Marguerite La Ferne and Joseph Lefebvre, the reasons for which involve a level of detail beyond the scope of this chapter.

9. The most complete treatments of marriage contracts and inventories appear in Susan C. Boyle, "Did She Generally Decide? Women in Ste. Genevieve, 1750–1805," *William and Mary Quarterly* 44 (1987): 775–89; and Ekberg, *François Vallé and His World*, 30, 35, 118–20, 193–94 (see chap. 3, n. 13). Studies of the Coutume

in colonial Lower Louisiana are limited in number and scope. See Sara Brooks Sundberg, "Women and Property in Early Louisiana: Legal Systems at Odds," *Journal of the Early Republic* 32 (Winter 2012): 637n5. This chapter cites relevant sections of the *Coutume*, but its provisions must be considered in light of their application in the documents.

10. *Coutume*, 2:5–6, Article CCXX.

11. Baade, "Marriage Contracts," 15. See also Carl J. Ekberg, Grady Kilman, and Pierre Lebeau, *Code Noir: The Colonial Slave Laws of French Mid-America*, Extended Publications Series 4 (Naperville, Ill.: Center for French Colonial Studies, 2005), 44–45.

12. For example, Marguerite La Ferne, FSA, no. 2014. See chapter 8.

13. *Coutume*, 2:156–157, Article CCLX.

14. Baade, "Marriage Contracts," 17; *Coutume*, 2:69, Article CCXXXVII. A widow had forty days after the completion of the inventory to decide whether to accept or renounce the division of the *communauté*.

15. Legal separation of persons and possessions was feasible under the *Coutume* but occurred rarely. Billon recounts a separation in 1789, *Annals*, 250–53, as well as the Volsey scandal, 435–37, in which a dissolution of marriage was granted in 1779. A notorious case also occurred in the Vallé family in Ste. Genevieve. Ekberg, *François Vallé and His World*, 128–34. Normally, inventories were done within three months of the death of the spouse. Under certain conditions the *communauté* could continue. *Coutume*, 2:94–97, Article CCXLI.

16. See below for the Laville inventory as an example. François Olivier-Martin, *Histoire du Droit Français des origins à la Révolution*, (n.p.: Éditions Domat Montchrestien, 1951), 653.

17. FSA, nos. 2021 and 2033. The smaller (without marriage contract) estate was of Laville; the larger had belonged to Guillaume Bizet, FSA, Box 32.

18. J. Thomas Scharf, *History of St. Louis City and County*, 2 vols. (Philadelphia: Louis H. Everts, 1883) 1:172–73. The account derived from an article in an unnamed newspaper.

19. FSA, no. 2007. According to her baptismal record, she was sixteen in 1766. See appendix A.

20. Janine M. Lanza, *From Wives to Widows in Early Modern Paris: Gender, Economy, and the Law* (Burlington, Vt.: Ashgate, 2007), 49, comments that families might limit the amount of money and goods that each spouse committed to the community property.

21. 2000-livre, FSA, no. 2014 and 2016. 150-livre, FSA, no. 2012.

22. Family relations, which might figure later in inheritance, were specified in many marriage contracts.

23. *VC,* 171.

24. Resident in Ste. Genevieve as per the May 1766 census (AGI, Audiencia de Santo Domingo, 2595). See Ekberg, *François Vallé and His World*, 45–46, concerning Antoine Heneaux/Hunaud in Ste. Genevieve.

25. In Labuxière's marriage contracts, women did not generally appear as witnesses.

26. His estate in 1772 was worth more than fifty-four thousand livres, twice the size of the Dodier estate (below), and one hundred times the 1764 estate of the master cobbler Laville (below). Bizet was from Canada and had family still there.

27. FSA, nos. 45 and 46. The *tuteurs* were appointed on September 25, 1769. The widow herself was likely their first *tuteur.* The role of tuteurs as financial administra-

tors is elucidated in Articles CCLXV–CCLXXI, 2:169–81, of the *Coutume,* including the general role of guardians and also curateurs. See also chapter 9 for the story of Jean Comparios.

28. FSA, no. 123. Toussaint and Marie-Josèphe had five children. They moved to Carondelet. Marie-Josèphe was murdered in 1799. *SRM,* 2:267.

29. FSA, no. 2009.

30. See appendix A. Pierre Laclède attended the marriages of the parents of the wives of both Auguste and Pierre Chouteau.

31. Natalia Maree Belting, *Kaskaskia under the French Regime* (Carbondale: Southern Illinois University Press, 2003), 62n83. Her name also appears with spellings of "Le Bonte" and "Le Bourg."

32. FSA, no. 2310. See chapter 9 for the long-term care arrangements of Jean Comparios.

33. SLAR, Baptism.

34. See chapter 8 for more on Angélique and St. Ange.

35. Guy Dufossat's exquisite color map done in October 1767 shows a church building. Rothensteiner, *History of the Archdiocese of St. Louis* (St. Louis: Blackwell Wielandy, 1928), 1:103, without citing a source, insisted that Father Meurin dedicated the first church in June 1770.

36. SLAR, interments March 9, 1771 (son), and May 9, 1772 (father).

37. FSA, no. 2310.

38. SLAR. "Gilette SansSoucy" was buried between August 8 and 16—this particular entry is undated.

39. FSA, no. 2580.

40. FSA, no. 1818.

41. See the inventory of the Barsalous estate, chapter 9.

42. Foley and Rice, *First Chouteaus,* 44 (see chap. 3, n. 10); FSA, no. 1647.

43. Marriage contract, April 3, 1769, FSA, no. 2021. Agnès Hulin married Louis Normant *dit* La Bruiere in 1747. She was the daughter of Pierre Hulin and Dorothée Accica, an Indian woman. Belting, *Kaskaskia under the French Regime,* 82.

44. Perhaps Labuxière had already gotten involved as notary in procedures in the adultery case involving Thérèse's mother Agnès Hulin, which François Vallé would deal with in Ste. Genevieve in April 1770. See Ekberg, *François Vallé and His World,* 226. Since Hervieux was not married, technically only Agnès had committed adultery.

45. FSA, no. 50.

46. FSA, no. 2688.

47. Neither Hervieux's natural daughter nor her husband had any legal claim to his estate. According to the *Coutume* (1:364–66, Article CLXVII), the local government had a right to sequester Hervieux's estate until a legitimate heir stepped forward to claim it.

48. See chapter 9 for more details on Hervieux's life and the disposition of his possessions after death.

49. SLAR, September 27, 1776.

50. FSA, no. 2330.

51. Hans Baade, "Women and the Law in Eighteenth Century Illinois Country," paper delivered at annual meeting of the Center for French Colonial Studies, October 2011; *Coutume,* 2:54–61, Articles CCXXXIV–CCXXXVI. Labuxière used the phrase "femme marchande" just once, in a real estate contract written for the widow Lobinois

in the summer of 1765. KM, 65-6-13-1. A husband had to have no stake in his wife's commerce as a *femme marchande*.

52. In earlier decades, for example, Hélène Danis, the métisse wife of Ignace Hébert, was frequently authorized by her husband to conduct business at Fort de Chartres. KM 30-04-10; and *VC,* 423–24, 432–33.

53. FSA, no. 2008. Madame Chouteau is designated *commerçante* only once, in the insinuation of FSA, no. 9B, Registre des Insinuations des Donations au Siège des Illinois, Perrin Collection, Illinois State Archives, Springfield. In Panissé's case, the word "commerçant" had been used in documents for La Giroflée and Panissé (his wife) from 1760, referring to one or both of them. The 1766 Panissé-Marcheteau marriage contract is unambiguous. See appendix A for further discussion of Panissé.

54. The flower Cheiranthus was favored by Charlemagne for its scent, according to tradition, and in a Scottish story of ill-fated lovers it represented "fidelity in adversity." Sheila Pickles, *Le Langage des Fleurs du Temps Jadis,* translated by Michel Beauvais and Salem Issad (Paris: Éditions Solar, 1992), 105. Thanks to Christine Knutson Beveraggi for this reference.

55. KM 58-4-12-1 Sometimes his name appears as "Brunet."

56. KM 59-12-21-1.

57. See Margaret Kimball Brown, *History as They Lived It: A Social History of Prairie du Rocher,* Ill. (Tucson- Patrice Press, 2005), 77, 92, for more on the widow Drouin.

58. KM 60-1-31-1.

59. KM 63-11-19-1. This property is now known as the Ghost Horse site. See Mazrim, *At Home in the Illinois Country,* 209–16 (see chap. 3, n. 20).

60. *VC,* 788–90. Jean Gerardin was a witness to this transaction. Labuxière had owned the property for ten days, selling the land and buildings to La Giroflée for the same price (10,150 livres) he paid for it. This short turnaround on property was not unheard of.

61. Boyle, "Did She Generally Decide?": 786.

62. KM 64-4-10-1.

63. The burial record in the Prairie du Rocher transcription for Jean Brunet (Prunet?), age forty-two, has the date written as September 1766, which was crossed out and 1767 written. The entry is found among other 1767 entries, but this later date is obviously problematic in relation to Panissé's remarriage in 1766. MHM.

64. FSA, nos. 2198 and 2203. In Spain civil law going back to Roman times stressed the importance of wills in the disposition of estates. This was much less true in France, especially northern France.

65. KM 68-9-10-1, Perrin Collection, Illinois State Archives. *Coutume,* 2:214–19, Article CCLXXX, deals with mutual donations between spouses without children.

66. FSA, no. 2879.

67. FSA, no. 305.

68. The extensive list of household items may have been from the Hervy purchase in 1759 rather than the Debary purchase in 1758.

69. See FSA, no. 9B; also by date in the Perrin Collection, Illinois State Archives.

70. See Ekberg, *Stealing Indian Women,* 87–88 (see chap. 1, n. 25); and chapter 8 below.

71. SLAR, 1768.

72. *VC,* 150.

73. The inventory also prevented claims from children of a first marriage to more than their legal right from the second marriage. FSA, no. 2295. *Coutume,* 2:114–19, Titre XI "Des Doüaires," especially Article CCXLVII.

74. Madame Duchemin was Marie-Jeanne Quebedot, Marie-Josèphe's sister, and their brothers Charles and Jacques Quebedot *dit* Lespagnol appeared on the militia muster roll.

75. FSA, no. 2847.

76. Hodes, *Beyond the Frontier,* 86 (see chap. 3, n. 37).

77. FSA, no. 2848.

78. FSA, nos. 2856 and 2840.

79. SLAR, marriage; St. Louis 1787 Census.

80. *Coutume,* 2:80–97, Articles CCXL and CCXLI. When there were minor children from the marriage, the *communauté* could continue.

81. Julie Hardwick, "Widowhood and Patriarchy in Seventeenth-Century France," *Journal of Social History* 26 (1992): 137–48. Hardwick concluded from her data on Brittany that the dominant patriarchy of French society prevented middling-status widows from exercising the promises of the law.

82. Hardwick detailed situations in which the male kin contested widows' competence as managers of their husbands' estates. No evidence of such conflict has come to light in the documents in St. Louis. Only the Panissé wills hint at this.

83. FSA, no. 2015.

84. See appendix A for details.

85. *Coutume,* 2:69, Article CCXXXVII. If a widow contemplated renouncing the *communauté,* time limits were invoked.

86. FSA, no. 1398. Bizet was a witness at Millet and Dodier's daughter's wedding in 1768 and was the *tuteur* for the minor Beaugenou children.

87. On the topic of single slaves in estate inventories, however, see chapter 8.

88. Only two daughters, Élisabeth and Thérèse, reached adulthood and married. See appendix A.

89. See Emmanuel Le Roy Ladurie, "A System of Customary Law: Family Structures and Inheritance Customs in Sixteenth-Century France," in *Family and Society: Selections from the Annales: Economies, Sociétiés, Civilisations,* edited by Robert Forster and Orest Ranum (Baltimore: Johns Hopkins University Press, 1976), for interesting observations on this egalitarian aspect of the *Coutume.*

90. See chapter 8 for more discussion of the *Code Noir.*

91. Only Baptiste and the Indian slave of Antoine Hubert, Joseph, whom Hubert apprenticed out to become a joiner, are mentioned as slave craftsmen in early St. Louis. FSA, no. 2840. No clear evidence of slaves' working for their own gain has yet emerged from these sources.

92. *VC,* 262–63.

93. *SRM,* 1:56.

94. FSA, no. 2015.

95. Cotté does not appear in *VC,* the Kaskaskia Manuscripts name index, the 1766 census or militia muster roll, or other documents prior to the marriage contract.

96. FSA, no. 134.

97. FSA, no. 2378.

98. In the 1772 report of the flour harvest, Cotté is credited with thirty-three quintals, an amount slightly less than Gabriel Dodier (thirty-eight), and just over half that of his mother-in-law (sixty-one). *SRM,* 1:56.

99. FSA, no. 2378. Boyle, "Did She Generally Decide?" documented women's participation in auctions without written permission from their husbands.

100. The actions of many St. Louisans of the time with regard to their slaves are complicated. The widow Dodier sold a métisse slave child in 1782, an act that was

illegal under both French and Spanish laws regarding Indian slaves. See Ekberg, *Stealing Indian Women*, 81; FSA, no. 331. See chapter 8 for further examples and discussion of O'Reilly's decree.

101. The widow Hébert, Hélène Danis, was also a decades-long manager of her husband's estate.

102. François Olivier-Martin, *Histoire de la Coutume de la Prévôté et Vicomté de Paris* (Paris: Éditions Ernest Leroux, 1926–30), 2:421, 503–5. Wills were used to designate executors, manumit faithful slaves, and distribute property that did not fall within the terms of the marriage contract.

103. Le Roy Ladurie, "System of Customary Law," 78, 83–84, 88, 97.

104. See marriage contract dated September 21, 1786, in Chouteau Collection, MHMA. The ms. contains a note certifying that the contract had been filed in the official records of St. Louis County, Missouri Territory, September 15, 1817. The court-ordered estate sale in 1830 after Chouteau's death cited the marriage contract for the six thousand dollars his widow should receive, and the remainder of the estate was divided, half to the widow and half shared among their children (http://www.nps.gov/jeff/historyculture/slave-sales.htm).

Chapter 8. Slaves: African and Indian

1. See Illinois census of 1725 in ANOM, G^1 464. This census is routinely identified as a 1726 census, but internal evidence demonstrates that it was compiled in 1725, likely in May. See Margaret K. Brown, "Who's Who in Illinois in 1726," paper presented at the annual meeting of the French Colonial Historical Society, Mackinac Island, Mich., May 1990. See also Ekberg, *Stealing Indian Women*, chap. 2 (see chap. 1, n. 25).

2. Studies of Indian slavery include James F. Brooks, *Captives and Cousins* (Chapel Hill: University of North Carolina Press, 2002); Juliana Barr, *Peace Came in the Form of a Woman* (Chapel Hill: University of North Carolina Press, 2007); Kathleen DuVal, *The Native Ground* (Philadelphia: University of Pennsylvania Press, 2006); and Alan Gallay, *The Indian Slave Trade* (New Haven, Conn.: Yale University Press, 2002).

3. Carl Masthay, ed. and comp., *Kaskaskia Illinois-to-French Dictionary* (St. Louis: published privately, 2002), 403, 479.

4. A. P. Nasatir, ed., *Before Lewis and Clark: Documents Illustrating the History of the Missouri, 1785–1804* (Norman: University of Oklahoma Press, 2002), 19–20; Ekberg, *Stealing Indian Women*, 17–24. John Joseph Mathews, *The Osages: Children of the Middle Waters* (Norman: University of Oklahoma Press, 1961), 154–63, relates the oral tradition of Osage slave raids on the Pawnees and Padoucas. Norman Gelb, ed., *Jonathan Carver's Travels through America, 1766–1768: An Eighteenth-Century Explorer's Account of Uncharted America* (New York: John Wiley & Sons, 1993), 74. See also chapter 1.

5. Studies of Indian slavery in St. Louis and the Illinois Country include Russell M. Magnaghi, "The Role of Indian Slavery in Colonial St. Louis," *Bulletin of the Missouri Historical Society* 31 (1975): 264–72; Ekberg, *Stealing Indian Women*; and Person, *Standing Up for Indians* (see chap. 1, n. 28).

6. Gwendolyn Midlo Hall, "Epilogue: Historical Memory, Consciousness, and Conscience in the New Millennium," in *French Colonial Louisiana and the Atlantic World*, edited by Bradley G. Bond (Baton Rouge: Louisiana State University Press, 2005), 300, discusses the African origins of Louisiana's slaves. See also Gwendolyn Midlo Hall, *Africans in Colonial Louisiana: The Development of Afro-Creole Culture in the Eighteenth Century* (Baton Rouge: Louisiana State University Press, 1992), 60.

7. See "État de la Louisiane au mois de juin, 1720," Archives de la Guerre, series A[1] 2592:93, Château de Vincennes, Paris.

8. Vaudreuil to Minister, December 6, 1744, C[13A] 28:248. In the eighteenth-century French ecclesiastical and civil records examined in this study, the words used to describe slaves were (here in their masculine forms) *nègre, sauvage, métis,* and *mulatre.* The authors acknowledge that twenty-first-century sensitivity to the vocabulary of race does not allow an easy rendering of these terms.

9. AGI, PC, 2357; 1732 census in ANOM, G[1] 464; 1752 census, HMLO 426.

10. Ekberg, *French Roots in the Illinois Country,* 215 (see chap. 1, n. 76).

11. For Bienvenu, see Cécile Vidal, "Antoine Bienvenu, Illinois Planter and Mississippi Trader," in *French Colonial Louisiana and the Atlantic World,* edited by Bond, 111–16; and Ekberg, *French Roots,* 153–66. The slave total is from the 1752 census, HMLO 426.

12. 1752 census, ibid.; 1766 census, AGI, Audiencia de Santo Domingo, 2595; *SRM,* 1:53–57.

13. Ekberg, *François Vallé and His World,* 172, 273 (see chap. 3, n. 13).

14. AGI, Audiencia de Santo Domingo, 2595. See Dufossat's 1767 map for the mill. *SRM,* 1:56.

15. ISC lists Indian slaves' monetary value.

16. FSA, no. 1398.

17. FSA, no. 434.

18. See David Brion Davis, *Inhuman Bondage* (Oxford: Oxford University Press, 2006), 181; and Winthrop D. Jordan, *White over Black* (Chapel Hill: University of North Carolina Press, 1968), 316–20.

19. Concerning Indian slaves involved in the fur trade, see chapter 10.

20. See Ekberg, Kilman, and Lebeau, *Code Noir,* 1–3 (see chap. 7, n. 11); Mathé Allain, *"Not Worth a Straw": French Colonial Policy and the Early Years of Louisiana* (Lafayette: Center for Louisiana Studies, University of Southwestern Louisiana, 1988), 15; and Vernon Valentine Palmer, *Through the Codes Darkly: Slave Law and Civil Law in Louisiana* (Clark, N.J.: Lawbook Exchange, 2012).

21. Guillaume Aubert, "'To Establish One Law and Definite Rules': Race, Religion, and the Transatlantic Origins of the Louisiana Code Noir," in *Louisiana: Crossroads of the Atlantic World,* edited by Cécile Vidal (Philadelphia: University of Pennsylvania Press, 2014), 21–43, discusses various influences on the development of the 1724 Louisiana *Code Noir.*

22. Ekberg, Kilman, and Lebeau, *Code Noir,* Article II, 24–25; Article VI, 26–27; Article VIII, 28–29; Article XXI, 34–35; Article XLIII, 44–45; Article L, 48–49.

23. FSA, no. 1. Also related in Ekberg, Kilman, and Lebeau, *Code Noir,* 8–9.

24. See examples cited from the Kaskaskia manuscripts (pre-1764) in Ekberg, Kilman, and Lebeau, *Code Noir,* 62–67. Jennifer M. Spear, *Race, Sex, and Social Order in Early New Orleans* (Baltimore: Johns Hopkins University Press, 2009), 89, notes that the Superior Council in 1735 put the authority for manumission in the hands of the governor and ordonnateur. She also notes that New Orleans slave owners sometimes designated individuals as free in baptismal registers, bypassing the legal requirements.

25. For Hall, see note 6 above; and Daniel H. Usner Jr., *Indians, Settlers, and Slaves in a Frontier Exchange Economy* (Chapel Hill: University of North Carolina Press, 1992). See also Laurent Dubois, *A Colony of Citizens: Revolution and Slave Emancipation in the French Caribbean, 1787–1804* (Chapel Hill: University of North Carolina Press, 2004); Rebecca Hartkopf Schloss, *Sweet Liberty: The Final*

Days of Slavery in Martinique (Philadelphia: University of Pennsylvania Press, 2009); Hall, *Africans in Colonial Louisiana*; and John D. Garrigus, *Before Haiti: Race and Citizenship in French Saint-Domingue* (New York: Palgrave Macmillan, 2006).

26. FSA, no. 2841. It misses, by less than three weeks, the distinction of being the earliest known document written and recorded in St. Louis.

27. The Condé–La Ferne marriage record shows both La Ferne parents were deceased. No inventory of the estate has been located. Fort de Chartres Register (parish of Ste. Anne), "Illinois, Diocese of Belleville, Catholic Parish Records, 1729–1956," images, Family Search (https://familysearch.org/pal:/MM9.3.1/TH-267-11882-156130-83?cc=1388122&wc=M99B-QMV:n408136662), Randolph > Fort de Chartres > St. Anne (transferred to St. Joseph) > 1721–1840 Baptisms, Marriages, Deaths, First Communion, Confirmations > image 110 of 603.

28. *VC*, 265–66.

29. SLAR, Old Cathedral Registers, Baptism. Lorine's term of indenture finished before Catherine was born, so Lorine was not taken on as a wetnurse.

30. FSA, no. 1512.

31. Belting, *Kaskaskia under the French Regime*, 96 (see chap. 7, n. 31). Bardet de la Ferne was the surgeon at Kaskaskia in 1752. Belting located Marianne (Barrois) Bardet de la Ferne in New Orleans in 1760. Henri Carpentier, the first guardian of Marguerite La Ferne, resided in Ste. Genevieve (FSA, no. 1783, dated 1766).

32. Marriage Contract, FSA, 2014. See chapter 9 for the story of their marriage. The designation of slaves as *propres*, belonging to Marguerite alone, may have violated several articles of the *Code Noir*. See Ekberg, Kilman, and Lebeau, *Code Noir*, 44–45. On the other hand, inherited movables were often written into marriage contracts as *propres*. See Lanza, *From Wives to Widows*, 166 (see chap. 7, n. 20).

33. SLAR, Baptism.

34. FSA, no. 1410, AGI, PC, 212A. See chapter 10. The godfathers were Jacques Chauvin and Lambert Bonvarlet, both unrelated to La Ferne or her husband.

35. A government seizure was likely treated differently from other creditors' claims. See Ekberg, Kilman, and Lebeau, *Code Noir*, Article XLII, 44–45.

36. FSA, no. 1412.

37. Jennifer L Morgan, *Laboring Women: Reproduction and Gender in New World Slavery* (Philadelphia: University of Pennsylvania Press, 2004), chap. 3, discusses slave women of childbearing age as heritable property. The girls' mother (and stepfather) would have retained Lorine on behalf of the minor daughters.

38. St. Louis History Collection, Box 1, folder 1, and Litigation Collection, Box 1, folder 2, MHMA. See also Cleary, *The World, the Flesh, and the Devil*, 203–8, 212–14 (see chap. 4, n. 46). She relates the trial and Marie-Anne's marital troubles with Roubieu.

39. Litigation Collection, Box 1, folder 2, MHMA.

40. In 1781 a comparable punishment was decreed by the lieutenant governor (succeeding de Leyba) for slaves who were found guilty of illegally assembling, fifty lashes for the first offense and one hundred for the second. St. Louis History Collection, Box, 1, folder 1, MHMA.

41. FSA, no. 433. The child's name was Joseph. FSA, no. 1410.

42. Ekberg, *Stealing Indian Women*, 111–13, relates this case. See also Ekberg, *Colonial Ste. Genevieve*, 219–20 (see chap. 3, n. 50), on the general lack of evidence of physical brutality to slaves.

43. FSA, no. 433. Charles Sanguinet was Marianne's husband. Married in 1779, by 1786 the couple had three young children. *Annals*, 450–51.

44. FSA, no. 2570.

45. Charles Taillon was identified as both sub-lieutenant in the Spanish royal army and as lieutenant in the St. Louis militia. FSA, no. 522.

46. The guarantee may have referred to the confused and confusing change of ownership when Condé bought Lorine and Julie back from the government after they had been seized. Condé died just two weeks after this transaction. Statements of slaves' health were also typically made in sale documents.

47. FSA, nos. 448 and 2617. This was comparable to the price of five hundred piastres for a black female slave with a daughter sold several years earlier.

48. Numerous notes in inventories document informal, short-term arrangements.

49. See chapter 7 for the Dodier inventory and partition, and St. Ange, who passed his Indian slave to his niece in his 1774 will. FSA, no. 2187.

50. Per the baptismal registers through 1779. The incompleteness of many of the records frustrates a more complete count.

51. The code's Article VI specified fines for producing children with slaves but did not specifically forbid sexual relations with slaves. In principle, ecclesiastical courts were intended to deal with issues of sexual morality, and of course no such courts existed in Upper Louisiana.

52. No reference to a midwife, methods of contraception, or abortion ("restoring menstruation") was found in any of the early St. Louis manuscripts, and women's burial records that followed closely after a birth never gave a cause of death. Susan E. Klepp, *Revolutionary Conceptions: Women, Fertility, and Family Limitation in America, 1760–1820* (Chapel Hill: University of North Carolina Press, 2009); chap. 6, and Morgan, *Laboring Women,* discuss these critical issues in other locations in the eighteenth century.

53. Hall (*Africans in Colonial Louisiana,* 175) commented on the high birthrate among slaves through the 1740s. See also Ekberg, *Colonial Ste. Genevieve,* 246–48 (see chap. 3, n. 50); and James Pritchard, "Population in French America, 1670 to 1730," in *French Colonial Louisiana and the Atlantic World,* edited by Bond, 184–85. Infant mortality rates in British America ranged from 20 to 25 percent, depending on social class and setting, urban or rural. Klepp, *Revolutionary Conceptions,* 292–93.

54. SLAR, Baptism.

55. Jeannette is a well-known figure in early St. Louis. See Christine Williams, "Prosperity in the Face of Prejudice: The Life of a Free Black Woman in Frontier St. Louis," *Gateway Heritage* 9, no. 2 (1998): 4–11.

56. Certificate of Burial, November 1796, Archdiocese of New Orleans Archives, states he was about twenty-eight years old, natural son of "Augusto Choutau, (mother unknown)."

57. See Ekberg, *Stealing Indian Women,* 83–87.

58. SLAR, Baptism. Uses of "infideles" with no additional description of parents in Indian slave baptismal records suggest that the child was alone.

59. For example, VC 311–12, a black slave of the widow Hébert, is godmother to a child of legitimately married black slaves of the widow Dodier.

60. Ekberg, Kilman, and Lebeau, *Code Noir,* Article VIII, 28–29; Article XLIII, 44–45.

61. The records examined extend from 1757 to 1779, with most falling between 1766 and 1770. No claim is made for statistical weight, however, since not every slave would appear in such records.

62. On St. Ange's slaves, see below.

63. The widow Dodier owned the black/Indian couple. FSA, no. 1398.

64. These couples are identified in the sacramental registers, SLAR.

65. Ekberg, *François Vallé and His World*, 168. The fact that it was usually the same priests performing the rituals makes a comparison of their records reasonably valid.

66. Philip D. Morgan, *Slave Counterpoint: Black Culture in the Eighteenth-Century Chesapeake and Lowcountry* (Chapel Hill: University of North Carolina, 1998), 501–2.

67. FSA, no. 2832. The family name also appears in records as Quebedeau, Quebedot, and *dit* L'Espagnol.

68. See appendix A. Chemin had reported no slaves on the 1752 census, HMLO, 426. Neither brother appears to have married.

69. SLAR, Marriage, May 16, 1783. Vaillancourt was a native of Montreal.

70. See chapter 1, especially on Bourgmont's diplomacy.

71. Census of 1732 [General Summary of the entire Illinois Country], in ser. G^1 464, Archives Nationales Coloniales, Paris. They had arrived at Chartres in 1730.

72. VC, 109. The makeshift surname Patoka (Padouca, or Plains Apache) is the only indication of the origin of any of the St. Ange family slaves. The name may be the origin of her captors if she was too young to remember her family origins.

73. 1752 census, HMLO, 426.

74. Homer, *The Iliad*, translated by E. V. Rieu (Harmondsworth, UK: Penguin Books, 1964), 23–24.

75. Hodes, *Beyond the Frontier*, 79.

76. Registre des Insinuations, Perrin Collection, 57-3-22-1, Illinois State Archives, named his uncle Louis St. Ange as an heir.

77. The baptisms of Lizette's first three children are in the Vincennes register. Only Jean-Baptiste, the first child, seems to have survived. Register, St. Françoise Xavier, Vincennes, Transcription, MHM Library.

78. SLAR, Baptism. FSA, no. 2187. It is possible that Charlotte and Constance are the same person.

79. For the story of Francisco Cruzat's slave Marie-Thérèse and Auguste Chouteau who purchased her unborn slave child, see Ekberg, *Stealing Indian Women*, 82–87.

80. SLAR, Burial, August 31?, 1774.

81. FSA, no. 2187.

82. Ignace was probably not part of St. Ange's slave families. Laclède's slave Antoine is also absent.

83. See Kimberly Hangar, *Bounded Lives, Bounded Places: Free Black Society in Colonial New Orleans, 1769–1803* (Durham, NC: Duke University Press, 1997), 36–37, on paternity and manumission in Spanish Louisiana.

84. SLAR, Burial.

85. S. White, *Wild Frenchmen and Frenchified Indians*, 77, 88–96 (see chap. 1, n. 53). The degree of consent by Indian women in the process of Frenchification must have been as varied as the individuals who experienced it. Indian slave women who became French wives surely went through a substantial part of the process of Frenchification during their time in bondage.

86. FSA, no. 2557.

87. The rate of illegitimate births increased sharply in eighteenth-century France as the moralizing effects of the Catholic Reformation receded. See Jean-Louis Flandrin, *Familles: Parenté, maison, sexualité dans l'ancienne société* (Paris: Hachette, 1976), 176–84.

88. See Ekberg, *Stealing Indian Women*, 82–88.

89. Memo books, Billon Collection, MHMA, 196.

90. FSA, no. 36B; Memo Books, Billon Collection, MHMA, 196.

91. Described in chapter 5.

92. She later appeared in a "duly authorized" transaction (see chapter 7), becoming the first freed Indian slave woman in St. Louis to take part in a notarial sale contract. FSA, no. 37.

93. See Person, *Standing Up for Indians,* 85–89; and Ekberg, *Stealing Indian Women,* 75–76.

94. Memo books, Billon Collection, MHMA, 196; Belting, *Kaskaskia under the French Regime,* 106–7. This may be the same Agnès that Métivier freed (with her two children) in 1774 so that she could marry Louis Lacroix in Prairie du Rocher. Ekberg, *Stealing Indian Women,* 79. Henrion likely lived with his sister, the widow Beaugenou. The exact terms of Marie's freedom, that is, whether she should be cared for until the age of fifteen (see Quevedot above), were not mentioned in the manumission.

95. There is one emancipation for an adult black woman, slave of Louis Villars, lieutenant of the infantry, 1771. Billon Memobook, MHM, 196. See also Ekberg, *François Vallé and His World,* 135.

96. FSA, no. 2167. The details of this fascinating, unusual document touch simultaneously on the topics of slavery, multiple wills and inheritance, and the role of wives in the legal system.

97. The couple eventually was granted a legal separation, a story worthy of reexamination. Memo books, Billon Collection, MHMA, 196. See also Cleary, *The World, the Flesh, and the Devil,* 146–50; and Judith A. Gilbert, "Esther and Her Sisters: Free Women of Color as Property Owners in Colonial St. Louis, 1765–1803," *Gateway Heritage* (Summer 1996): 14–23.

98. According to Billon, *Annals,* 448, Papin's legitimate son J. M. Papin was not in St. Louis when his father died, and so this manumission of property in the heir's absence needed to be handled carefully. Before his estate items were auctioned, several articles of clothing were given to Flora. FSA, no. 2309; Memo books, Billon Collection, MHMA, 197. Flora purchased her first property in 1774. FSA, no. 138.

99. St. Louis 1787 census.

100. Sharon Block, *Rape and Sexual Power in Early America* (Chapel Hill: University of North Carolina Press, 2006), 73. Block provides useful characterizations of situations that blurred the line between consent and coercion.

101. See chapter 9 for their story.

102. Ekberg, *Stealing Indian Women,* 128. See also Din, *Spaniards, Planters, and Slaves,* 86 (see chap. 4, n. 81). This is in contrast to Lower Louisiana, where there were armed camps of runaway slaves and Indians. See Usner, *Indians, Settlers, and Slaves,* 140–41; and Hall, *Africans in Colonial Louisiana,* esp. chap. 4.

103. Marie-Louise was likely taken by the Peorias as a slave (her SLAR burial record in 1801 names her a Peoria Indian, but this cannot be her tribe of origin) and sold to Taillon. Her sons appear in the 1770 Indian slave census, and their ages indicate they were born before St. Louis was founded. See also appendix A.

104. In 1806 Auguste Chouteau gave a deposition in one phase of the Scypion freedom case that stated that there was discussion by Labuxière, Jean-Baptiste Martigny, and Joseph Taillon about exactly which of Taillon's slaves to include and which to exclude on the 1770 census. Lucas Collection, MHMA.

105. "Marguerite v. Chouteau," in *Cases Argued and Determined in the Supreme Court of Missouri,* edited and annotated by Louis Houck (St. Louis: Gilbert Book, 1870–90), 2:50. This deposition was part of the Marie Scypion freedom suit.

106. Kinnaird, *SMV,* 1:125–126.

107. Lucas Collection, 1806, MHMA.

108. FSA, no. 2302.

109. The often-recounted escape of Indian slaves occurred almost twenty years later. See *Annals,* 233–43.

110. Ekberg, *Stealing Indian Women,* 46–47, 102. In addition, manumitted Indian slave women could become wives of Frenchmen. See S. White, *Wild Frenchmen and Frenchified Indians,* 119.

111. See, for example, the Papin manumission record. Memo books, Billon Collection, MHMA, 197.

112. Quoted in Eugene D. Genovese, *Roll, Jordan, Roll: The World the Slaves Made* (New York: Pantheon Books, 1972), xv.

Chapter 9. In Small Things Forgotten

The chapter title is taken from James Deetz, *In Small Things Forgotten: The Archaeology of Early American Life* (New York: Anchor Books, 1977).

1. See, for example, muster roll from December 1, 1764 (ANOM, D^{2C} 52).

2. Gasconade, Missouri, is supposedly named after boastful French farmers who settled the region. See Robert L. Ramsay, *Our Storehouse of Missouri Placenames* (Columbia: University of Missouri Press, 1952), 94.

3. Gregory P. Ames of St. Louis suggests that Comparios might derive from the Italian *compare*, meaning "old friend" or "old mate."

4. ANOM, D^{2C} 52.

5. FSA, no. 2181.

6. FSA, no. 167.

7. FSA, August 14, 1775, no. 1406.

8. FSA, no. 2351.

9. ANOM, D^{2C} 52.

10. *SRM,* 1:187, 194.

11. SLAR, St. Ferdinand Burial Register; also deposition of Jean-Baptiste Rivière, Antoine's son, in Theodore Hunt, "Minutes," typescript copy, 2:102–3, MHMA.

12. FSA, no. 2351.

13. Two traditional French words were used for kneading trough, *pétrin* and *huche*. These words seem to imply no distinction between these vessels in either shape or use.

14. Regarding St. Louis potters, see Charles van Ravenswaay, "Missouri Potters and Their Wares," *Missouri Historical Bulletin* 7 (July 1951): 453–57.

15. *Curateurs* play an important role in French customary laws (*Coutume de Paris*), somewhat different from that of *tuteurs*. Whereas *tuteurs* dealt only with young children, *curateurs* served as guardians in other circumstances. For a discussion of *tuteurs* and *curateurs*, see Lange, *La nouvelle pratique civile, criminelle, et bénéficiale*, 137–42 (see chap. 1, n. 81); and chapter 7.

16. SLAR.

17. St. Louis 1787 census named four children.

18. Marriage contract, FSA, no. 2014, and chapter 8.

19. See guardianship document in FSA, no. 1783.

20. Description of the residential property in AGI, PC, 212A. See also map in Hodes, *Beyond the Frontier,* 87 (see chap. 3, n. 37). The house, though substantial, may have been quite small. In 1767 Lefebvre had a house built (building contract in FSA, no. 2844) that measured only twenty-by-twenty-five pieds, although this did not include the "apenty" kitchen addition.

21. Original ms. in KM 70-5-28-1.

22. AGI, PC, 212A.

23. These black women were Marianne and Lorine, who appeared above, in chapter 8.

24. See also chapter 8.

25. The best black walnut in North America grew in Upper Louisiana. See also van Ravenswaay, "Creole Arts and Crafts," 213–48 (see chap. 5, n. 14).

26. See Ekberg, *Colonial Ste. Genevieve,* esp. 347–50 (see chap. 3, n. 50).

27. *Une culotte* in French, whereas in English the plural, *culottes,* is preferred.

28. In medieval times, *camelot* literally meant woven of camel hair. By the eighteenth century, however, it had come to mean fine wool, sometimes mixed with silk.

29. Gail Moreau-DesHarnais, "Edward Ciotte Ledger, 1749–1752: Containing Accounts of French Settlers at Detroit," *Michigan's Habitant Heritage* 29 (July 2008): 147–56.

30. See Suzanne Boivin Sommerville, "The True Wife of Louis Deshêtres in 1760 Detroit: Thérèse Damours de Louvières, Daughter of Marie-Josèphe de Tonty," *Michigan's Habitant Heritage* 28, no. 1 (2007): 33 37; Loraine M. DiCerbo, "The Rest of the Story: Louis [-Antoine] Deshêtres and Marie Thérèse Damours de Louvières," *Michigan's Habitant Heritage* 28, no. 1 (2007): 37–44. We are much indebted to independent scholars Suzanne Boivin Sommerville, Loraine M. DiCerbo, and Gail F. Moreau-DesHarnais for an extended exchange of e-mails in April and May 2012 that clarified for us many of the complexities in the Deshêtres and Damours de Louvière families. We could not have completed this section without their patient assistance.

31. Ernest J. Lajeunesse, ed., *The Windsor Border Region: Canada's Southernmost Frontier* (Toronto: Champlain Society for the Government of Ontario, University of Toronto Press, 1960), lv.

32. E-mail communications from Loraine M. DiCerbo and Suzanne Boivin Sommerville, April 30, 2012.

33. See John Campbell to William Johnson, May 21, 1765, in *The Papers of William Johnson*, digital version (Albany: State University of New York Press, 2008), 11:744–46.

34. DiCerbo, "Rest of the Story," 40.

35. Marie-Thérèse was a daughter of the deceased Louis Damours and Marie-Josèphe Tonty. Sommerville, "True Wife," 33–37.

36. Croghan's "Journal," *NR,* 35.

37. Regarding the Richardville family at Vincennes, see chapter 2; and *DGFQ,* 362.

38. Antoine Damours de Louvières, cousin to Marie-Thérèse Damours de Louvières Deshêtres, married Marie-Louise Godere native of Vincennes on February 4, 1766. "Illinois, Diocese of Belleville, Catholic Parish Records, 1729–1956," images, Family Search (https://familysearch.org/pal:/MM9.3.1/TH-267-11882-155778-47?cc=1388122&wc =M99B-QMV:n408136662), Randolph > Fort de Chartres > St. Anne (transferred to St. Joseph) > 1721–1840 Baptisms, Marriages, Deaths, First Communion, Confirmations > image 133 of 603.

39. Jacques Mathieu and Serge Courville, *Peuplement colonisateur au XVIIe et XVIIIe siècles* (Quebec: Celat, 1987).

40. Michael McCafferty of Indiana University (e-mail communication, May 4, 2012), an expert on early Illinois Country routes and waterways, thinks that it would have taken more than a month to get from Detroit to Prairie du Rocher by water.

41. The head of this family had been Michel Damours de Louvière (died 1757), who had been an officer in the militia. Michel was the brother of Louis, father of Marie-Thérèse Deshêtres. E-mail communication (May 4, 2012) from Loraine DiCerbo, president of the French Canadian Heritage Society of Michigan. Concerning Michel's life in the Illinois Country, see the various documents pertaining to him in *VC*.

42. Prairie du Rocher is suggested (not declared) as the place of birth in Meurin's baptismal record of May 16, the baptism having taken place in Prairie du Rocher (transcripts of Prairie du Rocher baptismal records in MHMA).

43. Meurin baptized a child in St. Louis on May 9, 1766. SLAR.

44. See appendix A.

45. Sommerville, "Wife of Louis Deshêtres," 35.

46. Nasatir, "Government Employees," 914 (see chap. 4, n. 24).

47. FSA, no. 11. The mill had one "meule" and one "lit," rather than two meules, revealing that it was not a gristmill.

48. *LT* 1:fol. 2.

49. *DGFQ*, 460.

50. FSA, no. 2013. Also cited in DiCerbo, "Rest of the Story," 41.

51. FSA, no. 2839.

52. *DGFQ*, 1014.

53. See Georges-Henri-Victor Collot, *A Journey in North America, Containing a Survey of the Countries Watered by the Mississippi, Ohio, Missouri, and Other Affluing Rivers; with Exact Observations on the Course and Soundings of These Rivers; and on the Towns, Villages, Hamlets and Farms of That Part of the New-World* (Paris: A. Bertrand, 1826), 1:126.

54. Bill of sale in FSA, no. 52. Dimensions of the house given as twenty-five-by-forty-two pieds.

55. FSA, no. 2302. Deshêtres performed both these tasks for Pierre Laclède. See also chapter 8.

56. Ibid.

57. Motard referred (ibid.) to "ma boutique," and in traditional French usage boutique meant a shop associated with a residence.

58. See Deshêtre's succession papers in FSA, no. 2302. *Cinchona* was Carolus Linneaus's appellation for the South American tree that provided the bark, which contains quinine and is useful in taming malarial fevers.

59. FSA, nos. 103 and 2302.

60. Ibid., no. 2302.

61. In principle, a *pot* was equal to two French *pintes*, thereby equaling nearly one-half an English gallon, but in practice the amount in a *pot* varied widely.

62. Paul Alliot, "Historical and Political Reflections on Louisiana," in *Louisiana under the Rule of Spain, France, and the United States, 1785–1807*, edited by James A. Robertson (Cleveland: Arthur H. Clark, 1911), 1:113.

63. Sergeant John Ordway's "Journal," http://lewisandclarkjournals.unl.edu/read/?_xmlsrc=1805-05-05.xml&_xslsrc=LCstyles.xsl.

64. Sociologists tend to be more concerned with nineteenth-century fashions than eighteenth-centurty fashions. See, for example, Diana Crane, *Fashion and Its Social Agendas: Class, Gender, and Identity in Clothing* (Chicago: University of Chicago Press, 2000), chap. 2.

65. See capots made of "cadiz" in Belting, *Kaskaskia under the French Regime*, 51 (see chap. 7, n. 31).

66. See inventory of Jacques Bourdon's estate in KM 23-7-1-1.

67. DGFQ, 568. See also, concerning Léonard Hervieux, Suzanne Boivin Sommerville, "Marie-Anne Magnan *dite* Lespérance, Called Hope: A Cautionary 'Tale,'" *Michigan's Habitant Heritage* 25, no. 1 (2004): 5.

68. "Illinois, Diocese of Belleville, Catholic Parish Records, 1729–1956," images, Family Search (https://familysearch.org/pal:/MM9.3.1/TH-267-11765-123759-29?cc=1388122&wc=M99B-QMN:n2031332824), Randolph > Kaskaskia Island > Immaculate Conception > 1741–1834 Marriages > image 22 of 118.

69. Louis was born in Canada, sometime before 1720, of the marriage of Louis Normand *dit* Labrière and Anne Bruneau (Suzanne Boivin Sommerville, e-mail communication, September 20, 2012).

70. "Illinois, Diocese of Belleville, Catholic Parish Records, 1729–1956," images, Family Search (https://familysearch.org/pal:/MM9.3.1/TH-267-11765-123425-64?cc=1388122&wc=M99B-QMN:n2031332824), Randolph > Kaskaskia Island > Immaculate Conception > 1741–1834 Marriages > image 12 of 118. Raimond married at Prairie du Rocher in 1777. Faribault-Beauregard, *Population des forts français*, 2:267 (see chap. 2, n. 56).

71. Thérèse married at St. Louis in 1769 (see FSA, no. 2021 and chapter 7).

72. See Ekberg, *François Vallé and His World*, 226. Agnès had apparently moved to Ste. Genevieve, and Lieutenant Governor Pedro Piernas was not at all pleased with adultery within his jurisdiction.

73. *VC*, 615, 673–74. The substantial property was part of the estate of the deceased royal storekeeper André Chevalier.

74. *CP*, 131.

75. See town plan in Hodes, *Beyond the Frontier*, 86–87.

76. *VC*, 803; baptismal record, July 7, 1765, "Illinois, Diocese of Belleville, Catholic Parish Records, 1729–1956," images, FamilySearch (https://familysearch.org/pal:/MM9.3.1/TH-266-11825-78896-83?cc=1388122&wc=M99B-QMJ:687691126), Randolph > Kaskaskia Island > Immaculate Conception > 1759–1815 Baptisms, Marriages, Deaths, Other > image 35 of 244.

77. FSA, no. 2330.

78. *LT*, 1:fol. 9.

79. FSA, no. 2330.

80. *Polonaise* (*polonesa* in Spanish) appears regularly in descriptions of clothing from the Illinois Country. The origin of the name is unclear, and how it was used in colonial Louisiana is even less clear. Professor Robert S. Duplessis of Swarthmore College adduces (personal communication) a Superior Council record at the Louisiana State Museum (LSM doc. no. 1766122301) containing the expression "coton ou polonaise," which is useful but not definitive. Elizabeth Hardouin-Fugier, Bernard Berthod, and Martine Chaient-Fusaro, *Les Etoffes: Dictionnaire Historique* (n.p. Editions de l'Amateur, 1994), 312, state that "*polonaise* was a half-silk, half-cotton fabric used for women's clothing and linings, particularly useful for millinery work and also for furniture." We are indebted to Gregory P. Ames of St. Louis for providing this last reference.

81. Concerning material culture in the Illinois Country, see especially Mazrim, *At Home in the Illinois Country* (see chap. 3, n. 20). We are grateful to Robert F. Mazrim, who provided invaluable expert opinion on these artifacts. Pipestone quarries are located and preserved in Pipestone National Monument outside Pipestone, Minnesota.

82. John Francis McDermott, *Private Libraries in Creole St. Louis* (Baltimore: Johns Hopkins University Press, 1938), somehow overlooked Hervieux's little library.

83. Concerning the property rights of illegitimate children, see Lange, *La nouvelle pratique*, 131.

84. FSA, no. 31. Concerning *en colombage* construction, see Edwards and Pecquet du Bellay de Verton, *Creole Lexicon*, 65 (see chap. 6, n. 9); and chapter 6.

85. FSA, nos. 2344A and 2344B.

86. FSA, no. 104. When St. Ange died in December 1774, he owed money to Laville for various articles of clothing, including a riding coat (FSA, no. 2187).

87. FSA, no. 2344A.

Chapter 10. Foundations of the St. Louis Fur Trade

1. Hiram Martin Chittenden, *The American Fur Trade of the Far West*, 3 vols. (New York: F. P. Harpter, 1902). Concerning Chittenden's relationship to the Chouteaus, see Jay Gitlin, "From Private Stories to Public Memory: The Chouteau Descendants of St. Louis and the Production of History," in *Auguste Chouteau's Narrative of the Settlement of St. Louis,* edited by Gregory P. Ames (St. Louis: Mercantile Library, 2010), 12–13. The renowned Chouteau Collection of manuscripts in the archives of the Missouri History Museum provides virtually no information about the fur trade during the 1760s, for the apparent reason that Auguste Chouteau was little involved in it.

2. Gordon claimed "that the whole Trade of the Missouri, that of the Mississippi Northwards, and that of the Nations of La Baye, Lake Michigan, St. Josephs, by the Illinois River, is entirely brought to him" ("Journal," August 31, 1766, *NR,* 300). See the most recent citations of Gordon in Cleary, *The World, the Flesh, and the Devil,* 71 (see chap. 4, n. 46); Jay Gitlin, *The Bourgeois Frontier: French Towns, French Traders, and American Expansion* (New Haven, Conn.: Yale University Press, 2010), 16.

3. "Peltries" in this chapter refers both to fur-bearing skins and those, especially of deer, that had been scraped clean ("rasée") and cured.

4. The standard study of the Canadian fur trade is Harold A. Innis, *The Fur Trade in Canada* (Toronto: University of Toronto Press, 1962). The more recent compendious study is Havard, *Empire et Métisssages,* (see chap. 4, n. 36).

5. Havard, *Empire et Métisssages,* 277–83 and passim. See also *DCB*, s.v. "La Forest, François Dauphin de" and "Tonti, Henri de."

6. Archives Civiles et Notariales, Bibliothèque et Archives Nationales du Québec, Montreal. See also Gratien Allaire, "Les engagements pour la traite des fourrure: Évaluation de la documentation," *Revue d'histoire de l'Amérique française* 34 (1980): 3–26.

7. KM 21-9-13-1 and 23-7-1-1.

8. Johnson to the Lords of Trade, November 16, 1765, *NR*, 117–18.

9. FSA, no. 2828. Jean may well have been the Jean-Baptiste Degaigné who was married to a *métisse* and was enumerated on the 1752 census of Kaskaskia. See Belting, *Kaskaskia under the French Regime,* 88 (see chap. 7, n. 31).

10. Finiels, *Account of Upper Louisiana,* 100 (see chap. 3, n. 24).

11. FSA, no. 2829.

12. FSA., no. 2831.

13. FSA, no. 2830.

14. Thomas Gage to Guy Johnson, May 29, 1768, in *Papers of Johnson,* 12:517 (see chap. 3, n. 61).

15. AGI, PC, 188A.

16. See *FFL*, s.v. "Fagot de la Garcinière, Daniel-François."

17. AGI, PC, 188A.

18. This according to master genealogist Winston De Ville, e-mail communication November 10, 2011.

19. AGI, PC, 188A. Devin died while trading on the Des Moines River in 1773. FSA, no. 2320.

20. AGI, PC, 188A. See also Nasatir, *Before Lewis and Clark*, 1:66–68 (see chap. 4, n. 92).

21. Nasatir, *Lewis and Clark*, 1:68–69. See also Foley and Rice, *First Chouteaus*, 19–20 (see chap. 3, n. 10).

22. Contract in FSA, no. 1502.

23. *Annals*, 33–36. Chickasaw Bluffs, located just upriver from present-day Memphis, was called either Écores de Prudhomme or Écores à Margot by the French.

24. St. Ange granted Lambert a double residential lot in St. Louis on July 1, 1767 (*LT,* 1:fol. 11).

25. FSA, no. 1512. Michel Rolet was a fusilier in the garrison at Fort de Chartres in June 1765 (ANOM, D^{2c} 52). He was the winning bidder for the slave Lorine in 1766; see chapter 8.

26. FSA, no. 1513.

27. ANOM, D^{2c} 52. After having promoted Montardy, St. Ange busted him for incompetence (St. Ange to Aubry, July 18, 1768, AGI, PC, 187A). Nevertheless, Montardy went on to live a long and active life in St. Louis and was still trading up the Missouri River in 1792 (Nasatir, *Lewis and Clark*, 1:162).

28. See Foley and Rice, *First Chouteaus*, 144–45, 170–71.

29. FSA, no. 1523. The name also appears as Desnoyers. See militia muster roll, volontaires section, appendix A.

30. FSA, no. 1539.

31. ISC; see appendix B.

32. FSA, no. 1514.

33. FSA, no. 2311. And this amount did not include his possessions in New Orleans, which included black slaves and a residence. The possessions that Lambert had with him in Ste. Genevieve when he died were inventoried there (Ste. Genevieve Civil Records, estates, no. 151, MHMA) and then added to the St. Louis inventory.

34. FSA, no. 2311.

35. See Foley and Rice, *First Chouteaus*, 21.

36. St. Ange to Aubry, July 18, 1769, AGI, PC, 187A.

37. This was obviously a nickname, and could have meant the difficult or obstinate one, one who stands athwart, or, alternatively, one who makes a crossing, who traverses a major body of water.

38. FSA, no. 1532.

39. FSA, no. 1534.

40. FSA, no. 2833.

41. FSA, no. 2861.

42. FSA, no. 2854. The Otos spoke a Siouan language of the Chiwere group and were a small tribe. Lewis and Clark met them in early August 1804, apparently west of where Omaha, Nebraska, now stands (http://lewisandclarkjournals.unl.edu/read). The Panis spoke a Caddoan language, and their villages were also located along the lower Platte River.

43. FSA, no. 2846.

44. Piernas seems to have established this licensing policy on his own, without instructions from O'Reilly (see Piernas's report of July 28, 1770 in AGI, PC, 188A).

45. AGI, PC, 188A.

46. *Chat* usually translates as "raccoon" in fur-trade contexts. See McDermott, *Glossary of Mississippi Valley French,* 49 (see chap. 6, n. 36).

47. AGI, PC, 188A, addendum to license drafted by Villars. Concerning Villars as commandant at Ste. Genevieve, see Ekberg, *François Vallé and His World,* chaps. 3 and 4 (see chap. 3, n. 13); and Ekberg, *Stealing Indian Women,* chaps. 7 and 8 (see chap. 1, n. 25).

48. Ste. Genevieve Civil Records, Contracts, no. 45, MHMA.

49. This may be the earliest commercial document signed by Chouteau.

50. FSA, no. 2863.

51. See license, dated July 19, 1771, issued by Lieutenant Louis Villars, AGI, PC, 188A.

52. Ibid.

53. AGI, PC, 110. Concerning flour shipments to New Orleans, see Ekberg, *French Roots,* chap. 6.

54. Addendum to license inscribed by Villars, AGI, PC, 188A.

55. FSA, nos. 1548, 1551, 1552, 1553.

56. FSA, no. 1548.

57. FSA, no. 1551.

58. FSA, no. 1554.

59. It is relevant that Perrault does not appear as a slave owner on the St. Louis Indian slave census of 1770, ISC. He had little or no use for such slaves as a *négociant.*

60. See Carl J. Ekberg, *A French Aristocrat in the American West: The Shattered Dreams of Delassus de Luzières* (Columbia: University of Missouri Press, 2010), 34, 56, 87, 94, 131, 162, 202.

61. AGI, PC, 111.

62. See McDermott, *Glossary of Mississippi Valley French,* 116–17.

63. FSA, no. 2311.

64. See, for examples of this common early usage, KM 23-7-1-1, 24-9-2-2, 25-3-15-1, 28-3-6-1.

65. Richter, *Before the Revolution,* 406 (emphasis in the original) (see chap. 4, n. 91).

66. See, for some examples, Havard and Vidal, *Histoire de l'Amérique française,* esp. chap. 6; Havard, *Empire et Métissages,* esp. chaps. 8 and 9; Tanis C. Thorne, *The Many Hands of My Relations: French and Indians on the Lower Missouri* (Columbia: University of Missouri Press, 1996), esp. chap. 2; Jennifer S. H. Brown: *Strangers in Blood: Fur Trade Company Families in Indian Country* (Norman: University of Oklahoma Press, 1996); and Susan Sleeper-Smith, *Indian Women and French Men: Rethinking Cultural Encounter in the Western Great Lakes* (Amherst: University of Massachusetts Press, 2001), esp. chap. 1.

67. Recounted above, in chapter 4.

Chapter 11. End of an Era

1. Ulloa to Grimaldi, August 4, 1768, AGI, Santo Domingo, legajo 2542, no. 20.

2. David E. Stannard, *American Holocaust* (New York: Oxford University Press, 1992), 118–21.

3. Sophie White's sophisticated analysis (*Wild Frenchmen and Frenchified Indians,* esp. chap. 2 [see chap. 1, n. 53]) is about as far as one can go in this direction.

4. Guillaume Aubert's arguments ("'The Blood of France': Race and Purity of Blood in the French Atlantic World," *William and Mary Quarterly* 61 [July 2004]:

452–53) about racialist attitudes in eighteenth-century France have little or no demonstrated relevance for the Illinois Country.

5. St. Ange to Aubry, May 16, 1768, AGI, PC, 187A.

6. Ríu to Ulloa, November 12, 1767, AGI, PC, 109.

7. Barr, *Peace Came in the Form of a Woman,* 10 (see chap. 8, n. 2).

8. David J. Weber, *Barbaros: Spaniards and Their Savages in the Age of Enlightenment* (New Haven, Conn.: Yale University Press, 2006), 15.

9. See *IOE,* 832.

10. Dunn, *Documents Relating to the French Settlements on the Wabash,* 5 (see chap. 2, n. 51).

11. St. Ange to Aubry, November 19, 1767, AGI, PC, 107.

12. St. Ange's countryman Charles-Louis de Secondat de Montesquieu helped to promote the notion that government was intended to served the greater public good. Montesquieu thought that "le bien commun" and "le bien public" were best served in small republics rather than in large republics or in monarchies (see *De l'Esprit des Lois,* bk. 8, chap. 16, first published in 1748). St. Ange, of course, remained a monarchist through and through and would have been horrified by the very thought of republican government.

13. Billon understood this and published an English translation of the will (*Annals,* 125–27). The original ms. is in FSA, no. 2187.

14. Pierre Laville was identified as a "tailleur habits" in 1770 (FSA, no. 104).

15. See, however, Ekberg, *Stealing Indian Women,* 29 (see chap. 1, n. 25).

16. FSA, no. 2187. The will was probated on September 2, 1776, and made official with the signature of Lieutenant Governor Francisco Cruzat (FSA, no. 1813).

17. Michel Rolet *dit* La Déroute bequeathed his Indian slave Piero to his son in his will in 1775 (FSA, no. 2194).

18. SLAR, Burial, December 27, 1774.

19. Jean-Baptiste Vallé, youngest son of François Vallé, kept vigil at his father's deathbed and noted the exact time of his death—5:00 a.m., September 28, 1783. See Ekberg, *François Vallé and His World,* 277 (see chap. 3, n. 13).

20. FSA, no. 2325.

21. Ekberg, *François Vallé and His World,* 277.

22. See note 18.

23. FSA, no. 2325.

24. Record of auction, FSA, no. 2557. In general, the appraisers, Sarpy and Segond, erred on the side of caution. Their total for St. Ange's physical possessions amounted to 2247 livres, 5 sols. At auction the effects brought 2977 livres, 5 sols, although a few items were sold that, for whatever reasons, had not been tallied in the inventory.

25. "Ordonnance du roy pour Deffendre à tous Négocians, Marchands, Bourgeois & autres qui ne sont pas Officiers de porter l'Epée, . . ." (Paris: L'imprimerie royale, 1720).

26. Benito Basquez, a relative newcomer to St. Louis, bought them (FSA, no. 2557).

27. Ibid. It seems virtually certain that St. Ange's books were Briquet, *Code militaire* (see chap. 1, n. 80); and Charlevoix, *Histoire de l'Isle espagnole ou de S. Domingue: Écrite particulièrement sur des mémoires manuscrits du p. Jean-Baptiste le Pers, jésuite, missionnaire a' Saint Domingue, & sur les pièces originales, qui se conservent au Dépôt de la marine / par le p. Pierre-François-Xavier de Charlevoix . . .* (Paris: Hippolyte-Louis Guerin, 1730–31).

28. Foley and Rice, *First Chouteaus,* 25 (see chap. 3, n. 10). When Laclède's estate was sold off, Auguste Chouteau bought eight books, which provided a nucleus for his eventual library of more than six hundred volumes (ibid.).

29. William R. Swagerty, *The Indianization of Lewis and Clark*, 2 vols. (Norman: Arthur H. Clark, 2012); Carolyn Gilman, *Lewis and Clark: Across the Divide* (Washington, D.C.: Smithsonian Books, 2003), 211.

30. "Ynstruccion a que se arreglaran los Tenientos de Governado." January 26, 1770, AGI, PC, 2357.

31. Numbers of documents drafted by Labuxière and Piernas between 1766 and 1775 may be seen in the FSA. The king of France was customarily called "His Christian Majesty."

32. *SRM*, 1:73.

33. See, for an excellent example, the marriage contract of Auguste Chouteau and Marie-Thérèse Cerré (September 21, 1786, Chouteau Collection, MHMA), which was drafted in French but made official with the signature of Spanish lieutenant governor Francisco Cruzat.

34. Piernas to Unzaga, July 19, 1772, AGI, PC, 81; Unzaga to Piernas, February 19, 1773, ibid.

35. FSA, no. 2885.

36. *SRM*, 1:139.

37. He drafted Kiery Marcheteau's will with Véronique Panissé in October 1780 (FSA, no. 305).

38. Clarence Walworth Alvord, ed., *Kaskaskia Records, 1778–1790*, Collections of the Illinois State Historical Library, no. 5 (Springfield: Illinois State Historical Library, 1909), 275, for example.

39. Ibid., 286–87.

40. Northwest Ordinance, sec. 2, July 13, 1787, http://www.ourdocuments.gov/doc.

41. John Francis McDermott, *Old Cahokia: A Narrative and Documents Illustrating the First Century of Its History* (St. Louis: St. Louis Historical Documents Foundation, 1949), 130–31n102.

42. Burial record at "Illinois, Diocese of Belleville, Catholic Parish Records, 1729–1956," images, FamilySearch (https://familysearch.org/pal:/MM9.3.1/TH-266-11132-133558-56?cc=1388122&wc=M99B-Q7X:893567332), St. Clair > Cahokia > Holy Family > 1783–1819 Deaths (originals) > image 9 of 57.

43. *VC*, 198.

44. McDermott, *Old Cahokia*, 130–40.

Conclusion

1. Thorne, *Many Hands of My Relations*, 84 (see chap. 10, n. 66).

2. See Robert Michael Morrissey, "Kaskaskia Social Network: Kinship and Assimilation in the French-Illinois Borderlands, 1695–1735," *William and Mary Quarterly* 70, no. 1 (2013): 103–46.

3. Peterson, *Colonial St. Louis*, 40 (see chap. 5, n. 2).

4. McDermott, *Glossary of Mississippi Valley French*, 60–62 (see chap. 6, n. 36).

5. FSA, no. 434.

6. Jay Gitlin coined the catchy phrase "Creole Corridor" and uses the expression frequently in his recent fascinating book, *The Bourgeois Frontier* (see chap. 10, n. 2). Les Amis, an organization in St. Louis that promotes regional French colonial history, has defined (borrowing from Gitlin) a one-hundred-mile swath of the Mississippi Valley as the "Creole Corridor" and is advocating that the National Park Service recognize the region as a definable and unique historical entity, worthy of protection and promotion.

7. Recent decades have witnessed a surge of literature on the topic of creolization. The subject is popular in Atlantic studies, diaspora studies, postcolonial studies, literary criticism, history, sociology, linguistics, and, particularly, anthropology. Fascination with creolization is pan-global and includes Louisiana architectural studies. See Jay D. Edwards, "Creolization Theory and the Odyssey of the Atlantic Linear Cottage," *Etnofoor* 23, no. 1 (2011): 50–83.

8. This does not conflict with Dawdy's capsule definition of "creolization as the birth of a new native society" (*Building the Devil's Empire,* 5 [see chap. 4, n. 61]).

9. Edwards and Kariouk, *Creole Lexicon,* 77 (see chap. 6, n. 9).

10. FSA, no. 231.

11. "Grande Chambre" could mean master bedroom or simply large room; in this case, the context suggests the latter.

12. Concerning craftsmen in early St. Louis, see chapter 9; and van Ravenswaay, "Arts and Crafts," 245. This document (FSA, no. 231) establishes beyond any doubt the important fact that craftsmen in early St. Louis were fashioning armoires.

13. Johnson to the Lords of Trade, November 16, 1765, New Regime, 117.

14. Daniel H. Usner Jr., "Between Yankees and Creoles: The Discursive Representation of Colonial Louisiana in American History," in *French Colonial Louisiana and the Atlantic World,* edited by Bond, 17 (see chap. 8, n. 6). On this same subject, see Emily Clark, "Moving from Periphery to Centre: The Non-British in Colonial North America," *Historical Journal* 42, no. 3 (1999): 903–10.

15. Review in *William and Mary Quarterly* 64, no. 2 (2007).

16. Usner, *Indians, Settlers, and Slaves* (see chap. 8, n. 25).

17. See, for examples, Thomas Benjamin, *The Atlantic World: Europeans, Indians, and Their Shared History, 1400–1900* (Cambridge: Cambridge University Press, 2009); Karen Ordahl Kupperman, *The Atlantic in World History* (Oxford and New York: Oxford University Press, 2012); John H. Elliot, *Empires of the Atlantic: Britain and Spain, 1492–1830* (New Haven, Conn.: Yale University Press, 2006). In fairness, it must be noted that Elliot does mention that Louisiana was controlled by France and then Spain during the eighteenth century (265, 272, 295, 373).

18. Jack P. Greene and Philip D. Morgan, eds., *Atlantic History: A Critical Appraisal* (Oxford and New York: Oxford University Press, 2009), 137–62.

19. Ibid., 148.

20. Ibid., 149.

21. Davis, *Inhuman Bondage,* 104 (see chap. 8, n. 18).

22. Ira Berlin, *Many Thousands Gone: The First Two Centuries of Slavery in North America* (Cambridge, Mass.: Harvard University Press, 1998), 90.

23. Ibid., 134.

24. Din, *Spaniards, Planters, and Slaves,* 3, 10 (see chap. 4, n. 82).

25. For Bienvenu, see Vidal, "Antoine Bienvenu," 111–16 (see chap. 8, n. 11); and Ekberg, *French Roots,* 153–66.

26. Hall, *Africans in Colonial Louisiana,* 175–76 (see chap. 8, n. 6). St. Louis numbers are from the 1766 census, appendix A, and the St. Louis 1787 Census.

27. Hall, *Africans in Colonial Louisiana,* 130.

28. The 1787 census categorized slaves by skin colors—blancos (whites), pardos (tans), and negros (blacks)—and Indians, métis, and mulattoes were encompassed within the pardo category.

29. Spanish census of 1796 in AGI, PC, 2364.

30. Peter H. Wood, "From Atlantic History to a Continental Approach," in *Atlantic History,* edited by Greene and Morgan, 279–98.

31. Daniel K. Richter, *Facing East from Indian Country: A Native History of Early America* (Cambridge, Mass.: Harvard University 2001), 1–3, 166, mentions "le pays des Illinois" in one sentence.

32. Mapp, *Elusive West,* 265 (emphasis added) (see chap. 3, n. 1).

33. Ibid., 200.

34. See Chouteau's account of Laclède's vision of St. Louis's future success. *ACJ,* facsimile ms., 2.

Appendix A. St. Louis Counts

1. Original in AGI, Audiencia de Santo Domingo, 2595.

2. St. Ange returned the census to Ulloa AGI, PC, 2357.

3. The census has been discussed in Ekberg, *François Vallé and His World,* 49–54 (see chap. 3, n. 13); Thomas N. Ingersoll, *Mammon and Manon in Early New Orleans* (Knoxville: University of Tennessee Press, 1999), 42- 43; and Paul LaChance, "The Growth of the Free and Slave Population of French Colonial Louisiana," in *French Colonial Louisiana and the Atlantic World,* edited by Bond, 204–43 (see chap. 8, n. 6). Different versions of the same census appear in the AGI collections, making it difficult to compare Ingersoll and LaChance to this study, and the data they likely used are from the summary page rather than the list of individuals, which comprises the treatment of the document here.

4. Ames, *ACJ,* 76, 91n71.

5. *Annals,* 17.

6. Only Judge Lefebvre, who died April 3, 1767, FSA no. 2297, Antoine Hubert, Antoine Rivière, and La Giroflée (his name is often awfully mistranscribed as "la Garosse") are on the census but not the militia muster roll. The *volontaires* list includes many men who later were called habitants. They married and settled in St. Louis.

7. The totals in this paragraph do not include the first column of the summarized chart "Vecinos." It is assumed that the 56 named residents were also enumerated in the proper column for militia or widow and should not be counted twice. The usual age for militia was approximately fourteen to fifty. Racial categories "white" and "black" appeared for the first time on the census in 1772.

8. LaChance, "Growth of the Free and Slave Population," 228–29, has a total of 713 residents in the Illinois Country in 1766. The version used in this study has a total of 879.

9. See *SRM,* 1:72, for the 1769 comment on population and 53–54 for the 1772 census totals, 597 for St. Louis and 691 for Ste. Genevieve. A different census, also dated 1772, in AGI, 2357, showed the total white (blancos) population of St. Louis at 373, with 124 black slaves, and Ste. Genevieve with 332 whites and 273 black slaves.

10. AGI, Audiencia de Santo Domingo, 2595.

11. Includes the outlying settlements at Mine la Motte and La Saline.

12. These "older" categories may represent children not yet of majority age, but above the age limit of the categories "niños" and "niñas." See Brooks, *Captives and Cousins,* 56 (see chap. 8, n. 2), for an interpretation of the same Spanish terms from a 1692 Spanish census.

13. Nasatir, "Government Employees," 914.

14. This may have been added purely for clarification, as there was another Louis Dubreuil in St. Louis who was not a négociant.

15. Identities of troops can often be gleaned from the FSA, Pierre Montardy and Jean Comparios, for example.

16. Jacques Noisé was not married in 1766, notwithstanding the mark in the "wife" column, so he is not included in this count.

17. Pierre Laclède being first among these, but see chapter 8 for other accounts.

18. One exception, for example, is Michel La Déroute and his wife, Marguerite LeGrain, married in 1765 at Fort de Chartres. "Illinois, Diocese of Belleville, Catholic Parish Records, 1729–1956," images, FamilySearch (https://familysearch.org/pal:/MM9.3.1/TH-267-11882-151767-50?cc=1388122&wc=M99B-QMV:n408136662), Randolph > Fort de Chartres > St. Anne (transferred to St. Joseph) > 1721–1840 Baptisms, Marriages, Deaths, First Communion, Confirmations > image 114 of 603.

19. *VC,* 254; FSA no. 2014. Their father died in 1762; their mother was buried January 1763. "Illinois, Diocese of Belleville, Catholic Parish Records, 1729–1956," images, FamilySearch (https://familysearch.org/pal:/MM9.3.1/TH-267-11882-154060-86?cc=1388122&wc=M99B-QMV:n408136662), Randolph > Fort de Chartres > St. Anne (transferred to St. Joseph) > 1721–1840 Baptisms, Marriages, Deaths, First Communion, Confirmations > image 124 of 603.

20. FSA, no. 1783.

21. Not all the ciphers for children could be associated with names, however.

22. See, for example, Piernas's report in *SRM,* 1:66–72, for a mixed assessment of the character of St. Louis and Ste. Genevieve.

23. Baptisms of twin daughters were recorded in Ste. Anne at Fort de Chartres on May 17, 1746; one died the next day, "Illinois, Diocese of Belleville, Catholic Parish Records, 1729–1956," images, FamilySearch (https://familysearch.org/pal:/MM9.3.1/TH-267-11882-152159-32?cc=1388122&wc=M99B-QMV:n408136662), Randolph > Fort de Chartres > St. Anne (transferred to St. Joseph) > 1721–1840 Baptisms, Marriages, Deaths, First Communion, Confirmations > image 36 of 603.

24. Her daughter married Louis Briard *dit* La Roche.

25. *Annals,* 39–40. See especially Williams, "Prosperity in the Face of Prejudice," 4–11 (see chap. 8, n. 55). Neither the French 1752 census nor the census summarized in *SRM,* 1:53–57, has a category for free blacks. Din, *Spaniards, Planters, and Slaves,* 39 (see chap. 4, n. 81), comments that free blacks were present but not counted in the 1766 census. The 1772 census draft had columns available for enumerating free blacks, but the totals for both Ste. Genevieve and St. Louis were zero. AGI, 2357.

26. S. White, *Wild Frenchmen and Frenchified Indians,* 25 (see chap. 1, n. 53). Originals in KPR, images 1–7, for examples.

27. Le Programme de recherche en démographie historique (PRDH) online. It is often assumed Hélène was the daughter of Dorothée Méchiperouta, but the authors agree with Danis descendant Pat Weeks (personal communication) that this assumption is problematic. Nevertheless, it is probable that Danis was *métisse* and until conclusive evidence to the contrary is found, the authors accept this. Danis also appears in Belting, *Kaskaskia under the French Regime,* 90 (see chap. 7, n. 31).

28. See chapter 1. There are several references to Indian slaves called "Patoka," for example, *VC* and in the Vincennes register: in 1757 Joseph Padouca and Marie-Louise Chicacha, slaves of Framboise married. Register, St. Françoise Xavier, Vincennes, Transcription, MHM Library.

29. See marriage contract, FSA, no. 2008.

30. In the east-side registers, especially Kaskaskia (Immaculate Conception) beginning around 1730, French-Indian marriages are apparent. By the time of the settlement of St. Louis, several generations later, Indian heritage was no longer noticeable unless a family name such as Patoka persisted. See Belting, *Kaskaskia Under the French Regime,* 10–16, 74–75; and Ekberg, *Stealing Indian Women,* 24–40 (see chap. 1, n. 25).

298   Notes to Appendix A

31. See FSA, nos. 2841 and 2302.

32. Jean Baptiste Langevin is recorded with sixty parcels of land, but this must be a transcribing mistake. He was never this prominent, and his name does not appear in any land transactions that might imply such a large holding; his 1792 inventory also indicates that he held only an ordinary amount of land. FSA, no. 2834.

33. KM 60-11-20-1 François Cottin Sr. was schoolmaster of Kaskaskia. The son François served as bailiff and clerk for Labuxière in St. Louis and sometimes drafted documents as well.

34. See chapter 5 and Ekberg, *French Roots in the Illinois Country*, 75, 97 (see chap. 1, n. 76). The royal land edict of 1716 was the basis for agricultural land grants in the Fort de Chartres area throughout the colonial period. The number of lots granted depended on "differing requests by the grantees, family size, variation in the quality of the respective tracts of land, or different degrees of political influence." It is reasonable to assume that comparable replacement of land lost in the move across the river and encouragement to resettle on the west side of the river were in play.

35. *NR*, 125.

36. The 1752 census (HMLO, 426) of the village of Chartres, the home of many who would move to St. Louis, enumerated 862 horses, oxen, cattle, and pigs; St. Louis had a total of 488 in 1766.

37. These paragraphs are limited tallies for those listed as residents on the census and their spouses. Birth dates could not be found for all residents and spouses.

38. It is possible that Judge Lefebvre was in the age cohort with Rivière and St. Ange. Louis Chancellier, "garçon habitant," or bachelor resident (the son, therefore), is the recipient of a grant in the Livres Terriens on November 15, 1766.

39. Belting, *Kaskaskia under the French Regime*, 108, cites Cyprien Tanguay, ed., *Dictionnaire généalogique des familles Canadiennes depuis la fondation de la Colonie jusqu'à nos jours*, 7 vols. (Montreal: E. Senécal, 1871–90).

40. Belting, *Kaskaskia under the French Regime*, 60.

41. See chapter 7.

42. *NR*, 107.

43. For example, KM 59-12-15-2 and 59-12-17-1

44. They had a falling-out later and moved out. FSA, no. 2201.

45. FSA, no. 1538.

46. "Illinois, Diocese of Belleville, Catholic Parish Records, 1729–1956," images, Family Search (https://familysearch.org/pal:/MM9.3.1/TH-267-11765-123279-72?cc=1388122&wc=M99B-QMN:n2031332824), Randolph > Kaskaskia Island > Immaculate Conception > 1741–1834 Marriages > image 33 of 118; FSA, no. 2009.

47. Genealogical information on this family is largely from Anton Pregaldin's unpublished genealogy compilations. Mercantile Library, University of Missouri–St. Louis. The family used the *dit* name Desnoyers.

48. *Annals*, 427, lists François Bissonet as a farmer and Routier as a mason.

49. SLAR, Burial, July 16, 1794, gives his age at death as fifty-eight.

50. FSA, no. 2028.

51. See chapters 5 and 6 for Hubert's purchase of a town lot and building contract.

52. *VC*, 326–27, baptism of Noël Blotte, *VC*, 270, burial of François Blot.

53. FSA, no. 2042. The widow Charon is found nowhere in Billon or Houck. Her name on this census and that in the marriage contract are perhaps the only records of her in St. Louis. Patricia Cleary (*The World, The Flesh, and the Devil*, 154–55) relates

the story about a slander case involving the daughter, Thérèse "Caron," Madame Petit, in 1778.

54. See chapter 11 for Labuxière's eventual move back to the east side of the river.

55. SLAR, Baptism, May 7, 1767, states she was born May 6, 1766.

56. Pregaldin's compilations were most frequently consulted in these cases.

57. See chapter 1 for a discussion of his birth date. SLAR, Burial, December 27, 1774.

58. See chapter 8 for details on St. Ange's slaves.

59. FSA, no. 2841. Died April 3, 1767 FSA, no. 2297. See chapter 4.

60. His son was approximately twenty-three years old. He must have been enumerated elsewhere.

61. Marriage, June 30, 1757, "Illinois, Diocese of Belleville, Catholic Parish Records, 1729–1956," images, FamilySearch (https://familysearch.org/pal:/MM9.3.1/TH-267-11882-153267-31?cc=1388122&wc=M99B-QMV:n408136662), Randolph > Fort de Chartres > St. Anne (transferred to St. Joseph) > 1721–1840 Baptisms, Marriages, Deaths, First Communion, Confirmations > image 88 of 603. Burial record April 29, 1791, at about age sixty-four. "Illinois, Diocese of Belleville, Catholic Parish Records, 1729–1956," images, FamilySearch (https://familysearch.org/pal:/MM9.3.1/TH-266-11132-133558-56?cc=1388122&wc=M99B-Q7X:893567332), St. Clair > Cahokia > Holy Family > 1783–1819 Deaths (originals) > image 9 of 57.

62. Marriage record: see previous note. Birth year from McDermott, *Old Cahokia*, 131n102 (see chap. 11, n. 41). She was born in the Illinois Country. Noted as parents in SLAR, Baptism, May 3, 1768.

63. FSA, 2019. Labuxière was the *tuteur* of his sister-in-law until she married Antoine Sans Soucy in 1769.

64. *SRM*, 1:184, 1780 Militia Roster, Joseph "Labuciera" is twenty-four years old, born in Illinois. Indiana, Marriages, 1780–1992, index, *FamilySearch* (https://familysearch.org/pal:/MM9.1.1/XF3B-Z7C), Charles Joseph La Buxiere and Genevieve Godere, Feb 13, 1786; Antoine-Joseph Labuxière signed a 1780 document together with his father, who wrote the document. FSA, no. 1818.

65. Baptism, April 28, 1765. "Illinois, Diocese of Belleville, Catholic Parish Records, 1729–1956," images, FamilySearch (https://familysearch.org/pal:/MM9.3.1/TH-266-11825-78976-86?cc=1388122&wc=M99B-QMJ:687691126), Randolph > Kaskaskia Island > Immaculate Conception > 1759–1815 Baptisms, Marriages, Deaths, Other > image 33 of 244.

66. "Illinois, Diocese of Belleville, Catholic Parish Records, 1729–1956," images, Family Search (https://familysearch.org/pal:/MM9.3.1/TH-267-11882-153554-29?cc=1388122&wc=M99B-QMV:n408136662), Randolph > Fort de Chartres > St. Anne (transferred to St. Joseph) > 1721–1840 Baptisms, Marriages, Deaths, First Communion, Confirmations > image 123 of 603, burial of a young Indian slave boy belonging to Labuxière in 1761; ISC, he owned Louison, a twenty-four-year old Indian woman.

67. This is the only document in which this title appears. Foley and Rice, *First Chouteaus*, 211, birth and death dates (see chap. 3, n. 10).

68. It is not clear who these men were.

69. Earliest slaves of Laclède's are in SLAR, Baptism 1767, one-month-old Antoine and his parents, Indians. Two of the three here are possibly Antoine's unnamed parents.

70. *Archdiocese of New Orleans Sacramental Records*, vol. 1, *1718–1750* (New Orleans: Archdiocese of New Orleans, 1987), 31. SLAR Burial, August 15, 1814.

71. *Archdiocese of New Orleans Sacramental Records*, 1:52; Baptismal record for "René" Chouteau, September 7, 1749.

72. This category must exclude the militia; otherwise, Auguste would be enumerated here, too. Nevertheless, there is likely some duplication between the militia column and the older males.

73. *Archdiocese of New Orleans Sacramental Records*, 2:57, born October 10, 1758.

74. Ibid., 57, born October 6, 1760.

75. Foley and Rice, *First Chouteaus*, 211.

76. *Archdiocese of New Orleans Sacramental Records*, 2:57, born March 23, 1764.

77. SLAR, Baptism, October 20, 1767. Marie-Catherine was the mother of Louis in that record.

78. SLAR, Burial, October 4, 1776, thirty-six years. FSA, no. 2197 for birthplace.

79. ISC.

80. FSA, no. 2350. He died on the descent to New Orleans. He is not listed on the militia muster roll.

81. FSA, no. 2840.

82. SLAR, Burial, November 29, 1776. Marriage record "Illinois, Diocese of Belleville, Catholic Parish Records, 1729–1956," images, FamilySearch (https://familysearch.org/pal:/MM9.3.1/TH-267-11882-156130-83?cc=1388122&wc=M65M-L2Q:13745501,14104601,14104602,14104603), Randolph > Fort de Chartres > St. Anne (transferred to St. Joseph) > 1721–1840 Baptisms, Marriages, Deaths, First Communion, Confirmations > image 110 of 603, native of Bordeaux.

83. FSA, no. 1410. Marriage record, July 18, 1763, gives her birthplace (see note 82).

84. FSA, no. 1783. Guardianship names them as sisters.

85. *Annals*, 390. She was brought to St. Louis as an infant. St. Louis 1787 Census, age twenty-three.

86. FSA, no. 1410. This 1778 partition document names slaves, but it is a little removed from 1766.

87. FSA, no. 2014. SLAR, Marriage, April 23, 1775, (second) marriage names her birthplace.

88. FSA, no. 2014.

89. AGI, 187A. St. Louis 1787 Census (living in Florissant), age sixty-four. SLAR, Burial, 21 September 1792, origin is Canada. "Illinois, Diocese of Belleville, Catholic Parish Records, 1729–1956," images, FamilySearch (https://familysearch.org/pal:/MM9.3.1/TH-267-11882-154486-36?cc=1388122&wc=M99B-QMV:n408136662), Randolph > Fort de Chartres > St. Anne (transferred to St. Joseph) > 1721–1840 Baptisms, Marriages, Deaths, First Communion, Confirmations > image 27 of 603, gives his origin as the parish of "Varenne" Canada. 1780 Militia Roster, age fifty. FSA, no. 1425, age in 1790 was seventy-eight.

90. KM 59-12-15-2 identifies them as brothers and partners. *DGFQ*, 713, birthplace was Cap St. Michel, Canada, in 1724. St. Louis 1787 Census, living in Florissant in the household of his brother, age sixty-three.

91. "Illinois, Diocese of Belleville, Catholic Parish Records, 1729–1956," images, Family Search (https://familysearch.org/pal:/MM9.3.1/TH-267-11882-154486-36?cc=1388122&wc=M99B-QMV:n408136662), Randolph > Fort de Chartres > St. Anne (transferred to St. Joseph) > 1721–1840 Baptisms, Marriages, Deaths, First Communion, Confirmations > image 27 of 603, marriage September 6, 1745. Jean-Baptiste Martigny and Marie Hebert were named in many transactions together (for example, FSA, no. 1424), but had

no children that survived past infancy. Baptisms of twin daughters at Fort de Chartres on May 17, 1746; one died the next day. "Illinois, Diocese of Belleville, Catholic Parish Records, 1729–1956," images, FamilySearch (https://familysearch.org/pal:/MM9.3.1/TH-267-11882-152159-32?cc=1388122&wc=M99B-QMV:n408136662), Randolph > Fort de Chartres > St. Anne (transferred to St. Joseph) > 1721–1840 Baptisms, Marriages, Deaths, First Communion, Confirmations > image 36 of 603. SLAR, Burial, February 25, 1802, seventy years. FSA, no. 2011, marriage contract of Thérèse Hébert, names Jean-Baptiste Martigny as the bride's brother-in-law.

92. ISC (below, appendix B) gives their ages as thirty-five and six.

93. Name appears sometimes as Bissette. Only the surname was on the census; Guillaume was more prominent than Charles. Birthplace, *Annals*, 439; SLAR, Burial, June 6, 1772.

94. Named as his brother in Guillaume Bizet's will and inventory FSA, no. 54. SLAR, Burial, May 26, 1780, "massacré(s) par les sauvages." This is the famous battle of 1780.

95. SLAR, Baptism, October 20, 1767 (Courtette). Bizet's 1772 Inventory and Sale, FSA, Box 32, lists fifteen slaves, nine of whom were old enough to have been present in 1766.

96. KM 24-1-24-1, marriage at age fifteen to Mathurin Chaput in 1724; KM 28-11-27, marriage to Ignace Hébert, November 27, 1728. SLAR, Burial, November 29, 1784; FSA, no. 2011, names Danis as the widow of Ignace Hébert, deceased officer of the militia.

97. FSA no. 2036, dated 1774, says he is twenty-four years old, born Fort de Chartres.

98. François and Auguste are on the 1766 Militia Muster Roll. François was killed in the battle of 1780. *Annals*, 431. *SRM*, 1:188, 1780 Militia Roster lists "Agustin Hever" as forty-four years old, born in Illinois, a hunter. St. Louis 1787 Census, "Agustin Ever," forty-eight years old. Pregaldin: Auguste interred in Florissant, May 1801, age fifty-nine. Auguste Hébert was a witness at Joseph's marriage in 1761, "Illinois, Diocese of Belleville, Catholic Parish Records, 1729–1956," images, FamilySearch (https://familysearch.org/pal:/MM9.3.1/TH-267-11882-154210-74?cc=1388122&wc=M65M-L2Q:13745501,14104601,14104602,14104603), Randolph > Fort de Chartres > St. Anne (transferred to St. Joseph) > 1721–1840 Baptisms, Marriages, Deaths, First Communion, Confirmations > image 100 of 603. Both Billon and Houck have information that conflicts with source documents concerning this family.

99. Ibid., marriage of Joseph Hébert, son of Hélène Dany and "Joseph" Hébert, February 2, 1761. SLAR, Baptism, May 7, 1767, a daughter of Joseph Hébert and Agnès Michel is baptized, with godparents François and Therese Hébert, "all of this parish." Joseph is not on the 1766 Militia Muster Roll. St. Louis 1787 Census, gives Joseph "Hever"'s age as forty-one. SLAR, Burial, January 28, 1801, Joseph Hébert, sixty years, son of Ignace Hébert and Hélène Danis. SLAR, Burial of Agnès Michel, seventy years, wife of Joseph, trader, March 23, 1814.

100. FSA, no. 2011, marriage contract, February 28, 1767, gives her age as approximately twenty-one. SLAR, Burial, February 2, 1772.

101. SLAR, Baptism, May 3, 1768 for Joseph, son of Janette négresse à Madame Veuve Hébert.

102. *VC*, 311–12. Godmother to a child of married slaves of widow Dodier in 1765. Madeleine was over fifty in 1784. FSA, no. 2389.

103. FSA, no. 2389, twenty years old in 1785.

104. Birth year and birthplace from Pregaldin. FSA, no. 1398. SLAR, Burial, February 10, 1783.

105. "Illinois, Diocese of Belleville, Catholic Parish Records, 1729–1956," images, Family Search (https://familysearch.org/pal:/MM9.3.1/TH-267-11882-156142-25?cc=1388122&wc=M99B-QMV:n408136662), Randolph > Fort de Chartres > St. Anne (transferred to St. Joseph) > 1721–1840 Baptisms, Marriages, Deaths, First Communion, Confirmations > image 87 of 603. Marie-Jeanne Dodier was godmother to Marie-Jeanne Dodier, daughter of Gabriel Jr. and Marie-Marguerite Bequette. Jeanne is named in FSA, no. 1398, the 1763 inventory of Gabriel Sr.'s estate, no age given. SLAR, Burial, October 9, 1775, Janette Dodier.

106. Élisabeth married Alexis Cotté FSA, no. 2015 in 1768, at about age fifteen. SLAR, Marriage, June 13, 1791, states that Élisabeth was born at Fort de Chartres. St. Louis 1787 Census, Isabel Cotte, forty-six?

107. SLAR, Burial, 1782. Her age at burial is illegible. FSA, no. 2032, Married Simon Coussot ca 1773. Original document missing.

108. FSA, no. 1398. Catteau is not mentioned again after the 1763 inventory. FSA, no. 2393.

109. No burial record located. *VC*, 704–5, he was in the village of Chartres in 1760.

110. SLAR, Baptism, May 9, 1766 of their daughter Marie (Louise).

111. SLAR, Marriage November 8, 1780 to Charles Tayon.

112. SLAR, Baptism, (undated first entry) 1766. St. Louis 1787 Census, Louise, twenty-three.

113. "Illinois, Diocese of Belleville, Catholic Parish Records, 1729–1956," images, Family Search (https://familysearch.org/pal:/MM9.3.1/TH-267-11882-155419-55?cc=1388122&wc=M99B-QMV:n408136662), Randolph > Fort de Chartres > St. Anne (transferred to St. Joseph) > 1721–1840 Baptisms, Marriages, Deaths, First Communion, Confirmations > image 93 of 603, marriage February 5, 1759 gives birthplace as Chateauguay Canada. *SRM*, 1:188, 1780 Militia Roster, age fifty, born Canada, habitant. SLAR, Burial, November 6, 1787. St. Louis 1787 Census, age fifty-seven.

114. SLAR, Baptism, May 9, 1766, daughter Véronique. "Illinois, Diocese of Belleville, Catholic Parish Records, 1729–1956," images, FamilySearch (https://familysearch.org/pal:/MM9.3.1/TH-267-11882-155419-55?cc=1388122&wc=M99B-QMV:n408136662), Randolph > Fort de Chartres > St. Anne (transferred to St. Joseph) > 1721–1840 Baptisms, Marriages, Deaths, First Communion, Confirmations > image 93 of 603, married February 5, 1759. She was the daughter of Louis Marcheteau and Françoise Le Duc. SLAR, Burial, January 3, 1773, Véronique Marcheteau.

115. St. Louis 1787 Census, age twenty-eight. *Annals*, 418–19, has Louis born 1762.

116. *Annals*, 418–19, has Laurent, born 1764, and Claude, born 1766 (the baptismal register has a torn entry for a "Claude" on June 20, 1767), SLAR, Burial, an unnamed seventeen-year-old son of Louis Ride was interred February 28, 1786, and a second unnamed son on January 25, 1793 or 1794. *SRM*, 1:188. There is a Lorenzo Ride on the 1780 Militia Roster, age twenty-four, born in Illinois, a rower. This would make the birth year 1756, three years before their marriage (not likely). St. Louis 1787 Census, has Lorenzo age twenty-five, more likely. (And "Claudio" age twenty.)

117. SLAR, Baptism, May 9, 1766. Billon did not list her in the family sketch in *Annals*, 418–19. Meurin noted the godfather was judged (by Meurin) not to be "capable" and perhaps this was a reference to her brother Louis, whom Billon remarked was deaf and dumb.

118. Pregaldin for birth year. SLAR, Burial, May 26, 1780, "massacré(s) par les sauvages." This was the famous battle of 1780.

119. Pregaldin for birth place, Michilimackinac. SLAR, Baptism, October 20, 1767, for Amable Jr. She was interviewed (as Mrs. Lecompt "said to have been the first

woman that came to St. Louis") by Wilson Primm in the 1830s, McDermott, *Early Histories*, 110–11 (see chap. 3, n. 40). SLAR, Burial, October 31, 1832, Marguerite Lecomte, age eighty-eight.

120. St. Louis 1787 Census, Amable Guion, twenty-four. SLAR, Burial, September 19,1813, age fifty. FSA, no. 2073 says he was born at Holy Family parish (Cahokia). 1780 Militia Roster, age sixteen, born in Illinois, a rower. *SRM* 1:188.

121. *Annals*, 430, gave a death date of Oct 21, 1797, age seventy-four, in St. Louis, but there is no burial record for this date for him in St. Louis in the Old Cathedral Register. St. Louis 1787 Census, "errero" forty-nine. This would make his birth year 1739 rather than 1725. *VC*, 9, son of Jean-Baptiste Becquet and Catherine Baron, named Jean-Baptiste, birth year missing, but assumed to be 1725.

122. Pierre Becquet is on the list of volontaires. He appears with the Becquet household on the 1787 census age forty-six. A Pierre "Bekiot" identified by Brown & Dean as *Becquet*, was a witness to a marriage in 1765. *VC*, 264–65.

123. FSA, no. 1398. *Annals*, 430, her age was forty-one at death. SLAR, Burial, April 19, 1785, says only "Mde Bequet," interpreted to be Marie-Françoise Dodier.

124. FSA, no. 2064. *SRM*, 1:188, 1780 Militia Roster, age twenty-two, born in Illinois, rower. St. Louis 1787 Census, age thirty.

125. FSA, no. 2048 She married in 1779 at twenty.

126. SLAR, Marriage, to Joseph Hortiz February 1, 1780.

127. FSA no. 1398.

128. Death information from Pregaldin.

129. Marked "absent" in the habitants section of the 1766 Militia Muster Roll. He does not otherwise appear in records.

130. SLAR, Baptism, Henry-François, their son, May 7, 1767. In 1757 they were married and living in Ste. Genevieve KM 57-11-25-1. *Annals*, 425, married in Mobile, 1755; she died by 1793.

131. *Annals*, 424–25, born Fort de Chartres 1760; married 1784 Marie Louise Cotté. FSA, no. 2116 Second marriage of Julien Roy, to Renée Guilgaut, widow of Alexis Marié, 1797. Both of Julien Roy's parents were dead by then.

132. SLAR, Marriage to Suzanne Dodier, July 3, 1779. Labuxière is his "cousin germain," first cousin, by marriage to Catherine Vifvarenne. St. Louis 1787 Census, Carlos Roy thirty-one and his wife, Susana, twenty-seven. *SRM*, 1:187, 1780 Militia Roster lists 1st Corporal Carlos Roy, age twenty-six, born in Illinois, habitant.

133. FSA, no. 2036 married François Hébert in February 1774. She was fifteen years old. Both parents were absent from the marriage contract ceremony.

134. His wife's burial in 1798, SLAR, refers to her as a widow.

135. SLAR, Baptism, May 3, 1768 both are mentioned in baptism of son Louis. SLAR Burial, May 28, 1798, Agnès Pichart Veuve Denoyers, fifty years old.

136. FSA, no. 2028, gives his birthplace and age, thirty-one in 1772; his wife was seventeen. St. Louis 1787 Census, he was fifty-one, his wife Susana thirty-two, with five children, the oldest twelve. SLAR, Burial, July 16, 1794, fifty-eight years.

137. FSA, no. 2499.

138. SLAR, Burial, February 24, 1792 Jacques "Noser . . . 50 and some years." *SRM*, 1:186, 1780 Militia Roster, "Jacobo Labe" is listed as a corporal, age forty, born in Illinois. St. Louis 1787 Census, Santiago Labe, thirty-nine, and Teresa, his wife, twenty-four.

139. No record has been found for him other than the militia muster roll.

140. This is either a transcription mistake or refers to another woman and child in the household. The only marriage record located for Noisé is from 1781, FSA, no. 2058, when he married Teresa Beaugenou, the widow of Hyacinth "Do" (D'Eau).

304   *Notes to Appendix A*

141. "Illinois, Diocese of Belleville, Catholic Parish Records, 1729–1956," images, Family Search (https://familysearch.org/pal:/MM9.3.1/TH-267-11882-152298-54?cc=1388122&wc=M65M-L2Q:13745501,14104601,14104602,14104603), Randolph > Fort de Chartres > St. Anne (transferred to St. Joseph) > 1721–1840 Baptisms, Marriages, Deaths, First Communion, Confirmations > image 102 of 603. His birthplace is given as Montréal in the 1761 marriage record of his daughter Elizabeth.

142. Pierre "Marchetaud" is marked "absent" in the habitants section of the 1766 Militia Muster Roll.

143. Joseph Marcheteau *dit* Desnoyers, see FSA, no. 1394, Donation to François Bissonet and his wife (Marcheteau's daughter), 1769.

144. Françoise Le Duc died sometime before the marriage of Elizabeth in 1764. Marriage record, "Illinois, Diocese of Belleville, Catholic Parish Records, 1729–1956," images, Family Search (https://familysearch.org/pal:/MM9.3.1/TH-267-11882-154988-23?cc=1388122&wc=M65M-L2Q:13745501,14104601,14104602,14104603), Randolph > Fort de Chartres > St. Anne (transferred to St. Joseph) > 1721–1840 Baptisms, Marriages, Deaths, First Communion, Confirmations > image 112 of 603.

145. FSA, no. 2008 Marriage contract. FSA, no. 2030 Marriage contract of Louis Marchetaud *dit* Desnoyers, a witness is "Louis Marchetaud *dit* Kiery son fils." *SRM*, 1:188, 1780 Militia Roster lists "Guiery Denoye," age forty-six, born in Canada, habitant. *Annals*, 417, Bazile Desnoyers was listed as Louis's son, but he is not included in a 1772 inventory FSA, no. 2313 as an heir of Françoise le Duc, Louis Sr.'s deceased wife.

146. These are unknown.

147. See marriage contract below. *VC*, 326–27, baptism of Noel Blot *dit* Charon in St. Philippe, December 25, 1762, son of François Blotte and Marie Françoise Pinot. A Noël Charon is mentioned as a hunter in Truteau's Journal of 1794 in Nasatir, *Before Lewis and Clark*, 280 (see chap. 8, n. 4).

148. FSA, no. 2042 Marriage Contract 1776. Her mother is Francesca Pineau, her father Francisco Charron. Thérèse was eighteen. SLAR, Burial, possibly February 2, 1785, "femme de petit," thirty years.

149. *SRM*, 1:188, 1780 Militia Roster, age forty-eight, born in Illinois, habitant. Billon, *Annals*, 429, has birth year 1740.

150. SLAR, Baptism, October 20, 1767 baptism of their son Gabriel, godparents are Louis Dodier (on *volontaire* list of 1766 militia muster roll) and Elizabeth Dodier. Also *VC*, 262–63: Marriage August 6, 1764. SLAR, burial 1813, age eighty-five. Birth information from Pregaldin.

151. No records for a son at this time. Gabriel was born August 10, baptized October 20, 1767. SLAR.

152. FSA, no. 2046 Suzanne, sixteen years old in 1779, married Charles Le Roy. Her parents married in 1764.

153. "Illinois, Diocese of Belleville, Catholic Parish Records, 1729–1956," images, Family Search (https://familysearch.org/pal:/MM9.3.1/TH-267-11882-156142-25?cc=1388122&wc=M99B-QMV:n408136662), Randolph > Fort de Chartres > St. Anne (transferred to St. Joseph) > 1721–1840 Baptisms, Marriages, Deaths, First Communion, Confirmations > image 87 of 603, baptism August 4, 1765.

154. FSA, no. 1398. Indian slave, eighteen years old in 1763 given to Gabriel Jr. in the partition of his father's estate.

155. Burial, Prairie du Rocher September 20, 1766. Register (Transcription), MHM. There is a notation that the year should be 1767, but that would mean that his wife remarried while he was still alive. He is not on the militia muster roll. Birth year from Pregaldin.

156. FSA, no. 2008. She is La Giroflée's widow.

157. ISC, Véronique Panissé owned a métis Indian slave named Joseph, thirteen years old, in 1770.

158. SLAR, Burial, November 23, 1773 for *Jean* Vaudris. Birth year from Pregaldin.

159. *VC*, 319, the baptism of an Indian, names Du Pré as Vaudry's wife, February 5, 1762. Birthplace, Montréal, and year from Pregaldin.

160. SLAR, Burial, November 13, 1773. FSA, no. 2326 inventory of the estate as his widow prepares to remarry, June 1774.

161. SLAR, Marriage, April 27, 1779 Ignace La Roche, son of Joseph and Marie La Pointe married Marie Becquet daughter of Jean-Baptiste Becquet and Marie Dodier.

162. A Joseph "Laroche" was granted a trading license for the Oto tribe in 1777, *SRM,* 2:139.

163. "Illinois, Diocese of Belleville, Catholic Parish Records, 1729–1956," images, Family Search (https://familysearch.org/pal:/MM9.3.1/TH-267-11882-155419-55?cc=1388122&wc =M99B-QMV:n408136662), Randolph > Fort de Chartres > St. Anne (transferred to St. Joseph) > 1721–1840 Baptisms, Marriages, Deaths, First Communion, Confirmations > image 93 of 603, marriage February 12, 1757, of Louis Briard (*dit* La Roche) of St. Philippe and Marie-Anne Jerome daughter of Jerome Roussilliet deceased, of St. Philippe. Vaudry is stepfather. St. Louis 1787 Census, Maria Larroche was fifty-eight.

164. Born November 8, 1763, baptized Ste. Genevieve May 14, 1764, SLAR, Ste. Genevieve Baptism Register.

165. FSA, no. 2038 Maria Anna, daughter of Louis La Roche and Marianne married Louis Dubreuil (the habitant) June 28, 1776. SLAR, St. Ferdinand Burial Register February 6, 1838, age eighty.

166. SLAR, Burial, May 17, 1771, fifty-five years.

167. They had a grown son, Charles, but there is only one Charles Parant on the 1766 Militia Muster Roll.

168. SLAR, Burial, April 20 1780, fifty-five years. Pregaldin, marriage contract Kaskaskia June 18, 1747.

169. FSA, no. 2007. Marie-Anne Henrion's birth year from Pregaldin. FSA no. 45 indicates she had died by September 25, 1769, when guardians for the minor children were appointed.

170. FSA, no. 1842. Charles Henrion is the uncle of Nicolas Beaugenou, 1786. SLAR, Burial September 1783, sixty years, Charlot Genrion. This is one of many versions of this family name.

171. Billon's Memobook, Billon Collection, MHMA, 194, died by 1768. There is another brother François, who is not on the census or militia muster roll, perhaps the older male. FSA, no. 2214 names François as the uncle of Nicolas Beaugenou.

172. Both Nicolas Jr. and Charles are named as heirs to Nicolas Beaugenou Sr. in 1799. FSA, no. 123; "Illinois, Diocese of Belleville, Catholic Parish Records, 1729–1956," images, FamilySearch (https://familysearch.org/pal:/MM9.3.1/TH-267-11882-155527 -48?cc=1388122&wc=M99B-QMV:n408136662), Randolph > Fort de Chartres > St. Anne (transferred to St. Joseph) > 1721–1840 Baptisms, Marriages, Deaths, First Communion, Confirmations > image 57 of 603, baptism April or May 1748, born 1747. *SRM,* 1:187, 1780 Militia Roster lists Nicolas as thirty-eight years old, born in Illinois, habitant. St. Louis 1787 Census, Nicolas Beaugenou, age thirty-nine.

173. Married at twenty, FSA, no. 2026 to Jacques Lasablonière in 1771. Baptism of daughter Angélique, "Illinois, Diocese of Belleville, Catholic Parish Records, 1729–1956," images, FamilySearch (https://familysearch.org/pal:/MM9.3.1/TH-267-11882-155522-27 ?cc=1388122&wc=M99B-QMV:n408136662), Randolph > Fort de Chartres > St. Anne

(transferred to St. Joseph) > 1721–1840 Baptisms, Marriages, Deaths, First Communion, Confirmations > image 177 of 603, burial in Prairie du Rocher in 1788, age thirty-five, just one month after the birth of her daughter Angélique. "Illinois, Diocese of Belleville, Catholic Parish Records, 1729–1956," images, FamilySearch (https://familysearch.org/pal:/MM9.3.1/TH-267-11882-154271-39?cc=1388122&wc=M99B-QMV:n408136662), Randolph > Fort de Chartres > St. Anne (transferred to St. Joseph) > 1721–1840 Baptisms, Marriages, Deaths, First Communion, Confirmations > image 271 of 603.

174. "Illinois, Diocese of Belleville, Catholic Parish Records, 1729–1956," images, Family Search (https://familysearch.org/pal:/MM9.3.1/TH-266-12115-120701-13?cc=1388122&wc=M659-72S:13745701,14604701,14604702,14692201 : St. Clair > Cahokia > Holy Family > 1819–1838 Deaths > image 11 of 53, "vieux garçon créol" age ca. sixty. September 20, 1821.

175. Married Alexis Loise, their daughter Victoire baptized in 1774. SLAR, Baptism.

176. SLAR, Marriage, September 3, 1776, to Joseph Hugé.

177. SLAR, Marriage, married first Joachim D'eau April 8, 1777, then Jacques Noisé FSA, no. 2058. Interred February 9, 1840, age one hundred, "Illinois, Diocese of Belleville, Catholic Parish Records, 1729–1956," images, FamilySearch (https://familysearch.org/pal:/MM9.3.1/TH-266-11779-36855-7?cc=1388122&wc=M99B-Q7T:n737385829), St. Clair > Cahokia > Holy Family > 1838–1850 Deaths > image 9 of 74. Burial record states she was born at Fort de Chartres.

178. The métis daughter of Nicolas Henrion was three years old. She may be the fourth "daughter" here. Billon Memobook, Billon Collection, MHMA, 196. See chapter 8.

179. Possibly "Vieux Henrion" SLAR, Burial, February 8, 1789.

180. SLAR, Burial, 11 November 1784, age 70. Marriage record gives birthplace as parish of St-Paul, Paris, France. "Illinois, Diocese of Belleville, Catholic Parish Records, 1729–1956," images, FamilySearch (https://familysearch.org/pal:/MM9.3.1/TH-267-11765-123877-24?cc=1388122&wc=M99B-QMN:n2031332824), Randolph > Kaskaskia Island > Immaculate Conception > 1741–1834 Marriages > image 15 of 118, marriage 22 September 1749.

181. See Chapter 8 for Jacques Quebedeau's métis child with an Indian slave of Chemin's. FSA, no. 2832.

182. Baptism of Charles, February 3, 1751, Fort de Chartres, "Illinois, Diocese of Belleville, Catholic Parish Records, 1729–1956," images, FamilySearch (https://familysearch.org/pal:/MM9.3.1/TH-267-11882-152298-54?cc=1388122&wc=M65M-L2Q:13745501,14104601,14104602,14104603), Randolph > Fort de Chartres > St. Anne (transferred to St. Joseph) > 1721–1840 Baptisms, Marriages, Deaths, First Communion, Confirmations > image 102 of 603.

183. "Illinois, Diocese of Belleville, Catholic Parish Records, 1729–1956," images, Family Search (https://familysearch.org/pal:/MM9.3.1/TH-267-11765-123877-24?cc=1388122&wc=M99B-QMN:n2031332824), Randolph > Kaskaskia Island > Immaculate Conception > 1741–1834 Marriages > image 15 of 118. SLAR, Baptism, June 30, 1770 (godparents). SLAR, Burial, August 7, 1783, "Madame Duchemin."

184. Their daughter Thérèse was already married to Pierre Montardy, active member of the military and not on the census. "Illinois, Diocese of Belleville, Catholic Parish Records, 1729–1956," images, FamilySearch (https://familysearch.org/pal:/MM9.3.1/TH-267-11882-152464-26?cc=1388122&wc=M99B-QMV:n408136662), Randolph > Fort de Chartres > St. Anne (transferred to St. Joseph) > 1721–1840 Baptisms, Marriages, Deaths, First Communion, Confirmations > image 84 of 603, baptism of Thérèse February 15, 1753. "Illinois, Diocese of Belleville, Catholic Parish Records, 1729–1956," images, Family

Search (https://familysearch.org/pal:/MM9.3.1/TH-267-11882-151767-50?cc=1388122&wc =M99B-QMV:n408136662), Randolph > Fort de Chartres > St. Anne (transferred to St. Joseph) > 1721–1840 Baptisms, Marriages, Deaths, First Communion, Confirmations > image 114 of 603, marriage to Pierre Montardy July 9, 1765. Charles is identified as her brother at the marriage.

185. She was the three-year-old child of Jacques Quevedot in 1767. FSA, no. 2832. See Chapter 8. SLAR, Marriage, Marianne Quevedot, daughter of Jacques Quevedot married Joseph Vaillancourt, May 16, 1783.

186. Pregaldin, birthplace and year of baptism. FSA, no. 2008, identified as uncle of Louis (Kiery) Marcheteau in marriage contract of Kiery and Véronique Panissé.

187. FSA, no. 2017 Marriage Contract of Jean-Baptiste Durand and Marie-Josèphe Marcheteau, daughter of François Marcheteau and the deceased Marie-Josèphe "Denoyelle," 1768.

188. Pregaldin, born December 31, 1750, baptized Detroit January 1, 1751. FSA, no. 2017 marriage contract of daughter Marie-Josèphe Marcheteau, 1768.

189. Pregaldin, baptized Detroit December 21, 1753. Died by 1795, married St. Louis, November 23, 1779, Charlotte-Ursule Cardinal. *SRM*, 1:185, 1780 Militia Roster, Joseph Marcheteau age twenty-five, a carpenter born in Illinois.

190. Pregaldin, born and baptized Detroit September 1757; Marriage contract Cahokia August 29, 1773, with Joseph Poirier *dit* Desloge.

191. SLAR, Marriage, June 9, 1782, to Pierre Papin.

192. He predeceased his wife, see below. FSA no. 2007, born La Prairie, Canada.

193. "Illinois, Diocese of Belleville, Catholic Parish Records, 1729–1956," images, Family Search (https://familysearch.org/pal:/MM9.3.1/TH-267-11882-150882-52?cc=1388122&wc =M99B-QMV:n408136662), Randolph > Fort de Chartres > St. Anne (transferred to St. Joseph) > 1721–1840 Baptisms, Marriages, Deaths, First Communion, Confirmations > image 66 of 603, baptism January 4, 1750. FSA, no. 2007. SLAR, Burial, July 8, 1799, the widow of Toussaint Hunaud.

194. Birthplace, "Illinois, Diocese of Belleville, Catholic Parish Records, 1729–1956," images, FamilySearch (https://familysearch.org/pal:/MM9.3.1/TH-267-11608-61313-16?cc =1388122&wc=M99B-Q78:1059079494), St. Clair > Cahokia > Holy Family > 1740–1839 Index Marriages > image 26 of 96. The first of his widow's wills was dated 21 July 1778, FSA, no. 2606. He was named as the uncle of Marie-Josèphe Taillon in FSA, no. 2009.

195. SLAR, Burial, December 24, 1789 (born in Canada), sixty-seven years.

196. See *volontaire* section of Militia Muster Roll.

197. FSA, no. 241 uses both names Langlois and LaCroix. SLAR, Burial, March 20, 1779, Madame Rondeau, sixty-seven years. Marriage Cahokia March 1, 1756, "Illinois, Diocese of Belleville, Catholic Parish Records, 1729–1956," images, FamilySearch (https://familysearch.org/pal:/MM9.3.1/TH-267-11608-61313-16?cc=1388122 &wc=M99B-Q78:1059079494), St. Clair > Cahokia > Holy Family > 1740–1839 Index Marriages > image 26 of 96.

198. Marie-Josèphe/Josephte appeared in the baptismal register and the 1770 Indian slave census. Marie-Josèphe was transferred by the widow Lacroix's 1778 will to Louis Robert. FSA, no. 241.

199. He signed his own name with this spelling. He was a sergeant in the marines when he married in 1756. SLAR, Burial, April 30, 1783.

200. SLAR Baptism, February 14, 1779, godfather. Pourée is not on the militia roster, which is to be expected for active troops, but why he was on the census is unclear.

308   *Notes to Appendix A*

201. SLAR, Baptism, June 27, 1770, godmother. "Illinois, Diocese of Belleville, Catholic Parish Records, 1729–1956," images, FamilySearch (https://familysearch.org/pal:/MM9.3.1/TH-267-11765-123619-72?cc=1388122&wc=M99B-QMN:n2031332824), Randolph > Kaskaskia Island > Immaculate Conception > 1741–1834 Marriages > image 23 of 118, marriage January 10, 1756. SLAR, Burial, May 2, 1785.

202. SLAR, Baptism, May 3, 1768, her child was baptized.

203. Eloy (Sr. or Jr.?) requested a lot grant from Commandant Neyon de Villiers in 1762 KM 62-4-29-1. *VC*, 753–54, April 2, 1762, he is twenty-four and a half, the brother of Marie-Barbe, wife of Antoine Rivière.

204. See chapter 9. SLAR, Burial, November 6, 1775.

205. Hervieux had an illegitimate daughter with Agnès Hulin. FSA, no. 2021.

206. SLAR, Baptism, May 11, 1771, Victor, a black slave of Hervieux was baptized.

207. Because there are no children mentioned, this must be Chancellier Jr. The father's death date is not known. Billon gives the father Chancellier's death year "by 1770," but Billon used documents like inventories and marriage contracts that confirm only the fact that someone had died, not the date of death. Marriage contract FSA, no. 2066. SLAR, Burial, April 9, 1785. Pregaldin for birth year.

208. KM 65-7-27-1 gives a François Cotin and Co.; the father, a schoolmaster is in KM 60-11-20-1. The census entry above may be either the father or the son, but there was no further record of the father in St. Louis. SLAR, Burial, April 5, 1810. François Cottin, (Canadian), sixty years.

209. *Annals*, 419, born Canada. SLAR, St. Ferdinand Burial Register, August 17, 1816, age 110. He may have been too old for the militia in 1766.

210. SLAR, Burial, March 8, 1823, age ca. seventy-eight. *SRM*, 1:188, 1780 Militia Roster listed him as fifty and born in Illinois, habitant. St. Louis 1787 Census, Antonio Bacane, fifty-eight (?).

211. "Illinois, Diocese of Belleville, Catholic Parish Records, 1729–1956," images, Family Search (https://familysearch.org/pal:/MM9.3.1/TH-267-11882-154431-29?cc=1388122&wc=M99B-QMV:n408136662), Randolph > Fort de Chartres > St. Anne (transferred to St. Joseph) > 1721–1840 Baptisms, Marriages, Deaths, First Communion, Confirmations > image 82 of 603, marriage January 15, 1753. SLAR, Baptism for Julie Rivière, February 11, 1778, named them as parents. SLAR, Burial, June 7, 1786, age sixty. She nevertheless appeared on the 1787 census as fifty-three years old.

212. Pregaldin, married February 13, 1786, Marguerite Vial at thirty-four. *SRM*, 1:188, 1780 Militia Roster listed him as twenty-six, born in Illinois, a rower.

213. If Billon, *Annals*, 419, is correct and he was born in 1757, he would be in this age category.

214. St. Louis 1787 Census, Joseph Riviere age twenty-one, and a Joseph Bacane age twenty-eight. Billon listed a son Joseph with no birth or death date.

215. "Illinois, Diocese of Belleville, Catholic Parish Records, 1729–1956," images, Family Search(https://familysearch.org/pal:/MM9.3.1/TH-267-11882-151923-24?cc=1388122&wc=M65M-L2Q:13745501,14104601,14104602,14104603), Randolph > Fort de Chartres > St. Anne (transferred to St. Joseph) > 1721–1840 Baptisms, Marriages, Deaths, First Communion, Confirmations > image 205 of 603. Marriage November 18, 1775, to François Maréchal. She was sixteen. The record states they were of the "paroisse de St. Louis."

216. SLAR, Burial, May 8, 1830, age seventy, Marie Riviere Henau (married to Louis Hunaud, son of Toussaint Hunaud and Marie-Josèphe Beaugenou).

217. The census said "el nombrado Taillon." St. Louis 1787 Census, age seventy. SLAR Burial, December 3, 1807. *Annals*, 414, he was born in Canada.

218. FSA, no. 2009 Marriage contract, Roger Jacques Taillon was the uncle of Marie-Josèphe.

219. FSA, no. 2009 named them as parents. St. Louis 1787 Census, age fifty-six SLAR, Burial, June 25, 1799, age sixty-nine. The 1787 census listed two sons, Juan, eighteen, and Francisco, sixteen.

220. *Annals*, 414–15, married Jacques Chauvin at Ft de Chartres (no b or d date) SLAR, Baptism, she was the godmother of St. Ange's (slave's) daughter Constance baptized May 7, 1767.

221. SLAR, Marriage, November 8, 1780, married Cécile Deschamps. SLAR, Baptism, June 25, 1770, godfather to Charles, a slave of Laclède.

222. FSA, no. 2055 Marriage contract Joseph Tayon and Marie Berger May 1, 1781. *SRM*, 1:186, 1780 Militia Roster Joseph Tayon, age twenty-eight, born in Illinois, a farm laborer.

223. SLAR, Marriage, baptized at Fort de Chartres, married August 5, 1777. SLAR Baptism, July 3, 1770, godmother of a Pawnee Indian (slave) girl.

224. "Illinois, Diocese of Belleville, Catholic Parish Records, 1729–1956," images, Family Search (https://familysearch.org/pal:/MM9.3.1/TH-267-11882-152464-26?cc=1388122&wc =M99B-QMV:n408136662), Randolph > Fort de Chartres > St. Anne (transferred to St. Joseph) > 1721–1840 Baptisms, Marriages, Deaths, First Communion, Confirmations > image 84 of 603, baptism January 26, 1753. SLAR, Baptism, July 3, 1770, she was the godmother.

225. ISC, SLAR, Burial, 1801. The designation of Peoria in her burial record likely indicates that she was taken slave by the Peoria tribe. A member of the Peoria tribe would not have been held as a slave in neighboring St. Louis.

226. ISC; Lucas Collection, 1806, MHMA.

227. SLAR, Baptism 1770, Lucas Collection, 1806, MHMA. KM 57-3-14-1 an unnamed black male slave was bequeathed by Father Gagnon to Joseph Taillon, his godson.

228. SLAR, Burial, January 10, 1797, sixty years. Born Fontenay en Brie, France, *VC*, 244–46, marriage record February 9, 1762. St. Louis 1787 Census, age forty-nine, Renée Guilgaut (Renata) thirty-nine, their son Alexis twenty-three.

229. KM 62-3-22-1 Registration of their marriage contract. *VC*, 244–46, marriage February 9, 1762. St. Louis 1787 Census, she was thirty-nine. FSA, no. 2116 She remarried in 1797, identified as his widow, to Julien Roy, of age, son of Julien Roy and Marie-Barbe Saucier.

230. FSA, no. 2075 Marriage contract, 1784. St. Louis 1787 Census, age twenty-three.

231. FSA, no. 2834.

232. SLAR, Burial, June 28, 1784 gives her name as Marianne Berri; Baptism Register May 7, 1767, says "Charbonet"; SLAR, Baptism, June 25, 1770, says "Le Male."

233. Baptism year from Pregaldin. "Illinois, Diocese of Belleville, Catholic Parish Records, 1729–1956," images, FamilySearch (https://familysearch.org/pal:/MM9.3.1/ TH-267-11882-154670-54?cc=1388122&wc=M99B-QMV:n408136662), Randolph > Fort de Chartres > St. Anne (transferred to St. Joseph) > 1721–1840 Baptisms, Marriages, Deaths, First Communion, Confirmations > image 55 of 603, first marriage February 3, 1748. St. Louis 1787 Census, Marie La Roche was still living, but her husband had died.

234. "Illinois, Diocese of Belleville, Catholic Parish Records, 1729–1956," images, Family Search (https://familysearch.org/pal:/MM9.3.1/TH-267-11765-123942-32?cc=1388122&wc =M99B-QMN:n2031332824), Randolph > Kaskaskia Island > Immaculate Conception > 1741–1834 Marriages > image 19 of 118, marriage September 4, 1752, Picard was a widower. SLAR, Burial, March 11, 1787 (1788?), La Veuve Pikart, sixty-six years.

235. St. Louis 1787 Census, put her birth date ca. 1760.

236. FSA, no. 2024 Married July 6, 1771, Charles Simoneau.

237. The two Jean Baptiste Becquets were always distinguished as "the miller" or "the blacksmith." *Annals*, 431, Becquet moved to Ste. Genevieve in 1777.

238. Pregaldin listed a Pierre as the brother of this Jean-Baptiste Becquet. There was one Pierre Becquet on the list of habitants on the 1766 Militia Muster Roll, and another (?) Pierre Becquet in the *volontaires* section.

239. Pregaldin, Marriage January 19, 1752, at Cahokia. SLAR, Baptism, June 25, 1770, their daughter Thérèse was baptized, born February 26 that year. FSA, no. 1390 named Elisabeth (Becquet), and Catherine Bissonet as daughters of Joseph Marchetaud and Françoise LeDuc. Baptism and death years from Pregaldin.

240. Pregaldin, born Fort de Chartres 1755, SLAR, Ste. Genevieve Burial Register, April 11, 1817; married Ste. Genevieve November 1778 Marie-Louise Lacourse.

241. Pregaldin, Joseph married 1780, died 1836 age eighty-eight; André born Cahokia ca. 1761, died 1806 age ca. forty; Charles born ca. 1763 per St. Louis 1787 Census.

242. FSA, no. 2079, marriage contract, 1786. She was nineteen in 1772 when she married Joseph Chancellier. FSA, no. 2029. Charles Routier was her uncle (by marriage).

243. Pregaldin, married Cahokia May 20, 1785, Antoine Lamarche. Later children were born in St. Louis through 1774.

244. SLAR, Burial, March 10, 1777, seventy-four years. Pregaldin, born Canada January 21, 1710.

245. Pregaldin, baptized Cahokia November 5, 1747.

246. *VC*, 260–61, married Cahokia January 7, 1747. SLAR, Baptism, June 25, 1770, named as spouses. Burial November 1773 "Jean" Denoyé Marcheteau. FSA, no. 1390, Jeanne was the daughter of Joseph and Madeleine Robert.

247. Pregaldin, baptized Cahokia April 6, 1749, FSA, no. 2027 m. St. Louis 1771 Louis Bissonet. SLAR, Baptism, June 25, 1770, godmother for Henri François Roy. St. Louis 1787 Census, Genoveva Visonet, forty-seven.

248. SLAR, Marriage, Langoumois's widow remarried in 1776. He was still alive in 1771, FSA, no. 2024 as a witness in a marriage contract.

249. Born Cahokia, Pregaldin, Perrin Collection 63:10:1:1 registration of their marriage. She was thirty-eight when she remarried in 1776, FSA, no. 2040.

250. SLAR, Burial, April 17, 1805, seventy-two years, Jean-Baptiste Gamache, Sr. FSA, no. 2013 Marriage Contract said he was born in Cap St. Ignace, Canada. He married Marie-Charlotte Louvière in 1767, and their first son Jean-Baptiste was born in 1768. Pregaldin, Gamache was baptized September 21, 1734.

251. DiCerbo, "Rest of the Story" (see chap. 9, n. 30), born and baptized Fort St. Joseph, January 26, 1731. FSA, no. 2032, for death date.

252. DiCerbo, "Rest of the Story," married February 8, 1760, Ste. Anne de Détroit. FSA, no. 2013 Marriage Contract of Jean-Baptiste Gamache and Charlotte d'Amour de Louvière, sister of Thérèse, 1767. Pregaldin, born Montreal. SLAR, Burial for Thérèse Labrosse, November 27, 1776.

253. FSA, no. 2013, for the name of Marie-Thérèse's mother, the widow of Louis d'Amour de Louvière. See chapter 9.

254. Prairie du Rocher Baptism Register, Transcription, MHM, born January 2 baptized May 16, 1766, son of Louis Deshêtres and Thérèse.

255. DiCerbo, "Rest of the Story," born July 11, 1763, on the South Coast of Detroit (Sandwich). DeCerbo stated that a daughter named Charlotte lived for at least one year. Charlotte, the daughter of Louis and Marie-Thérèse, must have died, and this

space is taken by Marie-Thérèse's sister Charlotte. Charlotte's marriage contract (FSA, no. 2013) states that she was living with Deshêtres and her sister.

256. SLAR, St. Ferdinand Burial Register November 16, 1798, "natif de Port Louis en Bretagne" sixty-five years.

257. Grégoire, "Illinois, Diocese of Belleville, Catholic Parish Records, 1729–1956," images, FamilySearch (https://familysearch.org/pal:/MM9.3.1/TH-267-11882-154431-29?cc=1388122 &wc=M99B-QMV:n408136662), Randolph > Fort de Chartres > St. Anne (transferred to St. Joseph) > 1721–1840 Baptisms, Marriages, Deaths, First Communion, Confirmations > image 82 of 603, baptism January 5, 1753.

258. FSA, no. 2009 Marriage contract.

259. Pregaldin, married February 11, 1747. SLAR, Baptism, February 7, 1769, they were parents of Marie-Josèphe. Burial, December (November?) 16, 1783.

260. SLAR, Marriage May 19, 1781, to François Coussot (index reference).

261. Pregaldin, born Pointe Claire, Canada March 14, 173? died after 1791 (SLAR, St. Ferdinand Burial Register, there was a Joseph Calvé buried at St. Ferdinand September 10, 1815). *SRM,* 1:184, 1780 Militia Roster gave his age as fifty and birthplace Canada.

262. SLAR, Burial, July 2, 1791. FSA, no. 2010 Joseph Calvé was the brother-in-law of the bride, Catherine Maréchal, September 1767. FSA, no. 2443, Marie Maréchal, wife of Joseph Calvé. St. Louis 1787 Census, Maria Calvé, forty-seven.

263. SLAR, Burial, May 26, 1780, Calvé fils "massacré(s) par les sauvages." *SRM,* 1:184. 1780 Militia Roster lists "Antonio Galve" Sr. and Jr. This must be Joseph Calvé and his son. The son's age was seventeen, born in Illinois. St. Louis 1787 Census named Joseph forty-nine, wife Maria forty-seven, Joseph? twenty-eight, Francisco twenty-five, and three children too young for the 1766 census.

264. SLAR, St. Ferdinand Burial Register d. December 8, interred December 10, 1828. SLAR, Marriage, St. Louis February 3, 1785. She did not appear on the 1787 census with the other children.

265. Birth year from Pregaldin. FSA, no. 2010, Identified as parents, 1767. Her father was already deceased as of the marriage contract date (contrast to Billon). SLAR, Burial, December 5, 1784.

266. FSA, no. 2010 witness. FSA, no. 2301 names Nicolas Maréchal Sr.'s eight children as heirs: Joseph, François, "Jacob," Calvé representing his wife (Marie), Elizabeth, Nicolas, Moreau husband of Catherine Maréchal, and Antoine. SLAR, Marriage, June 30, 1784, Jacques Maréchal son of Nicolas Maréchal and Marie-Jeanne Illeret married Genevieve Cardinal.

267. SLAR, Marriage, Antoine Maréchal is the son of Nicolas Maréchal and Marie-Jeanne. St. Louis 1787 Census, Antonio Marechal, forty-three, his wife Catarina thirty-one.

268. FSA, no. 2010 Marriage Contract of François Moreau and Catherine Maréchal. Belting, *Kaskaskia under the French Regime,* 119, noted her baptism as October 19, 1747.

269. St. Louis 1787 Census, François Maréchal was thirty-six, married to Teresa, twenty-five. The marriage record is cited in note 215.

270. FSA, no. 2037 She married Louis Martin still as a minor in 1774.

271. SLAR, Burial, January 1, 1787, age forty-six. *SRM,* 1:185, 1780 Militia Roster had a "Fran(cis)co Vizonete," age fifty, a habitant from Canada. St. Louis 1787 Census had Francisco age fifty-three; Catarina, forty-seven, and other children born after 1766.

272. François had a brother Louis who appears frequently in documents, but Louis is not on the militia roster.

273. SLAR, Burial, February 20, 1808. Born ca. 1740 per St. Louis 1787 Census. SLAR, Baptism, May 7, 1767, names them in the baptism of their daughter. Marriage

contract FSA, no. 2059. Also FSA, no. 1390, sisters, daughters of Joseph Marcheteau renounced their inheritance so he might use it in his old age.

274. FSA, no. 2059 Marriage Contract, 1781.

275. FSA, no. 2012 François and his wife were identified in their daughter's marriage contract, June 25, 1767.

276. *VC*, 165–66, February 9, 1750, marriage. His birthplace was Québec.

277. FSA, no. 2012. Marriage contract, 1767. She was seventeen years old.

278. "El nombrado Lorenzo" Marriage contract, FSA no. 2018. Marriage "Illinois, Diocese of Belleville, Catholic Parish Records, 1729–1956," images, FamilySearch (https://familysearch.org/pal:/MM9.3.1/TH-267-11882-156044-38?cc=1388122&wc=M99B-QMV:n408136662), Randolph > Fort de Chartres > St. Anne (transferred to St. Joseph) > 1721–1840 Baptisms, Marriages, Deaths, First Communion, Confirmations > image 140 of 603. Birthplace given as St. Laurent, Beaujolais, diocese of Lyon. His *dit* name appeared frequently in documents. *SRM*, 1:184, 1780 Militia Roster listed "Felizberto Gañon" age fifty, born in France, habitant.

279. "El nombrado Fran.co" Collet identified him as "Petit François." FSA, no. 2845 François Delin, master carpenter. See chapter 6. Delin was listed in the habitants section of the militia muster roll. FSA, no. 2234 Will of "Delon" identified by the WPA index at MHM as Delin, gave a birthplace of "Delimoche."

280. AGI, 187A. Spelling is preserved as it appeared on the document. Names in parentheses were added based on source documents. First names not in parentheses were on the original document, as were other notations like the *dit* names, ranks, and "present" or "absent."

281. An asterisk next to a name indicates that this person was a resident listed on the census or has been placed in the household of relatives on the census.

282. *VC*, 785–86, August 23, 1763, bought land from Louis Marcheteau in New Chartres.

283. *VC*, 784–85, bought land in New Chartres from Louis Métivier; FSA, no. 2022 Marriage Contract, February 1770; *SRM*, 1:185, 1780 Militia Roster, age forty, born Canada, habitant. St. Louis 1787 Census, Joseph Menville forty-two, sons Josef nineteen, Luis, sixteen, and daughter Teresa, eighteen. SLAR, Burial, March 1, 1795.

284. *VC*, 86, Father and son with the same name; son b. May 19, 1746, in St. Philippe.

285. FSA, no. 36B emancipation of his Indian slave, 1767.

286. Probably Joseph Marie Papin, who married Marie Louise Chouteau. Foley and Rice, *Chouteaus*, 211.

287. See Chapter 7 and FSA, no. 2009 Marriage Contract.

288. A Pierre Becquet was also on the volontaire list. A minor Pierre Becquet appeared in 1757 in a land sale at Chartres, *VC*, 630–32.

289. Baptism July 29, 1764, of Basil, son of Basil La Chapelle and Louise Lalumandière, "Illinois, Diocese of Belleville, Catholic Parish Records, 1729–1956," images, Family Search (https://familysearch.org/pal:/MM9.3.1/TH-266-11825-77941-71?cc=1388122&wc=M99B-QMJ:687691126), Randolph > Kaskaskia Island > Immaculate Conception > 1759–1815 Baptisms, Marriages, Deaths, Other > image 30 of 244.

290. *SRM*, 1:185, 1780 Militia Roster, Choret was forty-six, born in Canada, a rower.

291. SLAR, Burial, Joseph Pichet, April 17, 1789.

292. Belting, *Kaskaskia under the French Regime*, 97, notes that La Vigne was the *dit* name of several Illinois families.

293. FSA, no. 1523.

294. SLAR, Burial, 1813 Pierre Bequet, "vieux garçon" age seventy-nine.

295. St. Louis 1787 Census, Fran. Santaman, age forty-six.

296. SLAR, Burial, Louis Dufresne July 5, 1789.

297. SLAR, Burial, March 17, 1795, born in Canada. St. Louis 1787 Census, Bpta. Probanché was forty-six, his wife Maria forty-one, and children Antonio, Josef, Baptista, and Maria.

298. FSA, no. 2018. He was on the census, see above.

299. *SRM*, 1:186, 1780 Militia Roster. He was thirty-eight, a hunter born in Canada. SLAR, Burial, buried in St. Charles, fifty years, December 8, 1789. FSA, no. 2687 listed Laurant and Alexis Michon as brothers.

300. FSA, no. 2016. See Chapter 9.

301. There were several Pinot, Pineau names in the records.

302. FSA, no. 2012.

303. See chapter 5 for his grant of a town lot by St. Ange.

304. Marriage of Michel Rolet and Marguerite Le Grain June 1765, "Illinois, Diocese of Belleville, Catholic Parish Records, 1729–1956," images, FamilySearch (https://familysearch.org/pal:/MM9.3.1/TH-267-11882-151767-50?cc=1388122&wc=M99B-QMV:n408136662), Randolph > Fort de Chartres > St. Anne (transferred to St. Joseph) > 1721–1840 Baptisms, Marriages, Deaths, First Communion, Confirmations > image 114 of 603. He appeared in numerous documents, as did his children. SLAR, Burial, November 15, 1775. See also chapter 8.

305. Same as Joseph Deschênes, habitant? *SRM*, 1:185, 1780 Militia Roster had "Joseph Duchene" age forty from Canada, a farmer, and "Pedro Dechene" age thirty-six, a trader.

306. There was a Louis Gervais with St. Ange in Vincennes, 1745. Parish Registers of French North America, St. François Xavier, Vincennes, Indiana Register, witness at marriage that St. Ange also witnessed.

307. FSA, no. 2011.

308. KM 70-6-25-2 inventory of the late Jean-Baptiste Chartrand; *SRM*, 1:187, 1780 Militia Roster had Joseph Chartran, thirty-eight, from Canada, a habitant.

309. FSA, no. 2023.

310. There were numerous Texiers. See chapter 10 for Pierre Texier, FSA, no. 2833.

311. FSA, no. 6.

312. FSA, no. 2015, witness.

313. *VC*, 885–86, Pierre Dirouse *dit* St. Pierre Laverdure married Catherine Delauney. Their son was François. François received a gift in 1726; he was a child. Belting, *Kaskaskia under the French Regime*, 96–97: Pierre Derouse *dit* St. Pierre Laverdure was on the 1752 census of Kaskaskia. François married the métisse daughter of Louis Turpin and Dorothée in 1760.

314. *SRM*, 1:186, 1780 Militia Roster had François Cornaud "Corno," forty-three, born in Canada, a rower.

315. *VC*, 291, Etienne Chuinert *dit* Sanschagrin. His Indian wife died and was buried September 10, 1761. Belting, *Kaskaskia under the French Regime*, 96, listed Antoine Cheneau *dit* Sanschagrin, a master slater from the 1752 census of Kaskaskia. A Sanschagrin was also a witness at the marriage of Gilles Chemin and Marie-Jeanne Quebedot.

316. FSA, no. 2019; *SRM*, 1:185, 1780 Militia Roster "Antonio Sansy," forty, born in Canada, was a mason.

317. *SRM*, 1:188, 1780 Militia Roster, Jean-Baptiste Hortez, carpenter, as Houck noted "should not be confounded with Joseph Alvarez Ortiz, usually spelled Hortiz." Jean-Baptiste Hortez came from Béarn, France.

318. Jacques Boutilliet, "Illinois, Diocese of Belleville, Catholic Parish Records, 1729–1956," images, FamilySearch (https://familysearch.org/pal:/MM9.3.1/TH-267-11882-154270-26?cc=1388122&wc=M99B-QMV:n408136662), Randolph > Fort de Chartres > St. Anne (transferred to St. Joseph) > 1721–1840 Baptisms, Marriages, Deaths, First Communion, Confirmations > image 130 of 603, marriage in Prairie du Rocher, 1765.

319. *VC*, 323–24, Joseph Provost *dit* Blondin was godfather. Belting, *Kaskaskia under the French Regime*, 110, in 1745, a Nicolas Provot *dit* Blondin married Marie-Françoise Quebedot, daughter of Joseph and Marie-Anne Antoine Beau. Belting said that Joseph was likely a child of Nicolas Provot and Quebedot.

320. *Annals*, 158, François Villet/Viellette, 1779.

Appendix B. St. Louis Indian Slave Census, 1770

1. They were named Aiken and Julien. "Marguerite v. Chouteau" (2:50) (see chap. 8, n. 105).

2. Her age is given in her baptismal record, SLAR, Baptism, June 27, 1770.

INDEX

Abbreviations: I.C. = Illinois Country; La. = Louisiana; N.O. = New Orleans; S.G. = Ste. Genevieve; S.L. = St. Louis

d'Abbadie, Jean-Jacques-Blaise: as La. governor, 44, 47, 51–52, 56, 60, 62, 64, 65, 69, 98, 60, 65, 262n8; grants trading privileges, 51, 62; no interest in Laclède, 53, 56, 57–58, 60
Africans: as boatmen, 35, 191, 202–4; emancipated, 155, 162, 191, 224, 230–31, 285n98, 297n25; as slaves, 107, 125, 129, 139, 143, 144, 147–64 passim, 168–70, 172, 186, 217, 219, 223–24, 230, 235, 291n33, 295n28. *See also* slaves
Agamemnon: female slaves of, 158
agriculture: at S.G., 53, 105, 122, 148, 222; commons and common fields in S.L., 96, 105–6, 272n49; crops, 106, 235; in I.C., 6, 27, 28, 48, 57, 97, 105, 148, 223, 231, 234
alcohol: Indians and, 80, 81; prohibitions against, 81; S.L citizens' petition concerning, 81–82; uses of in trade, 80, 191, 192, 268n45
Alliot, Paul: remarks on bear's oil, 180
Alvord, Clarence W., 218, 251, 252
American expansion, 5–6
American Revolutionary War, 6, 45, 92, 119
Ames, Gregory P., 286n3, 289n80; discusses Chouteau "Journal," xiii, 252n6, 290n1
architecture: *apentis*, 114, 115, 168, 172, 179; Canadian, 118, 219, 232, 274n31; Creole, 117, 118, 218–21, 232; *galeries* and, 117–19, 219–21; at S.L., 111–26 passim, 218–21. *See also* building practices
Arkansas Post: receives foodstuffs from I.C., 202, 204
armoires: local fabrication of, 173, 186, 221, 295n12; ubiquity of in I.C., 173
Arnold, Morris S.: on legal nomenclature, xiii

d'Artaguiette, Pierre Diron, 17, 30, 31, 34, 35
Atlantic world, 222–24
Aubert, Guillaume: discussion of race, 292n4
Aubry, Charles-Philippe: acting governor at N.O., 47, 78, 80, 85, 88, 89, 196, 268n61; corresponds with St. Ange, 78, 79, 82, 83, 86, 89, 196, 208, 269n67; taken prisoner at Niagara, 46
auctions: of property, 55, 57, 117, 125, 132, 213, 285n98, 293n24; at S.L., 76, 101, 117, 121, 125, 151, 213; of slaves, 144–45, 150–51; on Sundays, 55

baptisms: first in S.L., 104; of slaves, 151–52, 154–55, 158
Baram, Martin, 198
Baron, Pierre Lupien *dit*, 122, 123, 221, 274n48
Barr, Juliana, 207
Barsalou, Madeleine: wardrobe of, 185–86
Barsalou (Barzalou), Nicolas: estate of, 165, 185–86
Baudouin (*engagé*), 203
Beaugenou, Marie-Josèphe, 131, 240
Beaugenou, Nicolas Sr., 131, 239
Beaugenou, Widow (Marie-Anne Henrion), 132, 229, 233, 239
Becquet, Jean-Baptiste (blacksmith), 238, 310n237
Becquet, Jean-Baptiste (miller), 142, 143, 233, 241, 310n237
Belestre, François-Louis Picoté de: resident of S.L., 76, 81, 112; wife of, 104, 112, 159
Belestre, Joachine Coulon de Villiers de: husband of, 112; inherits slaves of St. Ange, 159, 210
Belle Famille: French routed in battle of, 46, 59
Belle Fontaine Creek, 12

315

Bellerive. *See* St. Ange de Bellerive
Bellerive Country Club (St. Louis Field Club): named after Louis St. Ange de Bellerive, xii
Belting, Natalia M., 218, 288n65, 312n292, 313n315, 314n319
Beor, Louis, 100, 161
Bérard, Antoine, 200, 201, 210; major merchant, 233, 234; on militia roll, 243; on 1766 census, 236
Bienvenu, Antoine, 148, 223
Bienville, Jean-Baptiste Le Moyne de, 15, 16, 18, 30, 31, 33, 34, 35, 37, 44, 97, 257n63
Big Osages, 79, 83, 205, 215
Billaud, Guillaume (*dit* L'Esperance), 189
Billon, Frederic Louis, 61, 62, 72, 97, 107, 227, 228, 251, 263n34, 274n29
Bissonet, François, 106, 243, 298n48
Bissonet, Louis, 220, 221
Bizet (Bissette), Charles, 230, 233, 234, 237, 245
Bizet (Bissette), Guillaume, 132, 142, 143, 155, 156, 230, 233, 237, 245, 249, 276n26, 279n86
Black Legend (*la leyenda negra*): stigmatizes Spain, 94, 271n104
Blondeau, Marguerite, 233, 238, 302–3n9
Blondeau, Thomas: 114, 233; fur trade merchant, 193
Bloüin, Daniel, 49, 86, 87, 88, 195, 269n66
Bobé-Descloseaux, Jean-Valentin (La. administrator), 142
Boisbriant, Pierre Dugué de, 16–20, 148, 257n75
Boone, Daniel, 207
Bossett, Marie-Louise, 132, 234, 241
Boucher (*engagé*), 194, 195, 204
Bouquet, Antoine, 189
Bourdon, Jacques, 127, 145, 188
Bourgeois, Marie-Thérèse. *See* Chouteau, Marie-Thérèse Bourgeois
Bourgmont, Étienne Veniard de: builds Fort d'Orléans, 18; at Fort de Chartres, 16; Indian slavery and, 16, 17, 22; Missouri Indians and, 17, 20, 22, 23, 254n24; in Missouri Valley, 15; recruits Jean-Paul Mercier, 16, 19; relationship with Robert St. Ange, 16, 18–20 passim, 23, 254n22, 256n41; returns to France, 23; voyage from N.O., 16
Boyle, Susan, 137
Braudel, Fernand: comments on traditional village life, 119

Bray, Étienne: resides *chez* Comparios, 166–67
Brown, Margaret K., 258n75
Bruggeman, Jean, 275n49
Buet, René: contract with Laclède, 116–17
building practices: *poteaux-en-terre*, 112–16 passim, 120, 121, 168, 171, 179, 196, 219, 273n6, 273n12, 273n15; *poteaux-sur-sole*, 112, 115, 184, 185; roofing, 113–14, 120–22, 172, 184; stone used in, 104, 112–14, 116, 122, 172, 177, 178, 184, 220, 273n9, 274n29; timber used in, 112–14, 122, 125–26, 273n7. *See also* architecture
Buissonnière, Alphonse de la, 34

Cahokia (village): 1, 16, 41, 42, 61, 107, 127; Pontiac killed at, 86, 88
Cailhol, François. *See* Cayolle, François
Calvé, Joseph Sr., 62, 100–101, 105, 233, 242, 244
Carlos III, King of Spain, 76, 78, 90, 92, 97, 159, 270n100
Carondelet, François Louis Hector de, 217
Cayolle, François, 189
Cayton, Andrew R. L., 47
Cazeau (trader): seized by Indians, 193
Céloron de Blainville, Pierre-Joseph: explores upper Ohio Valley, 40
censuses: of the I.C., 38, 157, 224; of Indian slaves, 46, 149, 159, 163, 247–50; of S.L., 141, 157, 162, 224, 227–35, 236–43
Cerré, Gabriel: father-in-law to Auguste Chouteau, 57; major merchant of Kaskaskia, 55; marriage to Catherine Giard, 57; moves to S.L., 222
Cerré, Marie-Thérèse (wife of Auguste Chouteau), 57, 146
Chancellier, Louis, 81, 232, 240, 244, 298n38, 308n207
Charlevoix, Pierre-François Xavier de, 213, 253n8; Robert St. Ange and, 14, 26, 212; travels of, 14; views of Canadians, 14
Charon, Widow (Marie-Françoise Pinot), 229, 231, 234, 239, 298n53
Chartres, village of, 1, 20, 29, 38, 48; Laclède buys property at, 53, 56, 63, 137; militia of, 46; provides settlers for S.L., 59–60, 107, 131, 136, 142, 163, 170, 235. *See also* Fort de Chartres
Chauvin, Jacques, 115, 202
Chemin, Gilles, 131–32, 156–57, 240, 243

Chickasaw Bluffs (Écores de Prudhomme or Écores à Margot), 30, 291n23
Chickasaw campaign of 1736, 30–31; Bienville planned, 30; French defeat at, 31; Pierre St. Ange killed at, 31; François-Marie de Vincennes killed at, 31
Chickasaw Indians: interdict French commerce, 36–37, 193; traditional enemies of French, 30
children: 81, 95, 107, 130, 141, 145; mixed or inter-racial, 149, 151–52, 154, 156–58, 162; outside of marriage, 139–40, 135–36, 183; in 1766 census, 230. *See also* slavery; slaves
Chittenden, Hiram Martin (author): early historian of fur trade, 187, 290n1
Choiseul, duc Étienne-François de: diplomacy of, 50; minister of Louis XV, 47, 50
Chorel, Élisabeth. *See* St. Ange, Élisabeth Chorel
Chouteau, Antoine, 155
Chouteau, Auguste, xiii, 2, 4, 33, 58, 73, 103, 107, 125, 227; arrives in I.C., 53; fur trade and, 187, 201; lack of importance in early S.L., xi, 59, 76, 290n1; Laclède and, 56, 57, 139, 233; on 1766 militia roll, 243
Chouteau, Jean-Pierre (or Pierre), 61, 88, 132, 134, 139, 140
Chouteau, Marie-Louise, 139, 196
Chouteau, Marie-Pélagie, 139
Chouteau, Marie-Thérèse Bourgeois: 32, 61, 119, 121, 140, 209, 236; arrives in S.L., 61; commerçante, 136, 139, 278n53; consort of Laclède, 53, 61, 121, 139, 140, 229; personality of, 53, 61; slaves of, 149, 155, 160
Chouteau, Pierre-Sylvestre, 187
Chouteau, Victoire, 61, 139
Chouteau's *Journal*: problems with, 4, 33, 55, 59–60, 61, 101, 225, 227–28, 235, 252n6, 253n1, 262n3
church: built in S.L., 105, 133, 166
Clark, George Rogers, 67, 207
Clark, William, 2, 17; and Corps of Discovery, 180, 198, 214
Code Noir (Black Code), 89, 143; governs black slavery, 149, 163, 223; origins of, 149, 281n21; provisions of, 149, 154, 156, 162, 163
Collet, Oscar W., 1, 252n6, 271n4
colonialism, 5, 94, 95
commerçants: defined, 151, 189, 197; at S. L., 82–83, 103, 107, 193, 199, 221

commerce: based on paper bills, 178–79, 197; between I.C. and Canada, 36; between I.C. and N.O., 30, 147, 197, 204; between S.L. and N.O., 199–205, 222; Bourgmont's expedition and, 25; at Fort d'Orléans, 46; in furs, 81, 187–205 passim; in Indian slaves, 15, 89, 145, 147, 160, 180, 210; at Kaskaskia, 6; at Vincennes, 41
Compagnie des Indes. *See* Indies Company
Comparios, Jean (Kerseret, Carsseret, Gascon): death of, 165, 166, 170; French marine, 99, 165, 167; slave of, 162, 166, 167, 168, 170
Condé, André-Auguste, 76, 81, 104, 150–54, 171, 172, 229, 230, 236
contracts in S.L.: fur trade, 188–99, 202–5; marriage, 128–36, 146, 151–52, 170; indenture, 123, 141, 157; land sales, 98, 99, 100, 104, 119, 124, 139, 231; mills, 122–26, 177; slave sales, 144, 145, 149, 153, 219, 279n100
Cotté, Alexis, 143, 144, 279n95, 279n98, 302n106
Cotté, Joseph, 152, 153
Cottin, François: legal clerk at S.L., 76, 98, 179, 231, 232, 241, 267n20, 298n33, 308n208
Coulon de Villiers, François. *See* Villiers, François Coulon de
Coutume de Paris (customary law of Paris), 127–28, 146, 215–16; community property (*communauté*) and, 129–30, 136; *douaire préfix* and, 130–31; *femme marchande* and, 136; illegitimate children and, 139; inventories and, 130, 142, 278n73; inheritance under, 139, 144; marriage contracts and, 128–31, 146; *préciput* and, 130–31; renunciation clause, 130; widows and, 141, 145; wills and, 127, 166, 278n64, 280n102
Crevier, Marguerite-Louise, 11, 31
Croghan, George, 175; activities of, 68, 69; St. Ange and, 68
Cruzat, Francisco: lieutenant governor in S.L., 126, 167; slaves of, 284n79
Custer, George Armstrong, 206

Danis, Hélène. *See* Hébert, Hélène Danis
Datchurut, Jean-Baptiste: I.C. merchant, 62, 195, 264n50; sues Pierre Laclède, 195
Dawdy, Shannon Lee, 95, 103–4
Debruisseau (Desruisseau), Joseph (Pierre-François Brunot Joseph d'Inglebert Lefebvre), 151, 152, 170–74

Delin, François, 125, 243, 245
Denis, Jacques, 99, 100, 112, 113, 115, 221, 246
Denoyé (Desnoyers), Bazile: voyageur, 194, 195, 304n145
Desfond, Louis, 199, 246
Desgagné, Antoine, 188, 189, 197, 202
Desgagné, Jean, 188, 189
Deshêtres, Antoine (*dit* Tranquille), 174, 182
Deshêtres, Charlotte Chevalier, 174, 177, 242, 311–12n255
Deshêtres, Louis: 76, 81, 268n45; arrives from Detroit, 176; estate of, 179, 180–82; family of, 174–80, 242, 287n30, 288n41, 310–11n255; interpreter with Indians, 163, 176, 178, 180; slave catcher, 163, 178
Des Loriers, Louis, 177, 178
Desnoyers, Louis (husband of Agnès Pichart) 106, 233, 238
Desnoyers, Marcheteau *dit*. *See* Marcheteau (*dit* Desnoyers)
Detroit, 6, 27, 34, 36, 64, 69, 175, 171, 181
DeVille, Winston, 291n18
Devin (N.O. merchant), 192, 291n19
DiCerbo, Loraine M., 287n30
Dion (Gion, Guion), Nicolas François, 135–36
Dodier, Élisabeth, 143, 144
Dodier, Gabriel Jr., 143, 145, 233, 239, 245
Dodier, Gabriel Sr., 141, 142, 229
Dodier, Marie-Françoise (Millet, Widow Dodier) 141–45, 155, 229–30, 233, 237, 249, 283n63
Dodier, Marie-Françoise (wife of Jean-Baptiste Becquet), 142, 143, 238
Dodier, Thérèse, 143, 144, 145
Dubé, Joseph: 244; land grant of, 100; manumits Indian slave, 160–61
Dubois, Laurent, 223
Dubreuil, Louis Chauvet, 119, 134, 221, 229, 234, 238, 243, 248
Dubut (*engagé*), 203
Dufossat, Guy, 85, 91, 272n35; ascends Mississippi, 78; maps of, 103, 105, 112, 121, 124, 219, 277n35; work for Spaniards, 78, 83, 84
Dumay, Pierre: indenture contract of, 123
DuPré, Marianne, 232
Duralde, Martin Milony, 135, 185, 272n35; land surveyor, 103
Durcy, François, 204
DuVal, Kathleen, xiii, 280
Duverger, Jacques-François Forget, 230; describes Vincennes, 42, 43

Eddington, Lieutenant James: arrives in I.C., 67; comments about Fort de Chartres, 70, 72
education: Creole libraries, 289n82
Edwards, Jay Dearborn: authority on creolization, xiii, 219–20, 221
Edwards, Richard, 61
engagés: 17, 191; at S.L., 199; in fur trade, 151, 198, 202, 203, 204

fabrics: in clothing at S.L., 174, 181, 185, 186, 213
Fagot (de la Garcenière), Daniel-François, 116, 191
Farmar, Arthur, 69
Ferrière, Claude de: on *Coutume de Paris*, 127
Finiels, Nicolas de: comments on I.C., 56, 189, 266n87
flour: importance of, 28, 30, 37, 124, 148, 202; shipped from S.G., 122, 201, 202, 203. *See also* mills
Foley, William E., xiii, 134
Fontainebleau, Treaty of (1762): cession of La. to Spain, 50, 90, 97, 98, 217, 227, 262n7
food, 122, 165–66, 178, 199, 256n57; bread, 143, 168–69, 173–74; diet, 25, 151, 154, 169, 180, 186, 212; Laclède as quartermaster, 77, 229
Forchet (Forget), Jeannette, 230
Fort de Chartres: British occupy, 70–71; commandants of, 16, 25, 26, 30, 34, 38; descriptions of, 27, 70; Indian presence, 53, 60, 65, 84, 87; Neyon de Villiers commandant at, 47–52, 56, 60, 64; new fort built, 28, 38, 96; role in Laclede's trading expedition, 56–58, 60; St. Ange de Bellerive commandant of, 27, 49, 64–74, 90, 97; St. Ange *père*, commandant of, 27–30
Fort Don Carlos el Señor, Principe des Asturies: location of, 83–84; purpose of, 83
Fort d'Orléans: Bourgmont builds, 18; location of, 17, 18; purposes of, 16, 20, 23, 25; Louis St. Ange commandant at, 19, 25, 35, 46, 206, 257n63; Robert St. Ange commandant at, 19, 24–25; St. Ange family at, 18, 20, 23, 24, 157, 158, 254n22
Fort Duquesne, 68; strategic location of, 40, 69
Fort Niagara: French lose to British, 46, 59
Fort Pitt, 66, 68, 69, 176
Fort St. Joseph: location of, 12, 26; Robert St. Ange commandant at, 12–14, 206

Foucault, Denis-Nicolas, 262n3
Fourcelles, Olivier de, 192
Fournier and Saintpé (fur trade partners), 192
Fox Indians, 84; defeat of, 26, 257n64; persistent enemies of French, 25, 36
Fraser, Lieutenant Alexander, 72, 77–78; remarks on Pontiac, 67–68; visits I.C., 66–68
free black population: of N.O., 163, 224; of S.L., 155, 162, 224, 230, 231
French and Indian War: conclusion of, 47, 52, 107, 142, 145; French defeats at Niagara and Quebec, 46, 59; I.C. and, 46, 59, 188, 264n38
fur trade: competition with British, 91, 188, 190, 205, 221; contracts for, 188–99, 202–5; extent of, 187–88, 189–90, 221; Indian involvement in, 195, 205; origins of in S.L., 187–205, 222, 290n1
furniture: at Fort de Chartres, 27; at S.L., 168, 172–73, 180, 186, 212, 221

Gage, General Thomas: British commandant in North America, 49, 64, 68, 69, 87, 94, 232; remarks on fur trade, 190
Gagnon, Joseph, 36, 38, 157, 309n227
galeries (porches): as Creole features, 118; at S.L., 119, 219, 221. *See also* architecture
Gamache, Jean-Baptiste, 177, 242, 244, 310n250, 310n252
Gauvereau, Étienne, 182
Gayarré, Charles, 65
Gerardin, Jean, 137, 278n60
Germain (*engagé*), 204
Gibault, Pierre, 45, 151, 152, 154, 155, 179, 211, 215
Gibert (*dit* La Fontaine), Jean, 168
Gitlin, Jay: coins "Creole Corridor," 294n6; discusses zones of settlement, 253n8
godparenting, customs of, 155–56, 164
Gordon, Harry: comments on Fort de Chartres, 70; comments on fur trade, 187, 290n2
Greene, Jack P., 223
Gros Bled (Piankashaw chief), 42
Grotton St. Ange, Robert. *See* St. Ange, Robert Grotton
Guion, Amable, 233, 234, 238, 244, 303n21
Gulf Coast, 6, 112, 204

Haldimand, Frederick, 44
Hall, Gwendolyn Midlo, 150, 224, 280n6, 283n53, 295n26
Hamelin, Jean-Baptiste, 198, 205

Hardwick, Julie: on colonial family life, 279nn81–82
Hébert, François, 233, 237, 245, 303n133
Hébert, Hélène Danis (Widow Hébert), 59, 229, 231, 232, 237, 278n52, 280n101, 283n59, 297n27, 301n101; marries Ignace Hébert, 229, 301n96
Hébert, Ignace: captain of Chartres militia, 59; marries Hélène Danis, 229, 301n96, 301n99
Hébert, Marie, 59, 230, 232, 237; marries Martigny, 300n91
Henrion, Charles, 233, 239, 245, 305n170
Henrion, Nicolas, 132, 161, 162, 233, 239, 245
Hervieux, Catherine Magnan, 198
Hervieux, Jean-Baptiste: 240, 243, 277n44, 289n82; death of, 135, 139; inventory of, 184–85; as royal gunsmith, 76, 81, 182, 183, 184
Hervieux, Léonard, 182, 289n67
Hervieux, Thérèse (natural daughter of J-B. Hervieux), 135, 185
Historic American Buildings Survey, 111
Hodes, Frederick H., 59
Hopewell, M., 61
Houck, Louis, 218, 254 22, 313n317
houses. *See* architecture
Hubert, Antoine, 99, 113–15, 121–22, 148, 185, 233, 234, 236, 248, 279n91, 296n6
Hulin, Agnès: affair with Hervieux, 135, 183, 184, 277n44
Hunaud (Huneau), Toussaint, 131, 132, 240, 244
Hunt, Theodore, 61, 101
Huron (*dit* Lorette), Michel, 200, 204

Illinois Country: censuses of, 38, 148, 227–28, 230; convoys to N.O. from, 28, 35, 49, 199, 204; definition of, 1, 51; neglect of by historians, 222–24; settlement of, 1, 6, 100; S.L. and, 90, 96, 107; villages in, 1, 41, 48, 53, 80, 99, 120, 213
illiteracy, 14, 29, 55, 63, 139, 177, 183, 197
indentures: Pierre Dumay, 123; Joseph (slave), 115, 148, 149, 236; François Laville, 141; Madeleine Laville, 140
Indians: alliances with British, 59, 66, 68, 269n74; alliances with French, 22, 26, 31, 40, 42, 46, 47, 91, 147; alliance with Spain, 15, 79, 84; Arkansas, 30, 31; Big Osage, 79, 83, 192, 205, 215; Cahokia (Cahos), 63, 269n67; Cherokee, 30, 31, 36, 37; Chickasaw, 30, 31, 34, 36, 37, 193, 258n83;

Indians (*continued*): Chippewa, 26; Choctaw, 30; Comanche, 254n16; Delaware, 53; Fox, 24–27, 30, 36, 84, 257n62, 257nn64–65; Illinois, 31, 65, 84, 87, 205; inter-tribal alliances, 30, 87–88; inter-tribal warfare, 17, 26, 84; Iowa, 22, 217; Iroquois, 26, 30, 31, 53, 59, 86; Kansas, 22; Kaskaskia, 65, 66, 81; Kickapoo, 26, 40, 68, 87; Little Osage, 191; marriages with habitants, 28–29, 218, 297n30; Mascouten, 26, 40, 68, 87; Miami, 30, 31, 34, 35, 40, 87; Missouri, 15–23 passim, 24, 38, 65, 66, 81, 83, 84, 205, 215, 217, 254n24, 256n47; Ojibway (Sauteurs), 41, 87; Osage, 23, 65, 66, 81, 215, 217, 280n4; Ottawa, 26, 41, 68, 86, 87, 88, 175; Padouca (Plains Apache), 11, 15, 17, 22, 23, 254n16; Padouca as slaves, 16, 17, 231, 280n4, 284n72, 297n28; Pawnee (Pani, Panis) as slaves 15,16–17, 280n4, 309n223; Peoria, 65, 81, 84, 86–88, 178, 269n66, 285n103, 309n225; Piankashaw, 26, 40, 42, 43, 47, 87; Piankashaw abandon Vincennes, 35, 37; Pontiac (Ottawa), xii, 49, 50, 55, 57, 60, 64–69, 269n68, 269n74; Pontiac, death of, 86–88, 269n67, 269nn75–76; Potawatami, 87; Potawatami role in French and Indian War, 40, 42, 46; Sac (Sauk), 84; Shawnee, 53, 62, 63, 265n56; Sioux, 79, 83, 188, 217; Sioux as slaves, 17, 22, 147, 148, 164; surrounding S.L., 84, 86; Tamarois, 66

Indian Slave Census (1770), 46, 149, 159, 163, 247–50

Indian slave trade, 15, 89, 145, 147, 160, 180, 210

Indies Company, 15, 18, 25, 26, 34

interpreters of Indian languages: Deshêtres, Louis 163; Dodier, Gabriel, 141

Jesuits. *See* Society of Jesus

Jesuit's bark: for treating malaria, 179

Johnson, Sir William: British Indian agent, 188; suspicions of French, 221

Jolliet, Louis: descends Mississippi River, 1, 14, 56, 187

Jumonville. *See* Villiers, Joseph Coulon de

Kaskaskia (village): Cerré marriage at, 57, 58; Laclède and, 55, 56, 57, 58, 61; metropole of I.C., 6, 67; Society of Jesus and, 45, 53, 55, 104, 148, 263n17

Kennedy, Matthew, 195

Kerlérec, Louis Billouart de: approves of St. Ange, 42, 43; as La. governor, 41, 42, 43, 45, 46, 52, 262n8

Kiercereau, Paul Jr., 133

Kiercereau, Paul Sr., 132, 133, 242, 244

Kiercereau, Pélagie, 132–34

Kiercereau, René, 81, 133, 232, 242, 244

Labbadie, Sylvestre, 156, 198, 199

Labrosse, Joseph, 116, 118, 137, 250

Labuxière, Charles-Joseph: birth in France, 75, 215, 266n12; death and burial, 215, 216; importance of as notary, 4, 5, 75–77, 118 128, 131, 134, 136, 138–40, 144, 149, 151, 165, 168, 178, 183, 189, 197, 205, 214, 225, 227, 229, 277n51; marriage to Anne-Catherine Vifvarenne,75; returns to east side of Mississippi, 215; as scribe under Spanish government, 168, 170, 171, 202, 209, 211, 214; St. Ange and, 4, 5, 75–76, 80–82, 100, 101, 103, 106, 107, 126, 172, 179, 183, 209, 211, 214, 225, 227, 272n28; at Ste. Genevieve, 92, 277n44; writes to O'Reilly, 76, 92, 93

Laclède Liguest, Pierre, 2, 4; arrival in I.C., 53; at auction of Jesuit properties, 53, 55; auction of country residence, 121; country house of, 107, 120; death and estate, 125, 140, 213; family life in S.L., 132, 139, 140; at Fort Chartres, 56; friendship with St. Ange, 159; leaves N.O. for the I.C., 53; Madame Chouteau and, 53, 61, 121, 139; meets François Vallé, 53; as négociant, 62–63, 187, 192, 193, 196, 199, 200, 202, 203; partnership with Maxent, 51; purchase of Taillon's mill, 124–25; purchases property at Fort de Chartres, 53, 56; purported land grants of, 97; selects site for trading post, 56–57, 60; slaves of, 125, 149, 155, 160, 163, 299n69; trades with Shawnees, 62–63; witnesses Cerré marriage, 57

La Demoiselle (Miami chief), 40, 41, 42

Ladéroute, Pierre, 246

Ladurie, Emmanuel Le Roy (author), 279n89

La Ferne, Marguerite, 151, 152, 154, 170, 171, 174, 230, 232, 237, 275n8

La Ferne, Marie-Anne, 151, 153, 154, 171, 230, 236

Lafitte (La. merchant), 192

La Garcinière, Daniel-François Fagot de, 116

La Giroflée, Jean Prunet (Brunet) *dit*, 136, 137, 230, 239, 278n53, 296n6

Lambert, Catherine Lépine, 195, 204

Lambert *dit* Lafleur, Jean-Louis: death of, 115, 195, 196, 204, 291n33; house of, 114, 115, 118, 196, 291n24; major merchant, 181, 193–95, 199, 202–4, 222; officer in S.L. militia, 94
Lamy, Marie-Françoise, 24
land and land grants: agricultural land, 105, 106, 107, 231; homesteading provision, 100, 101, 106; records of, 97, 100; relative size of parcels,104, 105, 107; at S.L.,76, 97, 98; St. Ange's authority in S.L., 97, 98, 100; squatting, 100, 106; stipulations of, 99, 104; surveying, 103, 107; town lots, 97, 101, 103, 105; verbal, 44, 99, 100; at Vincennes, 43, 44, 97
Langlade, Charles-Michel de (*métis* partisan warrior), 41
Langlois, Alexandre, 232, 233, 240, 244, 248
Langlois, Noël, 233, 240, 244
Langoumois, Jean-Baptiste, 119, 120, 141, 242, 244
La Renaudière, Philippe de: joins Bourgmont expedition, 11, 20, 23; journal of, 20, 22, 23
La Salle, Robert Cavelier de: descends Mississippi River, 1, 15, 187
La Traverse, Louis, 196, 197, 202
Laville, Pierre, 186, 293n14
Law, John: financial schemes of, 16
Le Boure (Le Bourg), Gillette (Madame Kiercereau), 133, 134
Lecompte (bateau skipper), 202
Le Dee, Jean-François: partner of Laclède and Maxent, 51, 52
Lefevre (Lefebvre), Joseph-François (Desruisseau), 65, 70, 75, 76, 97–100 passim, 112, 149, 151, 170, 219, 229, 236, 271n20, 272n28, 274n29, 298n38
Lemoine-Martigny, Joseph, 59, 233, 237, 244
Lepage, Madeleine (Madame Barsalou), 134, 185, 186
Lépine, Catherine (Madame Lambert), 195, 204
Le Roy, Julien, 119, 185, 238, 244
l'Espérance, Guillaume Billaud *dit*, 187, 189
Lewis and Clark Expedition, search for Fort d'Orléans, 17
Leyba, Fernando de: battle of 1780 and, 84; commandant at S.L., 84, 167
Lisa, Manuel, 194
livestock, 96, 129, 132, 227, 228, 231, 232
Lorine. *See* slaves
Louis IX, King of France, 108

Louis XV, King of France, 15, 27, 40, 44, 47, 50–52, 55, 76, 78, 97, 100, 105, 107
Louvières, Marie-Thérèse Damours de, 175–77, 287n30

Macarty-Mactigue, Jean-Baptiste: commandant at Fort de Chartres, 38–40, 41, 261n45; compiles 1752 census, 38; reports casualties from Niagara, 46; St. Ange's superior, 261n45
Mackay, James: map of, 17, 255n29
Mainville (*dit* Deschênes), Joseph, 210, 244, 313n305
Malet, Antoine, 195
Mapp, Paul: comments on French colonies, 224; on Choiseul's diplomacy, 50
Marcheteau (*dit* Desnoyer), François, 233, 248
Marcheteau (*dit* Desnoyer), Joseph, 233,
Marcheteau (*dit* Desnoyer), Kiery (Louis Jr.), 138–39, 167, 232
Marcheteau (*dit* Desnoyer), Louis, 233, 238
Marcil, Pierre, 199
Marié, Alexis, 104, 141, 241, 243, 249
Marin, François, 200, 201
Marines, French, 12; at Fort de Chartres, 26, 30, 46, 47, 56, 70, 72; move to S.L., 72, 73, 90, 96, 140, 165; St. Ange de Bellerive commands, 45, 46, 91
Marquette, Father Jacques: descends Mississippi, 1, 14, 56
marriages: adultery or infidelity and, 135, 139–40, 162, 183, 277n44, 289n72; age disparities in, 232; *Coutume de Paris* and, 127–46; Frenchmen and Indian women, 27, 231, 297n30; Frenchmen and *métisse* women, 28–29; husband's rights and obligations in, 129, 130, 136, 277–78n51; legal separation/divorce, 130, 276n15; wife's rights and obligations in, 129–30, 136. *See also* children; sex; slavery; slaves; women
Martigny, Jean-Baptiste Lemoine: appears in Chouteau's "Journal," 263n34; captain of militia, 59, 94, 209, 237, 243; founding of S.L. and, 59–61, 98, 107; marriage of, 59, 230, 232, 300n91; militia officer at Chartres, 59, 60; prominence of in S.L., 59, 126, 155, 195, 237, 249
material culture: architecture, 111–26, 186, 218, 219–21, 274n31; building practices, 111–26, 177–78, 179, 218, 219; clothing, 24, 174, 181, 184, 185–86, 214, 289n80; household furnishings, 168, 172–73, 180, 186

Maxent, Gilbert-Antoine: historical comments of, 56; as Laclède's partner, 51, 56, 62, 192–93; as N.O. merchant, 192
Mazrim, Robert F., 258n75
McDermott, John Francis, 218, 219; describes founding of S.L., 58, 77
Ménard, Pierre, 121
Mercier, Jean-Paul: at Fort d'Orléans, 19, 23, 25; recruited by Bourgmont, 16
Meyer, Michael J., 273n6
métissage, 27, 28, 154, 218, 231
Métivier, Louis, 158, 161–62, 285n94
Meurin, Father Sébastien-Louis: former Jesuit, 76, 104, 272n41; serves at S.L., 72, 76, 105, 133, 155, 229; serves at Vincennes, 45, 46
Miami Portage, 34, 36
Michilimackinac, 41, 232
militia: at Battle of Belle Famille, 46, 59, 264n38; importance of, 48, 59, 60, 65, 77, 80, 94; in I.C., 26, 30, 53, 59, 65, 77, 92, 98; in S.L., 59, 60, 92, 94, 98, 168, 183, 211, 228, 233, 235; S.L. militia muster roll (1766), 228, 233, 243–46; officers of, 76, 77, 94, 131, 144, 195
Mill Creek (Petite Rivière): at S.L., 102, 121, 124–25, 152; slave brawl at, 152–53
Millet, Marie-Françoise (Widow Dodier): 141–45, 229, 237
mills: built by Taillon, 124, 125, 234; grist, 122, 124; horse-driven, 122; at S.L., 122–26; tannin, 123, 177; water-driven, 122, 125, 126
Mississippi River: as artery between S.L. and N.O., 35, 49, 96, 116, 188, 191–94, 199–200, 222; bateau traffic on, 190, 191, 193, 196, 202–4; as international frontier, 49, 50, 52, 55, 65, 72, 73, 89, 91, 92, 96, 171–72, 215, 225; Laclède ascends, 53, 56
Missouri Indians, 15–23 passim, 24, 38, 65, 66, 81, 83, 84, 205, 215, 217, 254n24, 256n47
Missouri River: Bourgmont ascends, 15, 17, 224; Fort d'Orléans on, 15, 17–18, 23, 55; fur trade up, 6, 62, 83, 192, 194, 198–99, 221
Mobile: British at, 65, 69; French post at, 6, 30, 188, 204, 232
Montardy, Pierre: French marine, 291n27; fur trader, 194–95
Montesquieu, Charles-Louis de Secondat, marquis de: philosopher of government, 293n12
Montreal, as center of fur trade, 188, 199

Moogk, Peter N., 274n31
Moreau-DesHarnais, Gail, 262n75, 287n30
Morgan, George, 86, 88
Morgan, Philip D.: discusses slavery, 156
Morice (*dit* La Fantazie), Urbin, 199
Motard, Joseph, 178, 181

Napoleon, 252n1
Natchitoches, 79, 192
Native Americans. *See* Indians
négociants: defined, 104, 188–89, 193; in fur trade, 82, 188, 194, 197, 198, 202–3; in I.C., 55, 188; at S.L., 82, 83, 114, 193–96, 222
New Orleans: diversity of, 163, 168, 217, 224; foundations of, 96, 107, 188; French rebellion against Spanish, 85, 89, 93; *négociants* in, 103, 114, 188, 191–93; as "rogue" colony, 95; trade with S.L., 178, 181, 186, 188, 190, 198, 200, 204, 221, 222; urban planning of, 101, 103–4
Neyon de Villiers, Pierre-Joseph. *See* Villiers, Pierre-Joseph Neyon de
Nicollet, Joseph N., 271n4
Northwest Ordinance of 1787, 215
notaries: *Coutume de Paris* and, 128, 215; importance of in I.C., 45, 55, 75, 77, 205; Labuxière as, 4, 5, 75–76, 99, 137, 149, 197, 227, 229, 277n44; suppression of by Spaniards, 93, 166, 171, 183, 214–15; training of, 75

oath of loyalty to Spain, 90–92
Ohio River Valley: Anglo-French competition in, 35, 40, 47, 67; importance of, 6, 36, 37
O'Reilly, General Alejandro: crushes anti-Spanish revolt, 89; interim governor of La., 73, 89, 90, 93–94; policies of, 89, 145, 214; slavery and, 145, 160, 163, 210; St. Ange and, 90–94
Oro, Antonio de, 172, 173
Osage Indians, 23, 65, 66, 79, 81, 83, 84, 191, 192, 205, 215, 217, 255n29, 280n4
Oto Indians, 15, 22, 23, 192, 199
Ottawa Indians, 26, 41, 68, 86, 87, 88, 175

Paincourt, nickname for S.L., 121, 124, 143, 206
Panissé, Véronique: *Coutume de Paris* and, 136–39; husbands of, 36, 138, 230, 239; marriages of, 138, 232; personality of, 139
Papin, Jean-Baptiste *dit* La Chanse, 81, 116
Papin, Joseph, 162, 196–97

Paris, Treaty of (1763): Choiseul and, 50; ends Seven Years' War, 50, 69, 91, 204, 221
Parkman, Francis, 1, 65, 86, 88, 222, 253n1, 269n76
Parks, Douglas: discusses western Indian tribes, 254n16
Pays d'en haut (Upper Canada), 12, 14, 34, 188, 221
Peckham, Howard Henry: on Pontiac, 86–87, 269n75
Peoria Indians: alcohol and, 81, 178; death of Pontiac and, 86, 87, 88, 269n66; presence at S.L., 87, 285n103; villages of, 84
Périer, Étienne: policies of, 25
Perin *dit* Boucher, Jean, 194
Perrault, Louis, 117, 196–97, 199, 202–3, 222, 292n59
Pery (*dit* La Pierre), Pierre, 76, 167–68
Peterson, Charles E.: and founding of HABS, 111; historian of architecture, 111, 118, 218; infatuated with S.G., 111; studies early S.L., 97, 101, 121–22
Peyser, Joseph L.: leading expert on Fox wars, 257nn65–66
Philibert, Étienne, *dit* Orléans, 44–46
Pichart, Agnès, 106, 231, 238
Piernas, Pedro: appointed to S.L., 75, 90, 93, 94, 103, 171, 183, 199, 214; criticism of S.L. and St. Ange, 93–94, 214
Pittman, Philip: in I.C., 122
Pontiac (Ottawa): drunkenness of, 67, 68, 88; at Fort de Chartres, 64, 65, 67; murder of, 86, 87; Neyon de Villiers rebuffs, 64; Pierre Chouteau and, 88; St. Ange and, 67, 86, 87, 88
Pontiac's Rebellion/War, 49, 50, 55, 58, 60, 64, 65–69, 175
Pourré (Pourée), Eugene, 94, 105, 144, 156, 230, 240, 248
Prairie de la Joie: associated with S.L., 121; location of, 122, 126
Prairie des Granges: associated with S.L., 119; location of, 119
Prairie du Rocher, 1, 41, 176, 272n41
Priests, Roman Catholic: Julien Devernay, 45; Jacques-François Forget Duverger, 42–43, 230; Joseph Gagnon, 36, 38, 157, 309n227; Pierre Gibault, 45, 151, 152, 154, 155, 179, 211, 215; Bernard de Limpach, 135, 156; Jean-Paul Mercier, 16, 19, 23, 25; Sébastien-Louis Meurin, 76, 104–5, 133, 154, 155, 176, 229, 272n41, 277n35; Valentin, 129,

155, 210, 211; Louis Vivier, 43, 45; René Tartarin, 36
Primm, Wilson, 303n119

Quebedot (Quebedeau, Quevedot), Marie-Josèphe, 140–41
Quevedot, Jacques, 156–57, 159, 162, 240

race, issues concerning, 154, 155, 163, 207, 218, 224, 258n77, 281n8, 292–93n4, 296n7
religion: baptism of slaves, 149, 154, 155, 164; burial practices, 45, 133, 186, 210, 211, 215, 234; conversions, 155; government announcements at church/mass, 55, 121; Jesuit missionaries, 27, 45, 55, 76, 104, 148, 258n74, 263n17; marriage rituals, 128–29, 171, 231; role of church in S.L., 105, 154–55, 230
Renault (*engagé*), 202
Renaut, Philippe, 28
Reynal, Antoine, 167
Rice, C. David, 134
Richardville, Joseph-Antoine Drouet de, 48, 176, 262n75
Richter, Daniel K.: comments on Mississippi frontier, 224
Ríu y Morales, Francisco: ineptness of, 80, 83, 84; relationship with St. Ange, 78–79, 86; removal from command, 84; voyage to S.L., 78
Rivet (*engagé*), 202
Rivière, Jean-Baptiste, 61, 106, 119
Rivière (*dit* Baccané), Antoine Sr., 61, 168, 232, 291
Rocheblave, Philippe Rastel de: commandant at Ste. Genevieve, 73, 92, 153; St. Ange's subordinate, 73
Rolet (*dit* La Déroute), Michel: as French marine, 291n25; as fur trader, 193; purchases black slave, 151
Ross, Lieutenant John, 65–66
Roussel (*dit* Sans Souci), Antoine, 123–24, 177–78, 246
Rôtisseur, Antoine Gilbert *dit*, 19, 255n34
Roubieu, Gaspard, 153
Rougeau (*dit* Berger), Pierre, 111, 114, 233, 246
Routier, Charles, 233, 242, 244
Roy, Pierre, 170
Royer (*dit* Sans Quartier), Nicolas, 203, 248

Saintous, Suzanne, 221, 234
Salmon, Edme-Gatien, 27–31, 35

Sanguinet, Charles, 234
Sans Souci. *See* Roussel (*dit* Sans Souci), Antoine
Sarpy, Jean-Baptiste, 104, 119, 178, 181, 211
Saucier, François, 38
Scypion freedom suit, 285nn104–5
Segond, Joseph, 195, 211
Seven Years War. *See* French and Indian War
sex: addressed in *Code Noir*, 149; and enslaved women, 95, 154, 155, 159, 162; extra-marital, 135, 183–84, 230; inter-racial/inter-cultural, 162
Shawnee Indians: at Ste. Genevieve, 62–64; in Ohio Valley, 62
Sheridan, Philip Henry, 206
Sioux: appear in S.L., 79; trade with, 83, 188
slavery: absence of slave families, 156; Africans, brought to La., 148; ban on trading of Indian slaves, 145, 160, 163, 210; baptism of slaves, 151–52, 155–56; comment by Boisbriant, 148; corporal punishment of, 153; emancipated slaves, 156, 159, 161, 164, 230; in the I.C., 147–48; of Indians, 147–48, 155–62, 163; inheritance of slaves, 131, 142–45; marriage, 156; proportion of owners, 230; proportion of S.L. population, 230; restrictions upon slaves, 162; runaway slaves (*marronnage*), 163; in S.L., 147–64, 230; value of slaves, 149. *See also* sex; slaves
slaves: Agnès (Métivier), 161–62; Aiken (Taillon), 163, 241, 314n1; Angélique (St. Ange), 133, 158–59, 160, 210–12, 236, 279; Antoine (Laclède), 155; Antoine (St. Ange), 159; Baptiste (Dodier), 142–43, 144, 148, 149, 237; Catteau (Dodier), 142, 145, 237; Charlotte (St. Ange), 159; Cirille (Chouteau), 149; Courtette (Bizet), 155, 237; Cupidon (Laclède), 149, 250; Flora (Papin, manumitted), 162; François (St. Ange), 159, 249; Françoise (De Volsey, manumitted), 162; Françoise (Dodier), 145, 249; Jacob (Dodier), 142, 149, 237; Jeannette (Forget, manumitted), 230; Joseph (Hubert), 148–49, 236, 248; Julien (Taillon), 163, 241, 314n1; Lizette (St. Ange), 46, 158–59, 236, 249; Lorine (La Ferne), 150–54, 237; Manon (Chouteau), 139, 160, 248; Marguerite (Comparios), 162, 166–70; Marguerite (Dubé, manumitted), 160–61; Marianne (de Leyba), 152–53; Marianne (Chemin), 156–57, 240; Marie (Métivier, manumitted), 161–62; Marie-Louise (Taillon), 163, 241, 248; Marie Patoka (St. Ange), 157; Marie Scypion (Taillon), 241; Thérèse (Chouteau), 139, 248. *See also* slavery
Society of Jesus, 14, 23, 27, 31, 43, 45, 53, 55, 76, 104, 148, 258n74, 263n17; importance of in I.C., 55, 263n17; mission at Kaskaskia, 148; priests in I.C., 45; properties of auctioned, 53, 55; suppressed by French crown, 76, 109
Sommerville, Suzanne Boivin (French colonial scholar), 262n75, 287n30
Soulard, Antoine, 103
Spain: acquires La., 50, 52–53, 78, 90, 227; ambitions in West, 16, 20–22, 91, 97, 215, 216; government in La., 73, 78, 85, 89–90
St. Ange, Élisabeth Chorel: at Fort de Chartres, 14, 25, 27, 157; at Fort d'Orléans, 20–24; Indian slaves of, 25; life of, 12, 14, 38; longevity of, 1, 157–58; marriage to Robert St. Ange, 12, 25
St. Ange, Pierre, 22–23; killed by Chickasaws, 31; marriage to *métisse*, 28–29
St. Ange, Robert Grotton: attack on Fox Indians, 25–26; background of, 11, 25; Bourgmont and, 16–19, 22; commandant at Fort de Chartres, 26–30; commandant at Fort d'Orléans, 19, 23–25; family of, 11, 12, 20, 23; at Fort St. Joseph, 12–14; marriage of, 12; orders execution of Frétel, 29; retires at Fort de Chartres, 30–31
St. Ange de Bellerive, Louis: assembles Indians at Fort de Chartres, 65–67; attitude toward Indians, 158, 206–7, 214; Aubry and, 47, 78–79, 89; birth of, 31, 259n92; character and personality of, 43, 207; commandant at Fort de Chartres, 47, 64, 65, 70; commandant at Fort d'Orléans, 19, 25, 35, 46, 206, 257n63; commandant at S.L., 73–95, 179, 227; commandant at Vincennes, 35–49 passim; concubines of, 46, 158–59; death of, 70, 211; death of Pontiac and, 86–88; diplomacy with Indians, 33, 35, 37–38, 40, 41–42, 47, 64, 65–66; diplomatic relations with Spanish, 78–79; establishes government at S.L. 72, 73–75; estate inventory of, 212–14; Indian slaves of, 46, 157–60, 201–11, 214, 236, 249; Laclède and, 77, 213; land grants and *Livres Terriens* (land books), 97–107, 124, 126; leaves Vincennes, 47–49; Madame

Chouteau and, 209; Missouri Indians and, 38; name of, 31–32; official correspondence of, 41, 64, 76, 84, 90–92; Piernas and, 73–74, 93–94; praised by superiors, 33, 34, 35, 38, 42, 43, 206; probity of, 42, 208; Ríu and, 78–79, 83–86

Ste. Genevieve: agriculture at, 53, 105, 122, 148, 222; architecture at, 112, 115, 116, 118; citizens swear allegiance to Spain, 92; compared to S.L. in 1766, 228; founding of, 3; François Vallé captain of militia at, 57, 59; Pierre Laclède at, 53–59; "pretty girls" at, 69; Rocheblave commandant at, 73, 92, 153; slave families in, 156

St. Ferdinand, 168

Stirling, Captain Thomas: assumes command at Fort de Chartres, 69–71, 72

St. Louis: Canadian population of, 96, 219, 232; censuses of (*see* censuses); citizens' petition against alcohol, 80–82; commons and common fields in S.L., 96, 106, 107; comparison to Ste. Genevieve in 1766, 228; debate about founders, xi–xii, 58, 63, 107; early surveying, 99, 103, 106–7, 124; first chapel built, 105; free blacks in, 191, 224, 230, 297n25; housing in, 111–26; imbalance in sex ratio, 230; labor shortages, 92; Laclède's Landing, 125; name first appears, 98; named, 107–8; nicknamed "Paincourt," 143, 206; physical configuration, 96, 101; salaries for government officials, 76–77; urban planning of, 96, 108; violence and disorder in, 89, 95

Stoddard, Amos: assumes command at S.L, 93, 101

St. Pierre, Charles, 193

Superior Council: decides against Laclède, 62–63; high court in N.O., 62, 85, 89, 149

Taillon, Charles, 153
Taillon, Joseph Michel *dit*, 81, 104, 124–25, 132–34, 143, 148, 152, 163, 230, 234, 241
Taillon, Marie-Josèphe, 132–34
Tamarois (Kaskaskia chief), 66
Tellier, Joseph, 202
Tessier, Louis, 28–29, 188
Texier, Joseph, 198, 205
Thorne, Tanis, C., 217
Thornton, John K., 222
Tinon, Claude, 140–41
Toulouse, Jean-Marie, 116, 189–90

trade: competition for, 221; Indian trading licenses/grants, 51; in Indian slaves, 15, 89, 145, 147, 160, 180, 210; Maxent, Laclède, and, 51, 53, 56, 62, 192, 193; of peltries, 196, 197, 199–203, 205, 221. *See also* commerce

translators. *See* interpreters

treaties: of Fontainebleau (1762), 50, 90, 97, 98, 217, 227, 262n7; of Paris (1763), 50, 69, 91, 204, 221

Turner, Frederick Jackson: frontier thesis and, 5–6

Ulloa, Antonio de: Aubry and, 78; ineptitude of, 78, 83; issues trading restrictions, 82–83; as La. governor, 73, 78, 79, 148, 192; requests census, 227; revolt against, 85, 89; restrictions on alcohol, 80–82

Upper Canada (*Pays d'en haut*), 12, 14, 34, 188, 221

Upper Louisiana, 1, 14, 34, 41, 53, 73, 76, 79, 84, 85, 90–93, 96, 108, 163, 180, 195, 196, 199, 210, 218

Usner Jr., Daniel H., 150, 222

Valentin, Father, 122, 129, 155, 210, 211, 156, 148
Vallé, François, 122, 148, 156, 211, 231, 270n98; captain of militia at S.G., 57, 59
de Vaudreuil-Cavagnal, Pierre de Rigaud, 38, 40, 41, 44, 97, 148
Vaudry, Toussaint, 230, 233, 239
Vien, Jean-Baptiste: billiard entrepreneur, 201; boatman, 200, 201, 204
Villars, Louis: commandant at S.G., 200–202, 203
Villiers, Élisabeth St. Ange: birth of, 20; marriage of, 36
Villiers, Élisabeth de (wife of de Volsey), 155, 162, 210
Villiers, François Coulon de; family of, 104; marriage of, 36; taken prisoner at Niagara, 46
Villiers, Joseph Coulon de: killed on Pennsylvania frontier, 36
Villiers, Louis Coulon de: avenges his brother's death, 36
Villiers, Pierre-Joseph Neyon de: accommodates British, 64; commandant at Fort de Chartres, 47, 56–57; departure for N.O., 49; and Laclède, 53, 60; rebuffs Pontiac, 64; St. Ange and, 49

Vincennes: as buffer against British, 40–42; Croghan at, 68; Forget Duverger describes, 43; fort at, 34, 41, 43; founded by François-Marie Bissot de Vincennes, 34; importance of, 41; moved to lower Wabash, 34; Piankashaw Indians at, 34–37, 41–42, 43, 47; St. Ange commandant at, 35–49 passim

Viviat, Louis, 264n50; Laclède seizes boat of, 62; prevails in lawsuit against Laclède, 62

Volontaires: definition of, 48, 114, 228; at S.L., 245–46

Volsey, Pierre-François Hautemer de: natural daughter of, 162; marine officer, 80, 267n24; marriage of, 76; serves St. Ange, 76, 80; at S.L., 104, 250

voyageurs: in fur trade, 34, 49, 62, 189–203 passim; status of, 103

Wabash (Ouabache) River: 34, 36, 37, 47, 68; French outposts on, 25; Vincennes and, 42, 49, 176

Washington, George, 36, 64, 174, 207

Weeks, Pat, 253n5, 256n47

White, Sophie : advocate for I.C., 222; discusses clothing, 24, 160

widows: Beaugenou (Marie-Anne Henrion), 229, 233, 239; Charon (Marie-Françoise Pinot), 229, 231, 234, 239; and *Coutume de Paris*, 140–45; Dodier (Marie-Françoise Millet), 141–45, 148–49, 155, 156, 229, 230, 233, 237, 249; Gouin (Marie-Josèphe Lacroix), 232; Hébert (Hélène Danis), 59, 229, 231, 237; importance of, 141; Laville (Marie-Josèphe Quevedot), 140–41; Maréchal (Marie-Jeanne Illeret), 229, 233, 242

Wilkins, John, 87–88, 171–72

women: as black slaves, 150, 152, 154, 155, 162, 164, 172; *Coutume de Paris* and, 129, 130, 136, 145; importance of in S.L., 235; as Indian slaves, 26, 147, 158, 160, 164, 231; widowed, 140–45, 229. *See also* marriage; sex; slavery; slaves

Wood, Peter H., 224, 225

Woodward, C. Van: remarks about slavery, 164

Carl J. Ekberg is a professor emeritus of history at Illinois State University. His many books include *A French Aristocrat in the American West: The Shattered Dreams of Delassus de Luzières* and *Stealing Indian Women: Native Slavery in the Illinois Country*, and he is a two-time winner of the Kemper and Leila Williams Prize.

Sharon K. Person is a professor of English specializing in English as a Second Language at St. Louis Community College, St. Louis, Missouri. She has written extensively on St. Louis's colonial history and received (as co-author) from the State Historical Society of Missouri the award for the best article of 2014 for "Tracking Pierre Laclède, 1763–66: A Trading Career Gone Wrong," which appeared in the *Missouri Historical Review*.

The University of Illinois Press
is a founding member of the
Association of American University Presses.

Designed by Jennifer S. Holzner
Composed in 10/13 ITC Garamond Std
by Lisa Connery
at the University of Illinois Press
Manufactured by Sheridan Books, Inc.

University of Illinois Press
1325 South Oak Street
Champaign, IL 61820-6903
www.press.uillinois.edu